THE WRITER'S DIGEST
Character Naming Sourcebook

THE WRITER'S DIGEST
Character Naming Sourcebook

Sherrilyn Kenyon
With Naming Strategies by
Hal Blythe and Charlie Sweet

WRITER'S DIGEST BOOKS
CINCINNATI, OHIO

The Writer's Digest Character Naming Sourcebook. Copyright © 1994 by Sherrilyn Kenyon. Printed and bound in the United States of America. All rights reserved. No part of this book may be reproduced in any form or by any electronic or mechanical means including information storage and retrieval systems without permission in writing from the publisher, except by a reviewer, who may quote brief passages in a review. Published by Writer's Digest Books, an imprint of F&W Publications, Inc., 1507 Dana Avenue, Cincinnati, Ohio, 45207. (800) 289-0963. First edition.

This hardcover edition of *Writer's Digest Character Naming Sourcebook* features a "self-jacket" that eliminates the need for a separate dust jacket. It provides sturdy protection for your book while it saves paper, trees and energy.

Other fine Writer's Digest Books are available from your local bookstore or direct from the publisher.

00   99   98   7   6   5

Library of Congress Cataloging-in-Publication Data

Kenyon, Sherrilyn, 1965-
    Writer's Digest character naming sourcebook / by Sherrilyn Kenyon, with naming strategies by Hal Blythe and Charlie Sweet.—1st ed.
        p.   cm.
    Includes index.
    ISBN 0-89879-632-6
    1. Characters and characteristics in literature. 2. Names, Personal—Dictionaries. I. Blythe, Hal. II. Sweet, Charlie. III. Writer's Digest Books (Firm) IV. Title.
PN56.4.K46   1994
929.4—dc20   93-35940
                                                                    CIP

Edited by Jack Heffron and Argie Manolis
Designed by Sandy Conopeotis

Dedication

In loving memory of my grandfather, who first taught me that names have meaning and whose scholarly ways inspire me still. And, of my brother, Buddy, who convinced me that even brats can fly. *Dormez dans paix, mon precieux frere*.

To:

My Mother, for all the years she kept me supplied with the notebooks where I diligently recorded my finds.

Diana Porter Hillock and Cathy Maxwell, who told me this was a good idea and kept my spirits soaring.

Cathe and Kimberley Watson and my father, who know why.

And to Ken, for everything and more.

ABOUT THE AUTHOR

Sherrilyn Kenyon has spent her life studying languages, mythology, fairy lore and history. She first started collecting names at age eight when her grandfather told her what her name meant. Rushing home with her newfound knowledge, she wrote down her own name as the first entry in what eventually became a mammoth collection of names. With a B.L.S. in Classics, she is currently working toward her M.A. in Medieval History.

She is a member of the Charles Homer Haskin Society for Medieval Historians, the Society for Creative Anachronism, and the Archaeological Institute of America. When not immersed in her studies or out collecting medieval books, she divides her spare time between her husband, her two cats and her fiction writing.

Introduction 1

PART ONE

The Craft of Naming 4
By Hal Blythe and Charlie Sweet

One   **THE IMPORTANCE OF NAMES** 5

Two   **CHARACTERNYMS** 9

Three   **TOPONYMS AND RESNYMS** 13

Four   **NAMING FOR THE GENRES** 17

PART TWO

The Name Lists 26

      ANGLO-SAXON 27

      ARABIC 35

      ARMENIAN 40

      ARTHURIAN LEGEND NAMES 42

      BASQUE 48

      CELTIC 50

      CZECHOSLOVAKIAN 58

      DANISH 60

      DUTCH 63

      EGYPTIAN 66

      ENGLISH 72

      FINNISH 100

      FRENCH 102

      GAELIC 112

      GERMAN 119

      GREEK 127

HEBREW 150

HUNGARIAN 161

INDIAN 164

IRISH 173

ITALIAN 183

LATIN 188

NATIVE AMERICAN 213

NORSE 224

PERSIAN 240

POLISH 242

RUSSIAN 246

SCANDINAVIAN 251

SCOTTISH 252

SLAVIC 259

SPANISH 261

SWEDISH 271

TEUTONIC 277

UKRANIAN 287

WELSH 289

OTHER 302

Index 305

Introduction

Since humans first learned to use their vocal cords to form words of association, we have been obsessed with naming everything from swords to teddy bears. This tendency has caused us to borrow names from mythology, from our ancestors, or from any other object, color or form we have ever heard mentioned.

When it comes to naming children, people have shown great imagination and love of variety. Though this work is extensive, it is not exhaustive. But this work is the culmination of over fifteen years of research, diligently penned and guarded for my own use. My sources have been as varied as the names themselves: old family Bibles, historical writings, literature, mythology, archaic birth recordings and literature.

In all cases, I have done my best to attribute the names to the countries where they originated and to give their meaning in that language. But, as with all historical research, there have been times when the information was either contradictory or diversified. In such cases, I have chosen the meaning that I found in two or more sources or used my best judgment. However, there are still names whose original meanings have eluded me. As this occurred, I listed the name in its country of origin without a definition. In the few cases where I couldn't locate the originating country, I have placed the name in the "Other" section. I apologize for any errors in my research or conclusions and take full responsibility for them.

Etymology has been a labor of love for me. The comparison of languages both current and dead has never been a dull study. It has always amazed me how the same word can have entirely different meanings in its own language as well as in another.

A word such as *dip*, in English, can pose a vexing dilemma for a student trying to learn the language or even for an experienced translator trying to find the author's or speaker's true intent. *Dip* can mean anything from a "stupid person" to a "hole in the road," "something one uses for potato chips," or a "dance step." In German, *cour* means "suitor," and in French it means "heart"—two vastly different though related nouns. The French word *dire* means "statement"; in English, it is more closely related to the Latin *dirus*, meaning "ominous." Names, like words, have often changed meanings and pronunciations as they crossed borders and were used in other lands.

The naming of children has not always been quite as demanding as it is today. Everywhere, expectant parents hound the local bookstore and library shelves and dig through tons of pages, trying to find the perfect name before they even know the gender of the child. In the past, parents had much more time to decide on the "perfect" name. Within my own family, in the second decade of this century, my grandmother's sister was allowed to name herself. Only with the coming of modern birth certificates and the need for a social security card has the immediate demand for a name come into fashion. In centuries past, parents would use names such as Jill, Laddie, Lassie, Baby, Sissy, Bambi, Bambino, Primus, Dixie, and so on to distinguish between their children until a name was settled on.

In archaic civilizations, predominately the Greek and Roman, it was quite common for the fathers to name all their children after themselves — a habit that has caused hours of aggravation for historians, since a family could consist of four daughters named Octavia and three sons, as well as the father, named Octavius.

During the Middle Ages, the eldest children were named after the father and mother, grandfather and grandmother, with one of the succeeding daughters occasionally given a variant of the father's name — hence Henrietta, Huette, Conradina, and so on.

And as the Middle Ages passed, man discovered the need for another name — the surname. When the middle class began to evolve, and mercantilism required licenses and other designations for tax purposes, the populace of Europe developed the custom of using surnames. Before this, men commonly used their given name with either their location (John of Hexham), their father's name (John Gilbert's son), a descriptive name (John Red-Beard), their occupation (John the Marshal), or a combination of the above (John Fitz Gilbert the Marshal). I chose this historical figure to demonstrate a point about the name Fitz. Fitz commonly designated the illegitimate children of the aristocracy; the father's name followed. Hence, the modern Fitzpatrick was at one time Fitz Patrick.

If a man changed location or occupation, his name might change. If John moved from Hexham to Pembroke, he would then be called John of Pembroke. The nobility often took their names from their castles or the territory they oversaw; for example, Robert of Huntington (territory) was also known as Robin of Locksley (castle) and finally as Robin O' the Hood (descriptive).

Many occupational names were used—Woodward, Baker, Tucker, Fuller and so forth. Place names continued to proliferate, yielding such surnames as London, Pembroke, Hastings and Hapsburg. Some again used their father's name, which became Jackson, Price, Harris, Rawlins, Bowen, Key, Maddox, McLucas, O'Brian—well, you get the picture.

Another tendency was to choose names based on a physical characteristic. Cecil meant blind, Claude meant lame, Russell meant red-haired, Cameron meant a crooked nose, Mary meant bitter, Kenneth meant handsome. For surnames, we see John Lackland, so called because he was without land, or Robert Curthose, who lacked height.

In addition, names were chosen to engender fear or respect. To this end, we see names such as Wolf, Ren (raven), Drake (dragon), Alfred (wise), Cenewyg (bold warrior), Hadwyn (friend in war) and so on.

As you peruse the lists in this book you'll see many such names from a variety of countries. Surnames came late; these names were already in use as given names centuries earlier.

As a writer, the task of choosing a name for the child you have created is far more laborious than it would be for the normal parent. I have pored over piles of reference materials myself, seeking the appropriate name. It was this eternal, time-gnawing chore that yielded the *Writer's Digest Character-Naming Sourcebook*.

One thing to remember as you search: Many countries borrowed names from their neighbors or invaders. In twelfth century England, it was common for children to be given Saxon and English names as well as Arthurian legend names or names from Gaelic, French, Welsh, Celtic, Norse, Teutonic, German, Latin, Greek, etc. In Scotland, parents borrowed from the English, Welsh, Irish, French, Celtic and Gaelic. Now—at last—you have a ready source for the countries, without all the hours of tedium.

PART ONE

The Craft of Naming

by Hal Blythe and Charlie Sweet

Chapter One

The Importance of Names

You're looking for a good read. You pick up a pile of paperbacks and pore over the first few pages of each. You come across this opening paragraph:

The young man hurried out of the restaurant, hopped into a sports car, and flipped on the radio. Then, gunning his engine, he swerved out of the parking lot, leaving several patches of burnt rubber, nauseous exhaust fumes, and a tearful girl screaming his name.

Think you'll read on? Probably not. Yet the basic situation is certainly intriguing—a boy-girl conflict, exploding emotions, initial action, a familiar setting. But something's wrong; something is keeping you from reading just one more paragraph. What is it?

John D. MacDonald, in his introduction to Stephen King's *Night Shift*, provides a key insight into fiction writing. "Story," MacDonald claims, "is something happening to someone you have been led to care about." The opening paragraph above is certainly a scene, but is it a story? Does it make you concerned about the plight of the young man or the girl? Why not?

To figure the answer out, let's look at another version of that opening:

The sweat still oozing from his acne-covered pores, C. Bryce Arthur ran out of the 10-4 Truck Stop, hopped into his new Patrizio Turbo, and flipped on his CD player. Instantly, six speakers asked him the same question, "Will you still love me tomorrow?" Tromping on the accelerator, he fishtailed out of the parking lot, never once noticing a tear-stained Hannah Lee standing in her food-stained uniform beside the WELCOME TO LESLIE, Y'ALL sign.

The content of the second paragraph is basically the same as the first, with one important difference: the detail is specific. The characters, setting and objects are all given names—precise names. These specific names have the collective effect of sharpening the focus on a fuzzy picture. Instead of forcing readers to view the scene from a distance, the second paragraph draws them closer. Rather than seeing any boy or girl, the audience, in effect, says, "Oh, that's the Arthur boy and Hannah Lee." Readers spotting a Patrizio Turbo are certain it's an expensive Italian sports car. The 10-4 Truck Stop is definitely not a five-star restaurant renown for its haute cuisine. And the welcome sign places the scene in the small-town South.

MAKING THE AUDIENCE CARE

In classic understatement, Robert Frost once said that it's difficult to hate someone up close. Specific detail about people and their immediate surroundings individualizes the characters. As a result, readers are led to care about what happens.

It's the same technique you see on the six o'clock news. If a local station were to show you shots of people living in cardboard boxes, panhandling for their next meal on some anonymous blacktop, would you be very interested? Suppose the same station focused on one woman living in a Frigidaire box down on Fourth Street. She's lost her job . . . can't afford a new coat . . . eats out of McDonald's trash cans . . . her name is Ruth. See how each successive detail pulls you closer to Ruth?

Specific names also suggest what else is going on in a story. Precise details invite readers to participate in the story, to read between and beyond the lines. By stimulating your readers' curiosity and inductive powers, you prod them into making conclusions.

A boy with a name like C. Bryce Arthur who drives an Italian sports car is probably rich. Thus, he probably doesn't dine often at chez 10-4. Hannah Lee's stained uniform makes it obvious she waits tables at this greasy spoon. C. Bryce probably doesn't. The odds are, then, that the tears came from an argument that had something to do with the gap between the boy's and girl's social status.

REAL OR FICTIONAL NAME?

Effective writers recognize the value of specificity. They aren't satisfied with ballpark figures, approximate descriptions, generalized locales or vague characters. They realize this desire for precision involves more than simply choosing the more detailed verb ("limped" instead of "walked") or exact time ("last Thursday evening" instead of "a while back"). They know specific names are especially important to communicate precise information to readers.

In choosing specific names, fiction writers have two options: They can use real names or make them up. For the most part, writers invent their characters and hence the names of their characters. Occasionally, real-life characters are thrown into fiction, as when Hawthorne surrounds his fictional Hester Prynne with historical personages such as Governor Winthrop. Hawthorne sets *The Scarlet Letter* in historic Salem, while Ed McBain places his 87th Precinct on the mythical island of Isola. Lawrence Block's creation, Bernie Rhodenbarr, can pick any lock, and Block often has him open what is supposedly the best lock in the world, the Rabson, a brand that is also a Block invention.

Why create a fictional character, place and brand name rather than use a real one? The main advantage of the real is that it is already familiar to the reader. If your heroine journeys to Hollywood in the 1950s and runs into John Wayne, you don't have to use much physical description or characterization of the Duke. If she travels to Paris, readers already know the city's atmosphere of love.

But this advantage is also a problem. Suppose you want your heroine to fall in love with a Hollywood leading man and have a grand affair. Readers will know that historically the Duke did not see her. And what about the Duke's living relatives? Do you think they'll be happy with your accusations of infidelity? When Frederick Forsyth wrote *The Day of the Jackal*, he decided to stage an assassination attempt on the life of a real person, General Charles de Gaulle. Everyone knows that de Gaulle was not assassinated, so Forsyth's novel suffered a loss of suspense.

Fictional names overcome this problem because they are not tied to historical reality. Since she never lived, Hester Prynne may or may not admit to an affair with the Reverend Arthur Dimmesdale—the results are not on historical record. Vampires may well have plagued Stephen King's New Jerusalem because the town doesn't exist. And if you want your terrorist group to take over a San Diego eatery you named Chicken Charlie's, you open yourself up to a lot of possibilities. But if the same group targets a San Diego McDonald's, readers are very much acquainted with the actual results.

To create fictional names, then, you can choose from three large categories: characternyms are character names chosen to reveal something significant about the bearer; toponyms are place names (e.g., countries, rivers, towns) selected to identify a specific characteristic of a particular locale and the people who live there; resnyms, deriving from the Latin word *res* for "things," are names (often brand names) of material objects.

WHAT'S IN A NAME?

Henry James is famous for the engaging names he gave his characters. But he didn't just spontaneously come up with Christopher Newman or Isabel Archer. James kept a notebook in which he did nothing but record the names of people he knew or names he dreamed up. When he started writing his stories, he thumbed through this personal encyclopedia of names until he came to a suitable one, such as Frederick *Winter*bourne for the emotionally cold suitor of *Daisy* Miller, a young American girl who is, indeed, fresh as a daisy.

Writers today draw names from various sources. Most have atlases and roadmaps for geonyms, catalogs for resnyms, as well as *What to Name the Baby* and phone books for characters' names. The problem with such sources—even Henry James's notebooks—is that they provide only random lists of people, places and things.

The Chinese have a proverb that says, "The beginning of wisdom is learning to call things by their right name." Implicit in this Oriental pearl is the notion that names have meaning in themselves, that each name has an origin and a significance. If you were to find the name Sweet, Charles, in the phone book, all you'd learn is his address and phone number. However, if you looked up Charles in this book, you'd find it is the Teutonic word for "manly."

Fiction, then, differs from real life in its compression of reality and its desire to communicate some insight, theme or world view beyond surface events. Fiction carefully chooses the names of characters, places and objects for their resonance, their significance. In short, a rose by any other name doesn't necessarily smell as sweet. This book provides you a quick, easy-to-use reference for those fictional names.

Ultimately, choosing the right name gives you greater control over your reader's response to your story. And that is your goal every time you sit down to write.

Chapter Two

Characternyms

Even before you watched your first episode of *Magnum, P.I.*, you had a good idea of what to expect from the show's hero. Power . . . size . . . wealth. Your anticipation was conditioned by the title character's name, Magnum. If the beginning of wisdom is learning to call things by their right name, then the beginning of successful fiction is learning to call your characters by their right names. But subtlety is important. Medieval playwrights, appealing to an uneducated audience, peopled their dramas with such obviously tagged characters as Good Deeds, Faith and Everyman. Writers addressing children also must be simplistic, so there's no mistaking the roles played by He-Man or Goldilocks.

Occasionally, even in more sophisticated fiction, names provide blatant clues to a character's background. Dino Manelli is obviously a male of Italian descent, Bubba and Bo are sons of the South, and Slim is so skinny he has only one stripe on his pajamas.

Some names, though, are more suggestive. By implying the character's major motivation or primary role in the story, they elicit response either consciously or subconsciously, thus involving the reader without insulting his or her intelligence. Don't you wish your annual checkup could be given by Dr. Welby (Well-be)? Could a lawyer with the surname Mason build anything other than a strong case for you?

Whereas the audience starts with the name and figures out the personality, you as a writer have to work the other way around. Here are a few guidelines for creating suggestive names.

Pinpoint what makes your character tick. If you have a character you want to come across as honest, play around with names. Candide? No, Voltaire already has dibs on that one. How about Frank? Maybe Mary Candhor. You want clever? We used Wiley. Insightful? Hawkeye Pierce is still *M.A.S.H.*-ing pretense in syndication. Of course, every person in your story doesn't require a characternym, but you can be a little more imaginative than Tom, Dick and Mary.

Choose a name with the right sound. Pronounce possible names out loud. Often how a name strikes the ear will carry more weight than its meaning. In a book in which one man is named Bond and the other Scaramanga, is there any doubt which one is the villain? Conversely, how can anybody be afraid of a woodland creature named Papa Smurf? The name is basically nonsense, but Smurf has a pleasant ring to it. Herb Resnicow often uses hard sounds, especially plosives, for tough or bad guys and soft, euphonious consonants for the good guys.

Also, a memorable character's name should be easy to pronounce. Rambo trips off the tongue, but Pryzloskivitch twists the tongue. Avoid comic book cognomens outside the medium. Alliteratives like Clark Kent, Bruce Banner and Peter Parker may be fine for the four-color medium, but they detract from the seriousness with which readers will regard your character.

If you have two characters with the same name or similar-sounding names, try again. Think about it—if you write a mystery, won't you needlessly confuse your audience by naming the suspects Porter, Potter and Peters?

Obviously, even in this age of talking books, most readers don't read everything out loud. Readers are, however, Sunday drivers. Tongue twisters and similar-sounding names act as roadblocks, causing readers to lose the narrative flow. So, when choosing a name for its sound, spell it as phonetically as possible unless it's a commonly recognized name.

Pay attention to the name's source. Another way names evoke response is by tying your characters to history, ethnic origin and etymology. Remember that anonymous, honest character of yours? You might tag him with the first name Lincoln. Allusions are equally effective. Biblical, literary and mythological sources provide a rich treasury from which to draw names. To indicate your character is honest in the face of danger, you might call on the Old Testament for Daniel Lyons.

"Using meaningful names is a great idea," you say, "but I don't happen to be a scholar or a historian." Not to worry. That's what this book is all about. It will provide you with many sources from which to choose.

Consider the name's connotations. Sometimes the current cultural connotations of a name are more important than its meaning, sound or source. In the early 1960s a character named Debbie, by reminding audiences of Debbie Reynolds, suggested cute, cuddly and vivacious. Today, names like Skippy and Tipper have preppy connotations.

Keep in mind, too, whether you are writing for a national or regional audience. Billy Bob may be endearing in Texas, but to a non-Western reader the name may seem somewhat derisive.

Use the appropriate degree of subtlety. The key once again is the audience for whom your work is intended. When you're writing for a juvenile market, you should make your characters' personalities crystal clear. What would you name the hero of a youth-oriented mystery? Private eye I.C. Klews or Inspector Solvitt might do. But your three-inch brush isn't as effective for a mass adult audience. Suppose you're targeting your book for the *New York Times* best-seller list and it's time to name your newly created detective hero. You certainly wouldn't want to insult your readers' intelligence with a broad stroke. The name of the fake character in *Sleuth*, Inspector Doppler, simultaneously refers to doppelgänger ("double") and "plodder." Sam Spade, Dashiell Hammett's gumshoe, attains success by "digging" for clues (spadework, if you will).

Literary audiences necessitate the artist's fine-point. What would you name a sleuth intended for more sophisticated readers? Robert B. Parker decided on Spenser. With its allusion to the sixteenth-century poet who wrote *The Faerie Queene*, the name fits Parker's contemporary knight and his quest for truth and justice.

Collect names from the world around you. How conscious are you of everyday names and their usage? Do you know a Bill, Billy, William, Wilhelm or Willie? How do the differing forms of the same basic name affect your perception of the bearers? Are you aware that in the past few years the most popular name for newborn girls has been Jennifer? That one of the most common surnames in the National Basketball Association is Johnson? That all Chinese surnames are monosyllabic? That Nathaniel Hawthorne added the *w* to his last name to disguise the fact that his ancestor presided over the Salem witchcraft trials?

Keep your eyes and ears open. The next time you meet a Lesley Byrd-Smith at a cocktail party, find out if she hyphenates her name because she's British or because she kept her maiden name upon marriage. The answer might help you create a memorable character in your next story.

Every day in the newspapers you confront names from different cultures. Haven't you ever wondered what Sinead (O'Connor) means? The Russian origin of Boris (Yeltsin)? The next time you run across one of these famous names, try checking out its meaning in this book. It might be appropriate for your future, if not your immediate, needs.

ILLUSTRATING THE CHARACTERNYM

How important is the naming process? A few summers ago we started a detective novel, but after 35,000 words we realized that it wasn't going anywhere — except maybe to the trash can. The problem? We had named our investigator Price simply because we liked the name. The fact that we didn't have any rationale for the name we'd given our P.I. was our strongest clue that we lacked a firm grip on his personality.

Later we went back to the manuscript and started over, this time asking ourselves what motivated our character. Above all, we decided, he should be a protector of the weak, a guide for the helpless through troubled times. Yet we wanted to avoid the tough-guy cliché, the man whose physical prowess à la Mike Hammer carried the day.

We're not sure if it was our religious background, a surname spotted in the paper, or the sign on a local store, but our character's name suddenly came to us. Shepherd. And the moment we had that name, all the separate strands of our P.I.'s personality came together. Our novel took off and we were able to complete it before the summer ended.

A TEST

Remember that revised version of a paperback opening in chapter one? The names involved were actually chosen for more than just their specificity. An alert reader might be aware that this version has greater depth and richness because of the names' etymological significance.

For instance, Patricio not only sounds Italian, but if you looked it up in this book under Italian Male, you'd find it means "noble" — the sports car has class. Hannah comes from the Hebrew Female for "grace" — though she works at a truck stop, she has hidden personality traits that her profession tends to obscure. Bryce's name suggests exactly what he is, "son of a noble" (Anglo-Saxon Male), while Arthur signifies "like an eagle" (Anglo-Saxon Male). Even the town's name, while seemingly common and innocuous, implies the locale is isolated and cut off, for Leslie means "from the gray fortress" (Gaelic Female).

Chapter Three

Toponyms and Resnyms

TOPONYMS

Place names deserve as careful consideration as character names. Instead of throwing darts at a map of the United States when you need a locale, ask yourself some key questions: What do I want the locale to suggest? Can it aid characterization? Can it contribute to atmosphere? Can it foreshadow plot? Can it underscore theme?

For example, in the late 1930s, Jerry Siegel and Joe Shuster wanted a hero who reflected the traditional passage of growing up in rural America and then moving to the big city. As a result, they depicted young Clark being reared in Smallville, Kansas, before heading for Metropolis. The toponyms are obvious, but they were perfectly understandable by adolescent readers being introduced to the comic-book superhero Superman.

Toponyms, then, like characternyms, should be appropriate to the audience. When Samuel Butler wanted to create a perfect society for a more educated nineteenth-century British audience, he called his utopia Erewhon. Since Butler's main point was that a utopia was impossible, he hinted at this theme by naming his locale Erewhon—which, spelled backwards, suggests "Nowhere." Butler figured that his literate readership, capable of heavy mental gymnastics, was apt to unscramble his toponym and get the subtle satire. Shady Hill, John Cheever's fictional milieu, has a generic suburban feel to it but also sounds like a rest home or even a cemetery. This name, then, reinforces the theme of the suburbs as a place of spiritual decay and death.

Our main point again is that effective writers gain extra mileage by consciously choosing a place name. Whether you select a place name to develop character, to create mood, to generate plot, or to undergird your central purpose, be mindful of a major principle: *Place names usually reflect the locale's origin.*

This principle comprises several guidelines. The original settlers could have named their new home for a number of reasons:

- Prominent geographical features: Dry Ridge, Kentucky; Pleasant

Valley, Connecticut; Salt Lake City, Utah
- Prominent founder: Boonesborough, Kentucky; Pittsburgh, Pennsylvania; Hitchcocksville, Connecticut; Baltimore, Maryland
- Original hometown of settlers: Bristol (Connecticut and England); Cambridge, Massachusetts
- Religious influence: Shakertown, Kentucky; New Harmony, Indiana; Satan's Kingdom, Connecticut; Santa Barbara, California
- Expectation: Concord, Massachusetts; Niceville, Florida
- Ethnic origin: cities in lower New England show the English influence; cities in upper New England, the French (ditto Louisiana and eastern Missouri); Spanish in Florida, California, and parts of the Southwest; Scandinavian in Minnesota and Wisconsin; Irish around major Eastern cities; and Native American throughout the country, depending on each tribe's original habitat.

As a writer, you have a major choice to make. You can set your story in one of these real locations to take advantage of their existing connotations. Perhaps, for instance, your protagonist is a Cajun with abusive parents, so you explain that he ran away from his hometown of Port Sulfur, Louisiana—that is, he is escaping from hell. To suggest, on the other hand, your heroine had a rather serene childhood, you could divulge that her place of birth was Lake Placid, New York.

The problem with real places? You must be aware of the extant associations your readers have with the place. You could pick a town with a beautiful, soft-sounding name like Salem if you weren't aware of the witchcraft trials in Massachusetts, but you would be calling up negative associations in your readers' minds. A city that to the uninformed sounds romantic might in reality have racial tensions, high unemployment, heavy pollution, and a famous murder in the very year you set your story. Also, as science fiction writer Orson Scott Card notes, "if you use a real place name, you have less freedom to invent major landscape features."

If you create your own place, however, you can control to some degree your readers' responses. Name it Pleasantville. Describe its pastoral beauty. Relate how it was settled by families seeking religious freedom in the seventeenth century. Show its rich soil that allows for abundant growth.

This book can help you create an appropriate place. Let's say you need a locale for a story involving the Irish-American community where your protagonist grew up. Look under Irish or Gaelic. Select a male or female name that suggests the place's characteristic you wish to emphasize. You could call it Gothfraidh (peaceful), Nevyn (holy) or Teague (poet).

Traditionally, American locations are named by adding suffixes such as -ville, -burg, -ton, -town, -caster, -bury, -shire, -borough/boro, -field, City, -land or Corners. Some names graft on a description of the topography (Cape, Hills, Grove, Shore, Island, Ground, River, Creek, Lake, Valley, Springs, -ridge, -dale). Your fictional setting could be Teaguesboro, Massachusetts, which you inform your readers is a wealthy suburb of Boston. You would also be implying that the town's inhabitants are artistically inclined. And you've accomplished these associations subtly.

Finally, toponyms aren't limited to the names of towns and cities. You can create mountain ranges, deserts, rivers, lakes, roads, forests, even parks.

RESNYMS

Almost everybody has watched Wile E. Coyote's long-frustrated pursuit of his elusive quarry, the Roadrunner. Thus, we all know about the American conglomerate that has supplied Wile with products, devices and technology—Acme, makers of mechanisms from missiles to mousetraps. Warner Brothers couldn't have chosen a real manufacturing company for legal and practical reasons. No one company could possibly construct such a variety of defective devices and stay in business, so Warner Brothers invented Acme. In so doing, they chose a name that means "the best." This name suggests, on one hand, that even the cleverest technology is no match for the physical and mental speed of the Roadrunner. On the other hand, it is used ironically, given the quality of its products.

Resnyms, as mentioned, are names of imaginary products and companies, things that exist only in your fictional universe. Sometimes writers create resnyms for legal reasons; their plot involves something derogatory about a product. The movie *Class Action* centers on a trial over a make of automobile that tends to burst into flames on impact. However, had Gene Hackman uttered the word Pinto on-screen, Ford's lawsuits would have made the press quicker than the reviews. Similarly, if you want to have a bank launder Mafia moolah, you probably won't want to take on CitiCorp or Wells Fargo.

Even if your story presents a company/product in a favorable light, you can't rewrite history. If your hero founds and develops an automobile manufacturing company, you probably wouldn't call the owner Reggie Ford. History books are pretty clear on Henry's life and what he named his car. The solution? To write his inside look at the automobile industry, Arthur Hailey had to invent his own car company for *Wheels*. To check if your imaginary company is using the name of a company that really exists, you can consult Standard & Poor's *Register of Corporations, Directors and Executives*.

The basic principle for creating resnyms is essentially the same as that for toponyms. Say you decide you want to show your heroine conquering the restaurant industry with a chain of popular five-star eateries. You've already decided your heroine, Arabella, is the only daughter of poor German immigrants. Through cleverness, courage and good taste, she raises the capital to start the first restaurant. What do you call it? Start with your heroine's ethnic origin and look under German Male. How about Errando, which means "bold venture"?

Chapter Four

Naming for the Genres

H ow would you feel if you picked up a romance and discovered that the heroine and hero were Betty Lou and Waldo? How about a hardboiled P.I. named Percy? A western hero named J. Alfred De La Mare? A science fiction novel wherein the archon of Antares IV is Fred "The Hammer" Johnson?

APPROPRIATENESS

As a writer you must not only consider the general suitability of a name (its characternymic, toponymic or resnymic value), but also its generic appropriateness. Each specific category (science fiction, romance, mystery, comic book, western) has a particular makeup and trades on names that fit into its fictional arena. Readers of these genres have certain expectations that must be fulfilled or they will feel betrayed. Some of these conventions are admittedly artificial, but they have been, to a certain extent, validated by history and their repeated, successful use.

Think of these naming conventions as more than suggestions, perhaps as boundaries within which you still have a great deal of choice. Can you trespass? Probably not as a beginner. We remember reading an interview with a well-known editor of a romance line. She claimed that she had just turned down a manuscript because although the story was engaging and the historical period rendered with fair accuracy, every character in the book was given a monosyllabic name.

There's a principle larger than fiction writing involved here. You don't go to McDonald's because you crave Chateaubriand with sauce Bernaise. No matter how good the steak, it's not what you expect to find under the golden arches. Mack Bolan's war on the Mafia is not *War and Peace*. Readers coming to John D. MacDonald's *The Scarlet Ruse* do not expect the style, plot or characterization of *The Scarlet Letter*. The same expectations govern naming.

SCIENCE FICTION

To the outsider, many science fiction names seem alien — extraterrestrials whose names appear to be a random string of letters (Xmygrlyz) and distant worlds with more syllables than moons. The truth is, successful science fiction writers devote a lot of time to precise, meaningful nomenclature.

A case in point is Ben Bova, longtime editor of *Omni* and author of over seventy novels. When asked where he gets his names for hardware, planets and astronauts, Bova starts with a general explanation—"Same place as other writers"—and then explains his process. Although names occasionally pop magically into his head, much of his work is conscious. His home libraries in West Hartford and Naples contain books about technology and science, reference books, biographies of famous scientists, and even a few *What to Name the Baby*s.

Fantasy writers, Bova believes, tend to rely too heavily on J.R.R. Tolkien—Frodo lives, again and again. Interestingly, Tolkien himself cut his teeth on Old English epics, so his fantasy world resembles Anglo-Saxon mythology. Rather than turning to rehashed Tolkien, writers ought to seek out the original source of these names in this book. Simply look at "myth names" under various cultures (for example, Anglo-Saxon or Hebrew).

As a science fiction writer, Bova follows several principles of naming. An avid reader of scientific journals, he loves to use the latest jargon as well as arcane knowledge for place names. For instance, he might name a distant world after a scientist who recently made a leap in quantum physics. He also names characters after specific geographical locales. Alci, the mountains on the Russian-Chinese border, is also the name of a character who is headstrong and unbudging. Other favorite sources for names include historical astronomers and figures from Greek and Roman mythology (which is, after all, how our solar system was named). This book contains a pantheon of such legendary names. For the hero of this latest novel, *Mars*, Bova turned to Native American lore to come up with Jamie Waterman. To insure authenticity, Bova contacted Tony Hillerman, who writes mysteries centering on the Navaho population in New Mexico.

Bova also offers some specific advice about the naming of characters, places and things:

• Pay more attention to minor characters' names than those of major characters. The name may be the sole method you have of suggesting, for instance, a minor character's personality.

• Consider the nature/gist of your story. In a story about New Age believers, for example, Bova named his characters after jewels and crafted their personalities respectively on the supposed qualities of each stone.

• Rely more on obscure historical personages for names than on paying literary homage. Harlan Ellison claims that most beginning science fiction writers rip off Kafka's "Metamorphosis" (in other words, don't name your buglike creature Gregor).

• When creating resnyms, consider the object's function. Phasers and photon torpedoes sound like believable weapons, but butterfly bolts do not.

• Be consistent with your naming. For a distant planet story, don't have a couple named Peter and Qwo'lib (unless you're dealing with the problem of miscegenation). George Lucas achieved a strange consistency in his feature *THX 1138* by naming all his characters after California license plates. You'll never be able to create your own grammar with workable rules as well as sufficient vowels and consonants, so stick to borrowing one type of name.

Certain other tendencies dominate science fiction nomenclature. Characters on TV and in movies usually have broader, more obvious, easy-to-pronounce names. Darth is a combination of "death" and "dark" while Vader echoes both the Latin *pater* ("father") and "invader." Captain Picard is easy to say; *picaro* is Spanish for "knight" (appropriate for someone going boldly where no one has gone before).

Isaac Asimov tried to create names that were not present-day, but that sounded like they were real names. One of his most famous characters is R. Daneel (not "Daniel") Olivaw, where the R. stands for robot.

Tuckerisms abound in science fiction. Named for science fiction writer Bob Tucker, Tuckerism refers to the process of naming characters for friends/writers (that is, in jokes). Therefore, the distant sun Bova goes nova, on a far star Lord Burroughs goes ape, and future space explorers train at Camp DeSprague.

This book can help you with ethnic names. If you place a colony on the moon circa 2993, it shouldn't be populated with all Anglo-Saxon names. The settlement should be more representative of a cultural mix.

Men are usually known by their last name (on some primitive worlds they have only one name); women, by their first. But this principle is changing. Note how the heroine of the three *Alien* pictures is named simply Ripley.

Make the names, especially alien ones, pronounceable. Many Americans are sight-readers. If they can't pronounce a name, they won't read it, and you don't want to tie them up in the attempt.

Have the names reflect the prevailing cultural ethos. People escaping from a prison planet probably have harsh names if they're hardened criminals; softer names if they are oppressed. If these same people found a colony, names of places and offspring will suggest hope (for example, New Freedom, Phoenix, Second Chance). On the other hand, a new colony settled as a capitalist venture would probably have easy-to-remember, cut-and-dry, unemotional names (Hallas III, Rondal IV).

ROMANCE

Every word in a romance is geared to achieving a single effect — to elicit an emotional response from the reader. Most romance writers seem to do this instinctively. There are a number of social and psychological reasons for this, such as it is traditionally the woman who names the child. And so most women automatically know the importance of choosing the right name.

But that instinct is not quite enough. When crafting a well balanced romance, other factors play a vital role. The writer must be aware of every social factor that shapes and molds the characters of the story.

Here names can be of vital importance.

Take for example, Remington Steele. Perfect name for a British-born private investigator — strong, yet it hints at a certain sophistication. A heroine wouldn't expect Remington Steele to be a slightly overweight, Bronx-born detective in need of a shave. A name like Lumpy Kincaid would be more in keeping with the latter. But notice the hard consonant sounds of Kincaid. Even with the first name Lumpy, there's a sense that this character may be harsher than he appears — certainly more so than a man named Lumpy Bromley. Thus the heroine might be surprised to find out Lumpy isn't quite the pushover she first suspected, and that he's hiding many secrets from her.

In the same order, who would be the best woman C.E.O. — Lisa-Anne Cassidy, J.T. Crosby, or Racquel Dupres?

Actually, all three can be used depending on what the writer has in mind. Lisa-Anne Cassidy might do well in a southern corporation, especially a family business. J.T. Crosby sounds like the type of woman who rose through hard work and diligence, and one who may hold a grudge against a male-dominated workplace. Racquel Dupres would probably be the woman who used her wiles and sex appeal to get where she is. Or, she could easily be a nice girl from Louisiana or Southern Mississippi with Cajun roots. But what if she nicknamed herself Rockie, or Ellie? Two different images come to mind, one of a fierce tomboy, the other of a sweet, caring woman; and each of these types would have had a different experience rising through a modern corporation.

Also, ethnic roots will definitely flavor a character, no matter the occupation. But a writer must decide to hide the character's roots, or relish them. If the character is Jewish and working in a Jewish community, he might want to use the name Josias Shim'on, whereas if he grew up in an area that was hostile to his culture and he now worked in a similarly hostile area, he might use the name Joe Simmons instead.

Just as a writer wouldn't want a contemporary character to be laughed at over his/her name (unless that is the intent), there are important factors to think of when naming historical characters. During the Reformation period of England, the Puritans or Round-heads had names very different from the Cavaliers. Where a Cavalier might have a romantic name such as Amanda or Thorne, a Round-head would prefer a Biblical or Virtue name such as Honor, Innocent, Barnabus or Joseph.

But remember past prejudices. In the Middle Ages, traditional Jewish or Old Testament names such as Rebecca, Miriam and Isaac, would not have been used by Christians. Yet the Christians did prefer other Biblical (New Testament) names such as John, Peter or Mary.

In choosing a surname, lilt and balance play an important role. A name should have a complimentary syllable balance between the first and last name; i.e. if the first has one syllable, the last name should have two or more, if the first has two, then the last should be one or three syllables, etc.

After all, Jerry McCartney has a better sound to it than Jerry Cartney. Also keep in mind the way the consonants strike one another. Kyle Kenyon has a very harsh sound to it. If that is the impact the writer wants, then the name is fine, but said aloud, it just doesn't have as good a ring as Christopher Kenyon.

Focus on the way the letters and syllables blend together, not clash. The harder sounding letters: S, K, (hard) C, D, B, F, (hard) G, J, P, Q, T, V, Z, denote strength. The softer letters: A, (soft) C, (soft) R, (soft) G, L, N, H, I, E, O, M, U, Y, denote malleability. But even a soft letter can have a harsher effect depending on the other syllables of the name. Ashlyn will never be as strong a heroine as Adelaide. And by the same token, a man named Bob will never be as strong as Brader or Brent.

Also keep in mind the mental pictures a reader will have with certain names. Sasheen or Cenobia would be perfect choices for villainesses.

These names conjure up a slithering snake. The names Frost or Winter would not be as good for a heroine as Summer.

Remember, names stick with readers forever when they're done correctly. What romance reader can't name the book and author who used: Aislin and Wolfgar, Ruark and Shanna, Bronwyn and Stephen or Rhett and Scarlet.

MYSTERY

The two major subgenres of the mystery category have different views of the fictional world and of naming. The so-called classic/cozy/English/ locked-room school is more artificial with its isolated locales, its limited set of characters, and its incredible plots (from the dying clue to the red herring to the "I guess you're wondering why I've called you all together" scene). The characters' names reflect this artificiality—Hercule, Nero, Philo, Auguste, Lord Peter Wimsey.

On the other hand, the hard-boiled American school attempts to reproduce the gritty reality of life's mean streets. As such, the characters' names purport to be those of real people. In truth, however, even these names have a certain artificial quality to them. Hard-boiled writers, for instance, love characternyms, and the favored choices are heroes named after weapons: Hammer, Magnum, Cannon.

Another tendency with heroes' names is allusions. Ever since Raymond Chandler viewed his P.I.s as tarnished knights, detectives' names have followed the same path. Lew Archer is Ross Macdonald's homage to Sam Spade's dead partner, Miles Archer. Albert Samson's name (Sam's son) makes him sound like a literal descendant of Sam Spade, not to mention the strong man of Hebrew mythology.

Some names, like the soft-boiled Hercule and the hard-boiled Hunter, suggest strength. Jonathan Valin has Harry Stoner, and Burt Reynolds has played TV tecs named Stryker and Hawk. Some writers have suggested a subtle way to create strength through sound: Use a multisyllabic name that breaks between the double consonant—Hammer, Dan Tanna, Joe Mannix, Frank Furillo, Harry Callahan, Dave Brandstetter, Matt Scudder.

A new direction is ethnic names. Sara Paretsky's V.I. Warshawski is Polish; Tony Hillerman's Joe Leaphorn, Navaho; James Lee Burke's Dave Robicheaux, Cajun. While Anglo-Saxon names used to predominate (Nick and Nora Charles, Perry Mason), democratization has taken over, and now you will find Easy Rawlins and Kinsey Milhone.

Denver-based mystery writer Ann Williams has a few simple suggestions about characters' names. Since names make a first impression, she argues, "Make the names believable and manageable (easy-to-pronounce) or you turn off your readers. Stay away, too, from strange spellings. Don't reach for gimmicks." For Ann, the most jarring note is names that don't fit the character's ethnic origins, generation or locale. Also, "Writers who populate their books with people of ethnic groups other than their own had better do some serious research to seem credible."

Longtime writer Herb Resnicow offers a few basic naming tips for mystery writers:

• Give a character a nickname: Tom "Horsethief" Jonas and Tam "Haggismaker" Jones.

• Tie a physical description to a character's name: Big Hank, Skinny Henry and Moustache Pete. This lets you use "The big man said . . ." "The skinny lad whimpered . . . ," and "The moustachioed rascal drew his gun."

• Attach an occupation to the name: Sergeant Willis and Captain Corcoran. Again: "The Sergeant pulled out . . ." and "The Captain came in . . ."

• Call some characters by their position in the pecking order: Sir, Madame, Boss, Number One, Champ.

• When names become a problem, call some characters by their family relationship: Uncle, Gramps, Number-One Son, Sis.

• Name characters by their land of origin: the Pole, the Israeli, the Dutchman.

• Have some characters called by an outstanding or unusual physical characteristic: Baldy, Blondie, Gimp, Popeye.

• Give some characters names implying nobility: Lili von Schtupp, van der Mieste, de Provenzo, Count Cagliostro.

• Name them by age: the Old Man, the Kid, Boy, Baby.

• Call them by cultural or religious characteristic: The Sikh, the Chassid, the Vegetarian.

Randy Russell, a Kansas City writer, echoes Ann's point about avoiding names that are difficult to pronounce. He even confesses, "My own inability to pronounce the name of a central character to my own satisfaction has caused me to abandon novels I might otherwise have enjoyed reading." Names, Randy stresses, convey the tone of a book. "How seriously do you take a vampire-slayer named Buffy?"

In other words, at the moment the mystery field is wide open. What we suggest, though, is that you search for a characternym that encapsulates your protagonist's personality. Ian Fleming chose to name his hero after the ornithologist who lived in a nearby Jamaica estate. While James Bond is a real person's name, the double monosyllabic sound suggests strength, and "bond" is positive, being something of value (my word is my bond, a monetary bond).

WESTERNS

Texas author Bill Crider thinks names in fiction are very important. "I often sit and stare at my computer screen for a long time trying to come up with just the right one. It has to sound right to me, if not to anyone else." Where does Bill get these names? The phone book, other westerns, baby books and Tuckerisms. "I just pick out things I think sound Western and that fit the character."

Western characters tend to be named after places (the Durango Kid), physical appearance (Slim, Four-Fingers Jackson), professions (Cookie), local phenomena (Cactus Jack, Saleratus Bill, Dungaree Bob), religious influences (Micah, Jeremiah), and ethnic cultures (Cajun Bill, Injun Joe, or Zorro, which is Spanish for fox). Because of this book's ethnic organization and its many religious names, it is particularly helpful in this category.

James Reasoner writes series westerns (e.g. *Abilene, Cody's Law*), and thus the names of the major characters as well as supporting characters already are chosen by an editor before James sits down to write. James admits to using *4000 Names for Your Baby* (but not a phone book) and to a preference for the name Cody. Because he cross-refers his characters, creating fictional lineages (for example, the grandfather of a character in Series A may appear in Series B), he is especially careful of the names he chooses. James also has a fondness for names from classical mythology, such as Castor and Pollux Gilworth. Like the other categorists, he Tuckerizes. One of his favorite characters is named Doc and comes from a town called Ryanville, Texas. The explanation? James's buddy Dr. Bill Crider is from Alvin, Texas, home of Major League pitcher Nolan Ryan.

HORROR AND FANTASY

Horror/fantasy draw on historical/mythological/biblical sources for a great percentage of their names. These genres deal constantly with the universal struggle of good versus evil and the course of human history. The stories are effective in part in proportion to their readers' recognition of their supernatural elements. Stephen King's short story (not the

movie) "The Lawnmower Man" makes sense only if the audience real-
izes the strange figure "mowing" the front yard is Pan, from classical
mythology; with its mother of all battles against the father of all vampires, *Salem's Lot* plays upon its readers' knowledge of biblical struggles.

Since this genre often deals with aboriginal monsters and cultures,
older names are very important. Ardath Mayhar claims that one of the
main categories of imaginary beings is "the semioriginal being with its
roots and mythological sources." Thomas Millstead writes in *How to
Write Tales of Horror, Fantasy & Science Fiction* that "this genre,
above all others, thrusts below the surface to touch the subterranean
depths that lie within us all . . . to awaken that which was hidden and
secret. . . . In this effort, names have power — sometimes almost mysti-
cal power. They can be a formidable tool to reach those depths. When
properly chosen, they can guide the reader insinuatingly and almost
subliminally into the journey of illusion. Ineptly chosen, they can botch
the trip and dispel the magic."

If a particular category of names appeals to you (for example, Hindu),
you can check for myth names in this book under that heading.

ACTION-ADVENTURE

The key in this category, as in others, is tone. If you're writing a flamboy-
ant spy story à la Ian Fleming, you can choose broad, perhaps outlandish
names — Auric Goldfinger, Odd Job or Pussy Galore. On the other hand,
when John le Carré wrote serious explorations of the intelligence community, he gave his characters more commonplace, normal names such
as George Smiley and Alex Leamas. Michael Newton, who writes for the
Mack Bolan series, argues that the name's sound shapes the audience's
perception of the characters even before they get going.

OTHER CATEGORIES

Obviously many other genres exist, and each has its own tendencies.
Comic books today, for instance, are dominated by superheroes/metahu-
mans. Most are male, possess alliterative names (Peter Parker, Clark
Kent, Billy Batson, Bruce Banner), have violent noms du guerre (Wol-
verine, Cyclops, Pantha), and belong to groups with militant names (New
Warriors, Brigade, Team Titans).

Our major point is that each category has favored sources for names.
Once you have learned your category's inclinations, this book becomes
a quick reference tool for obtaining effective names.

PART TWO

The Name Lists

Anglo-Saxon

The hereditary surnames that we take for granted today were once unknown to the Anglo-Saxon population of England. In fact, very few people had any form of identification other than their given name. Occasionally, the names of nobility would include an epithet or description, such as Alfred the Great, Aethelflaed Lady of the Mercians, Harald Bluetooth, Edward the Confessor, or Harold Godwineson (son of Godwine).

In the century before the Norman invasion in 1066, more and more of the English were referred to by their occupation, a distinguishing feature, or their home — for example, Aiken the Miller, Sherard the Bald, or Aisley of York.

Anglo-Saxon parents searched hard to find distinctive names for their children, names that hadn't been used by an ancestor and weren't being used by anyone in the village or town. To aid in this endeavor, they turned to literature and also combined words and names to form unique names. Edwyn, for example, is a combination of the prefix Ed-, which means rich or noble, and Wyn, which means friend.

FEMALE

Acca — from Acca
Aedre — stream
Aefentid — evening
Aefre — forever
Aethelflaed — sister of King Edward
Aethelthryth — wife of King Ecgfrith
Alodie, Alodia — rich
Andswaru, Andsware — answer
Anlicnes, Anlicnisse — image
Annis — unity
Ar — mercy
Ardith — good war
Arianrod — silver wheel

Ashley, Aisley, Aisly — dwells at the ash-tree meadow
Audrey — noble strength
Bearrocscir — from Berkshire
Bernia, Beornia — battle-maid
Bisgu — cares
Bletsung — blessing
Bliss — happy
Blythe — happy
Bodicea, Bodiccea, Bodicia, Boadicea, Boudicea, Boudicca — victory, also queen of the Iceni
Brigantia — Yorkshire goddess
Brimlad — sea-way

Bysen — unique

Cartimandua — name of a queen of Brigantes

Catherine, Cathryn, Catheryn, Cate — innocent

Cearo — sorrow

Chelsea — port

Claennis — purity

Clover — clover

Coventina — name of a nymph

Cwen, Cwene — queen

Cyst — best

Daedbot — penance

Daisy — the day's eye

Darlene, Darline, Darelene, Darelle, Daryl, Darel — tenderly loved

Dawn — awakening

Devona — protector

Diera — from Diera

Dohtor — daughter

Don — mother goddess

Eacnung — bears children

Eadgyth — wife of Edward the Confessor

Eadignes — bliss

Easter, Eostre — myth name (goddess of the dawn)

Eda, Edina — wealthy

Edith, Editha, Edita, Edit, Edyt, Edyth — joyous

Edlyn, Edlynne, Edlynn, Edla, Eadlin, Edlin — princess

Edmee, Edmunda, Edmonda — wealthy defender

Edris, Edrys — wealthy ruler

Eldrida, Elda, Eldride — wise or prudent advisor

Elene — name of a poem

Elga — elf's spear

Ellenweorc — famous courage

Ellette — little elf

Elswyth — elf from the willow trees

Elva, Elvia — elf

Elvina, Elwine, Elwyna — friend of the elves

Engel — angel

Erlina, Erline, Erlene, Aerlene — elfin

Esma, Esme — kind defender

Estra — myth name

Etheswitha — name of a princess

Freya — queen of the gods

Garmangabis — a goddess worshipped in Lanchester

Hamia — a Syrian goddess

Harimilla — a Tungrian goddess

Hilda, Hild — war

Ifield — meaning unknown

Juliana — name of a poem

Kendra — prophetess

Linette, Lynet, Lynette — bird

Lora, Loretta — small sage one

Lyn, Lynn, Linn, Lynna, Lynne — a cascade

Mae, May — kinswomen

Maida, Mayda — maiden

Megan, Meghan — strong and capable

Mercia — from Mercia

Mildred — gentle advisor

Moira, Moire — bitter

Nelda — from the elder trees

Nerthus — name of a goddess

Odelia, Odella, Odelina, Odelinda, Odilia, Otha, Othilia, Odette, Ottilie, Odelyna, Odelyn — little, wealthy one

Ora — money

Orva—brave friend
Osberga, Osburga—name of a
    queen
Rheda—a goddess
Rowena—white-haired
Sibley—friendly
Silver—white
Shelley, Shelly—from the ledge
    meadow
Sulis—goddess who watched
    over Bath

Sunniva, Synne, Synnove,
    Sunn—gift of the sun
Taite, Tayte, Tate, Tait—
    pleasant and bright
Udele, Udela—wealthy
Viradecthis—a Tungrian
    goddess
Whitney—from the white island
Wilda—wild
Willa—desired
Wilona, Wilone—hoped for

MALE

Aart, Arth, Arthur, Artair—like
    an eagle
Abeodan—announce
Ablendan—blind
Abrecan—storm
Ace, Acey—unity
Acennan—brings
Acwellen, Acwel—kills
Adamnan—name of an abbot
Aelle—name of several kings
Aethelbald—a king of Mercia
Aethelbert—name of a king
Aethelfrith—name of a king
Aethelhere—name of a king
Aethelred—name of a king
Aethelwulf—name of a king
Agiefan, Agyfen—gives
Agilberht—name of a bishop
Aglaeca—fighter
Aheawan—cuts down
Ahebban—wages war
Ahreddan—rescues
Aidan—name of a saint
Aiken—oaken
Albinus—name of an abbot
Alchfrith—meaning unknown

Alden, Aldin, Alwin, Aldwyn—
    defender
Aldfrith—name of a king
Aldhelm—name of a bishop
Aldred—old advisor
Alfred—name of a king
Alger, Algar—noble spearman
Almund—defender of the temple
Alwalda—all-ruler
Amaethon—god of agriculture
Anbidian—patient
Ancenned—only child
Andettan—confesses
Andsaca—enemy
Andswarian, Andswaru—
    answers
Andweard, Andwearde,
    Andwyrdan—present
Anfeald—simple
Anhaga—solitary
Ann, Ane—graceful
Anna—name of a king
Anson—Ann's son
Anwealda—ruler
Archard, Archerd—sacred
Archibald—bold
Arian—spares

Arlice, Arlyss, Arlys, Arwyroe —
  honorable
Astyrian — remove
Atelic — horrible
Athelstan, Aethelstan — name of a
  king
Atol — hateful
Attor, Ator — venom
Atyhtan — entice
Audley — from the old meadow
Averil, Averill — born in April
Avery — rules the elves
Awiergan — cursed
Baecere — baker
Baldlice — bold
Bana, Banan — slayer
Banning — one who reads the
  banns
Bar — boar
Bawdewyn, Bawdewyne — bold
  friend
Bayen, Benwick, Benoic — from
  Ban
Beadurinc — warrior
Beadurof — bold in war
Bealohydig — enemy
Bearn — son
Bebeodan — commands
Bede — name of a historian
Beircheart, Bertie — intelligent
  army
Bellinus — name of a king
Beorn — warrior
Beornwulf — name of a king
Beowulf — intelligent wolf
Berkeley, Barclay — from the
  birch meadow
Bestandan — stands beside
Besyrwan — ensnares
Betlic — splendid

Birdoswald — from Birdoswald
Bliss — happy
Boniface — name of a saint
Borden, Bordan — from the boar
  valley
Bowden, Boden, Boyden,
  Bowdyn — messenger
Brecc — name of a king
Brice, Bryce — son of a nobleman
Broga, Brogan — terror
Bronson — son of the dark man
Brun, Bron — brown or dark
Byrtwold — meaning unknown
Cadman — warrior
Cadwallon — name of a king
Caedmon — poet
Caedwalla — name of a king
Caflice — brave
Camden, Camdene — from the
  winding valley
Ceawlin — name of a king
Cedd — name of a bishop
Cenwalh — name of a king
Ceolfrith — name of an abbot
Ceolwulf — name of a king
Cerdic — name of a king
Chad — name of a saint
Chapman — merchant
Cnut — name of a king
Colby — from the dark village
Corey — chosen
Courtland, Courtney, Courtnay —
  from the enclosed land
Cuthbert — famous, intelligent
Cynegils — name of a king
Cyneheard — meaning unknown
Cynewulf — name of a king
Cynn — family
Cynric, Cyneric — powerful
Cyst — best

Daegal, Dougal, Douglas —
  dweller by the dark stream
Dalston — from Dougal's place
Deman — judge
Denby — from the Danish
  settlement
Denisc — Danish
Deogol — secret
Derian — harm
Desmond — gracious defender
Devon, Devyn — from Devon
Drefan — trouble
Dreng — warrior
Dreogan — suffers
Drew — wise
Druce — son of Drew
Durwin, Durwyn — dear friend
Eadbert — name of a king
Eadig — blessed
Ealdian — live long
Earh — coward
Earl, Earle, Eorl — chief
Earm — wretched
Ebissa — meaning unknown
Ecgfrith — name of a king
Edgar, Edgard, Eadgard — lucky
  spearman
Edlin, Edlyn, Eadlyn — wealthy
  friend
Edmund, Edmond, Eamon —
  wealthy defender
Edred — name of a king
Edric — wealthy ruler
Edsel — from Ed's hall
Edson, Eddison — Ed's son
Edward, Eadward — guardian
Edwin, Edwyn, Eadwyn — valued
Edwy — name of a king
Egbert — name of a king
Egesa, Egeslic — terror

Eldred, Eldrid, Eldwin, Eldwyn —
  wise advisor
Ellen, Elne — courage
Elmer — noble
Erconberht — name of a king
Erian — ploughs
Ethelbald — name of a king
Ethelbert — name of a king
Ethelred — name of a king
Ethelwulf — name of a king
Fairfax — blond
Faran, Feran — advances
Farmon, Firman — traveler
Felix — name of a saint
Finan — name of a bishop
Fleming — from Flanders
Fraomar — name of a king
Freeman — free man
Fugol — bird
Fyren — wicked
Gaderian — gathers
Galan — sings
Gar, Garr — spear
Garberend — spear-bearer
Garrett, Gareth — strong spear
Geoffrey, Geoff — peaceful gift
Geraint — name of a king
Gifre — greedy
Gildas — name of a historian
Gimm — gem
Godric — rules with God
Godwine — friend of God
Gordon, Gordie, Gordy — from the
  cornered hill
Govannon — god of the forge
Graham, Grahem, Graeme,
  Gram — warring
Gremian — enrages
Grendel — legend name
Grimbold — fierce, bold

Grimm, Grimme — fierce
Grindan — sharp
Halig — holy
Halwende — lonely
Ham — home
Hengist — son of Wodan
Heolstor — darkness
Heorot — deer
Hererinc — hero
Heretoga — commander
Hilderinc — warrior
Hlaford — master
Hlisa — fame
Holt — wood
Hrothgar — legend name
Hrypa — the shouter
Ida — name of a king
Iden — wealthy
Ine — name of a king
Irenbend — iron bend
Irwin, Irwyn — sea lover
Isen — iron
Iuwine — friend
Jeffrey — peaceful gift
Kenric, Kendrick, Kendryck — fearless leader
Kent — white
Kenway — brave in war
Kimball, Kim — noble, brave
Landry — ruler
Lang, Lange, Leng — long
Lar — teaches
Larcwide — counsel
Lathrop — meaning unknown
Leanian — reward
Leax — salmon
Leof — beloved
Lidmann — sailor
List — cunning
Lucan — joins

Lufian — love
Lunden — from London
Lynn, Linn, Lyn, Lin — dwells by the torrent
Maccus — son of Gus
Magan — competent
Mann — vassal
Manton — from Mann's castle
Maponus — god of youth and music
Mars Leucetius — god worshipped at Bath
Maxwell — from Maccus's pool
Merton — from the farm by the sea
Modig — brave
Nechtan — name of a king
Nerian — protects
Newton — from the new estate
Nodens, Nodons — a British god
Norton — from the north farm
Norville, Norvel — from the north state
Nyle — desire
Octa, Octha — a son of Hengist
Odell, Odel — wealthy
Odon, Odin, Odi, Ody — wealthy defender
Offa — name of a king
Ord — spear
Ordway — warrior armed with a spear
Orlege — battle strife
Ormod — sad
Orvin, Orvyn — brave friend
Osric — divine ruler
Oswald — name of a king
Oswine — name of a king
Oswiu — name of a king
Oswy — name of a King

Oxa — ox
Page, Paige — page
Peada — name of a prince
Penda — name of a king
Pendragon — from the dragon's enclosed land
Penrith — from Penrith
Perry — pear tree
Piers, Pierce, Pearce — rock
Pleoh — danger
Prasutagus — name of a king
Putnam — dwells by the pond
Raedan, Raedbora — advises
Raedwald — name of a king
Ramm — ram
Rand — shield
Rawlins — son of Rolfe
Recene — quick
Renweard — guardian of the house
Rheged — from Rheged
Rice, Ryce — powerful
Rinan — rain
Rinc — warrior
Ripley — from Hrypa's meadow
Rodor — sky
Rowe, Roe, Ro, Row — red-haired
Roweson, Rowson, Ruadson — Rowe's son
Russell — fox
Rypan — plunders
Sar, Sarlic — pain
Scand — disgrace
Scead, Sceadu — shade
Sceotend — archer
Scowyrhta — shoemaker
Scrydan — clothes
Scur — storm
Seamere — tailor
Seaton — from Sai's estate

Seaver, Seber, Sever — fierce stronghold
Selwyn, Selwin — friend at court
Seward — guards the coast
Shelby — from the ledge farm
Sheldon — from the hill on the ledge
Shelley — from the ledge meadow
Shephard, Shepard — shepherd
Sheply — from the sheep meadow
Sherard — of glorious valor
Sherwin, Sherwyn — quick as the wind
Sibley — friendly
Sigebert — name of a king
Sihtric — name of a king
Slean — strikes
Slecg — hammer
Snell — bold
Stearc — severe
Stedman, Steadman — dwells at the farm
Stefn — stem
Stepan — exalts
Stewert, Stewart, Stuart — steward
Stillman — gentle
Stilwell — from the tranquil stream
Storm — storm
Strang — strong
Swift — swift
Swithun — name of a saint
Synn — sin
Tamar — from Tamar
Tedman, Tedmund, Theomund — wealthy defender
Tellan — considers
Temman — tame
Teon — harms

Tilian — strives

Tobrecan, Tolucan — destroys

Tobrytan — crushes

Toland, Tolan — from the taxed land

Torht, Torhte — bright

Torr — tower

Tracy, Trace, Tracey — brave

Tredan — tramples

Treddian — leaves

Trymian — encourages

Trymman — strengthens

Upton — from the high town

Verge — owns four acres of land

Wacian — watchful

Wade — moving

Waelfwulf — wolf of slaughter

Wallace, Wallis — stranger

Wann — dark

Ware — wise

Warian — attend

Wellington — from the wealthy estate

Werian — defends

Whitney — from the white island

Wilbur — dearly loved stronghold

Wilfrid — name of a saint

Willan — wishes

Winchell, Wynchell — drawer of water

Wine, Wyne — friend

Winter — year

Wirt, Wurt — worthy

Wissian — guide

Woden — king of the gods

Worthington — from the river's side

Wregan — accuses

Wright — tradesman

Wulf — wolf

Wulfgar — wolf spear

Wulfhere — name of a king

Wylie — enchanting

Wyman — fighter

Yrre — anger

Arabic

Arabic names are patronymic in origin, meaning that they are taken from the name of the father, but religious names are also extremely popular. Additionally, names can be descriptive and occupational. Adults are seldom called by their given name except by close friends and family. It is insulting to call any parent or older person by his or her given name.

Moslem names are taken from the names of the prophet Muhammad's immediate family and from the Koran. To help in this endeavor, Muslims combine names that incorporate the necessary religious names.

An Arab's complete name follows this order: professional title, given name, title (Inb, Bin or Binte), name of father and possibly a few ancestors (genitive indicator dropped), Abu or Um, followed by the name of the eldest son (if they have one), then a trade, place or tribe name. Sometimes, names are shorter and are made up of some combination of the above.

An example of a male name would be Katib Bahir Ben Kalil Kadir Hassan Abu Lufti Riyad. Translation: the Writer Bahir, son of Kalil, grandson of Kadir, great grandson of Hassan, father of Lufti, from the garden or tribe of Riyad. To most he would simply be known as Katib Ben Kalil Abu Lufti. A female name would be Najjareh Binte Nur Um Lufti. Translation: Najjareh, daughter of Nur, mother of Lufti.

Common genitive articles are:

Ibn — son of
Ben — son of
Binte — daughter of
Abu — father of
Um — mother of
Abd — servant
Al, El — definite article

FEMALE

Abia — great
Abir — fragrant
Abra — lesson
Adara — virgin
Adiba — polite
Adila — similar
Adiva — gentle
A'ishah, Aisha, Ayisha, Ayska, Asia, Ashia, Asha — lively
Akilah — wise
Ali — lion of God
Alima — knows dance and music
Almira — princess
Altair, Altaira — bird
Alula — first born
Alzena, Alzan, Alzina, Alzena — woman
Amal, Amala — bird
Amber — jewel
Ameerah, Amira — princess
Amineh — faithful
Amir — commanding
Ara — opinionated
Arub, Aruba — loves her husband
Asfoureh — bird
Asima, Azima — defender
Atia — ancient
Atiya — gift
Azhar, Azhara — flower
Azizah, Aziza — cherished
Bab — from the gateway
Bahira — sparkling
Baraka — white
Bashiyra, Bashira — joyful
Batul, Batula — virgin
Bibsbebe — lady
Buthaynah — of a beautiful body
Cantara — bridge

Fadilah — virtue
Faridah — unique
Fatima — meaning unknown
Fatin, Fatinah, Fatina — captivating
Halah — nimble
Hasna — beautiful
Iamar — moon
Intisar, Intisara, Intizara — triumphant
Jamilah, Jamila — beautiful
Jumanah — a silver pearl
Kalila — dearly love
Kamilah, Kamila — perfect
Karimah — giving
Khalidah — eternal
Leila, Laila — born during the night
Lina — delicate
Makarim — honorable
Manal — achieve
Manar, Manara — light
Mariam — Arabic form of Mary (bitter)
Maysun — has a beautiful face
Melek — angel
Meryl, Meriel, Muriel — myrrh
Muna — desire
Nada — giving
Nawar — flower
Noura, Nureh — light
Nudar, Nudara — gold
Oma — commanding
Rabi — spring
Rafa — happy
Rahimateh — grace
Raja — hope
Rana — behold

Rasha — gazelle
Rima — white antelope
Sabirah — of great patience
Sadira — ostrich running from water
Safa — innocent
Safiyyah — tranquil
Sagirah — little one
Sahar — awakening
Saidah — fortunate
Samar — conversations at night
Sameh — forgiver
Samirah — woman who entertains
Sara — from Sarah in the Bible (princess)
Sarsoureh — bug
Sharifah — noble

Shunnareh — pleasant
Tahirah — virginal
Talibah — scholar
Tarub — happy
Thurayya — star
Vega — falling
Waqi — falling
Widad — love
Yasmin, Yasmina, Yasmeen — jasmine
Zada, Zayda, Zaida — lucky
Zafirah — victory
Zahirah — dazzling
Zahrah, Zahra — white
Zara — princess
Zayna — beauty
Zenobia — father's ornament
Zuleika — fair, intelligent

MALE

Aban — meaning unknown
Abba — father
Abbas — lion
Abd al'alim — servant of the all-knowing
Abd al Bari — servant of Allah
Abd al Hakim — servant of the wise
Abd al Jabbar — servant of the mighty
Abd al Matin — servant of the strong
Abd al Qadir — servant of the capable
Abd al Rashid — servant of the guided
Abd al Sami — servant of the all-hearing
Abdel — servant
Abd-er-Rahman, Abdalrahman —

servant of the merciful one
Abdullah, Abdul — servant of God
Abu Bakr — companion of Muhammad
Adil — judicious
Adnan — meaning unknown
Ahmed — praiseworthy
Akil — intelligent
Akram — generous
Al'alim — omniscient
Altair — flying eagle
Amin — honest
Amir — prince
Ammar — builder
Arif — knowing
Asad — lion
Asfour — bird
Ashraf — honorable
Asim — defender
Aswad — black

Avicenna — myth name
Azzam — determined
Baghel — ox
Bahir — sparkling
Barakah — blessed
Bari — of Allah
Bashshar — brings good news
Boulus — Arabic form of Paul
　(small)
Bruhier — name of a Sultan
Butrus — Arabic form of Peter
　(stone)
Dabir — teacher
Dawud — Arabic form of David
　(beloved)
Diya al din — faithful
Eisa — Arabic form of Jesus
Fadil — generous
Fahd — lynx
Fakhir — proud
Farid — one of a kind
Faris — knight
Farran — baker
Faruq — wise
Fatin — intelligent
Ferran — baker
Gadi — my wealth
Gadiel — God is my wealth
Haddad — smith
Hakeem — ruler
Hakim — wise
Halim — gentle
Hamal — lamb
Hanna — Arabic form of John
　(gracious God)
Harb — war
Haroun, Harun — superior
Haroun al Rachid, Harun al
　Rachid — Aaron the upright
Hashim — destroys evil

Hassan — handsome
Husain — small beauty
Husam al Din — sword of faith
Ibrahim — Arabic form of
　Abraham (father of many)
Jabbar — mighty
Jabir — comforts
Ja'far — meaning unknown
Jamal, Jamil — handsome
Jawhar — jewel
Jedidiah — the hand
Jibril — archangel
Kadar, Kedar — strong
Kadin, Kaden, Khalil — companion
Kadir — green
Kalil — good friend
Kaliq — creative
Kamal, Kamil — perfection
Kardel — meaning unknown
Karif, Kareef — born during
　autumn
Karim, Kareem — generous
Kasib, Kaseeb — fertile
Kasim, Kaseem — divided
Kateb — writer
Khaldun, Khalid — eternal
Kharouf — lamb
Khayri — generous
Khayyat — tailor
Khoury — priest
Lufti — kind
Mahir — skilled
Makin, Makeen — strong
Malik — master
Marid — rebellious
Marwan — meaning unknown
Matin — strong
Moukib — last of the prophets
Mudawar — round
Muhammad, Hamid, Hammad,

Hamden, Hamdun, Humayd,
Mahmoud, Mahmud,
Mehemet — praised
Muhunnad — sword
Mukhtar — chosen
Munir — sparkling
Musa — Arabic form of Moses
(taken from the water)
Nabil — noble
Nabi Ulmalhamah — prophet of
war
Nadim — friend
Nadir — dearly loved
Najjar — carpenter
Nasim — fresh
Nasser — victorious
Nour, Nur — light
Omar, Omer, Ommar — first son
Qadir — capable
Qasim, Qaseem — divides
Rabi — breeze
Rahimat — grace
Ra'id — leader
Rakin — respectful
Rashad, Rashid — integrity
Riyad — garden
Sabih — handsome
Sabir — patient
Sadiq — friend
Saghir — short
Sahir — wakeful
Salim, Saleem, Salem — peace
Sami — all hearing

Samman — grocer
Saqr — falcon
Sarsour — bug
Sayyid — master
Shakir — grateful
Sharif — honest
Shunnar — bird
Sulaiman — Arabic form of
Solomon (peaceful)
Tabari — meaning unknown
Tahir — pure
Tamir — owns palm trees
Tarafah — tree
Tarif — unique
Tarik — meaning unknown
Taweel — tall
Taysir — makes easier
Umar, Umarah — meaning
unknown
Wafiyy — loyal
Wasim — handsome
Xavier — intelligent
Yacoub — Arabic form of Jacob
(supplants)
Yaman — meaning unknown
Yasin — rich
Yasir — rich
Yusuf — Arabic form of Joseph (He
adds)
Zafir — victorious
Zahid — altruistic
Zahir, Zuhayr — sparkling
Zaki — smart
Zero — empty

Armenian

Armenian surnames are chosen from place names and occupational names. They also can be patronymic and descriptive.

A few surnames:

Abovian
Bedrosian
Draskhankertsi
Haig
Hovhaness
Izmirlian

Karayan
Khodijian
Kooyumjian
Missirian
Narekatsi

FEMALE

Anahid — Armenian form of Diana (moon goddess)

Ankine — valuable

Anoush — sweet tempered

Armenouhie — woman from Armenia

Gadara, Gadarine — from the top of a mountain

Gayane — meaning unknown

Lucine — moon

Margarid — Armenian form of Margaret (pearl)

Miriam — biblical name (rebellious)

Nairi — from Armenia

Serpuhi, Sirpuhi — holy

Shakeh — meaning unknown

Shoushan — Armenian name for Susan (lily)

Siran — beautiful

Sirvat — beautiful rose

Takouhi — queen

Vartoughi — rose

Voshkie — golden

Zagir, Zagiri — flower

MALE

Antranig — first born

Ara — legend name

Armen — Armenian

Arshavir — meaning unknown

Artaxiad — name of a king

Athangelos — name of a historian

Avarair — from Avarair

Avedis — brings good news

Bedrosian — descended from Peter (rock)

Boghos — Armenian form of Paul (small)

Dickran, Dikran — name of a king

Eznik — name of a fifth-century philosopher

Garabed — forerunner

Ghoukas — Armenian form of Luke (light)

Hagop — Armenian form of James (supplants)

Haig — from the hedged field

Haroutyoun — resurrection

Hovan, Hoven, Hovhaness — God's gift

Hovsep — Armenian form Joseph (He adds)

Izmirlian — from Izmir

Jirair — hard-working

Karayan — dark

Kevork — farmer

Khachig — small cross

Kolb — from Kolb

Korian — name of a historian

Krikor — Armenian form of Gregory (watchful)

Magar — meaning unknown

Mesrop — name of a saint

Nishan — sign

Parounag — grateful

Sahak — Armenian form of Isaac (laughs)

Tiridates — name of a king

Vartan — giver of roses

Yervant — meaning unknown

Zeroun — wise

Arthurian Legend Names

From the twelfth through the fifteenth century, when many of the Arthur legends were written, surnames were usually given only to noblemen as a way of distinguishing them. The surnames were not hereditary. Given names only were used predominantly in Germany, Wales, England, France, Scotland and Ireland.

FEMALE

Acheflour, Blancheflor, Blancheflour — white flower

Ade — a mistress of Lancelot

Albiona — white

Angharat, Angharad — a love of Peredur

Anglides — mother of Alexandre (twelfth century)

Anna — Arthur's sister (twelfth century)

Argante — name of a queen (thirteenth century)

Astolat — Lady of Shalott; kills herself for the love of Lancelot (thirteenth century)

Avalon, Avilon, Avaron, Avarona — Arthur's burial place

Bedegrayne — name of a castle

Belakane — an African queen (thirteenth century)

Branwen, Branwyn — daughter of Llyr

Brengwain — meaning unknown

Camelot — Arthur's castle (twelfth century)

Chelinde, Chelinda — Tristan's grandmother

Clarine — mother of Lancelot

Clarissant — sister of Gawain

Condwiramurs — wife of Percival

Cotovatre — name of a lake

Creiddyladl — daughter of Llud

Cundry, Cundrie — woman who condemns Percival

Dechtire, Dechtere — meaning unknown

Deira — meaning unknown

Dummonia — meaning unknown

Elaine, Elayne, Helain — mother of Lancelot

Elizabeth — sister of Mark

Elsa — rescued by Percival

Enid, Enite, Enide — faithful/abused wife

Enygeus — grandmother of Percival

Ettard, Ettare — lover of Pelleas

Fenice — meaning unknown

Floree — meaning unknown

Florete — meaning unknown

Galiene — a lady

Ganieda — Merlin's sister

Graine, Grainne — taken from Igraine

Grisandole — a princess who dresses as a man

Guenloie — a queen

Guinevere, Guanhamara, Gvenour, Wenhaver, Quinevere, Guanhumora — Arthur's queen

Gwenddydd — Merlin's sister

Gwendolen — Arthur's wife

Gwendoloena — Merlin's wife

Gwenhwyfach — Guinevere's sister

Herzeloyde — Percival's mother

Iblis — wife of Lancelot

Igraine, Igerne, Ygerne, Igrayne — mother of Arthur

Isabella — meaning unknown

Isolde, Isoud, Ysolde, Isoude — lover of Tristan

Kundry — meaning unknown

Laudine — a widow

Lausanne — Lake Geneva

Lidoine — daughter of Cavalon

Llamrei — Arthur's horse

Luned, Lunet, Lunete — servant of Laudine

Lynet, Lynette — sister of Lyonors

Lyonesse, Lyones — wife of Gareth

Lyonet — sister of Lyones

Lyonors, Lysanor — mother of Boore

Maledysaunte — meaning unknown

Matilda — mother of Merlin

Melissa — meaning unknown

Modron — goddess; possible precursor of Morgan le Fey

Morcades — sister of Arthur

Morgan, Morgana — half-sister of Arthur, enchantress

Morguase, Morgawse, Margawse — mother of Gawain

Nineve, Nimue, Nimiane, Vivien, Viviane, Nyneve — the Lady of the Lake

Olwyn — daughter of a giant

Orguelleuse — an arrogant lady

Pridwyn, Prydwyn — name of Arthur's ship

Ragnall — Gawain's wife

Saveage — sister of Lyones

Sebille — a fairy

Shalott — land of Astolet

Sigune — Percival's cousin

Soredamors — Gawain's sister

Tryamon — a fairy princess

Yserone — meaning unknown

MALE

Aballach, Avalloc — father of Modron

Accalon — lover of Morgan le Fay (fifteenth century)

Aglaval, Aglarale, Aglaral — brother of Percival (fourteenth century)

Agravain — brother of Gawain (thirteenth century)

Alain — from Alain le Gros, one of the Fisher kings (thirteenth century)

Albion — Britain

Alexandre, Alixandre — nephew of

King Mark (twelfth century)

Aleyn—a Fisher king

Alis—brother of Cliges (twelfth century)

Amr, Anir—son of Arthur (ninth century)

Andret—King Mark's nephew (twelfth century)

Anguysh—father of Isolde

Antfortas—keeper of the grail (thirteenth century)

Antor, Auctor—foster father of Arthur (thirteenth century)

Apollo—uncle of Tristan

Arden—meaning unknown

Arthgallo—high honor

Arthur—king of Britain

Augwys—brother of Lot (thirteenth century)

Awarnach—a giant

Bagdemagus—father of Meleagant (twelfth century)

Baldulf—a knight (thirteenth century)

Balin, Balen—brother of Balaan (fifteenth century)

Ban—father of Lancelot (thirteenth century)

Beal—meaning unknown

Beaumains—white hands

Bedivere, Bedver, Bedwyr— returns Excalibur to the Lady of the Lake (thirteenth century)

Bellangere—son of Alixandre

Benigied Vran—meaning unknown

Benoyce—name of a kingdom (thirteenth century)

Bernlak, Bercilak, Bredbeddle— the Green Knight

Bersules—a knight

Bertram—a knight (twelfth century)

Bicoir—father of Arthur (seventh century)

Bladud—meaning unknown

Blaise—a cleric (thirteenth century)

Blamor—meaning unknown

Bleoberis—meaning unknown

Bliant—healer (thirteenth century)

Bodwyn—brother of Mark

Bohort, Bors—uncle of Arthur (thirteenth century)

Borre, Boarte, Lohoot—son of Arthur

Brademagus—meaning unknown

Bran—meaning unknown (sixth century)

Brandeles, Brandelis—a knight (fifteenth century)

Brangore, Brangorre, Brangoire—meaning unknown (thirteenth century)

Branor—a knight (thirteenth century)

Brennus, Brenius—a supposed king of Britain (fifteenth century)

Breuse, Brehus—a knight

Breri—a messenger

Briefbras—meaning unknown

Bryan—Lord of Pendragon

Cabal, Cafall—Arthur's dog (ninth century)

Cacamwri—servant

Cador—nephew of Arthur (thirteenth century)

Cadwallon—seventh-century king

Caerleon—name of a battle site

Cai, Che, Ke—variant of Kay, Arthur's brother

Caliburn, Caliborne, Caliborn, Caliburnus, Calibor—various names for Arthur's sword

Calles—meaning unknown

Calogrenant—a knight (twelfth century)

Camlann, Camelon—site of Arthur's last battle

Caradoc, Caradawc—son of Bran

Carmelide—Guinevere's father (thirteenth century)

Carrado—a knight

Catterick, Catterik—name of a battle

Cavalon—name of a king

Caw—name of a giant

Celidone, Celidon—meaning unknown

Chapalu, Cath—name of a monster

Clamedeus—name of a king

Clarion—name of a king

Claudas—name of a king

Corbenic—where the grail was kept

Crudel—name of a king

Culhwch—Arthur's nephew

Custennin—meaning unknown

Cymbeline—meaning unknown

Cynfarch—meaning unknown

Daguenet, Dagonet—Arthur's fool

Dinadan—friend of Tristan

Dinas—meaning unknown

Dodinel—meaning unknown

Domingart—meaning unknown

Dristan, Drystan—an advisor to Arthur

Druas—a murderer

Drudwyn—a knight

Drust—meaning unknown

Dudon—meaning unknown

Dynadin—a knight

Echoid—meaning unknown

Ector, Ektor—father of Arthur (fifteenth century)

Edern—meaning unknown

Eliaures—meaning unknown

Elidure—meaning unknown

Emyr—meaning unknown

Engres—a usurper

Erbin—meaning unknown

Erec, Erek—meaning unknown

Escalibor, Excalibur—Arthur's sword

Escanor—knight slain by Gawain

Escorant—meaning unknown

Evadeam—a dwarf

Evelake, Evalac—name of a king

Evrain—name of a king

Evrawg—meaning unknown

Feirefiz—a mulatto heathen who becomes Christian

Flollo—meaning unknown

Florence—son of Gawain

Frollo, Froille—killed by Arthur

Gahariet, Gaheris—sons of Lot

Gahmuret—Percival's father

Galahad—son of Lancelot

Galahalt, Galahault—name of a prince

Galatyn, Galantyne—Gawain's sword

Galeron—a knight
Gallehant—meaning unknown
Galvarium—a knight
Gareth—son of Lot
Gawain, Gauvain—eldest son of Lot
Gesnes—meaning unknown
Giflet, Girflet, Griflet—returns Excalibur to the lake
Gildas—meaning unknown
Girard—meaning unknown
Glais, Gais—Percival's grandfather
Glewlwyd—meaning unknown
Gorlois—Igraine's husband
Gorre, Gore—a kingdom
Gouvernail, Governayle, Gorvenal—a knight
Griffith, Griffyth—a murderer
Gringolet, Gringalet—Gawain's horse
Gryfflet—killed by Lancelot
Guerehes—brother of Gawain
Guiderius—meaning unknown
Guivret—a dwarf king
Gurgalan—a pagan king
Gwyr—meaning unknown
Hebron—meaning unknown
Hellekin—French lover of Morgan le Fay (thirteenth century)
Hoel—father of Isolde
Houdain, Houdenc—Tristan's dog
Howel—killed by Arthur
Huon—meaning unknown
Isdernus—knight of Arthur
Ither—killed by Percival
Johfrit—a knight
Kadyriath—meaning unknown

Kaherdin—brother of Isolde
Kanelingres—father of Tristan
Kardeiz—son of Percival
Kay, Kei—son of Ector
Kyner—meaning unknown
Lailoken—a fool
Lamorak, Lamorat—brother of Percival
Laodegan—meaning unknown
Laudegrance, Leodegraunce—father of Guinevere
Launcelot, Lancelot—knight of Arthur, lover of Guinevere
Launfal—a knight
Leodegan—Guinevere's father
Lionel—cousin of Lancelot
Llacheu—Arthur's son
Llew—meaning unknown
Lludd—name of a king
Llychlyn—meaning unknown
Loc—father of Erec
Lohengrin—son of Percival
Lot—name of a king
Lucan—brother of Arthur
Lucius—a Roman emperor
Mabon—a knight
Mabonagrain—a knight
Mabuz—ruler of Death Castle
Madoc—meaning unknown
Mador—accuser of Guinevere
Maheloas—lord of the Isle of Glass
Malduc—a wizard
Mariadok—King Mark's servant
Maris—meaning unknown
Mark—Tristan's uncle
Marrok—a knight thought to be a werewolf
Medrod—meaning unknown
Melchior—meaning unknown

Meleagant — kidnapped Guinevere

Melechan — Mordred's son

Meliadus, Meliodas — Tristan's father

Melwas — name of a king

Melyon — son of Mordred

Merlin — Arthur's tutor

Moraunt — meaning unknown

Mordrain — name of a king

Mordrayans — meaning unknown

Mordred, Modred — son/nephew of Arthur

Morgan Tud — a physician

Morholt, Morold — prince killed by Tristan

Nafiens — meaning unknown

Nantres, Nentres — name of a king

Nascien — meaning unknown

Nudd — a knight

Octha — enemy of Arthur

Ocvran — father of Guinevere

Osla — meaning unknown

Owain — son of Urien

Ozanna — meaning unknown

Padarn — meaning unknown

Palomydes, Palamedes — a knight

Pant — father of Lancelot

Passebreul — meaning unknown

Pellam — father of Pelles

Pellanor, Pellinore — name of a king

Pellean — Percival's father

Pelleas, Pelles — a Fisher king

Pendragon — meaning unknown

Percival, Perceval, Percyvelle, Parzifal, Parsifal — hero of several Arthurian stories

Peredur — meaning unknown

Peredurus — name of a king

Petrus — one of Joseph's disciples

Phelot — meaning unknown

Pheredin — meaning unknown

Rhongomyant — meaning unknown

Rhydderch — meaning unknown

Rion — a pagan giant

Rivalen — Tristan's father

Ron — meaning unknown

Ryence, Ryons, Royns — a Welsh king

Saffire — meaning unknown

Sagramour, Sagremor — a knight

Taliesin — sixth-century poet

Tentagil, Tintagel — land of Igraine

Tor — son of Pellinore

Tortain — meaning unknown

Trevrizent — Percival's uncle

Tristram, Tristan — a knight

Turquine — meaning unknown

Uriens, Urien — name of a king

Uther — Arthur's father

Uwaine, Uwayne — meaning unknown

Vortigern — name of a king

Vortimer — Vortigern's son

Yder, Ider — meaning unknown

Ysbaddaden — a giant

Basque

The Basques prefer religious and biblical given names. Most surnames are place names. Many of the modern surnames now have French or Spanish spellings and forms.

A few Basque surnames:

Barrena	Jauregi
Basterra	Mateo
Bilboa	Pasquale
Constano	Toussaint
Cristobal	Zdenek

FEMALE

Agurtzane, Ainhoa, Aitziber, Alona, Arama, Arrate — refers to the Virgin Mary

Aintzane — glory

Alazne — miracle

Alesandese — Basque feminine form of Alesander (helper of man)

Amaia — end

Andere — feminine form of Ander (masculine)

Argi — light

Arrosa — rose

Balere — strong

Barkarne, Barkarna — lonely

Bixenta — victory

Catalin — form of Katherine (pure)

Danele — feminine form of Danel (judge)

Edurne — snow

Eguskine, Eguskina — sunshine

Garaitz — victory

Gechina — graceful

Gotzone — angel

Igone — refers to Christ's Ascension

Kontxesi — refers to the Immaculate Conception

Mirari — miracle

Naiara, Naiaria — refers to the Virgin Mary

Nerea, Neria — mine

Osane — health

Tote — meaning unknown

Yanamari — bitter grace

Yera — reference to the Virgin Mary

Zurine, Zurina — white

MALE

Adiran—from the Adriatic
Ager—gatherer
Aingeru—messenger
Akil—from the Akil
Ander—Basque form of Andrew (manly)
Antton—praiseworthy
Asentzio—ascending
Benat—bear
Bingen, Bittor—conquers
Danel—Basque form of Daniel (judge)
Deunoro—all saints
Dunixi—Basque form of Dionysus (god of wine)
Edorta—Basque form of Edward (rich guardian)
Edrigu—Basque form of Richard (strong ruler)
Edur—wine
Elazar—help of God
Erromon—from Rome
Etor—steadfast
Gabirel—Basque form of Gabriel (God-given strength)
Gaizka—savior
Gentza—peace
Gotzon—messenger

Gurutz—Holy Cross
Iker—visits
Inaki, Inigo—ardent
Ixaka—laughs
Jakome—Basque form of James (supplanter)
Kemen—strong
Kerbasi—warrior
Mikel—godlike
Mikolas, Mikolaus—of the conquering people
Ortzi—meaning unknown
Palben—blond
Txanton—Basque for Joseph Anthony (He adds/priceless)
Txomin—like God
Ugutz—name for John the Baptist
Unai—shepherd
Urtzi—sky
Xabier, Xavier—owns a new house
Xanti—named for Saint James
Ximon, Ximun—God is heard
Yosu—God saves
Yuli—youthful
Zadornin—Saturn
Zigor—punishes
Zorion—happy

Celtic

There aren't any Celtic surnames per se. Surnames developed in the lands settled by the Celts—Manx, Wales, Scotland, Ireland, etc. The surnames (some of which are in part Celtic) of those areas developed separately and are listed by country in this book.

FEMALE

Adsaluta—myth name

Aife—a great warrior woman of myth

Aifric, Afric, Africa, Aphria—agreeable

Aigneis—pure

Ailidh—kind

Aina, Aine—joy

Aingeal—angel

Aithne, Aine—fire

Alanna, Alane, Alina, Aline, Alene—fair

Alastriona, Alastrine, Alastrina—defends mankind

Alice, Alys, Ailis, Elsha—noble

Alma—good

Andraste—victory

Annwn, Annwfn—myth name (the Otherworld)

Ardra—noble

Arienh—oath

Arlana, Arlene, Arela, Arleen, Arleta, Arlette, Arlina, Arline—an oath

Bab, Bav—meaning unknown

Berit, Birgit, Berta, Birte—splendid

Betha, Beatha—life

Blair—from the plain lands

Brangaine—character from Isolde legend

Branwen—sister of Bendigeidfran

Brenna—raven

Bretta, Bret, Brit, Brite, Brittany, Brita—from Britain

Briana—strong

Bricta—meaning unknown

Brid, Bride, Brighid, Breeda, Brigid, Brigitta, Brigitte, Birgit, Britta, Brietta, Brita, Brites, Brygid, Bridget, Birkita, Brit—strong

Brina—defender

Caoilfhionn, Keelin—slender and comely

Cara—friend

Carmel—from the vinyard

Cary, Carey—the dark one

Cinnia, Cinnie—beauty

Cordelia—of the sea

Coventina—water goddess

Daghda—meaning unknown

Dana—from Denmark

Dechtire — myth name (a nursemaid)

Deirdre — sorrowful

Deoch — myth name (a princess of Munster)

Diva, Deva, Devona, Divone, Deheune — divine one

Donella — dark-haired elfin girl

Donia — dark-skinned

Doreen, Doreena — moody

Edana, Ena — passionate

Edna, Ena, Ethne — fire

Enid — geist (spirit)

Epona — meaning unknown

Erina, Erin, Erie, Erea — from Ireland

Etain — a fairy

Evelyn, Engl, Evelina, Eveline — light

Fedelm — myth name (wife of Loegaire)

Fenella — of the white shoulders

Fianna — legendary tale

Findabair — myth name (daughter of Medb)

Fingula — myth name (daughter of Lyr)

Fiona — white or comely

Genevieve — white wave

Germaine — loud of voice

Gilda, Gildas — serves God

Ginerva, Ginebra, Ginessa — white as foam

Gitta — strong

Grania — love

Guennola — white

Guinevere, Guenevere, Gwenyver — white lady

Gwendolen, Gwendolin,

Gwyndolin, Gwenn, Gwynn — of the white brow

Gwenneth, Gweneth, Gwynith, Gwenith — blessed

Iona, Ione — from the king's island

Isold, Isolde, Isolda — the fair

Jennifer, Jennyfer, Jennyver, Jenny — white wave

Joyce — feminine of Jodoc

Keelin, Keely, Keelia — slender, comely

Kennocha — lovely

Lavena — joy

Leslie, Lesley — from the gray fortress

Linette, Linnette, Lynette, Lynet — grace

Lyonesse — little lion

Maureen, Moreen — great

Mavis, Mavelle, Mavie — songbird

Meadghbh, Maeveen, Mabina — nimble

Medb, Maeve — mythical queen

Melva, Melvina, Malvina — handmaiden

Meredith — protector of the sea

Moina, Moyna — mild

Morgan, Morgance, Morgane, Morgana — dweller of the sea

Morna — dearly loved

Morrigan — a war goddess

Moya, Moira, Mor — exceptional

Myrna, Merna, Mirna, Moina, Morna, Moyna — tender

Nantosuelta — meaning unknown

Neala, Nealie — ruler

Nola — famous

Oifa — myth name (sister of Ove)

Oilell — a mythical queen

Olwen, Olwyn — myth name
(daughter of Yspaddaden)

Oppida — meaning unknown

Oriana — blond

Ove — myth name (daughter of
Dearg)

Penarddun — myth name
(daughter of Beli)

Regan, Reaghan — nobility

Rhiannon — myth name (daughter
of Hefeydd)

Ronat — seal

Rowena — white, comely

Selma — comely

Ula — sea jewel

Una — white wave

Venetia — blessed

Wynne, Winnie, Wynnie — white
or fair

Yseult — fair

Zenevieva, Zinerva — pale

MALE

Adair — from the ford by the oak
trees

Ahern, Ahearn — lord of the
horses

Aiden, Aidan, Aodhan, Aodh — fire

Ailbe — meaning unknown

Ailill — myth name (king of
Connaught)

Airell — nobleman

Alan, Allen, Allan, Allyn —
handsome

Alanson — son of Allan

Angus, Anghus, Aengus,
Aonghus — exceptionally
strong

Annan, Anant — from the stream

Ansgar — warrior

Anwell, Anwyl — beloved

Anyon — anvil

Aod — myth name (son of Lyr)

Ap Owen — son of Owen

Arawn — myth name (king of the
Underworld)

Argyle — from the land of the Irish

Arlen, Arlin, Arlyn, Arlan — oath

Arthur, Artur, Art, Atty, Attie,

Arturo — strong as a bear

Baird — bard

Barry, Bairrfhionn, Barra,
Bearach, Bearchan — good
marksman

Beacan, Becan — small

Bedwyr — Arthurian legend name

Bendigeidfran — name of a king

Bevan, Bevin, Bevyn — young
soldier

Blaine, Blayne, Blane, Blainey,
Blayney — slender

Blair — from the plain

Boadhagh — meaning unknown

Bowden, Bowdyn, Boden, Bodyn,
Boyden, Boyd — blond

Bowen, Bowyn — son of Owen

Boynton — from the white river

Bran, Brann — raven

Brasil, Breasal, Basil — battle

Breanainn, Breandan, Bredon,
Brandan — sword

Brendan, Bran, Bram, Broin,
Brennan — raven

Brett, Bret — a Breton

Brian, Bryan, Bryant, Briant —
strong

Brice, Bryce — swift

Bricriu — myth name (the poison-
tongued)

Britomartus — meaning unknown

Burgess — citizen

Cachamwri — legend name (a
servant of Arthur)

Cadell — warring

Cadman — fighter

Calder — from the stony river

Calum — dove

Cameron, Camero, Camey —
crooked nose

Caoimhghin — gentle

Caradoc — dearly loved

Cardew — from the black fort

Carew, Carey, Cary — from the
fortress

Carney, Car, Carr, Cathaoir,
Cathair — fighter

Carrol, Carroll — champion

Casey — brave

Cassivellaunus, Caswallan —
Arthurian myth name

Cathal, Cahal, Conall, Connell —
strong in battle

Cathbad — meaning unknown

Cedric — chief

Celyddon — myth name (father of
Culhwch)

Chad — defence

Clust — myth name (son of
Clustfeinad)

Clustfeinad — myth name

Cocidius — myth name (a hunter
god)

Coinneach — handsome

Conall — myth name (Ulster
chieftain)

Conall Cernach — myth name
(Ulster chief)

Conan, Conant, Con, Conn,
Cuinn — wise

Conchobar — myth name (a hero)

Condan, Condon — dark-haired
wise man

Conlaoch — meaning unknown

Conn — myth name (son of Lir)

Connla — myth name (son of
Conn)

Conroy — persistent

Conway — hound of the plain

Corann — myth name (a druid)

Cormac, Cairbre, Carbry —
charioteer

Cradawg — myth name (son of
Bran)

Cuchulain — myth name (the
Hound of Ulster)

Culain, Culann — myth name (the
smith)

Culhwch — meaning unknown

Cullen — cub

Custennin — myth name (a giant)

Cynyr — meaning unknown

Dallas — dwells by the waterfall

Daman — demon

Darcy — dark

Dearg — son of Daghda

Dermot — free

Desmond — from south Munster

Devin, Devyn — poet

Dillion — faithful

Dinsmore — from the hill fort

Doane — from the sand hill

Donald, Don, Doyle, Doy,

Dughall, Dougal, Doughal—dark stranger

Donat, Donal, Domhnall, Donall, Doran, Dorran—stranger

Donnally, Donnelly—brave, dark man

Donnchadh, Donogh, Donaghy, Donovan—strong fighter

Doughlas, Douglas—dwells by the dark stream

Drem—myth name (son of Dremidydd)

Driscoll, Driscol, Driskell—interpreter

Druce—wise

Drudwyn—myth name (Mabon's dog)

Drummond—lives on the hill top

Duane, Dewain, Dwayne—song

Duer—hero

Duff, Dubv, Duffy—dark-faced

Duncan, Dunham—dark-skinned fighter

Dyfed—from Dyfed

Ea, Edan—fire

Eburacon—lives near the yew-tree estate

Efnisien—myth name (son of Euroswydd)

Egan, Eghan—ardent

Egomas—meaning unknown

Einion—anvil

Elidor—myth name (a monk)

Emrys—Celtic form of Ambrose (immortal)

Erim—meaning unknown

Evan—young fighter

Evnissyen—meaning unknown

Ewen, Ewan, Ewyn, Eoghann, Eoin—young

Farrel, Farrell—brave

Ferchar—myth name (son of Uisnech)

Ferdiad—meaning unknown

Ferghus, Fergus, Fearghus—manly

Ferris—rock

Fiacre, Fiacra—eagle

Fiallan—meaning unknown

Fiamain—meaning unknown

Finbar, Finnbar, Fynbar, Finnobarr—blond

Finian—handsome

Finn, Fingal—myth name

Floyd—gray

Forsa—meaning unknown

Gall—stranger

Galvin, Galvyn—sparrow

Gelban—meaning unknown

Gildas—serves God

Gilmore—serves Mary

Gilroy—serves the red-haired lord

Girard—meaning unknown

Glen, Glyn, Glenn—from the valley

Glifieu—myth name (son of Taran)

Gorsedd—myth name (from Arberth)

Gruddieu—myth name (son of Muriuel)

Guy—sensible

Gwalchmai—myth name, Arthurian legend (Gawain)

Gwawl—myth name (son of Clud)

Gwefl—myth name (son of Gwastad)

Gwern—myth name (son of Matholwch)

Gwernach — myth name

Gwri — of the golden hair

Gwynham — myth name (father of Teithi)

Hafgan — myth name

Halwn — meaning unknown

Hefeydd — myth name (father of Rhiannon)

Heilyn — myth name (son of Gwyn)

Henbeddestr — fastest man

Henwas — myth name (brother of Henbeddestr)

Herne — myth name (a hunter god)

Hoel — meaning unknown

Huarwar — myth name (son of Halwn)

Hueil — myth name (son of Caw)

Huon — meaning unknown

Iden — wealthy

Innis, Inness — from the island

Irvin, Irven, Irvyn, Irving — white

Kane, Kayne — intelligent

Karney, Kearney — fighter

Keane, Keene — tall and handsome

Kegan, Keegan, Keaghan — son of Egan

Keir — dark-skinned

Kelvin, Kelvyn, Kelwin, Kelwyn — from the narrow river

Kendall, Kendal, Kendhal — from the bright valley

Kenneth — handsome

Kent, Kentigern — head chief

Kermit, Kermode — son of Diarmaid

Kerry, Keary — dark

Kerwin, Kerwyn, Kirwin, Kirwyn, Kieran — dark-skinned

Kevin, Kevyn, Kevan — gentle

Killian, Kilian — blind

Kunagnos — wise

Kynthelig — myth name (a guide)

Lairgnen — myth name (of Connaught)

Lee, Leigh — healer

Leith — meadow

Lesley, Leslie — from the gray fortress

Lincoln — from the settlement by the pool

Lir — a mythical king

Llewelyn — ruler

Lloyd — gray

Llyr — a mythical king

Luxovious — myth name (god of Luxeuil)

Mabon — myth name (god of youth)

Mac, Mack — son of

Maccus — hammer

Macklin, Macklyn — son of Flann

Maddox, Maddock — beneficent

Malcolm — servant of Saint Columba

Malvin, Malvyn, Melvin, Melvyn, Melville — leader

Matholwch — myth name

Medr — myth name

Medredydd — myth name (son of Medredydd)

Menw — myth name (a wizard)

Merlin, Merlyn — from the hill over the sea

Morfran — myth name (an ugly demon)

Morgan, Morven, Morvyn, Mariner, Marvin, Marvyn, Moryn, Murray, Murry—lives by the sea
Mungo—lovable
Murdoc, Murdoch, Murdock—seaman
Murtagh—protects the sea
Mynogan—myth name (father of Beli)
Naois—myth name (a warrior)
Neal, Neil, Nealon, Nell, Neale, Niall, Neill, Niallan, Nyle—champion
Nels—chief
Nelson—son of Neil
Nemausus—myth name (god of Nimes)
Newlin, Newlyn—from the new spring
Niece, Neese—choice
Nisien—myth name (son of Euroswydd)
Nolan, Noland—noble
Orin, Oran—white
Oscar, Oskar, Osker, Osckar—jumping fighter
Ossian, Oisin—meaning unknown
Owen, Owin, Owyn—young fighter
Pendaran—meaning unknown
Perth, Pert—from the thorn-bush thicket
Phelan—wolf
Powell—son of Howell
Pryderi—care
Pwyll—myth name (lord of Annwn)
Quin, Quinn—wise

Regan, Reghan, Reagan, Reaghan—regal
Rivalin—meaning unknown
Ronan—oath
Roy—red-haired
Sativola—name of a saint
Sawyer—cuts timber
Scilti—legend name (messenger of Arthur)
Setanta—myth name (son of Sualtam)
Sheridan—untamed
Sidwell—meaning unknown
Sloan, Sloane—fighter
Sugn—myth name (son of Sugnedudd)
Tadhg—myth name (a prince of Munster)
Taliesin—myth name (a bard)
Tanguy—fighter
Taran—meaning unknown
Teague, Teaghue—bard
Teirtu—meaning unknown
Teithi—myth name (son of Gwynham)
Tegid—meaning unknown
Teyrnon, Tiernan, Tiernay—regal
Torrey, Tory—lives by the tower
Trahern—strong as iron
Tremayne, Tremaine—from the town encircled by stone
Trevor—wise
Tuireann—meaning unknown
Turi—bear
Twrch Trwyth—myth name
Uchdryd—myth name (Cross-beard)
Uisnech, Usenech—meaning unknown

Usk-water — meaning unknown

Varden, Vardon — from the green
    hill

Varney — from the alder grove

Vaughn — small

Weylin, Weylyn — son of the wolf

Wynne — fair

York — yew-tree

Yspaddaden — myth name (father
    of Olwyn)

Czechoslovakian

Czechoslovakian names are taken from descriptive, patronymic, occupational and place names. Overall, they tend to be short, and female surnames always end in -ova or -a.

A few Czech surnames:

Chaloupek	Krizova
Demetr	Leva
Demkakova	Tesar
Divis	Tichacekova
Kopecky	Zeleny

FEMALE

Alzbeta — Czechoslovakian form of Elizabeth (consecrated to God)

Anezka, Anicka — Czechoslovakian for Agnes (pure)

Bela, Bel, Belia, Bell — white

Bozena — meaning unknown

Capeka — little stork

Cermaka — robin

Frantiska — free

Jana — God's gift

Jirina — feminine form of Jirka (farmer)

Krasava, Krasna — beautiful

Libuse — myth name

Ludmila — loved by the people

Marenka, Maruska — bitter

Milada — my love

Milka, Mila — industrious

Miroslava, Mirka — tranquil

Otka — lucky

Pavla — feminine form of Pavlov (small)

Rusalka — wood sprite

Ruza — rose

Svetla — gift

Vlasta — myth name

Zelenka — little green one

Zophie — Czechoslovakian form of Sophie (wise)

MALE

Bednar — cooper

Benes — Czechoslovakian for Benedict (blessed)

Bily, Bilko — white

Bohumil, Bohous — God's peace

Brlety — searcher

Buciac — thick
Capek — little stork
Cermak — robin
Cerny — black
Cestmir — fortress
Chval — flattery
Damek — of the earth
Dudek — bagpiper
Eda — wealthy guardian
Ferda — brave
Fleischaker — butcher
Franta — free
Greguska — watchful
Hlinka — burns lime
Hnedy — brown
Holic — barber
Honza — gift from God
Hrusosky — dwells near the pear
    tree
Hudak — blond
Jarda — myth name
Jaroslav — myth name
Jirka — farmer
Jozka — God will multiply
Kafka — bird
Kopecky — hill
Kovar — smith
Kozel — goat
Kral — king
Kramoris — merchant
Krany — short
Krejci — tailor
Krocka — moves slowly
Kubas — supplanter
Kusner — furrier
Laco — famous ruler
Ladislav, Lada — meaning
    unknown
Lev — lion
Lojza — famous warrior

Martinek — warring
Miloslav — loves glory
Mirek — peace
Miroslav — peaceful glory
Mlynar — miller
Molner — miller
Mroz — walrus
Novak — newcomer
Ondrus — manly
Otik — wealthy
Pavlov, Pafko — Czechoslovakian
    for son of Paul (small)
Pekar — baker
Pepik — God will add
Peterka — stone
Petrov — Peterka's son
Polak — from Poland
Praza, Lomsky, Lomy — from
    Prague
Reznik — butcher
Risa — Czechoslovakian form of
    Richard (strong ruler)
Rostislav — meaning unknown
Ryba — first
Rybar — fisherman
Silny — strong
Siman — heard
Slansky — salt
Standa, Stanislav — camp glory
Svec — shoemaker
Tesar — carpenter
Tomik, Toman —
    Czechoslovakian form of
    Thomas (twin)
Tonda — meaning unknown
Vargovic — has big lips
Vasek — victorious
Vrba — willow
Zapotocky — from beyond the
    brook
Zeleny — green

Danish

Danish surnames began in the late Middle Ages, but not until the nineteenth century were they used regularly as hereditary names. Even in the nineteenth century, most people continued to use just their given name without any other title.

In fact, the government was forced to intervene to get people to use surnames. In 1828, the government declared that children should receive both a given and family name at birth. An 1860 act made surnames permanent.

Unfortunately, most of the Danish people simply added son (-sen) or daughter (-datter) to the father's name, which produced an inordinate number of -sen names. To help counteract this trend, in 1904 the government began encouraging Danish people to change their surnames. As a result, many kept their -sen suffixes and just added a hyphen along with their occupation.

A few Danish surnames:

Andersen	Fabricus
Bang	Frederiksen
Christiansen	Kirkegard
Dinesen	Kristoffersen
Dyhr	Larsen

FEMALE

Abellona — mannish

Agneta — pure

Ailsa — Danish form of Elizabeth (consecrated to God)

Almeta — pearl

Andrea — feminine form of Anders (masculine)

Annelise — graceful light

Annemette — bitter pearl

Arvada — eagle

Astrid — divine strength

Bergitte, Britta — Danish form of Bridget (strong)

Bitten — good

Clady — Danish form of Claudia (lame)

Dagmar — glory of the Danes

Dana — from Denmark

Dorothea — Danish form of Dorothy (God's gift)

Ebba — strength

Else — Danish form of Elizabeth (consecrated to God)

Eva — Danish form of Eve (life)

Federikke — feminine form of Frederik (peaceful ruler)

Gelsomina — jasmine

Gjerta — protection

Gudrun — wise

Gytha — warring

Hanne — feminine form of Hans (God's gift)

Hedvig — meaning unknown

Inga, Inger — daughter of a hero

Ingeborg — Ing's protection

Ingelise — Ing's grace

Jensine — God is generous

Karen, Katrine — pure

Kirsten, Kristine — Christian

Kolinka — born to the conquering people

Laila — night

Larine, Larina — feminine form of Lars (laurel)

Lisbet, Lise — Danish form of Elizabeth (consecrated to God)

Margarethe, Meta — Danish form of Margaret (pearl)

Mettalise — graceful pearl

Nielsine — feminine of Neils (champion)

Petrine, Pedrine — feminine of Pedar (rock)

Rigmor — myth name

Saffi — wise

Sigrid — victorious counselor

Sorine, Sorina — feminine form of Sorin (of Thor)

Stinne, Stina — Christian

Thora, Thyra — feminine form of Thor (thunder)

Trudel — strong

Vibeke — little woman

Wilhelmine — resolute protector

MALE

Anders, Anker — Danish form of Andrew (manly)

Aren — eagle

Arend — Danish form of Arnold (eagle)

Argus — vigilant

Axel — father of peace

Balduin — bold

Bardo — Danish form of Bartholomew (farmer)

Bent — blessed

Berde, Brede — glacier

Bodil, Bo — commanding

Caesar — long hair

Christian — believes in Christ

Christiansen — son of the Christian

Christoffer — Christ-bearer

Christofferson — son of Christoffer

Dane — from Denmark

Ejnar — warrior

Enok — meaning unknown

Erik — powerful

Eskild — meaning unknown

Frans, Franz — free

Frederik — peaceful ruler

Fritz — free

Gregos — watchful

Hans — God's gift

Harald—war chief

Henrik, Henning—Danish form of Henry (rules the home)

Hjalmar—meaning unknown

Holgar, Holger—meaning unknown

Jakob—Danish form of Jacob (supplanter)

Jens, Jen, Joen—Danish form of John (God is gracious)

Joren, Joris, Jory, Jorgen—farmer

Josef—Danish form of Joseph (He adds)

Karl—manly

Klaus—Danish form of Nicholas (people's victory)

Knud—kind

Kolinkar—born to the conquering people

Lars, Lauritz—laurel

Magnus—great

Mikkel—Danish form of Michael (God-like)

Mogens—powerful

Niel—champion

Niels, Niles, Nils—son of Niel

Olaf, Ole—family

Pedar—rock

Poul—little

Soren—Danish form of Thor (thunder)

Svend—young man

Tage—day

Thor—myth name (god of thunder)

Ulrik—ruler of all

Vilhelm—Danish form of William (determined protector)

Dutch

Hereditary surnames began in the thirteenth century. By the seventeenth century, the lower classes were also using surnames. Most surnames began as patronymics but now encompass occupational, place and descriptive names.

Common articles are:

van (unlike *von* in German, *van* does not indicate nobility) — of
de — the (used with nicknames and, on occasion, occupational names)
van den — from the (used with place names)
van der — from the
ver — combination of van and der
ter, tor, ten, tom — at the (used with place names)
-sen, -sze, -sz, -se — son
het — the
't — the
op, on — from a farm
-man — used with place names, indicating the bearer is from there

Some Dutch surnames:

Carstens	Kersten
Christoffels	Korstiaan
Citroen	Rossevelt
Dekens	Vander Klei
Dekker	Van Dych

FEMALE

Adrie — from the Adriatic
Aleen, Alene, Aline, Alina — alone
Alida — noble
Alva — meaning unknown
Anke, Anika, Anki — Dutch form
   of Anne (graceful)

Annemie — bitter grace
Arabella — beautiful
Betje — devoted to God
Brandy, Brande — meaning
   unknown
Edda — poetic

Francisca—free
Grishilde, Griseldis, Grushilda—
gray battle-maid
Gusta, Gust—feminine form of
Gustaaf (staff of God)
Hendrika—rules the home
Lina, Lien—pure
Mahault—Dutch form of Matilda
(strong battle-maid)

Mina—protector
Rozamond—known defender
Saskia—meaning unknown
Skye, Skyla, Schyler, Skylar—
sheltering
Sofie—wise
Sybylla, Sibylla—prophet
Wigburg—young

MALE

Ambrosius—divine
Barend—bear
Bartholomeus—farmer
Basilius—kingly
Berg—mountain
Bleecker—bleacher of cloth
Bonifacius—does good
Bram—father
Cecilius—blind
Claudios—lame
Clementius—merciful
Dehaan—cock
Deman—tame
Devisser—fisherman
Devoss—fox
Devries—Frisian
Dewitt—white
Dirck, Dirk—Dutch forms of
Theodoric (God's gift)
Dwight—blond
Egidius—youthful
Espen—bear of God
Eugenius—noble
Eustatius—peaceful
Everhart—boar brave
Geldersman—from Guelders
Godewyn—good friend
Gottfried—divinely peaceful
Gotthard—divine, firm

Gregor—vigilant
Groot—large
Harold—strong fighter
Henrick—rules the home
Jan—Dutch form of John (God is
gracious)
Jilt—money
Karel—strong
Koenraad—bold
Krisoijn—curly-haired
Lange, Lang—tall
Larry, Lars, Larz, Lauritz—laurel
Mogens—power
Narve—strong
Nicolaas—victorious army
Noach—comfort
Roosevelt—from the rose field
Schuyler—shelter
Smedt, Smid, Smit—smith
Stille—silent
Ten Eyck—lives at the oak
Ter Heide—lives at the heath
Theodorus—gift from God
Tiebout—bold
Van—of
Van Aken—from Aachen
Vanderbilt, Vandenberg—from
the hill
Vanderpool—from the pool

Vanderveer—from the ferry
Vandyke—from the dike
Van Eych—from the oak
Van Ness—of the headland
Verbrugge—from the bridge
Vogel—bird

Vromme—wise
Wevers—weaver
Wit—white
Woudman—forester
Zeeman—sea man

Egyptian

The Ptolemaic rulers, Roman Emperors and Pharaohs of Egypt could have a series of names and titles, but usually a two- or three-name system went as follows:

1. A name relating to the god Horus (names that end with -re or -ra) that also represented the bearer as a ruler of Earth and a divine spirit, and ruler of all Egypt, both North and South.

2. The individual's given name.

An example of a full name would be *Sahura Amen*.

The Moslem settlers of the region use the rules listed in the sections of this book on Indian and Arabic names. Other settlers use the naming system of their native tribe or land. Thus, there are no purely Egyptian surnames.

FEMALE

Ain—priceless
Akila—intelligent
Amunet—myth name (goddess of mystery)
Anat—myth name (a wife of Seth)
Anippe—daughter of the Nile
Astarte—myth name (a wife of Seth)
Auset—myth name (another name for Isis)
Aziza—precious
Bahiti—fortune
Bast—myth name (personification of the heat of the sun)
Bastet—myth name (cat)
Bennu—eagle
Chione—myth name (daughter of the Nile)
Cleopatra—name of a queen

Dendera—from Dendera
Dalila—gentle
Echidna—myth name (a monster)
Edjo—myth name (another form of Uadjit)
Eshe—life
Femi—love
Fukayna—intelligent
Habibah—loved
Hafsah—married to the prophet
Halima—gentle
Haqikah—honest
Hasina—good
Hathor, Hathor-Sakmet—myth name (goddess of destruction)
Hatshepsut—name of a queen
Hehet—myth name (goddess of the immeasurable)

Heqet — myth name (a frog-headed goddess)

Ife — love

Isis — myth name (goddess of magic)

Jamila — beauty

Jendayi — thankful

Kakra — a twin

Kamilah — perfection

Kanika — black

Keket — myth name (goddess of darkness)

Kesi — born of a troubled father

Khepri — morning sun

Kissa — sister of twins

Lapis — named for the lapis stone

Layla — born at night

Lotus — lotus flower

Maat — myth name (goddess of order and justice)

Mafuane — soil

Maibe — grave

Mandisa — sweet

Masika — born during rain

Meht-urt — represented by a cow

Memphis — myth name

Mert, Mert-sekert — lover of silence

Mesi — water

Meskhenet — destiny

Monifa — lucky

Mosi — born first

Moswen — white

Mukamutara — daughter of Mutara

Mukantagara — born during war

Mukarramma — revered

Muminah — pious

Mut — myth name (mother)

Naunet — myth name (goddess of the ocean)

Nebt-het, Nephthys — myth name (nature goddess)

Nefertari — name of a queen

Nabirye — mother of twins

Naeemah — benevolent

Nailah — successful

Nathifa — pure

Neema — born to wealthy parents

Nefertiti — name of a queen

Nekhbet — myth name (vulture-goddess)

Nephthys — myth name (daughter of Nut and Geb)

Net, Neith — the divine mother

Nile — from the Nile

Nit — myth name

Niut — myth name (goddess of nothingness)

Nourbese — wonderful

Nubia — from Nubia

Nuru — born during the day

Nut — myth name (sky goddess)

Ode — from the road

Olabisi — brings joy

Olufemi — beloved of the gods

Omorose — beautiful

Oni — wanted

Oseye — happy

Panya — mouse

Pili — born second

Quibilah — peaceful

Rabiah — born in the spring

Ramla — prophetess

Rashida — righteous

Raziya — agreeable

Rehema — compassionate

Renenet — myth name (goddess of fortune)

Sabah—born in the morning
Safiya—pure
Sagira—little one
Sakhmet—myth name (goddess
 worshipped in Memphis,
 lioness)
Salama—peaceful
Salihah—agreeable
Sanura—kitten
Sechet—myth name
Sekhet—wife of Ptah
Selma—secure
Serq, Selk—myth name (another
 form of Isis)
Shani—wonderful
Sharifa—respected
Shukura—grateful
Siti—lady
Subira—patient
Suma—ask
Tabia—talented
Tahirah—pristine

Tale—green
Talibah—seeks knowledge
Tauret—myth name (goddess of
 pregnant women)
Tefnut—myth name
 (atmospheric moisture)
Thema—queen
Theoris—great
Thermuthis—myth name
 (another form of Renenet)
Uadjit—myth name (cobra-
 goddess)
Uatchit—myth name (another
 form of Hathor)
Umayma—little mother
Umm—mother
Urbi—princess
Walidah—newly born
Yaminah—meaning unknown
Zahra—flower
Zalika, Zaliki—well-born
Zesiro—a twin

MALE

Abasi—stern
Abayomi—brings joy
Abubakar—noble
Adeben—born twelfth
Adio—righteous
Adofo—fighter
Adom—receives help from the
 gods
Agymah—meaning unknown
Akhenaten—devoted to Aten
Akiiki—friendly
Akil—intelligent
Akins—brave
Amen, Amun, Ammon—myth
 name (god of a united Egypt)
Amenhotep—name of a pharaoh

Amenophis—name of a pharaoh
Amen-Ra—myth name (personi-
 fication of the power of the
 universe)
Amsu, Amsi—myth name (per-
 sonification of reproduction)
Amun—myth name (god of
 mystery)
An-her, Anhur—myth name
Anubis, Anpu—myth name (god
 of the dead)
Anum—born fifth
Anzety—myth name (god of
 Busiris)
Apis—myth name (dead bull
 thought to be Osiris)

Apophis — meaning unknown

Asim — protector

Aswad — black

Ata — twin

Atemu — myth name (great god of Annu)

Aten — myth name (sun-disk)

Atsu — twin

Atum — whole

Ausar — myth name (another name for Osiris)

Azibo — earth

Azizi — precious

Baal — meaning unknown

Babafemi — loved by his father

Badru — born during the full moon

Bakari — noble oath

Bankole — meaning unknown

Baruti — teacher

Beb, Bebti, Babu, Baba — myth name (Osiris's firstborn)

Behdeti — myth name

Bes — myth name (dwarf god, brings joy)

Bomani — warrior

Chafulumisa — fast

Chatha — ends

Chatuluka — departs

Chenzira — born on a journey

Cheops — name of a pharaoh

Chibale — kinsman

Chigaru — hound

Chike — power of God

Chisisi — secret

Chuma — wealthy

Dakarai — happy

Darius — name of a pharaoh

Darwishi — saint

Djoser — name of a pharaoh

Donkor — humble

Ebo — born on Tuesday

Edfu — from Edfu

Fadil — generous

Faki — meaning unknown

Fenuku — born late

Fenyang — conquers

Funsani — a request

Gahiji — hunter

Garai — settled

Geb — myth name (earth-god)

Gyasi — wonderful

Haji — born during the pilgrimage

Hakizimana — God saves

Hamadi — praised

Hanbal — pristine

Hanif — believes

Hapi — a god of the Nile

Hapu — name of a pharaoh

Harakhty — myth name (disguise of Horus)

Hasani, Husani — handsome

Heh — myth name (god of the immeasurable)

Heru — myth name (sun-god)

Hondo — war

Horemheb — name of a pharaoh

Horus — myth name (god of the sky)

Hu — myth name (a nature god)

Idogbe — brother of twins

Ini-herit — he who brings back the distant one

Ishaq — laughs

Issa — God saves

Jabari — brave

Jafari — creek

Jahi — dignified

Jibade — related to royalty

Jumoke — loved by all

Kafele — would die for

Kamuzu — medical
Kaphiri — hill
Kasiya — departs
Kazemde — ambassador
Kek — myth name (god of darkness)
Khafra — name of a pharaoh
Khaldun, Khalid — immortal
Khalfani — shall rule
Khentimentiu — myth name (god of the dead's destiny)
Khepri — meaning unknown
Khnemu — to model
Khnum — myth name (reborn sun)
Khons — myth name (god of the moon)
Khufu — name of a pharaoh
Kneph — meaning unknown
Kontar — only son
Kosey — lion
Lateef — gentle
Lisimba — lion
Lukman — a prophet
Luzige — locust
Madu — of the people
Makalani — clerk
Manu — born second
Maskini — poor
Masud — lucky
Matsimela — root
Mbizi — water
Memphis — from Memphis
Menes — name of a king
Menkaura — name of a pharaoh
Mensah — born third
Min — myth name (god of fertility)
Minkah — justice
Month — myth name (god of Thebes)

Mosegi — tailor
Mosi — born first
Moswen — light skin
Msamaki — fish
Msrah — born sixth
Mudada — provider
Mukhwana — twin
Musa — of the water
Muslim — believer
Naeem — benevolent
Najja — meaning unknown
Narmer — name of a king
Nassor — victor
Neb-er-tcher — myth name (god of the universe)
Nefertum — myth name (worshipped in Memphis)
Nephthys — myth name
Nexeu — meaning unknown
Ngozi — blessed
Niu — myth name (god of nothingness)
Nizam — disciplined
Nkosi — rules
Nkrumah — born ninth
Nkuku — rooster
Nun — myth name (god of the ocean)
Nuru — born during the day
Oba — king
Odion — born of twins
Okpara — firstborn
Omari — high born
Onuris — brings back the distant one
Osahar — God hears me
Osaze — loved by God
Osiris, Un-nefer — myth name (god of the dead)
Ottah — born third

Oubastet, Bastet — myth name (cat)

Paki — witness

Petiri — meaning unknown

Pili — born second

Psamtic — name of a pharaoh

Psusennes — name of a pharaoh

Ptah — myth name (god worshipped in Memphis)

Ptolemy — name of pharaoh

Qeb — father of the earth

Quaashie — born on Sunday

Ra — the sun

Ramses — name of a pharaoh

Rashidi — wise

Re — midday sun

Re-Harakhty — myth name (Horus of the horizon)

Reshef — myth name

Runihura — destroyer

Saa — myth name (a nature god)

Sabola — pepper

Sadiki — faithful

Salih — upright

Seb — myth name (god of the earth)

Sebak — myth name (companion of Set)

Sefu — sword

Sekani — laughs

Shakir — grateful

Senusnet — name of a pharaoh

Sept — meaning unknown

Serapis — myth name (another name for Apis)

Set, Sutekh — myth name (son of Seb and Nut)

Seth — myth name (murdered Osiris)

Sethos — name of a prince

Shabaka — name of a king

Shu — myth name (air)

Sifiye — meaning unknown

Sneferu — name of a pharaoh

Sobk — myth name (worshipped in Faiyum)

Sudi — lucky

Tabari — meaning unknown

Tarik — name of a warrior

Tau — lion

Tehuti — myth name (god of earth, sky, air and sea)

Teremun — loved by his father

Thabit — strong

Thoth, Astennu — myth name (god of the moon)

Thutmose — name of a pharaoh

Tor — king

Tsekani — close

Tum — myth name (great god of Annu)

Tumaini — hope

Tutankhamun — name of a pharaoh

Typhon — meaning unknown

Ubaid — faithful

Ufa — flour

Umi — life

Unika — meaning unknown

Ur, Ur-Atum — myth name (great)

Usi — smoke

Uthman — a friend of Muhammad

Wamukota — left-handed

Yafeu — bold

Yahya — given by God

Yazid — meaning unknown

Zahur — flower

Zaid, Ziyad — He shall add

Zuberi — strong

Zuka — meaning unknown

English

English surnames began as epithets or as place, occupational and patronymic names. They can be traced back for centuries. By 1290 even peasants had surnames, but the surnames didn't become hereditary until much later.

A great influx of names accompanied the Norman Conquest of 1066. Traditional Hebrew (Old Testament) names such as Mary, Joseph, Miriam, Rebecca and so on, were not used until the late Middle Ages. New Testament biblical names such as John and Peter became popular around the twelfth and thirteenth centuries.

Common English surnames:

Baker	Smith
Brown	Taylor
Butler	Walker
Jones	White
Martin	Williams

FEMALE

Ada, Aida, Adda, Adia — wealthy
Alberta, Adalbeorht, Albertina, Albertyna, Albertine, Alberteen, Albertyne, Adalbrechta, Aldora, Aeldra — noble
Aldercy — chief
Aldis, Aldys — from the old house
Aleda, Aleta, Alita — winged
Afreda, Aelfraed, Alfrida — elf counselor
Altheda, Altha, Althia — healer
Alura, Alhraed, Alurea, Allura — divine counselor
Alvina, Aethelwine, Aethelwyne, Aelfwine — friend of the elves
Amorica — ancient name for Britain
Anora — light
Arda, Ardelia, Ardi, Ardys, Ardine, Ardene, Ardeen, Ardella, Ardyne — warm
Arietta, Ariette — melody
Ashley, Aisley — from the ash-tree grove
Attheaeldre, Atilda, Athilda — at the elder tree
Audrey, Audra, Audie, Audre —

noble strength

Aurea, Auria, Aria — gentle music

Autumn — born in the fall

Avis — refuge in battle

Avril, Averil, Averyl, Avryl — born in April

Beda, Beadu — warrior maid

Berengaria, Berangari — bear-spear maid

Bertilde, Beorhthilde, Bertilda — shining battle-maid

Bertrade, Beorthtraed — bright counselor

Bethia, Betia — house of God

Beverly, Beverley — woman from the beaver meadow

Birdie, Birdy — birdlike

Blessing, Bletsung — consecrated

Bliss, Bliths — joy

Blossom, Blostm — fresh

Blythe, Blithe — cheerful

Bonnie, Bonny, Bonie — good

Brande — firebrand

Brooke — stream

Cadena, Cadyna — rhythmic

Callie, Cally, Calli — lark

Cambria — myth name

Carmia, Carmya, Carmina, Carmine, Carmita, Charmaine — song

Carol, Caroline, Carolyn, Carolina, Carrie — joy

Chelsea — seaport

Claresta — brilliant

Cleantha — glory

Cleva — dwells at the cliffs

Clover, Claefer — clover

Cody, Codie, Codi — cushion

Cordelia — myth name

Corliss — good-hearted

Cwen — queen

Cyne, Cym, Cim — ruler

Cyneburhleah, Cynburleigh, Cymberly, Cimberleigh — from the royal meadow

Daisy, Daesgesage — day's eye

Dale, Dayle, Dael — lives in the valley

Daryl — loved dearly

Dawn, Dagian — dawn

Dena, Deanna, Deana, Deane, Dina — from the valley

Devona, Defena, Devonna, Devyna — from Devonshire

Eadda, Ede, Eda, Eada — wealthy

Eadwine, Edwina, Edina — wealthy friend

Earlene, Erleen — noblewoman

Eartha, Ertha — worldly

Earwine, Earwyn, Erwina, Erwyna — friend of the sea

Easter, Eastre — born at Easter

Ebba — flowing tide

Edith, Edyth, Eadgyth — happy warfare

Edlyn, Eathelin, Eathelyn, Edlin, Edlen — noble waterfall

Edmonda, Eadmund, Edmunda, Edmanda, Eduarda — rich benefactress

Edrea, Earric, Edra — powerful

Eferhild, Eferhilda — bear, warrior-maiden

Egberta, Egbertina, Egbertine, Egbertyne — shining sword

Elberta, Elberte, Elbertina, Elbertine, Elbertyna — noble, glorious

Eldrida, Eldreda — sage

Elethea, Elthia, Elethia — healer

Elfrida, Elfreda, Elfrieda, Elva,
Elvie — good counselor
Elida, Elita, Elyta — winged
Ella, Elle — beautiful fairy
Elmira, Elmyra — noble
Elva, Elvia, Elvie, Elfie, Elivina,
Elvine, Elvyne, Elvin, Elvina,
Elvena — good elf
Enid, Enit, Enyd — fair
Erna, Earna — eagle
Ernestine, Enerstyne, Enerstina,
Earnestyna — serious
Erwina, Erwyna, Earwyna,
Aerwyna — friend of the sea
Ethelreda, Aethelreda,
Eathelreda — noble maiden
Faith, Faithe, Fayth — faithful
Fayre — beautiful
Felabeorht, Filberta, Felberta —
brilliant
Fern — fern
Fleta, Flyta — swift
Fonda — tender
Gay, Gayle, Gail, Gale — lively
Gijs — bright
Gilda, Gylda, Gyldan, Golda,
Goldie, Goldy, Gildan — gilded
Glad, Gleda — happy
Gloriana, Glorianna, Gloriane —
glorious grace
Godiva, Godgifu — gift from God
Goneril, Gonerilla — myth name
Gracia, Grace, Gracie — grace
Guendolen — white
Gypsy — wanderer
Gytha, Githa — gift
Hayley — from the hay meadow
Hazel, Haesel — nut
Heallfrith, Hallfrita, Halfryta,
Halfrith — peaceful home

Heather — heather
Hertha — of the earth
Hilda, Hildie, Hild, Hilde — battle-
maid
Hlynn — waterfall
Holly, Holea, Halig — holy
Honey, Hunig, Honbria,
Honbrie — sweet
Hope — hope
Hrothbeorhta, Hrothberta,
Hrothnerta, Hrothbertina —
bright, famous
Huette, Huetta, Hughette,
Hugiet, Hughetta — little Hugh
Ilde, Idla — battle
Irvette, Irvetta — friend of the sea
Ivy, Ivey, Ifig — ivy
Jill — girl
Jocelyn, Joscelyne, Josceline,
Jocelyne — playful
Kermeilde, Kermilda, Kermilla,
Kermillie — gilded
Kerrie, Kerry — ruler
Kimberly, Kim, Kimbra — from
the royal fortress meadow
Kimbrough, Kimbro — from the
royal field
Lark, Larke — lark
Lassie, Lasse, Lass — girl
Leigh, Ley, Lee, Lea, Leah,
Leia — meadow
Leoma — bright
Levina, Levene, Levyna — flash
Liberty — free
Lindsay, Lindsey — from the
linden-tree island
Lissa, Lyssa — honey
Lodema, Lodima, Lodyma — guide
Lona, Loni — solitary
Love, Lov — affection

Luella, Louella, Luell — famous elf

Luvena, Luvina, Luvyna — little beloved one

Lynn, Lyn, Lin, Linne — waterfall

Madra, Madre — mother

Maida, Maegth, Maidie, Mady, Maidel, Mayda, Mayde — maiden

Maitane, Maite, Maitena — dearly loved

Mercia — from Mercia

Mercy — merciful

Merry — happy

Mertice, Maertisa, Mertysa, Mertise — famous

Mildred, Mildraed, Mildrid, Mildryd — mild of strength

Nara, Nearra — nearest

Neda — wealthy guardian

Nelda — by the alder tree

Nellwyn, Nelwin, Nelwina, Nelwyna — bright friend

Oleda, Oleta, Olita — winged

Ora, Orabelle, Orabel — beautiful seacoast

Oralie, Orelia — golden

Orva, Ordwin, Ordwyn, Ordwyna, Ordwina — spear friend

Peace, Pax — peaceful

Philberta — brilliant

Piper, Pipere — piper

Poppy — flower

Portia — meaning unknown

Queena, Queenie — queen

Ra, Rae — doe

Radella, Raedself — elfin counselor

Raven, Ravyn — dark-haired, wise

Regan — myth name

Ricarda — strong ruler

Rillette, Rilletta — stream

Roberta, Robertia — famous

Sabrina — legendary princess

Saxona, Saxonia — a Saxon

Scarlett, Scarlet — red

Shelley, Scelfleah — from the edge meadow

Sherry, Sherri, Shirley — from the white meadow

Starr, Starla, Star — star

Stockard, Stockhart, Stockhard, Stokkard — hardy tree

Storm, Stormy, Stormie — tempest

Summer, Suma — born during the summer

Sunny — cheerful

Tangerine, Tangerina — from Tangiers

Tatum, Tayte, Tait, Tate — brings joy

Tuesday, Tiwesdaeg — born on Tuesday

Twyla — woven

Tyne, Tyna, Tina — river

Velvet, Velouette — soft

Wallis, Waleis — from Wales

Wanetta, Wann — pale

Welcome — welcomed

Welsa, Welsie — from the west

Wenda — comely

Willa — resolute

Withypoll — twig head

Yedda — beautiful voice

Yetta — generous

Zavrina, Zabrina — taken from Sabrina (name of a princess)

MALE

Abbot, Abbott—abbey father

Acker, Akker—from the oak tree

Ackerley, Ackley—from the oak-tree meadow

Ackerman—man of oak

Adam—of the red earth

Addis, Adamson—son of Adam

Addison—descendent of Adam

Addy—ardent

Adkins, Attkins, Atkinson, Atkinsone—son of Aiken

Adney, Addaneye, Addney, Adny—lives on the noble's island

Aeldra—lives at the elder tree

Aelfdane—Danish elf

Aelfdene—from the elfin valley

Aethelisdun, Athelston, Aetheston—from the noble's hill

Aiken, Adken, Adkyn, Aikin, Aickin—oaken

Ainsley, Ainslie—from Ann's meadow

Ainsworth—from Ann's estate

Albern, Aethelbeorn, Alburn—noble warrior

Albert, Alburt, Aethelberht, Aethelbert—noble, bright

Alcott—from the old cottage

Alden, Aldwine, Aldwyn, Aldwin—wise friend

Alder, Aler—from the alder tree

Aldis, Aldus, Aldous—from the old house

Aldo—archaic

Aldrich, Aldric, Aldrik—wise ruler

Alford, Alvord, Avery—from the old ford

Alfred, Alfredo, Aelfraed, Alfrid—sage

All—handsome

Allard, Alhhard, Aethelhard—brave

Allred, Aldred, Aldrid—wise, red-haired man

Almo, Aethelmaer, Athemar, Athmarr—noble, famous

Alson, Alison, Adalson, Aliceson, Alycesone—son of All

Alston, Aethelstun—from the elf's home

Alton, Alden, Aldan, Aldtun—from the old manor

Amsden—from Ambrose's valley

Anglesey—from Anglesey

Ann, Ain—merciful

Anna—name of a king

Anscom, Aenescumb, Anscomb—lives in the valley of the majestic one

Ansley, Ainsley, Aenedleah, Ansleigh—from the awe-inspiring one's meadow

Archer, Archere—bowman

Ardell, Ardel—from the hare's dell

Ardley, Ardaleah, Ardleigh—from the home-lover's meadow

Ardolf, Ardwolf, Ardolph—home-loving wolf

Aric, Alhric, Arik, Alhrick, Alhrik—sacred ruler

Arkwright—makes chests

Arledge—lives at the hare's lake

Arley, Arlie, Arleigh—from the hare's meadow

Arlo—fortified hill

Armstrong, Armstrang—strong-armed

Arnett, Arnet, Arnatt, Arnott—little eagle

Arthgallo—myth name

Arundel, Arndell—from the eagle's dell

Ascot, Ascott—lives at the east cottage

Ashburn, Aesoburne—lives near the ash-tree brook

Ashby, Aescby—from the ash-tree farm

Ashford, Aisford, Aescford—lives by the ash-tree ford

Ashley, Ashly, Aisley, Aescleah—lives in the ash-tree ford

Ashlin, Aesclin—lives at the ash-tree pool

Ashton, Aiston, Aesctun—from the ash-tree farm

Ashwin, Aescwine, Ashwyn, Aescwyn—spear friend

Atherton, Aethretun—lives at the spring farm

Athmore, Attmore, Atmore—from the moor

Atwater, Attewater—from the waterside

Atwell, Attwell, Attewell—lives by the spring

Atwood, Attewode—lives in the forest

Atworth, Atteworthe—lives at the farmstead

Aurick—noble valor

Averil, Averill, Averell—wild boar

Avery, Aelfric, Aubrey—elf ruler

Axton, Aeccestane—swordsman's stone

Aylmer, Almer, Aethelmaere, Aegelmaere—infamous

Aylward, Aegelweard, Aethelweard, Athelward—noble protector

Bainbridge, Banbrigge, Bainbrydge—lives near the bridge over the white water

Balder, Baldhere—bold army

Banaing, Banning—son of the slayer

Bancroft, Benecroft—from the bean field

Barclay, Berkeley, Berkley, Bercleah—lives at the birch-tree meadow

Barden, Bardan—lives near the boar's den

Bardolf, Bardawulf, Bardolph, Bardulf, Bardalph, Barwolf—ax-wolf

Bardrick, Bardaric, Bardarik—ax-ruler

Barlow, Baerhloew, Barhloew—lives on the bare hill

Barnett, Beornet—leader

Barnum, Beornham—from the nobleman's home

Baron, Barron—warrior

Barr, Barre—gateway

Barth—son of the earth

Bartley, Bartleah, Bartleigh—from Bart's meadow

Barton, Bart, Beretun—from the barley farm

Bartram, Beorhthramm, Barthram — glorious raven

Baxter, Baker, Backstere, Bax — baker

Bayhard, Bay — reddish-brown hair

Beacher, Beceere, Beecher — lives by the beech tree

Beadutun, Beaton — from the warrior's estate

Beaman, Beomann — beekeeper

Beamer, Bemeere — trumpeter

Beck, Bek — brook

Bede — prayer

Belden, Beldan, Beldene, Beldon, Beldane — lives in the beautiful glen

Bentley, Bentleah, Bentleigh — from the bent grass meadow

Benton — lives on the moor

Beresford, Berford — from the barley ford

Bert, Burt, Beorht — glorious

Berton, Burton, Beorhttun, Burhtun — from the fortified town

Bertram, Beorhthram — bright raven

Berwick, Berwyk — from the barley grange

Beverly, Beverley — from the beaver meadow

Bickford, Biecaford, Bick — from the hewer's ford

Bink — lives at the bank

Birch, Beore, Birk — birch tree

Birkett, Birkhead, Birkhed — lives at the birch headland

Birkey — from the birch-tree island

Birley, Byreleah — from the cattle shed on the meadow

Birney, Burneig, Burney — lives on the brook island

Birtle, Birtel, Byrtel, Birdhil, Birdhill — from the bird hill

Bishop — overseer

Bitanig — from the preserving land

Black, Claec — dark

Blade, Blaed — wealthy glory

Blagdon, Blagdan, Blagden — from the dark valley

Blaise, Blaze — stutters

Blake, Blaec — black or white

Blakeley, Blakely, Blaecleah — from the dark meadow

Blakemore — from the dark moor

Blakey, Blacey — blond

Blanford, Blandford — gray-haired

Blayne — twin

Bliss — happy

Blyth, Blythe — merry

Bolton — from the manor farm

Bond — tied to the land

Booth, Boothe, Bothe — lives in a hut

Borden, Bardene, Barden — from the boar valley

Bors — myth name

Bosworth — lives at the cattle enclosure

Botolf, Botewolf, Botwolf — herald wolf

Bradburn, Bradbourne — from the broad brook

Braden, Bradyn, Brad, Bradan, Bradene — from the broad valley

Bradford — from the broad ford

Bradley, Bradly, Bradleah—from the broad meadow

Bradwell—from the broad spring

Brady, Bradig—from the broad island

Brainard, Branhard, Brainerd—bold raven

Bramwell, Braemwiella—from the bramble bush spring

Brandon, Branddun—from the beacon hill

Brantley, Brant, Brand—proud

Brawley, Brawleigh, Braleah—from the hillslope meadow

Brent, Brentan—from the steep hill

Brewster, Brewstere—brewer

Bridger, Brydger, Bryggere, Briggere—lives at the bridge

Brigham, Briggeham—lives by the bridge

Brinton—from Brinton

Britto—myth name

Brock, Brok, Broc—badger

Brockley, Brocleah, Brocly, Brocleigh—from the badger meadow

Broderick, Brodrig, Brodrik, Broderik—from the broad ridge

Bromley, Bromleah, Bromleigh, Bromly—from the broom-covered meadow

Brook, Brooke—lives by the stream

Brooks, Brooksone, Brookson—son of Brooke

Brougher, Burghere—lives at the fortress

Broughton, Burgtun—from the fortress town

Brown, Brun—dark-skinned

Brutus—myth name

Buck, Boc—male deer

Buckley, Bocleah, Bocley—lives at the buck meadow

Budd, Buddy, Boda—herald

Bundy, Bondig—free

Burbank, Burhbank—lives on the castle's hill

Burch, Birche, Birch—birch

Burchard, Burghard—strong as a castle

Burdon, Burhdon—lives at the castle

Burford, Burhford—lives at the castle ford

Burgess, Burgeis—lives in town

Burl, Byrle—cup-bearer

Burley, Burhleag, Burleigh, Burly—lives at the castle's meadow

Burn, Byrne, Bourne, Burne, Bourn—from the brook

Burnett, Burnet—meaning unknown

Burney, Bureig—lives on the brook island

Burns, Bursone, Byrnes—son of Byrne

Burton, Burhtun—lives in the fortified town

Byford, Biford—lives at the river crossing

Byram—from the cattle yard

Byrd, Bird, Birde—bird

Byron—bear

Cadby, Cadabyr—from the warrior's settlement

Caindale — from the clear river valley

Calder, Caldre, Calldwr — cold brook

Caldwell, Caldwiella — from the cold spring

Cale, Cal, Cayle — bold

Calvert, Calbert, Calfhierde — shepherd

Camber — myth name

Carleton, Carlton, Carlatun — from Carl's farm

Carlisle, Carlyle — from the walled city

Carson — son of Carr

Carswell, Caersewiella — lives at the watercress spring

Carter, Cartere — drives a cart

Cartland — from the land between the streams

Carvell, Carvel — from the villa by the march

Carver — carves wood or sculpts

Cassibellaunus — myth name

Caster — from the Roman camp

Cedric, Caddarik, Caddaric — battle leader

Cenehard, Cynhard — bold

Ceneward, Cynward — bold guardian

Cenewig, Cenewyg — bold warrior

Chad, Cadda — warring

Chadburn, Chadburne, Chadbyrne — from the wildcat brook

Chadwick, Chadwyk, Chadwik, Caddawyc — from the warrior's town

Chapman, Ceapmann — merchant

Charleton, Charlton — from Charles's farm

Chatham, Caddaham — from the soldier's land

Chatwyn, Chatwin — warring friend

Chauncey, Chance, Chancey, Chaunce, Chancellor, Chaunceler — chancellor

Chester, Ceaster — lives at the camp

Cheston, Ceastun — camp

Chetwyn, Chetwin, Cetewind — from the cottage on the winding path

Chilton, Celdtun — from the farm by the spring

Churchill, Circehyll, Churchyll — lives at the church hill

Cingeswiella, Cingeswell, Cinwell — lives at the king's spring

Clay, Claeg, Clayton, Claegtun — mortal

Clayborne, Claiborn, Claegborne, Claybourne, Clayburn — from the clay brook

Cleveland, Clifland, Clyfland, Clevon, Cleon — from the cliffs

Clifford, Cliff — lives by the ford near the cliff

Cliffton, Clifton, Cliftun, Clyftun, Clyffton — from the farm near the cliff

Clinton, Clint, Clinttun — from the headland estate

Clive, Clyve, Cleve — lives at the cliffs

Cody, Codi, Codie — a cushion

Colbert, Culbert, Culbart,

Ceolbeorht, Colvert—seaman

Colby—from the black farm

Coleman, Colemann—dark-skinned

Collier, Colier, Collyer, Colyer—charcoal merchant

Collis, Colis, Colys—son of the dark man

Colter, Coltere—horse herdsman

Colton, Colt, Coletun, Cole—from the dark town

Cooper, Cupere, Coopersmith—makes barrels

Corwin, Corwyn, Corwine, Corwan—friend of the heart

Courtland—lives at the farmstead

Covell, Covyll, Cofahealh—lives at the cave slope

Crandall, Crandell—from the crane valley

Cranley, Cranleah, Cranly—from the crane meadow

Cranston, Cranstun—from the crane estate

Crawford—from the crow's ford

Creighton, Creketun—lives at the creek town

Crichton—from the town by the creek

Croften, Crofton—from the enclosed town

Crompton—from the winding farm

Cromwell, Crombwiella—lives by the winding stream

Crosley, Crosleah, Crosly, Crosleigh—from the cross meadow

Culver, Colver, Colvyr, Colfre—dove

Cuthbert, Cuthbeorht—noted splendor

Cutler—makes knives

Cwentun—from the queen's estate

Cymbelline—myth name

Cyneleah, Cyneley—lives in the royal meadow

Cyning, Cyneric, Cynerik, Cynric, Cynrik—royal

Dagwood—from the bright one's forest

Dalbert, Delbert, Dealbert, Dealbeorht—proud

Dale, Dael, Daley, Dayle—lives in the valley

Dalton—from the farm in the dale

Darnell, Darnall—from Darnall

Darrell, Daryl—dearly loved

Darton, Deortun—from the deer park

Davis, Davidson, Davidsone—David's son

Dean, Deanne, Dene, Dino—from the dene

Dearborn, Dearbourne, Derebourne—from the deer brook

Deems, Demason, Demasone—judge's son

Dempsey—from the judge's meadow

Dempster—judicious

Denley—from the valley meadow

Denton—from the valley farm

Denver—lives at the valley's edge

Derwin, Derwyn, Derwan—friend of the deer

Derward, Deorward, Deerward—
guardian of the deer
Diamond, Deagmund, Diamont—
bridge protector
Dickson, Dixon, Dikesone—son
of Dick
Doane, Doune—from the down
hill
Drake, Draca—dragon
Dryden, Driden, Dridan,
Drygedene—from the dry
valley
Dudley—from the people's
meadow
Dunley, Dunleigh, Dunly,
Dunleah—from the hill
meadow
Dunn—dark-skinned
Dunstan—hill of stone
Dunton—from the farm on the
hill
Durward—gatekeeper
Durwin, Durwyn, Deorwine—
friend of the deer
Earl, Eorl, Earle—nobleman
Eaton, Eatun—from the riverside
village
Edbert, Eadburt, Eadbeorht—
wealthy
Edelmar, Edelmarr, Eadelmarr—
noble
Edgar, Eadger—wealthy spear
Edison, Eadwardsone,
Edwardson, Eddis—son of
Edward
Edmund, Edmond, Edmondo,
Eadmund—happy defender
Edric, Edrik, Edwald, Edwaldo,
Eadweald, Eadric—wealthy
ruler

Edsel, Eadsele—from Edward's
estate
Edward, Eduard, Eda, Edvard,
Ede, Eideard, Eadward,
Eadweard—wealthy guardian
Edwin, Edwyn, Eadwyn,
Eadwine—wealthy friend
Egbert, Ecgbeorht—intelligent
Egerton—from the town on the
ridge
Eibhear, Ever, Evert, Everet,
Everhard—strong as a boar
Elden, Eldan, Eldon, Ealhdun,
Ealdun—from the elves' valley
Elder, Ellder, Eldur—from the
elder tree
Elidure—myth name
Ellard, Eallard, Ealhhard—brave
Ellison, Eallison—son of Elder
Elmore, Elmoor, Elmer—lives at
the elm-tree moor
Elsdon—from the noble's hill
Elsworth—from the noble's
estate
Elton—from the old town
Elvy, Elvey—elf warrior
Elwald, Elwold—old Welshman
Elwell, Eadwiella—from the old
spring
Elwood, Ellwood, Ealdwode—
from the old forest
Elwyn, Elwin, Elwen—old friend
Emery, Emeric, Emerick—
meaning unknown
Eoforwic—from the bear estate
Erland, Eorlland, Eorland—from
the nobleman's land
Erling, Eorlson, Earlson—
nobleman's son
Erwin, Earwyn, Earwine,

Erwyn—friend of the sea

Esmond, Estmund, Esmund—protected by God

Estcott, Estcot—from the east cottage

Ethelbert, Aethelbeorht—splendid

Everard, Eferhard, Ever—brave

Everly, Eferleah, Everley, Everleigh—from Ever's meadow

Ewald—powerful

Ewert, Eawart, Eweheorde—shepherd

Ewing—lawyer

Fairfax—blond

Fane, Fayne, Fain, Faegan, Fagan—joyful

Farley, Farleigh, Farly, Faerrleah, Fairlie—from the bull's pasture

Farnell, Fearnhealh, Farnall, Fernald—from the fern slope

Farnham, Fearnhamm—from the fern field

Farnley, Farnly, Fearnleah—from the fern meadow

Farold, Faerwald—powerful traveler

Farr, Faer—traveler

Farson, Farrs, Fars—son of Farr

Felton, Feldtun, Feldun, Feldon—from the field estate

Fenton—from the farm on the fens

Ferrex—myth name

Fielding, Felding—lives in the field

Filbert, Filburt, Felabeorht—brilliant

Filmer, Filmore, Filmarr, Felamaere—famous

Finn—blond

Firman—fair

Fiske—fish

Fitch, Fitche, Fytch—ermine

Fitz—son

Fitz Adam, Fitzadam—son of Adam

Fitzgerald, Fitz Gerald—son of Gerald

Fitzgibbon, Fitz Gibbon, Fitzgilbert, Fitz Gilbert—son of Gilbert

Fitzhugh, Fitz Hugh—son of Hugh

Fitzjames, Fitz James—son of James

Fitzpatrick, Fitz Patrick—son of Patrick

Fitzsimon, Fitz Simon, Fitzsimmons, Fitzsimons—son of Simon

Fitz Water, Fitzwater, Fitz Walter, Fitzwalter—son of Walter

Fleming—Dutchman

Flint, Flynt—a stream

Ford—river crossing

Foster, Forest, Forrester—keeps the forest

Fowler—game warden

Frayne, Fraine, Freyne—foreigner

Freeland—from the free land

Frewin, Frewyn, Frewen, Freowine—noble friend

Frey—lord

Frick, Frika, Freca—bold

Fridolf, Fridolph, Fridwolf,

Friduwulf—peaceful wolf
Frisa—curly-haired
Fuller, Fullere—cloth thickener
Fulton, Fugeltun, Fulaton—from
the people's estate
Gail, Gayle, Gale—lively
Galt—from the high ground
Galton, Galeun—from the town
on the high ground
Garr, Gar—spear
Gardner, Gardiner—gardener
Garfield, Garafeld—from the
triangular field
Garland, Gariland—from the
spear land
Garman, Garrman, Garmon,
Garmann—spearman
Garmond, Garmund, Garm—
spear protector
Garnett, Garnet—armed with
spear
Garrett, Garrard, Garet—spear-
brave
Garrick—rules by the spear
Garroway, Garwig—spear-fighter
Garson, Garrson, Garsone—son
of Gar
Garton, Garatun—lives in the
triangular farmstead
Garvin, Garvyn, Garwin, Garwyn,
Garwine—spear friend
Garwood, Ayrwode, Arwood—
from the fir forest
Gary—carries spears
Gaukroger—Roger the clumsy
Gawain, Gawen, Gawyn—battle
hawk
Geary, Gerry—flexible
Gehard, Gerd, Gerrit, Gerardo,
Gherardo—spear-hard

Geol—born at Christmas
Gervase—serves
Gibson, Gibbesone—Gilbert's
son
Gifford, Gifuhard—gift of bravery
Gijs—intelligent
Gilbert, Gilburt, Guilbert,
Giselbert, Gilpin—trusted
Gildas—gilded
Gilford—from Gill's ford
Gilmer, Gilmar, Giselmaere—
famous hostage
Gladwin, Gladwyn, Glaedwine—
happy friend
Godwin, Gowyn, Godwine—
God's friend
Gold, Golden—blond
Golding—son of Gold
Goldwin, Goldwyn, Goldwine—
golden friend
Goodwin, Goodwine, Goodwyn—
good friend
Gorboduc—myth name
Gordon, Garadun, Garadin,
Garadyn, Garaden—from the
three-cornered hill
Graeham, Gram, Graeghamm—
from the gray home
Granger, Grangere—farmer
Grant, Graent—great
Grantham, Graham—from the
great meadow
Grantland, Grantley—from the
large meadow
Grayson, Grayvesone—son of the
reeve
Greeley, Greely, Graegleah—
from the gray meadow
Gresham, Grisham—from the
grazing

Grover, Grafere — lives in the grove

Guiderius — myth name

Hadden, Haddon, Heath, Hadon, Haden, Heathdene — from the heath

Hadley, Heathley, Heathleah — from the heath-covered meadow

Hadrian — son of Adrian

Hadwin, Hadwyn, Haethowine — war friend

Hagley, Hagly, Hagalean, Haig — from the hedged enclosure

Halbert, Halburt, Halbart, Halebeorht — brilliant hero

Hale, Hayle, Haele — lives in the hall

Halford — from the hall by the ford

Hall, Heall — from the manor

Hallam, Healum — lives at the hall's slopes

Halley, Healleah — from the manor house meadow

Halliwell, Haligwiella, Hallwell, Holwell — lives by the holy spring

Halsey, Halsig — from Hal's island

Halstead, Heallstede — from the manor house

Halton, Helton, Healhtun — from the hillslope estate

Hamilton, Hamelatun — from the grassy estate

Hand — worker

Hanford, Heanford — from the high ford

Hanley, Heanleah, Hanly — from the high meadow

Harden, Hardin, Hardyn,

Harding, Heardind — from the hare's valley

Hardwin, Hardwyn, Heardwine — brave friend

Hare — rabbit

Harelache, Harlak, Harlake — lives at the hare's lake

Harford, Haraford — from the hare ford

Hargrove — from the hare grove

Harlan, Harland — from the hare's land

Harley, Harleigh, Hareleah — from the hare's meadow

Harlow, Harlowe — from the hare's hill

Harper, Hearpere — harpist

Harrison, Harris — son of Harry

Hart, Heort — stag

Hartford, Harford — from the stag's ford

Hartley — from the stag's meadow

Hartwell, Heortwiella — lives near the stag's spring

Hartwood, Heortwode — from the stag forest

Harvey, Houerv, Herve — bitter

Haslet, Haslett — from the hazel-tree land

Hastings, Haestingas — violent

Haven, Havyn, Haefen — safety

Hawley, Hawly, Hagaleah — from the hedged meadow

Hayden, Haydon — from the hedged-in valley

Hayes — from the hedged land

Hayward, Hagaward — keeper of the hedged enclosure

Haywood, Heywood — from the hedged forest

Healy—from the slope land

Hearne, Hern, Herne—myth name (a hunter)

Heathcliff, Heathclyf, Hetheclif—from the heath cliff

Hillock, Hillocke—from the small hill

Hilton—from the hall on the hill

Histion—myth name

Holbrook—from the brook

Holcomb—from the deep valley

Holden, Holdin, Holdyn—from the hollow in the valley

Hollis—lives by the holly trees

Holmes—from the river island

Holt—from the forest

Horton, Hartun—from the gray estate

Houghton—from the estate on the bluff

Howard, Heahweard—chief guardian

Howland—from the chief's land

Hraefnscaga—from the raven forest

Hring—ring

Hristun—from the brushwood estate

Hroc—crow

Hrocby—from the crow's estate

Hrocesburh—from the crow's forest

Hrycg—from the ridge

Hrychleah—from the meadow's edge

Hrypanleah, Hrapenly—from the shouter's meadow

Hrytherford—from the cattle ford

Hwaeteleah—from the wheat meadow

Hweolere—wheel maker

Hwertun—from the estate at the hollow

Hwistlere—piper

Hwitby—from the white farmstead

Hwitcomb, Hwitcumb—from the white hollow

Hwitford—from the white ford

Hwithloew—from the white hill

Hwitloc—from the white fortress

Hud, Hod—hooded

Hudson, Hodsone—son of the hooded man

Hugh, Huey, Hugi—intelligent

Humility—humble

Hunt, Hunter—hunter

Huntingdon, Huntingden—from the hunter's hill

Huntingtun, Huntington—from the hunting farm

Huntley, Huntly—from the hunter's meadow

Hurlbert, Hurlbart, Herlbert, Herlebeorht—army strong

Hurst, Hurste—lives in the forest

Hutton—from the estate on the ridge

Huxford, Huxeford—from Hugh's ford

Huxley, Huxly—from Hugh's meadow

Hyatt, Hiatt—from the high gate

Hyde, Hid, Hide—from the hide

Innocent—innocent

Irving, Irwin, Irwyn—sea friend

Isham, Isenham—from the iron one's estate

Ives—little archer

Iwdael, Idal—from the yew-tree valley

Jack—replace (derivative of James)

Jackson—son of Jack

Jagger, Jager—carter

James—replace

Jasper—English form of Casper (master of the treasure)

Jefferson—son of Geoffrey

Keane, Keene, Keenan, Keanan—sharp

Kemp, Kempe—warrior

Kendall—from the clear river valley

Kendrick, Kendrik, Kendryk—son of Harry

Kenelm—defends the family

Kenley, Kenly—from the king's meadow

Kennard—bold

Kenneth, Ken—royal obligation

Kenrick, Kenrik, Kenryk—royal ruler

Kent—from Kent

Kenton—from a farm in Kent

Kenward—bold guardian

Kenway—bold warrior

Kester—from the Roman camp

Kim—ruler

King—royal

Kingdon—from the king's hall

Kingsley—from the king's meadow

Kingston—from the king's village or estate

Kingswell—lives at the king's spring

Kinsey—victorious

Kipp, Kip, Kippar, Kippie—from the pointed hill

Kirk, Kyrk—church

Kirkley, Kirkly—from the church's meadow

Kirkwood, Kyrkwode—from the church's forest

Kleef—from the cliff

Knight—noble, soldier

Knox, Knocks—from the hills

Kyne, Ken—royal

Lach, Laec, Lache—lives near water

Ladd, Lad, Ladde—attendant

Laibrook, Ladbroc—lives by the path by the brook

Laidley, Laidly—from the creek meadow

Lander, Launder—from the grassy plain

Landon, Langdon—from the long hill

Lane, Laine—from the long meadow

Langford—lives near the long ford

Langley, Langleah—from the long meadow

Lanston—from the long estate

Langston—from the long enclosure

Lathrop—from the barn farmstead

Latimer—interprets Latin

Law, Lawe—from the hill

Lawford—from the ford at the hill

Lawley, Lawly—from the hill meadow

Lawson—son of Law or Lawrence

Lawton—from the hillside farm

Lawton—from the hillside farm
Leal, Lele—loyal
Lear, Lir—myth name
Lee, Lew—shelter
Leicester—from Leicester
Leigh, Leo—from the meadow
Leighton, Layton, Lay—from the
    meadow farm
Leland—from the meadow land
Leverton, Laefertun—from the
    rush farm
Lincoln—from the colony by the
    pool
Lind, Lynd—lives by the linden
    tree
Lindell, Lindael—lives by the
    linden-tree valley
Lindisfarne—from Lindisfarne
Lindley, Lindleigh, Lindly—from
    the linden-tree meadow
Linford, Lynford—from the
    linden-tree ford
Link, Line, Hline, Hlink—from
    the bank
Linley, Linly, Linleah—from the
    flax field
Linton, Lintun—from the flax
    enclosure
Litton, Hlithtun, Lifton—from the
    hillside town
Livingston—from Lyfing's town
Locke, Loc—lives by the
    stronghold
Lockwood—from the enclosed
    wood
Locrine—myth name
Lorimer, Lorimar—saddle maker
Lorineus—myth name
Lowell, Lovell, Lyfing, Loefel—
    dearly loved

Lud—myth name
Ludlow—from the prince's hill
Lydell—from the open dell
Lyman, Leman, Leyman—from
    the valley
Lyndon, Linddun—lives by the
    linden tree
Madison—son of a mighty
    warrior
Maitland—from the meadow
Malin, Malyn—little warrior
Malvin, Malvyn, Maethelwine—
    council friend
Manfred, Manfrid—hero's peace
Manley, Manly, Mannleah—from
    the hero's meadow
Mann—hero
Manning—son of a hero
Mansfield, Maunfeld—from the
    field by the small river
Manton—from the hero's town or
    farm
Marden, Mardon—from the
    valley with the pool
Marland, Marchman,
    Marchland—from the march
Marley, Marly—from the march
    meadow
Marlow, Marlowe, Merlow—from
    the hill by the lake
Marsden—from the marsh valley
Marsh, Mersc—from the marsh
Marshall, Marschall, Marshal—
    steward
Marston, Merestun—from the
    farm by the pool
Marwood, Merewood,
    Merewode—from the lake
    forest

Mather, Maetthere — powerful army

Matherson, Mathers — son of Mather

Maxwell — capable

Mayfield — from the warrior's field

Mead, Maed — from the meadow

Medwin, Medwyn, Medwine — strong friend

Melbourne, Melburn, Melbyrne, Mylnburne, Melborn — from the mill stream

Meldon — from the hillside mill

Meldrick, Meldryk, Meldrik, Mylnric — from the powerful mill

Melvin, Melvyn, Maelwine — strong friend

Mercer — merchant

Merritt, Maeret — little famous one

Merton — from the estate by the lake

Mervin, Mervyn, Maerewine, Merwyn — famous friend

Milburn, Milbyrne — from the mill stream

Milford — from the mill's ford

Miller — miller

Millman, Milman — mill worker

Milton — from the mill farm

Milward — keeper of the mill

Mitchell, Mitchel — like God

Mordred, Modraed — brave

More, Moreland, Morland — from the moors

Moreley, Morlee, Morly — from the meadow on the moor

Morse, Morris, Morrisey, Morrison — son of More

Morton — from the farm near the moor

Moulton — from the mule farm

Montgomery, Monte, Monty — from the wealthy man's mountain

Napier — in charge of royal linens

Newell, Niewheall — from the new hall

Newland — lives on the new land

Newman — newcomer

Newton — from the new farm

Nixon, Nixen, Nicson, Nikson — son of Nick

Norcross — from the north crossroads

Northcliffe, Northclyf, Northclif — from the north cliff

Northrop, Northrup — from the north farm

Norton, Nortin, Northtun — from the north farm

Norvin, Norvyn, Norwin, Norwyn — friend of the north

Norward — northern guardian

Norwell, Norwel — from the north spring

Norwood, Northwode — from the north forest

Nyle, Nye — island

Oakes, Okes — from the oak

Oakley — from the oak-tree meadow

Ocelfa — from the high plain

Odell, Odale, Odayle — of the valley

Odom, Odam — son-in-law

Odwulf, Odwolf, Odwolfe — wealthy wolf

Ogden, Oakden, Ogdon—from the oak-tree valley

Ogelsby, Oegelsby, Ogelsvy, Ogelsvie—fearsome

Olney, Ollaneg—from Olney

Onslow, Onslowe—from the zealous one's hill

Oram, Orahamm, Orham—from the riverbank enclosure

Orford—from the cattle ford

Orlan, Ordland, Orland—from the pointed hill

Orman, Ordman—spearman

Ormeman—ship man

Ormemund, Ormund, Ordmund, Ormond—spear-defender

Orrick, Orik, Orick, Orrik, Harac—from the ancient oak tree

Orson, Orsen, Ordsone— Ormond's son

Orton, Ortun, Oratun—from the shore farm

Orval, Orvil, Orville, Ordwald, Orwald—spear-strength

Orvin, Orvyn, Ordwin, Ordwine—spear-friend

Os, Oz—divine

Osbert, Osburt, Osbart, Osbeorht—divinely brilliant

Osborn, Osburn, Osbourne, Osbeorn—divine warrior

Osmar, Osmarr—divinely glorious

Osmond, Osmund, Osmont— divine protector

Osred, Osrid, Osryd, Osraed— divine counselor

Osric, Osrik, Osrick—divine ruler

Oswald, Osweald, Oswell— divinely powerful

Oxford, Oxnaford—from the ox ford

Oxley, Oxnaleah—from the ox enclosure

Oxton, Oxnatun—from the ox farm

Palmer, Palmere—pilgrim

Park, Parke, Pearroc—of the forest

Parker—keeper of the forest

Parkin, Perekin, Parle, Pierrel, Parnall, Pernel, Pernell, Pollock, Pauloc, Perkin, Perekin—little rock

Parkins, Parkinson—son of Parkin

Parr—from the cattle enclosure

Parrish, Parisch—lives near the church

Parsefal, Percival, Parsifal, Perceval—valley piercer

Patton, Patten, Pattin, Paton— from the warrior's town

Paxton, Pax, Paxtun—from the peaceful farm

Payne, Paine—pagan

Payton, Paegastun, Peyton, Payden—from the fighter's farm

Pell, Paella—mantle

Pemton, Pelltun—from the pool farm

Penley, Penleigh, Pennleah— from the enclosed pasture meadow

Penn, Pyn—from the enclosure

Penton—from the enclosed farm

Perkins, Perkinson—son of Perkin

Perry, Perye—from the pear tree

Phelps, Phillips, Philips—son of Philip

Philip, Phillip—lover of horses

Pickford, Picford—from the peak ford

Pickworth, Picaworth—from the woodcutter's estate

Pierce, Pearce, Peirce—rock

Pierson, Piers, Pearson—son of Pierce

Pit, Pyt—from the pit

Pitney—from the preserving land

Porrex—myth name

Prentice, Prentiss—scholar

Prescott, Prescot, Preostcot—from the priest's dwelling

Presley, Pressley, Priestly—from the priest's meadow

Preston, Prestin, Preostun—from the priest's farm

Prior, Pryor—servant of the priory

Putnam—from the commander's estate

Quentin, Quinton—from the queen's estate

Rad, Raed—red

Radbert, Radburt, Redman, Redamann, Readman—red-haired counselor

Radburn, Radbyrne, Radbourne, Raedburne—lives by the red stream

Radcliffe, Radclyf, Raedclyf, Radcliff—from the red cliff

Radford, Raedford, Redford—from the red ford

Radley, Redley—from the red meadow

Radnor, Raedanoran—from the red shore

Radolf, Radolph, Raedwolf—red wolf

Raedeman—red-haired horseman

Raleigh, Rally, Raleah, Raley, Rawley—from the roe deer meadow

Ralph, Ralf, Raff, Rolf, Rolfe—red wolf

Ralston—from Ralf's farm

Ram, Ramm—ram

Ramsay, Ramsey—from Ram's island

Ramsden—from the ram's valley

Randolph, Randal, Randall, Rafe—shield wolf

Randy—coarse

Ranfield, Renfield—from the raven's field

Rankin, Randkin—little shield

Rans, Raven, Rand, Ren—raven

Ransey, Ransy—from raven's island

Ransford—from the raven ford

Ransley—from the raven's meadow

Ransom, Randson—son of Rand

Rawson, Rawlins, Rawls—son of Rawley or Raleigh

Rayburn, Reyburn, Raybourne—from the deer's stream

Read, Reed, Reid—red-haired

Reading, Redding—son of Reed

Redmond, Redmund, Radmund, Raedmund—red-haired defender

Redwald—strong counsel
Reeve, Reve, Reave—steward
Reeves, Reaves—son of Reeve
Reginald, Regenweald—strong
Remington, Renton—from the
   raven farm
Renfred, Renfrid, Regenfrithu—
   peaceful raven
Renshaw—from the raven forest
Rexford—from the king's ford
Rexley—from the king's meadow
Rexton—from the king's farm
Rhodes, Rodes—lives near the
   crucifix
Rich—wealthy
Richard, Rikkard—strong ruler
Richman, Ricman, Rickman—
   powerful
Ricker—strong army
Rickward, Rikward, Ricweard—
   strong guardian
Rider, Ryder, Ridere—knight
Ridge, Rydge—from the ridge
Ridgely, Ridgeley—lives at the
   meadow's ridge
Ridley, Redley, Raedleah—from
   the red meadow
Ridpath, Raedpath—lives near
   the red path
Rigby, Ricadene—lives in the
   ruler's valley
Rigg—lives near the ridge
Riggs—son of Rigg
Ring—ring
Ripley—from the shouter's
   meadow
Risley—from the brushwood
   meadow
Riston—from the brushwood
   farm

Roan, Rowan—from the rowan
   tree
Rodman—lives by the road
Rodwell—lives by the spring near
   the road
Roe, Row—deer
Romney—from Romney
Ronald—powerful
Ronson—son of Ronald
Roper, Rapere—maker of rope
Rover, Rovere—wanderer
Rowell, Rawiella—from the deer
   spring
Rowley, Ruhleah—from the
   rough meadow
Roxbury—from the raven's
   fortress
Royce, Royse—royal
Royden—from the royal hill
Ruck, Rook—raven
Rudd, Ruddy, Reod—ruddy-
   colored
Rudyard, Ruhdugeard—from the
   rough enclosure
Ruford, Rufford—from the red
   ford
Rugby—from the raven's estate
Rumford—from the wide ford
Rune—a rune
Rush, Rysc—rush
Rushford, Ryscford—lives near
   the rush ford
Russell—fox
Rutherford—from the cattle ford
Rutledge—from the red pool
Rutley—from the root meadow
Rycroft, Rygecroft—from the rye
   field
Ryland, Rygeland—from the rye
   land

Ryman, Rygemann — rye merchant

Ryton, Rygetun — from the rye farm

Safford, Salford, Salhford — from the willow ford

Salisbury — from the fortified keep

Salton, Salhtun — lives near the willow farm

Sanborn, Sanbourne — from the sandy brook

Sanders, Sanersone, Saunders, Saunderson, Sanderson — Alexander's son

Sandon — from the sandy hill

Sanford — from the sandy ford

Santon — from the sandy farm

Sawyer, Sawyere — saws wood

Sawyers — son of Sawyer

Saxon, Saxan — sword

Scott, Scottas — from Scotland

Seabert, Seaburt, Seabright, Sebert, Saebeorht — glory at sea

Seabrook, Saebroc — from the brook by the sea

Seadon — from the hill by the sea

Seaton, Seeton, Seton — from the farm by the sea

Sedge, Secg — swordsman

Sedgeley — from the swordsman's meadow

Sedgewic, Sedgewick, Secgwic, Sedgewik — from the sword grass place

Seely, Selig, Saelig, Sceley, Sealey — from the happy meadow

Sefton — from Sefton

Seger, Seager, Segar, Saeger — seaman

Selby, Seleby, Shelby — from the manor house

Seldon, Selden, Salhdene — from the willow valley

Selwyn, Selwine, Selwin — good friend

Severin — boundary

Seward, Saeweard, Seaward — sea guardian

Sewell, Sewall, Sewald, Saewald — sea powerful

Sexton, Sextein — meaning unknown

Seymour — tailor

Shadwell, Scadwiella — from the shed spring

Shandley, Scandleah — from the loud meadow

Shandy, Scandy — boisterous

Shattuck, Shaddock, Shaddoc, Schaddoc — shad-fish

Shawn, Shaw — from the shady grove

Sheffield, Scaffeld — from the crooked field

Sheldon — from the shield farm

Shelley — from the ledge meadow

Shelton, Scelftun — from the ledge farm

Shepherd, Shepard — shepherd

Shepley, Sheply, Sceapleigh — from the sheep meadow

Sherborne, Sherbourne, Sherbourn, Sherburne — from the clear brook

Sherlock, Scirloc — blond

Sherman — cuts the nap of woolen cloth

Sherwin, Sherwyn — swift

Sherwood, Scirwode — from the bright forest

Shipley — from the sheep meadow

Shipton — from the sheep farm

Siddell, Sidell, Siddael — from the wide valley

Sidney, Sydney — from Sidon

Sidwell — from the broad well

Sigehere — victorious

Silsby — from Sill's farm

Skeet, Skete, Skeat, Sketes — swift

Skelton — from the estate on the ledge

Skipper, Skippere — captain

Skipton — from the sheep estate

Slade, Slaed — from the valley

Slaton, Slayton — from the valley farm

Smedley, Smetheleah — from the flat meadow

Smith, Smyth, Smythe — tradesman

Snowden — from the snowy hill

Somerset — from the summer settlers

Somerton, Sumertun, Sumerton — from the summer estate

Southwell — from the south spring

Spalding, Spelding — from the split meadow

Spark, Sparke — gallant

Spear, Spere — spear

Speed, Sped — success

Spencer, Spenser — keeper of provisions

Sproule, Sproul, Sprowle — active

Squire, Squier — shield bearer

St. Alban — from St. Alban

Stafford, Steathford — from the landing ford

Stanbury, Stanburh, Stanberry — from the stone fortress

Stancliff, Stanclyf — from the rocky cliff

Standish, Stanedisc — from the stony park

Stanfield, Stanfeld — from the stony field

Stanford, Sanford, Stamford — from the stony ford

Stanhope, Stanhop — from the stony hollow

Stanley, Stan, Stanly — lives by the stony grove

Stanton, Staunton, Stantun — from the stony farm

Stanway, Stanweg — lives by the stony road

Stanwick, Stanwyk, Stanwik, Stanwic — from the stony village

Stanwood, Stanwode — from the stony forest

Starbuck — star-deer

Starling, Staerling — bird

Starr — star

Stedman, Stedeman — owns a farm

Sterling, Stirling — of honest value

Sterne, Stern, Stearn — austere

Stewert, Stewart, Stuart, Steward — bailiff

Stillman, Stilleman, Stillmann — quiet

Stock, Stok, Stoc — from the tree stump

Stockley, Stocleah — from the tree-stump meadow

Stockwell, Stocwiella — from the tree-stump spring

Stod, Stodd — horse

Stoddard — keeper of horses

Stoke — from the village

Storm, Storme — tempest

Stowe — place

Stratford — from the river ford on the street

Strong, Strang — powerful

Stroud, Strod — from the thicket

Styles, Stiles, Stigols — stiles

Suffield, Suthfeld — from the south field

Sully, Suthleah, Suthley — from the south meadow

Sumner, Sumernor — summoner

Sutcliff, Sutclyf, Suthclif, Suttecliff — from the south cliff

Sutton — from the south farm

Swain, Swayn — knight's attendant

Swinton, Swintun — from the swine farm

Symington, Symontun — from Simon's estate

Taburer, Tab — drummer

Talon — claw

Tanner, Tannere — leather maker

Tanton, Tamtun — from the quiet river farm

Tarleton, Thoraldtun — from the thunder estate

Tate, Tayt, Tayte, Tait — cheerful

Tearle, Thearl — stern

Tedmond, Theomund, Tedmund — national protector

Templeton, Tempeltun — from the temple farm

Tennyson — son of Dennis

Terrell, Tirell, Terrill, Tirell, Tyrell — thunder ruler

Terris, Terrys, Teryysone — son of Terrell

Thain, Thane, Thegn, Thayne, Thain — follower

Thatcher, Thacher, Thaxter, Thacker, Thackere — roofer

Thaw, Thawain — thaw

Thorley, Torley, Thurleigh, Thurleah — from Thor's meadow

Thormond, Thurmond, Thormund — Thor's protection

Thorn, Torn, Thorne — from the thorn tree

Thorndyke, Thorndike, Thorndic — from the thorny dike

Thornley, Thornly — from the thorny meadow

Thornton, Thorntun — from the thorn-tree farm

Thorpe, Thorp — from the village

Thunder — stormy tempered

Thurlow, Thurhloew — from Thor's hill

Thurston, Thurstun, Thurstan — Thor's stone

Tila, Tyla — good

Tilden, Tiladene — from the fertile valley

Tilford — from the fertile ford

Tilman, Tillman — virile

Tilton — from the good estate

Toft — from the small farm

Toland, Tolland—owns taxed land

Tolman—collects taxes

Tomkin, Thomkins—little Tom

Tomlin—little twin

Torr—tower

Tostig—name of an earl

Towley, Townly, Tunleah—from the town meadow

Townsend—from the end of the town

Tredway, Treadway, Thrythwig—strong warrior

Trent—from the river Trent

Tripp, Trip, Trypp, Tryp, Tripper—traveler

Trowbridge, Trowbrydge, Treowbrycg—from the tree bridge

True, Treowe—loyal

Truesdale, Truitestall, Truesdell—from the beloved one's farm

Trumble, Trumbald, Trumball—strong, bold

Trumen, Truman, Treoweman—loyal

Tucker, Toukere, Tuckere—tucker of cloth

Tupper, Tuppere—ram herder

Turner, Tournour—lathe-worker

Twain, Twein—cut in two

Twitchell, Twitchel—lives on a narrow passage

Twyford, Twiford—from the double river ford

Tye, Tyg, Teyen—from the enclosure

Tyler, Tylere—maker of tiles

Tyson, Tyesone—son of Tye

Udell, Udale, Udayle, Udall—from the yew-tree valley

Udolf, Udolph—wealthy wolf

Ulfred—wolf of peace

Ulger—wolf spear

Ullock, Ullok, Ulvelaik—wolf sport

Ulmar, Ulmarr—wolf famous

Unwin, Unwyn, Unwine—unfriendly

Upchurch—from the upper church

Upton, Uptun—from the upper farm

Upwood, Upwode—from the upper forest

Vail, Vayle, Vale—lives in the valley

Valiant—brave

Vance, Vannes—grain fans

Varik, Varek, Varyk, Vareck—from the fortress

Vingon, Vinson, Vinsone—son of Vinn

Vinn—conqueror

Wade, Wada, Waed—advancer

Wadley—from Wade's meadow

Wadsworth—from Wade's estate

Wainwright—wagon maker

Waite, Wait, Wayte—guard

Wake, Wacian—alert

Wakefield, Wacfeld—from Wake's field

Wakeley, Wacleah—from Wake's meadow

Wakeman, Wacuman—watchman

Walbridge, Walbrydge—from the Welshman's bridge

Walby—from the Welshman's dwellings

Walcot, Walcott, Weallcot — lives in the Welshman's cottage

Walden — from the Welshman's valley

Waldon, Waldron — from the Welshman's hill

Walford — from the Welshman's ford

Walker — thickener of cloth

Wallace, Waleis, Wallis, Walsh, Welch, Welsh — from Wales

Waller, Weallere — mason

Walton, Walworth, Wealaworth — from the Welshman's farm

Walwyn, Wealaworth — Welsh friend

Ward, Warde, Warden, Worden, Weard — guard

Wardell, Weardhyll — from the guardian's hill

Wardley, Weardleah — from the guardian's meadow

Ware, Waer — wary

Wareine, Warren — gamekeeper

Warfield, Weifield — from the field by the weir

Warford, Weiford — from the farm by the weir

Warley, Warleigh, Weirley — from the weir meadow

Warrick, Warwick, Warwyk, Waeringawicum — fortress

Warton, Wartun — from the farm by the weir

Washburn, Washbourne, Washburne, Waescburne — from the flooding brook

Washington — from the intelligent one's farm

Watford, Watelford — from the hurdle ford

Watkins, Wattkins, Wattikinson, Wattekinson — son of Watt

Watson, Wattesone, Watts, Wattson — son of Walter

Watt, Wat — hurdle

Waverly, Waefreleah — from the quaking-aspen tree meadow

Wayland, Wegland, Weyland — from the land by the highway

Wayne, Wain — craftsman

Webley, Webbeleah — from the weaver's meadow

Webster, Webb, Webbe, Webbestre — weaver

Weddell, Wadanhyll — from the advancer's hill

Welborne, Welburn, Welborn, Wiellaburne — from the spring brook

Welby, Wiellaby — from the spring farm

Weldon, Wielladun — from the spring hill

Welford, Wiellaford — from the spring by the ford

Wellington, Weolingtun — from the wealthy estate

Wells, Welles — lives by the spring

Welton, Wiellatun — from the spring farm

Wentworth, Wintanweorth — from the white one's estate

Wesley, Westley, Westleah — from the west meadow

West, Wes — from the west

Westbrook, Westbroc — from the west brook

Westby—from the west farm

Westcott, Westcot—from the west cottage

Weston, Westun—from the west farm

Wetherby, Weatherby, Wethrby—from the wether-sheep farm

Wetherly, Weatherly, Wethrleah—from the wether-sheep meadow

Wharton—from the estate at the hollow

Wheatley—from the wheat meadow

Wheeler—wheel-maker

Whistler—piper

Whitby—from the white farm

Whitcomb—from the white hollow

Whitelaw, Whitlaw—from the white hill

Whitfield—from the white field

Whitford—from the white ford

Whitley—from the white meadow

Whitlock, Whytlok—blond

Whitman—white-haired

Whitmore, Whitmoor—from the white moor

Whitney—from the white-haired man's estate

Whittaker—from the white field

Wickam, Wiccum, Wichamm, Wickley, Wicleah—from the village meadow

Wilbert, Wilburt—intelligent

Wilbur, Willaburh—from the strong fortress

Wildon—from the wooded hill

Wilford, Wylingford—from the willow ford

Wilfrid, Wilfred, Wilfryd—peace

Will, Willa—resolute

Willard, Willhard—resolute, brave

William—resolute protector

Willis, Wilson, Willesone, Williams, Williamson—son of William

Willoughby, Wyligby—from the willow farm

Wilton, Wylltun—from the farm by the spring

Wichell, Wincel—from the bend in the road

Windsor, Winsor, Wendlesora—from Windsor

Wine, Wyne, Win, Winn—friend

Winfield, Wynfield, Winefield—from a friend's field

Winfred, Wynfrid, Winfrid, Winefrith, Winfrith, Wynfrith—friend of peace

Wingate, Windgate—from the winding gate

Winslow, Winslowe—from Wine's hill

Winston, Winton, Wynston—from Wine's farm

Winter, Wynter—born in the winter

Winthrop, Wynthrop, Winthorp, Winetorp—from Wine's estate

Winward, Wynward, Winswode, Winwood, Winwodem, Wynwode—from Wine's forest

Witt, Witta—wise

Witter, Wittahere—wise warrior

Witton, Wittatun — from the wise man's estate

Wolcott, Woolcott, Wulfcot, Wolfcot — lives in Wolfe's cottage

Wolfe, Wolf, Wulf — wolf

Woodley, Wodeleah — from the wooded meadow

Woodman — hunter

Woodrow — from the hedgerow by the forest

Woodruff — bailiff

Woolsey, Wulfsige — victorious wolf

Woodward, Wudoweard — forester

Worcester, Wireceaster — from the alder forest, army camp

Worden — defender

Wordsworth, Wulfweardsweorth — world guardian

Worrell, Waerheall — from the true man's manor

Worth, Weorth — from the farm

Worton, Wyrttun — from the vegetable farm

Wright, Wryhta — craftsman

Wulffrith — wolf of peace

Wulfgar — wolf spear

Wyatt, Wiatt — guide

Wycliff, Wyclyf — from the white cliff

Wyman, Wigman — warrior

Wymer, Wigmaere — famous in battle

Wyndham, Windham — from the windy village

Wythe, Wyth — from the willow tree

Yale — from the slope land

Yardley, Yardly — from the enclosed meadow

Yates — lives by the gates

Yeoman, Yoman — retainer

York — from the bear estate

Yule, Yul — born at Christmas

Finnish

Surnames are mostly patronymic (-nen), but the Finns also use descriptive, occupational and place names.

Some Finnish surnames:

Heikkinen	Kivi
Hietamaki	Miettlinen
Joki	Mustanen
Kipelainan	Seppanen
Kirkkomaki	Valkoinen

FEMALE

Annikki — bitter
Antti — legend name
Anttiri — mannish
Dorotea — Finnish form of Dorothy (God's gift)
Eeva — life
Helli — Finnish form of Helen (light)
Ilmarinen — legend name
Ingria, Inkeri — hero's daughter
Jaakkina, Janne — feminine form of Jukka (God is gracious)
Jurma — legend name
Kalwa — heroine
Katrina, Kaisa, Katri, Katrikki — pure

Kerttu — Finnish form of Gertrude (spear)
Kyllikki — woman of strength
Laila — light
Leppa — legend name
Liisa — consecrated to God
Maikki, Maiju — bitter
Mielikki — pleasant
Mirjam — Finnish form of Miriam (rebellious)
Parttyli — meaning unknown
Rikka — feminine form of Rikkard (strong ruler)
Russu, Ruusu — rose
Rute, Ruta — beautiful
Vellamo — protector

MALE

Antti — Finnish form of Andrew (manly)
Eikki — powerful

Heikki — Finnish form of Henry (rules the home)
Heikkinen — son of Henry

Hietamaki — meaning unknown
Jani, Johan, Jussi, Jukka — Finnish form of John (God is gracious)
Jarvi — lake
Joki — river
Joosep, Joosef — Finnish form of Joseph (He adds)
Jorma — farmer
Kaarle, Kaarl, Kaarlo, Kalle, Kal — strong
Kalevi — hero
Kirkkomaki — meaning unknown
Kivi — stone
Lippo — legend name
Maki — hill
Mustanen — black
Niles — people's victory
Oskari — leaping warrior
Paavo, Paaveli — Finnish form of Paul (little)

Pekka — stone
Rikkard — Finnish form of Richard (strong ruler)
Risto — form of Christopher (Christ-bearer)
Seppanen — smith
Severi — legend name
Taavi, Taavetti — beloved
Talo — house
Taneli — form of Daniel (judge)
Tapio — legend name
Teppo — victorious
Tuomas — Finnish form of Thomas (twin)
Vaino — legend name
Valkoinen — white
Vappu — legend name
Viljo — resolute protector
Yrjo — Finnish form of George (farmer)

French

There are two types of French surnames: those coming from the Frankish Empire and those brought in by the Norman settlers in the tenth century. Last names began as epithets attached either after the name or to the name, e.g., Pepin the Short or Charlemagne (Charles the Great). This tendency goes back to the Dark Ages but was restricted to the aristocracy.

When the Normans invaded England in 1066, they added epithets that named their estates in Normandy—Robert de Montgomerie, for example. If they didn't have an estate, they took the name of the province or town from whence they came—Piers de Paris.

By the twelfth century, some names had become hereditary, and by the thirteenth they had become common. The handing down of name from father to son was firmly established by the fifteenth century.

One interesting point about the Normans is that before hereditary surnames became commonplace, families stuck to a few names that alternated by generation. George would name his son after his own father, Gilbert, and when Gilbert grew to manhood and had a son, that son would be named George.

Surnames are descriptive, patronymic, or based on place or occupation.

In the twelfth and thirteenth centuries, biblical names became very popular: Peter, John, Jean, Luke and so on. After the French Revolution, names were restricted to a list of French names that bore no resemblance to foreign words or names. Throughout French history, Teutonic, Norse, Slavic, Latin and Danish names have been used.

The article *de* (meaning of) between names was usually reserved for the nobility and denoted lands or estates the man held. *Le* means simply the and has been used with occupation or descriptive names.

A few French surnames:

Bettencourt	Dutetre
Billaud	Fortier
Cuvier	Guignard

Heuse   Raison
Olivier   Severin

FEMALE

Abella — breath
Aceline — noble
Adele, Adela — good humor
Adorlee — adored
Adrienne — dark
Afrodille — daffodil
Agathe — kind
Aida — help
Aiglentine, Aiglentina —
    sweetbrier rose
Aimee, Amata, Amy, Ami — dearly
    loved
Alacoque — meaning unknown
Albertine, Albertina — feminine
    form of Albert
Albracca — legend name
Alcina — legend name
Alexandrine, Alexis — feminine
    form Alexandre
Allegra — cheerful
Allete, Alita — winged
Amabelle, Amabella — lovable
Amarante — flower
Ambre, Ambra — jewel
Amedee — loves God
Amelie — hard working
Amity, Amite, Amitee — friend
Ancelin, Ancelina — handmaiden
Andree, Andrea — feminine form
    of Andre (manly)
Angelette, Angeletta — little angel
Angelique, Angela, Angilia, Ange,
    Angeline, Angelina,
    Angelika — angel
Annette — little Ann

Antoinette — beyond praise
Apolline, Apollina — gift from
    Apollo
Aubine, Aubina — blond
Aude, Auda — old, wealthy
Aveline, Avelaine — nut
Avice — warlike
Aya — legend name
Azura — blue
Babette — stranger
Belda — fair maiden
Belisarda — legend name
Berangaria — name of a princess
Bernadette — feminine form of
    Bernard (bear)
Bertha — legend name
Blanch, Blanche — white
Blanchefleur — white flower
Bonny, Bonnie — sweet
Bradamate — legend name
Brucie — forest sprite
Brunella — brown-haired
Cadence, Cadencia — rhythmic
Calandre — lark
Calanthe, Calantha — beautiful
    flower
Capucine, Capucina — cape
Caresse — endearing
Carine, Carina, Cateline — pure
Carnation — flesh-colored
Carola, Carolina, Caroline, Carol,
    Carole — song of happiness
Chantel — song
Charlotte, Carlotta — tiny and
    feminine

Charmaine, Charleen, Charlene, Charline — manly

Cherry, Cherie, Cher, Cheree, Cheri, Cherise — dear

Cinderella, Cendrillon — of the ashes

Claire, Clarette — clear

Clarice — famous

Clarimunda — legend name

Claudette, Claudine — lame

Clementina — merciful

Colette, Collette — necklace

Comfort, Comforte — strength

Coralie — coral

Corette, Coretta — little maiden

Cosette — victorious

Crescent, Creissant — to create

Daisi — daisy

Damien, Damiane, Damia, Damiana — untamed

Darcy, D'Arcy — from Arcy

Delight, Delit — pleasure

Delmare — of the sea

Demi — name taken from heraldry

Denise, Denice — feminine form of Denys (named for the god of wine)

Desiree, Desire, Desirat, Desideria — desired

Diamanta — diamond

Diane, Diana — from the Greek goddess of the moon

Dixie — born tenth

Dominique — feminine form of Dominic (born on Sunday)

Dorene, Dory, Doreen, Dorine, Dore — blonde

Durandana, Durindana — legend name

Edmee — feminine form of

Edmund (rich protector)

Eglantine, Eglantina — wild rose

Elinore, Elienor, Eleanor, Ellinor — light

Elisa, Elise, Eliza, Elisabeth — consecrated to God

Elita, Eleta — chosen

Eloise, Eloisa, Eloisee — famous in war

Emmeline — industrious

Erembourg — meaning unknown

Ermengardine — meaning unknown

Esmeraude, Emeraude — emerald

Esperanza — hope

Estelle — star

Eugenia — noble

Eulalie — well-spoken

Fabienne — bean grower

Falerina — legend name

Fanchon, Fanchone — free

Fanette, Fanetta — crowned with laurels

Fantine, Fantina — childlike

Favor — approval

Fawnia, Faunia, Faun, Fauna — fawn

Fay, Faye, Fae — fairy

Fayette — little fairy

Fayme — famed

Fealty — faithful

Felicienne, Filicia, Felicia, Felicity — great happiness

Fifi, Fifine — nickname for Josephine

Fleur — flower

Fleurette — little flower

Flordelis — legend name

France — from France

Fusberta — legend name

Gaetane, Gaetana — from Gaete
Galatee — white
Gallia, Gala, Galla — from Gaul
Garland — crowned with flowers
Gay — light-hearted
Gemma — jewel
Geneva, Genevre — juniper
Genevieve — white wave
Georgette, Georgitte — feminine form of George (farmer)
Germana, Germaine, Germain — from Germany
Gyongy — meaning unknown
Halette — little Hal
Harriet, Hanriette, Hanrietta, Harriette, Harrietta — rules the home
Hedvige — fighter
Heloise — French form of Louise (famous warrior maiden)
Henriette, Henrietta — keeper of the hearth
Hilaire — French form of Hilary (happy)
Holly — shrub
Honore — honor
Huette, Huguetta, Hugette — feminine form of Hugh (intelligent)
Ila — from the island
Iva — from the yew tree
Jacqueline — feminine form of Jacques (supplanter)
Jacquenette, Jacquenetta — little Jacques
Jeanette, Jeanetta — little Jean
Jeanne, Jehane — feminine form of Jean (God's gift)
Jessamine, Jessamina — jasmine
Jewel, Jule — jewel

Joanna — God's gift
Jolie — beautiful
Josette, Josephine, Josepha, Josephe — feminine form of Joseph (He adds)
Joy — jewel/delight
Julie, Julia, Juliette, Juliet, Julietta, Julita — youthful
Julienne — feminine form of Julian (youthful)
Karla — strong
Karlotta, Karoline, Karolina — tiny and feminine
Karoly, Karcsi, Kari — joyful song
La Roux — red-haired
Laurel, Lauren, Laurene — laurel
Laurette — little laurel
Laverna, Lavernia, La Verne, La Vergne — born in the spring
Leala, Liealia, Lealia — loyal
Leona, Leonie, Leone, Leonelle, Leonarda — lion
Liane, Liana — bond
Liriene, Lirienne — reads aloud
Logistilla, Logestilla — legend name
Lorraine, Loraine — from Lorraine
Lotye, Letya, Letje — tiny and womanly
Lucille, Lucile — light
Lundy — born on Monday
Lynnette, Linette, Lyonette, Lyonette — little lion
Madeleine, Madeleina, Madie, Madolen — tower
Magnolia — flower
Manette, Mariette, Marietta, Marian, Marianne, Maria, Marie — bitter

Marcelle, Marcella, Marcellia — warring

Margo, Margaux, Margot, Marguerite, Marjori, Margery — pearl

Marjolaine, Marjolaina — flower

Marphisa — legend name

Marvel, Marveille, Marvella, Marvelle — miracle

Mathilde, Matilda, Mathilda, Mattie, Matty, Maud, Maude — strong in war

Maura, Maureen, Moreen, Maurine, Maurina — dark-skinned

Maurelle — dark and elfin

Mavis, Mavise — joy

Melisande — honey-bee

Melodie — melody

Melusina — dark-skinned

Merci, Mercy — merciful

Methena, Methina — meaning unknown

Mignon, Mignonette — delicate

Millicent, Millicente — of a thousand saints

Mimi, Minna, Minnie, Minette, Minetta — form of Williamina (resolute protector)

Mirabelle, Mirabella — of incredible beauty

Mireille — miracle

Monique, Moniqua — wise

Morgana — legend name

Musetta, Musette — a song

Nadine — from Nada

Nanna — legend name

Natalii, Natalie, Natuche — born at Christmas

Nicola, Nicolette — people's victory

Ninette, Ninon, Nanon — grace

Noel, Noelle, Noella — Christmas

Odelette, Odeletta — little spring

Olympe, Olympia — from Olympus

Ophelie, Ophelia — serpentine

Orane — rising

Oriel — bird

Orlena, Orlene, Orlina — gold

Ormazd — legend name

Orva — worth gold

Paige, Page — attendant

Pansy — flower

Parnella — rock

Pascale, Pascala, Pascaline, Pasclina — born at Easter

Patience — enduring

Patrice — noble

Pensee — thoughtful

Phillipa — loves horses

Pierrette, Pierretta — feminine form of Pierre (rock)

Prunella, Prunellie — color of plum

Rachelle — lamb

Raina, Reine, Reina — queen

Raissa, Raison — thinker

Renee, Rene — reborn

Rive, Riva — from the shore

Robinette, Robinetta — small robin

Romaine, Romana — from Rome

Rose, Rohais, Roesia, Rosamonde — rose

Rosemarie, Rosemaria — bitter rose

Roux — red

Roxane, Roxanne — dawn

Royale, Roial — regal

Ruby, Rubie — jewel

Searlait — tiny and womanly

Sidonie, Sidonia, Sydney — follower of Saint Denys

Simone — heard

Slania, Slainie, Slanie — health

Solange, Silana, Solaine, Solaina — dignified

Stephanie, Stefania — crowned in victory

Suzanne, Suzette — lily

Sibyla — prophetess

Tempeste — stormy

Tilda, Tilly — mighty in war

Trinette, Trinetta — little innocent

Valerie, Valere, Valara, Valeraine — brave

Vedette, Vedetta — from the guard tower

Veronique — honest

Victorine, Victorina — victory

Vignette, Vignetta — little vine

Villette, Villetta — from the country estate

Viollette, Violetta — little violet

Vivienne — lively

Voleta, Voletta — veiled

Xavierre, Xavierra — owner of a new home

Yolanda, Yolande, Yolanthe — strong

Yolette — meaning unknown

Yseult — fair

Yvette, Yvonne — archer

Zara — light

Zuria, Zuri, Zurie — white and lovely

MALE

Agramant — myth name

Agrican — from the field

Ahriman — legend name

Alain — handsome

Aleron — knight

Alexandre — French form of Alexander (defends mankind)

Algernon, Algrenon — bearded

Aloin, Aluin — noble friend

Amaury — name of a count

Ansel, Ancil, Acel, Ansell — adherent of a nobleman

Arber — dealer of herbs

Archaimbaud, Archambault, Archenbaud — bold

Archard — powerful

Armand — French form of Herman (soldier)

Arnaud — eagle ruler

Arno — little eagle

Arnou, Arnoux — eagle wolf

Arridano — legend name

Artus — noble

Ashtaroth — legend name

Astolpho — legend name

Atlantes — legend name

Aubert — noble

Aubin — fair

Aubrey, Albaric — blond ruler

Audric, Aldrick, Aldrich — old, wise ruler

Auriville — from the gold town

Avenall, Avenelle, Aveneil — lives near the oatfield

Avent, Advent — born during Advent

Aymon—legend name
Bailey, Bayley—steward
Balisarda—myth name
Barry, Barrie—lives at the barrier
Bartlett—ploughman
Bayard—legend name
Beaufort—from the beautiful
    fortress
Bellamy, Bell—handsome
Beltane—legend name
Bertrand—intelligent
Bevis, Beauvais—from Beauvais
Brice—from Brieuxtown
Brigliadoro—legend name
Bruce, Brys—from Brys
Brunelle—dark-haired
Burkett, Burcet—from the little
    stronghold
Burnell, Burel—reddish-brown
    hair
Burrell—reddish-brown skin
Byron, Buiron—from the cottage
Campbell—from the beautiful
    field
Carolos, Carlo, Carolus, Carlos,
    Carel—strong
Chandler, Chanler—maker of
    candles
Channing—member of the
    bishop's council
Chapin—clergyman
Chappell, Chappel—from the
    chapel
Charles, Cearbhall—manly
Charlot—name of the son of
    Charlemagne
Cheney—from the oak wood
Christien, Cretien—Christian
Cloridan—myth name
Clovis—name of a king

Courtland, Courtney, Court, Curt,
    Courtnay, Cort—from the
    court
Curtis, Curtice, Curcio—
    courteous
Darcy, D'Arcy—from Arcy
Davet—beloved
Delmar, Delmer—mariner
Denis, Dennis, Denys, Dennet—
    named for Saint Denys
Desire, Didier—desired
Dexter—name taken from
    heraldry
Donatien—gift
Eliot, Eliott, Elliot—believes in
    God
Etienne—French form of
    Stephen (crowned)
Ferragus—legend name
Ferrau—legend name
Fitz—son of
Fletcher—feathers arrows
Florismart—legend name
Florus—flower
Forrest—from the woods
Fortun, Fortune—lucky
Frontino—legend name
Gaetan—from Gaete
Ganelon, Gan—legend name
Gano—legend name
Garland—crowned in victory
Gaspar, Gaspard—French form of
    Caspar (guardian of the
    treasure)
Gaston, Gascon—from Gascony
Gauthier, Gautier—French form
    of Walter (strong warrior)
Geoffrey—divine peace
Germain, Germano—German
Gifford, Guifford—chubby cheeks

Gill, Gil — French form of Julius (youthful)

Gradasso — legend name

Granville, Grenville — from the large town

Grosvenor — great hunter

Guerin — legend name

Guy — guide

Hamilton — from the mountain town

Harbin — glorious warrior

Harcourt — from the fortified farm

Hardouin — name of a count

Henry — rules the home

Hugh — intelligent

Ignace — fiery

Iven — little archer

Jacques, Jacquelin — French form of Jacob (supplanter)

Javier — born in January

Jay, Jaye — bluejay

Jean — French form of John (God is gracious)

Jean Baptiste — named for John the Baptist

Jeoffroi, Jeffrey — divine peace

Jesper, Jasper — jasper stone

Jules, Julian, Jullien — youthful

Karel, Karl, Kaarlo, Kalle, Kaarle, Karlis, Kalman, Karoly, Kari, Karcsi, Karlens, Karlitis — strong and masculine

Kerman — German

Lance, Lancelot, Launcelot, Lancelin — servant

Landers, Landis — from the grassy plain

Langley, L'Angley — Englishman

Latimer — interprets Latin

Leal — faithful

Legget — delegate

Leon, Leone, Leonce, Leocadie, Leodegrance — lion

Leroy — regal

Leverett, Leveret — young rabbit

Loring — from Lorraine

Lothair — fighter

Louis — famous in war

Lowell, Lovell, Lowe, Louvel — little wolf

Loyal — true

Lyle, Lisle — from the island

Malagigi — legend name

Mallory, Mailhairer — ill-fated

Mandel, Mantel — makes garments

Manville, Manneville — from the great estate

Marlon — little falcon

Marmion — small one

Marshall, Marshal, Marsh — steward

Marsilius — legend name

Maslin, Masselin — little Thomas

Mason, Masson — stone worker

Mayhew, Mahieu — gift of God

Medoro — legend name

Melville, Malleville — from Malleville

Mercer — merchant

Merle — blackbird

Merlin, Merlion — falcon

Michel, Michele — French form of Michael (God-like)

Millard — strong

Montague, Montaigu — from the pointed hill

Moore, More, Moor — dark-skinned

Namo—legend name

Neville, Neuveville—from the new town

Noel—Christmas

Normand, Norman, Norm—from the north

Norris, Norice, Noreis—caretaker

Nouel—a kernel

Octave—born eighth

Odo—name of a bishop

Ogier—legend name

Oliver—legend name

Olivier—from the olive tree

Onfroi—peaceful Hun

Orson, Ourson—little bear

Orville—from the gold town

Page, Paige, Padgett, Paget—attendant

Paien—name of a nobleman

Parfait—perfect

Pascal, Pascual, Pasquale—born on Easter

Peppin, Pippin—name of a king

Percy, Percival—pierce

Perrin, Perren, Perryn, Perry, Pierre—rock

Peverell, Piperel, Pepperell—piper

Philip, Philippe, Phillipe—loves horses

Pierpont, Pierrepont—lives by the stone bridge

Pinabel—legend name

Platt, Plat—from the flat land

Pomeroy, Pommeraie—lives near the apple orchard

Porter, Portier, Porteur—gatekeeper

Prewitt, Pruitt, Preruet, Pruet, Pruie—brave

Pryor, Priour—head of a priory

Quennel, Quesnel—from the little oak tree

Quincy, Quincey—from the place owned by the fifth son

Rabican—legend name

Ranger, Rainger—ward of the forest

Raoul—wolf

Ray, Roy, Rey, Rui, Royal—regal

Remy, Remi—rower

Rene—reborn

Robert—bright, famous

Roch, Roche, Rocke—rock

Romain—a Roman

Roslyn, Roslin, Roselin, Roselyn, Rosselin, Rosselyn, Ruff, Ruffe, Rush, Rushe, Rousse, Rushkin, Rousskin, Rust, Rousset—red-haired

Royce—son of Roy

Royden—from the king's hill

Rule, Ruelle, Reule—famous wolf

Russell, Roussel—reddish

Saber—sword

Sacripant—legend name

Sargent—a squire

Satordi—Saturn

Saville, Sauville—from the willow farm

Scoville—meaning unknown

Searlas, Searle, Searlus—manly

Senapus—legend name

Senior, Seignour—lord of the manor

Sennet, Senet—wise

Seymour—from St. Maur

Sidney, Sydney—from St. Denys

Somer — born in summer

Somerville, Sumarville — from the summer estate

Soren, Sorel, Sorrell — reddish-brown hair

Sumner — a summoner

Tabor — tabard

Talbot, Talebot — bloodhound

Talon — sharp

Taylor — a tailor

Tearlach — manly

Telford, Telfer, Taillefer, Telfor, Telfour — works in iron

Thierry, Thibaud, Tibault — rule of the people

Toussaint — all saints

Travers, Travis — from the crossroads

Troy, Troyes — curly-haired

Turner — champion in a tournament

Tyson, Tyeis — son of a German

Vachel — little cow

Vaden — meaning unknown

Vail, Vayle — from the vale

Valiant — brave

Vallis, Vallois — a Welshman

Varden, Vardan, Vardon, Verddun — from the green hill

Verney, Vernay — from the alder grove

Vernon — from Vernon

Verrill, Verel, Verrall, Verrell, Veryl — true

Vick, Vic, Vicq — from the village

Warrane — warden of the game

William — determined protector

Wyatt, Wiatt — guide

Xarles — manly

Yves — little archer

Yvon, Yvet — archer

Zdenek — follower of Saint Denys

Zerbino — legend name

Gaelic

As in the case of the Celtic surnames, Gaelic surnames are found in the countries where the Gaelic language is spoken, such as France, Ireland and Scotland.

FEMALE

Africa, Affrica, Apirka — pleasant

Aigneis, Una — Gaelic forms of Agnes (pure)

Ailis — Gaelic form of Alice (honest)

Aimil — Gaelic form of Amelia (industrious)

Aingealag — angel

Airleas — oath

Alanna, Alain, Alayne, Allene, Allyn, Alina, Alana — bright

Amber — fierce

Amhuinn — lives at the alder-tree river

Annabel, Annabelle, Annabella, Anabal — joy

Arienh — meaning unknown

Aselma — fair

Barabell, Barabal — stranger

Bebhinn — harmony

Beitris — Gaelic form of Beatrice (makes others happy)

Breandan, Brenda — little raven

Brighde — myth name

Cairistiona, Ciorstag, Ciorstan — Christian

Carling — little champion

Cassidy, Casidhe — clever

Cathasach, Caci, Casey — brave

Catriona, Ceit, Cait, Caitlin — pure

Ceallach — warrior maid

Ceara — spear

Ciarda — dark

Coleen, Colleen — girl

Con — exalted

Cuini — queen

Deirdre, Deidra, Deardriu — raging

Diorbhall — Gaelic form of Dorothy (God's gift)

Donalda, Domhnulla, Donia — rules all

Doreen, Dorene, Doire-ann, Doireann — sullen

Dymphna — little poet

Ealasaid — devoted to God

Edana, Eideann — fiery

Eibhlin — Gaelic form of Eileen or Evelyn (light, or life-giving)

Eilidh — light

Eilionoir — Gaelic form of Eleanor (light)

Erin — peace

Erlina, Erline — girl from Ireland

Fionnghuala — flower

Frangag — free

Ghleanna — lives in the valley

Giorsal — Gaelic form of Grizel (gray battle-maid)

Glen, Glenn, Glenna, Glennis, Glynnes, Glynnis, Glynis — from the glen

Grainne — grace

Iseabal, Isobail — devoted to God

Ita — thirsty

Kerry, Keriam — dark-haired

Kyna — intelligent

Laoidheach — from the pasture meadow

Leitis — happy

Leslie, Lesley — from the gray fortress

Lili — lily

Liusaidh, Kelly, Kellie — warrior woman

Mairearad, Mairghread — pearl

Maolmin — polished chief

Marsali — pearl

Mildread — Gaelic form of Mildred (mild counselor)

Moibeal — Gaelic form of Mabel (lovable)

Mor, Mairi, Muireall — bitter

Morag — Gaelic form of Sheila (blind)

Muadhnait — noble

Nara — happy

Nuallan — famous

Odharnait — pale

Onora — honor

Peigi — peg

Raonaid, Raonaild — ewe

Ros, Rois — rose

Seana, Seonaid — gift from God

Sile, Silis, Sighle — Gaelic form of Sheila (blind)

Sine — feminine form of Sean (God is gracious)

Siubhan — Gaelic form of Joan (God is gracious)

Siusan — lily

Taithleach — quiet

Tara — from the crag of a tower

Toirdealbach — myth name

MALE

Abboid — abbey father

Adair, Athdara, Athdar — from the oak-tree ford

Adhamh — Gaelic form of Adam (man of the red earth)

Ahern, Aherin, Aherne — owns many horses

Ailin, Ailen, Ailean — handsome

Aindreas — manly

Airdsgainne — from the height of the cliff

Airleas, Arlen — pledge

Allister, Alaster, Alai — defender of man

Alroy — red-haired

Aod — myth name

Aodh — spirit

Aodhhan, Aidan, Aodhagan — ardent

Aonghus, Angus — superior strength

Arregaithel — from the land of the Gaels

Artur, Art — rock

Bacstair — baker

Baillidh — steward

Bain, Bharain, Bheathain — lives near the clear stream

Bainbridge, Bainbrydge — lives by the bridge over the stream

Baird, Bard — poet

Balfour, Bailefour — from the pasture land

Banain, Banning — little blond one

Baran — noble warrior

Batair — strong warrior

Beagan, Beagen — little one

Bealantin — Gaelic form of Ballantine (brave)

Bearach, Barry, Barra — spear

Bearnard — Gaelic form of Bernard (bear warrior)

Beattie, Beatie, Beatty, Biadhaiche — blesses

Bebhinn — harmony

Bhruic — badger

Blair — child of the fields

Bowie, Bow, Bowen, Bowyn, Boyd, Buidhe — blond

Boyne, Bofind — white cow

Boynton — from the white river

Brady, Bradach — spirited

Brendan, Breandan, Brennan, Brendon — brave

Brothaigh — from Brodie

Brus — from Bruys

Buadhachan — victorious

Cailean, Cailen, Caillen, Colin, Colan, Collin, Coll — child

Caley, Caolaidhe — slender

Calhoun, Coillcumhann — from the narrow forest

Calum, Colm — servant of Saint Columba

Camden, Camdene — from the crooked valley

Cameron, Camshron — crooked nose

Campbell, Caimbeul — crooked mouth

Caolabhuinn — from the narrow river

Carlin, Carlie, Cearbhallan, Carling — small champion

Carmichael, Caramichil — friend of Saint Michael

Carney, Cearnach — victorious

Carrick, Carraig, Charraigaich — rocky headland

Carroll, Carol, Carly, Carolus — champion

Casey, Cathasach — brave

Cassidy, Casidhe — clever

Cathmor, Cathmore, Cathaoirmore — great warrior

Cavan, Caomhan — handsome

Ceallach — warrior

Ceannfhionn — blond

Ceileachan — little champion

Cerin — little dark one

Cian, Cein — ancient

Ciardubhan — little black one

Cinnard — from the high hill

Cinneididh — helmeted

Cinnfhail — from the head of the cliff

Cleary, Cleirach — scholar

Cluny, Clunainach — from the meadow

Coigleach — distaff

Coilleach, Choilleich — guards the forest

Coinleain — well-shaped

Coinneach — handsome

Colin, Coilin — virile

Colum, Columbanus, Calum — dove

Comhghan — twin

Comyn, Cuimean—meaning unknown

Conlan, Connlan, Conlin—hero

Conroy, Conaire—wise

Conway—hound of the plain

Corcoran, Corcurachan—reddish-skinned

Corey, Cori, Cory, Coire—ravine

Cormac, Cormick, Cormack—charioteer

Cowan, Cobhan—dwells by the hillside hollow

Coyle—searches for battle

Craig, Creag—dwells at the crag

Criostoir, Crisdean—Christ-bearer

Cronan—dark brown

Cuilean—cub

Cuinn—wise

Cullan, Cullin, Cully—handsome

Culley, Colle, Cully—dwells at the woodland

Curran, Curr, Curney, Curadhan—hero

Daibhidh—beloved

Dall, Dallas—wise

Daly—counselor

Darby, Diarmaid, Dermot, Dermod, Dermott, Diarmid, Diarmad—free man

Darren, Daryn, Daron, Dearan—great

Darry, D'Ary, Dar, Darce—dark

Deasach, Dacey, Dacy—southerner

Delano—healthy black man

Dempsey, Diomasach—proud

Deorsa—farmer

Derry—red-haired

Desmond, Deasmumhan,

Desmon—man from south Munster

Devlin, Devlyn, Dobhailen—fierce

Devyn, Devin, Devan, Daimhin—servant

Dillon, Diolmhain—faithful

Domhnull, Donald—dark stranger

Donahue, Duncan—dark warrior

Dooley, Dubhloach—dark hero

Duff, Dubhthach, Duffy, Dugan, Dubhgan—dark-skinned

Dugald, Dughall—dark stranger

Duncan, Donnchadh—dark warrior

Eachann—steadfast

Eachthighearn—horse lord

Ealadhach—genius

Eamonn, Eamon—rich protector

Eanruig—ruler of the home

Earvin—handsome

Earnan—earnest

Eideard—rich guardian

Eoghan, Egan, Egon, Eoghann—young fighter

Erin—peace

Fagen, Faodhagan, Fagin—ardent

Faolan—little wolf

Farrell, Fearghall—victorious

Fearcher, Farquhar—very dear

Fergus, Fearghus, Ferghus—rock

Finlay, Fionnlaoch, Fionn, Findlay, Finn, Fionnlagh—small, blond soldier

Flann—red-haired

Flynn, Flin—son of the red-haired man

Forbes, Fearbhirigh—wealthy or stubborn

Frang, Frannsaidh—frank

Gabhan—Gaelic form of Gavin (from the hawk field)

Gaelbhan—sparrow

Gair, Gear—short

Galen, Gaylen, Galyn, Gaelan—tranquil

Gall—stranger

Gallagher, Galchobhar—eager helper

Galloway, Galaway, Galway, Gallgaidheal—of the strange Gauls

Galvin, Gaelbhan—white

Gannon, Gannie, Gionnan—fair-skinned

Garvey, Gairbhith, Garbhach—rough

Gaynor, Gayner—son of the blond man

Gearald—Gaelic form of Gerald (spear mighty)

Gilleasbuig—sacred and bold

Gille-Eathain—Gaelic form of Gillian (youthful)

Gilmore, Giollamhuire—devoted

Gilroy, Giollaruaidh—serves the redhead

Giollanaebhin—worships the saints

Girven, Gervin, Girvyn, Garbhan—rough

Glen, Glenn, Gleann—from the glen

Glendon—from the dark glen

Goraidh, Godfrey—God's peace

Gordan, Gordain—hero

Gorman—little blue-eyed one

Gow—a smith

Grady, Gradey—noble

Guin—blond

Guthrie, Gaothaire—free wind

Hogan, Hagan—young

Hurley, Hurly, Hurlee—tide

Iain—Gaelic form of John (God is gracious)

Iomar—archer

Irving—handsome

Kane, Kayne, Kaine—tribute

Keefe, Keifer—cherished

Keegan, Kegan—small and fiery

Keller—little champion

Kelly, Kelley—warrior

Kelvin—from the narrow river

Kendrick—son of Harry

Kennedy—helmeted

Kenyon—blond

Kermichael, Kermichil—from Michael's fortress

Kermit—free

Kern, Kerne, Kearn—little dark one

Kerr—spear

Kerry—son of the dark-haired man

Kerwin, Kerwyn, Kerwen—little black one

Kevin, Kevyn—attractive

Key—son of Aidan

Kieran—black

Kinnard—from the high hill

Kinnell—from the head of the cliff

Kyle—handsome

Labhruinn—laurel

Lachlann—from Scandinavia

Lawler—mumbles

Lennon, Leannan—little cloak

Lennox, Leamhnach—lives near

the place abounding in elm trees

Leslie, Lesley, Liosliath—from the gray fortress

Liam—helmeted

Logan, Loghan—from the hollow

Lon, Lonn—fierce

Lucas—light

Luthais—famous in battle

Mac a'bhaird—son of Baird

Mac a'bhiadhtaiche—son of Bhiadhtaiche

Mac Adhaimh, MacAdam, MacAdhaimh—son of Adam

Mac Ailean, MacLean, MacAilean, MacAllen—son of the handsome man

Mac Alasdair, MacAladair, MacAllister—son of Alasdair

Mac an Aba, MacNab—father's son

Mac an Bhaillidh—son of the steward

Mac an Bharain—son of the noble warrior

Mac an Bhreatannaich—son of the Briton

Mac an Tsagairt—son of the prelate

Mac an t-Saoir—son of the carpenter

Mac Artuir, MacArthur, MacArtuir—son of Arthur

Mac Asgaill—son of Asgaill

Mac Bheathain—son of the man who lives by the clear stream

Mac Bhriain—son of the strong

Mac Daraich—son of the man from the ford by the oak trees

Mac Ghille Aindreis—son of the one who served the manly one

Mac Ghille-bhuidhe—son of the one who serves the blond

Mac Ghille-dhuibh—son of the one who serves the dark man

Mac Ghille-dhuinn—son of the one who serves Brown

Mac Ghille-easpuig—son of the one who serves the sacred and bold

Mac Ghille-laider—son of the one who serves the strong armed

Mac Ghille Mhicheil, Carmichail—son of the one who served Saint Michael

MacNair—son of an heir

Malcolm—Colum's servant

Maloney, Maoldhomhnaigh—devoted to God

Malvin, Maolmin—polished chief

Manus, Mannis—great

Maoltuile—quiet

Marcus—hammer

Martainn—warlike

Mayo—lives near the yew trees

Micheil—Gaelic form of Michael (godlike)

Monroe—from the red swamp

Morvan, Morven, Morvyn, Morfinn, Morvin—pale

Muireach—Moorish

Mungan—Gaelic form of Mungo

Murchadh—protector of the sea

Murthuile—sea tide

Neacal—people's victory

Neall, Niall, Neil—champion

Nevin, Nevyn, Nevins—worships the saints

Nolan, Noland, Nuallan—famous

Odharnait, Oran, Odran, Oren,

Orin, Orran, Orren, Orrin —
pale

Padruig — Gaelic form of Patrick
(noble)

Parthalan — son of the furrows

Peadar — Gaelic form of Peter
(rock)

Phelan — little wolf

Piaras — rock

Pol — little

Proinsias — frank

Quigley — distaff

Quinlan — well-shaped

Quinn — wise

Rafferty, Rabhartach — wealthy

Raghnall, Raonull — mighty power

Raibeart — Gaelic form of Robert
(shining fame)

Riley, Raghallach — valiant

Riordan, Rioghbhardan — royal
bard

Risteard — Gaelic form of Richard
(strong ruler)

Rooney, Ruanaidh — red-haired

Rory — ruddy

Roy — red

Ruairidh — famous ruler

Ryan — little king

Scully — town crier

Seorus — farmer

Seosamh — He shall add

Seumas — supplanter

Sholto, Siolat — teal duck

Sim — heard

Skelly, Skelley, Sguelaiche —
storyteller

Slevin, Slevyn, Slavin, Slaven,
Sleven, Slaibhin — mountain
man

Sloan, Sloane, Sluaghan — warrior

Somhairle, Somerled — asked of
God

Stiabhan — Gaelic form of Stephen
(crowned)

Taggart — son of a prelate

Taithleach — quiet

Teague, Taidhg, Tadhg — poet

Tearlach, Tearley, Tearly —
manly

Tioboid — bold

Toirdealbhach — myth name

Tomas — twin

Tormod — from the north

Torrance, Terrence — from the
knolls

Tully, Tulley, Tuathal — peaceful

Tynan, Teimhnean — dark

Uilleam — helmeted

Uisdean — intelligent

German

German surnames began in the south during the late twelfth century and moved north. By the sixteenth century, the names had become hereditary. Surnames derive from occupational, patronymic, descriptive and place names.

Common suffixes are:

-sohn — son
-er, -mann — denote occupational names
-ke, -isch, -usch — are from Slavic influences on the language

Common articles:

von — can mean either from or owner
zu — reserved for aristocrats and used with a title

In some cases, both zu and von are used along with titles.
Some German surnames:

Altbusser	Elend
Braun	Finster
Breit	Hall
Dengler	Hirsch
Eisenbein	Rahn

FEMALE

Ada — joyful
Adalia, Adali, Adalie — noble
Adele, Adela — pleasant
Adeline, Adelinda, Adette, Adelheide, Adelle, Adelina, Adelita, Adelheid, Adal, Adelaide, Adalheida — sweet, noble
Adelyte — has good humor

Adolpha, Adalwolfa — noble she-wolf
Adrian, Adriane — dark
Agathe, Agatha — good
Alarice, Alarica — all-ruler
Alberta, Albertine, Albertyne, Albertina — intelligent
Alda — old
Alfonsine, Alphonsine — noble

Alice, Alys, Alison, Alisz, Aliz, Ailis, Alicia, Ailse, Aili — sweet, noble

Alida, Aleda, Alyda, Aldona — archaic

Alonsa — eager

Aloysia, Aloisia — famous fighting woman

Alvar, Alva, Alvie, Alvara, Alvarie — army of elves

Amalasand, Amalasanda — industrious

Amara — eternal

Annemarie, Annamaria — bitter grace

Antonie — priceless

Arabella — eagle heroine

Ararinda — tenacious

Armina — warrior maid

Arnalda — eagle, strong

Ballard, Baldhart — bold, strong

Bathilda, Bathild, Bathilde — heroine

Berdine, Berdina — glorious

Berit — intelligent

Bernadette — has the courage of a bear

Berta, Bertha, Bertina — intelligent

Binga, Binge — from the kettle-shaped hollow

Blas, Blasa — firebrand

Bruna, Brune — of the dark hair

Brunhilde, Brunhilda, Brunhild — dark, noble

Cheryl — feminine form of Charles (manly)

Chriselda — strong

Clarimond, Clarimonda, Clarimonde — brilliant protectress

Clotilda, Clotilde — heroine

Conradina, Conradine — bold

Dagmar, Dagomar — glorious day

Della — bright

Didrika — folk rule

Eadaion — joyous friendship

Ebba — strength

Edda — pleasant

Edeline, Ediline, Edelina — gracious

Else, Elsie, Elsa, Elsha, Elica, Ilse, Ilyse, Elyse, Elsje — noble

Emilie — German form of Emily (industrious)

Emma — universal

Engleberta, Engelbertha, Engelbertine, Engelbertina — bright angel

Eraman, Eramana — honorable

Erma — war goddess

Erna, Ernestine, Ernestina — serious

Ethelinda, Ethelinde — noble serpent

Etta — little one

Felda — from the field

Felisberta — intelligent

Franziska — free

Frieda — peaceful

Fritzi — peaceful ruler

Gaelle — stranger

Galiena, Galiana — haughty

Genevieve, Genowefa, Genoveva — white wave

Geraldine, Gerwalt, Gerwalta, Gerhardine, Gerhardina, Geraldina — mighty with a spear

Gerda, Gerde, Gerdie — protected

Gertrude, Gertrut, Gertrud, Gertruda — myth name

Ghislaine, Guilaine — pleasant oath

Gilberta, Gisilberhta — hostage

Gretchen — little pearl

Griselda, Grisjahilde, Griselde — gray battle-maid

Griswalda, Griswalde — from the gray forest

Gudrun, Gudruna — divine knowledge

Guida — guide

Gunilla, Gunnel — battle-maid

Gustel — noble

Halfrida, Halifrid, Halfrid — peaceful heroine

Hannelore, Hannelora — meaning unknown

Harimanna, Harimanne — warrior maid

Hedda, Hadu — vigorous battle-maid

Hedwig, Haduwig — strife

Heidi, Heida, Hild, Hilda, Hilde — nobility

Helene — German form of Helen (light)

Helga, Halag — pious

Helma, Hilma — protective

Herta, Hertha — of the earth

Hida, Hide — warrior

Hildegard, Hildimar, Hildemar, Hildemara — glorious

Hildreth, Hildireth — battle counselor

Holda, Holde, Holle, Hulda, Hulde — beloved

Huberta, Hugiberahta — intelligent

Ida, Idaia, Idna, Idalie — active

Idette, Idetta — hard-working

Ilse — noble

Irma, Irmine, Irmina, Irmigard, Irmgard, Irmuska — war goddess

Isa, Isane, Isana — strong-willed

Isolda, Isole, Isold — rule of ice

Jakoba, Jakobe, Jakobie — feminine form of Jakob (supplanter)

Johanna — German form of Joanna (God's gracious gift)

Jolan, Jolanka, Joli — country

Karola, Karolina, Karla, Karoline — feminine form of Karl (manly)

Katharina, Katchen, Kathe — German form of Katherine (pure)

Kuonrada — wise

Leoda, Luete, Leota, Leopoldine, Leopolda, Leopoldina — of the people

Linda, Lind, Lindie — snake

Lisa, Lise, Lisette — devoted to God

Lorelei, Lurline, Lurlina, Lurleen, Lurlene — temptress

Lorraine, Loraine — made famous in battle

Lotte — masculine

Louise, Louisane, Luise, Lovisa, Lujza, Luijzika, Loyce — renowned warrior

Luana, Ludkhannah, Luane — graceful battle-maid

Magd, Mady, Magda — maiden

Magnilda, Maganhildi, Magnhilda, Magnild, Magnilde—strong battle-maid

Mallory, Madelhari—army counselor

Malene, Maddalena, Maddalene, Maddalen, Maddalyn—magnificent

Marelda, Marilda, Marhildi, Marhilda—famous battle-maid

Marlis, Marlisa, Maria—bitter

Mathilda, Mathilde, Mathild—mighty battle-maid

Millicent—industrious

Minna, Mina, Minne, Mindy—love

Nadette, Nadetta, Nadine, Nadina—the courage of a bear

Nixie—little water sprite

Norberta, Norberaht, Norberte—bright heroine

Nordica, Nordika—from the north

Odile, Odelina, Odiane, Odiana, Odette, Oda, Odila, Ordella, Ordalf—elfin spear

Olinda—defender of the land

Otka, Otthild, Otthilde, Otthilda, Ottila, Otilie, Ottilia, Otylia—fortunate heroine

Perahta—glorious

Petronille, Petronilla—rock

Philippine, Philipinna—loves horses

Rachel—lamb

Ricarda—ruler

Rikka—mistress of all

Rilla, Rille, Rillia, Rillie—brook

Roch—glory

Roderica, Roderika—famous ruler

Rolanda, Rolande—from the famous land

Romilda, Ruomhildi, Romilde, Romhilda, Romhilde, Romhild—glorious battle-maid

Rosamund, Rozomund, Rosemunda, Rosemonde, Rozmonda, Rosa—noted protector

Rudelle, Rudella, Rupetta, Rupette—famous

Senta, Sente—assistant

Serilda, Sarohildi, Serhilda, Serihilda, Serihilde, Serhilda, Serhild—armored battle-maid

Sigfreda, Sigfrieda, Sigfriede—victorious

Solvig, Sigilwig—champion

Suzanne—lily

Tibelda, Tibelde, Tibeldie—boldest

Truda, Trude, Trudchen—fighting woman

Tugenda—virtue

Ulla—has willpower

Ulrike, Ulrica, Ulka, Uli—mistress of all

Valborga—protecting ruler

Vanda, Vande—wanderer

Verena, Verina, Verene—protector

Vibeke, Viveka—little woman

Walda, Welda—ruler

Waldburga, Walborga—protecting ruler

Wanda, Wande, Wandy—wanderer

Warda—guardian

Wido—warrior maiden

Wilda, Wilde—untamed

Wilhelmina, Wilhelmine—
  resolute protector
Winifred, Winifrid, Winifrida,

Winifride—peaceful friend
Winola—gracious friend
Yseult—ruler of ice

MALE

Abelard, Adelhard—resolute
Adal, Adel—noble
Adalard, Adalhard—brave
Adalwine, Audwin, Audwine,
  Adalwen—noble friend
Adler, Adlar, Ahren, Aren—eagle
Adolf, Adalwolf, Adolph—noble
  wolf
Alaric, Alarick, Alarik, Alrik,
  Aurik, Aric, Arick, Arik,
  Aurick—noble leader
Albrecht, Adelbert, Adalbert,
  Albert, Ailbe, Alvy, Ardal—
  intelligent, noble
Aldo, Ald—old, wise
Alemannus—myth name
Alfonso, Alphonso—ready
Alger, Adalgar—noble spearman
Alhsom—sacred fame
Alois—famous warrior
Altman, Altmann—wise man
Alvin, Alhwin, Alwin, Adalwin—
  noble friend
Amory, Amery, Alhmarric—
  divine
Andreas—German form of
  Andrew (manly)
Ann—name of a king
Anson—son of Ann (grace)
Anton—German form of Anthony
  (beyond praise)
Archard—strong
Archimbald, Archibald—bold
Armand—protective
Arndt, Arnaud, Arnot, Arnoll,

Arnott, Arnet, Arnett, Arnald,
  Arnold, Arnd, Arend, Arno,
  Arnell, Arnhold, Arnall—
  power of an eagle
Arne, Are, Adne, Arney, Arni,
  Arnt—eagle
Arnwolf—eagle wolf
Arvin—friend of the people
Audric, Audrick, Adalric, Aldrik,
  Adalrik—noble friend
Axel, Apsel, Aksel—father of
  peace
Baldemar—princely
Baldric, Baldrik—bold
Baldwin, Baldwyn, Balduin—bold
  friend
Baltasar—protected by God
Bannan—commander
Bannruod—famous commander
Barret, Berowalt—mighty as a
  bear
Berdy—intelligent
Berg—mountain
Bern, Berne, Ber, Berrin—bear
Bernard, Bernon, Bernot,
  Barnard, Benat, Barrett,
  Bernhard, Bernd, Berend,
  Berinhard, Barney, Bernardo,
  Bernardyn—brave as a bear
Berthold, Berchtwald—bright
  ruler
Bing, Binge—from the kettle-
  shaped hollow
Bittan, Bitten—desire
Bogart, Bogohardt—bowstring

Brandeis — dwells on a burned
    clearing
Brendan, Bren, Brendis — flame
Bruno, Brunon — brown
Burhardt, Burkhart — strong as a
    castle
Clovis, Chlodwig — famous
    warrior
Conrad, Conradin, Cord, Cort,
    Conrado — honest advisor
Corrado — bold
Dagoberto — glorious day
Derry, Dearg — red-haired
Dick — strong leader
Diederich, Dietrich, Dedrick,
    Dedrik, Derrick, Dieter, Dirk,
    Derek, Dierck, Dietz —
    people's ruler
Drugi, Drud — strong
Dutch, Deutsch — a German
Eberhard, Eberhardt, Eburhardt,
    Eward, Edward, Evrard —
    strong as a boar
Edel — brave
Edingu — famous ruler
Eduard — German form of Edward
    (rich guardian)
Edwin, Edwyn — happy friend
Eginhard, Eginhardt, Einhard,
    Egon, Enno, Eno, Einhardt —
    strong with a sword
Ehren — honorable
Ellery — lives by the alder tree
Eloy, Ely — famous fighter
Emory, Emery — joint ruler
Englbehrt, Englebert — bright
    angel
Erchanbold — sacred, bold
Erchanhardt, Ekhard, Ekerd,
    Eckerd, Erkerd — sacred

Erhardt, Erhard — honor
Erich — German form of Eric
    (forever strong)
Ernest, Earnest, Ernst, Erno —
    serious
Errando — bold venture
Eugen — noble
Franz — German form of Frank
    (free)
Friedrich, Fritz — German form of
    Frederick (peaceful ruler)
Fremont, Frimunt — noble
    protector
Georg — German form of George
    (farmer)
Gerhard, Gerard, Goddard — hard
    spear
Gerlach — spear thrower
Ghislain — oath
Gilleasbuig — bold
Godfrey, Godfried, Gottfried —
    peaceful god
Griswold, Griswald — from the
    gray forest
Hackett, Hacket — little hacker
Hamlet, Hamlett, Hamoelet —
    from the little home
Hamlin — loves the little home
Hans, Hann, Hanno, Han, Hanz —
    gift from God
Hardy, Harti — daring
Hariman, Harimann — protective
Hartman, Hardtman, Hartmann —
    strong
Harvey — soldier
Heinrich — German form of Henry
    (rules the home)
Helmut, Helmutt — brave
Hernando — adventuresome
Herrick — army leader

Hewett, Hewitt, Hewlitt, Hewlett — little Hugh

Hildebrand, Hildbrand — war sword

Hobart, Hobbard, Hobard, Hohberht — high, bright

Howe, How, Hoh — high

Hulbert, Huldiberaht, Hubbard, Hulbard, Hulbart — graceful

Humphrey, Hunfrid, Hunfried — peaceful Hun

Ingel, Engel, Ingall, Ingalls — angel

Ingelbert — bright angel

Jakob — German form of Jacob (supplanter)

Japhet — myth name

Jarman, Jarmann — a German

Jarvis — sharp spear

Jay, Jaye — swift

Johan, Johann, Johannes — German form of John (God is gracious)

Josef — German form of Joseph (He adds)

Jurgen — German form of George (farmer)

Karl — German form of Charles (manly)

Klaus — German form of Nicholas (victory of the people)

Konrad, Kurt, Kuno, Konni, Kunz, Kord, Koenraad, Koen — honest advisor

Kuhlbert, Kulbert, Kulbart — calm, bright

Lamar, Lamarr, Landmari — land famous

Lambrecht, Lambert, Lambart,

Lambret, Lambrett — light of land

Leopold, Leopoldo — prince of the people

Lindberg, Lindeberg — from the linden-tree hill

Lorenz, Loritz — laurel

Loring, Lotharing, Lothar, Lothair — famous in battle

Ludwig, Lutz, Ludwik, Luki, Louis, Luis, Luduvico, Lughaidh, Lewy, Luigi, Luiginw — famous fighter

Mallory, Madelhari — war counselor

Mandel — almond

Manfred, Manfried, Manfrit — peaceful

Meinhard, Meinke, Meino, Maynard, Meinyard — firm

Meinrad — strong advisor

Nefen, Nefin, Nef, Neff — nephew

Orbert, Odbert, Orbart, Odbart — wealthy

Oswald — power of God

Othman, Otto, Otho, Othmann, Othomann — wealthy

Otto — born eighth

Ottokar — happy fighter

Penn — commander

Penrod — famous commander

Pepin, Peppi — petitioner

Ragnorak — myth name

Rainart, Rainhard, Reinhard, Renke — strong judgment

Rainer, Reiner — counsel

Rambert, Reginberaht, Rambart — mighty, intelligent

Raymond — strong defender

Reginald, Reggie, Rich, Rikard,

Richard, Riocard, Rickard, Ryszard, Risteard, Riccardo, Ricardo — powerful ruler

Reynard, Reginhard, Reinhard — mighty brave

Richmond — strong protector

Ritter — knight

Roald, Rald — famous leader

Roch, Rico — glory

Rosswald, Roswell, Roswalt, Roswald — horse mighty

Roth — red-haired

Rune — secret

Rutger, Rudiger — German form of Roger (famous spearman)

Ruodrik, Rodrik, Roderick — famous ruler

Rupert, Ruprecht — bright fame

Selig, Saelac, Selik — blessed

Siegfried, Sigifrith, Sigfrid, Sigifrid — victorious

Sigwald, Sigiwald, Sigwalt — victorious ruler

Spangler, Spengler — tinsmith

Stein — stone

Tab, Tabbert, Tabbart — brilliant

Tibalt — prince of the people

Treffen — meets

Trennen — divides

Tretan — walks

Ubel — evil

Ulrich, Uli, Ulz — noble leader

Valdemar, Valdemarr — famous ruler

Vernados — courage of a bear

Volker — people's guard

Volney, Vollny — people's spirit

Wagner — wagon maker

Waldemar, Waldemarr — famous ruler

Waldo — ruler

Waldron, Waldhramm, Waldrom — ruling raven

Walfred, Waldifrid, Walfrid — peaceful ruler

Wallache, Wallace — a Welshman

Waller — army ruler

Walmond, Waldmunt — mighty protector

Walter, Walthari — powerful ruler

Walton, Walten — ruler

Warren, Waren — loyal

Weber, Webber — weaver

Wendell, Wendel — wanders

Werner, Warner, Warenhari — defending warrior

Wilbur, Willaperht, Wilpert, Wilburt, Wilbert, Wilbart — resolute, brilliant

Wilfred, Willifrid, Wilfrid — peaceful, resolute

Wilhelm, Williamon — German form of William (resolute protector)

Wilmer, Willamar, Willmar, Wilmar, Willmarr — resolute, famous

Wilmot, Willimod, Wilmod — resolute spirit

Wolfgang — advancing wolf

Wolfric, Wolfrick, Wolfrik — wolf ruler

Wotan — myth name

Zelig — happy

Greek

Greek names are, for the most part, patronymic in origin. In ancient Greece, son-of suffixes (-opoulos, -akis, -adhis, -idhis, -ides) were attached to the father's name if the bearer needed more identification in addition to his given name.

Present-day surnames are taken from occupational, patronymic, descriptive and place names.

Most Greeks have a given and surname only. When Greek children are given a middle name, they are usually given the name of their father. A married woman changes her middle name to her husband's name and adds an *a* to feminize the name. A woman's surname is always listed in a feminine form.

The prefix Papa- is a reference that the bearer is related to a priest, which lends prestige to the name.

A few Greek surnames:

Anaghnostopoulos	Mylonas
Arvanitidhis	Nikolaidhis
Christofides	Panopoulos
Dhimitrakopoulus	Papandreou
Kaloyeropoulos	Spaneas

FEMALE

Abdera — from Abdera

Abellona, Abellone — masculine

Acacia, Akakia — guileless

Acantha, Akantha — thorn

Adara — beautiful

Adelpha, Adelphie, Adelphe — dear sister

Admeta — myth name (from a tale of Hercules)

Adonia — feminine form of Adonis (lover of Aphrodite)

Aeaea — myth name (island of Circe)

Aedon — myth name (daughter of Pandareos)

Aegina — meaning unknown

Aello — myth name (a Harpy)

Aethra — myth name (mother of

Theseus)

Aetna — from Aetna

Agafia, Agave, Agaue — good

Agalaia — myth name (splendor)

Agalia — happy

Agatha, Agathi, Agate, Agotha, Agata — good

Agave — myth name (mother of Pentheus)

Aglauros — myth name (turned into stone by Hermes)

Agnes, Agna, Aigneis, Agnese, Agneta, Agnek, Agnella — pure

Agueda — kind

Aidoios — honored

Airlia, Airla — ethereal

Alcestis — myth name (gave her life to save her husband)

Alcina — feminine of Alcinous (king who entertained Odysseus)

Alcippe — myth name (daughter of Ares)

Alcmene — myth name (mother of Hercules)

Alcyone — feminine form of Alcyoneus (fought against Athene)

Aldora — winged gift

Alena, Alina — light

Aleris, Alerissa — meaning unknown

Alesandese, Alexandra, Alexandina, Alexine, Alexina — defender of mankind

Alesia — helper

Alethea, Althaia, Alethia, Aletheia, Alecta — honesty

Alexia, Alexa, Aleka, Alexis — aid

Alicia — honest

Alpha — firstborn

Althaea, Althea, Altheda — pure

Alysia — bond

Alyssa — rational

Amalthea, Amalthia — myth name (nursed Zeus)

Amara — unfading

Amarantha, Amarande, Amaranda — flower

Amaryllis — sparkling

Ambrosia — myth name (food of the gods)

Ambrosine, Ambrotosa — immortal

Amethyst — jewel

Amphitrite — myth name (a sea goddess)

Amymone — myth name (murdered her husband)

Anastasia, Anstice, Anstace — one who will be reborn

Anatola, Anatolia — from the east

Anaxarete — myth name (cruel woman punished by the gods)

Andrea, Andreas — masculine

Andromache — myth name (wife of Hector)

Andromeda — myth name (princess saved by Perseus)

Anemone — myth name

Anezka — gentle

Angeliki, Angela, Angel, Angelique, Angelina, Angeline — angel

Annis, Annys — whole

Antea — feminine form of Antaeus (son of Poseidon)

Anthia, Anthea — flower

Anticlea — myth name (mother of Odysseus)

Antigone — myth name (daughter of Oedipus)

Antiope — myth name (daughter of Asopus)

Anysia — complete

Aphrodite — myth name (goddess of love)

Apollina, Apollonia, Apollinaris — from Apollo

Ara — myth name

Arachne — myth name (changed into a spider by Athena)

Arene, Arena, Ariane, Ariana — holy one

Arete, Areta, Aretha — beauty

Arethusa — myth name (nymph)

Aretina — virtuous

Argie, Argia — all-seeing

Ariadne — very holy

Artemia, Artemisia — gift from Artemis

Artemis — myth name (goddess of the hunt)

Aspasia — welcomed

Astra, Astrea, Asta — star

Astraea — myth name (justice)

Atalanta, Atlanta, Atalante — myth name (a huntress)

Ate — myth name (goddess of irrationality)

Athanasia — immortal

Athena, Athene — myth name (goddess of wisdom)

Atropes, Antropas — myth name (a Fate)

Aure, Aura — soft breeze

Autonoe — myth name (mother of Actaeon)

Autumn — myth name

Baptista — baptizer

Barbara, Bairbre, Baibin, Basham, Babita — stranger

Basilia — regal

Baucis — myth name (wife of Philemon)

Berdine, Berdina — intelligent maid

Berenice, Bernice — brings victory

Beroe — myth name

Beryl — crystal

Briseis — myth name (slave of Achilles)

Caeneus — myth name (a woman who asked to become a man)

Caitlin, Caitilin, Caitlyn, Caitrin, Caitryn, Caitriona, Catia, Catalin, Catalyn, Catherine, Catheryn, Cathryn, Catherin, Catharina, Catarina, Catheryna — pure

Calandra — lark

Calantha — lovely blossom

Calida, Calli, Callie, Calla, Callista — the most beautiful

Callia — beautiful voice

Calligenia — born of beauty

Calliope — myth name (muse of epic poetry)

Calliste — myth name (another name for Artemis)

Callisto — myth name (mother of Arcas)

Calypso — myth name (daughter of Atlas)

Canace — myth name

Candance, Candice, Cadis — sparkling

Cassandra, Cassondra — myth

name (a prophetess no one
believed)

Cassie — purity

Cassiopeia — myth name (mother
of Andromeda)

Casta — meaning unknown

Castalia — myth name (sacred
fountain of the Muses)

Cathleen, Cathlin, Cathlyn — pure

Celaeno — myth name (a Harpy)

Celandine, Celandina — swallow

Celena, Celina — myth name
(goddess of the moon)

Celosia — burning

Cenobia — stranger

Ceres — myth name (another
name for Demeter)

Cestus — myth name (Aphrodite's
girdle)

Ceto — myth name (goddess of the
sea)

Charis — myth name (grace and
beauty)

Charissa — loving

Chloe — blooming

Chloris, Cloris, Cloria — myth
name (goddess of spring)

Christa — anointed

Christine, Christen, Christiane,
Christiana, Christian —
Christian

Chryseis — myth name (prisoner
of Agamemnon)

Cinyras — myth name (founded
the cult of Aphrodite)

Cipriana — myth name

Circe — myth name (a witch)

Clematis — flower name

Cleo — famed

Cleopatra — her father's fame

Cliantha, Clianthe — glory

Clio — celebrate

Clotho — myth name (a Fate)

Clymene, Clymena — myth name
(mother of Atalanta)

Clytemnestra — myth name
(murdered Agamemnon)

Clytie, Clyte — myth name (a
water nymph)

Colette — people's victory

Cora, Corella — maiden

Coral, Coralie, Coraline, Coralina,
Coralin — from the coral of the
sea

Corinna, Corinne, Corin, Coretta,
Corette — maiden

Coronis — myth name (mother of
Aesculapius)

Cosimia, Cosma — of the universe

Creusa — myth name (daughter of
Erechtheus)

Crocale — myth name

Crystal — sparkling

Cybele — myth name (mother of
the Olympians)

Cyma — flourish

Cynara — myth name

Cynthia, Cinthia — moon

Cypris — from Cyprus

Cyra — myth name

Cyrene, Cyrena — myth name
(mother of Aristaeus)

Cyrilla — noble

Cythera — from Cythera

Cytherea, Cytheria — myth name
(another name for Aphrodite)

Daffodil — flower

Damaris, Damara — gentle

Damia — myth name

Danae — myth name (mother of Perseus)

Daphne — bay tree

Deianira — myth name (wife of Hercules)

Delbin, Delbina, Delbine — flower

Delia, Della — myth name

Delphine, Delphina, Delfine, Delfina, Delphia — from Delphi

Delta — born fourth

Demas, Demos — popular

Demetria, Demeter — myth name (goddess of the harvest)

Desma — oath

Desmona, Desdemona — unlucky

Dia — myth name (daughter of Eineus)

Dianthe, Diantha — flower

Dice, Dike — myth name (justice)

Dido — myth name (queen of Carthage who killed herself)

Dino — myth name (sister of the Gorgons)

Dione, Diona — myth name (mother of Aphrodite)

Dionysia, Dionysie — named for Dionysus, god of wine

Dirce — myth name (killed for abusing children)

Dora, Dorette, Doralie, Doralia, Dorelia, Doralis, Doralice, Doretta — gift

Dorcas, Dorkas — gazelle

Dordie, Dordei — divine gift

Doreen — beautiful

Dorinda — beautiful gift

Doris, Dorice, Doria, Dorea, Dorian, Dorien, Doriana — of the sea

Dorothy, Dorothea, Dollie, Dolly, Doll, Dorita, Dorlisa, Dorte, Drew — a vision

Dryope — myth name (a nymph)

Ecaterina, Ekaterina, Ecterine — innocent

Echidna — myth name (a child of the Titans)

Echo — myth name (attended Hera)

Ede, Eda — generation

Effie — fair flame

Egeria — myth name (a water nymph)

Eidothea — myth name (a sea nymph)

Eileithyia — myth name (goddess of childbirth)

Eirene — myth name (peace)

Elaine, Elena, Eleanor, Eleanora, Eleanore, Ellen, Elnora, Elora, Endora, Eleni, Elenitsa — light

Eldoris — of the sea

Electra — sparkling

Elefteria, Elepheteria, Elephteria — free

Elisabet, Elisabeth, Elissa, Elisia, Ellice — devoted to God

Elma — friendly

Elpida, Elpide — hope

Ennea — born ninth

Enyo — myth name (goddess of war)

Eos — myth name (the dawn)

Erato — myth name (muse of erotic poetry)

Erianthe, Eriantha, Erianthia — sweet

Erigone — myth name (daughter of Icarius)

Erinyes — myth name (a Fury)

Eriphyle — myth name (wife of Amphiaraus)

Eris — myth name (goddess of discord)

Errita — pearl

Erytheia — myth name (one of the Hesperides)

Esmerelda, Esmeralda — emerald

Eudosis, Eudoxia, Eudocia, Eudosia, Eudocia, Eudokia — highly regarded

Eugenia, Evgenia — well-born

Eulallia — well-spoken

Eunice — joyous victory

Eunomia — myth name (order)

Euphemia, Euphemie, Ephie — well-spoken

Euphrosyne — good cheer

Europa — myth name (mother of Minos)

Eurayle — wanders far

Eurycleia — myth name (nurse of Odysseus)

Eurydice — myth name (wife of Orpheus)

Eurynome — myth name (goddess of all)

Eustella — fair star

Euterpe — myth name (muse of the flute)

Evadne — myth name (wife of Capaneus)

Evangeline, Evangelia — bringer of good news

Evania — peaceful

Evanthe, Evanth — flower

Fate — myth name (destiny)

Fedora — God's gift

Fern — feather

Filia — amity

Filipina — lover of horses

Filomena, Filomenia — lover of man

Gaea, Gaia — myth name (mother earth)

Galatea — white as milk

Gelasia — inclined to laughter

Georgia, Georgiana, Georgine, Georgette — farmer

Geranium — crane

Giancinta, Giancinte — hyacinth

Gina — well-born

Glauce — myth name (murdered by Medea)

Gregoria, Gregoriana — observant

Greta, Gretal, Grete, Gretel, Gredel, Gryta, Ghita, Gretchen — pearl

Haidee — modest

Halcyone, Alcyone — myth name (daughter of Aeolus)

Halimeda — thinking of the sea

Harmonia — myth name (daughter of Ares)

Hebe — myth name (goddess of youthful beauty)

Hecate — myth name (a Titan)

Hecuba, Hekuba — myth name (mother of Paris and Hector)

Hedia, Hedy, Hedyla — pleasant

Helen, Helena, Helli, Helene, Helenka, Halina — light

Helia — of the sun

Helice, Helike — from Helicon

Helle — myth name (daughter of Athamas)

Hemera — myth name (day)

Henrika — mistress of the hearth

Hera, Here — myth name (wife of Zeus)

Hermione, Hermandine, Hermia, Hermandina — well-born

Hero — myth name (priestess of Aphrodite)

Hesione — myth name (daughter of Laomedon)

Hesper, Hester — evening star

Hesperia — myth name (one of the Hesperides)

Hestia — myth name (goddess of hearth and home)

Hilaeira — myth name (girl carried off by Pollux and Castor)

Hippodamia — myth name (wife of Pirithous)

Hippolyte, Hippolyta — myth name (queen of the Amazons)

Horae — myth name (goddess of the season)

Hyacinthe, Hyacinth — purple

Hyades — myth name (name for the nymphs)

Hydra — myth name (a dragon killed by Hercules)

Hygeia, Hygieia — myth name (goddess of health)

Hypatia, Hypate — exceptional

Hypermnestra — myth name (refused to kill her husband on their wedding night)

Hypsipyle — myth name (daughter of Thoas)

Ianthe, Iantha, Ianthina — flower

Iasius — myth name (mother of Atalanta)

Ida — myth name (name of a mountain)

Idalia — myth name

Idola — a vision

Ileana, Iliona — from Troy

Ilithya, Ilithia — myth name

Ilona, Ilke, Ilka, Ica, Ilay, Ilon, Ilonka, Ilu, Iluska — light

Inesa, Inese, Ines, Inez — kind, innocent

Ino — myth name (daughter of Cadmus)

Iola, Iole — myth name (sister of Iphitus)

Iolanthe, Iolantha — violet

Iona, Ione, Ionia, Ionessa — amethyst

Iphegenia — myth name (daughter sacrificed by Agamemnon)

Irena, Irene, Irini, Irina, Irinia, Iryna, Irynia — peace

Iris, Irisa — rainbow

Irta — pearl

Isadora, Isidora, Isadore — gift of Isis

Isaura, Isaure — gentle breeze

Ismene, Ismini — myth name (daughter of Oedipus)

Ivanna — gift of the gods

Ivy — ivy

Jacinta, Jacintha, Jacinthe — beautiful

Jarina, Jarine — farmer

Jocasta — myth name (a queen of Thebes)

Kaia — from the earth

Kairos — myth name

Kalliope — beautiful voice

Kalonice — victory of beauty

Kalyca, Kaly, Kali, Kalie, Kalika — rosebud

Kandake — glittering

Kanake — myth name

Katherine, Kathrine, Katheryn, Kethryn, Katrina, Katarina,

Katarin, Kate, Kit, Kitty,
Karen, Karin, Koren, Karena,
Kara, Kasia, Kassia, Kaisa,
Kasen, Kasin, Katie, Katy,
Katri, Kaethe, Katja, Katya,
Kolina, Koline, Kora, Katakin,
Katoka, Katica, Katus, Koto,
Katinka, Kasienka, Kaska,
Katarzyna, Kolina, Kore—
pure
Kay—glory
Keleos—flaming
Kepa, Kepe—stone
Keres—evil spirits
Kineta, Kinetikos—active
Kirsten, Krista, Kristina,
   Khrustina, Kirsty, Kristell,
   Kristel, Kirstie, Krisztina,
   Kriszta, Kriska, Krysta,
   Krysia—Christian
Kleopatra—glory of the father
Kolete, Kolette, Klazina—
   people's victory
Kore—myth name (another name
   for Persephone)
Kosmo, Kosma, Kasma, Kasmo—
   universal
Kristin, Kristen—the anointed
Kynthia—moon
Lachesis—myth name (a Fate)
Lais—favorite name with poets
Lalage, Lalia—verbose
Lamia—myth name (an evil spirit
   who abducts and murders
   children)
Lampetia—myth name
Lana, Lenci, Lena, Lina, Lenore,
   Leonora, Leora, Leonore,
   Leonarda—light

Laodamia—myth name (wife of
   Protesilaus)
Larissa, Larisse—cheerful
Leda—myth name (mother of
   Helen)
Lelia—well-spoken
Lethe—myth name (river of
   oblivion)
Lethia, Letha, Leitha—forgetful
Leucippe—myth name (mother of
   Teuthras)
Leucothea, Leucothia—myth
   name (a sea nymph)
Lexine, Lexina—defender of man
Lia, Lea—bringer of good news
Ligia—beautiful voice
Lilis, Lilia, Lillis, Lili, Lily, Lilch,
   Lila, Lilla—lily
Loni—short form of Apollonia
Lotus—flower
Luigina—well-born
Lycoris—twilight
Lydia, Lydea—from Lydia
Lyris, Lyra—lyrical
Lysandra—defends man
Madge—approval
Madora, Medora—ruler
Magaere, Megara—myth name (a
   Fury)
Maia—myth name (mother of
   Hermes)
Malinda, Melinda—gentle
Malva, Malvina, Malvine—soft
Margaret, Margeret, Maggie,
   Margery, Marjorie, Marjory,
   Margolo, Margalo, Margarita,
   Margareta, Margaretta,
   Marketa, Mairead, Megan,
   Meghan, Meagan—pearl
Marmara, Marmee—shining

Marpessa — myth name (daughter of Evenus)

Mathilde, Matilda — brave in war

Medea — myth name (wife of Jason who murders her children)

Medusa — cunning

Melania, Melanie — dark

Melantha, Melanthe — dark flower

Melantho — myth name (a serving girl)

Melina, Melena — yellow as a canary

Melissa, Melisse, Mellisa — honey bee

Melita, Melleta, Meleta, Meleda — sweet as honey

Melpomene — myth name (muse of tragedy)

Merope — myth name (foster mother of Oedipus)

Metanira — myth name

Metea — gentle

Metis — myth name (resourcefulness)

Minerva — wise

Minta, Mintha — plant name

Mnemosyne — myth name (goddess of memory)

Moerae, Moirai — myth name (a Fate)

Moira, Moirai — merit

Moly — myth name (an herb Hermes gives to Odysseus to protect him)

Mona — solitary

Monica, Moniqua, Monika, Monique — advisor

Musidora, Musadora — gift of the Muses

Myra, Mira, Mirias — abundance

Myrtle, Mytra, Merta, Myrtis, Myrtice, Myrtisa, Myrtia, Myrta — myrtle

Narkissa, Narcissa, Narcisa — daffodil

Nathacha, Natasha, Natassia — born at Christmas

Nausicaa — myth name (princess who finds Odysseus)

Nella, Nell, Nelly, Nellie, Nellis, Nelma — light

Nemesis — myth name (goddess of vengeance)

Neola — youthful

Neoma, Neomia, Neomenia, Neomea — new moon

Nephele — myth name (the cloud Hera made by Zeus that birthed the Centaurs)

Nerine, Nerina, Neried — myth name (the sea nymphs)

Nerissa, Nerita, Nireta, Nerice — from the sea

Neysa, Nessa, Nessia — pure

Nicia, Nicea, Nicolette, Nicoletta, Niki, Nikolia, Nicola, Nicole — feminine form of Nicholas (people's victory)

Nike — myth name (goddess of victory)

Niobe — fern

Nitsa — peace

Norah, Nora — light

Nox — myth name (night)

Nympha — bride

Nysa, Nyse, Nyssa — goal

Nyx — night

Obelia, Obelie — pointed pillar

Ocypete — myth name (a Harpy)

Odele, Odelle — harmonious
Odelet, Odelette — little singer
Odessa, Odysseia — wrathful
Oenone — myth name (lover of
    Paris)
Oighrig — well-spoken
Oleisia — protector of man
Olympia, Olympe — from
    Olympus
Omphale — myth name (a queen
    of Lydia)
Onella, Olena, Olina — light
Ophelia — serpentine
Ophelie — wisdom
Orea, Oria — from the mountain
Orithyia — myth name
Ortygia — myth name (Calypso's
    island)
Page — child
Pamela — made from honey
Panagiota — holy
Pandora — myth name (released
    misery and hope into the
    world)
Panphila — all-loving
Pansy — flower
Panthea — all the gods
Parthenia, Parthenie — chaste
Pasha, Pesha — born at Easter
Pasiphae — myth name (wife of
    Minos)
Peg, Peggy, Pegeen — pearl
Pelagia — dweller by the sea
Pelicia — weaver
Pelopia — myth name (mother of
    Aegisthus)
Pemphredo — myth name (sister
    of the Gorgons)
Penelope — myth name (faithful
    wife of Odysseus)

Penthea, Penthia — born fifth
Penthesilea — myth name (a
    queen of the Amazons)
Peony, Penny — flower
Pephredo — myth name (dread)
Persephone, Persephonie — myth
    name (wife of Hades)
Persis — from Persia
Petrina, Pierette, Petronella,
    Perrine, Petronelle, Petra,
    Petrine — rock
Phaedra — myth name (daughter
    of Minos)
Phaethusa — myth name
Phemie — well-spoken
Pheobe, Phebe — sparkling
Pheodora, Phedora — supreme
    gift
Phila — loving
Philana — lover of man
Phillida, Phillina, Philina,
    Philida — loving
Phillipa, Philippa — lover of horses
Philomela, Philomel — nightingale
Philomena, Philomina — greatly
    loved
Philothea — loves of God
Phoebe — myth name (mother of
    Leto)
Phoenix — heron
Phyllis, Phillis, Phylis, Philis —
    green bough
Pleasure — myth name
Podarge — myth name (a Harpy)
Polyhymnia — myth name (muse
    of sacred song)
Polyxena — myth name (daughter
    of Priam)
Procne — myth name (wife of
    Pandion)

Psyche — myth name (lover of Cupid)

Pyrena, Pyrene, Pyrenie, Pyrenia — ardent

Pyrrha — myth name (daughter of Epimetheus)

Pythia — prophetess

Rena, Rina — peaceful

Resi, Rezi — gatherer

Rhea — myth name (wife of Cronus)

Rheta, Rita, Rhete, Reta, Reit — speaker

Rhoda, Rhodanthe, Rhodantha, Rhodia — rose

Ritsa, Ritza — protector of man

Saba — from Sheba

Sandra, Sandrine, Sondra — protector of man

Sapphira, Sapphire — jewel

Scylla — myth name (a sea monster)

Sebastene, Sebastienne, Sebastiana — adored

Selena, Selene, Selina, Selia — moon

Semele — myth name (mother of Dionysus)

Sibley, Sibyl, Sybyl, Sibylla, Sybilla — oracle

Sinovia, Sinobia — stranger

Sirena, Sirina — named for the Sirens

Solon, Solonie, Solona, Solone — wise

Sophia, Sophie, Sofia, Sofronia, Sofi, Saffi — wise

Sophronia — of judicious mind

Stasia, Steise, Stacie, Stacy, Stacey — shall be reborn

Stephana, Stephania, Stephanie, Stephene, Stefina, Stefinia, Stevie — crowned in victory

Stheno — mighty

Strephon, Strephonn, Strep — one who turns

Styx — myth name (a river of the underworld)

Suadela — myth name (goddess of persuasion)

Symaethis — myth name

Syna — together

Syrinx — myth name (a nymph)

Tabitha — gazelle

Terentia — guardian

Teresa, Terese, Teresina, Terisita, Therese, Theresa, Tess, Tessie, Tressam, Terry, Tracy, Tassos, Tosia — reaper

Terpsichore — myth name (muse of dance and lyric poetry)

Tessa — born fourth

Tethys — myth name (wife of Oceanus)

Thaddea, Thaddia — brave

Thais — beloved

Thalassa — from the sea

Thalia, Talia, Thaleia — joyous (muse of comedy)

Thea, Thia, Theola — divine

Thecla, Thekla, Tecla, Tekla — renowned fame

Thelma — nursing

Themis — myth name (righteousness)

Theodora, Theda, Tedra, Tedre, Theodosia — supreme gift

Theone, Thenoma, Thenomia, Theona — God's name

Theophania, Theophaneia — God appears

Theophilia, Tesia — loved by God

Theora, Theore, Thora — watcher

Thera, Thira, Thyra, Tyra — untamed

Thetis — myth name (mother of Achilles)

Thisbe — myth name (lover of Pyramus)

Tienette, Tynet — crowned in victory

Timothea, Timothia — honoring God

Tiphanie, Theophanie, Theophane, Tifany, Tiffany, Tiffeny — gods incarnate

Tisiphone — myth name (a Fury)

Titania — giant

Trina, Trine, Tryn, Taryn, Taren, Terran, Terrian, Terriana, Tryna, Tryne — innocent

Tyro — myth name (a nymph)

Urania — heavenly

Ursa, Ursel, Ursula — myth name

Vara, Varvara, Vavara — stranger

Venessa, Vania, Vanny, Vanna — butterfly

Veronica, Veronika, Veronicha — honest image

Xanthe, Xantha, Xanthia — blond

Xenia — welcome

Xylia, Xylina, Xylona, Xyliana, Xylinia — from the woods

Yalena, Yalene — light

Yolanda, Yolande — violet

Zandra, Zondra — defender of man

Zelia, Zelina, Zelinia — zealous

Zenaide, Zenaida — myth name

Zenia, Zena, Zene — friendly

Zenobia, Zenobe, Zena, Zenna, Zenina, Zenda, Zenaida — born of Zeus

Zephyr, Zyphire, Zefiryn, Zephyra, Zephira — of the west wind

Zeta — born last

Zeva — sword

Zoe, Zoelie, Zoelle, Zoel, Zoya, Zoia — alive

Zsofia, Zsofie, Zofia, Zofie — wisdom

Zyta, Zita — reaper

MALE

Abderus — myth name (a friend of Hercules)

Absyrtus — myth name (brother of Medea)

Abydos — from Abydos

Acastus — myth name (an Argonaut)

Acestes, Agestes — myth name

Achates — myth name (companion of Aeneas)

Achelous — myth name (a river god)

Acheron — myth name (river of woe)

Achilles — lipless

Acis — myth name (lover of Galatea)

Aconteus — myth name

Acrisius — myth name (grandfather of Perseus)

Acteon, Actaeon — myth name (a hunter torn apart by his own dogs)

Admetus — myth name (a king of Pherae)

Adonis — myth name (lover of Aphrodite)

Adrastus — myth name (one of the attackers in "The Seven Against Thebes")

Aeacus — myth name (grandfather of Achilles)

Aeetes — myth name (Medea's father)

Aegeus — myth name (second husband of Medea)

Aegis — myth name (shield of Zeus)

Aegisthus — myth name (cousin of Agamemnon)

Aegyptus — myth name (father of the Danaides)

Aeneas — praiseworthy

Aeolus — myth name (god of the winds)

Aesculapius, Asklepios — myth name (god of medicine)

Aeson — myth name (father of Jason)

Agamedes — myth name (murdered by his brother for theft)

Agamemnon — myth name (leader of the Greek forces against Troy)

Agenor — myth name (son of Poseidon)

Ajax — eagle

Akil — from the river Akil

Alastair, Alastor, Alasdair — avenger

Alcides — descended from Alcaeus

Alcinous, Alcinoos — myth name (helps Odysseus return home)

Alcmaeon — myth name (one of the Thebes attackers)

Alcyoneus — myth name (fought against Athena)

Alexander, Alexis, Alec, Alex, Aleksandur, Alessandro, Alexandros, Alexandras, Alexandrukas, Alix, Aleksandr, Aleksy, Alexio, Alexei, Alyosha, Alyoshenka — defender of man

Aloeus — myth name (father of giants)

Alphenor — myth name

Alpheus — myth name (river god)

Ambrose, Ambrus, Ambrocio, Athan, Athanasius, Anstice — immortal

Amphiaraus — myth name (one of the attackers of Thebes)

Amphion — myth name (son of Zeus)

Amphitryon — myth name (husband of Alcmene)

Ampyx — myth name (father of Mopsus)

Amycus — myth name (son of Poseidon)

Anastasius, Anasztaz, Anastagio, Anastasio — reborn

Anatole, Anatoli, Anatolio, Anatolijus, Anatol — easterner

Ancaeus — myth name (an Argonaut)

Anchises—myth name (father of Aeneas)

Anderson, Anders, Papandrou—son of Ander

Andraemon—myth name

Andrew, Ander, Andres, Anker, Antti, Adras, Andor, Aindreas, Aindriu, Androu, Aniol, Anndra, Andrea, Andries—manly

Androgeus—myth name (son of Minos)

Angell, Angel, Angelo—messenger

Anibal—graced by God

Anstice, Anastasios, Anstiss—resurrected

Antaeus—myth name (killed by Hercules)

Anteros—myth name (mutual love)

Anthony, Anton, Antony—priceless

Anthor—myth name

Antilochus—myth name (son of Nestor)

Antinous—myth name (one of Penelope's suitors)

Antiphates—myth name (a Cyclops)

Aonghas, Angus—unique choice

Apollo, Apoloniusz—manly beauty

Arcas—myth name (son of Zeus)

Archemorus—myth name (son of Lycurgus)

Ares—myth name (god of war)

Argo—myth name (name of Jason's ship)

Argus, Argos—all-seeing

Arion—myth name (horse of Adrastus)

Aristaeus—myth name (son of Apollo)

Aristid—son of a great man

Aristotle—best of thinkers

Arsene, Arsenio—strong

Artemas, Artemus, Artemesio—gift from Artemis

Ascalaphus—myth name (turned into an owl by Persephone)

Asopus—myth name (a river god)

Astyanax—myth name (son of Hector killed at Troy)

Athamas—myth name (father of Phrixus and Helle)

Athanasios—noble

Atlas—myth name (a Titan)

Atreides—descended from Atreus

Atreus—myth name (father of Agamemnon)

Attis—myth name (son of Manes)

Auster—myth name

Autolycus—myth name (son of Hermes)

Avernus—myth name (portal to Hades)

Balasi—flat-footed

Baltsaros—Greek form of Balthazar

Baptiste—baptizer

Baruch—goodly

Basil, Basile, Basilio, Bazyli—royal

Bastien, Bastiaan, Baste—revered

Baucis, Baccus, Baccaus—myth name (name of Dionysus)

Bellerophon — myth name (slew Chimera)

Biton — myth name (son of a priestess)

Boethius — myth name

Boreas — myth name (the north wind)

Briareus — myth name (a Titan)

Cadmon — myth name

Cadmus — from the east

Calais — myth name (son of Boreas)

Calchas — myth name (a seer)

Capaneus — myth name (one of the attackers against Thebes)

Castor — myth name (brother of Helen)

Cebriones — myth name

Cecrops — myth name (founder of Athens)

Celeus — myth name (father of Triptolemus)

Cenon — friendly

Cephalus — myth name (husband who killed Procris)

Cepheus — myth name (father of Andromeda)

Cerberus — myth name (guardian to the gate of Hades)

Cercyon — myth name (name of a king)

Cesare, Caesare, Caseareo — long-haired

Cetus — myth name (sea monster of Poseidon)

Ceyx — myth name (husband of Alcyone)

Charon — myth name (ferryman across the river Styx)

Charybdis — myth name (a deadly whirlpool)

Chimera — myth name (the monster killed by Bellerophon)

Chiron — myth name (a centaur)

Christian, Cretien, Chris, Christiano — Christian

Christopher, Cristophe, Christobel, Christoph, Christophoros, Cristoforo, Christoffel — Christ-bearer

Christos — Christ

Chryses — myth name (a priest of Apollo)

Chrysostom — golden-mouthed

Claus, Claas, Colum, Cole — people's victory

Cleobis — myth name (son of a priestess)

Cletus — summoned

Cocytus — myth name (river of lamenting)

Coeus — myth name (father of Leto)

Corineus — myth name

Corybantes — myth name (priest of Rhea)

Corydon, Coridan — ready to fight

Cosmas, Cosmo, Cosima, Cos — order

Cottus — myth name (a Titan)

Creon — myth name (Jocasta's brother)

Cronus — myth name (a Titan)

Ctesippus — myth name (one of Penelope's suitors)

Cycnus — swan

Cyprian — from Cyprus

Cyr, Cyril, Cyryl, Cyrek, Coireall, Cirilo, Ciro, Cirio — lordly

Cyrano—from Cyrene

Cyrus, Ciro, Cy—sun

Daedalus—myth name (killed his nephew)

Daemon—myth name (guardian spirit)

Damaskenos, Damaskinos—from Damascus

Damian, Damen, Damae—tame

Damocles—myth name (a tyrant of Syracuse)

Danaus—myth name (father of the Danaides)

Daphnis—myth name (blinded for his infidelity)

Dardanus—myth name (founder of Troy)

Deiphobus—myth name (a son of Priam)

Delphinus—myth name (a scout of Poseidon)

Demetrius, Demetri, Demetre, Demetrios—gift from Demeter

Demodocus—myth name (a blind bard)

Demogorgon—myth name (thought to be the name for Satan)

Demophon—myth name (son of Theseus)

Deucalion—myth name (son of Prometheus)

Dhimitrios—myth name

Diomedes—myth name (an evil king)

Dionysius, Denes, Dion, Dunixi, Denys, Dionysios, Dionysus—myth name (god of wine)

Dolius—myth name (a shepherd)

Doran—a gift

Dorian—a Dorian

Echion—myth name

Egidio—shield-bearer

Elek, Eli—defender of man

Eleutherios, Eleftherios—free

Elpenor—myth name (one of Odysseus's men)

Enceladus—myth name (a giant)

Endre—manly

Endymion—myth name (a shepherd)

Enea—born ninth

Eneas—praised

Epeius—myth name (maker of the Trojan horse)

Epopeus—myth name

Erasmus—worthy of love

Ercole—gift from God

Erebus—myth name (father of Charon)

Erechtheus—myth name (a king of Athens)

Erichthonius—myth name (a king of Athens)

Erymanthus—myth name (son of Apollo)

Erysichthon—myth name (cursed with an insatiable hunger that caused his death)

Estebe, Estevao—victorious

Eteocles—myth name (son of Oedipus)

Etor, Ettore, Eachann—steadfast

Eubuleus—myth name (told Demeter about her daughter)

Eugene, Eugen, Eugenios, Eugenio, Evasn, Eoghan—wellborn

Eumaeus—myth name (a

swineherd who fought with Odysseus)

Eupeithes — myth name (father of a suitor for Penelope)

Eurus — myth name (god of the east wind)

Euryalus — myth name (taunted Odysseus)

Eurylochus — myth name (turned into a pig by Circe)

Eurymachus — myth name (suitor of Penelope)

Eurypylus — myth name (a soldier against Greece in the Trojan War)

Eurystheus — myth name (a cousin of Hercules)

Euryton — myth name (a giant)

Eusebius — pious

Eustace, Eustis, Eustachy — fruitful

Evzen — noble

Farris — rock

Fedor, Feodor — divine gift

Feodras — stone

Filippo, Fulop, Flip, Filips — lover of horses

Galen — meaning unknown

Galinthias — myth name (servant of Alcmene)

Ganymede — myth name (cup-bearer to the gods)

Gelasius — laughter

George, Georg, Georges, Georget, Gorka, Gyorgy, Gyoergy, Gyuri, Gyurka, Geordie, Goran, Gheorghr — farmer

Geryon — myth name (monster killed by Hercules)

Giles, Gilles — shield-bearer

Glaucus — myth name (son of Minos)

Gregory, Gregoire, Gregorie, Gregor, Grigor, Gruev, Grigorov, Gregos, Gergely, Gergor, Gregorior — vigilant

Guilio — young

Gyes — myth name (a Titan)

Haemon — myth name (son of Creon)

Hali — sea

Halirrhothius — myth name (son of Poseidon)

Halithersis — myth name (seer who warns Penelope's suitors)

Haralambos — meaning unknown

Hasione — myth name

Hector — steadfast

Helenus — myth name (son of Priam)

Helios — myth name (god of the sun)

Hephaestus — myth name (god of the crafts)

Hercules, Heraklesr — myth name (son of Zeus)

Hermes — myth name (messenger of the gods)

Hesperos — evening star

Hieronim — meaning unknown

Hipolit, Hippolytusr — freer of horses

Hippocampus — myth name (a horse of Poseidon)

Hippogriff — myth name (part horse, part griffen)

Hippolytus — myth name (son of Theseus)

Hippomenes — myth name (winner of Atalanta)

Homer, Homerus, Homeros — security

Hyancinthe, Hyacinthusr — hyacinth

Hylas — myth name (son of Theiodamas)

Hymen — myth name (god of marriage)

Hyperion — myth name (a Titan)

Hypnos — myth name (god of sleep)

Hyrieus — myth name

Iapetus — myth name (a Titan)

Iasion — myth name (father of Plutus)

Iasius — myth name

Iason — healer

Ibycus — myth name (a bard)

Icarius — myth name (gave wine to the citizens of Athens who mistook it for poison and killed him)

Icarus — myth name (son of Daedalus)

Icelos — myth name (son of Hypnos)

Idas — myth name (an Argonaut)

Idomeneus — myth name (a king of Crete)

Ignatius — fiery

Inachus — myth name (a river god)

Iobates — myth name

Ion — myth name (son of Apollo)

Iorgas, Igorr — farmer

Iphicles — myth name (Hercules' twin brother)

Iphis — myth name (hanged himself over unrequited love)

Iphitus — myth name (brother of Iole)

Irus — myth name (challenged Odysseus on his return to Ithaca)

Isidore, Isadorer, Ixidorr, Isidoror, Isidrro — strong gift

Istvan — victorious

Ivan, Ivanetsr, Ivankor — glorious gift

Ixion — myth name (father of the centaurs)

Jacinto — hyacinth

Jason, Jasunr, Jayr — healer

Jeno, Jencir — well-born

Jerome, Jeroenr — holy name

Jiri, Jirkar, Jurgisr, Jorisr, Jerzyr, Jorgenr, Jornr, Jorgr, Jorenr — farmer

Julian, Juliusr — youthful

Kadmus — from the east

Kaj — earth

Karsten, Kristr — anointed

Kedalion — myth name

Keril, Kirilr, Kyrillosr, Kirilr, Kuirilr, Kirylr — lordly

Kester, Kestorr, Kitr, Kipr, Krisr, Kristor, Kristofr, Krystupasr — Christ-bearer

Khristos — Christ

Klaus, Klaasr — people's victory

Kolya — victorious army

Korudon — helmeted

Kosmy, Kosmosr — order

Kratos — strength

Krikor — vigilant

Kristian, Krischanr, Krzysztofr, Khrystiyanr — Christian

Kyrillos — lordly

Kyros — master

Ladon — myth name (dragon of Hera)

Laertes — myth name (father of Odysseus)

Laestrygones — myth name (a tribe of giants)

Laius — myth name (father of Oedipus)

Laocoon — myth name (son of Priam)

Laomedon — myth name (father of Priam)

Lasse — people's victory

Leander, Lander, Leandro — lion

Leksi — defender of man

Lethe — myth name (river of oblivion)

Lichas — myth name (Hercules' friend)

Lidio — meaning unknown

Linus — flaxen-haired

Lippi, Lipp, Lippio — lover of horses

Loxias — crooked

Lycaon — myth name (a king of Arcadia)

Lycomedes — myth name (a king of Scyros)

Lycurgus — myth name (a king of the Edones)

Lynceus — myth name (an Argonaut)

Lysander — liberator

Macaire, Makarioa, Marcario — blessed

Machaon — myth name (son of Aesculapius)

Marsyas — myth name (a satyr)

Maur, Maurice — dark

Medus — myth name (son of Medea by Aegeus)

Melampus — myth name (seer)

Melanippus — myth name (helps defend Thebes against the attackers)

Melanthius — myth name (sides with Penelope's suitors against his master Odysseus)

Meleager — myth name (an Argonaut)

Melecertes — myth name (son of Ino)

Meletios — meaning unknown

Menelaus — myth name (brother of Agamemnon)

Menoeceus — myth name (father of Jocasta)

Mentor — wise counselor

Mette — pearl

Mezentius — myth name

Midas — myth name (turned everything he touched to gold)

Mikolas — people's victory

Mimis — myth name

Minos — myth name (son of Zeus)

Momus — myth name (god of ridicule)

Mopsus — myth name (a seer)

Morpheus — myth name (bringer of dreams)

Myles, Miles, Milo — destroyer

Myron — myrrh

Nape — myth name

Napolean, Napoleon — of the new city

Narcissus, Narkis, Narcisse — daffodil

Nauplius — myth name (an Argonaut)

Nectarios—name of a saint

Neleus—myth name (son of Poseidon)

Nemo, Nemos—from the glen

Neotolemus—myth name (son of Achilles)

Nereus—myth name (father of the Nereids)

Nestor—wisdom

Nicholas, Nicholaus, Nicolas, Niles, Nils, Nikolai, Nik, Nick, Nicodemus, Nikodem, Nicole, Nicolaus, Nicol, Nilo, Nikita, Nikolos, Nilos, Niocole, Niocol, Niklaus, Nikolajis—people's victory

Nisus—myth name (father of Scylla)

Notus—myth name (the south wind)

Obiareus—myth name (a Titan)

Oceanus—myth name (father of the Oceanids)

Ocnus—incompetent

Odysseus—wrathful

Oedipus—swollen foot

Oeneus—myth name (king of Calydon)

Oenomaus—myth name (son of Ares)

Oighrig—well-spoken

Oles—defender of man

Ophion—myth name (a serpent)

Orestes, Oreste, Oreias—from the mountain

Orion—son of fire

Orpheus—myth name (son of Apollo)

Orthros—myth name (guardian of Geryon)

Otis, Otos, Otus—keen of hearing

Owen—well-born

Palaemon—myth name (a sea god)

Palamedes—myth name (son of Nauplius)

Pan—myth name (god of flocks)

Panagiotis—all-holy

Pancratius—supreme ruler

Pandareos—myth name (a thief)

Pandarus—myth name (killed for breaking a truce)

Panteleimon—merciful

Parthenios—virgin

Paris—myth name (son of Priam)

Patroclus—myth name (Achilles' best friend)

Pegasus—myth name (winged horse)

Peisistratus—myth name (son of Nestor)

Peleus—myth name (father of Achilles)

Pelias—myth name (son of Poseidon)

Pelops—myth name (father of Atreus)

Peneus—myth name

Pentheus—myth name (a king of Thebes)

Perdix—myth name (killed by his uncle)

Pericles—myth name

Persius, Perseus—myth name (son of Danae)

Peter, Pedro, Petr, Piotr, Peder, Perrin, Pekka, Petros, Panos, Pierro, Pietro, Pero, Peterke, Piero, Pello, Peru, Piarres, Preben, Per, Petter, Pierre,

Pertras, Petrukas, Petrelis,
Piet, Pieter, Pietr, Pedar,
Peadair, Prophyrios, Piaras —
rock

Phaethon — myth name (son of
Helios)

Phantasos — myth name (son of
Hypnos)

Phaon — myth name (a ferryman)

Phemius — myth name (a bard)

Pheobus — shining

Philander — lover of man

Philemon — loves thought

Philip, Pippo, Philippe, Phillip,
Philipp, Pilib — lover of horses

Philo, Phylo — friend

Philoctetes — myth name (killed
Paris)

Philoetius — myth name (a
cowherd)

Phineas, Phinees, Phineus —
mouth of brass

Phlegethon — myth name (river of
fire)

Phoenix — myth name (a bird that
built its own pyre and then was
reborn from the ashes)

Phrixus — myth name (son of
Nephele)

Phorbas, Phorbus — myth name

Phorcys — myth name (a sea god)

Pirithous — myth name (friend of
Theseus)

Pirro — red-haired

Pittheus — myth name (king of
Trozen)

Pityocamptes — pine-bender

Plato — broad

Plexippus — myth name (an
Argonaut)

Plutus — myth name (wealth)

Polites — myth name

Pollux — myth name (brother of
Helen)

Polycarp — much fruit

Polydamas — myth name (a
Trojan warrior)

Polydeuces — myth name (Pollux)

Polydorus — myth name (son of
Priam)

Polyeidus — myth name (a seer)

Polymestor — myth name
(Priam's son-in-law)

Polynices — myth name (uncle of
Oedipus)

Polyphemus — myth name (son of
Poseidon)

Pontus — sea

Porfirio — purple stone

Poseidon — myth name (god of the
sea and ocean)

Priam — myth name (king of Troy)

Priapus — myth name (god of
fertility)

Procrustes — myth name
(stretcher)

Prokopios — declared leader

Prometheus — myth name (gave
fire to man)

Protesilaus — myth name (offered
himself as a sacrifice for the
Greeks when they arrived at
Troy)

Proteus — myth name (a sea god)

Pygmalion — myth name (king of
Cyprus)

Pylades — myth name (friend of
Orestes)

Pyramus — myth name (lover of
Thisbe)

Pyrrhus—myth name (king of Epirus)

Rasmus—amiable

Rhadamanthus—myth name (a judge in the underworld)

Rhesus—myth name (king of Thrace)

Rhoecus—myth name (saved Hamadryad)

Risto—Christ-bearer

Rodas—rose garden

Salmoneus—myth name (during Trojan War, pretended to be Zeus)

Sanders, Saunders, Sander, Sandor—defender of man

Sarpedon—myth name (killed by Patroclus during the Trojan War)

Sebastian, Sebasten, Sebestyen, Sebastiano—revered

Seoirse, Seorsa—farmer

Sidney, Sydney—from Sidon

Simon, Simeon, Symeon—sign

Sinon—myth name (convinced the Trojans to pull the horse inside the city walls)

Sisyphus—myth name (son of Aelous)

Socrates—name of a philosopher

Soterios—savior

Spyridon—round basket

Stamitos—enduring

Stephen, Steven, Stefan, Stefano, Stephano, Steverino, Stavros, Stefanos, Steafan, Staffen—victorious

Stoffel—Christ-bearer

Tadhg, Teague, Taidgh, Tiege—honor

Takis—all-holy

Talus—myth name (mechanical man made by Hephaestus)

Tantalus—myth name (condemned to eternal torment)

Taxiarchai—archangel

Telamon—myth name (father of Ajax)

Telegonus—myth name (son of Odysseus)

Telemachus—myth name (son of Odysseus)

Telephus—myth name (son of Hercules)

Tereus—myth name (king of Thrace)

Teucer—myth name (an archer)

Teuthras—myth name (king of Mysia)

Thamyris—myth name (a musician punished for hubris)

Thanatos—myth name (death)

Thanos, Thanasis—noble

Thaumas—myth name (father of the Harpies)

Theoclymenus—myth name (befriended by Telemachus)

Theodore, Theodosios, Teadoir, Teodors, Theodrekr, Todor, Tuder, Tudor, Tivadar—gracious gift

Theon—godly

Theophile, Teofile—divinely loved

Theron—hunter

Thersites—myth name (soldier in the Trojan War)

Theseus—myth name (son of Aegeus)

Thyestes — myth name (brother of Atreus)

Tigris — myth name

Timothy, Timon, Timun, Timotheos, Timothea, Tiomoid, Tymon, Tymek, Tymoteusz — God-fearing

Tiresias — myth name (a blind seer)

Titos, Tito, Titus — of the giants

Tityus — myth name (a giant)

Toxeus — myth name (brother of Althaea)

Tracy, Tracey — harvester

Triptolemus — myth name (taught agriculture by Demeter)

Triton — myth name (son of Poseidon)

Trophonius — myth name (brother of Agamedes)

Tydeus — myth name (father of Diomedes)

Tyndareus — myth name (father of Castor)

Typhon, Typhoeus — myth name (a child of the Titans)

Tyrone, Turannos — lord

Ulysses — wrathful

Uranus — myth name (sky)

Urian — from heaven

Vanko — gracious gift

Vasilis, Vasos, Vasileios, Vasyl, Vasylko, Vasyltso — regal

Xanthus — myth name (a river god)

Xuthus — myth name (son of Helen)

Xenophon, Xeno — strange voice

Xenos — stranger

Xerxes — leaving

Xylon — from the forest

Yrjo, Yurii, Yura, Yurochka, Yure, Yuri, Yehor — farmer

Zale — power of the sea

Zarek — God protect the king

Zelotes — zealous

Zelus — myth name

Zenas — living

Zeno, Zeus — myth name

Zenon — friendly

Zephyrus — myth name

Zetes — myth name (son of Boreas)

Zoltan, Zoltar — life

Zotikos — meaning unknown

Hebrew

Since the Hebrews have no single national identity, surnames developed at odd intervals in communities throughout the world. Most last names were patronymic in a fashion similar to Arabic names. Now they tend to be more place oriented. Before hereditary surnames, Hebrews used Ben (son of), then their father's name, the name of their home, or a name from the Bible.

The first Hebrew surnames occurred in Spain. During the Middle Ages, Hebrews in Germany used the name of their houses for a surname. In 1785 in Austria, they were required to take surnames, and in 1787 they were restricted to using biblical names only.

In 1804, Russia prevented the Hebrews from altering their names. And in 1844, Russia compelled them to adopt surnames.

Poland passed laws in 1821 to require Hebrews to choose surnames. As late as 1942, France forbade them to change their names.

Again, there is wide variety in Hebrew surnames, when they came into being, and what form they took. I would caution writers to do more research on the nomenclature of the region and branch the of Hebrews they are interested in.

A few surnames:

Altschul	Kleinlerer
Benjamin	Levy
Herzhaft	Mindel
Isaac	Reis
Joseph	Tischler

FEMALE

Abarrane — feminine form of Abraham (father of many)

Abelia, Abelie — breath

Abigail, Abegayle, Abaigael, Abaigeal, Abby, Abbie, Avichayil, Abichail, Avigail — gives joy

Abra — mother of many

Adah — beautiful

Adar, Adara — fire

Adine, Adinam, Adena, Adene — tender

Admina—of the red earth

Afra—doe

Ahuva, Ahava, Ahuda, Ahave—
dearly loved

Ailat, Ayalah—behind

Ailsa, Ailsie—devoted to God

Akiva, Akibe, Akiba—protected

Aleeza, Aliza, Alizah, Alitza,
Aleezah—joyous

Alona, Allona, Allonia, Alonia—
strong as an oak

Alumit, Aluma—girl

Amaris, Amariah, Amarisa,
Amarise, Amarissa—given by
God

Anamari, Annamarie, Anamarie—
grace, bitter

Anat, Anate, Anata, Anatie—a
singer

Ann, Anne, Ane, Annie, Anny,
Ayn—prayer

Anna, Ana, Annette, Anetta,
Anita, Anitra, Annora,
Annorah, Anora, Anais, Antje,
Ance, Aneta, Anka, Asenka,
Anyuta, Asenke, Annze, Anica,
Anichka, Asya, Anku—grace

Anneliese, Annaliese, Annalisa,
Analise—grace, devoted to
God

Annikki, Aniki, Aniko, Annikka,
Anika, Annikke—grace

Annot—light

Aoife—life

Araminta, Araminte—lofty

Ardath, Aridatha—flowering field

Ariel, Areille, Ariela, Ariellel,
Athaleyah—lioness of God

Ashira—wealthy

Ateret, Atarah, Atara—crowned

Athalia, Athalie, Atalia, Atalie—
God is great

Atira, Atera—pray

Avera—transgresses

Avivit, Avivi, Aviva—innocent

Axelle, Axella—peace

Aya, Aiya—bird

Azalea, Azelia, Azelie, Aziel—
flower

Aziza—meaning unknown

Bathsheba, Bethsheba—oath

Battseeyon, Battzion—daughter
of Zion

Batya, Bitya—daughter of God

Beathag—to serve God

Becky—captivating

Beruriah—selected by God

Bethel, Betheli—house of God

Bethseda, Bethsaida—merciful

Bettina, Bettine, Betti, Betty,
Bozi, Bella, Betje, Betsy—
devoted to God

Beulah, Beula—to marry

Brachah—blessed

Carmel—vineyard

Carmella, Carmela, Carmeline,
Carmelina—garden

Carmen—guard

Chanah, Chana—graceful

Chasidah—pious

Chasya, Chasye—shelter

Chava, Chaya, Chabah, Chaba,
Chayka, Chaka—life

Chaviva, Chavive—dearly loved

Chedva—joyous

Chephzibah—she is our delight

Cochava—star

Csilla—defender

Daganyah, Daganya—
ceremonial grain

Dalit, Dalis — drawing water

Daliyah, Daliah — tree branch

Danette, Daniela, Danita, Danele, Danelle, Danielle, Danae, Danya, Danila, Dania, Danetta, Danit — God is my judge

Daphna, Daphnah, Daphne — victory

Davina, Davinia, Davinah, Davida, Davi, Davite, Davitah — cherished

Debora, Deborah, Debra, Devora, Devoria — bee

Delilah, Delila, Dalila — desired

Dena, Dina, Dinah — avenged

Derora, Derorit, Derorice — free

Divsha, Divshah — honey

Eden, Edan — perfect

Edra, Edrea — powerful

Eliora, Eleora, Elora — God is light

Elka, Elke — oath to God

Ellice, Eliane, Elia, Eliana — Jehovah is God

Elspeth, Elli, Elizabeth, Elisabeth, Elisabet, Elsie, Eliza, Erzsebet, Elisheva, Els, Elzira, Elizaveta, Elisaveta, Elisavet — devoted to God

Emmanuelle, Emunah, Emmanuella — faith

Erelah, Erela — angel

Erith, Eritha — flower

Ester, Eszter, Esther, Estrela — star

Etel, Etilka, Ethel — noble

Eva, Eve, Eeva, Evika, Evike, Evacska, Ewa — life

Fifne, Fifna, Fina — He shall add

Gabrielle, Gabriella, Gavra, Gavrila, Gavrilla, Gabriele — God gives strength

Galia, Gallia, Galilah, Galila, Galya, Galina, Galenka, Galochka — God shall redeem

Galit, Gali, Galice — fountain

Ganit, Ganet, Gana, Ganice — garden

Gazit, Gisa, Giza — cut stone

Gilah, Gila, Gilit, Geela, Gilia, Gili, Gilala, Gilal, Gilana, Gilat — eternal joy

Giovanna — gracious gift from God

Grazyna, Grazina, Grazinia — grace

Guiditta — praise

Guiseppina, Guiseppie — He shall add

Gurit, Gurice — cub

Hadar, Hadara — spectacular ornament

Hadassah — myrtle

Hagar — flight

Hannah, Hanna, Hanne, Hannele, Hannela — grace

Haya — life

Helsa — devoted to God

Hephzibah, Hepsiba, Hepzibeth — she is my delight

Hulda, Holda — weasel

Ilana, Ilanit — tree

Ilia — God is Lord

Ilse — God's word

Ionanna — grace

Iris — flower

Isabel, Izabella, Isabelle, Isabella, Isibeal — devoted to God

Ivana, Ivane, Iva, Ivanna — gift from God

Izso — God's salvation

Jacoba, Jakoba, Jakobah,
  Jaquenette, Jaquetta, Jocelin,
  Joceline, Jocelyn, Jaqueline,
  Jaquelina — supplanter
Jael — goat
Jaffa, Jafit, Jafita — beauty
Janet, Jane, Jayne, Janetta,
  Janette, Janice, Janis, Joan,
  Joanna, Johanna, Jone, Jan,
  Jenda, Jana, Jaine, Janie, Janne,
  Janine, Janka, Janina, Janita,
  Jansje, Jans, Jaantje, Juana,
  Juanita, Joka — gift from God
Jardena, Jardina — meaning
  unknown
Jemima, Jonati — dove
Jemina — listened to
Jensine, Jensina — God has
  blessed
Jerusha — married
Jessica, Jessie — rich
Jobina, Jobyna — persecuted
Jochebed — God's glory
Joelle, Joella, Joelliane, Joelliana,
  Jola — Jehovah is God
Jokine, Jokina, Joaquina,
  Joaquine — God shall establish
Jordane, Jordan — descended
Josepha, Josephine, Josette,
  Josetta, Josephina, Joxepa,
  Josebe, Jose, Josie, Josee,
  Jozsa — God will add
Judith, Judy, Judie, Jodie, Judit,
  Juci, Jutka, Jucika — praised
Kalanit — flower
Karmia, Karmit, Karmelit,
  Karmelita, Karmelite — Lord's
  vineyard
Kefira — lion cub
Kelilah, Kelula, Kyla — victorious

Keren, Keryn, Keran — horn
Ketura — incense
Kinneret, Kinnette — harp
Kiva, Kivi, Kiba — protected
Ksena — praise be to God
Laila, Lailie, Laili, Laylie —
  nightfall
Lea, Leah — tired
Lemuela, Lise, Liza, Lisabette,
  Lisabet, Lisavet, Liesbeth,
  Liesbet, Lizbeth, Lizbet —
  devoted to God
Lesham — precious
Lewanna — the moon
Levia — join
Lilith, Lily, Lilie, Lilah — lily
Lirit, Lirita — poetic
Livana — white
Magda, Magdalen, Magdalene,
  Magdala, Magdalena, Madalen,
  Maialen, Matxalen, Madel,
  Maidel, Madeleine, Madelaine,
  Madelene, Madelena,
  Madalyn, Malina, Marlene,
  Marlena — from the tower
Mahala, Mahalia — tender
Malak — messenger
Malcah, Malkah, Milcah — queen
Manuela — God is among us
Mariamne, Miriam — rebellious
Maribel, Maribelle, Maribella —
  bitter, beautiful
Mary, Mara, Mae, Maria, Maren,
  Miren, Mariette, Marika,
  Mallaidh, Marie, Marion,
  Mariska, Molly, May, Marily,
  Marthe, Martha, Mirit, Miri,
  Mira, Marisha — bitter
Matea, Mattea, Matthea, Matthia,
  Mathea, Mathia — God's gift

Mava — pleasant

Mayah, Maia, Michelle, Micheline, Michaele, Michalin, Mikele, Micheala, Michaelina — close to God

Mazel — luck

Mehetabel, Mehitabelle, Mettabel, Meheytabel — God's favor

Meira — light

Menachemah, Menachema — consolation

Mitzi, Mieze — small, bitter

Moriah, Morit, Moriel, Morice, Morise — God teaches

Moselle — from the water

Naamah, Naomi, Neomi, Navit — pleasant

Naamit — bird

Naavah, Naava — beautiful

Nathania — God's gift

Nechama, Nehama — comfort

Nedivah, Nediva — giving

Neorah, Nora, Norah — light

Neta, Nita — grace

Nili — success

Nina, Nana, Nan, Nanna, Nancy, Nanelle, Nanelia, Nanette, Nanetta, Nanine, Nanny, Nannie, Nancsi, Ninacska, Nusi, Nusa, Nainsi, Nin — grace

Niria, Nira — plow

Nirit, Nurit, Nurita, Nureet — plant

Nitzanah, Nizana, Nitza — blossom

Noga — sparkle

Noy — decoration

Odeda, Odede — strong

Ofra — fawn

Ona, Onit — graceful

Ophra, Ophrah, Oprah — fawn

Ora, Orah, Oralee, Orali, Orlee — light

Ornah, Ornette, Ornetta, Orna — cedar tree

Orzora — God's strength

Orzsebet — devoted to God

Paili, Polly, Pall, Poll — bitter

Pazit, Pazia, Pazice, Paz, Paza — golden

Peninah, Penina — pearl

Perzsike, Perke, Perzsi — devoted to God

Qeturah — incense

Raananah — unspoiled

Rachel, Rachele, Rakel — ewe

Ranit, Ranita, Ranice, Ranica — lovely tune

Raphaella, Rafela — healer

Raquel, Rahil, Raonaid — innocent

Reba, Rabah — fourth born

Rebecca, Reveka, Rebekah, Rivka — captivating

Rena, Rina, Rinna, Rinnah — joyous song

Rimona — pomegranate

Ronli, Rona, Ronia — my joy

Rosanne, Rosana — graceful rose

Ruth, Ruta — friend

Sabra — to rest

Sadie, Sara, Sarah, Sally, Sallie, Sarita — princess

Salome, Salomeaex1, Saloma, Selima, Schlomit, Shulamit — tranquil

Samantha — name of God

Samara, Shemariah — protected by God

Samuela — asked of God
Sapphira, Sapphire — beautiful
Sarai — argumentative
Segulah — precious
Sela, Sele, Seleta — rock
Semadar — berry
Semira, Sheiramoth — from heaven
Seraphina, Seraphine, Serafine, Serefina — burning fire
Sharon — from the land of Sharon
Sheena — God's gift
Shifra — beautiful
Shira, Shiri — tune
Sidonia, Sidonie — captivates
Simcha — joyous
Simona, Simone — loud
Sinead, Siobhan — kind
Sippora — bird
Susan, Sue, Susie, Susy — lily
Susanna, Susannah, Suzanna — graceful lily
Suzette, Suzetta — little lily
Talia, Talya, Tal — dew of heaven
Talori, Talora — morning's dew
Tamara, Tamar, Tamarah — palm tree
Tamma, Teme, Temima — without flaw
Temira — tall
Thadine, Thadina — given praise
Thirza — delightful
Thomsina, Thomasin, Tomasina, Tomasine — twin
Tikva — hope
Tivona — love's nature
Tova, Toba, Toibe — goodly
Tsifira — crown
Tzilla — defender
Tzippa, Tzzipporah — bird

Tzivia — doe
Tziyona — of Zion
Urit, Urice — light
Uzziye — God's strength
Vania, Vanna — God's gift
Varda, Vardit, Vadit, Vared — rose
Vida, Vidette — dearly loved
Ya-akove — replaces
Yachne — kind
Ya-el — goat
Yaffa, Yaffit — beautiful
Yardenah — from the river Jordan
Yarkona — green
Yedidah — friend
Yehudit, Yuta, Yuhudit — praise
Yelizavetam, Yelysaveta — devoted to God
Yeva, Yetsye, Yevunye — life
Yocheved — God's glory
Yona, Yonina, Yonita — dove
Yordana — descended from
Yoseba, Yosebe, Yosepha, Yosephina — God will multiply
Yovela — rejoice
Zahavah, Zehave, Zehuva, Zehavit, Zehavi — golden
Zaneta, Zanna — God's gift
Zara, Zarah — day's awakening
Zehira — protected
Zemira, Zemirah — joyous melody
Zera, Zera'im — seed
Zerlinda, Zarahlinda — beautiful dawn
Zibiah, Zibia — doe
Zilla, Zillah — shadow
Zimra, Zimria, Zemira, Zemora, Zamora — praised
Zippora, Zipporah — beauty
Ziva — splendid
Zohar, Zoheret — sparkle

MALE

Aaron, Aron — high mountain

Abbot, Abbott — father

Abbotson — son of Abbot

Abel — breath

Abijah, Abisha — the Lord is my father

Abir, Aitan, Avniel — strong

Abner — father of light

Abraham, Abram, Abramo, Avraham, Aram, Abarron, Avidor — father of a multitude

Adam — man of the red earth

Adamson — son of Adam

Adar, Adir — noble

Aderet — crown

Adin, Adiv — delicate

Adlai — witness

Adley — judicious

Adon — the Lord

Adriel, Adriyel — of God's flock

Ager, Asaph, Asaf — gathers

Akiba, Akub, Akiva — replaces

Akim — God will establish

Alon — oak

Alter — old

Alva — exalted

Amasa — burden

Amichai — my parents are alive

Amiel, Ami-el — of the Lord's people

Amikam, Amram — rising nation

Amir — proclaimed

Amiram — of lofty people

Amita, Amiti, Ammitai — truth

Ammi — my people

Amnon, Amon — faithful

Amos — brave

Ari, Arie, Ariel, Aryeh, Arye — lion of God

Arion — melodious

Arnon — roaring stream

Arvad — wanderer

Asa — healer

Asher — happy

Avi, Avidan, Avidor, Aviel, Avniel — father

Avichai — my father is alive

Avidan — God is just

Avigdor — father protection

Avimelech, Abimelech — father is king

Avinoam — pleasant father

Aviram, Abiram — father of heights

Avisha, Avishai — gift from God

Avital — father of dew

Aviv — young

Avner, Abner — father of light

Axel, Aksel, Absalom, Avshalom, Avsalom — father of peace

Azarious, Azaryah, Azaria, Azaryahu, Azriel — God helps

Baram — son of the nation

Barnabas, Barnaby, Barnabe, Barna — son of prophecy

Bartholomew, Bart, Bartel, Bartley, Benkamin, Binyamin — ploughman

Baruch — blessed

Bela — destruction

Ben — son

Ben-ami — son of my people

Ben-aryeh, Benroy — son of a lion

Benedictson — son of Benedict

Benjamin, Beniamino — son of the right hand

Benoni — son of my sorrows

Benson — son of Benjamin

Ben-tziyon, Benzion — son of Zion

Berakhiah — God blesses

Betzalel — in God's shadow

Binah — understanding

Boas, Boaz — swift

Bogdan, Bohdan — gift from God

Cain — possessed

Caleb — bold

Carmel — garden

Carmi, Carmine — vine dresser

Chagai — mediates

Chaim, Chayim — life

Chanan — cloud

Chanoch — initiating

Chavivi, Chaviv — dearly loved

Che, Chepe, Chepito — God will multiply

Chiram — noble

Choni — gracious

Dagan — grain

Daniel, Danel, Danil, Dan, Dani, Daniele, Dane, Danny, Deen, Danila — God will judge

Dar — pearl

David, Davin, Davey, Davi, Dabi — dearly loved

Deron — free

Dor — a home

Doren — gift

Dovev — speaks in a whisper

Eben, Eban — rock

Ebenezer — rock of help

Efrat — honored

Ehud — meaning unknown

Elan — tree

Elazar — God helps

Eleazar, Elazaro, Eliezer — God has helped

Elhanan — God is gracious

Elias, Elihu, Elijah, Ellis, Eliot, Ely, Eli, Elisha, Eliseo — Jehovah is God

Elishama — God hears

Elisheva, Elisheba — God is my wrath

Elkanah — possessed by God

Elrad — God rules

Emmanuel — God is with us

Enoch — consecrated

Ephrem, Ephram, Ephraim, Efrayim — fruitful

Errapel — divine healer

Esdras — help

Eshkol — grape cluster

Ethan, Etan — strong

Evelyn — life

Eyou — symbol of piety

Ezechiel — strength of God

Ezra — helper

Foma — twin

Gabriel, Gavi, Gavriel, Gabriele, Gabrielo, Gabor, Gabi — God is my strength

Gal — wave

Gamaliel — God's reward

Gedalya, Gedaliah, Gedalyahu — God has made great

Gedeon, Gideon — destroyer

Geremia — God is high

Gersham, Gershom — exiled

Giacomo — replaces

Gian, Giovanni, Giannes — gift from God

Gil, Gilli, Gili — happiness

Guiseppe — God will multiply

Guri, Gurion — my lion cub

Guy — valley
Habib — dearly loved
Hadar — glory
Hanan — grace
Hananel — God is gracious
Hans, Hansel — gift from God
Harel, Harrell — mountain of God
Harrod — heroic
Hayyim, Hyman — life
Herschel, Hershel — deer
Hezekiah — God is my strength
Hieremias — God will uplift
Hiram — exalted
Hod — vigorous
Honi — gracious
Hosea — salvation
Iakovos — supplanter
Iaokim, Iov — God will establish
Ichabod — the glory has departed
Illias, Ilias — Jehovah is God
Imanol — God is with us
Ioseph, Iosep — God will multiply
Ira — descendant
Isaac, Izaak, Isaakios, Ixaka —
   child of laughter
Isaias, Isaiah, Isiah — God's helper
Iseabail — devoted to God
Isreal, Izreal — ruling with the
   Lord
Itai — friendly
Ittamar — island of palms
Ivan, Ioan, Ian, Iban, Ionnes — gift
   from God
Jacob, Jack, Jock, Jake, Jacobe,
   James, Jim, Jamie, Jimmy, Jem,
   Jakome, Jaques, Jacot, Jaap,
   Jov — supplanter
Jael — mountain goat
Japhet — handsome
Jared, Jori — descending

Jasper — jewel
Jedidiah, Jed, Jedi — beloved by
   God
Jephtah — first born
Jeremias, Jeremiah, Jeremy,
   Jeremi, Jeremie — exalted of
   the Lord
Jesse, Jessie — wealthy
Joachim — God prepares
Job — persecuted
Jocheved — God is glorious
Joel — strong-willed
John, Juan, Jens, Jonam, Jonathan,
   Jonatan, Jon, Jan, Jenda, Joen,
   Jani, Janie, Johan, Jussi, Jukka,
   Juha, Jean, Jeannot, Jancsi,
   Jonas, Jankia, Janko, Janos,
   Jantje, Jannes — gift from God
Jokin — God will establish
Jordan — flowing down
Joseph, Joosef, Jooseppi,
   Josephus, Joop, Jopie, Joseba —
   God will multiply
Joshua, Josue, Josias — God is
   salvation
Josiah — God heals
Josu — God saves
Judd, Judy, Jude, Judah, Judas,
   Jud — praised
Jurrien, Jurre, Jore, Jorie, Jory —
   God will uplift
Karmel — vineyard
Laban, Lavan — white
Lapidos, Lapidoth — torch
Lazarus, Lazzaro, Lazar — God
   will help
Leb — heart
Lemuel — dedicated to God
Levi, Lev, Levey, Lewi — united
Lot — veiled

Machum, Menachem — comfort

Mai-ron, Miron, Myron — holy place

Malachy, Mal, Malachi — messenger of God

Manasses, Menassah — forgetful

Manuel — God is with us

Marnin — one who creates joy

Mathew, Matthias, Mattias, Mate, Matyas, Matai, Mathews, Mads, Mikael, Mikkel, Matthieu, Mathe, Matz, Michael, Mitchell, Mikel, Mikko, Michel, Michon, Michele, Machau, Makis, Misi, Mikhail, Mikhalis, Mikhos, Maichail, Mihaly, Miska, Mika, Micah — gift from God

Mayir, Meir — enlightens

Meilseoir, Melchoir — king

Mordechai, Mordecai — warrior

Moses, Mosheh — saved from the water

Naaman — pleasant

Nadav — gives

Nadiv — noble

Naftali, Naftalie — wreath

Nahum, Nachman — compassionate

Nathan, Nathaniel, Nathanael, Natanael, Nethanel — gift from God

Nehemiah, Nechemya — comforted by God

Nissim — wonders

Noe, Noah, Noach — comfort

Nuri — my fire

Obadiah, Ovadiah, Ovadya, Obediah — serves God

Oded — encourages

Ofer — fawn

Ophir — meaning unknown

Oren, Orin, Oris — tree

Ori, Orneet, Ornet — my light

Osip — God will multiply

Oved, Ovid — worker

Ozi, Ozzie, Ozzi — strong

Palti, Palt-el — God liberates

Pascal, Paschal — born on Passover

Paz — golden

Pessach, Pesach — spread

Phineas — oracle

Pinochos — dark-skinned

Raanan — fresh

Ranit, Ronit, Rani, Roni, Ron — song

Ranon, Ranen — joyful

Raphael, R'phael, Rafal — God's healer

Ravid — wanderer

Rechavia — broad

Reuben, Ruben, Rueban, Rouvin, Re'uven — behold a son

Saadya — God's helper

Sakeri — remembered by God

Samson, Sampson, Shimshon — bright sun

Samuel, Schmuel — asked of God

Sanson — the sun's man

Sasson, Simcha — joy

Saul, Sha-ul — longed for

Schmaiah — God hears

Seanan, Senen, Sinon, Shane — gift from God

Seosamh, Seosaph — God will multiply

Seraphim, Serafin, Serafim — seraph

Seth — anointed

Shet, Set — compensation
Simeon, Simon, Symeon, Siomon, Simen, Simao — obedient
Simpson, Simson, Shim'on — son of Simon
Sinai — from the clay desert
Solomon, Salamon, Shelomo, Shalom — peaceful
Taaveti, Taavi — dearly loved
Taneli — judged by God
Tapani, Teppo — victorious
Thaddeus — wise
Thomas, Tomas, Tuomas, Thoma, Tamas, Tomek — twin
Tobias, Tobin, Toby, Tovi, Tuvya, Tobiah, Turyahu — goodness of God
Tsidhqiyah — God's justice
Tzadok — just
Tzefanyah, Tzefanyahu — treasure by God
Tzion — sunny mountain
Tzuriel — God is my rock
Tzvi — deer
Uriah, Uri, Uriel — God is my light
Uzziel, Uzziah — God is mighty
Veniamin, Venamin, Venjamin — son of the right hand
Ximen, Ximon, Ximun — God has heard
Yaakov — held by the heel
Yagil — He will rejoice
Yair — enlighten
Yakov, Yago — supplanter
Yannis, Yehoash, Yehonadov — gift from God
Yaphet — handsome
Yardane — descendent

Yaron — singer
Yavin — understanding
Yedidyah, Yedidiah, Yerucham — beloved by God
Yeeshai — rich gift
Yehoshua — God's help
Yehuda, Yehudi — praised
Yerachmiel — loves God
Yerik, Yarema, Yaremka — appointed by God
Yeshaya — God lends
Yechurun — meaning unknown
Yiftach — opens
Yigil, Yigol — shall be redeemed
Yisreal — God's prince
Yissachar — reward
Yitzchak — humorous
Yo-el, Yoel — God prevails
Yonah — dove
Yusef — God shall multiply
Zacharias, Zachariah, Zachary, Zachery, Zachaios — remembered by God
Zadok — just
Zared, Zarad — ambush
Zayit — olive
Zebadiah, Zebediah, Zane, Zani — gift from God
Zebulon — from the dwelling place
Zedekiah — God's justice
Zephaniah, Zephan — treasured by God
Z'ev, Ze'ev — wolf
Zevulun, Zebulun, Zebulon — habitation
Zimra — song
Ziv — bright
Zohar — sparkles
Zuriel — stone

Hungarian

In Hungary, the surname is placed before the given name. When traveling abroad, Hungarians will often reverse the order. Surnames are taken from descriptive, place, occupational and patronymic names.

An interesting fact is that a woman, instead of using Mrs., will add -ne to her husband's given name. For example, Mrs. Biro Dessewffy would be Birone Dessewffy.

Suffixes often give a clue about the social standing of the bearer:

Aristocratic suffix:	Corresponding suffix for the lower classes:
-cz	-c
-th	-t
-eo	-o
-ss	-zs
-ew	-o
-ff	-f
-gh	-g
-oo	-o
-y	-i

The suffixes -i and -y are resident names showing the bearer is from a particular city, village, town, etc.

A few Hungarian surnames:

Balogh	Domokos
Boldizsar	Domotor
Deak	Fabin
Deme	Kalman
Dkany	Kelemen

FEMALE

Agotha, Agoti, Agi, Aggie — Hungarian form of Agatha (kind)

Alberta — bright, noble

Alexandra, Alexa — defender of man

Aliz, Alisz — Hungarian form of Alice (honest)

Anasztaizia—Hungarian form of
Anastasia (she shall rise again)
Anci—graceful
Angyalka—messenger
Aurelia, Aranka—gold
Bella, Bela, Belle—intelligent
Bertuska, Berta—brave
Borbala, Borsala, Bora, Borka,
Brosca, Broska, Boriska—
Hungarian forms of Barbara
(stranger)
Cili—Hungarian form of Cecilia
(blind)
Czigany—gypsy
Darda—dart
Dorika, Dorottya—Hungarian
form of Dorothy (God's gift)
Duci—wealthy gift
Erika—powerful
Ernesztina, Erna—serious
Erssike, Erzsi, Erzsok, Erzebet—
Hungarian form of Elizabeth
(consecrated to God)
Eszti—star
Etilka, Etel—Hungarian form of
Ethel (noble)
Evike, Evacska—life
Ferike, Fereng, Franciska—
Hungarian form of Francisca
(free)
Firenze, Florka—flower
Frici—Hungarian form of
Fredrika (a peaceful ruler)
Gisella, Gizi—pledge
Gitta—pearl
Hajna—grace
Ibolya—violet
Ica, Ilona, Ilka—light
Irenke—peaceful

Janka—Hungarian form of
Joanna (God is gracious)
Jucika, Juci—praised
Juliska, Julcsa—youthful
Karolina, Karola—feminine
form of Karl (manly)
Katinka, Katakin, Kat, Katalin,
Katarina—pure
Krisztina, Kriszta—Christian
Lenci—light
Linka—mannish
Liza—consecrated to God
Lujza—myth name
Malika, Malcsi—industrious
Marcsa, Mara, Marika, Martuska,
Marianna—bitter, grace
Nancsi, Nusa, Ninacska, Nusi—
graceful
Orzsebet—form of Elizabeth
(consecrated to God)
Paliki—little
Piroska—Hungarian form of
Priscilla (ancient)
Rez—copper-haired
Rozalia, Roza—lily, rose
Sarika, Sasa—princess
Teca, Treszka—Hungarian form
of Teresa (reaper)
Tunde—meaning unknown
Tzigane—gypsy
Vicuska, Viva—life
Viktoria—Hungarian form of
Victoria (victorious)
Virag—flower
Zigana—gypsy
Zsa Zsa, Zsuzsanna, Zsuzsi,
Zsuska—lily
Zsofia, Zsofika—Hungarian form
of Sophia (wise)

MALE

Adelbert, Albert — bright, noble

Adorjan — Hungarian form of Adrian (from the Adriatic)

Agoston — Hungarian form of Gustaaf (staff of the gods)

Ambrus — Hungarian form of Ambrose (immortal)

Andor — manly

Arpad — wanderer

Attila — myth name

Bartalan — Hungarian form of Bartholomew (farmer)

Bela — nickname for Albert (noble)

Benci — blessed

Bodi, Boldizsar — God bless the King

Csaba — myth name

Endre — manly

Ervin — mariner

Ferenc, Ferko — Hungarian form of Francis (free)

Fredek — Hungarian form of Frederick (peaceful ruler)

Fulop — Hungarian form of Philip (loves horses)

Gabor — Hungarian form of Gabriel (strength from God)

Gazsi — protects the treasure

Gergo — watchful

Gyurka — farmer

Gyuszi, Gyala — youthful

Imre — innocent

Istvan — Hungarian form of Stephen (crowned with victory)

Izsak — Hungarian form of Isaac (laughter)

Jenci — well-born

Jozsef, Joska, Jozsi — Hungarian form of Joseph (God is gracious)

Kelemen, Kellman — gentle

Kristof — Hungarian form of Christopher (Christ-bearer)

Laszlo — famous ruler

Lorant — victory

Lorencz — Hungarian form of Lawrence (laurel)

Lukacs — Hungarian form of Lucas (light)

Moricz — Moorish

Mozes — Hungarian form of Moses (from the water)

Neci — fire

Oszkar — Hungarian form of Oscar (leaping warrior)

Peterke — Hungarian form of Peter (rock)

Pista, Pisti — victorious

Poldi — patriotic

Rendor — peacekeeper

Rez — copper-headed

Rikard — Hungarian form of Richard (strong ruler)

Samuka — God hears

Sandor — defender of man

Sebestyen, Sebo — revered

Soma — horn

Tabor — camp

Tass — myth name

Vencel — victorious

Vidor, Viktor, Vincze — Hungarian form of Victor (victorious)

Indian

Due to the variety of languages (over two hundred spoken) and cultures of India, it would be impossible to list all the various naming taboos, customs and history in this work.

The most common language in India is Hindi, which is why there is a separate listing for Hindi in this section.

One prevalent custom is that of giving a child two or three names, one of which is never to be told (to prevent bad luck). When a child enters puberty, a new name is often chosen.

Surnames are not used in business affairs. Patronymic, occupational, caste or place names are substituted for identification at such times.

Children are never named after a parent. Often, children are given offensive names, especially if a sibling has already died, to make the demons think this child is beneath their notice and not worth taking.

The gamut of naming practices and rules is far too extensive to cover here. I would encourage any writer working on this culture to research the nomenclature of the language, caste and area of the story's setting.

A few Indian surnames:

Balin	Kistna
Dalal	Sahir
Dandin	Takeri
Kedar	Vasin
Kesin	Yamuna

FEMALE

Abhirati — myth name (mother of five hundred children, a mother goddess)

Aditi — free

Adya — born on Sunday

Ahalya — night

Ahisma — gentle

Akshamala — meaning unknown

Amaravati — full of ambrosia

Amba, Ambi, Ambika — mother

Ambrosia — food of the gods

Amrita, Amritha — meaning unknown

Anahita — myth name (goddess of the waters)

Anasuya — charitable

Anga—from Anga
Angirasa—myth name (of the Luminous Race)
Annapurna—myth name (goddess of bread)
Anumati—myth name (moon)
Apala—myth name (woman cursed with a skin disorder)
Apsaras—from the water's stream
Arundhati—morning star
Arya—myth name (noble goddess)
Behula—myth name (a perfect wife)
Bha—star
Bhadraa—cow
Bhagiratha—goddess
Bhairavi—meaning unknown
Bhikkhuni—a nun
Bhimadevi—myth name (a frightening goddess)
Bhu, Bhudevi—myth name (earth)
Chamunda—myth name (a form of Durga)
Chanda, Chandi—fierce
Channa—chickpea
Charumati—daughter of Buddha
Chhaya—shade
Daeva, Div—myth name (an evil spirit)
Dakini—myth name (a demon)
Dakshina—competent
Damayanti—name of a princess
Danu—meaning unknown
Deva—superior
Devaki—black
Devamatar—myth name (mother of the gods)

Devayani—myth name (daughter of Shukra)
Dharani—myth name (earth)
Diti—myth name (daughter of Daksha)
Drisana—myth name (the sun's daughter)
Gandhari—name of a princess
Garudi—bird of prey
Gauri—shining
Gatha, Gita—song
Gayatri—a singer
Haimati—myth name (snow queen)
Hariti—myth name (goddess of smallpox)
Indrani—myth name (goddess of the sky)
Indumati—myth name (daughter of Vidarbha)
Ishani—lady
Jaganmata—myth name (mother of the world)
Janna—paradise
Jarita—myth name (a bird)
Jayanti—victory
Jivanta—gives life
Jyotis—light of the sun
Kadru—myth name (daughter of Daksha)
Kailasa—silver mountain
Kalindi—myth name (daughter of the sun god)
Kamala—lotus
Karma—destiny
Karuna—compassion
Kawindra—meaning unknown
Kerani—sacred bells
Khasa—myth name (daughter of Daksha)

Kirati—from the mountain
Krodha—anger
Kumari—princess
Kumudavati—owns lotuses
Kunti—myth name (lover of the
    sun god)
Lajila—shy
Lakshmi—myth name (goddess
    of fortune)
Lakya—born on Thursday
Leya—lion
Madri—myth name (wife of
    Pandu)
Mahadevi—myth name (great
    goddess)
Mahamari—killer
Maheshvari—great lady
Mahila—woman
Marisha—myth name (dew)
Matrika—myth name (divine
    mother)
Mehadi—flower
Mira—myth name (name of a
    princess)
Nidra—myth name (goddess of
    sleep)
Nipa—stream
Nirveli—from the water
Odra—from Odra
Padma—lotus
Pandara—wife
Pishachi—shrew
Pithasthana—myth name (wife of
    Shiva)
Pramlocha—myth name (a
    nymph)
Rana—royal
Rashmika—sweet
Rati—myth name (wife of
    Pradyumna)

Ratna—a jewel
Ravati—myth name (a princess)
Riddhi—wealthy
Rudrani—meaning unknown
Ruma—myth name (queen of the
    apes)
Sakari—sweet
Sakra—from India
Sakujna—bird
Samvarta—myth name (a mare)
Sandhya—twilight
Sanjna—conscientious
Sanya—born on Sunday
Sara—soul
Sarama—quick
Sati, Satyavati—true
Saura—of the Saura
Savarna—same color
Savitari—myth name (daughter of
    Ashvapati)
Sevti—white rose
Shaibya—myth name (faithful
    wife)
Shakini—myth name (a demon)
Shakra—owl
Shanta—meaning unknown
Shapa—cursed
Sharada—lute
Sharama—myth name (dog of
    dawn)
Shashi—moon
Shasti—myth name (goddess of
    childbirth)
Shitala—(goddess of smallpox)
Shraddha—faithful
Shri—wealthy
Sita—furrow
Sitara—morning star
Sur—sharp-nosed

Tapati—myth name (daughter of the sun god)

Tara—myth name (goddess of the sea)

Taraka—myth name (a demon)

Trisna, Trishna—desired

Tulsi—basil

Uma—bright

Upala—opal

Usha—myth name (daughter of Bana)

Ushas—myth name (dawn)

Vach, Vac—well-spoken

Varaza—boar

Vineeta—simple

Varunani—myth name (goddess of wine)

Vema—myth name (goddess of sex)

Vina—vina (a stringed instrument)

Vinata—myth name (daughter of Daksha)

Vivika—wisdom

Yamuna—from the Yamuna river

Yasiman, Yasmine, Yasmina—jasmine

Zudora—labors

MALE

Abhaya—has no fear

Abhimanyu—myth name (killed by Lakshmana)

Abjaja—born of a lotus

Acharya—spiritual teacher

Achir—new

Adharma—lawless

Adi—myth name (a form of Vasishtha)

Aditya, Arun—sun

Agastya—name of a wise man

Agneya—son of Agni

Agnimukha—face of fire

Ahriman—myth name (an evil spirit)

Airavata—child of water

Aja—goat

Akshobhya—myth name (one of the Dhyani-Buddhas)

Ameretat—immortal

Amitabha—myth name (one of the Dhyani-Buddas)

Amma—myth name (supreme god)

Ananda—a half-brother of Buddha

Ananga—without body

Anish—born without a master

Aruna—myth name (god of the dawn)

Asad—lion

Ashoka—name of an emperor

Asipatra—meaning unknown

Asura—myth name (a demon)

Ayodhya—from Ayodhya

Bhaga—myth name (god of luck)

Balarama, Balahadra—myth name (brother of Krishna)

Bali, Balin—mighty warrior

Bhagwandas—serves God

Bhaskar—sun

Bhavaja—myth name (god of love)

Bhavata—dearly loved

Bhikkhu—a monk

Bhima, Bhishma—terrible

Bodhi — awakens
Brahman, Brahma — absolute
Brahmaputra — son of Brahma
Chakra — myth name (symbol of the sun)
Chandaka — myth name (charioteer of Buddha)
Chandra — moon
Chinja — son
Daksha — brilliant
Das, Dasa — a slave
Dasras — handsome
Dasya — he serves
Deven — for God
Dhenuka — myth name (a demon)
Dhumavarna — the color of smoke
Duhkha — sorrowful
Durvasas — myth name (son of Atri)
Dushkriti — sum of all sins
Dyaus — sky
Ekadanta — has one tooth
Frashegird — wonderful
Gada — mace
Gadhi — myth name (father of Vishvamitra)
Gajra — garland of flowers
Garuda — myth name (the god who carried Vishnu)
Girisha — myth name (a storm god)
Guga — myth name (serpent god)
Gulab — rose
Haidar — lion
Halim — kind
Hari — tawny
Haripriya — loved by Vishnu
Harischandra — name of a king
Hasin — laughs
Hastimukha — face of an elephant

Hemakuta — from Hemakuta
Indra — myth name (supreme god)
Isha, Ishana, Ishvara — lord
Jafar — little stream
Jahnu — name of a sage
Jambha — jaws
Jambhala — myth name (god of wealth)
Jatinra — legend name
Javas — quick
Jivin — gives life
Josha — satisfied
Jyotish — moon
Kabandha — myth name (an ugly giant)
Kabir — meaning unknown
Kakar — grass
Kala, Kali — black
Kalari — myth name (a form of Shiva)
Kalki, Kalkin — white horse
Kami — loving
Kanaka — gold
Kanishka — name of a king
Kantu — myth name
Karu — legend name
Kashi, Kasi — meaning unknown
Kavi — poet
Kedar — meaning unknown
Keshi — long-haired
Kesin — long-haired almsman
Kintan, Kiritan — crowned
Kotari — unclothed
Kritanta — myth name (god of death)
Kumar — prince
Kumara — youthful
Lais — lion
Lakshmana — lucky omen

Lusila — leader
Madhava — myth name (god of spring)
Mahakala — myth name (a form of Shiva)
Malajit — victorious
Manoj — meaning unknown
Matsya — fish
Mehtar — prince
Mesha — ram
Mithra, Mitra — myth name (god of the sun)
Mukul — blossoming
Muni — silent
Nadisu — meaning unknown
Nandin — myth name
Nara — man
Nehru — canal
Nila — blue
Omparkash — light of God
Palash — flowering tree
Panchika — myth name (husband of Abhirati)
Pandu — pale
Pani — pagan
Pavaka — purifies
Pavit — pious
Pitamaha — grandfather
Pitar, Pitri — father
Poshita — dearly loved
Priyamkara — myth name (favorite son of Abhirati)
Pumeet — innocent
Rajak — meaning unknown
Raji — name of a king
Rajnish — myth name (king of the gods)
Rakshasa — myth name (a demon)
Raktavira — myth name (a demon)
Raktim — bright red

Ranjan — delights his parents
Ravana — an unjust king
Ravi — sun
Rishi — name of a priest
Rohin — meaning unknown
Rudra — howls
Sachi — myth name (descended from the sun god)
Sahan — falcon
Sahen — above
Sahir — friend
Sajag — watchful
Samantaka — destroys peace
Sanjiv — long life
Saubhari — name of a hermit
Shaitan, Shetan — myth name (demon)
Shaka, Saka — from the Shaka
Shaktar — name of a hermit
Shakti — powerful
Shalya — throne
Shamba — myth name (son of Krishna)
Shami — husband
Shankara — grand
Shashida — ocean
Shesha — myth name (king of serpents)
Shiva — myth name (god of the moon)
Shudra — born to the lowest caste
Skanda — myth name (god of war)
Sunreet — pure
Taj — crown
Takshaka — carpenter
Tandu — myth name (god of dancing)
Tathagata — walks the straightway
Tayib — good

Tripada — myth name (god of
  fever)
Uja — grow
Utathya — name of a wise man
Valmiki — name of a poet
Varuna — infinite
Vasin — ruler
Vasistha, Vasu — wealthy

Vasuki — myth name (king of the
  serpents)
Vibishana — frightening
Visha — poison
Vivek — wise
Vrishni — manly
Vritra — myth name (a demon)
Vyasa — name of a poet

Hindi Female

Aditi — free
Ahisma — not violent
Ajaya — invincible
Alka — long hair
Ambar — sky
Ambika — myth name (goddess of
  the moon)
Amritha — precious
Anala — fiery
Ananda — bliss
Ananta — myth name (name of a
  serpent)
Anila — meaning unknown
Arpana — dedicated
Aruna — radiant
Avasa — independent
Avatara — descending
Baka — crane
Bakula — meaning unknown
Bela — jasmine
Bharati — India
Chaitra — meaning unknown
Chandi — angry
Chandra — moon
Changla — active
Chitra — bright
Corona — kind
Daru — pine
Deepa — meaning unknown
Devi — myth name (noble)

Divya — divine
Drisana — meaning unknown
Durga — impenetrable
Ellama — meaning unknown
Ganesa — from Ganas
Garuda — myth name (the sacred
  bird that carries Vishnu)
Gauri — gold
Girisa — meaning unknown
Hanita — divine grace
Hara — myth name (form of Shiva)
Hema — golden
Indi — Indian
Indra — myth name (king of the
  gods)
Jarita — myth name (a bird)
Jaya, Jayne — victory
Kala — black
Kalinda — sun
Kamala — lotus
Kantha — wife
Kanya — virgin
Karka — crab
Kasi — from Kasi
Kaveri — from the sacred river
  Kaveri
Kesava — of the beautiful hair
Kiran — ray
Kumuda — flower
Lakini — meaning unknown

Lakshmi — myth name (wife of Vishnu)
Lalasa — love
Lalita — named for the Lalita-Vistara
Lanka — from Lanka
Latika — meaning unknown
Madhur — gentle
Mahesa — myth name (wife of Shiva)
Makara — meaning unknown
Malini — meaning unknown
Manda — pivotal
Mandara — from Mandara
Matrika — myth name (Divine Mother)
Mythili — meaning unknown
Nandini — myth name (a cow)
Narmada — gives us pleasure
Natesa — dancer
Neerja — lily
Nishkala — meaning unknown
Padma — lotus flower
Pandita — studious
Pavithra — meaning unknown
Pinga — tawny
Prabha — light
Radha — myth name (a cowgirl)
Rajni — night

Ramya — beautiful
Rani, Ranee, Rania, Ran — queen
Ratna — jewel
Rekha — fine
Rohana — sandalwood
Rohini — woman
Sandhya — twilight
Sarisha — sophisticated
Seema — limit
Shanata — tranquil
Shashi — moonlight
Sita — myth name (goddess of the land)
Sitara — the morning star
Soma — moon
Subha — beautiful
Supriya — beloved
Sur — knife
Tira — arrow
Tirtha — ford
Trisha — thirst
Uma — bright
Usha — myth name (a princess)
Vairocana — myth name (king of the demons)
Varouna — infinite
Vayu — myth name (vital force)
Vedas — myth name (eternal laws)
Vijaya — victory

Hindi Male

Adri — rock
Agni — fire
Anand — happy
Arun — sun
Ashwin — meaning unknown
Atman — self
Avatar — descending
Bharani — meaning unknown
Bharat — name of a saint

Bhaskar — sun
Brahma — born to the highest caste
Chander — moon
Darshan — meaning unknown
Ganesh — myth name (lord of the dwarves)
Girish — lord of the mountains
Hansh — meaning unknown

Hanuman — monkey
Hari — golden
Hastin — elephant
Hiranyagarbha — myth name (a golden egg)
Inay — meaning unknown
Inder, Indra — myth name (Supreme god)
Iswara — myth name (a personal god)
Jalil — meaning unknown
Kabir — meaning unknown
Kala — myth name (god of time)
Kalkin — white horse
Kamal — lotus
Kapil — from Kapila-Vastu
Karthik — meaning unknown
Kesin — long-haired beggar
Kintan, Kiritan — royal
Kistna — meaning unknown
Lal — beloved
Loknoth — meaning unknown
Mahadeva — great god
Manu — myth name (a ruler of the earth)
Markandeya — myth name (name of a sage)
Marut — myth name (a storm god)
Matsya — fish

Mohan — delightful
Murali — meaning unknown
Nandin — named for Shiva's bull, Nandi
Narain — meaning unknown
Naraka — hell
Narayan — moving water
Natesha — myth name (lord of dance)
Onkar — meaning unknown
Purdy — recluse
Ravi — myth name (sun)
Salmalin — claw
Sanat — ancient
Sarad — born during the fall
Srinath — meaning unknown
Surya — myth name (god of the sun)
Timin — meaning unknown
Vadin — speaker
Valin — meaning unknown
Varun — infinite
Vasuki — myth name (another name for Ananta)
Vijay — victory
Vishnu — myth name (protector of the worlds)
Yama — myth name (god of death)

Irish

Ireland has some of the oldest surnames. Almost all are patronymic. Surnames became popular in the tenth and eleventh centuries and by the twelfth century were widespread. Names that derive from place or occupation are much newer than the older, patronymic ones.

Common prefixes:

M', Mc, Mac — son of
O — grandson or descendant of
ni — daughter of
ban — wife of
giolla — follower of
moal — servant of

In the original Gaelic, the apostrophe isn't used after O- or M-. Women were never referred to as Mac or Mc, but always by -ni if they were unmarried, -ban if they were married.

The fitz suffix is not traditionally Irish but was brought in by Anglo-Norman invaders. *K* was also imported by the invaders; the letter in a name indicates a foreign name or spelling.

Common Irish surnames:

Byrne	O'Neill
Connor	Ryan
Kelly	Smith
Murphy	Sullivan
O'Brien	Walsh

FEMALE

Abiageal — Irish form of Abigail (brings joy)
Adara, Athdara — from the ford at the oak tree
Africa, Afric, Aifric — pleasant

Agata, Agate — kind
Aghadreena — from the field of the sloe bushes
Aghamora — from the great field
Aghaveagh, Aghavilla — from the

field of the old tree

Aghna—Irish form of Agnes
(kind)

Ahana—from the little ford

Aidan, Adan, Adeen, Aideen—
little fire

Aigneis—pure

Aileen, Ailey, Aili, Ailia—light

Ailis, Ailise, Ailisa—noble

Aine—ardent

Aingeal—angel

Aislinn, Aislin, Aisling, Ashling—
vision

Alanna, Alaine, Alayne, Allene,
Allyn, Alina, Alana—beautiful

Alastrina, Alastriona—feminine
form of Alastair (avenger)

Alison, Allsun, Allison, Alyson,
Ailis—honest

Alma—all good

Alvy—olive

Annabla—Irish form of Annabel
(lovable)

Aodhnait—meaning unknown

Aoibheann—fair

Aoife—Irish form of Eve (gives
life)

Ardala—high honor

Arleen, Arlene, Airleas, Arlena,
Arleta, Arlette, Arline,
Arlyne—oath

Assane, Assana—waterfall

Asthore—loved one

Attracta, Athracht—saint name

Augusteen—feminine form of
Augustine (great)

Aurnia—golden lady

Avonmora—from the great river

Bab, Babe—meaning unknown

Baibre—strange

Banba—myth name

Barran—little top

Bebhinn, Bevin—singer

Bellinagara—meaning unknown

Benvy—meaning unknown

Berneen—feminine form of
Bernard (courage of a bear)

Blathnaid—flower

Blinne—meaning unknown

Bluinse—white

Brenda, Breandan—little raven

Brenna, Brann—raven

Brianna, Briana, Breanne,
Brianne, Brina, Bryana,
Bryanna, Bryna—strong

Brighid, Bidelia, Biddy, Bidina,
Breeda, Bride, Brid—
protective

Brona—sorrow

Buan—goodness

Cadhla—beautiful

Caffara, Caffaria—helmet

Cahira—warrior

Cailin—girl

Cait, Caitie, Caitlin, Caitlan,
Catlee, Cattee, Cat—pure

Caoimhe, Kevay—lovely and
charming

Caraid—friend

Carleen—feminine form of
Charles (manly)

Casey, Cathasach—brave

Cassidy, Casidhe—clever

Cavana—from Cavan

Christian, Cristin, Christa—
servant of Christ

Ciannait, Keenat, Kinnat—
archaic

Ciar, Ciara, Ceire, Keara—saint
name

Clodagh — from Clodagh
Colmcilla — dove of the church
Comyna — shrewd
Concepta — refers to the
    Immaculate Conception
Conchobarre, Conchobarra,
    Conchobara — feminine form of
    Connor (strong-willed)
Congalie, Connal — constant
Cumania — saint name
Damhnait, Devent, Downeti,
    Dymphna, Devnet, Downett —
    bard
Dana — a Dane
Darerca — saint name
Dearbhail, Derval — true desire
Decla — feminine form of Declan
    (saint name)
Dervla, Dearbhail, Derval,
    Dervilia — true desire
Dervorgilla, Derforgal,
    Derforgala — servant of Dervor
Dierdre, Dedre — myth name
    (sorrowful)
Doireann, Doreen — sullen
Dominica — saint name
Donelle — feminine form of Donal
    (rules the world)
Doon — from Doon
Duana, Dubhain — dark
Duvessa, Dubheasa — dark beauty
Dympna, Damhnait — saint name
Ealga — noble
Eavan — fair
Edana, Ena, Ethna, Eithna,
    Etney — feminine form of
    Aidan (fire)
Eileen, Eibhlhin, Eily — light
Eilinora — Irish form of Eleanor
    (light)

Eilis — Irish form of Elizabeth
    (consecrated to God)
Eistir — Irish form of Esther (star)
Eithne, Ethna, Etney — core
Elan — Irish form of Helen (light)
Emer — myth name
Ena, Enat, Eny — ardent
Ennis, Inis — from Ennis
Erin, Erina — from Ireland
Eveleen — Irish form of Evelina
    (light, giver of life)
Etain — sparkling
Ethna, Eithne — graceful
Fainche — free
Faoiltiarna — wolf lady
Feenat, Fianait — deer
Fenella, Fionnghuala, Finella —
    white-shouldered
Fineena — beautiful child
Fiona, Finna, Fionn — fair
Fionnuala, Finola, Nuala,
    Fynballa — fair shoulders
Flanna — red-haired
Gearoidin — meaning unknown
Glenna, Glynna — of the glen
Gobinet, Gobnait, Gobnat,
    Gubnat — Irish form of Abigail
    (brings joy)
Gormghlaith, Gormly, Gormley —
    sad
Grainne — charming
Grania, Granna — myth name
Hiolair — Irish form of Hilary
    (happy)
Hisolda, Izett — Irish form of
    Isolda
Hodierna — meaning unknown
Honor, Honoria, Honora — honor
Ibernia — from Ireland
Ide, Ida, Ita — thirsty

Ierne — from Ireland

Isibeal — Irish form of Isabel
(consecrated to God)

Isleen, Islene — vision

Ismey, Ismenia — meaning
unknown

Jana — feminine form of John
(God is gracious)

Kathleen — innocent

Keara, Kiara — saint name

Keavy — mild, lovely grace

Keely — beautiful

Kinnat, Keenat — archaic

Labhaoise — warrior-maid

Laetitia — Irish form of Letitia
(happy)

Leila, Lil — saint name

Luighseach — torch bringer

Mab, Mabbina, Meadhbh —
happiness

Macha — plain

Mada — from Mathilda

Madailein — Irish form of
Madeleine (magnificent)

Maeve, Mave — joy

Maible — lovable

Maighdlin — magnificent

Maille, Mailsi — pearl

Mairead, Margaret — saint name

Maitilde, Maitilda, Maude, Maud,
Maiti — strong battle-maid

Majella — saint name

Malvina — sweet

Maoli, Maola — handmaiden

Maureen, Maurine, Moire, Maire,
Mare, Maura, Mearr, Moira,
Moya, Maurya, Muire,
Mairona, Mairia — bitter

Meadhbh, Meghan, Megan —
pearl

Meara — happy

Melva — ruler

Merna, Myrna, Morna, Muirne —
beloved

Mide, Meeda — thirsty

Moina, Moyna — noble

Mona — noblewoman

Monca — wise

Moncha — alone

Mor, More, Moreen — great

Muadhnait — little, noble one

Mugain — myth name

Muireann, Morrin — long-haired

Muirgheal, Murel, Muriel —
knows the sea

Nainsi — Irish form of Nancy
(graceful)

Neala, Nelda — champion

Niamh — myth name

Noirin — meaning unknown

Nuala — lovely shoulders

Obharnait, Orna, Ornat — the
color of olive

Ohnicio, Onora — honor

Oilbhe, Olive — olive

Oona, Oonagh, Ona — one

Orghlaith, Orlaith, Orlaithe,
Orla — golden

Orna — pale

Padraigin — noble

Paili — meaning unknown

Phiala — saint name

Ranait, Renny, Ranalt,
Rathnait — wealthy, charming

Richael, Raicheal — saint name

Rioghnach, Riona — royal

Rois — horse

Sadbh, Sive — good

Sadhbh, Sadhbba — wise

Samhaoir — myth name

Saraid — excellent

Scota — myth name (named for Scotland)

Searlait — feminine form of Charles (mannish)

Seosaimhthin, Seosaimhin — fertile

Shawn, Shauna, Seana — present

Sheila, Sheelah — Irish form of Cecilia (blind)

Sile — youthful

Sinead, Sineidin, Sine, Siobhan — praise

Slaine, Slany, Siany — good health

Sorcha — intelligent

Sosanna — lily

Sybil, Sibeal — prophetess

Tara, Teamhair — myth name (where the kings met)

Treasa, Treise, Toireasa — strong

Tullia — peaceful

Una, Uny, Unity — together

Ulicia — feminine form of Ulik

Vevila — harmony

Vevina — sweet lady

Zaira — Irish form of Sara (princess)

Zinna — meaning unknown

MALE

Abban — abbot

Abracham, Bram — Irish form of Abraham (father of many)

Adamnan, Awnan — little Adam

Adare — from the ford of the oak tree

Addergoole — from between two fords

Aderrig, Aghaderg — from the red ford

Adhamh — of the earth

Aengus, Angus, Aonghus, Oengus, Ungus, Enos, Hungas — one vigor

Aghamore — from the great field

Aghy — friend of horses

Aguistin — majestic

Ahane — from the little ford

Ahern, Ahearn — lord of the horses

Aichlin — meaning unknown

Aidrian — from the Adriatic

Ailfrid — wise

Ailin — handsome

Aindreas — strong

Aineislis — glorious stand

Ainmire — great lord

Airleas, Arlen, Arlyn — pledge

Alabhaois — famous soldier

Alban — pale

Alphonsus — noble, ready

Alroy — red-haired

Alsandair — defender of man

Amalgith — meaning unknown

Amblaoibh — relic

Ambros — divine

Anguish — myth name

Anlon, Anluan — champion

Anmcha, Amnchadh — brave

Annaduff — from the black marsh

Anntoin, Ann — priceless

Aodhfin, Aodhfionn — white fire

Aralt — leader

Ardagh — from the high field

Ardal, Artegal, Arthgallo — high honor

Ardkill — from the high church

Artur, Art — noble bear

Assan — waterfall

Auley, Auliffe, Amhlaoibh — Irish form of Olaf (ancient)

Avonmore — from the great river

Baethan, Beolagh — foolish

Bailintin — valiant

Baird — bard

Ballinamore — from the great river

Ballinderry — from the town of oak wood

Banan — white

Banbhan — piglet

Barram, Bairrfhoinn — handsome

Bearnard — brave as a bear

Beartlaidh — from Bart's meadow

Bellinagar — meaning unknown

Benen — kind

Birr — from Birr

Blaine, Blian — thin

Blair, Blar — from the fields

Blathma — flower, sun

Boynton — from the town by the river Boyn

Brady, Bradaigh — spirited

Bran — myth name

Brandan — saint name

Branduff, Brandubh — black raven

Breandan — prince

Breasal — pain

Breen, Braoin — sadness

Brennan — little drop

Brody — from the muddy place

Brone — sorrowful

Buagh, Buach — victorious

Buckley — boy

Cacanisius — son of Nis

Cadhla — handsome

Caffar — helmet

Cahir, Cathaoir — warrior

Cairbre — myth name

Caith — from the battlefield

Caley, Caly, Caolaidhe — slender

Calhoun, Coillcumhann — from the narrow forest

Callaghan, Ceallachan — strife

Callough, Calvagh, Calbhach — bald

Canice — handsome

Caolan — slender

Caomh — lovable

Carlin — little champion

Carney, Cearnach — victorious

Carrick, Carraig — from the rocky headland

Carroll, Cearbhall — manly

Carthage, Carthach — loving

Cashel, Caiseal — from Cashel

Cathal — battle strong

Cathmor, Cathmore — great fighter

Cavan — from Cavan

Celsus — saint name

Cian, Cein, Cain, Cianan — archaic

Ciarrai — county

Cillian — battle

Cinneide — helmeted

Clancy — ruddy warrior

Cleary — scholar

Cluny — from the meadow

Coghlan, Cochlain, Coughlan — hooded

Coinneach, Canice — handsome

Coireall — lordly

Colla, Conary, Conaire — ancient Irish name

Collin, Coilin — virile

Colm, Colman, Coleman, Columbo — dove

Colmcille — dove of the church

Coman — bent

Comhghan, Cowen, Cowan, Cowyn — twin

Comyn — shrewd

Conchobhar, Conor, Connor, Conny, Connie, Cornelius — strong-willed, wise

Conlan — hero, wise

Connlaio, Conley, Conleth — ardent, wise

Connolly, Connacht — brave, wise

Conroy, Conaire — wise, red

Conway — hound of the plain

Cooney, Cuanaic — handsome

Corcoran — reddish-skin

Corey, Cori, Cory — from the round hill

Cormac, Cormick, Corbmac, Cormic — charioteer

Crevan — fox

Crogher, Crohoore — loves hounds

Cronan — little dark one

Crowley, Cruadhlaoich — hunch-backed

Cuinn — intelligent

Cumhea, Cooey, Covey — hound of the plains

CuUladh, Cooley, Coolie, Cullo — hound of Ulster

Cuyler — chapel

Daghda — myth name

Daibheid — dearly loved

Daire, Dary, Darragh, Darry — wealthy

Daithi, Dahy — quick and agile

Dallan — blind

Damhlaic — meaning unknown

Damon, Daman — tame

Daithi — beloved

Declan, Deaglan — saint name

Delaney — from the river Slaney

Dempsey — proud

Dermot, Dermod, Darby — free

Desmond — from south Munster

Devine, Daimhin — bard

Donnan, Donn — brown

Doran, Deoradhain — exile

Dougal, Dubhghall, Douglas, Doyle, Dowle — dark stranger

Dow, Dubg — black-haired

Driscol, Driscoll — mediator

Dubhan, Dowan, Duggan, Dubhagain — black

Dwyer — black

Eachan — horseman

Eamon — guardian

Earnan — knowing

Egan, Egon, Eagon — fiery

Eimhin, Eimar, Evin — swift

Elhe — legend name

Elroy — red-haired youth

Enan, Eanan — meaning unknown

Enda — saint name

Eoghan, Eoin — God's gift

Eoin Baiste — named for John the Baptist

Erc, Earc — red

Ernan — Irish form of Ernest (serious)

Eth — fire

Evoy — blond

Fachnan — saint name

Fagan, Hagan — little Hugh

Fahey, Fahy — from the green field

Fallon, Fallamhain — ruler

Faolan, Felan — wolf

Fardoragh — dark

Farry — manly

Fay, Feich—raven
Fiachra, Feary, Fiach—myth
    name
Fineen—beautiful child
Finghin, Fineen, Finnin, Fionan,
    Finian, Fionn, Fionnbarr,
    Finbar—handsome
Flann, Flainn, Floinn, Flannan,
    Flanagan, Flannagain, Flynn,
    Floinn—ruddy
Fogarty, Fogerty, Fogartaigh—
    exiled
Foley—plunders
Forba—owns the fields
Gaffney—calf
Gale, Gael, Gaile—stranger
Gall—rooster
Gara, Gadhra—mastiff
Garbhan, Garvan—rough
Garvey, Gairbith—rough peace
Gearoid—spear brave
Geraghty—from the court
Geralt—farmer
Gilchrist, Giolla Chriost, Gil,
    Gilley, Gilvarry—serves
    Christ
Gilibeirt—pledge
Giollabrighde, Gilbride—serves
    Saint Bridget
Giollabuidhe—blond
Giolladhe, Gildea—golden
Glaisne, Glasny—meaning
    unknown
Glaleanna—dwells in the glen
Gofraidh, Godfrey, Gorry,
    Gorrie—peace from God
Gogarty—banished
Gorman, Gormain—blue
Gothfraidh—peaceful
Grady—noble

Greagoir, Grioghar—watchful
Gruagh—giant
Haley—ingenious
Hanraoi—rules the home
Hegarty—unjust
Heremon—myth name
Hewney—meaning unknown
Hickey—healer
Hiero—saint name
Higgins—intelligent
Hoireabard—soldier
Hrothrekr—famous ruler
Hurley—sea tide
Iarfhlaith—meaning unknown
Inerney—steward of church lands
Innis, Inis, Inys, Innes, Iniss—
    from the river island
Irial—meaning unknown
Jarlath—tributary lord
Justin—judicious
Kealan, Kelan—slender
Keallach, Killian—battle
Keefe—handsome
Keegan, Keagan—fiery
Keely, Kealy—handsome
Keenan, Keanan—ancient
Keith—from the battlefield
Kellach, Killian, Ceallach—strife
Kelleher—loving husband
Kennedy—helmeted
Kenny, Kavan, Kaven—
    handsome
Kerry, Keary—from county
    Kerry
Kerwin, Kerwyn—small, black
    one
Kian, Kean, Kienan, Kenan—
    archaic
Kieran, Kyran, Kieron—dark

Killdaire, Kildare, Kildaire — from county Kildare

Kinsella, Kinsale — meaning unknown

Lalor, Leathlobhair — half-leper

Laoghaire — shepherd

Laughlin, Lany, Leachlainn, Loughlin — servant

Leary — cattle keeper

Lee, Laoidhigh — poetic

Lochlain, Lakeland, Lochlann — home of the Norse

Loman — bare

Lorcan — little wild one

Lugaidh — famous warrior

Lugh — myth name

Lunn, Lun — strong

Macartan — son of Artan

MacAuley, MacAuliffe — son of Olaf

MacBride — son of Bridget, Bride

MacCormack — son of Cormac

MacElroy — son of Elroy

MacMurra, MacMaureadhaigh — son of Murray

MacQuaid — son of Quaid

Madden — small dog

Maeleachlainn, Malachy, Milos, Miles, Myles — servant

Maelisa — serves Christ

Mago, Mane — great

Maher — generous

Mahon — bear

Malone, Maloney — serves Saint John

Mannix, Mainchin — monk

Mannuss — great

Maolruadhan, Melrone — serves Saint Ruadhan

Maughold — saint name

Meara, Meadhra — happy

Melchior — meaning unknown

Melvin, Melvyn, Malvin, Mal — chief

Miach — myth name

Mogue — saint name

Molan — servant of the storm

Molloy, Malloy — noble chief

Monohan — monk

Mooney, Maonaigh — wealthy

Moran, Morain — great

Moriarty, Muircheartaigh — expert seaman

Morolt — legend name

Morrissey — choice of the sea

Muireadhach, Murry, Murray — lord of the sea

Mulcahy — battle chief

Mulconry — hound of prosperity

Mundy — from Reamon

Murchadh, Murrough, Morgan — fighter of the sea

Murphey, Murchadh, Murphy — sea warrior

Naal — saint name

Nally — poor

Naomhan, Nevan, Nevyn — holy

Neason, Nessan — saint name

Nolan — noble

Nulty, Nulte — from Ulster

Odanodan — of the red earth

Odhran, Oran, Odran — pale green

Ossian — fawn

Owney, Oney — meaning unknown

Padriac, Padraig — noble

Parlan, Patholon — legend name

Phelan — joyful

Quaid — Irish form of Walter (strong warrior)

Queran — dark
Quigley — unruly hair
Quinlan — graceful
Quinn, Quin — intelligent
Raghnall — strong
Regan, Riagan — little king
Renny, Raighne — mighty
Riddock, Reidhachadh, Riddoc —
  from the smooth field
Riobard — bright
Riordan, Riordain — royal bard
Roark, Ruarc, Ruark, Rorke,
  Ruaidhri — famous ruler
Rogan, Ruadhagan, Rowe,
  Rowen, Rowyn, Rowin,
  Rowan, Ruadhan — red-haired
Roibhilin, Ravelin, Ravelyn,
  Revelin — meaning unknown
Roibin, Roibeard — robin
Ronan — little seal
Rooney, Ruanaidh — hero
Rory, Ruaidhri — red
Ruadhan — saint name
Ryan, Rian — little king
Scanlon, Scannalan, Scanlan —
  scandal
Scully, Scolaighe — herald
Seafra, Sheary, Seafraid — peace
  from God
Searbhreathach — judicious
Shamus, Seamus, Shemus —
  supplanter
Shanahan, Seanachan — wise
Shanley, Seanlaoch — old hero
Shannon, Seanan — little old wise
  one

Shaughnessy, Seachnsaigh —
  meaning unknown
Shea, Seaghda — majestic
Sheary, Sheron — Irish form of
  Geoffrey (peace of God)
Sheehan, Siodhachan — little
  peaceful one
Sheridan, Seireadan — untamed
Sorley — Viking
Strahan, Sruthan — poet
Struthers, Sruthair — from the
  stream
Sullivan, Suileabhan — black-eyed
Sweeney, Suidhne — little hero
Tadhg, Tadleigh — bard
Teague, Teaghue — poet
Terrence — tender
Terriss, Teris — son of Terrence
Tiarchnach, Tierney, Tier,
  Tighearnach, Tiernan — regal
Tibbot — Irish form of Theobald
  (strong for the people)
Torin, Toryn — chief
Tormey, Tormaigh — thunder
  spirit
Torrance, Torrence, Torrans,
  Tory — from the knolls
Treacy, Treasigh, Treasach —
  fighter
Trevor, Treabhar — prudent
Tully, Taicligh — peaceful
Uaid — Irish form of Walter
  (strong warrior)
Uaine — meaning unknown
Ualtar — strong fighter
Uther — myth name
Ward — bard
Whelan — joyful

Italian

Italian surnames came into use at the end of the tenth century. They became hereditary much later. Patronymic and descriptive names are most common, but surnames were also taken from place and occupation. Nicknames provided the most common pool from which surnames were drawn.

It is common for the surname to come first, followed by the given name, then father's name (the prefix fu- is used if the father is deceased). *Di* and *de* mean son of. All surnames end in a vowel.

Some Italian surnames:

Baldovino	Donatelli
Calabria	Fabrizio
Calendri	Faggini
Casale	Gallo
DeMitri	Minimi

FEMALE

Adriana, Adreana — dark

Agata — kind

Agnella, Agnese — pure

Aida — happy

Albinia — white

Alessandra, Alexandra — defender of man

Aletta — winged

Allegra — joyful

Alonza — ready for battle

Amalea, Amalia — hard-working

Andreana — feminine form of Andrea (manly)

Angelia, Angela — angel

Anita — grace

Annuziata — named for the Annunciation

Antonietta, Antonia — priceless

Aria — melody

Balbina — stammers

Bambi — child

Battista, Bautista, Baptiste — named for John the Baptist

Beatricia, Beatrice — blesses

Belinda — serpentine

Benedetta — blessed

Benigna — benign

Bianca, Bellance, Blanca — white

Brunetta, Bruna — dark-haired

Cadenza — rhythmic

Cameo, Cammeo — sculptured jewel

Caprice — fanciful

Cara, Carina — beloved

Carlotta — Italian form of Charlotte (manly)

Carmela, Carmelina, Carmelita — garden

Carolina — feminine form of Carlo (manly)

Catarina, Catarine, Caterina — pure

Cerelia — fertile

Cira — sun

Clarice, Clarissa, Clariss — clear

Concetta — from the Immaculate Conception

Constanza, Constansie, Constanzie, Stansie, Constantia, Constantina — constant

Clorinda — meaning unknown

Claudina — feminine form of Claude (lame)

Columbine — dove

Consolata — consolation

Dona, Donna — lady

Donata — gift

Edita, Editta — wealthy

Elda — warrior

Elena, Elene, Elenora, Eleanora, Elenore — light

Elisabetta, Elizabetta — Italian form of Elizabeth (consecrated to God)

Emilia — Italian form of Emily (industrious)

Enrichetta — ruler

Esta — from the east

Evelina — Italian form of Evelyn (light, gives life)

Fabiana, Fabia — feminine form of Fabio (bean farmer)

Fausta, Fortuna — lucky

Filomena — loves mankind

Fiorenza — flower

Flavia, Fulvia — blond

Francesca — Italian form of Frances (free)

Gabriella — feminine form of Gabriele (God-given strength)

Gaetane, Gaetana — from Gaete

Geltruda — meaning unknown

Gemma — jewel

Genevra — Italian form of Genevieve (white wave)

Ghita — pearl

Gianna, Gianina — God is gracious

Giovanna — feminine form of Giovanni (gift from God)

Giuditta — Italian form of Judith (praised)

Giulia — Italian form of Julia (youthful)

Grazia — grace

Gulielma, Guillelmina — feminine form of William (resolute protector)

Iniga — fiery

Isabella — Italian form of Isabel (consecrated to God)

Leola — lion

Leonora — light

Letizia — glad

Liliana — lily

Lucianna, Lucia — graceful light

Lucrezia — benefit

Luisa — Italian form of Louise (reknowned warrior)

Lunetta — little moon
Maria, Marea, Mara, Marietta, Maurizia, Margherita — bitter
Massima — great
Maura — dark skin
Mercede — merciful
Mona — lady
Natala — born at Christmas
Nicia — people's victory
Octavia — born eighth
Olympia — from Olympus
Oria, Oriana — golden
Ottavia — born eighth
Paola — little
Patrizia — noble
Pia — pious
Pietra — rock
Pippa — lover of horses
Rachele — lamb
Regina — queen
Renata — rebirth
Ricadonna, Ricarda — ruling lady
Roma, Romia — from Rome
Rosalie, Rosalia, Rozalia, Rosa — rose
Rosetta — little rose

Rufina — red-haired
Sabrina — from the border
Sancia — holy
Sebastiana, Sebastiene — feminine form of Sebastiano (revered)
Serafina — from the seraph
Serena — serene
Simona — Italian form of Simone (one who hears)
Speranza — hope
Teodora — gift from God
Teresa — harvester
Terza — born third
Tiberia — from the Tiber
Traviata — astray
Trilby, Trillare — sings with trills
Trista — sad
Valentina — brave
Vedette, Vedetta — guardian
Violet, Violetta — flower
Virginia — pure
Viviana — alive
Volante — flying
Ysabel, Ysabelle — Italian form of Isabel (consecrated to God)

Male

Aberto — Italian form of Albert (noble)
Abramo — Italian form of Abraham (father of many)
Adriano — from the Adriatic
Aldo — rich
Alessandro — Italian form of Alexander (defender of man)
Alfredo — Italian form of Alfred (counselor of the elves)
Amadeo — loved God

Ambrosi — Italian form of Ambrose (immortal)
Anastagio — divine
Andrea — Italian form of Andrew (manly)
Angelo — angel
Antonio — Italian form of Anthony (beyond praise)
Armanno — soldier
Arnaldo — Italian form of Arnold (eagle)

Arrigo, Aroghetto, Alrigo — rules the estate

Arturo — bear

Baldassare, Baldassario — Italian form of Bathalsar

Beniamino — Italian form of Benjamin (son of the right hand)

Bernardo — brave as a bear

Bertrando, Brando — Italian form of Bertrand (brilliant raven)

Biaiardo — reddish-brown hair

Bruno — brown-haired

Calvino — bald

Carlino, Carlo — manly

Caseareo, Ceasario, Cesare — long-haired

Cecilio — blind

Constantin — firm

Corrado, Corradeo — bold, sage counselor

Cristoforo — Italian form of Christopher (Christ-bearer)

Daniele — Italian form of Daniel (God is my judge)

Dante — lasting

Davide — Italian form of David (beloved)

Donatello, Donato — gift

Edmondo — Italian form of Edmund (prosperous)

Eduardo, Edoardo — Italian form of Edward (rich guardian)

Egidio, Egiodeo — squire

Elmo — worthy to be loved

Emmanuele — Italian form of Emmanuel (God is with us)

Enea — born ninth

Enrico, Enzo — Italian form of Henry (rules the home)

Ermanno — Italian form of Herman (warrior)

Ernesto — serious

Este — from the east

Ettore — loyal

Eugenio — noble

Fabio, Fabiano — bean grower

Fabrizio — craftsman

Fabroni — blacksmith

Faust, Fausto, Felicio — lucky

Federico — Italian form of Frederick (peaceful ruler)

Ferdinando — Italian form of Ferdinand (adventurer)

Fidelio — fidelity

Filippo, Filippio — Italian form of Philip (loves horses)

Fiorello — little flower

Flavio — blond

Francesco — free

Gabriele — Italian form of Gabriel (God-given strength)

Gaetano — from Gaete

Georgio, Giorgio — Italian form of George (farmer)

Gerardo — spear hard

Geronimo, Geremia — Italian form of Jerome (sacred)

Giacomo — supplanter

Gian, Giovanni — Italian form of John (God is gracious)

Giancarlo — God's gracious gift, manly

Gilberto — Italian form of Gilbert (pledge)

Gino — Italian form of Louis (famous)

Giorgio — Italian form of George (farmer)

Giovanni — gift from God

Giuliano, Giulio—youthful

Giuseppe—He shall add

Gregorio—Italian form of Gregory (watchful)

Gualtiero, Galtero, Galterio—Italian form of Walter (strong warrior)

Guglielmo—resolute protector

Guido—guide

Ignazio, Ignacio—fiery

Ilario, Ilari—cheerful

Innocenzio—innocent

Kajetan—from Gaete

Leonardo, Leone—bold lion

Lorenz, Lorenzo—laurel

Luciano, Lucan, Lucio, Lucca—light

Luigi—famous warrior

Marcello, Marco—warring

Mario—bitter

Matteo—gift of God

Maurizio—Italian form of Maurice (dark-skinned)

Michelangelo—who is like God, angel

Michele, Michel—Italian form of Michael (God-like)

Orlando—heroic

Paolo—Italian form of Paul (little)

Pasquale, Pascal, Pascual—born on Passover

Patrizio—noble

Piero, Pietro—Italian form of Peter (rock)

Pio—pious

Pippino, Peppino—Italian form of Joseph (He adds)

Primo—first born

Rafaele, Raphael, Rafaello—God has healed

Raimondo—Italian form of Raymond (mighty protector)

Renzo—laurel

Ricardo, Riccardo, Ricciardo—firm ruler

Rinaldo—wise power

Roberto—wide fame

Romano—from Rome

Romeo—pilgrim from Rome

Ruggero—Italian form of Roger (famous spear)

Salvatore, Salvatorio—savior

Santo—sacred

Sebastiano—Italian form of Sebastian (revered)

Sergio—attendant

Silvio—silver

Stefano—Italian form of Stephen (crowned with laurels)

Tiberio—from the Tiber

Tito—giant

Tommaso—Italian form of Thomas (twin)

Ugo—intelligent

Valentino, Valerio—brave, strong

Vincenzio, Vittorio, Vito—victor

Latin

The Romans were one of the first cultures to develop complex surnames. Unfortunately, after the decline of the empire (approximately A.D. 400), the nomenclature disappeared, not to be duplicated until hundreds of years later.

In the beginning, Romans had only a given name. Later, they added the father's or husband's name. The suffix -ius was added to indicate family. By 100 B.C. the long name was the norm.

Standard format for a name would be Praenomen (given), Nomen (clan or race), cognomen (surname). Most Romans were called by their cognomen.

Girls received given names on the eighth day after birth and boys on the ninth. The eldest son was usually given the name of the grandfather. Girls often took the feminine form of their father's name.

Women had two names, usually taken from the names of male relatives, and always in the genitive case. Military men were often given agnomina that were taken from the names of victorious battles.

Surnames were common by 100 B.C. By the time of the empire's decline in the fourth century A.D., one name had become the norm.

A few surnames:

Crescens	Rufus
Fortunatus	Sabinus
Hilarus	Secundus
Maximus	Tertius
Primus	Vitalis

FEMALE

Academia — named for Cicero's villa

Acarnania — from Arcanania

Accalia — myth name, possibly from Acca Larentia, the she-wolf who nursed the twins Remus and Romulus

Acidalia — myth name (named for Venus)

Adamina — of the red earth

Adora, Adoria, Adoree — glory

Adorabelle, Adorabella — adored

beauty

Adrasteia — unyielding

Adria, Adrian — dark

Adrie — of the Adriatic

Aea — from Aea

Aegaea — from the Aegean sea

Aegates — from the Aegates

Aegina, Aeginae — myth name
(mother of Aeacus)

Aeolia — myth name (daughter of
Amythaon)

Agrafina, Agrafine — born feetfirst

Agrippina, Agrippinae — colonist

Albina, Alba, Alva, Albinia,
Alvinia — white

Albula — from the Tiber

Albunea — meaning unknown

Alcimede — myth name (mother
of Jason)

Alcippe — mighty mare

Alcmena, Alcumena, Alcamene —
myth name (mother of
Hercules)

Aleria, Alera — eagle

Aleta, Aletta, Alida, Alaida,
Aluld — winged

Alexandre, Alexine, Alexina,
Alexis, Alexandrine,
Alexandria, Alexandrina,
Alexandriana, Alexandrea —
defender of man

Alma — loving

Almeta — driven

Alta — lofty

Alvita — lively

Amabel, Amabelle, Amabella,
Amabilis — beautiful, loving

Amadis, Amadea, Amadee — loved
by God

Amanda, Amadine, Amadina —
worthy of God

Amare, Amara — beloved

Amarna — meaning unknown

Amata — treasured

Amelia, Amalie, Amilia, Amalea,
Amelita, Amelinda — hard-
working

Aminta, Amyntas, Amynta —
protector

Amity — friendly

Amorette, Amoretta — little love

Amorita — dearly loved

Amphitrite — myth name (aunt of
Achilles)

Amymone — myth name (one of
the Danaides)

Anabel, Annabelle, Anabella —
lovely grace

Anahid — meaning unknown

Anaxarete — myth name
(unfeeling woman who caused
her lover to hang himself)

Ancyra, Ankara — from Ankara

Andes — from the Andes

Andreana, Andria, Andriana —
feminine of Andrew (manly)

Andromache, Andromacha —
myth name (wife of Hector)

Andromeda — myth name
(daughter of Cassiopeia)

Anemone — meaning unknown

Angerona — myth name (goddess
of anguish)

Angela, Angel, Angelica, Anjelika,
Angelina, Angelita, Angeline —
angel

Anna Perenna, Anna — myth
name (possibly the daughter of
Dido)

Annunciata—announces
Anona, Annona—myth name
Ansa, Anse—constant
Antandra—myth name (an Amazon)
Antigone—myth name (sister of Priam)
Antonia, Antonina, Antoinette, Antoinetta—praiseworthy
Apollonis—myth name (one of the muses worshipped at Delphi)
April, Aprille, Averil, Averyl—open
Apulia—from the river Apulia
Aquilina, Aquiline, Akilina—eaglelike
Aquitania—from Aquitaine
Arabia—from Arabia
Araceli, Aracelia—treasure
Arachne—myth name (turned into a spider by Minerva)
Arcadia—adventuresome
Arcanania—from Arcanania
Ardea—from Ardea
Ardelis, Ardelle, Ardella, Ardis, Ardine, Ardene, Ardinia, Ardra, Ardeen, Ardina—ardent
Arethusa—myth name (daughter of Poseidon)
Argenta, Argentina, Argentia—silver
Argolis—from Argos
Argous—myth name
Ariadna, Ariadne—myth name (daughter of Minos)
Ariana, Ariadne—pleases
Aricia—from Aricia
Aristodeme—myth name (daughter of Priam)

Armenia—from Armenia
Armida—little armed one
Armilla—bracelet
Arne—myth name (mother of Aeolus III Boeotus)
Arrosa, Arrose—rose
Arva, Arvia—from the seashore
Ascra—from Ascra
Asia—myth name (mother of Atlas)
Assa—myth name (mother of Sithon)
Asta—holy
Astarte—myth name (the Phoenician goddess of love)
Asteria—star
Astraea—myth name (surname for Artemis)
Astynome—myth name (daughter of Chryses)
Atalanta—myth name (a huntress)
Atella—from Atella
Atropos—myth name (one of the Moirae)
Atthis, Attica—from Attica
Attracta—drawn to
Augusta, Augustine, Augustina, Austine, Austina—majestic
Aulaire—well-spoken
Aulis—myth name (a Praxidicae)
Aura—gentle breeze
Aurelia, Aurelie, Aurea, Aurum, Aureline—golden
Aurore, Aurora—dawn
Automatia—Fortuna
Autonoe—myth name (mother of Hercules)
Avena, Avina—from the oat field

Averna—myth name (queen of the underworld)

Avis—bird

Aviva, Avivah, Auvita—youthful

Azalea—dry earth

Balbina, Balbine—strong

Balere, Balara, Balera—strong

Beata, Beate—merry

Beatrice, Beatrix, Bee, Beatriz—brings joy

Bella, Belle—beautiful

Bellona—myth name (goddess of war)

Benedicta, Benita, Benetta, Benedikta, Bente—blessed

Benigna—gracious

Beroe—myth name (traveled with Aeneas)

Bibiana, Bibine, Bibiane—animated

Bithynia—myth name (mother of Amycus)

Bittore—victor

Blanche, Blanka, Biana, Bianca—white

Blandina, Blanda, Blandine—mild

Blasia—stammers

Bolbe—myth name (a nymph)

Bona Dea—myth name (related to Faunus)

Bonnie, Bonny—beautiful

Borbala, Borsala, Bora, Borska, Borsca, Borka—stranger

Bremusa—myth name (an Amazon)

Britannia—from Britain

Bryce—myth name (wife of Chthonius)

Bubona—myth name (goddess of cattle)

Cacia, Caca—myth name (daughter of Vulcan)

Cadence—rhythmic

Caenis—myth name (daughter of Atrax)

Caieta—myth name (nursed Aeneas)

Cairistiona, Christine, Christina, Cristin, Christian, Cristiona—Christian

Caledonia—from Scotland

Calendae—first

Cales—from Cales

Calida, Callida—fiery

Calliope—myth name (muse of epic poetry)

Callista—chalice

Callisto—myth name (a nymph)

Callula—beautiful

Calva—myth name (a name referring to Venus)

Calybe—myth name (a nymph)

Calyce, Calcia—myth name (mother of Cycnus)

Calydona—from Calydon

Calypso—myth name (a nymph)

Camella—goblet

Camilla, Camille—servant for the temple

Candice, Candace—shining

Candida, Candide—dazzling white

Canens—myth name (wife of Picus)

Cantabria—from Cantabria

Cantilena—song

Cantrix—singer

Capita, Capta—myth name (a name referring to Minerva)

Cappadocia—from Cappadocia

Cara—doe

Cardea—myth name (protectress of hinges)

Caries, Caria—rotten

Carina, Carin, Caryn, Caryna—keel

Carisa, Carissa—artistic

Carissima—dearest

Caritas, Charity, Charissa, Carissa, Carita—giving

Carmen, Carmin, Carmia, Carmea—song

Carmenta, Carmentis—myth name (a healer)

Carna—myth name (protectress of vital organs)

Carya—myth name (daughter of Dion)

Casperia—myth name (second wife of Rhoetus)

Cassandra—myth name (a prophetess)

Cate—wise

Catena—retrained

Cecilia, Cecile, Cecily, Cili—dim-sighted

Cegluse—myth name (mother of Asopus)

Celaeno—myth name (one of the Pleiades)

Celeste, Celesta, Celestine, Celestina, Celia, Celine—of the heavens

Celine, Celina—hammer

Cerelia—of the spring

Ceres—myth name (goddess of the harvest)

Chalciope—myth name (daughter of Eurypylus)

Charybdis—myth name

(daughter of Poseidon)

Christabel, Christabella—beautiful

Chryse—myth name (daughter of Pallas)

Chryseis—myth name (daughter of a priest of Apollo)

Chrysogeneia—myth name (daughter of Halmus)

Chrysonoe—myth name (daughter of Cleitus)

Cilla—myth name (daughter of Laomedon)

Cinxia—myth name (a name referring to Juno)

Clara, Clare, Clareta, Clarice—distinguished

Clarabelle, Claribel, Claribelle, Claribella, Clarinda, Clarinde—shining

Clarissa, Clarisse—famous

Claudia, Clady—lame

Clarita, Clarine, Clareta—clarity

Clementina, Clementine—merciful

Clonia—myth name (an Amazon)

Clorinda—renowned

Clotho—myth name (one of the Moirae)

Clymene—myth name (an Amazon)

Columba—dove

Conception—understanding

Concordia, Concordea—harmony

Constance, Constanze, Constancia, Constantina, Connie, Constantia—firm of purpose

Consuela—consolation

Cornelia—horn

Courtney—born at court
Crescentia—growing
Crispina—curly-haired
Cyprien, Cyprienne—from Cyprus
Cyrilla, Cyrillia—noble
Dacia—meaning unknown
Damiana, Damone, Damia—untamed
Davida—dearly loved
Dea Roma—myth name (goddess of Rome)
Decima—born tenth
Deidameia—myth name (daughter of Bellerphon)
Delicia, Deliciae, Delicea—delightful
Delora, Deloras, Deloros—from the seashore
Demonassa—myth name (wife of Hippolochus)
Derimacheia—myth name (an Amazon)
Derinow—myth name (an Amazon)
Desirata—desired
Deverra—myth name (goddess of birthing)
Devota—devoted
Dextra—skillful
Diana, Diane—divine
Dido—myth name (queen of Carthage)
Diella, Dielle—worships God
Digna, Digne—worthy
Dionysia—named for Dionysus
Dioxippe—myth name (an Amazon)
Dirce—myth name (mother of Lycus)

Discordia—myth name (goddess of war)
Docilla, Docila—calm
Domela, Domele—mistress of the home
Domiduca—myth name (Juno's surname)
Dominica, Dominique, Domitiane, Domitiana—belongs to God
Domino, Damina—lady
Donata, Donica—give
Donelle—small mistress of the home
Donna, Dona—lady
Doris—myth name
Dorote, Dorothy, Dorothee, Dorothea, Dorika, Dorottya, Dorotea—God's gift
Drusilla, Drucilla—strong
Dryope—myth name (a nymph)
Dulcinia, Dulcine, Dulcine, Dulcia, Duclea, Dulcie, Dulcy—sweet
Dyna—myth name (sister of Roma)
Echidna—myth name (a monster)
Edulica—myth name (protectress of children)
Egeria, Aegeria—myth name (one of the Cumaean)
Egesta, Segesta—myth name (daughter of Phoenodamas)
Eirene—myth name (daughter of Poseidon)
Elata—glorified
Electa, Elekta—selected
Eloine, Eloina—worthy
Elvera, Elvira—white

Emera, Emira — worthy of merit

Empanda, Panda, Padana — myth name

Entoria — myth name (lover of Saturn)

Enyo, Enya — myth name (one of the Graeae)

Eos — myth name (goddess of dawn)

Ephyra — myth name (daughter of Oceanus)

Epione — myth name (wife of Asclepius)

Epona — myth name (protectress of horses)

Equestris — myth name (Venus's surname)

Eriboea — myth name (wife of Aloeus)

Ermina — noble

Espe — hope

Estelle, Estella, Essie — star

Euadne — myth name (daughter of Poseidon)

Euandra — myth name (an Amazon)

Euryale — myth name (mother of Orion)

Euryanassa — myth name (mother of Pelops)

Eurybia — myth name (an Amazon)

Eurydice — myth name (wife of Aeneas)

Euryganeia — myth name (wife of Oedipus)

Eurymede — myth name (mother of Bellerphon)

Eurynome — myth name (daughter of Nysus)

Eustacia — tranquil

Fabiana, Fabia — bean grower

Fabiola — bean

Faith — trust

Fama — myth name (rumor)

Fani, Fania — free

Fauna, Faula — myth name (lover of Hercules)

Faustina, Faustine, Fausta, Fauste, Faust, Fortunata, Fortune, Fortuna — fortunate

Felicia, Felice, Felise, Felita, Felicity, Feleta, Felisa, Felicitas — happy

Fidelity, Fidelia, Fides — faithful

Filomena, Filomina — lover of man

Flaminia, Flamina — Roman priestess

Flavia, Fulvia — yellow

Flora, Floris, Florice, Floria, Flor, Fiorenza, Forenza — flower

Florence, Florentina, Florentine, Florella, Floria, Florida, Florenza, Florentyna — blooming

Fluonia — myth name (Juno's surname)

Fornax — myth name (goddess of bread)

Fortuna — myth name (goddess of luck)

Fronde, Fronda — leafy branch

Fronia — wise

Furina, Furrina — myth name (a Fury)

Gala — from Gaul

Galatea — myth name

Garabi, Garbi — clear

Genetrix — myth name (Venus's surname)

Gill, Gillian, Gillien, Guilia, Guilie — young

Ginger — from the ginger flower

Gladys — sword

Glauce — myth name (wife of Upis)

Gloria, Gloriosa — glory

Graca, Gracinha, Grace, Grazia, Grata, Gratia, Gratiana, Graciana, Graciene — grace

Gregoria — watchful

Gryne — myth name (an Amazon)

Gustel, Gustelle, Gustella — majestic

Gymnasia — myth name (one of the Horae)

Hadria, Hadrea — dark

Hajnal — dawn

Harmony, Harmonia — concord

Harpinna — myth name (a mare of Oenomaus)

Hecuba — myth name (wife of Priam)

Helen — myth name (most beautiful woman in the world)

Henicea — myth name (daughter of Priam)

Hermippe — myth name (daughter of Boeotus)

Hero — myth name (daughter of Priam)

Herophile — myth name (priestess of Apollo)

Hersilia — myth name (married a follower of Romulus)

Hesperia, Hespera, Hesperie — myth name (daughter of Cebren)

Hibernia — from Ireland

Hibiscus, Hibiskus — flower name

Hilaeira — shining

Hilary, Hilaria, Hillary — happy

Hippodameia — myth name (daughter of Briseus)

Hippolyte — myth name (queen of the Amazons)

Hippothoe — myth name (an Amazon)

Honorine, Honorina, Honorata, Honoria, Honor, Honora — honor

Horacia, Horatia — timekeeper

Hortense, Hortencia, Hortenciana — gardener

Humility — humble

Hyale — myth name (a nymph)

Hyria — myth name (daughter of Amphinomus)

Iaera — myth name (a nymph)

Ibolya — flower

Ida — myth name (a nymph)

Ierne, Ierna — from Ireland

Ignacia, Igantia — fiery

Ilia — myth name (mother of Remus and Romulus)

Iliona — myth name (daughter of Priam)

Immaculata — reference to the Immaculate Conception

Imogene, Imogenia, Imogen — image

Imperia — commanding

Ina — meaning unknown

Inferna — myth name (Proserpina's surname)

Iniga — fiery

Intercidona — myth name (goddess of birthing)

Invidia — envious

Inyx — spell

Iphimedeia — myth name
(daughter of Triopas)

Iphinome — myth name (an
Amazon)

Irma, Irmine, Irmina — noble

Iulia — young

Iulius — youthful

Jacoba — supplanter

Jana — myth name (the moon)

Jette, Jetta — jet-black

Jewel — precious

Jinny — virgin

Jinx, Jynx — spell

Jocelyn, Jocelin, Joscelin, Joyce,
Joy — happy

Juga, Jugalis — myth name
(goddess of marriage)

Julia, Juliet, Judith, Juliette,
Julietta, Julie, Jill, Juliana,
Julianna, Julianne, June,
Julene, Junia, Julinka, Juliska,
Juli, Julesa, Jude — young

Juno — myth name (wife of
Jupiter)

Justa, Justina, Justine — fair

Juturna — myth name (a nymph)

Juventas — myth name (youth)

Juverna — from Ireland

Kalare, Kalara — shines

Kamilla, Kamilka, Kamille —
servant for the temple

Katalin, Katalyn, Katlyn — pure

Kira, Kirie, Kyra — light

Kirsten, Kirsty, Kirstie —
Christian

Klara, Klarissa, Klarisza, Klari,
Klarika — clear

Klaudia — lame

Konstanze, Konstanza — firm

Kornelia, Kornelie — horn

Lachesis — myth name (a Fury)

Lacinia — myth name (Juno's
surname)

Lamia — myth name (daughter of
Poseidon)

Lampeto — myth name (an
Amazon)

Laodamia — myth name (daughter
of Bellerophon)

Lara — famous

Laraine, Lorraine, Larina,
Larine — sea gull

Larentia, Laurentia — myth name
(the wolf who nursed Remus
and Romulus)

Larissa — myth name (a lover of
Poseidon)

Larunda — myth name (a nymph)

Latona, Latonia — named for
Latium

Laura, Laurette, Laurel, Laurella,
Laurentia, Laurene, Laureen,
Laurin, Lauren, Lauryn,
Laurena, Laurina, Laurica,
Loris, Lorena, Lorinda, Lorita,
Lorena, Lorna, Lora, Laurie,
Lavra, Laurissa — laurel

Laveda, Lavare, Lavetta,
Lavette — purified

Lavinia, Lavina — myth name
(wife of Aeneas)

Lelia, Lela, Lelah — from Laelius

Leda — myth name (mother of
Helen)

Ledaea — myth name
(granddaughter of Leda)

Leiriope, Leirioessa, Liriope —

myth name (mother of Narcissus)

Leis — myth name (mother of Althepus)

Lena, Lina — alluring

Lenita, Leneta, Lenis, Lenet, Lynet, Lynette — mild

Leonce, Leonita, Leontin, Leontina, Leontine, Leontyne, Leandra, Leodora, Leoine, Leoline, Leonlina, Lyonene, Leona, Leone, Leoarrie, Leonelle — lioness

Lerola — blackbird

Leta, Lita, Letitia, Lettie, Letty, Larissa — joyful

Leuconoe — myth name (daughter of Poseidon)

Levana — uplifting

Leverna, Lativerna — myth name (goddess of thieves)

Libentina, Lubentia — myth name (Venus's surname)

Libertas, Libera — liberty

Libitina — myth name (protectress of the dead)

Lida — sparkle

Lila, Lilian, Liliane, Liliana, Lily, Lilika, Lillian — lily

Lilybelle, Lilybel, Lilybella — beautiful lily

Lilybeth, Lilybet — graceful lily

Lima, Limentina — myth name (goddess of the threshold)

Linda — beautiful

Livia, Livie — olive

Lorelle, Lorella, Lorilla — little laurel

Lucania — myth name (mother of Roma)

Lucerne, Lucerna, Luceria — circle of light

Lucia, Lucy, Luciana, Lucille, Lucilla, Lucinda, Lukene, Lucie, Lucine, Lucina — light

Lucrece, Lucretia — profit

Luella, Louella — make amends

Luna — moon

Luperca — myth name (nursed Romulus and Remus)

Lysimache — myth name (daughter of Priam)

Lysippe — myth name (an Amazon)

Mabel, Mabelle, Manda — lovable

Madonna — my lady

Maera — myth name (daughter of Atlas)

Maia, Maya, May — myth name (daughter of Atlas)

Malache — myth name (a Lemnian woman)

Malvina, Malvinia — sweet friend

Majesta — majestic

Mana — myth name (protectress of stillborn babies)

Mania — myth name (mother of souls)

Manto — myth name (a prophetess)

Marica — myth name (a nymph)

Marina, Marea, Marnia, Meris, Merise, Merissa, Marine — of the sea

Marpe — myth name (an Amazon)

Marpesia — myth name (an Amazon)

Marpessa — myth name (daughter of Alcippe)

Martina, Martine, Martella,

Marcia, Marsha, Marcie, Marcy, Marcella, Marciane, Marcelline, Marcellina, Marsil, Marsile, Marsilla, Marsila — warring

Matuta — myth name (goddess of the morning)

Maura, Maure, Maureen, Maurine, Maurita — dark

Mavra — Moorish

Maxina, Maxime, Massima, Maxine — the best

Medea — myth name (wife of Jason)

Medesicaste — myth name (daughter of Priam)

Meditrina — myth name (goddess of healing)

Melanippe — myth name (a nymph)

Melia — myth name (a nymph)

Melissa — myth name (a nymph)

Mellona — honey

Mercedes — merry

Merle, Meryl, Merula, Merlina, Myrlene, Merrill, Merolla — blackbird

Messina, Messena, Messinia — middle child

Meta — goal

Miranda, Mirande — deserves admiration

Minerva — myth name (goddess of wisdom)

Modesta, Modesty, Modeste — modest

Moirae, Moira — fate

Molpe — myth name (a Siren)

Monica, Monika — counselor

Morag — blind

Muta — myth name (goddess of silence)

Myra, Mira, Merta, Merte, Myrilla, Mirilla, Mirillia — marvelous

Myrina — myth name (an Amazon)

Myrtoessa — myth name (a nymph)

Naenia — myth name (lamenting)

Naida, Naia, Naiadia — named for the nymphs

Napea, Napia — myth name (a nymph)

Narda, Nardia — fragrant

Nascio — myth name (goddess of childbirth)

Natalie, Nathalie, Natalia — born at Christmas

Nautia — from the sea

Nebula, Nebulia — misty

Neci — ardent

Nelia, Nelly, Nellie, Nella — horn

Neptunine — myth name (Thetis's surname)

Nerine, Nerina, Neris — named for the Nereides

Nerio — myth name (wife of Mars)

Nevada — snowy

Nixi — myth name (goddess who helped with childbirth)

Nila, Nilia, Nilea — from the Nile

Nola — olive

Noleta, Nolita — unwilling

Nona — born ninth

Nonna — sage

Nora, Norah, Norina, Norine — honor

Norma — typical

Nortia — lucky

Novia, Novea, Nova—young

Nox—myth name (goddess of
night)

Numeria—myth name (goddess
who assisted with childbirth)

Nunciata, Nunzia—announces

Nydia—refuge

Nyx—blond

Octavia, Octavie—born eighth

Ocyale—myth name (an Amazon)

Oenone—myth name (daughter
of Cebren)

Olethea, Olithia, Olethia,
Olethe—honest

Olinda—fragrant

Olive, Olivia, Olivie—olive

Oma—named for Bona Dea

Ona—only child

Ops—myth name (goddess of
plenty)

Ora—pray

Oralie, Oriel, Oralia, Oriana, Oria,
Orial, Orlena, Orlene—golden

Orbona—myth name (protectress
of sick children)

Orella, Oracula—divine message

Oribel, Oribelle, Oribella—
beautiful, golden child

Oris—myth name (mother of
Euphemus)

Ornora, Ornoria—honor

Orphe—myth name (lover of
Dionysus)

Ortensia, Ortensie, Ortensiana—
farmer

Otrera—myth name (mother of
the Amazons)

Ovia—egg

Pales—myth name (goddess of
shepherds and flocks)

Pallantia—myth name (daughter
of Hercules)

Pallas—myth name (daughter of
Triton)

Palma, Palmira, Palmyra—a palm
tree

Pamela, Pammeli, Pamelina,
Pameline, Pamella—made of
honey

Pantxike, Pacquita—free

Panya—crowned in victory

Paola, Paula, Paulina, Pauline,
Paulette, Pauletta, Paulita,
Pauleta, Pauli, Pavlina, Pavla—
small

Paphos—myth name (mother of
Cinyras)

Parcae, Parcia, Parca—myth
name (named for the Furies)

Pasithea—myth name (mother of
Pandion)

Patience, Patientia, Patiencia—
patient

Patricia, Patrice—noble

Pax—myth name (peace)

Peace—tranquil

Pearl, Pearla, Pearline, Pearlina,
Pearle—precious

Peirene—myth name (lover of
Poseidon)

Pellkita, Pellikita—happy

Pellonia—myth name (invoked to
ward off enemies)

Penthesilea—myth name (queen
of the Amazons)

Perdita—lost

Perdix—myth name (sister of
Daedalus)

Peregrine, Peregrina—wanderer

Pero—myth name (mother of Asopus)

Perpetua—continual

Persis—from Persia

Pertunda—myth name (Juno's surname)

Petra, Petronia, Petronella, Petronilla—rock

Phaedra—myth name (daughter of Minos)

Phoebe—myth name (daughter of Leda)

Phoenice—myth name (mother of Torone)

Phrygia—myth name (head goddess of Cybele)

Phylo—myth name (handmaiden of Helen)

Pia—pious

Pilumnus—myth name (goddess of birthing)

Placida, Placidia—tranquil

Polemusa—myth name (an Amazon)

Polyxena—myth name (daughter of Priam)

Pomona, Pomonia—fertile

Pompeia—from Pompey

Poppy—flower

Portia—an offering

Potina—myth name (blesses the food of children)

Praenestins—myth name (Fortuna's surname)

Prima, Primalia—firstborn

Primavera—born at the beginning of spring

Primrose—first rose

Priscilla, Prisca, Piroska, Piri—archaic

Procris—myth name (lover of Hercules)

Proserpina—myth name (goddess of the underworld)

Prosperia, Prospera—prosper

Prudence, Predentia—prudent

Prunella, Prunellia—plum

Quies—myth name (tranquility)

Quintina—born fifth

Raidne—myth name (a Siren)

Regina, Regine, Reginy—queen

Renee, Renelle, Renella, Renata, Renate—rebirth

Renita, Reneta—dignified

Reselda, Reseda—healer

Reva, Rive, Riva—regain strength

Rexana, Rexanne, Rexanna—royal grace

Rhea—myth name (mother of the gods)

Rhea Silva—myth name (a Vestal Virgin)

Rhode—myth name (daughter of Poseidon)

Rhodos—myth name (daughter of Poseidon)

Risa—laughter

Roma—myth name (Rome)

Romana, Romania, Romola—from Rome

Rosa, Rose, Ruzena, Rosie, Ruusu, Rosaline, Rosaleen, Rosalyn, Rosalina—rose

Rosabel, Rosabelle, Rosabella—beautiful rose

Rosalba—white rose

Rosemary—bitter rose

Rubette, Rubetta—little, precious jewel

Ruby—precious jewel
Rufina, Rufine—red-haired
Rumina—myth name
   (protectress of sleeping babes)
Runcina—myth name
   (protectress of crops)
Sabina, Sabine, Savina—a Sabine
Sabria, Sabrina—from Cyprus
Salacia—myth name (wife of
   Neptune)
Salina, Salena, Saline, Saleen—
   from a salty place
Salvia, Salva, Salvina, Salvinia,
   Sage—wise
Samia—myth name (wife of
   Ancaeus)
Sancta, Sancia—sacred
Saturnia—myth name (Juno's
   surname)
Scholastica—scholar
Scota—from Ireland
Season—fertile
Sebastiane, Sebastiana—majestic
Secuba—born second
Semele—myth name (mother of
   Dionysus)
Sena, Sina—blessed
Septima—born seventh
Serena, Serina, Serene—tranquil
Side—myth name (wife of Orion)
Sidero—myth name (an evil
   nymph)
Sidra, Sidera, Sideria, Siderea—
   luminous
Signa, Signe, Signia—sign
Silke, Silka, Silkie—blind
Silvia, Sylvia, Silva, Sylva,
   Sylvana, Sylanna, Sylvania—
   from the forest

Sinope—myth name (daughter of
   Ares)
Solita—accustomed
Speranza—hope
Spes—hope
Stella, Stelle, Star, Stanislava—
   star
Stimula—myth name (another
   name for Semele)
Suada—persuasion
Syllis—myth name (a nymph)
Symaethis—myth name (mother
   of Acis)
Tacita—silent
Tanaquil—myth name
   (worshipped in the home)
Tansy—tenacious
Tarpeia—myth name (killed for
   an act of treason against her
   father)
Telephassa—myth name (wife of
   Agenor)
Teles—myth name (a Siren)
Tellus, Terra—myth name
   (earth)
Templa—sanctuary
Tertia—born third
Tethys—myth name (daughter of
   Gaea)
Thalassa—myth name
   (Mediterranean)
Thelxiepeia, Thelxepeia—myth
   name (a Siren)
Tiberia—from the Tiber
Tigris, Tigrisia, Tigrisa—from
   the Tigris
Timandra—myth name (sister of
   Helen)
Tiryns—myth name (aunt of
   Hercules)

Tita — honored

Toinette, Tonia — praiseworthy

Topaz — jewel

Tosca, Toscana — meaning unknown

Trinity — unity

Triste, Trista — full of sorrows

Trivia — myth name (another name for Diana)

Trixy, Trix, Trixie — happy

Tryphena, Tryphana, Tryphaena — delicate

Tuccia — myth name (a Vestal Virgin)

Tullia, Tulia — meaning unknown

Tulliola — little Tullia

Tutilina — myth name (goddess of harvest)

Una — one

Undine, Undina, Undinia — of the waves

Urbana, Urbania — born of the city

Ursule, Urzula, Ursola, Urselina, Urseline, Ursula — bear

Vacuna — myth name (victory)

Val, Valentina, Valeria, Valery, Valorous, Valari, Valarie, Valencia, Valentia, Valeda, Valora — brave

Valonia, Vallonia — from the vale

Vega — star

Venessa, Vanessa — myth name (named for Venus)

Venilia — myth name (of the sea and winds)

Venus, Venita — myth name

(goddess of love and beauty)

Vera, Veradis, Veradisia — true

Verbane, Verbena, Verbenae, Verbenia — sacred limb

Verda — unspoiled

Verna, Vernita — born in the spring

Veronica, Veronika — honest

Vespera, Vespira, Vesperia — evening star

Vesta — myth name (goddess of the hearth)

Victoria, Vincentia, Viktoria, Vittoria, Victrix, Victrixa — triumphant

Vigilia — alert

Viola — flower

Virdis, Virdia, Virdisia, Virdisa — young and budding

Virgilia — staff-bearer

Virginia — blossoming

Virilis — myth name (Fortuna's surname)

Virtus — virtue

Vita, Veta, Vitia — life

Vivian, Viviana, Vivienne, Vavay — lively

Volupia — myth name (sensual pleasure)

Xanthe — myth name (an Amazon)

Yuliya, Yulenka, Yulenke, Yulene, Yulia — young

Zeuxippe — myth name (daughter of Lamedon)

Zezili, Zezilia — gray eyes

MALE

Abantiades — descendant of Abas

Abas, Abasantis — meaning unknown

Absyrtus — myth name
(murdered by his sister
Medea)

Academicus — name of a
philosopher

Acarnanus — from Acarnania

Acastus — myth name (son of
Pelias)

Accius — a Roman poet

Ace — first in luck

Acestes — meaning unknown

Achaemenius, Achaemenes — a
Persian

Achaeus, Achaean, Achivus — a
Greek

Achates — myth name (a friend of
Aeneas)

Acheron, Acheros — myth name
(river of sorrow)

Achilles — myth name (hero of the
Greeks)

Achillides — descendant of
Achilles

Acis — myth name (son of Faunus)

Acrisioniades — descendant of
Acrisius

Acrisius — myth name (father of
Danae)

Actaeon, Actaeonis — myth name
(a hunter)

Actaeus — from Athens

Actor, Actoris — myth name (son
of Azeus)

Adrian, Adrien, Adok, Adriano,
Adrik, Andrion — of the
Adriatic

Aeetes — myth name (Medea's
father)

Aegaeus, Aegeus — from the
Aegean sea

Aegides — meaning unknown

Aegisthus — myth name (cousin of
Agamemnon)

Aegyptus — myth name (brother
of Daunus)

Aeneades — descended from
Aeneas

Aeneas — excellent

Aeolius, Aeolus — myth name
(keeper of the winds)

Aeschylus — Athenian poet

Aesclapius, Asclepius,
Aesculapius — myth name (god
of medicine)

Aeson — myth name (father of
Jason)

Aethiops — an Ethiopian

Agenor — myth name (son of
Poseidon)

Agrippa — colonist

Ajax — myth name (a Greek at
Troy)

Alair — happy

Alban, Avaro, Albin, Albion,
Aubin, Aubyn, Albano, Alvar,
Alver, Albinus, Alva, Albus —
white

Albion — from Britain

Alcaeus — a Greek poet

Alcibiades — name of an Athenian
politician

Alcides — descended from
Alcaeus

Alcinous — myth name (father of
Nausicaa)

Aleron, Alerio — eagle

Aloysius, Alois — meaning
unknown

Alroy — regal

Amadeus, Amadis, Amadeo,

Amadio, Amado—loves God

Americus, Amerigo—meaning unknown

Amiphitryon—meaning unknown

Amphiaraus—name of a Greek prophet

Amphitryo, Amphitryon—myth name (husband of Alcmene)

Amory, Amery—meaning unknown

Amulius—myth name

Amyas, Amias—loves God

Anacreon—name of an ancient poet

Anaxagoras—name of a Greek philosopher

Anaximander—name of a Greek philosopher

Anaximenes—name of a Greek philosopher

Anchises—myth name (father of Aeneas)

Ancile—myth name (a king of Rome)

Andoni, Antton, Antonin, Antal, Antoine, Antoin, Antanas, Ante, Antanelis, Antanukas, Antoniy—beyond praise

Andronicus—name of a Roman poet

Anguis—dragon

Anius—myth name

Antenor—myth name (an elder of Troy)

Anteros—myth name (brother of Eros)

Antilochus—myth name (son of Nestor)

Antiphates—myth name (king of the Laestrygones)

Antisthenes—name of a philosopher

Apelles—name of an artist

Apollo—myth name (god of the sun)

Apollodorus—name of a Greek writer

Aquilino—eagle

Arar, Araris—from the Arar

Aratus—name of a Greek author

Arber, Arbor—sells herbs

Arcas—myth name (son of Callisto)

Archer—bowman

Archimedes—name of a scientist

Arcitenens—archer

Arctophylax—myth name

Arctos—myth name

Arcturus—myth name

Arden, Ardin—fervent

Ardmore—ardent

Ares—myth name (Greek god of war)

Argus—myth name (a monster)

Aries—ram

Ariobarzanes—name of a king

Arion—name of a Greek poet

Aristarchus—severe critic

Aristophanes—name of a poet

Aristoteles—Latin form of Aristotle (intelligent)

Arruns, Aruns—myth name (killed Turnus)

Arval, Arvalis—from the cultivated land

Ascanius—myth name (son of Aeneas)

Astyanax—myth name (son of Hector)

Atabulus—southeastern wind

Athamas — myth name (brother of Sisyphus)

Atlas — myth name (a Titan)

Atreus — myth name (father of Agamemnon)

Atrides — descended from Atreus

Attalus — name of a king

Attis — name of a priest

Aufidus — from the river Apulia

Augeas — myth name (king of Elis)

Augustus, Augusty, Augustine, August, Augustin, Austin, Agoston — majestic

Aurelian, Aurelien, Auerlio — golden

Auriga, Aurigo — wagoner

Avernus — myth name (gate to Hades)

Axenus — from the Black Sea

Bacchus, Bromius — myth name (god of wine)

Balbo, Balbas — speaker

Balendin, Balen — brave

Balint, Baline — strong and healthy

Bellerophon — myth name (son of Glaucus)

Belus — myth name (king of Tyre)

Benedict, Benedicte, Bennett, Benin, Bent, Benoit, Benedikte, Benedetto, Benedek, Benke, Bence, Benci, Benen, Beinean, Binean, Bendik, Bengt — blessed

Binger, Bittor — conqueror

Blaise, Blase, Ballas, Balaza, Braz — stutters

Blandon, Bland — gentle

Bonaventure — lucky

Boniface, Bonifacy, Bonifacio — good

Boreas — myth name (north wind)

Brencis — victorious

Brutus — stupid

Bucer — horned

Cacus — myth name (son of Vulcan)

Cadmus — myth name (son of Agenor)

Caduceus — myth name

Caesar, Cesar, Cesario, Cezar — long-haired

Cajetan — rejoiced

Calais — myth name (son of the north wind)

Calchas — myth name (a prophet)

Caligula — name given to Gaius Ceasar when he was a child

Calix, Callixtus — chalice

Calleo — knowing

Callimachus — name of a poet

Callosus — callous

Calvin, Calvinus — bald

Camillus, Camilo — temple servant

Canis — myth name

Cantor — singer

Capys — myth name

Carcer — prisoner

Carmine — crimson

Carneades — name of a philosopher

Carsten, Christiann, Cristiano, Christian, Carston — Christian

Cassius, Cass, Cash — vain

Castor — myth name (brother of Helen)

Cato, Catus, Caton — shrewd

Catullus — name of a poet

Cavillor — critical

Cecil, Cecilio, Caecelius — blind

Cecrops — name of a king

Celeres — paladin

Celestin, Celistine, Celestun — heavenly

Centaurus — myth name (half-man, half-horse)

Cephalus — myth name (husband of Procris)

Cepheus — myth name (father of Andromeda)

Cerberus — myth name (guard of Hades)

Chauncey, Chaucor, Chaucer, Chauncory — chancellor

Chester — camp

Chryses — myth name (priest of Apollo)

Ciceron, Cicero — chickpea

Clarence, Clare, Clarensis — illustrious

Claud, Claude, Cladian, Claus, Claudio, Claudion, Clodius, Claudius — lame

Clement, Clemence, Clem, Clemente — merciful

Cocles — myth name (a hero who saved Rome)

Collatinus — myth name

Colon — dove

Constantine, Constant, Constantios, Constantino — constant

Corbin, Cowin — raven

Cornelius, Cornelio — horn

Crispin — curly-haired

Curt — short

Damon — loyal friend

Danaus — myth name (king of Argos)

Daphnis — myth name (a shepherd)

Dardanus — myth name (father of Erichthonius)

Deiphobus — myth name (son of Priam)

Delmar, Delmer — mariner

Demodocus — myth name (a blind bard)

Deucalion — myth name (son of Prometheus)

Dexter — right

Dezso — desired

Dis — myth name (Hades)

Dolon — myth name (a Trojan spy)

Domiducus — myth name (Jupiter's surname)

Dominic, Dominick, Domeka, Domiku, Dominico, Domokas, Domo, Dome, Dom, Dedo — the Lord's

Donato, Donatello — gift

Dorjan — dark

Duke — leader

Durant, Duran, Durand — enduring

Eligius — worthy

Elvio — blond

Emil, Emilian, Emile — excellent

Erichthonius — myth name (founder of Troy)

Errol — wandering

Euphorbus — myth name (a Trojan soldier)

Eurus — myth name (east wind)

Eurypylus — myth name (a Trojan)

Eurystheus — myth name (cousin of Hercules)

Evander — myth name (fought with Aeneas)

Fabian, Fabiano, Fabiyan — bean grower

Fabrice, Fabrizio — craftsman

Fabron — mechanic

Faunus — myth name (god of forests)

Fausto, Faust — lucky

Favonius — myth name (west wind)

Felician, Felix, Feliks, Felice, Felicio — happy

Ferenc, Feri, Ferke, Ferko — free

Fidelio, Fidelis, Fidel, Fedele — faithful

Flavian, Flavio, Flawiusz — yellow

Florian, Florentin, Floren, Florentyn — flowering

Forrest — dwells in the forest

Foster — keeper of the forest

Ganymede — myth name (cup-bearer to the gods)

Garai — conqueror

Genius — myth name (a guardian spirit)

Germain — has the same parents

Giles — kind

Gilroy — serves the king

Giuliano — youth

Glaucus — myth name (son of Minos)

Graham, Graeme, Gram — grain

Grant — great

Gratian — grateful

Gustave, Gusztav — majestic

Guy, Guido, Gwidon — life

Gyala — young

Halirrhothius — myth name (son of Poseidon)

Harpocrates — myth name (Horus, Egyptian god of the sun)

Hector — myth name (brother of Paris)

Helenus — myth name (son of Priam)

Hercules — myth name (god of physical strength)

Herminius — myth name (a hero who saved Rome)

Hieronymous — sacred

Hilary, Hillary, Hillery, Hilarion — happy

Hippocampus — myth name (Neptune's horse)

Honorato — honor

Horace, Horatio, Horaz, Horacio — timekeeper

Horatius — myth name (a hero who saved Rome)

Idaeus — meaning unknown

Idomeneus — myth name (king of Crete)

Ignatius, Inaki, Inigo, Ignac — ardent

Ilari, Ilarion, Ilarius — cheerful

Illan, Illian, Illius — youth

Ilus — myth name (founder of Troy)

Inachus — myth name (father of Io)

Ince, Innocenty, Innocent — innocent

Inek — small

Inuus — myth name (god of fertility)

Iphicles — myth name (twin of Hercules)

Iphis — myth name (lover who hanged himself)

Iphitus — myth name (brother of Iole)

Iulus — myth name (son of Aeneas)

Janus — myth name (god of beginnings)

Jerolin, Jerome — holy

Jove — myth name (another name for Jupiter)

Julius, Julen, Jules, Juliusz, Julian, Jullian, Jullien, Junus, Junius, Julio — youthful

Jupiter — myth name (supreme god)

Justin, Justus, Joost, Justyn — just

Kasen — helmeted

Kauldi, Klaudi, Klaudius, Klaude — lame

Kelman, Klemens, Klemenis, Kliment — merciful

Kerstan — Christian

Kester — from the Roman camp

Killian, Kilian — blind

Kinden, Kindin — born fifth

Konstantin, Kostas, Konstantinus, Konstanz, Konstancji, Konstanty — constant

Korneli, Kees, Krelis, Kornel — horn

Lacy — from Latius's estate

Laocoon — myth name (son of Priam)

Laomedon — myth name (father of Priam)

Lapis — myth name

Lares — myth name (god of the household)

Lars — myth name (a Roman hero)

Lartius — myth name (a hero who saved Rome)

Latinus — myth name (king of Latium)

Laudalino, Lino — praise

Laurence, Lawrence, Laurel, Lorin, Loren, Lauren, Lorne, Lars, Laurentzi, Lauran, Lorentz, Loritz, Lauritz, Lawron, Lawrie, Laurie, Laurent, Laurentios, Lenci, Lorant, Loreca, Lorencz, Lorenc, Lorine, Labhras, Lorenzo, Loretto, Labrencis, Laiurenty, Laurencho — laurel

Leo, Leon, Leone, Leonidas, Leonide, Leonid, Lyonya, Lyonechka, Lee, Lev, Levka, Levushka, Lew, Lon, Leontis, Leander, Leandros — lion

Leroy — regal

Lester, Leicester — from the Legion's camp

Liber — myth name (another name for Dionysus)

Lichas, Lycus, Licus — myth name (friend of Hercules)

Lionel — little lion

Lombard, Longobard — long beard

Lorimer, Lorrimer — harness maker

Lucious, Lucian, Lucien, Luke, Lucas, Lucaas, Luken, Luk, Lukas, Loukas, Luciano, Lucio, Liuz, Lukyan, Lukasha, Luka — light

Lysander — liberator

Magnus, Max, Maximilian, Maximillian, Maximos, Maghnus, Manus, Miksa, Maksym, Makimus, Maxime, Maksymilian, Maximus — greatest

Mallory — ill-fated

Manvel, Manvil — from a great estate

Marcel, Marcellus, Marcian, Marco, Marcus, Mario, Marius, Mark, Marc, Markus, Marcellin, Markos, Markus, Marci, Marcilka, Marcely — hammer

Maren, Marinos — of the sea

Mars — myth name (god of war)

Martial, Martin, Martinus, Marcel, Martinien, Marceau, Martel, Marton, Martino, Mairtin, Marek, Marion, Marian — warring

Maurice, Moritz, Morie, Morris, Maury, Mauritz, Mauritins — dark-skinned

Mayer, Mayor — great

Mazentius — meaning unknown

Memnon — myth name (killed by Achilles in the Trojan War)

Mercer — merchant

Mercury — myth name (messenger of the gods)

Metabus — myth name (father of Camilla)

Miles, Myles — soldier

Miller — miller

Minos — myth name (king of Crete)

Misenos, Misenus — myth name (drowned for hubris)

Modeste, Modestus — modest

Moneta — admonishes

Montague — from the peaked mountain

Morrell, Morel — swarthy

Mortimer — dwells by the still water

Mulciber — meaning unknown

Munroe, Munro, Monroe — from the red marsh

Nelek — horn

Nemesio, Nemesus — just

Neon — strong

Neptune — myth name (god of water)

Nereus — myth name (a god of the sea)

Neville — from the new town

Nigel — dark

Nikki, Niki — of the lord

Noble, Nobilus — noble

Notus — myth name (south wind)

Numa — myth name (a king of Rome)

Nuncio, Nunzio — messenger

Octavian, Octavius, Octavio, Ottavio — born eighth

Oistin — revered

Oliver, Ollie, Olvan, Olliver, Olivier, Oliverio, Oliverios — peaceful

Orban — born in the city

Orcus — myth name (the underworld)

Orson — bear

Ovid — name of a poet

Paganus — villager

Paine, Payne — rustic

Pales — myth name (god of cattle)

Palinurus — myth name (pilot of Aeneas's boat)

Palmer — pilgrim

Pandarus — myth name (a Trojan soldier)

Paris — myth name (abductor of Helen)

Parnassus — from Parnassus

Pastor — shepherd

Patrick, Patrice, Paddy, Padraig, Padhraig, Padriac, Patricio, Patryk, Patrizio, Payton, Paton, Peyton — regal

Patroclus — myth name (a friend of Achilles)

Paul, Paulin, Pauli, Pavel, Poul, Pavlus, Pal, Palika, Paaveli, Paavo, Pawel, Paola, Pauls, Paulus, Pavlis, Pawelek, Pol, Pablo — small

Pax — peace

Peli — happy

Penates — myth name (god of the household)

Pephredo — dreaded

Percival, Parzifal — destroyer

Periphetes — myth name (son of Hephaestus)

Phoebus — shining

Picus — myth name (father of Faunus)

Pierpont, Pierrepont — dwells by the stone bridge

Pius, Pio, Pious — pious

Placyd, Placid, Placidio — tranquil

Pluto — myth name (god of the underworld)

Plutus — wealthy

Pluvius — meaning unknown

Pollux — myth name (brother of Helen)

Polydamas — myth name (a Trojan soldier)

Polydorus — myth name (son of Priam)

Polyeidus — myth name (a prophet)

Polymestor — myth name (son-in-law of Priam)

Pompilius — meaning unknown

Pontifex — priest

Porter — gatekeeper

Portumnus — myth name (a god of the sea)

Prentice — scholar

Priam — myth name (king of Troy)

Prince — prince

Prior, Pryor — head of a monastery

Proctor, Procurator — manager

Prosper, Prospero — fortunate

Publius — myth name (a hero who saved Rome)

Pygmalion — myth name (king of Cyprus)

Quartus — born fourth

Quintus, Quentin, Quincy, Quinton — born fifth

Quirinus — myth name (a lesser war-god)

Ray — radiant

Remus — myth name (founder of Rome)

Renato — reborn

Renzo — laurel

Rex — king

Rhadamanthus — myth name (an underworld judge)

Rhesus—myth name (king of Thrace)

Rodhlann, Roland, Rowland—famous

Romain, Romney, Romano—Roman

Romeo—pilgrim to Rome

Romulus—myth name (founder of Rome)

Royal, Royce—regal

Rufus, Russell, Rufin, Rufeo, Rufio—red-haired

Rule—ruler

Sabino, Sabin, Sabinus—a Sabine

Salmoneus—myth name (king of Elis)

Salvador, Salvator—savior

Sargent—military attendant

Sarpedon—myth name (a Trojan soldier)

Saturn—myth name (god of the harvest)

Savill—from the willow farm

Sebastian, Sebastianus—august

Segundo—born second

Septimus—born seventh

Sereno, Serenus—calm

Sergius, Sergios, Sergiusz, Serguei, Seriozha, Seriozhenka, Sergio, Serge—attendant

Severin, Seweryn—severe

Sibley—prophetic

Sichaeus—myth name (husband of Dido)

Silas, Silos, Sylvester, Silvester, Silvanus, Sylvanus, Sill, Sil, Silio, Silvain, Silvius, Sylvan, Silvanos—of the forest

Sinclair—hard-working

Sinon—myth name (a Trojan soldier)

Siseal—blind

Sisyphus—myth name (son of Aeolus)

Sixtus, Sextus—born sixth

Sol—sun

Somnus—myth name (sleep)

Spurius—myth name (a hero who saved Rome)

Stacy, Stacey—dependable

Tarchon—meaning unknown

Tavey—born eighth

Terence, Terrence, Terry—smooth

Terminus—myth name

Tertius—born third

Tithonus—myth name (a lover of Aurora)

Titus, Tito—saved

Tony—above praise

Tracy, Thrasius—bold

Trent, Torrentem—swift

Tristan, Tristam, Tristram—full of sorrows

Triton—myth name (a sea god)

Troilus—myth name (son of Priam)

Tros—myth name (founder of Troy)

Tulio—lively

Tullius—name of a king

Tully, Tullus—meaning unknown

Turner—works on the lathe

Turnus—myth name (killed by Aeneas)

Txanton—meaning unknown

Txomin—like unto the lord

Tyre—from Tyre

Uiseann—conqueror

Ulysses—myth name (Odysseus)

Urban, Urbain—of the city

Valens, Valentine, Valentino, Valerian, Valerius, Val, Valerio, Valentin, Valerijs, Valentijn, Valentyn, Valerii, Valera, Valerik—valiant

Varian—fickle

Venedictos—blessed

Vergil, Virgil, Virgilio—flourishing

Verne, Vernus—youthful

Vernon—flourishing

Vertumnus—myth name (god of seasons)

Viator—traveler

Victor, Victorin, Victorien, Viktor, Vidor, Vitenka, Vincent, Vincente, Vincien, Vincens, Vinzenz, Vincze, Vinci, Vince, Vincenzio, Vincenzo, Vinnie, Vittorio, Vito, Viktoras, Viktoryn—conqueror

Vital, Vitus, Veit, Vitale, Vito, Vivien—lively

Vulcan—myth name (god of fire)

Walerian—strong

Waring—true

Wincent, Wicek, Wicus, Wicenty—conqueror

Wit—life

Xanthus—myth name (a river god)

Yuli—young

Zephyrus—myth name (west wind)

Zethus—myth name (brother of Amphion)

Zeuxippus—myth name (son of Apollo)

Zorian—happy

Native American

In this section I have listed given names by tribe, when the tribe of origin is known. But each gender list begins with names whose tribes of origin are difficult (or impossible) to determine. Since many tribes were migratory, they passed on and borrowed names from other tribes, making it difficult for us to know in which tribe a name originated.

Names were bestowed upon a person at the various epochs of life after careful consideration and, in some cases, with extreme ceremony. Native Americans took pride in their names and in their meanings. Once Native Americans learned to speak English, they automatically translated their names; because certain phrases and distinctions didn't translate verbatim, many Native Americans were left with names that sound odd to most Euro-descendants. Indeed, in a similar fashion, many Blancs became Whites and Schmidts became Smiths after migrating to America.

Once more, I would encourage writers not to generalize; names and habits changed profoundly from one group to the next, even within a single nation.

During the nineteenth century, many nations and tribes were forced by law to take on Christian names and surnames. Often they chose the names of soldiers or towns. One tribe of the Apaches was so adamant in their refusal that they were issued numbers by the government to serve as names.

Today, there are still problems with hereditary surnames among certain tribes and nations. Depending on the nation/tribe and individual, a last name may be either a translated version of a native name (such as White-Cloud), a Christian name (Smith), or a native name in its original form (Eponi).

FEMALE

Adoette—large tree	Amitola—rainbow
Aiyana—eternal blossom	Anevay—superior
Alameda—grove of cottonwood	Angeni—spirit
Alaqua—sweet gum tree	Aponi—butterfly
Algoma—valley of flowers	Aquene—peace

Awendela — morning
Awenita — fawn
Ayita — worker
Bena — pheasant
Bly — tall
Chenoa — dove
Chilaili — snowbird
Chimalis — bluebird
Chitsa — fair
Cholena — bird
Cocheta — stranger
Dena — valley
Dyani — deer
Enola — solitary
Etenia — rich
Eyota — great
Flo — arrow
Gaho — mother
Halona — of happy fortune
Imala — disciplines
Istas — snow
Ituha — sturdy oak
Izusa — white stone
Kachina — sacred dancer
Kineks — rosebud
Leotie — flower of the prairie
Lomasi — pretty flower
Lulu — rabbit
Luyu — wild dove
Magena — moon
Mahal — woman
Mai — coyote
Maralah — born during an
      earthquake

Mausi — plucks flowers
Meda — prophetess
Memdi — henna
Miakoda — power of the moon
Mika — intelligent raccoon
Minal — fruit
Mona — gathered of the seed of a
      jimson weed
Nara — from Nara
Nashota — twin
Nata — speaker
Nina — strong
Nituna — daughter
Nuna — land
Ogin — wild rose
Olathe — beautiful
Onawa — wide awake
Onida — the one searched for
Petunia — flower name
Rozene — rose
Satinka — magical dancer
Shada — pelican
Sihu — flower
Sisika — bird
Taima — thunder
Tala — wolf
Tama — thunder
Tehya — precious
Utina — meaning unknown
Waneta — charger
Wenona — firstborn daughter
Winema — chief
Wyanet — beautiful
Yepa — snow woman
Zaltana — high mountain

Algonquin

Alawa — pea
Alsoomse — independent
Anna — mother

Chepi — fairy
Hausis, Hausisse — old woman
Hurit — beautiful

Kanti — sings
Keegsquaw — virgin
Kimi — secret
Makkitotosimew — she has
large breasts
Nadie — wise
Nijlon — mistress
Nittawosew — she is not sterile
Numees — sister

Nuttah — my heart
Oota dabun — day star
Pauwau — witch
Pules — pigeon
Sokanon — rain
Sokw — sour
Sooleawa — silver
Tahki — cold
Wikimak — wife

Blackfoot

Koko — night
Peta — golden eagle

Sinopa — fox

Cherokee

Adsila — blossom
Amadahy — forest water
Awenasa — my home
Awinita — fawn

Ayita — first to dance
Galilahi — attractive
Salali — squirrel
Tayanita — young beaver

Cheyenne

Tis-see-woo-na-tis — she who
bathes with her knees

Chippewa

Abedabun — sight of day
Abequa, Abeque — stays at home
Ayashe, Ayasha — little one
Keezheekoni — burning fire
Kiwidinok — of the wind
Meoquanee — wears red

Migisi — eagle
Namid — star dancer
Nokomis — grandmother
Odahingum — rippling water
Ominotago — beautiful voice
Sheshebens — small duck

Choctaw

Atepa — wigwam
Fala — crow
Isi — deer

Nita — bear
Poloma — bow
Talulah — leaping water

Dakota

Wicapi wakan — holy star

Zitkala — bird

Hopi

Angwusnasomtaqa — crow mother spirit
Ankti — repeat dance
Catori — spirit
Cha'kwaina — one who cries
Cha'risa — elk
Chochmingwu — corn mother
Chosovi — bluebird
Chosposi — bluebird eye
Chu'mana — snake maiden
Chu'si — snake flower
Hakidonmuya — time of waiting moon
Hehewuti — warrior mother spirit
Honovi — strong deer
Humita — shelled corn
Kachina — spirit
Kakawangwa — bitter
Kasa — dressed in furs
Kaya — elder sister
Kokyangwuti — spider woman at middle-age
Kuwanlelenta — to make beautiful surroundings
Kuwanyamtiwa — beautiful badger going over the hill
Kuwanyauma — butterfly showing beautiful wings
Lenmana — flute girl

Lomahongva — beautiful clouds arising
Mahu — myth name
Mansi — plucked flower
Muna — overflowing spring
Nova — chases butterfly
Nukpana — evil
Pakwa — frog
Pamuya — water moon
Pavati — clear water
Polikwaptiwa — butterfly sitting on a flower
Powaqa — witch
Shuman — rattlesnake handler
Sihu — flower
Soyala — time of the winter solstice
Sunki — to catch up with
Tablita — tiara
Takala — corn tassel
Tansy — name of a flower
Tiponi — child of importance
Tiva — dance
Totsi — moccasins
Tuwa — earth
Una — remember
Waki — shelter
Wuti — woman
Yamka — blossom
Yoki — rain
Zihna — spins

Iroquois

Onatah — of the earth

Orenda — magic power

Miwok

Amayeta — meaning unknown
Awanata — turtle
Helki — touch

Huata — carrying seeds in a basket
Huyana — falling rain

Kaliska—coyote chasing deer
Kolenya—coughing fish
Liluye—singing chicken hawk
that soars
Litonya—darting hummingbird
Malila—fast salmon swimming
up a rippling stream
Mituna—wraps salmon in willow
leaves
Omusa—misses with arrows
Oya—jacksnipe

Pakuna—deer jumping downhill
Papina—vine growing around an
oak tree
Pati—break by twisting
Posala—farewell to spring
flowers
Sanuye—red cloud at sundown
Sitala—of good memory
Suletu—flies
Taipa—spread wings
Tolinka—coyote's flapping ear
Wauna—singing snow goose

Navajo

Altsoba—all war
Anaba—returns from war
Asdza—woman
At'eed—girl
Dezba—goes to war
Dibe—sheep
Doba—no war
Doli—bluebird
Haloke—salmon
Kai—willow tree

Manaba—return to war
Mosi—cat
Nascha—owl
Ooljee—moon
Sahkyo—mink
Shadi—older sister
Shideezhi—younger sister
Shima—mother
Shimasani—grandmother
Sitsi—daughter
Yazhi—little one

Omaha

Abetzi—yellow leaf
Abey—leaf
Abeytu—green leaf
Donoma—sight of the sun
Migina—returning moon
Mimiteh—new moon

Nidawi—fairy
Tadewi—wind
Tadita—one who runs
Taigi, Taini—returning moon
Urika—useful to all

Osage

Misae—white sun

Niabi—fawn

Shoshone

Kimama—butterfly

Sioux

Anpaytoo — radiant
Chapa — beaver
Chumani — dewdrops
Ehawee — laughing maiden
Hantaywee — faithful
Kimimela — butterfly
Macawi — generous
Maka — earth
Magaskawee — graceful
Makawee — mothering
Mapiya — sky

Nahimana — mystic
Ptaysanwee — white buffalo
Takchawee — doe
Talutah — blood-red
Wachiwi — dancer
Wakanda — possesses magical power
Weeko — pretty
Wihakayda — little one
Winona, Wenona, Wenonah — giving
Witashnah — virginal

Zuni

Liseli — meaning unknown
Malia — bitter

Mankalita — meaning unknown
Meli — bitter

MALE

Ahanu — laughter
Ahmik — beaver
Akando — ambush
Akule — looks up
Anoki — actor
Apenimon — worthy of trust
Awan — somebody
Bemossed — walker
Bimisi — slippery
Bodaway — fire-maker
Chesmu — gritty
Delsin — he is so
Demothi — talks while walking
Dichali — speaks a lot
Dohosan — bluff
Dyami — eagle
Elan — friendly
Elsu — flying falcon
Enyeto — walks as a boar
Etu — sun
Ezhno — solitary

Gosheven — leaper
Guyapi — frank
Hahnee — beggar
Hakan — fire
Helaku — full of sun
Hinun — myth name
Honovi — strong
Hototo — he who whistles
Igasho — wanders
Inteus — has no shame
Istu — sugar
Iye — smoke
Jacy — moon
Jolon — valley of the dead oaks
Kaga — chronicler
Kajika — walks without sound
Knoton — wind
Langundo — peaceful
Lenno — man
Lonato — flint
Manipi — amazing

Maska — strong
Masou — myth name
Melvern — meaning unknown
Milap — charitable
Mingan — gray wolf
Mojag — never silent
Motega — new arrow
Muraco — white moon
Nahele — forest
Nawat — left-handed
Nayati — he who wrestles
Neka — wild goose
Nigan — ahead
Nikiti — round, smooth
Nitis — friend
Nodin — wind
Ohanko — reckless
Ouray — arrow
Paco — eagle

Pallaton — warrior
Pat — fish
Patamon — tempest
Patwin — man
Payat, Pay, Payatt — he is coming
Pinon — myth name
Sahale — falcon
Sakima — king
Siwili — tail of the fox
Songan — strong
Taima — thunder
Tate — he who talks too much
Wakiza — desperate warrior
Wapi — lucky
Wemilat — of wealthy parents
Wilny — meaning unknown
Wynono — firstborn
Yoskolo — meaning unknown
Yuma — chief's son
Yancy — Englishman

Algonquin

Abooksigun — wildcat
Abukcheech — mouse
Achak — spirit
Ahanu — he laughs
Anakausuen — worker
Aranck — stars
Askook — snake
Askuwheteau — he keeps watch
Chansomps — locust
Chogan — blackbird
Eluwilussit — holy one
Enkoodabooaoo, Enkoodabaoo —
   one who lives alone
Etchemin — canoe man
Etlelooaat — shouts
Hassun — stone
Huritt — handsome
Keme — secret

Kesegowaase — swift
Kestejoo — slave
Kitchi — brave
Machk — bear
Makkapitew — he has large teeth
Matchitehew — he has an evil
   heart
Matchitisiw — he has bad
   character
Matunaaga — fights
Matwau — enemy
Megedagik — kills many
Melkedoodum — conceited
Mukki — child
Nixkamich — grandfather
Nootau — fire
Nosh, Noshi — father
Pajackok — thunder

Pannoowau — he lies
Powwaw — priest
Rowtag — fire
Segenam — lazy
Sucki — black

Sunukkuhkau — he crushes
Taregan — crane
Tihkoosue — short
Togquos — twin
Wematin — brother

Cherokee

Adahy — lives in the woods
Dustu — meaning unknown

Tooantuh — spring frog

Cheyenne

Ahtunowhiho — one who lives below
Avonaco — lean bear
Hahkethomemah,
  Harkahome — little robe
Heammawihio — wise one above
Heskovizenako — porcupine bear
Hevataneo — hairy rope
Hevovitastamiutsto — whirlwind
Hiamovi — high chief
Hohnihohkaiyohos,
  Neeheeoeewootis — high-backed wolf
Honiahaka — little wolf
Hotuaekhaashtait — tall bull
Kohkahycumest — white crow or white antelope
Kuckunniwi — little wolf
Mantotohpa — four bears
Meturato, Mokatavatah,
  Moketavato, Moketaveto,
  Moketoveto, Mokovaoto,
  Motavato — black kettle
Minninnewah — whirlwind
Nahcomence — old bark

Nahiossi — has three fingers
Ocumwhowurst,
  Ocunnowhurst — yellow wolf
Ohcumgache, Okhmhaka — little wolf
Otoahhastis — tall bull
Otoahnacto — bull bear
Shoemowetochawcawewahcatowe — high-backed wolf
Tahkeome — little robe
Tahmelapachme — dull knife
Vaiveahtoish, Vaive atoish — alights on the cloud
Viho — chief
Vipponah — slim face
Vohkinne — Roman nose
Voistitoevitz, Voisttitoevetz — white cow
Vokivocummast — white antelope
Wahanassatta — he who walks with his toes turned outward
Waquini — hook nose
Wohehiv — dull knife
Wokaihwokomas — white antelope

Dakota

Ciqala — little one
Hinto — blue

Maza blaska — flat iron
Tasunke — horse

Tatanka-ptecila — short bull
Tokala — fox

Wambli-waste — good eagle
Wicasa — sage

Hopi

Ahiliya — meaning unknown
Ahote — restless one
Alo — spiritual guide
Alosaka — myth name
Aponivi — where the wind blows down the gap
Ayawamat — one who follows orders
Cha'akmongwi — crier chief
Cha'tima — the caller
Chavatangakwunua — short rainbow
Cheveyo — spirit warrior
Chochmo — mud mound
Chochokpi — throne for the clouds
Chochuschuvio — white-tailed deer
Choovio — antelope
Choviohoya — young deer
Chowilawu — joined together by water
Chu'a — snake
Chuchip — deer spirit
Chunta — cheating
Hania — spirit warrior
Hawiovi — going down the ladder
Honani — badger
Honaw — bear
Hototo — warrior spirit who sings
Istaqa — coyote man

Kachada — white man
Kele — sparrow
Kolichiyaw — skunk
Kotori — screech owl spirit
Kwahu — eagle
Kwatoko — bird with big beak
Lansa — lance
Lapu — cedar bark
Len — flute
Machakw — horny toad
Makya — eagle hunter
Masichuvio — gray deer
Mochni — talking bird
Moki — deer
Mongwau — owl
Nukpana — evil
Omawnakw — cloud feather
Pachu'a — feathered water snake
Pahana — lost white brother
Pivane — weasel
Qaletaqa — guardian of the people
Qochata — white man
Sikyahonaw — yellow bear
Sikyatavo — yellow rabbit
Sowi'ngwa — black-tailed deer
Tangakwunu — rainbow
Tocho — mountain lion
Tohopka — wild beast
Wikvaya — one who brings

Miwok

Elki — meaning unknown
Helki — touch
Hesutu — yellow jacket's nest

rising out of the ground
Howi — turtle-dove
Honon — bear

Kono—meaning unknown

Kosumi—fishes for salmon with spear

Lanu—meaning unknown

Leyati—shaped like an abalone shell

Lise—salmon's head rising above water

Liwanu—growl of a bear

Lokni—rain falls through the roof

Misu—rippling brook

Molimo—bear walking into shade

Momuso—meaning unknown

Mona—gathers jimson weed seed

Muata—yellow jackets inside a nest

Oya—meaning unknown

Sewati—curved bear claw

Telutci, Tuketu—bear making dust

Tupi—to pull up

Uzumati—bear

Wuyi—soaring turkey vulture

Navajo

Ahiga—he fights

Ashkii—boy

Ata'halne'—he interrupts

Bidziil—he is strong

Bilagaana—white person

Gaagii—raven

Gad—juniper tree

Hastiin—man

Hok'ee—abandoned

Naalnish—he works

Naalyehe ya sidahi—trader

Nastas—curve like foxtail grass

Niichaad—swollen

Niyol—wind

Sani—the old one

Shilah—brother

Shiye—son

Shizhe'e—father

Sicheii—grandfather

Sike—he sits at home

Sik'is—friend

T'iis—cottonwood

Tse—rock

Tsiishch'ili—curly-haired

Yanisin—ashamed

Yas—snow

Yiska—the night has passed

Pawnee

Kuruk—bear

Shiriki—coyote

Sioux

Akecheta—fighter

Chankoowashtay—good road

Chayton—falcon

Enapay—brave

Hotah—white

Howahkan—of the mysterious voice

Kangee—raven

Kohana—swift

Lootah—red

Mahkah—earth

Mahpee—sky

Matoskah—white bear

Napayshni—strong, courageous

Odakota — friend
Ogaleesha — wears a red shirt
Ohanzee — shadow
Ohitekah — brave
Otaktay — kills many
Paytah — fire
Skah — white
Takoda — friend to everyone
Teetonka — talks too much
Wahchinksapa — wise

Wahchintonka — has much practice
Wahkan — sacred
Wamblee — eagle
Wambleeska — white eagle
Wanageeska — white spirit
Wanahton — charger
Wanikiya — savior
Weayaya — setting sun
Yahto — blue

Winnebago

Chas-chunk-a — wave
He-lush-ka — fighter

Nawkaw — wood

Norse

The Normans used epithets, or added -son, -sen, -dotter or -datter to the father's name. Their nomenclature is discussed more fully in the sections on French and English names. In Norway, traditional surnames started in urban areas around the sixteenth century and spread to the rural areas in the late nineteenth century. Most names were taken from farms or were patronymic. Only rarely did they derive from nicknames or epithets.

Surnames were used first by the nobility and military officers and then spread down the social ladder. The first surnames were patronymic and included the suffixes -sen (son) or -datter (daughter).

Before surnames became common, people were identified by their given name plus their father's name, the name of their residence or a distinctive trait. Later, rural people were identified by their given name along with their father's, followed by the name of their residence.

The prefix Fitz originated in Norway during the early and mid-Middle Ages. It was usually given to illegitimate children and was followed by the name of the father.

Given names were handed down even in the earliest times in a specific order: the eldest daughter received the name of the paternal grandmother, and the eldest son was named after the paternal grandfather. The next children born were named after the maternal grandparents, and the rest were given names of other relatives.

In 1964 the Name Act was passed, which required legitimate children to take their father's surname and illegitimate children to take their mother's surname. Married women were required to take their husband's name unless they obtained special permission to retain their maiden or previous married name.

A few Norse surnames:

Anderson	Kerr
Ansgar	Kirby
Booth	Magnor
Crosby	Odell

Sutherland   Wray

FEMALE

Aase — tree-covered mountain

Aegileif — saga name (daughter of Hrolf Helgason)

Alfdis — spirit

Amma — grandmother

Andras — breath

Angerbotha, Angerboda, Angrboda — myth name (a giant)

Anrid — saga name (wife of Ketil Fjorleifarson)

Anselma — protected by God

Arna — eagle

Arnbjorg — eagle protection

Arndis — eagle spirit

Arnora — light eagle

Arnthrud — meaning unknown

Asdis — divine spirit

Ase, Asta — tree

Ashild, Ashilde, Ashilda — god-fighting

Aslaug — devoted to God

Astrid, Astra, Astred, Astryd, Astryr, Astrud — divine strength

Asvor, Asvora — saga name (wife of Asrod)

Aud, Auda — wealthy

Audhild, Audhilde, Audhilda — rich, warrior-woman

Audhumbla, Audumla — myth name (a giant cow that nursed Ymir)

Audney — newfound wealth

Audun, Auduna — deserted

Bera — spirited

Bergdis — spirit protection

Bergthora — Thor's spirit

Bestla — myth name (mother of Odin)

Bifrost — myth name (a bridge)

Bjork — meaning unknown

Bodil, Bodile, Bodilla — fighting woman

Borgny — help

Borghild, Borghlide, Borghilda — myth name (wife of Sigmund)

Botilda — directing heroine

Brenda — sword

Brisingamen — myth name (Freya's necklace)

Brita, Britta, Brit — from Britain

Bryngerd — saga name (mother of Tongue-Stein)

Brynhild, Brynhilde, Brunhilda, Brunhild, Brunnehilde — armored, fighting woman

Brynja — dark

Dagny — joy of the Danes

Dahlia, Dalr — from the valley

Dale — a valley

Dalla — saga name (mother of Kormak)

Disa, Diss — spirited

Draupnir — myth name (Odin's magic ring)

Dyrfinna — deer, Finn

Edda, Eda — poetry

Eir — peace

Eldrid — fiery spirit

Elin — saga name (daughter of the Russian king Boleslaw)

Elle — old age

Elli — myth name (a giant)

Ellisif—consecrated to God

Embla—from an elm

Erica, Erika, Ricci, Rika—forever strong

Erna—myth name (wife of Jarl)

Fjarskafinn—meaning unknown

Fjorgyn—myth name (mother of Thor)

Freya, Freydis—noblewoman

Frida, Frieda—beautiful

Frigga—myth name (goddess of matrimonial love)

Frikka, Frika—peaceful ruler

Frodis—meaning unknown

Fulla—myth name (one of Frigga's ladies-in-waiting)

Gala, Gale—lovely voice

Geirbjorg—saga name (sister of Bersi the Godless)

Geirrid—saga name (sister of Geirrod)

Gerd, Gerda, Gerdie, Garthf— protection

Gimle—myth name (new heaven)

Ginnungagap—myth name (the abyss that births all living things)

Gjaflaug—meaning unknown

Gjalp—myth name (a giant)

Gna—myth name (one of Frigga's ladies-in-waiting)

Greip—myth name (a giant)

Grid—myth name (a wife of Odin)

Grima—feminine form of Grim

Grimhild, Grimhilda, Grimhilde— myth name (mother of Gudrun)

Gro, Groa—gardener

Gudrun, Guro, Gudrid—divinely inspired wisdom

Gullveig—myth name (a witch)

Gunhilde, Gunnhild, Gunhilda, Gunnhildr—battle-maid

Gunnlod—myth name (mother of Bragi)

Gunnvor—meaning unknown

Guri—lovely

Gutrune—myth name

Gyda, Gytha, Guthr—warlike

Hakan—noble

Haldana—half-Dane

Haldis, Halldis—firm helper

Haldora, Halldora—half-spirited

Halfrid, Hallfrid, Halfrida—half- beautiful

Halla, Hallgerd, Hallgerda—half- protected

Halveig, Hallveig—meaning unknown

Haralda—army ruler

Heidrun—myth name (the goat who supplies mead for the gods)

Hekja—saga name

Hel, Hela—myth name (goddess of the underworld)

Helga, Helge—holy

Helle—meaning unknown

Herdis—saga name (Bolli's daughter)

Hilde, Hild, Hilda, Hildur—myth name (a Valkyrie)

Hildegunn, Hildigunn—warrior- woman

Hiordis—myth name (second wife of Sigmund)

Hlif—saga name (mother of Atli)

Hrefna—saga name (daughter of Asgeir)

Hrodny — saga name (mother of Hoskuld)

Hulda — hidden

Hvergelmir — myth name (the home of Nidhug)

Hyndla — myth name (a giant)

Hyrna — saga name

Hyrrokkin — myth name (an ogre)

Idona, Idun, Iduna, Idunn — active in love

Ingeborg, Injerd, Ingibjorg — under Ing's protection

Ingemar — of the sea

Ingigerd — saga name (sister of Dagstygg)

Ingrid, Ingrit, Ingrida — beauty of Froy

Ingunn — loved by Froy

Jarngerd — saga name

Jarnsaxa — myth name (a giant)

Jofrid — saga name

Jord — myth name (daughter of Night)

Joreid — Saga name

Jorunn — chief's love

Katla — meaning unknown

Kelda — fountain

Kelsey, Kelci, Kelda — from the ship's island

Kirsten — Christian

Kjolvor — saga name

Kolfinna — saga name

Kriemhild, Kriemhilda, Kriemhilde — myth name (wife of Siegfried)

Lene, Line — distinguished

Lin — myth name (one of Frigga's ladies-in-waiting)

Linnea — lime-tree

Liv — life

Ljotunn — saga name

Lofn — myth name (goddess of lust)

Lofnheid, Lyngheid — myth name (sister of Otter)

Lopthaena — saga name

Maeva — saga name

Magna — strong

Magnild, Magnilde, Magnilda — strong fighter

Maria — name not originally Norse, but it appears in several sagas, and is the name of King Harald Sigurdsson's daughter (bitter)

Marianne — bitter grace

Melkorka — saga name (a deaf and mute concubine)

Menglad — myth name (won by Svipdag)

Mildri — mild and lovely

Mista — myth name (a Valkyrie)

Nanna — myth name (wife of Balder)

Nerthus — myth name (mother of earth)

Norberta, Njorthrbiartr — heroic

Norna, Norn — fate

Noss — myth name (daughter of Frey)

Oda, Odd — point

Oddfrid — beautiful point

Oddny — new point

Oddveig, Oddnaug — pointed woman

Ola — descendant

Olaug — of the ancestors

Olga — holy

Osk — saga name (mother of Hild)

Otkatla — saga name

Ragnfrid, Ragni, Randi—lovely, goddess

Ragnild, Ragnilde, Ragna, Ragnhild—goddess, warrior

Ran—myth name (a sea goddess)

Rana, Rania—nobility

Ranveig, Rannveig, Ronnaug— house-woman

Reidun—lovely in the nest

Rinda, Rind—myth name (a giant)

Rona, Runa—mighty strength

Ronalda—strong

Saehild—saga name

Saeunn—saga name (mother of Bergthora)

Saga—myth name (drank with Odin in her hall)

Sangrida—myth name (a Valkyrie)

Sif—myth name (Thor's second wife)

Sigrid, Sigrath—conquering advisor

Sign, Sigun, Signy—myth name (daughter of Volsung)

Sigyn—myth name (wife of Loki)

Sinmora—myth name (wife of Surt)

Sissel—without sight

Siv—kinswoman

Skade—myth name (goddess of skiers)

Skalm—saga name

Skuld—myth name (Norn of the future)

Snor, Snora—myth name (wife of Karl)

Snotra—myth name (self-discipline)

Solveig—house-woman

Steinunn—saga name

Steinvorr—saga name

Svanhild, Svanhile, Svenhilda, Svenhilde—swan, warrior

Swanhild, Swanhilda, Swanhilde—myth name (daughter of Sigurd)

Syn—myth name (invoked during trials)

Thaukt—myth name (a giant)

Thir—myth name (wife of Thrall)

Thjodhild, Thjodhilda—saga name

Thokk—myth name (a female disguise Thor used to keep Balder from returning to life)

Thorarin—saga name

Thorberta, Thorbiartr, Torberta—brilliance of Thor

Thorbjorg—protected by Thor

Thordis, Thordissa, Thoridyss, Thordia—spirit of Thor

Thorfinna—saga name (wife of Thorstein Kuggason)

Thorgerd—Thor's protection

Thorgunna, Torgunna, Thorgunn—Thor's fighter

Thorhalla—saga name (daughter of Asgrim)

Thorhild, Thorhilda—Thor's maiden

Thorkatla—Saga name (wife of Mord)

Thorunn, Thorunna, Torunn— saga name (mother of Bishop Bjorn)

Thrud—myth name (promised to Alvis)

Thurid—saga name (wife of Thorstein the Red)

Tora, Tordis, Thora, Thorir — Thor, goddess

Toril — Thor-inspired fighting woman

Torne, Torny, Torney — Thor, new

Torunn — Thor's love

Tove — good

Trine — pure

Trude, Truda — strong

Uald — ruler

Unn, Unne — love

Urd — myth name (Norn of the past)

Vaetild, Vaetilda — saga name (mother of the Skraeling children)

Valda — rules

Valdis — saga name (daughter of Thorbrand)

Valgerd — ruling protection

Valkyrie — myth name (Freya's priestesses)

Var — myth name (punishes adulterers)

Velaug — saga name (wife of Bjorn Buna)

Verdandi — myth name (Norn of the present)

Vigdis — saga name (wife of Killer-Hrapp)

Villborg — saga name

Volva — myth name (a prophetess)

Vor — myth name (an omniscient goddess)

Woglinda — myth name

Yggsdrasil — myth name (the tree that binds heaven, hell and earth)

Yngvild — saga name (mother of Bishop Brand)

Yule — born during Yule

MALE

Aage, Age, Ake — ancestors

Aesir, Aegir — of the gods

Aevar — saga name (son of Ketil)

Afi — grandfather

Alberich — myth name (a dwarf)

Alf — dead and living in the underworld

Alfarinn, Alfarin — saga name (son of Hlif)

Alfgeir — elfin spear

Alfrigg — myth name (a dwarf)

Alfrothul — of the sun

Alvis, Alviss — wise

Amhlaoibh, Auliffe — relic from the ancestor

Amund, Amundi — bridal gift

An — saga name (son of Grim Hairy-Cheek)

Ander — Norse form of Andrew (manly)

Anderson — son of Ander

Andvaranaut — myth name (Brunhild's ring)

Andvari — myth name (treasure guardian)

Annar — father of the world

Aren — rule of the eagle

Aricin, Arkin, Arkyn — eternal king's son

Arild — battle-commander

Armod — saga name (blood brother of Geirleif)

Arngeir — eagle spear

Arngrim — saga name

Arni — saga name (in Njal's saga, killer of Althing)

Arnlaug — eagle, devoted

Arnljot — frightens eagles

Aros — from the river's mouth

Arvakl — myth name (a horse)

Arvid, Arve — eagle tree

Asbiorn, Asbjorn — divine bear

Asgard — myth name (city of the gods)

Asgaut — divine Goth

Asgeir, Ansgar, Asgerd — spear of the gods

Asgrim — saga name (in Njal's saga, chieftain of Tongue)

Ashiepattle — legend name

Asi — saga name

Ask — from the ash tree

Askel, Askell — saga name (son of Dufniall)

Aslak — saga name (a supporter of Thorgest)

Asolf — saga name (a kinsman of Jorund)

Asrod — saga name (husband of Asvor)

Asvald — saga name (son of Ulf)

Atli — myth name (king of the Huns)

Aud — myth name (son of night)

Audolf — wolf's friend

Audun — friend of wealth

Avaldamon — saga name (name of a king)

Avang — saga name (an Irishman)

Balder, Baldur, Baldr — myth name (son of Odin)

Balki — saga name (son of Blaeng)

Balmung — myth name (Siegfried's sword)

Bard — good fighter

Bardi — saga name (son of Gudmund)

Baug — saga name (son of Raud)

Beinir — saga name (name of a smith)

Bekan — meaning unknown

Bergelmir — myth name (a giant)

Bergthor — Thor's spirit

Bersi — saga name (son of Balki)

Bifrost — myth name (the bridge from earth to Asgard)

Birger — rescue

Bjarne, Bjorn, Bjarni — bear

Bjolf — saga name (blood brother of Lodmund)

Bjornolf — bear-wolf

Blund — saga name

Bodil — leader

Bodmod — saga name (son of Oleif)

Bodolf — wolf leader

Bodvar — saga name (son of Thorleif)

Bolli — saga name (son of Thorleik)

Bolthor — myth name (a giant)

Bolverk — myth name (a disguise of Odin)

Booth, Bothi, Bothe — herald

Bor — myth name (father of Odin)

Borg — from the castle

Bori — myth name (father of Bor)

Bork — saga name (killed by Gunnar)

Bragi — myth name (god of poetry)

Brand, Brander, Brandr —
firebrand

Branstock — myth name (a tree in
Volsung's palace)

Brede — broad

Bresi — saga name

Brian, Bryan — strong

Brisingamen — myth name
(Freya's necklace)

Brokk — myth name (dwarf)

Brondolf — saga name (son of
Naddodd)

Bruin — legend name

Bruni — saga name (son of Earl
Harek)

Brynjolf — saga name (killed Atli)

Buri — meaning unknown

Burnaby, Bionbyr — warrior's
estate

Burr — young

Busby, Busbyr — dwells at the
village

Cadby — from the warrior's
settlement

Canute, Cnute, Cnut — knot

Carr — from the marsh

Cawley, Cauley — relic

Cort, Cortie — short

Crosby — dwells at the shrine of
the cross

Crow-Hreidar — saga name (son
of Ofeig Dangle-Beard)

Dag — day

Dain — myth name (a dwarf)

Dana, Dain, Dane, Denby, Danb,
Den, Denny, Derby, Danby,
Denby — from Denmark

Darby — from the deer estate

Davin, Davyn — intelligent

Delling, Dellingr — shining

Desiderio — desired

Digby, Dikibyr — from the dike
settlement

Donner — meaning unknown

Draupnir — myth name (armlet of
Odin)

Dreng — brave

Duartr — rich guard

Durin — myth name (a dwarf)

Dyre, Dyri — dear

Ederyn — myth name

Eggther — myth name (guardian
for the giants)

Egil, Eigil — inspires fright

Eilif — saga name (wounded in an
attack on Hlidarend)

Einar, Enar — fighter

Eirik, Erik — forever strong

Eitri — myth name (a dwarf)

Eldgrim — saga name (killed by
Hrut Herjolfsson)

Elphin — meaning unknown

Elvis — sage

Eric, Erik, Erick, Eirik, Eryk,
Eikki — eternal ruler

Erland — leader

Erling — chief's son

Erp — saga name (son of Meldun)

Esbjorn — bear of the gods

Eske — spear of the gods

Eskil — vessel of the gods

Etzel — myth name (Atila the
Hun)

Eyfrod — saga name (farmed at
Tongue)

Eyjolf — saga name (killed by
Kari)

Eystein, Eistein — lucky

Eyvind — saga name (son of
Lodin)

Fafnir, Fafner—myth name (a dragon)

Fasolt—myth name (killed by Fafnir)

Faste—firm

Fell, Fjall—from the rough hill

Fenrir, Fenris-wolf, Fenris— myth name (a monster wolf)

Finn—finder

Finnbogi—saga name (a merchant)

Floki—saga name (a heroic Viking)

Flosi—saga name (a chieftain)

Forseti—myth name (son of Balder)

Freki—myth name (Odin's wolf)

Frey, Freyr—myth name (god of weather)

Freystein—rock-hard, Frey (a goddess)

Freyvid—saga name

Fridleif—saga name (father of Ari)

Frode—wise

Galm—saga name (father of Thorvald)

Ganger—Saga name (a founder of Normandy)

Gardar—saga name (son of Svafar)

Gardi—saga name (a ghost)

Garm—myth name (guards the gate of Hel)

Garth, Garrett, Garet—defender

Gaute—great

Geir, Geiri—spear

Geirleif—spear descendant

Geirmund—saga name (son of Gunnbjorn)

Geirolf—wolf spear

Geirrod—myth name (brother of Geirrid)

Geirstein—rock-hard spear

Gest—saga name (son of Oddleif)

Gjallar—myth name (horn sounded for Ragnorok)

Gjest—stranger

Gilby—pledge

Gils—saga name (father of Hedin)

Gimle—myth name (new heaven)

Gizur—saga name (leader of the attack on Hlidarend)

Gleipnir—myth name (magic net woven to hold Fenrir)

Glistenheath—myth name (the place where Sigurd killed Fafnir)

Glum—saga name (an outlaw)

Gnup—saga name (took refuge in Iceland after several killings he performed)

Gram—myth name (Sigurd's sword)

Grani—Saga name (son of Gunnar)

Grenjad—saga name (son of Hermund)

Greyfell—myth name (Sigurd's horse)

Grim—saga name (son of Njal)

Grimkel—saga name (son of Ulf)

Gris—saga name (a man freed by Skallagrim)

Gudbrand, Gudbrande—weapon of the gods

Gudlaug—saga name (son of Asbjorn)

Gudmund—saga name (a chieftain)

Gullinbursti — myth name (the boar ridden by Freyr)

Gulltopp — myth name (the horse of Heimdall)

Gungir — myth name (Odin's spear)

Gunlaug, Gunnlaug — saga name (son of Illugi)

Gunnar — fighter

Gunnbjorn — fighting bear

Gunnolf — fighting wolf

Gunther — myth name (brother of Kriemhild)

Guttorm — myth name (brother of Gudrun)

Gymir — myth name (father of Gerd)

Gynt — legend name

Gyrd — saga name

Hafgrim — saga name (a settler of Greenland)

Hafnar — saga name (father of Thorgeir Cheek-Wound)

Hafthor — saga name

Hagen — myth name (killed Siegfried)

Haki — saga name (name of a slave)

Hakon, Haaken — of the chosen race

Hall — saga name (son of Helgi the Godless)

Hallbjorn — rock bear

Halldor — saga name (son of Gunnbjorn)

Hallfred — saga name (son of Ottar)

Hallkel — saga name (brother of Ketilbjorn)

Hallstein — saga name (Thorolf)

Hallvard — saga name (fought in the Battle of Hafursfjord)

Halvdan, Halden — half-Dane

Halvor, Halvard — rock defender

Hamar, Hammer — hammer

Hamund — saga name (son-in-law of Helgi the Lean)

Hans — legend name

Harald, Harold, Herrick, Harry, Hal, Herryk — war-chief

Hardar — saga name

Hardbein — saga name (son of Helga)

Hastein — saga name (son of Atli)

Hauk — hawk

Havelock, Hafleikr — sea war

Hedin — saga name (son of Thorstein Troll)

Heimdal — myth name (guardian of Bifrost)

Helgi — holy

Herjolf — saga name (father of Vapni)

Hermod — myth name (messenger of the gods)

Hermund — saga name (brother of Gunnlaug)

Hersir — saga name (a chieftain)

Hilario — cheerful

Hoder, Hodur, Hodr — myth name (a blind son of Odin)

Hoenir, Honir — myth name (brother of Odin)

Hofud — myth name

Hogna, Hogni — saga name

Holmstein — saga name (supported Flosi)

Hord — saga name (father of Asbjorn)

Hoskuld—saga name (son of Thorstein)

Hrafn—saga name (son of Hrafn)

Hrani—meaning unknown

Hrapp—saga name (father of Hrodgeir)

Hreidmar—myth name (dwarf king)

Hrifla—saga name

Hrimfaxi—myth name (a horse of night whose bridle drips the morning dew)

Hringham—meaning unknown

Hroald—saga name (brother of Eyvind Weapon)

Hrodgeir—saga name (son of Hrapp)

Hrolf—wolf

Hrolleif—old wolf

Hromund—saga name (son of Thori)

Hrosskel—saga name (son of Thorstein)

Hrut—saga name (son of Herjolf)

Hugi—myth name (a giant)

Hugin—thoughtful

Hunbogi—saga name (son of Alf)

Hvergelmir—myth name (home of Nidhug)

Illugi—saga name (son of Aslak)

Im—myth name (a giant)

Ing—myth name

Inger, Ingharr—son's army

Inghram, Ingram—Ing's raven

Ingimund—saga name

Ingjald—saga name (son of Helga)

Ingmar, Ingemar, Ingemur—famous son

Ingolf—Ing's wolf

Isleif—saga name (brother of Isrod)

Isolf—saga name (son of Hrani)

Isrod—saga name (brother of Isleif)

Johannes, Johanne—legend name

Jolgeir—saga name (brother of Radorm)

Jormungand—myth name (the serpent who encircles the earth)

Jorund—saga name (son of Hrafn the Foolish)

Jostein—saga name

Kalf—saga name (son of Asgeir)

Kali—meaning unknown

Kalman—saga name (a man from Ireland)

Kare, Kari—tremendous

Karli—manly

Karr, Kerr, Kiarr—from the marsh

Kell, Keldan—from the spring

Kelsey, Kiollsig, Kelsig—from the ship's island

Ketil—saga name (son of Thori)

Kirby, Kirkjabyr—from the church village

Kirk—dwells at the church

Kjarr, Kjartan—saga name (son of Olaf the Peacock)

Kleng—has claws

Klepp—saga name

Knud—kind

Knut, Knutr—knot

Kodran—saga name (father of Thjodgerd)

Kol—dark

Kolbein — saga name (son of Sigmund of Vestfold)

Kolbyr — from the dark settlement

Kolgrim — saga name (son of Hrolf)

Koll, Kolli — dark

Kollsvein — dark, young

Kolskegg — meaning unknown

Konal — saga name

Kort — short

Kotkel — saga name (a sorcerer)

Krossbyr — dwells at the shrine of the cross

Kuanbyr — from the woman's estate

Kveld — saga name

Kvist — saga name

Kylan — saga name (son of Kara)

Lambi — saga name (son of Thorbjorn the Feeble)

Lamont, Lamond, Lagmann — lawyer

Lang — tall

Leidolf — wolf descendant

Leif — descendant

Lidskjalf — myth name (throne of Odin)

Lodmund — saga name (blood brother of Bjolf)

Lodur — myth name (giver of senses)

Loki — myth name (god of destruction)

Lunt — from the grove

Lyting — saga name (brother of Thorstein Torfi)

Magni — myth name (one of the seven gods of the Aesir)

Magnor, Magnild, Magne, Magnus — fighter

Mani — saga name (father of Ketil)

Mar — saga name (son of Naddodd)

Mikkel — Norse form of Michael (godlike)

Mjolnir, Miolnir — myth name (Thor's hammer)

Modan — saga name

Modi — myth name (son of Thor)

Modolf — saga name

Mord — saga name

Mottul — saga name

Munin — myth name (memory)

Myrkjartan — saga name

Nagelfar — myth name (the ship that will carry the dead to Ragnarok)

Narfi — meaning unknown

Nidhug, Nidhogg — myth name (a dragon)

Nithhogg — myth name

Njal, Njall — saga name (son of Thorgeir)

Njord — myth name (father of Freya)

Norbert, Norberto, Njorthrbiartr — hero

Odd — point

Oddleif — point descendant

Oddvar — pointable

Odell — wealthy

Odin, Othin — myth name (god of the sky)

Olave, Oilibhear, Olaf, Olin, Olyn, Olen, Ola, Ole, Olav, Olof — relic

Oleif — relic descendant

Oliver, Olvaerr, Olvir — affectionate

Onund — saga name (son of Viking)

Orebjorn — saga name

Orlyg — saga name (son of Valthjof)

Orm — saga name (son of Ulf)

Orn — saga name (father of Idunn)

Ornolf — saga name (son of Armod)

Os — divine

Oscar, Oskar — divine spear

Osgood — divine Goth

Ospak — saga name (brother of Gudrun)

Osvif — saga name (father of Gudrun)

Otkel — saga name

Ottar — fighter

Ovaegir — saga name (father of the Skraeling children)

Ove — ancestors

Oysten, Ostein, Osten — happy

Ozur — saga name (son of Thorleif)

Quimby — from the woman's estate

Radorm — saga name (brother of Jolgeir)

Ragi — saga name

Ragnarok — myth name (the final battle of the gods)

Ragnor, Ragnar, Raynor, Rainer — warrior from the gods

Raud — saga name (father of Ulf)

Ref — saga name

Regin — myth name (a blacksmith)

Reidar, Reider — fighter of the nest

Reist — saga name (son of Bjarn-Isle)

Reynard — legend name

Roar — fighter of praise

Rognvald — saga name (earl of Orkney)

Rolf — wolf

Roscoe, Raskogr — from the deer forest

Rothwell, Rauthuell — dwells near the red spring

Royd, Riodhr — dwells in the clearing in the forest

Rungnir — myth name (a giant killed by Thor)

Runolf — saga name (son of Ulf)

Rutland, Rotland — from the root land

Saehrimnir — myth name (a magic boar)

Siggeir — myth name (king of the Goths)

Sigmund — saga name (son of Volsung)

Sigurd, Sigvard, Sigurdhr, Siv, Sijur, Syver, Sigvat — victorious defender

Sindri — myth name (a dwarf)

Sinfiotli — myth name (son of Siggeir)

Skagi — saga name (son of Skopta)

Skalla — saga name

Skallagrim — saga name

Skamkel — saga name

Skapti — saga name

Skarp, Skarphedin — saga name

Skefil — saga name

Skeggi — saga name (son of Bodolf)

Skerry, Skereye — rocky island

Skidbladnir — myth name (the magical ship of Freyr)

Skinfaxi — myth name (stallion of the daylight)

Skipp — shipmaster

Skirnir — myth name (a servant of Freyr)

Skorri — saga name

Skrymir — myth name (king of the giants)

Skule, Skuli — hide

Skum — saga name

Sleipnir — myth name (Odin's horse)

Snaebjorn — saga name (son of Eyvindar)

Snorri — saga name (son of Thorfinn)

Solmund — saga name

Solvi — saga name (a farmer)

Soren — of Thor

Starkad — saga name

Starkadhr — myth name (a fierce warrior)

Stein — rock-hard

Steinar — rock-hard fighter

Steinbjorn — rock bear

Steinolf — rock wolf

Steinthor — Thor's rock

Stian — swift

Stigandi — saga name (son of Kotkel)

Storr — great

Strifebjorn — saga name (father of Ornolf)

Sturla — saga name

Styr — saga name (a supporter of Erik)

Sumarlidi — saga name (son of Killer-Hrapp)

Surtr — myth name (a giant)

Sutherland, Suthrland — from the south

Svaldifari — myth name (a stallion)

Svan, Svann — swan

Svart, Svartkel — saga name (father of Thorkel)

Svend, Svein, Svewn, Sveyn — young

Sverting — saga name (son of Runolf Ulfsson)

Tait, Tayte — happy

Tanni — saga name

Tarnkappe — myth name (a cloak that renders its wearer invisible)

Terje, Torgeir, Torger, Tarjei — spear of Thor

Thangbrand — saga name (a missionary)

Thialfi, Thjalfi — myth name (a servant of Thor)

Thor, Tor — myth name (god of thunder)

Thorald, Thorualdr, Torald — Thor ruler

Thorarin — saga name (son of Thorkol)

Thorbert, Thorbiartr — the glorious, Thor

Thorbjorn, Thorburn — bear of Thor

Thord — saga name (son of Viking)

Thorfinn — saga name (killed Einar)

Thorgils—saga name (father of Ingjald)

Thorgrim—saga name (brother of Onund Bild)

Thorhadd—saga name (son of Stein)

Thorhall, Thorhalli—saga name

Thorir—saga name (son of Asa)

Thorkel—saga name (a sorcerer)

Thorlak—saga name (bishop of Skalholt)

Thorleif—Thor's descendant

Thorleik—saga name (son of Bolli)

Thormod—saga name (son of Odd)

Thorolf—Thor's wolf

Thororm—saga name

Thorstein—Thor's rock

Thorvald—saga name (son of Asvald)

Thorvid—saga name (son of Ulfar)

Thrain—saga name

Thrand—saga name (brother of Eyvind the Easterner)

Thrasi—saga name (son of Thorolf)

Throst—saga name (son of Hermund)

Thrym—myth name (a giant)

Thurlow—from Thor's hill

Tind—saga name

Tjasse—myth name (a giant)

Torfi—saga name

Torgny—clamor of weapons

Torrad—saga name (son of Osvif)

Trigg, Trygg, Tryggr—true

Trond, Tron—growing

Trygve—brave victory

Turfeinar—saga name (son of Rognvald)

Turpin, Thorfinn—thunder Finn

Tuxford—from the spearman's ford

Tyr, Tiu—myth name (god of war)

Tyrkir—saga name (a German)

Uigbiorn, Ugbjorn—war bear

Ulf—wolf

Ulfar—saga name

Ull—myth name (god of skiers)

Ulmer, Ulfmaerr—famous wolf

Uni—saga name (a Dane)

Ura—from the corner property

Utgard-Loki—myth name (a king of the giants)

Valbrand—saga name

Valgard—saga name

Vali—myth name (son of Odin)

Valthjof—saga name (son of Orlyg)

Vandrad—saga name (son of Osvif)

Vanir—myth name (a god of rain)

Ve—myth name (giver of feeling)

Vegard—protection

Vegeir—great sacrificer

Velief—saga name

Vestar—saga name (son of Thorolf)

Vestein—saga name (son of Vegeir)

Vibald—saga name

Vidar—tree-fighter

Vifil—saga name (father of Thornbjorn)

Vigfus—saga name

Vigrid—battleground

Vigsterk—saga name

Viking—saga name (father of Thord)

Vili—myth name (giver of reason)

Volsung—saga name (ruler of the Huns)

Wray—from the corner property

Wyborn, Wybjorn—war bear

Ymir—myth name (a giant)

Yngvar—saga name

Yrar—saga name

Persian

Persian surnames were not used until 1926, when new laws forced everyone to register a surname and all married women to take the name of their husband's family. Nicknames were not tolerated. Only two names are used, the given and the surname. Many citizens added a place name to their surname with a hyphen. The place name is usually followed by the suffix -i.

A few Persian surnames:

Borzorg	Guebers
Borzorg-Alavi	Mehran
Caspari	Pahlavi
Feroz	Shabouh
Gazsi	Vali

FEMALE

Amira — feminine form of Amir (king)
Azar, Azara — scarlet
Azura, Azur — blue
Cyra — moon
Daria, Darya — preserver
Darice — queen
Esther — star
Farah — happy
Farideh — delightful
Gatha — song
Golnar — fire
Hester, Hetty, Hestia — star
Jaleh — rain
Jasmine, Jessamine — jasmine
Laleh — flower
Lila, Lilac — lilac
Marjan — coral
Minau — heaven
Mitra — angel's name
Nahid — myth name
Narda — anointed
Pari — myth name
Parvaneh — butterfly
Roxana, Roxanne — bright
Sadira — dreamy
Shabnan — raindrop
Shahdi — happy
Shahin — eagle
Sholeh — fire
Simin — silver
Soraya — name of a princess
Soroushi — happiness
Taraneh — song
Vashti — beautiful
Zenda — womanly

MALE

Ahura Mazda — wise lord
Amir — king
Asha — myth name (protector of fire)
Assim — great one
Bahram — name of a Persian king
Balthasar — war advisor
Behrooz — lucky
Caspar, Casper — treasure
Cyrus — sun
Dareh — rich
Darioush — name of a king
Darius — preserver
Feroz — lucky
Gaspar, Gazsi — treasure master
Ghebers, Guebers — followers of ancient Persian religion
Jamsheed — a Persian
Jasper — treasurer
Kansbar — treasure master
Kaveh — name of a hero
Ksathra — ruler
Kurush — myth name
Majeed — superior
Majnoon — a historical name
Mehrdad — gift from the sun
Melchior — king
Nasim — breeze
Saeed, Said, Soroush — happy
Shabouh — meaning unknown
Shatrevar — myth name (power)
Sohrab — name of a hero
Soroush — happiness
Val — high hill
Xerxes — prince

Polish

Polish surnames are patronymic, occupational or descriptive. Place names are also used. By 1500, most of the nobility had surnames ending with -ski or -ska that were distributed by the king as a way of honoring them. Surnames derived from saints' names were used by the urban classes. Polish names are used in the genitive case.

Common suffixes:

-yk, -ak, -ek, -czyk, -czak, -czek — little
-slaw (males), -slawa (female) — glory
-dski, -cki, -ski (male), -ska (female) — these suffixes linked aristocrats' names with the estates they owned.

When used with a Christian name by the lower classes, these suffixes meant son or daughter of.

-owski — place name
-lis — male
-lisowa — married woman
-lisowna — unmarried female

A few Polish surnames:

Cegielski	Dlugosz
Chodakowsk	Dolinski
Chudzik	Klimas
Dekownik	Klimek
Denys	Kryszka

FEMALE

Adelajda — Polish form of Adelaide (noble)

Albinka — blond

Aldona — old

Alina — beautiful

Alka — intelligent

Anastazja — Polish form of Anastasia (reborn)

Ania, Anka — grace

Anieli — masculine

Antonina — Polish form of Antonia (priceless)

Balbina — stammers
Basha — stranger
Beate, Beata — blesses
Bodgana, Bohgana, Bogna — gift of God
Celinka, Celek — myth name
Doroata — Polish form of Dorothy (gift from God)
Edyta — Polish form of Edith (wealthy gift)
Elwira — Polish form of Elvira (white)
Elzbieta — Polish form of Elizabeth (consecrated to God)
Euzebia — pious
Ewa — Polish form of Eva (brings life)
Felka, Fela — lucky
Franciszka — free
Gizela — pledge
Grazyna — grace
Gutka — good
Halina — light
Henka, Heniuta — Polish form of Henrietta (rules the home)
Hortenspa — Polish form of Hortensia (farmer)
Iwona — Polish form of Yvonne (bow of yew)
Jadwiga — refuge in war
Janecska, Jana, Jasia, Joanka — Polish form of Joanna (God is gracious)
Jolanta — violet
Kamilka, Kamilla — ceremonial attendant
Kassia, Kasienka, Kaska — pure
Katarzyna, Katrine, Katya, Katine — Polish form of Katherine (pure)

Krystynka, Krysta, Krystka, Krystyn — Christian
Kunigunde, Kunegundy — name of a queen
Lechsinska — wood nymph
Lidia — from Lydia
Lila — of the people
Lilka, Ludka, Lodoiska, Luisa — famous battle-maid
Lucja, Lucyna — Polish form of Lucille (light)
Malgorzata, Margisia — Polish form of Margaret (pearl)
Marta, Masia, Marysia, Macia — bitter
Marzina — warlike
Matyidy — Polish form of Matilda (mighty battle-maid)
Mela, Melka — dark
Minka — strong
Morela — apricot
Nadzia, Nata, Natia — hope
Nelka — stone
Olesia — Polish form of Alexandra (defends mankind)
Otylia — lucky heroine
Paulina — little
Petronela, Petra — stone
Rahel — Polish form of Rachel (lamb)
Rasia — regal
Rasine — rose
Roch — glory
Rozyczka, Roz, Rozalia — rose
Sylwia — Polish form of Sylvia (from the woods)
Tekli — Polish form of Tekla (divine fame)
Teodory, Teodozji — gift from God
Tesia — farmer

Vanda — Polish form of Wanda (wanders)
Weronikia — Polish form of Veronica (brings victory)
Wikitoria, Wiktorja, Wikta — Polish form of Victoria (victory)

Wirke, Wira — white
Yachne — gracious
Zanna — God's gracious gift
Zefiryn — zephyr
Zuzanny — Polish form of Suzanne (lily)
Zytka, Zyta — strong

MALE

Adok — dark
Adolf — noble wolf
Albin — white
Aleksandr, Aleksy — Polish form of Alexander (defends mankind)
Andrzej — Polish form of Andrew (manly)
Apoloniusz — Polish form of Apollo (god of the sun)
Armand, Armandek — soldier
Aron — exalted
Artur — Polish form of Arthur (bear)
Augustyn — Polish form of Augustus (majestic)
Aurek, Aureli — blond
Bazyli — kingly
Bendyk, Bendek — Polish form of Benedict (blessed)
Bialy, Bialas — white-haired
Bogumil — God's peace
Boguslaw — God's glory
Borys — stranger
Boryslaw — stranger, glory
Casimir, Kazmer — announcing peace
Cyprian — from Cyprus
Cyrek, Cyryl — lordly
Czeslaw — fortress glory
Dionizy — Polish form of

Dionysus (god of wine)
Dobieslaw — glory of Dionysus
Dobry — goodly
Dodek — hero
Donat — gift
Dorek — gift from God
Dymitr — meaning unknown
Elek — blond
Emmilian — active
Erek, Eryk — lovable
Feliks — Polish form of Felix (lucky)
Flawiusz — blond
Florian — flowering
Franciszk — Polish form of Francis (free)
Fryderyk — Polish form of Frederick (peaceful ruler)
Gerik — wealthy spearman
Gerwazy — warrior
Grzegorz — Polish form of Gregory (watchful)
Henryk — Polish form of Henry (rules the home)
Hieronim — Polish form of Jerome (sacred)
Holleb — dove
Jack, Janek, Jan — God's gracious gift
Jarek, Januarius — born in January
Jedrik, Jedrus — strong

Jerzy — Polish form of George (farmer)

Josep — Polish form of Joseph (God shall add)

Kazimierz — declares peace

Konstancji — constant

Krzysztof — Polish form of Christopher (Christ-bearer)

Laiurenty — Polish form of Lawrence (laurel)

Liuz — light

Lubomir — loves peace

Lucjan — Polish form of Lucian (light)

Ludoslaw, Luboslaw — loves glory

Ludwik — renowned warrior

Lukasz — Polish form of Lucas (light)

Maksym, Maksymilian — Polish form of Maximillian (great)

Mandek — warrior

Marek, Marcinek — warlike

Maury, Maurycy — Moorish

Mikolaj, Mikolai — Polish form of Nicholas (victory of the people)

Miron — peace

Nelek — horn

Nikodem — conqueror of the people

Oles — Polish form of Alexander (defends mankind)

Onufry — meaning unknown

Patryk — Polish form of Patrick (noble)

Pawelek, Pawel, Pawl — Polish form of Paul (little)

Piotr, Pietrek — Polish form of Peter (rock)

Radoslaw — loves peace

Rafal — Polish form of Raphael (God heals)

Rajmund — Polish form of Raymond (mighty)

Rufin — red-haired

Ryzard — Polish form of Richard (strong ruler)

Sergiusz — Polish form of Sergio (attendant)

Seweryn — severe

Stefan, Szczepan — crown

Telek — cuts iron

Teodor — Polish form of Theodore (ruler)

Tomislaw — glory of the twin

Tolek, Teos — gift of God

Waldemar — mighty, famous

Walerian, Waleron — brave, strong

Wienczyslaw — victory

Wiktor — Polish form of Victor (victor)

Wincent, Wicus — Polish form of Vincent (victor)

Wit — life

Zarek — God protect the king

Ziven — alive and vigorous

Zygmunt — conquering protection

Russian

Russian began to use surnames in the fifteenth century. The name format is surname first, then the given name and a name in genitive case referring to the father. The naming system was originally used only by princes; then it was adopted by the rest of the nobility. Commoners used their given name combined with a nickname.

Certain suffixes were controlled by the Czar or Czarina. Under Empress Catherine, for example, the right to use -ovich was extended to include the first five grades of civil servants. The sixth to the eighth grades could use -ov (-ova) or -ev (-eva). Later, the rest of the populace was allowed to use -ev (-eva) and -ov (-ova).

Common suffixes:

-sky, -ski, -ska — nature of or like
-ov, -ova, -ovna, -ev, -eva, -evna — of
-oy — used for nicknames
-ik — occupational names

Married couples decide which surname to use. If the wife's surname is chosen, the couple will later decide which name their children will use. Women use the -a suffixes.

A few Russian surnames:

Babin	Ivanov
Baklanov	Krestyanov
Balakirev	Petrov
Chapaev	Smirnov
Dyakonov	Varvarinski

FEMALE

Agafia — Russian form of Agatha (good)

Agrafina — born feetfirst

Agnessa — meek

Akilina — eagle

Alena — Russian form of Helen (light)

Alexandra, Aleksandra — defender of man

Alina — beautiful

Alla, Allochka — meaning unknown

Amaliji — Russian form of Amelia (industrious)

Anastasia, Stasya, Nastya — reborn

Antonina — feminine form of Anton (beyond praise)

Anya, Anitchka, Anna, Anechka, Asenka — grace

Arkadina — meaning unknown

Avdotya — meaning unknown

Charlotta — masculine

Dasha, Doroteya — God's gift

Devora — Russian form of Debra (bee)

Dimitra — from Demeter

Dominika — born on Sunday

Dunyasha — meaning unknown

Duscha — geist

Ekaterina — Russian form of Katherine (pure)

Elga — holy

Evelina, Eva — life

Evgenia — Russian form of Eugenia (noble)

Feodora — feminine form of Feodor (gift from God)

Galenka, Galine, Galya — God has redeemed

Helenka — light

Helga — holy

Ilia — the Lord is God

Irena, Irina — peace

Irisa — rainbow

Ivana, Ivane — feminine of Ivan (God's gracious gift)

Kira, Kirochka — Russian form of Helen (light)

Kisa — kitten

Kiska, Katya, Katarina, Katyenka, Katyuska, Katherina — pure

Ksana, Ksanochka — praise be to God

Lada — myth name

Lara, Larisa, Lanassa — cheerful

Lenusya — flower

Lidija, Lidia, Lidiya, Lidochka, Lida — from Lydia

Lubmilla — loving

Lyudmila, Lyuba, Lyubochka, Luda, Ludmila — love of the people

Margarete, Margosha — Russian form of Margaret (pearl)

Marianne, Marianna — rebellious

Marinochka, Marina — from the sea

Masha, Mara, Marisha, Manya, Mura, Maruska, Marusya — bitter

Mavra — dark

Milena, Mila — people's love

Nadia, Nadezhda, Nadyenka, Nadenka — hope

Narkissa — daffodil

Natasha, Natascha, Nitca, Natassia, Natalia, Natyashenka — born at Christmas

Nesha, Nessa, Nesya — Russian form of Agnes (pure)

Nikolaevna, Nika — belongs to God

Ninockha, Nina — grace

Oksanochka, Oksana — praise be to God

Olena — light

Olga, Olya, Olenka, Olechka — holy

Orlenda — eagle
Parasha, Parashie, Pasha — born
on Good Friday
Pauline, Paulina — little
Rahil — Russian form of Rachel
(lamb)
Ranevskaya, Ranya — meaning
unknown
Sabina — a Sabine
Sacha, Sasha, Sashenka —
defender of man
Sinovia, Sinya — stranger
Sonia, Sonya, Sonechka — wise
Stephania, Stefanya, Stesha,
Panya — feminine form of
Stephan (crowned with
laurels)
Svetlana, Sveta — luminescent
Tanya, Tania, Tanechka,
Tatyana, Tatiana, Tanichka —
myth name
Tasya — resurrected
Theodosia, Theda, Thedya —
God's gift
Ursola, Ursula — little bear
Valentina — brave

Valeska — victorious leader
Vania, Vanya — gift of God
Varvara, Varya, Varinka,
Varushka — stranger
Vassillissa, Vasilissa, Vasya —
royal
Velika — wonderful
Verochka, Vera — true
Viveka — beautiful voice
Vilma — Russian form of Wilma
(determined protector)
Yalena, Yalenchka — Russian
form of Helen (light)
Yelizaveta — Russian form of
Elizabeth (consecrated to God)
Yuliya, Yulenka — Russian form of
Julia (youthful)
Zaneta — gift from God
Zenevieva — Russian form of
Genevieve (white shoulders)
Zenochka, Zena — from Zeus
Zenya, Zenechka — Russian form
of Eugenia (noble)
Zinerva — Russian form of
Minerva (wise)
Zoyechka, Zoyenka, Zoya — life

MALE

Adrik — dark
Alek, Alik, Aleksandr, Aleksis,
Aleksi, Alexei — helper of man
Aloyoshenka, Aloysha — defends
mankind
Anatolii — from the east
Andrusha, Andrya, Andrei —
Russian form of Andrew
(manly)
Antosha, Antinko, Anton —
inestimable
Arman — protective

Bogdashka, Bohdan — gift from
God
Bolodenka — peaceful
Borya, Boryenka, Boris — fighter
Brencis — Russian form of
Stephen (crowned with
laurels)
Brody — from Brody
Burian — lives near the weeds
Cheslav — lives in a strong camp
Danya — God's gift
Deniska — myth name

Dima — strong fighter

Dimitri — from Demeter

Edik, Eduard — rich protector

Egor — Russian form of George (farmer)

Evgenii — Russian form of Eugene (noble)

Fabiyan, Fabi — Russian form of Fabian (bean farmer)

Fadeyka, Fadey, Faddei — brave

Fedor, Fedya, Fyodor, Fedyenka — God's gift

Fedyenka, Fyodor — Russian form of Theodore (gift from God)

Feliks — Russian form of Felix (lucky)

Fiers — meaning unknown

Filip — Russian form of Philip (loves horses)

Foma — twin

Fredek — Russian form of Frederick (peaceful ruler)

Gavril, Ganya, Gav, Gavrel, Gavrilovich — worships God

Gayeff — meaning unknown

Grisha, Grigori, Grigorii, Grisha — watchful

Hedeon — destroyer

Helge — holy

Igoryok, Igor — farmer

Ilya — meaning unknown

Ioakim, Iov — from Job

Ivan — Russian form of John (gracious gift from God)

Jasha — supplanter

Jermija — Russian form of Jeremiah (God's appointed one)

Jov — form of Job (persecuted)

Jurg, Jeirgif — Russian form of George (farmer)

Karolek, Karol — strong

Kiryl, Kiril — noble

Kolenka, Kolya — of the conquering people

Kostenka, Kostya, Konstantine — constant

Laurentij — Russian form of Lawrence (laurel)

Leonide, Lenya, Lyonechka, Levushka, Levka, Lyonya, Lev, Levka — lion

Lopahin — meaning unknown

Lukasha, Lukyan, Luka — Russian form of Lucas (light)

Maks, Maksimillian — great

Matvey, Motka, Matyash — God's gift

Mishenka, Mishe, Misha, Mikhail — Russian form of Michael (God-like)

Moriz — Moorish

Nicolai, Nikita — Russian form of Nicholas (victory of the people)

Oleg, Olezka — holy

Pashenka, Pavlushka, Pavlushshenka, Pavlusha, Pavla, Pavlya, Pavel, Pavlov — little

Petenka, Pyotr, Petya — stone

Romochka, Roman — a Roman

Rurik — noted ruler

Sacha, Sasha, Shura, Shurochka, Sanya, Shurik, Shashenka — defender of man

Semyon — Russian form of Simon (God is heard)

Seriozha, Seriozhenka, Serge, Serguei — an attendant

Stanislov, Slavik—glory

Stefan, Stepka, Stephan—
Russian form of Stephen
(crowned with laurels)

Tolenka, Tolya—from the east

Tosya, Tusya—beyond
expectation

Trofimoff—meaning unknown

Valerik, Valerii—brave

Vanechka, Vanyusha—God's gift

Vassily, Vassi, Vasya, Vas,
Vasilii—royal

Vitenka, Viktor—victor

Vladislav, Vladik, Vyacheslav—
has glory

Vladmir, Vladmiri—has peace

Vladsislas—meaning unknown

Volodya, Vladik, Vladya—
peaceful

Yakov—supplanter

Yaremka, Yerik—appointed by
God

Yasha—defends man

Yermolay—meaning unknown

Yuri, Yurii, Yurik, Yura,
Yurochka—farmer

Zhenechka, Zhenya—noble

Zhorah, Zorya—farmer

Ziven, Zivon—alive

Scandinavian

Scandinavian surnames are dealt with in the sections on current names in Norway, Sweden, Finland and so on.

FEMALE

Dana — myth name
Darda — a dart
Donalda — feminine form of Donald (dark one)
Edda — myth name
Frigga, Frig — myth name
Inga, Inge, Ingunna, Ingaborg — hero's daughter
Iwona — archer

Katrina, Karen — pure
Kirsten — Christian
Nada — hope
Nissa, Nisse, Nysse, Nyssa — friendly elf
Quenby — womanly
Ray, Rae — doe
Viveca, Viveka — life

MALE

Apsel — father of peace
Arles — pledge
Ashby — from the ash tree
Bergen, Bergin — mountain dweller
Bergren, Berggren — from the mountain branch
Carrson — son of Carr
Daegal — dawn
Dana, Dane, Dain — from Denmark
Davin, Daven, Dagfinnr — bright Finn
Denby — from the Danish settlement
Igor — hero
Ing — myth name
Ingvar — Ing's army

Ivor, Ivar, Iver — archer
Jens — God is gracious
Knut — knot
Lamont — lawyer
Lars — victorious
Larson — son of Lars
Latham — from the barns
Niels, Nils — champion
Paavo — little
Pedar — stone
Quinby — from the woman's estate
Royd — from the forest clearing
Tait — mirth
Thurston — Thor's stone
Welby — from the farm by the spring
Whitby — from the white dwelling

Scottish

Almost all surnames are clan and sept names that originated as patronymic names with the prefixes Mack-, Mac-, Ap- and P-, which mean son of. Members of clans belong to one of two categories: native men (men born to the clan and related by blood) and broken men (men from other clans who are under the Laird's protection).

Like Irish names, Scottish surnames are among the oldest in Europe. Highlander surnames developed separately from those in the lowlands. The lowlander surnames were more like the English and borrowed many English descriptive and place names.

In retaliation for acts by the clan against the crown, the name MacGregor was abolished from 1617 until 1661—to bear that name during the ban invited execution.

A few surnames:

Highlands:
Macauley	MacEwen
Maccallum	MacIntyre
MacDonald	MacKay
MacDougall	MacKinnon
MacDuff	MacLean

Lowlands:
Anderson	Grant
Crawford	Henderson
Douglas	Lawson
Gibson	Marshall
Gordon	Russell

FEMALE

Akira—anchor

Aila—from the strong place

Aileana, Aileen—from the green meadow

Alison—Scottish form of Louise (battle famous)

Alpina—blond

Anice—Scottish form of Ann (grace)

Annabel, Annabella—beautiful

grace

Athdara, Adaira, Adairia—from the oak-tree ford

Beathas—wise

Bonnie, Bonny—beautiful

Bradana—salmon

Cadha—from the steep place

Cailleach, Caillic—hag

Caroline—feminine form of Charles (manly)

Christel, Christal—Christian

Coira, Cora—seething pool

Colina—victory of the people

Cullodena, Cullodina—from the broken, mossy ground

Cumina—from Comines

Daracha—from the oak

Eara, Earie—from the east

Edina, Edine, Edeen—from Edinburgh

Eiric, Eirica—ruler

Erskina—from the top of the cliff

Evanna, Evina—right-handed

Fearchara, Fearcharia—dear one

Fenella—Scottish form of Finola

Fia—dark of peace

Firtha—arm of the sea

Forba, Forbia—headstrong

Fyfa—from Fifeshire

Gara, Garia, Gaira—short

Gavina, Gavenia—white hawk

Gilbarta—pledge

Gordania, Gordana—heroic

Grizel, Grizela—Scottish form of Grizelda (gray-haired)

Gunna—white

Inghean, Inghinn—daughter

Isobel, Iseabal—Scottish form of Isabel (consecrated to God)

Jean—Scottish form of Joan (gracious gift from God)

Lainie, Leana—serves John

Lair, Laire, Lara—mare

Larena, Laren, Laria—serves Lawrence

Lioslaith, Leslie—dwells at the gray fortress

Machara—plain

Mairi, Moire, Muire—bitter

Maisie, Mai, May, Maggie—Scottish form of Margaret (pearl)

Malmuira, Malmuirie—dark-skinned

Marcail—pearl

Moibeal—lovable

Moireach—lady

Muira, Muire—from the moor

Nairne, Nairna—dwells at the alder-tree river

Nathaira, Nathara—snake

Nessa, Nessia—from the headland

Nighean, Nighinn—young woman

Odara, Odaria—meaning unknown

Raoghnailt—lamb

Robena, Robina—robin

Rose—flower

Sileas—youthful

Sima—listener

Siubhan—praised

Siusan—lily

Skena—from Skene

Struana—from the stream

Tara—myth name (hill where the kings met)

Tavia, Teva—twin

Tira, Tyra—land

Torra—from the castle
Vika—from the creek

Wynda—from the narrow passage

MALE

Abhainn, Aibne—river
Acair, Akir, Acaiseid—anchor
Achaius—friend of a horse
Adhamh—of the earth
Ailbert—noble
Ailean—handsome
Ailein—from the green meadow
Aillig, Ail—from the stony place
Aindreas—strong
Alastair, Alasdair—defender of man
Albanact—myth name
Alpin—blond
Amhuinn—from the alder-tree river
Angus, Aengus, Aonghus—unnaturally strong
Aoidh—spirited
Argyle, Arregaithel—from the land of the Gauls
Armstrong, Armstrang—strong arm
Artair—bear
Athdar, Adair—from the oak-tree ford
Bac, Bhaic—bank
Baird—from Baird
Balfour—from the pastureland
Balgair, Balgaire—fox
Balloch—from the pasture
Balmoral—from the majestic village
Barclay—from Berkeley
Bean, Baen—fair-skinned
Bearnard—bear strong
Beathan—son of the right hand

Beth—lively
Bhaltair—strong fighter
Biast, Beiste—beast
Birk—from a birch tree
Blair—peat moss
Both, Bothan, Bothain—from the stone house
Braden, Bhradain—salmon
Braigh, Bhraghad—from the upper part
Breac, Bhreac, Brice, Bryce, Bhric—speckled
Broc—badger
Brochan, Brochain—broken
Brodie—from Brodie
Bruce—from Bruys
Buchanan—from the cannon's seat
Busby—meaning unknown
Cailean, Caillen—virile
Caladh—harbor
Callum—bald dove
Cam, Chaim, Crom, Cruim—crooked
Camden, Camdin, Camdan, Camdyn—from the winding valley
Cameron, Camshron—crooked nose
Campbell, Cam, Camp, Cambeul—crooked mouth
Carlton, Caraidland—from the land between the streams
Carmichael—friend of Saint Michael

Carr, Cathair—from the broken, mossy ground

Cat, Chait—catlike

Cawley, Cauley, Camhlaidh—relic

Ceard, Ceardach—smith

Chalmer, Chalmers—rules the home

Chattan—clan of the cats

Chisholm—from Chisolm

Christie, Christy—Christian

Clach—stone

Cleit—rocky eminence

Clennan—Finnian's servant

Colin—victory of the people

Colquhoun—from Colquhoun

Corey, Cory, Coire—seething pool

Craig—dwells at the crag

Crannog—lake dweller

Creighton—from the farm by the creek

Cromwell—from the crooked well

Culloden—from the nook of the marsh

Cumin, Comyn, Cumming—from Comines

Cunningham—from Cunningham

Dallas, Daileass—from the waterfall

Dalziel, Dalyell—from the little field

Damh, Daimh—ox

Darach—oak

Davis, Dave, Davidson, MacDaibhidh—David's son

Dearg—red

Doire, Dhoire—from the grove

Donel, Donell, Domhnull—all-ruler

Doughall, Dougal—black stranger

Douglas, Dubhglas—from the dark water

Dour—from the water

Drummand, Drummond—at the ridge

Duff, Dubh—black

Duncan, Donnchadh, Donnachadh—brown warrior

Dunmore, Dunmor—from the great hill fortress

Eanruig—rules the home

Ear, Earie—from the east

Eigg—meaning unknown

Eilig—from the deer pass

Elliot—old Welshman

Erskine—from the top of the cliff

Evan—right-handed

Fang, Faing—from the sheep pen

Farlan, Farlane—son of the furrows

Farquharson—son of the dear one

Feandan—from the narrow glen

Fearchar—dear one

Fergus—first choice

Fergusson, Ferguson—son of the first choice

Fie—dark of peace

Firth—arm of the sea

Fletcher—maker of arrows

Forbes—headstrong

Fraser—strawberry flowers

Fyfe, Fibh—from Fifeshire

Gare, Gair—short

Gavin, Gawain, Gawen, Gawyn, Gaven—white hawk

Gilleabart—pledge

Gilleasbuig—bold

Gillecriosd — Christ-bearer
Gillivray — servant of judgment
Goraidh — peaceful
Gordan, Gordain — hero
Gow, Gobha, Gowan — a smith
Graham — from the gray home
Grant — great
Gregor, Griorgair — vigilant
Gunn — white
Hamilton — from Hameldone
Harailt — leader
Hay, Haye — from the stockade
Henson, Henderson,
   MacKendrick — son of Henry
Home, Hume — from the cave
Houston — from Hugh's town
Ian, Iain — gift from God
Innes — from Innes
Irvin, Irving — from the city
Iver — archer
Johnson — son of John
Johnston — from John's farm
Kay, Kai — fire
Keith — from the battleground
Kermichil — from Michael's
   fortress
Kennedy — ugly head
Kenzie — fair
Kerr — man of strength
Kinnon — fair born
Kinny, Kin — from the top of the
   cliff
Kirk, Kerk — from the church
Lachlan, Laochailan — warring
Laine, Lean, Leane — serves John
Laird — lord
Lamont — man of law
Laren — serves Lawrence
Leith, Leathan — river
Leod — ugly

Leslie — from Leslie
Lindsay — from the island of the
   lime tree
Livingstone — from Livingston
Logan — Finnian's servant
Lundie, Lundy — from the island
   grove
Luthais — famous warrior
MacAdam, MacAdhamh — son of
   Adam
MacAlister — son of Alasdair
MacAlpine, MacAlpin — son of
   Alpine
MacAndrew, Anderson — son of
   Andrew
MacArthur — son of Arthur
MacAulay — son of Olaf
MacAuslan — son of Absalon
MacBean, MacBain — son of
   Beathan
MacBeth — son of Beth
MacCallum — son of Callum
MacColl — son of Coll
MacClennan — son of Finnian's
   servant
MacDonald, MacDomhnall,
   MacDonell — son of the world's
   ruler
MacDougal, MacDubhgall,
   MacDoughall — son of Dougal
MacDuff, MacDhuibh — son of the
   black man
MacEwen — son of Ewen
MacFarlane — son of Farlan
MacFie — son of the dark of peace
MacGillivray — son of the servant
   of judgment
MacGowan — son of the smith
MacGregor — son of a shepherd
Machar, Machair — plain

MacInnes — son of the unique choice

MacIntyre — son of the carpenter

MacIver — son of an archer

Mack, Mac — son of

MacKay — son of fire

MacKenzie — son of the fair man

MacKinley, MacCinfhaolaidh — son of Kinley

MacKinnon — son of the fair born

MackIntosh, MacIntosh — son of the thane

MacLachlan — son of Lachlan

MacLaine, MacLean — son of the servant of John

MacLaren — son of Laren

MacLeod, McCloud — son of the ugly man

MacMillan — son of the bald man

MacNab — son of the Abbot

MacNaughton, MacNachtan — son of the pure one

MacNeill, MacNiall — son of the champion

MacNicol — son of the conquering people

MacPherson — son of the parson

MacQuarrie — son of the proud man

MacQueen — son of the good man

MacRae, MacRay — son of grace

Malcolm, Mealcoluim — follower of Saint Columba

Maolmuire — dark-skinned

Math, Mathe — bear

Matheson — bear's son

Maxwell — from Maxwell

Menzies — from Mesniers, Normandy

Moncreiffe — from the hill of the sacred bough

Montgomery — from Montgomerie

Morrison — son of the servant of Mary

Muir — from the moor

Muirfinn — dwells near the beautiful sea

Munro, Munroe — man from Ro

Murdoc, Murdock, Murdoch — protector of the sea

Murray, Morogh — man of the sea

Nab — abbot

Nairne — from the alder-tree river

Nathair, Nathrach, Nathraichean — snake

Naughton, Nachton, Nechtan — pure

Nealcail — victorious people

Ness — from the headland

Niall — champion

Norval — from the north valley

Odar — meaning unknown

Ogilvie, Ogilbinn — from the high peak

Oidhche — night

Oliphant — great strength

Padruig — royal

Parlan — farmer

Payton, Paden, Paton, Peyton — royal

Pherson — Parson

Quarrie, Quarry — proud

Rae, Ray — grace

Ramsey — from Ramsey

Robertson — son of Robert

Rob Roy — red Rob

Ronald — mighty, powerful

Rose — flower

Ross, Ros—from the peninsula

Roy—red

Sandy—defender of man

Scrymgeour—fighter

Scot, Scott—wanderer

Shaw, Shawe—terse

Sheiling—from the summer pasture

Sim—listener

Sinclair—from Saint-Clair-sur-Elle

Skene—from Skene

Struan—stream

Sutherland—from Sutherland

Tarsuinn—meaning unknown

Tavis, Tavey, Tevis, Tamnais, Tavish—twin

Tearlach—strong

Todd—fox

Urquhart—from the fount on the knoll

Wallace—Welsh

Slavic

Slavic surnames are dealt with by country (Russia, Norway, Sweden, Finland, etc.) rather than by language.

FEMALE

Danica, Danika — morning star
Fania, Fanya, Fanny — free
Fedosia, Feodora — God's gift
Gavrila, Gavrilla — God give me strength
Hedy — strife
Ilka — flattering
Katarina — pure
Kasmira, Kazatimiru — commanding peace
Lala — tulip
Ludmilla, Ljudumilu — beloved
Marya — bitter
Milka — industrious
Nada, Nadia, Nadege, Nadezhda, Nadya, Nadyenka, Nadyuiska, Nadine — hope
Neda — born on Sunday
Radinka — active
Radmilla, Radilu — works for the people
Sonja — wise
Valeska, Valdislava — glorious ruler
Varvara, Varina — foreigner
Velika — great
Zora, Zorah, Zorana — dawn

MALE

Anatol — from the east
Andrej — strong
Boguslaw — God's glory
Bohuslav — God's glory
Boleslaus — sorrowful
Bolodenka, Dimka — universal
Boris, Borysko — fighter
Bronislaw — weapon of glory
Casimir — peaceful
Cestmir — fortress
Karel, Karol — manly
Kazatimiru, Kasimer — commands peace
Kersten — Christian
Laci, Laszlo, Lacko, Lazlo — famous ruler
Ladislas — good ruler
Lew — lion
Milos — pleasant
Nicholai, Nikolai — victorious
Pavel — little
Pjotr, Pyotr — stone
Rostislav — glory
Rurik — red
Sandor — defender of man
Slava, Slavochka — glory

Stanislaus, Stanislas, Stannes, Slavik, Stanislav, Stas — military glory

Stasio — stand of glory

Tibor — holy place

Vaclar, Vasek, Vladik, Vladya — wreath of glory

Vassily — Slavic form of Basil (kinglike)

Vladimer, Vimka, Vladimir, Volodya, Vova, Vladimiru — universal ruler

Vladislava, Vyacheslav, Vladislav — glory

Wenceslaus, Wenceslava — great glory

Zakarij — meaning unknown

Ziven, Ziv, Zivon — lively

Spanish

Surnames began in the mid–ninth century and became hereditary in the thirteenth century. Before they were used, the father's name was listed in the genitive form after the given name.

Most given names came from the Visigoths and the Moors. The majority of surnames derived from descriptive or occupational names, but there are still some patronymic and place names.

As was customary in most of Europe, the nobility took the names of the estates they owned. Occasionally, the father's name and the estate name were used in conjunction.

For the last two hundred years, the standard format of a Spanish full name has been given name first, then the father's name, y (and), and the mother's name.

A few articles and suffixes:
-ez, -es — son of
y — and
viuda — widow of
de — of
la, le — the
de la, de le, de los, del — of the

Married women add their husband's name to their own with the article *de*. Example: Agueda Padilla y de la Fuente de Chavez. Translated: Agueda (given name) Padilla (father's surname) y (and) de la Fuente (mother's maiden name) de (of) Chavez (husband's name). If viuda came before de Chavez, it would indicate that this woman was a widow. Names are always traced through the father.

A few Spanish surnames:

Aznar	Gonzalez
Chavez	Lopez
Fernandez	Menendez
Garcia	Ramirez
Gomez	Rodriguez

FEMALE

Adelina, Adelita — noble, kind

Adoracion — adoration

Adriana — dark

Agnese — Spanish form of Agnes (pure)

Agueda, Agata, Agacia — kind

Agurtzane — meaning unknown

Aida, Aidia — help

Ainhoa, Ainhoe — meaning unknown

Aintzane — glorious

Aitziber — meaning unknown

Alameda — promenade

Alazne — miracle

Albertine, Albertina — noble

Aldonza, Aldonsa — nice

Alegria — merry

Alejandra, Alejandrina — defender of man

Aleta, Adelita, Adelina — winged

Aletea, Aletia — honest

Alfonsa — feminine form of Alfonso (noble)

Alfreda — feminine form of Alfredo (counsels the elves)

Alicia — Spanish form of Alice (honest)

Alita — noble

Alma — geist (spirit)

Almira — from Almeira

Almunda, Almundena, Almundina — reference to the Virgin Mary

Alona — light

Alonsa — ready, noble

Alva — white

Amaia — end

Amalia — Spanish form of Amelia (industrious)

Amalur, Amalure — homeland

Amanda — lovable

Amaranta — flower

Amata — lovable

Amor, Amora — love

Andeana — leaving

Andere, Andera, Andrea — feminine form of Andrew (manly)

Angela, Angelina, Angelia — angel

Anitia, Anita, Anica — grace

Antonina, Antonia — feminine form of Antonio (beyond praise)

Anunciacion — of the Annunciation

Aquilina — eagle

Aracelia, Araceli — alter of heaven

Arama — reference to the Virgin Mary

Arcadia — adventurous

Arcelia — treasure

Arrate — meaning unknown

Artemisia — perfection

Ascencion — reference to the Ascension

Asuncion — born during the Feast of Assumption

Atalaya, Athalia — guard tower

Aureliana, Aurelia — golden

Aurkene, Aurkena — present

Beatriz, Beatrisa — brings happiness

Belinda — attractive

Bella — beautiful

Benigna — kind

Benita — blessed
Bibiana — lively
Bienvenida — welcome
Blanca — white
Blasa — stutters
Brigidia, Brigida — Spanish form
   of Bridget (strong)
Buena — good
Calandria — lark
Calida — ardent
Calvina — feminine form of
   Calvino (bald)
Camila — attendant
Candida — pure, white
Carilla, Carla, Carlita, Carletta,
   Carlotta, Carlota — feminine
   form of Charles (manly)
Carmelita, Carmela — garden
Carmencita, Carmen, Carmina —
   song
Carmita — rosy
Carona — crowned
Casild, Casilda — meaning
   unknown
Casta, Catalina — pure
Cenobia — Spanish form of
   Zenobia (born of Zeus)
Cesara — long-haired
Charo — nickname for Rosario
Chiquita — little one
Cipriana — from Cyprus
Clareta — brilliant
Clarinda — beautiful
Clarissa — clear
Claudia — lame
Clementina — merciful
Clodovea — feminine form of
   Clodoveo (famous warrior)
Concepcion, Concetta, Conchetta,
   Conshita — reference to the

Immaculate Conception
Constanza — constant
Consuelo, Consuela, Consolacion,
   Consolata, Chela — consolation
Corazon — heart
Cristina — Christian
Dalila — delicate
Damita — little noble
Danita — God judges
Daria — rich
Deiene, Deikun, Deina —
   religious holiday
Delcine, Dulcine, Dulcina, Dulce,
   Dulcinea, Dulcinia — sweet
Delicia — charming
Delma, Delmar, Delmara — of the
   sea
Desideria — desire
Devera — task
Dia — day
Diega — feminine form of Diego
   (supplanter)
Digna — worthy
Dionis, Dionisa — myth name
   (from Dionysus, god of wine)
Dolores, Doloritas — sorrow
Dolorita, Dolores — full of sorrows
Dominga — born on Sunday
Dorbeta — reference to the Virgin
   Mary
Doroteia, Dorotea — Spanish form
   of Dorothy (gift from God)
Duena — chaperon
Dulcinea — sweet
Elbertina — noble
Eldora — blond
Elena — Spanish form of Helen
   (light)
Elisa — Spanish form of Elizabeth
   (consecrated to God)

Elsa—truth
Elvira—white, beautiful
Ema—grandmother
Emilia, Emilie—flattering
Encarnacion—reference to the Incarnation
Engracia—graceful
Enriqueta, Enriqua—ruler
Erendira, Erendiria—name of a princess
Ernesta—serious
Eskarne, Eskarna—merciful
Esma, Esme, Esmerelda—emerald
Esperanza—hope
Estebana, Estefana, Esteva—crowned with laurels
Estella, Estrella, Ester—star
Eva, Evita—Spanish form of Eve
Exaltacion—reference to the cross
Faqueza—weakness
Fe—trust
Fermina—strong
Filipa—Spanish form of Phillipa (loves horses)
Florentina, Florida, Florinia, Flor, Florencia—blooming
Fonda—profound
Fortuna, Fausta, Faustina, Felisa—lucky
Francisca—free
Freira—sister
Frescura—freshness
Gala—from Gaul
Galena, Galenia—small, intelligent one
Garaitz—victory
Garbine, Garbina, Garabine, Garabina—purification

Gardotza—meaning unknown
Gaspara—treasure
Gechina—grace
Generosa—generous
Gertrudes, Gertrudis—Spanish form of Gertrude (spear)
Gezane, Gezana—reference to the Incarnation
Ginebra, Ginessa—white
Gitana—gypsy
Godalupe, Guadalupe—reference to the Virgin Mary
Gorane—holy cross
Gotzone—angel
Gracia, Graciana—grace
Gregoria—vigilant
Guadalupe—named for the Virgin Mary
Guillelmina—resolute protector
Gustava—staff of the gods
Henriqua—feminine form of Henrique (rules the home)
Herminia—myth name
Hermosa—beautiful
Honor, Honoria, Honoratas—honor
Idoia, Idurre, Iratze, Izazkun—reference to the Virgin Mary
Ignacia—fire
Igone—Ascension
Ikerne—visitation
Iluminada—illuminated
Immaculada—reference to the Immaculate Conception
Inez, Ines—meek
Inocencia, Inocenta—innocent
Irene—peace
Irmina—meaning unknown
Irune—reference to the Holy Trinity

Isabella, Isabel — devoted to God
Isidora — gifted with many ideas
Itsaso — sea
Itxaro — hope
Izar, Izarre, Izarra — star
Jacinta — purple
Jade — jewel
Jaione — reference to the Nativity
Jakinda, Jacinta — hyacinth
Jasone — assumption
Javiera — owns a new house
Jesusa, Josune — named for Jesus
Jimena — heard
Joaquina — prepared
Josefa, Josefina — Spanish form of Josephine (God shall add)
Juana, Juanita — God's gift
Kemena, Kemina — strong
Kesare, Kesara — youthful
Landa, Legarre, Leira, Lera, Lorda, Lourdes, Louredes, Lucita — reference to the Virgin Mary
La Reina — queen
Laura, Larunda, Laurencia — crowned with laurels
Leonora, Leonor — Spanish form of Eleanor (light)
Letitia — happy
Leya — loyalty
Liana — youthful
Linda — pretty
Lola, Lolita, Loleta, Lolitta — feminine form of Carlos (manly)
Lore, Lora — flower
Loretta — pure
Lucita, Lucrecia, Luz — brings light

Luisa — Spanish form of Louise (famous in war)
Lupe — wolf
Lur — earth
Madra, Madre — mother
Maite, Maitea — love
Manda — battle-maid
Manuela — God is with us
Marcela — warring
Margarita — pearl
Mariquita, Marquilla, Marisa, Marisol, Madalena, Maria, Marietta — bitter
Marta — Spanish form of Martha (lady)
Melisenda, Melosa, Melosia — sweet
Mendi, Molara — reference to the Virgin Mary
Mercedes — mercy
Milagros, Milagrosa, Milagritos, Mirari, Mireya — miracle
Miranda — admirable
Modesta, Modeste — modest
Monica — advisor
Mora — little blueberry
Naiara — reference to the Virgin Mary
Nalda — strong
Narcisa — daffodil
Natalia — born at Christmas
Natividad — reference to the Nativity
Nekane, Nekana — sorrows
Nelia — yellow
Nerea — mine
Neta, Nita — serious
Neva, Nieve, Nevada — snowy
Nicanora — victorious army
Nina — girl

Oihane — from the forest
Olinda — protector
Oliveria — affectionate
Olivia — olive
Ora — gold
Orlanda — famous land
Orquidea, Orquidia — orchid
Osane, Osana — health
Pabla — little
Paciencia — patient
Palba — blond
Palmira — from the city of palms
Paloma — dove
Paquita — free
Pastora — shepherdess
Patricia — noble
Paulita — little
Paz — peace
Pedra — stone
Perfecta — perfect
Pepita — He shall add
Pia — pious
Pilar — pillar
Placida — tranquil
Primavera — springtime
Prudencia — prudent
Puebla — from the city
Pureza, Pura, Purisima — pure
Querida — beloved
Quinta — born fifth
Ramira — judicious
Ramona — mighty
Ramona, Raimunda — wise
    defender
Raquel — lamb
Reina, Regina — queen
Remedios — remedy
Ria — from the river's mouth
Rica, Ricarda — rules the home
Rio — river

Rita — pearl
Roana — reddish-brown skin
Rocio — dew-drops
Roderiga — notable leader
Roldana — famous
Romana — from Rome
Rosalind, Rosalinda, Rosalinde,
    Roslyn, Rosario — beautiful
    rose
Rosamaria, Rosemarie — bitter
    rose
Rufa, Rufina — red-haired
Sabina — a Sabine
Salbatora, Salvatora — savior
Salvadora — savior
Sancia, Sancha — holy
Sarita, Sara — princess
Saturnina — gift of Saturn
Savanna, Savannah, Sabana —
    from the open plain
Segunda — born second
Seina — innocent
Senalda — sign
Senona — lively
Serafina — seraph
Serena — serene
Shoshana, Susana — lily
Simona — God is heard
Socorro — help
Sofia — wise
Solana — sunshine
Soledad, Soledada — solitary
Suelita — little lily
Tabora — plays a small drum
Terceira — born third
Trella — star
Ursulina — little bear
Usoa — dove
Valentina — brave
Ventura — good fortune

Verdad — honest
Veta — intelligent
Vicenta — victor
Vina — from the vineyard
Virginia — virgin
Vittoria — victor
Xalbadora, Xalvadora — savior
Xevera, Xeveria — owns a new
house

Yanamaria, Yanamarie — bitter
grace
Yoana — God's gift
Yolanda — violet
Zamora — from Zamora
Zita — little hope
Zurine, Zurina — white

Male

Adriano — dark
Alano — handsome
Alarico — rules all
Alberto — Spanish form of Albert
(noble)
Alejandro — Spanish form of
Alexander (defends mankind)
Alfonso — Spanish form of
Alphonse (eager for war)
Alfredo — Spanish form of Alfred
(counsels the elves)
Alonso, Alonzo — eager for battle
Aluino — noble friend
Amadeo, Amado — loves God
Ambrosio — divine
Anastasio — resurrected
Andres — Spanish form of Andrew
(manly)
Angel, Angelo — angel
Anibal — grace of God
Anselmo — divine helmet
Antonio, Anton — Spanish form of
Anthony (beyond praise)
Aquilino — eagle
Archibaldo — bold
Arlo — the barberry
Armando — protective
Arturo — handsome
Aurelio — gold

Bartolo, Bartoli, Bartolome —
ploughman
Basilio — noble
Beltran — bright raven
Benedicto — blessed
Bernardo — brave as a bear
Bernbe — Spanish form of
Barnaby (prophet)
Berto — intelligent
Beinvenido — welcome
Blanco — blond
Blas — stutters
Bonifaco, Bonifacio — benefactor
Calvino — bald
Camilo — meaning unknown
Carlomagno — Charles the Great
Carlos — manly
Casimiro — peaceful
Cesar, Cesaro — long-haired
Chico, Currito, Curro — free
Ciceron — chickpea
Cipriano — from Cyprus
Cirilo — noble
Ciro — sun
Claudio — lame
Clodoveo — famous warrior
Conrado — Spanish form of
Conrad (able counsel)
Constantino — constant

Cornelio—horn
Cristiano—Christian
Cristobal—Spanish form of Christopher (Christ-bearer)
Cuarto, Cuartio—born fourth
Curcio—polite
Damian—tame
Dario—rich
Delmar—of the sea
Desiderio—desired
Diego—supplanter
Domingo—born on Sunday
Edmundo—wealthy protector
Eduardo—wealthy guardian
Eloy—renowned warrior
Elvio—blond
Emilio—flattering
Eneas—praised
Enrique—rules the home
Erasmo—friendly
Ernesto—serious
Esteban, Estefan—crowned in victory
Eugenio—noble
Fabio—bean grower
Farruco, Frasco, Frascuelo—free
Fausto, Felix—lucky
Federico—Spanish form of Frederick (peaceful ruler)
Felipe—Spanish form of Phillip (loves horses)
Fermin—strong
Fernando—brave
Fidel, Fidele—faithful
Flaminio—meaning unknown
Flavio—blond
Florentino, Florinio—blooming
Fraco—weak
Francisco, Cisco—Spanish form of Francis (free)

Franco—frank
Fresco—fresh
Gabino, Gabriel, Gabrio—God is my strength
Galeno—small, intelligent one
Garcia—brave in battle
Gaspar, Gaspard—treasure
Generoso—generous
Gerardo—Spanish form of Gerard (spear courageous)
Geronimo—Spanish form of Jerome (sacred)
Gervasio, Gervaso, German—warrior
Gil—squire
Gilberto—Spanish form of Gilbert (hostage)
Godofredo, Godfredo—Spanish form of Godfrey (friend of God)
Gregorio—watchful
Gualterio, Galtero—Spanish form of Walter (strong warrior)
Guido—guide
Gustavo—staff of the gods
Hector—tenacious
Heriberto—Spanish form of Herbert (shining warrior)
Hernando—adventuresome
Hilario—happy
Honorato—honor
Horacio—Spanish form of Horace (timekeeper)
Humberto, Hugo—intelligent
Iago—supplanter
Ignacio, Ignazio, Incendio—fire
Inocencio, Inocente—innocent
Isidoro, Isidro—gifted with many ideas
Ivan—archer
Jacinto—hyacinth

Jago, Jaime — supplanter
Javiero — born in January
Jeronimo — Spanish form of
   Jerome (sacred)
Jesus — named for Jesus
Joaquin — prepared
Jonas — dove
Jorge — Spanish form of George
   (farmer)
Jose — God will increase
Josue — Spanish form of Joshua
   (He shall add)
Juan, Juanito — Spanish form of
   John (gracious gift from God)
Julian, Julio — youth
Kemen — strong
Lazaro — help of God
Leandro, Leonardo, Leon,
   Leonides — lion
Lorenzo — Spanish form of
   Lawrence (laurel)
Lucio, Lucero — Spanish form of
   Luke (light)
Macario — happy
Manuel — God is with us
Marco, Marcos, Mario, Martin,
   Martino, Martinez — warring
Mateo, Matro — God's gift
Mauricio, Mauro — Moorish
Miguel — Spanish form of Michael
   (God-like)
Moises — Spanish form of Moses
   (from the water)
Naldo — strong
Natal, Natalio — born at Christmas
Natanael, Nataniel — gift from God
Nemesio — named for Nemesis
   (goddess of vengeance)
Neron — strong
Nestor — wise

Neto, Nesto — serious
Nicanor — victorious army
Noe — peace
Norberto — heroic
Oliverio, Oliverios — affectionate
Orlando — famous land
Oro — gold
Pablo — little
Paco, Pacorro, Pacho — free
Palban, Palben — blond
Patricio — noble
Paz — peace
Pedro — stone
Pepe, Pepillo — Spanish form of
   Joseph (He shall add)
Pirro — red-haired
Placido — tranquil
Platon — broad-shouldered
Ponce — born fifth
Porfirio, Porfiro — purple
Primeiro — born first
Prospero — wealthy
Pueblo — from the city
Quinton — born fifth
Rafael — God has healed
Ramiro, Ramirez — judicious
Ramon, Raimundo — wise
   defender
Raul, Raulo — wise
Rey — king
Rico, Ricardo — strong ruler
Roano — reddish-brown skin
Roberto — Spanish form of Robert
   (shining fame)
Rodas — roses
Roderigo, Rodrigo — notable
   leader
Rodolfo — Spanish form of
   Rudolph (famous wolf)
Rogelio — famous soldier

Roldan — famous
Roman, Romeo, Romano — from
     Rome
Ruben — son
Rufo, Rufio — red-haired
Sabino — a Sabine
Salbatore, Salvatore, Salvadore,
     Salvador — savior
Salomon — peaceful
Sancho, Santos — saint
Santiago — named for Saint James
Saturnin — gift of Saturn
Saul — asked for
Sebastiano — Spanish form of
     Sebastian (revered)
Segundo — born second
Sein — innocent
Senon — lively
Serafin — seraph
Stefano — crown of laurels
Tabor — plays a small drum
Tadeo — praise

Tajo — day
Teodoro — Spanish form of
     Theodore (gift from God)
Terciero — born third
Tito — giant
Tobias — God is good
Toli — ploughman
Tomas — twin
Tulio — lively
Turi — bear
Urbano — from the city
Veto — intelligent
Vincente, Victor, Victoro — victor
Virgilio — Spanish form of Virgil
     (profiting)
Vito, Vidal — vital
Xalbador, Xalvador, Xabat —
     savior
Xavier, Xever — owns a new
     house
Yago — supplanter
Zacarias — remembered by God

Swedish

Swedish surnames appeared in the seventeenth century and were first used by the military for administrative purposes. By the eighteenth century, others began using hereditary surnames, but these names weren't standardized until the nineteenth century.

Before the nineteenth century, most Swedes used their given name with their father's name, to which they attached the suffix -son or -dotter. In 1901, laws were enacted to regulate surnames. Under these laws, only the king could change names. In 1946, the National Bureau of Statistics was granted the right to make name changes.

The suffix -son was used mostly by the lower classes. The upper classes preferred: -berg, -gren, -lund, -quist, -strom -in and -man.

A few Swedish surnames:

Dolk	Linberg
Eriksson	Lundquist
Hanson	Olsson
Johansson	Pettersson
Kristofferson	Svensson

FEMALE

Adrian — dark

Agda, Agata, Agaton, Agneta — pure

Aina — joy

Alexandra — defender of man

Algot — pearl

Alicia — truth

Alma — loving

Amalia — Swedish form of Amelia (industrious)

Anna, Annika, Annike — grace

Anna Cristina — graceful Christian

Annalina — graceful light

Anneli, Annalie, Annali — graceful meadow

Antonetta — priceless

Astrid — divine strength

Atalie, Atali — pure

Barbro — Swedish form of Barbara (stranger)

Beata — blessed

Berit, Berta — intelligent

Blenda — heroine

Botilda — commanding

Brigetta, Birgitta, Birget, Britta, Britt, Brite—strong

Carina, Carine, Caren—pure

Cecilia—blind

Cristina, Christina—Christian

Dagmar—Dane's joy

Ebba, Ebbe—strong

Edit—Swedish form of Edith (wealthy gift)

Eleonora, Elin—light

Elisabet—Swedish form of Elizabeth (devoted to God)

Elsa—truth

Emilia—industrious

Emma—universal

Erika—feminine form of Erik (rules forever)

Eva, Evelina—life

Filippa—loves horses

Frederika—feminine form of Frederik (peaceful ruler)

Freya—myth name

Frida, Frideborg, Fritjof—peaceful

Gabriella—strength from God

Gala—singer

Gerda—protector

Germund—defender of man

Gertrud—warrior-maid

Gote, Gota, Gotilda—strong

Greta—pearl

Guda—supreme

Gudny—unspoiled

Gudrun, Gudruna—wise

Gunilla, Gunnel—battle-maid

Gustava—divine staff

Hakan, Hakana—noble

Hanna—gracious

Hedwig—peace in battle

Helena—light

Helga—holy

Henrika—feminine form of Henry (rules the home)

Hildegard, Hilda—fighter

Hulda—hidden

Inga, Ingrid, Inge, Inger—Ing's daughter

Ingaborg, Ingeborg, Ingegard—Ing's helper

Ingalill—Ing's lily

Johanna—gracious

Judit—Swedish form of Judith (praised)

Julia—youth

Karin, Karen—pure

Karla, Karolina—feminine of Karl (manly)

Katarina, Katrina, Katrine, Kaysa—Swedish form of Katherine (pure)

Kate—legend name

Kerstin, Kristina—Christian

Klara—clear

Lage—from the sea

Laura—laurel

Lena, Lina—light

Lotta—masculine

Lovisa—renowned battle-maid

Lydia—from Lydia

Maj, Maja—pearl

Malena, Malene, Malin—from the tower

Margareta, Margit—pearl

Maria, Marita—bitter

Marta—lady

Martina—warring

Matilda—brave in war

Mikaela—feminine form of Mikael (God-like)

Monika—advisor

Nanna — graceful

Olga — holy

Olivia — olive

Paulina, Paula — little

Petra, Petronella — stone

Pia — pious

Quinby, Quenby — womanly

Ragnara, Ragnhild — feminine form of Ragnor (strong army)

Rakel — Swedish form of Rachel (lamb)

Rigmor, Rigmora — name of a queen

Rosel, Roselle, Rosa — rose

Rut — beautiful

Sibylla — prophetess

Signe, Signild, Signilda, Sigrid — victorious

Soasan — legend name

Solveig — house woman

Sonya, Sonja — wise

Stella — star

Stina — pure

Svante — myth name

Svea — myth name

Tekla — divine fame

Teresia — reaper

Tilda — heroine

Tora — victor

Trilby — meaning unknown

Trind, Trina, Trine — pure

Ulla, Ulrika — will

Vedia, Vedis — myth name

Vega — star

Viktoria — Swedish form of Victoria (victory)

Vilhelmina, Vilma — determined protector

Viola — violet

Virginia — virgin

Viveka — little woman

Male

Adolphus, Adolph, Dolph — noble wolf

Ake — ancient

Alberik — blond ruler

Albert — strong as a bear

Alexander — defender of man

Alf, Alfred — wise

Alfonso, Alfons — noble, ready

Alrik — all-ruler

Alvar — dwarf shrub

Ambrosius — divine

Anderson — son of Ander

Andreas, Anders — strong

Ansgar — warrior

Antonius, Anton — priceless

Arn, Arne, Arnold — eagle

Aron — illuminated

Artur — bear

Arvid — of the people

Axel — father of peace

Baltasar — protected by God

Bartholomeus — farmer

Basilius — kingly

Beck — from the brook

Bengt, Benedikt — blessed

Beowulf — myth name

Berg — mountain

Bergren, Bergron — from the mountain brook

Bertil — intelligent

Birger — rescuer

Bjorn — bear

Blasius — stutters

Bodil, Bo — commander

Borg, Borje — from the castle
Burr — young
Caesar — long hair
Cowbelliantus — legend name
David — beloved
Davin — pride of the Finns
Eddy — unresting
Edvard — Swedish form of Edward
    (rich guardian)
Emil — lively
Enar — warrior
Erik — forever strong
Erling, Erland — stranger
Ernst — earnest
Esbjorn — bear of God
Eskil — vessel of God
Eugen — Swedish form of Eugene
    (noble)
Evert — bear
Fabian — bean grower
Felix — lucky
Filip — Swedish form of Phillip
    (loves horses)
Fisk — fisherman
Frans, Franz — free
Fredrik, Fredek, Frederek —
    peaceful ruler
Gabriel — strength from God
Garth — protector
Georg, Goran, Gorin — Swedish
    form of George (farmer)
Gerhard — Swedish form of
    Gerard (spear courageous)
Greger — Swedish form of
    Gregory (watchful)
Gunner, Gunnar — battle strong
Gustav — noble staff
Hadrian — dark
Halvard — rock enclosure

Hans, Hansel — Swedish form of
    John (gift from God)
Harald — war commander
Helmer, Helmar — fighting fury
Hemming, Harry, Henrik,
    Henning, Hendrik — Swedish
    form of Henry (rules the home)
Herbert — intelligent warrior
Hermann — soldier
Hilmar, Hjalmar — name of a
    noble
Hugo — intelligent
Humfrid — peaceful Hun
Ingmar, Ingemar — famous
Ingvar — famous fighter
Isak — laughs
Ivar — archer
Jakob — supplanter
Jan, Jonam, Jens, Johan — Swedish
    form of John (gift from God)
Jesper — jasper
Jonas — dove
Justus — just
Kalle, Kjell, Karl — Swedish form
    of Charles (manly)
Klas — people's victory
Knut — knot
Kolbjorn — black bear
Konrad — Swedish form of Conrad
    (counselor)
Konstantin — firm
Krister, Kristar, Krist, Kristian —
    Christian
Kristofer — Swedish form of
    Christopher (Christ-bearer)
Lang — tall
Lars, Larry, Larz, Lorenz,
    Lorens — laurel
Leif — dearly loved

Lennart—Swedish form of Leonard (lion)

Lucio, Lukas—brings light

Ludvik—famous warrior

Lunt—from the grove

Magnild, Magnus—strong warrior

Malkolm—Swedish form of Malcolm (serves Saint Columba)

Manfred—peaceful

Markus, Mark—warring

Matteus, Mattias, Mats—Swedish form of Mathew (gift from God)

Melker—king

Mikael—Swedish form of Michael (God-like)

Nansen—Nancy's son

Natanael—Swedish form of Nathaniel (gift from God)

Nels, Nils—chief

Niklas, Nikolaus—Swedish form of Nicholas (victory of the people)

Noak—rest

Olof, Olaf—ancient

Oskar—leaping warrior

Otto—rich

Ove—egg

Patrik—Swedish form of Patrick (noble)

Per, Peder, Petter—stone

Perchnosius—legend name

Poul, Pol—little

Ragnar, Ragnor—strong army

Ragnvard—powerful fighter

Rikard—Swedish form of Richard (strong ruler)

Roald—Swedish form of Ronald (powerful)

Roland—famous

Rolf—wolf

Rune—secret

Rurik—famous

Rutger—Swedish form of Roger (renowned spear)

Samson, Simson—son of Samuel (heard)

Samuel—God listens

Saul—desired

Saxe—legend name

Set—compensation

Sigurd, Sigvard—victorious

Skamelson—legend name

Soren—reddish-brown hair

Staffan, Stefan—Swedish form of Stephen (crowned with laurels)

Sten—stone

Stig—from the mount

Sven, Svend, Svens—young

Svenbjorn—young bear

Tage—day

Tait—happy

Tobias—God is good

Tor, Thor, Tore—myth name

Torbjorn, Torborg—thunder bear

Torgny—Thor's loud weapon

Torkel—Thor's kettle

Torsten—Thor's stone

Ture—meaning unknown

Twigmuntus—legend name

Ulf—wolf

Valborg—powerful mountain

Valdemar—powerful

Valentin—brave

Valfrid—powerful peace

Valter—Swedish form of Walter
(strong fighter)
Vatt—legend name
Verner—friend protector

Vilhelm—Swedish form of
William (determined
protector)
Yngve—master

Teutonic

Teutonic surnames are dealt with under the country names, e.g., Germany, France, England and so on. During the period when the Teutonic tribes flourished, surnames were not hereditary.

FEMALE

Ada — happy
Adabel, Adbelle — lovely, happy
Adela, Adel, Adeline, Adelina, Adaline, Adalina, Adelicia, Adalia, Adalie, Adal — noble
Adolphina, Adolphine — feminine form of Adolph (noble wolf)
Ailsa, Alyssa, Alisa — good humor
Aimiliana, Amialiona, Aimilionia — hard-working
Alarica, Alaricia — universal ruler
Alberta, Alberte, Albertine, Albertina — feminine form of Albert (intelligent, noble)
Alda, Aldea — wealthy
Alfonsa, Alphonsa, Alphonza, Alphosine, Alonza, Alphosina — eager for war
Alfred, Alfreda, Alfrieda — oracle
Algiane, Algiana — spear
Alice, Alix, Allis, Alys, Alyce, Alicia, Alisa, Alissa, Alithia, Allys, Alicea — noble humor
Aline, Alina — noble
Alison, Allison — divine fame
Aloysia — famous in battle
Alvernia, Alverna, Alvina, Alvinia, Alvira, Alvera — dearly loved

Amelia, Amalie, Amalia, Amelie, Amalija — defender
Anselma — divine defender
Ara, Aria — intelligence of an eagle
Arabella — eagle, heroine
Ardith — wealthy gift
Arilda, Arilde — hearth maiden
Armilda, Armilde — armored battle-maiden
Arnoldine, Arnoldina — strong like an eagle
Astrid, Astred — impulsive
Asvoria — divine wisdom
Auberta — intelligent
Audris, Audrisa — rich
Audrey — strong
Bathilda, Bathilde, Bathild — commanding
Bera — bear
Bernadine, Berdine, Bernardina, Bertine — intelligent maiden
Beronika — honest
Bertha, Berta — sparkling
Bertild, Bertilde, Bertilda — commanding battle-maiden
Bertilla, Bertille — outstanding warrior-maiden

Blenda — glory
Brend, Brenda — sword
Bruna — dark-haired
Brunhild, Brunhilda, Brunhilde —
armored battle-maiden
Burga, Burgha — from the town
Carly — womanly
Clotild, Clotilde, Clotilda —
renowned for war
Dagmar — Dane's joy
Dagna — as beautiful as the day
Eberta, Elberta — intelligent
Edburga, Edra, Edrea — wealthy
defender
Edeline, Edelina — noble
Edith, Editta, Edyte, Edyta —
wealthy present
Edolie, Edolia — good humor
Edwige — refuge from war
Elda, Elde — warrior
Eldora — gift of wisdom
Elfreda, Elfrida — threatens the
elves
Elga — holy
Elke — industrious
Elmina, Elmine — intimidating
fame
Eloise — famous in war
Elsa — noble maid
Emily, Emlyn, Emeline, Emiline,
Emelina, Emelin, Emilie —
hard-working
Emma, Ema — nurse
Enrica, Enrika, Enriqueta — ruler
of the home
Erica, Erika — noble
Ermelinda, Ermelinde, Erma —
serpent
Ernestina, Ernestine, Ernesta,
Erna — directed

Ethel — noble
Ethelda, Ethelde — wise advisor
Ethelinda, Ethelind, Ethelinde —
intelligent
Etta — ruler of the home
Fanny, Fannie, Frances,
Francine, Fanchon, Franziska,
Franze, Frantiska, Francoise,
Francique, Francesca,
Francisca, Fotina, Franci,
Fereng, Ferike, Ferika — free
Felda — from the field
Fernande, Fernanda —
adventuresome
Fleda, Flede, Fleta, Flita — swift
Freda, Frida — tranquil
Frederica, Fredrika, Farica,
Fryda, Fritzi, Fritzie, Farica,
Farika, Friederike, Friederika,
Friedegard, Friedegarde —
tranquil leader
Frideborg, Fritjof — tranquil aide
Frodine, Frodina — sage friend
Garda, Garde, Gerda, Gerde —
guarded
Gari — spear-maid
Gay — happy
Geralda, Geraldine, Geraldina,
Girelda — capable with a spear
Germaine, Germane — armed
Gertraud, Gertraude, Gerte,
Gerta — warrior
Gertrude, Gertrud, Gertruda —
strong with a spear
Gilberta, Gilberte — hostage
Gisele, Gisel, Gizela, Gizi, Gizike,
Gizus — oath
Griselda, Griselde, Griseldis,
Grissel, Grizel — gray-haired
heroine

Gusta, Gustaafa, Guusa, Gustha,
Gustava — God's staff

Haldis, Haldisa — spirit of stone

Harriet, Harriette, Harrietta,
Henriette, Henrietta, Hatty,
Hattie, Henrika, Henie,
Hennie, Hen, Henny, Henka,
Henia, Henuita, Henuite —
ruler of the home

Harelda, Harelde, Harolda,
Harolde, Hally, Hallie — strong
in war

Hazel — commander

Hedwig, Hedy, Hadwig, Hedda —
refuge from battle

Hertha, Herthe, Heartha —
mother earth

Hilda, Hilde, Hild — battle-maiden

Hildegard, Hildegarde —
defending battle-maiden

Huberta, Huberte — intelligent

Huette — small, wise one

Ida, Ide — work

Idaline, Idalina — working noble

Idelle, Idette, Idetta — merry

Idona, Ilke, Ilka, Idone — hard-
working

Ilda — heroine

Ildiko — warrior

Ilsa, Ilse — noble maid

Inge, Inger, Ingeborg, Inga,
Inkeri, Ingria — hero's
daughter

Ingrid, Ing — myth name

Isa — devoted to God

Jadryga, Jada, Jadriga — refuge in
war

Jetje — ruler of the home

Kelly — born on the farm during
the spring

Kerttu, Kerta — warrior

Koldobike, Koldobika —
renowned holy

Kundegunde, Kundegunda —
name of a princess

Laobhaoise, Loes, Lois — holy

Lelia — loyal

Leola — dear

Lorelle, Lorrella, Lorilla — elfin
Laura

Lou, Louisa, Louise, Lulita,
Lulu — famous in war

Marcella — warring

Marelda, Marelde — elfin Mary

Matilda, Mathilda, Matilde,
Mathilde, Mathild — battle-
maiden

Maude, Maud — strong in war

Melcia — ambitious

Milia, Malia — hard-working

Milicent, Millicent, Milicente,
Melicent, Mellicent — strong

Mimi, Minka — resolute

Minna, Minnie, Minny — loving
memory

Mona — loner

Nette, Nettie — clean

Odile, Odelia, Odila — wealthy

Oktobriana, Octobriana — myth
name

Olga — holy object

Orlanthe, Orlantha — renowned
fame

Ortrud, Ortrude, Ortruda —
serpentine

Ottilie, Ottillia — lucky battle-
maiden

Pastora, Pastore — shepherdess

Proinnseas — free

Queena, Queeny, Queenie — wife

Ragnild, Reinheld, Renilde, Renilda, Renilde, Ragnilde, Renild, Reinhelda—wise strength

Raina, Raine—strong

Ramona—wise defender

Ricarda—strong leader

Rikka—tranquil leader

Roberta, Robina, Robine—sparkling fame

Roderica—princess

Rolanda, Rolande, Rollande, Rollanda—renowned

Romilda, Romilde, Romelde, Romelda—glorified battle-maiden

Ronalda, Ronalde—powerful

Rosamund, Rosemond, Rosamunde—famous defender

Selma—helmet

Serildá, Serilde—armored battle-maiden

Sigismonda, Sigismunda—victorious defender

Sunhild, Sunhilde, Sunhilda, Sonnehilda, Sonnehilde—sun battle-maiden

Swanhilda, Swanhilde—swan battle-maiden

Thora, Tora—thunder

Tilda, Tilde, Tille—battle-maiden

Uald, Ualda—brave

Ulrica, Ulrika—universal ruler

Valda—spirited in war

Vedia, Vidis, Vedis—holy spirit of the forest

Veleda, Velda—inspired intelligence

Verena, Verina—defending friend

Vigdis—myth name

Vilhelmina, Vilma—firm defender

Walburgha, Walburga—strong defender

Wandis, Wanda, Wenda, Wende, Wendelin, Wendeline, Wendelina—wander

Wilhelmina, Wileen, Willa, Willette, Wilmet, Wilhemine, Wilhemina, Wilna—firm defender

Wilva—determined

Winifred, Wynifred, Winifrid, Winfreda, Wynfreda—peaceful

Zelda, Zelde—gray-haired battle-maiden

Zerelda, Zerelde, Zereld—armored battle-maiden

Zissi, Ziske, Ziska—free

MALE

Abelard, Allard, Alard—resolute

Adal, Adel—noble

Adalard, Adelard, Adler, Adlar—brave noble

Adalbert, Adelbert, Ambert—intelligent

Adolf, Adolph, Adolphus—noble wolf

Adelric, Adalric, Aric, Arik—noble commander

Alajos—famous holiness

Alaric, Alirick, Alric, Alrik—universal ruler

Alberic—skillful ruler

Albern—noble bear

Albert—illustrious

Alcuin — noble friend

Aldo, Audwin, Audwyn — rich

Aldrich, Aldridge — sage

Alfred — supernaturally wise

Alger — noble spear

Alison, Allison — of holy fame

Alonso, Alonzo, Alphonse, Alphonso, Alfonso — eager for war

Aloysius, Alaois, Aloys — famous in war

Alvin, Alvyn, Alvan, Alwin, Alwyn — loved by all

Amerigo, Amery, Amory — hard-working

Annraoi, Arrigo, Arrighetto, Alrigo — rules an estate

Anselm, Ansel, Ancil, Anzelm, Anzel, Amselmo — divine helmet

Ansgar — divine spear

Archibald — holy prince

Ardmore — fervent

Armon, Armin, Armonno, Armino, Armando — warrior

Arnold, Arnaldo, Aroldo — strong as an eagle

Arvin — friend of the people

Aubrey, Aubrian — rules the elves

Aylmer, Aylmar — of awe-inspiring fame

Aylsworth — of awe-inspiring worth

Aylward — awe-inspiring guard

Aylwin, Aylwyn — awe-inspiring friend

Baldwin, Baldwyn — noble friend

Barrett — bear

Barron, Barin, Barrin, Baron, Baran — noble fighter

Bayard — reddish-brown hair

Belden, Beldan, Beldane — from the beautiful valley

Bert, Bertold — shines

Bertin, Berton, Bertwin, Bertwyn — shining friend

Bertram, Bertrand, Bartram, Bertok — shining raven

Bevis — archer

Booth — from the market stall

Boyce — dwells in the woods

Brainard — bold raven

Brandon — from the beacon hill

Brant, Brantley — firebrand

Bruno — dark-skinned

Burke — stronghold

Burleigh, Burley — from the meadow by the hill

Byron — from the cottage

Canute — hill

Cavell — bold

Chalmer, Chalmar, Chalmers — lord of the home

Charles — manly

Clay, Clayborn, Claybourne — mortal

Clayton — from the town on the clay bed

Clinton — from the headland farm

Conrad, Cort — bold speech

Crosby — dwells by the town cross

Culbert, Colbert — cool and intelligent

Dale — dwells in the dale

Dannel — Teutonic form of Daniel (God is my judge)

Darrick, Derek, Dedrick, Dedrik, Dedric, Dick — rules the people

Delwyn, Delwin — valley friend

Derwin, Derwyn — friend of the wild

Dirk — dagger

Dixon, Dickson — strong leader

Dolph — wolf

Dustin — valiant

Dwight — white

Edrigu — famous leader

Egan, Egon — formidable

Egbert — formidably intelligent

Einri — intelligent

Elbert — nobly intelligent

Elden, Eldon — the elder

Eldred, Eldridge — battle counselor

Elgar — shining spear

Ellard — nobly brave

Ellery, Ellary — dwells by the alder trees

Elmar, Elemer, Elmer — awe-inspiring

Emeric, Emrik, Emric — leader

Emilian, Emil, Emile — excellent

Emory, Emery — industrious ruler

Enrico, Enzo, Enrique — rules an estate

Erramun, Erroman, Ermanno — mighty defender

Everard — strong boar

Evgenii — noble

Ewald — wealthy prince

Faxon — thick-haired

Ferdinand — dwells by the alder trees

Fitz — son of

Fitz Gerald, Fitzgerald — son of Gerald

Fitz Patrick, Fitzpatrick — son of Patrick

Fletcher — fledger of arrows

Folke — people's guard

Francis, Franchot, Frank, Franklin, Frantisek, Franta, Francois, Franz, Franziskus, Franciscus, Frantisek — free

Frederic, Frederick, Fred, Fredi, Fritz, Frits, Friedel, Friedrich, Fredek, Frigyes, Frici, Fryderyk, Fredrick, Fredrik — peaceful ruler

Friedhelm — true peace

Fydor, Fedya, Fadyenka — divine gift

Gardell, Garner — defender

Gardener, Gardiner — farmer

Garrick, Garek — spear king

Garvin — friendly warrior

Gautier, Gauthier — powerful ruler

Gavin — battle hawk

Geoffrey, Gottfrid, Godfrey, Godfried, Gottfried, Goffredo, Godofredo, Giotto — God's peace

Gerald, Gerry, Gerold, Geraud, Giraud, Gerard, Girard, Garrett, Garret, Gearoid, Garcia — spear strength

Gervais — serves the spear

Gifford — brave

Gilamu, Gillen, Guillame, Gellert, Guilerme — resolute fighter

Gilbert, Gilberto, Gilburt, Gilen — oath

Gilfred, Gilfrid — oath of peace

Gilmer — famous hostage

Goddard, Gotthard — divinely stern

Goodwin, Godwyn, Godwin —
God's friend

Govert — divine peace

Graham — from the gray house

Griswald — from the gray forest

Gualtiero, Galtero — powerful
ruler

Guglilmo, Gwilym — resolute
guardian

Gunner, Gunnar — bold warrior

Gunther — battle army

Gustave, Gustavus, Gustaof,
Gusztav — staff of the Goths

Guy, Gert, Gerwazy, Gervasy,
Gervazy, German, Gervasio —
warrior

Hadwin, Hadwyn — friend in war

Hagan, Hagen — strong defender

Haines, Hanes, Hane, Haine —
dwells in the hedged enclosure

Halbert — shining jewel

Halden, Haldan — half-Dane

Hale — robust

Hallam — from the hillside

Hamlin — rules the home

Hardie, Hardy — strong

Harlan, Harland — from the land of
strength

Harold, Hal, Harry — mighty in
war

Harris — son of Harry

Harte, Hart — deer

Hartwell — from the deer's well

Hartwig, Hass — strong advisor

Harvey, Herman, Hermann,
Harm, Harme, Herve —
warrior

Haydon, Hayden — from the
hedged hill

Helmer — warrior's wrath

Hendrik, Henrik, Henerik, Harry,
Henning, Henri, Heinroch,
Heike, Harro, Hinrich,
Henrich, Hannraoi, Hank,
Henryk, Heromin, Henry —
rules an estate

Herbert, Heribert, Heriberto —
shining fighter

Herwyn, Herwin — loves war

Hildebrand, Hildebrandt — battle-
sword

Hilliard — defender in war

Hobart, Hubert, Hugo, Hugh,
Hugues, Huberto, Humberto,
Huw — intelligent

Holden — gracious

Holman — from the river island

Holmes — son of Holman

Howard — defender

Hrorek — famous ruler

Humbert — shining support

Humfried, Hunfredo, Hunfried —
peaceful Hun

Humphrey, Humfrey — supports
peace

Ibon, Ivar, Ivor, Ive, Iver, Iomhar,
Ives, Ifor — archer

Imre — hard-working

Ingram — Ing's raven

Jarvis, Jervis — sharp as a spear

Jerrold, Jarold — strong with a
spear

Jeffrey — God's peace

Kelby, Kilby — from the farm by
the spring

Kelsey, Kelcey — dwells by the
water

Kerbasy, Kerbasi — warrior

Kirby, Kerby — from the church
village

Kirk — dwells near the church

Koldobika — famous in war

Konrad — strong advisor

Lali, Lajos, Lajcsi, Laji — famous holiness

Lambert, Lamberto — light of the land

Latham — dwells by the barn

Learoyd, Leroy — from the cleared meadow

Ledyard — nation's defender

Leonard, Len, Leonardo, Leonaldo, Lennart, Leonhard — lion

Leopold, Leo, Leupold, Luitpold, Leorad — bold for his people

Liam — resolute defender

Lindsay, Lindsey — from the island of the snakes

Lombard — long-beard

Lopolda, Lopold, Lopoldi, Lipot — patriotic

Lothar, Lothair — fighter

Louis, Lewis, Luther — famous in war

Lydon — from the linden-tree hill

Madison — son of Maud

Manfred, Manfrid — mighty peace

Marvin, Marwin, Marwyn, Mervin, Merwin, Merwyn — mariner

Mason — works in stone

Maynard, Meinrad — brave

Medwin, Medwyn — powerful friend

Merrell, Merrill — famous

Merrick, Merek — strong ruler

Naldo — wise power

Nevin, Nevyn — nephew

Norbert, Norberto — shines like the sea

Norman, Norris, Norvin, Norvyn — from the north

Norward — guardian of the north road

Notker, Notcher — compelling spear

Odo, Odilo, Otto, Ota, Otik, Oto, Otokars, Otomars, Ode, Orton — rich

Olaf — relic

Orlando, Orland — fame of the land

Ormond, Orman — mariner

Osborn, Osbourne — divine bear

Osgood — divine creator

Osmund, Osmond — God's protection

Osric, Osrik — divine ruler

Oswald, Oswaldo, Osvald — divine power

Othmar — happy fame

Otway, Ottoway — lucky in war

Outram — wealthy raven

Patxi, Proinnsias, Paquito, Panchito — free

Paxton, Paxon — trader

Philibert — sharp-willed

Pippen — father

Podi — bold for the people

Pollard — short-haired

Raghnall, Ragnol, Randal, Randahl, Renaud, Rinaldo, Ranaldo, Randolf, Randolph, Rendell — wise power

Ram — raven

Ramsey, Ramsay — from Ram's island

Raoul, Ralph, Raul — strong

Rawdon — from the hill

Raymond, Raymund, Raimund,
Reamonn, Raimondo,
Raimundo, Rajmund, Ramon,
Redmond, Redmund,
Richmond, Ramone,
Reinhold — wise protector

Reginald, Reynold — strong
judgment

Renfred, Renfrid — peacemaker

Renwick, Renwyk — where the
ravens nest

Richard — powerful ruler

Robert, Roberto, Robin, Rob, Rab,
Robby, Raibert, Robinet,
Roibeard, Riobart, Rupert —
bright fame

Roderick, Roderic, Rodrick,
Rurik, Ruaidhri, Ruairidh,
Roderigo, Rogelio — noted
ruler

Roger, Rudger, Rutger, Rotger,
Rudiger, Rogerio, Ruggero,
Ruggiero, Rodrigue — famous
fighter

Roland, Rowland, Rolando,
Rolden, Rodney — famous

Rory — famous ruler

Roscoe — from the roe

Roswell, Roswald, Ross — mighty
horse

Rudolph, Rudolf, Rollo, Rolf,
Rolfe, Rolph, Rolphe, Rollin,
Rollins, Rezso — famous wolf

Saxon — swordsman

Searle, Serle — armed

Selby — from the manor farm

Seldon, Selden — from the manor
valley

Sewell, Seymour — mighty at sea

Siefried, Sigfrid, Sigfried,
Seifred — victorious peace

Sigmund, Sigmond, Sigismund,
Seigmund, Sigismondo —
victorious defender

Sprague — alert

Steen, Sten — stone

Stig — mount

Swain — young

Tage, Tag, Tajo — day

Tedman, Tedmund, Theomund —
defender of the nation

Terrill, Tirell, Terrell — martial
ruler

Terriss, Terris — son of Terry

Thayer — nation's army

Theobald — people's prince

Theodoric, Theodric, Theodrik,
Thierry, Terry, Till, Tillmann,
Tilman, Thilo, Til — people's
rule

Thorley — from Thor's meadow

Thorpe — from the hamlet

Torbert, Thorbert — glorious as
Thor

Tormod — from the north

Torquil, Torkel — from Thor's
cauldron

Torsten, Thorsten, Thurston —
Thor's stone

Traugott — God's truth

Tyson — son of a German

Ugo — spirit

Uilliam, Uileog, Ulik — resolute
defender

Uistean, Ustean, Uisdean,
Uberto, Ubert — intelligent

Uland — from the noble land

Ulrik, Ulric — noble ruler

Uther — myth name

Uwe, Udo — universal ruler
Valdis — spirited in war
Valter, Vater — powerful ruler
Varick, Varik — defending ruler
Verner — protecting friend
Vilhelm, Viljo, Vilho, Vilhelms,
     Vilis — resolute defender
Vilmos, Vili — resolute fighter
Volker — people's defender
Volney — of the people
Waldram — mighty raven
Wallace, Wallis — from Wales
Walter, Walt, Walther, Wlader,
     Wat, Watt, Wouter, Waldemar,
     Waldemarr, Walden, Waldo —
     strong fighter
Ward — guard
Waring — heedful
Warner, Werner, Wuhur,
     Werhar — protecting army
Warren — protecting friend
Warrick, Warwyk, Warwick —
     protecting ruler
Washington — active
Weldon — from the spring by the
     hill

Wendel, Wendell — wanderer
Wies — famous fighter
Wilfrid, Wilfred — resolute peace
Willard — brave
William, Will, Wilhelm,
     Wilhelmus, Willem, Wim —
     strong helmet
Wilmer, Wilmar — famous and
     loved
Wilmot — beloved heart
Wilson — Will's son
Windsor, Winsor — from the bend
     of the river
Winefeld, Winfield — friend of the
     soil
Winfred, Wynfred, Winfryd —
     friend of peace
Winthrop — from the friendly
     village
Wolfe, Wolf — wolf
Wolfgang — wolf's way
Wolfgar — wolf spear
Wolfram — wolf-raven
Zsigmond, Zsiga, Zygmunt —
     victorious defender

Ukrainian

Some Ukrainian surnames are patronymic. Others refer to place or occupation or are descriptive. A sequence of three names is the standard: given name, father's name (in the genitive case) and surname.

Common suffixes:

-enko, -vych, -ovych, -uk, -iuk, -yshyn—son of
-oviat, -iat—ancient forms of son of
-ivna—daughter of
-kha—widow of
-ska, -cka—female
-skyi, -ckyj, -ec, -iak, -ianyn—from

A few Ukrainian surnames:

Demidas	Klimus
Denisovich	Petriv
Dyachenko	Teslenko
Khristin	Tesler
Kimko	Volynskji

FEMALE

Aleksandra—defender of man
Alisa—noble
Aneta, Anita, Anichka—grace
Ionna—God's gift
Katerina, Katrya—Ukrainian form of Katherine (pure)
Klarysa—clear
Lavra—laurel
Leysa, Lyaksandra—defender of man
Marynia, Maryska—bitter

Nastasiya, Nastunye—rebirth
Nyura—graceful
Orynko—peace
Pavla—little
Sofiya, Sofiyko—wisdom
Yaryna—peaceful
Yelysaveta—Ukrainian form of Elizabeth (devoted to God)
Yevtsye, Yeva—Ukrainian form of Eve (life)

MALE

Aleksander — defender of man

Bohdan, Bohdanko, Bogdan, Bodashka — God's gift

Borysko — warrior

Burian — dwells near the weeds

Danya — God's gift

Danylets, Danylko — Ukrainian form of Daniel (judge)

Dymtrus — Ukrainian form of James (supplanter)

Fadey, Faddei, Fadeyka, Fadeyushka — brave

Hadeon — destroyer

Heorhiy — farmer

Ivan — God's gift

Krystiyan — Christian

Lyaksandro — defender of man

Matviyko — God's gift

Mychajlo, Mykhaltso — Ukrainian form of Michael (God-like)

Osip — Ukrainian form of Joseph (God shall add)

Petruso — stone

Vanko — God's gift

Vasylko — noble

Yevheniy, Yevhen — noble

Yure — farmer

Welsh

Despite evidence in medieval records that some Welsh border dwellers used their father's name as a surname as far back as the twelfth century, Wales was one of the last countries in Europe to adopt the use of hereditary surnames. In the sixteenth century, Welshmen who dealt regularly with the English began to use surnames, as did some of the nobility. However, it was not until the nineteenth century that surnames became common throughout the country.

Even today, in remote Welsh districts, some individuals cling to the old custom of adding ap- or ab- to their father's name rather than using a true hereditary surname.

Most surnames are patronymic in origin, but some are related to place, description or occupation.

Patronymic names are prefixed by Mab-, Map-, B-, P-, Ap- or Ab-, or suffixed with -s.

Originally, a Welshman used his given name followed by a list of all his male ancestors' names, which he linked with ap- or ab-.

A few surnames:

Brice	Madoc
Carne	Price
Crowther	Prosser
Don	Pugh
Glace	Teague

FEMALE

Aberfa — from the mouth of the river
Abertha — sacrifice
Adain, Adenydd — winged
Adara — catches birds
Addfwyn — meek
Addiena, Addien — beautiful
Adyna — wretched
Aelwyd — from the hearth
Amser — time
Anghard — loved greatly
Argel — refuge
Arglwyddes — lady
Argoel — omen
Argraff — impression
Arial — vigorous

Ariana, Arian—silver
Arianrhod—myth name
    (daughter of Don)
Arlais—from the temple
Armes—prophetess
Artaith—torment
Arthes—she-bear
Arwydd—sign
Asgre—heart
Atgas—hateful
Awel—breeze
Banon—queen
Berth—beautiful
Berthog—wealthy
Blodwen, Blodwyn—white flower
Braith—freckled
Bregus—frail
Briallan—primrose
Bronwen, Bronwyn, Brangwen,
    Brangwy, Branwenn—dark
    and pure
Buddug—Welsh form of Victoria
    (victory)
Cadi, Catrin—pure
Cadwyn—chain
Caethes—slave
Cafell—oracle
Caniad—song
Cath—cat
Cordelia, Creiddylad—jewel of
    the sea
Corsen—reed
Cragen—shell
Cymreiges—Welsh woman
Dee, Du, Dierdre, Delia—dark
Dera, Daere—fiend
Derwen—from the oak tree
Dicra—slow
Difyr—amusing
Drysi—thorn

Ebrill—born in April
Efa—Welsh form of Eve (life)
Eheubryd—legend name
    (daughter of Kyvwlch)
Elen—Welsh form of Helen
    (light)
Ellylw—legend name (daughter
    of Neol Hang Cock)
Eneuawg—legend name
    (daughter of Bedwyr)
Enit, Enid—woodlark
Enrhydreg—legend name
    (daughter of Tuduathar)
Erdudvyl—legend name
    (daughter of Tryffin)
Eres—wonderful
Esyllt—Welsh form of Isolda
    (fair)
Eurneid—legend name (daughter
    of Clydno)
Eurolwyn—legend name
    (daughter of Gwydolwyn)
Eyslk—fair
Ffanci—fancy
Ffraid—Welsh form of Bridget
    (strong)
Garan—stork
Gladys, Gwladys, Gleda—lame
Glan—from the shore
Glenda, Glyn—from the glen
Goewin—legend name (daughter
    of Pebin)
Goleuddydd—bright day
Gorasgwrn—legend name
    (daughter of Nerth)
Gorawen—joy
Gwaeddan—legend name
    (daughter of Kynvelyn)
Gwanwyn—spring
Gwen, Gwyn, Guinevere,

Gwenhwyvar, Gwyneth, Gwynedd, Gwynne — white

Gwenabwy — legend name (daughter of Caw)

Gwendoline, Gwendolen, Gwyndolen — white-browed

Gwener — Welsh form of Venus (goddess of love)

Gwenledyr — legend name (daughter of Gwawrddur Hunchback)

Gwenn Alarch — legend name (daughter of Kynwal)

Indeg — legend name (daughter of Garwy)

Iola — valued by the Lord

Isolde, Isolda — fair

Kelemon — legend name (daughter of Kei)

Kieve — myth name

Kigva — legend name (wife of Partholon's son)

Lilybet — God's promise

Lowri — Welsh form of Laura (laurel)

Mabli — Welsh form of Mabel (lovable)

Mair — bitter

Mali — Welsh form of Molly (bitter)

Marged, Margred, Mererid, Meghan — pearl

Mercia — from Mercia

Meredith, Maredud, Meredydd — magnificent

Modlen — Welsh form of Magdalene (tower)

Morgan, Morgana, Morgant — from the shore of the sea

Morvudd — legend name (daughter of Uryen)

Myfanawy — my fine one

Neued — legend name (daughter of Kyvwlch)

Olwen, Olwyn, Olwina, Olwyna — white footprint

Penarddun — legend name (daughter of Beli)

Rathtyen — legend name (daughter of Clememyl)

Rhan — fate

Rhawn — coarse, long hair

Rhedyn — fern

Rhiain — maiden

Rhiannon — pure maiden

Rhianwen, Rhianwyn — comely maiden

Rhonwen — Welsh form of Rowena (white-haired)

Rhosyn — rose

Saeth — arrow

Saffir — sapphire

Sarff — snake

Seren — star

Sian, Sioned — Welsh form of Jane (God's gift)

Talaith — diadem

Talar — from the headland in the field

Tangwen — legend name (daughter of Gweir)

Tarian — shield

Tarren — from the knoll

Teleri — legend name (daughter of Peul)

Telyn — harp

Terrwyn — brave

Toreth — abundant

Torlan — from the river bank

Torri — break
Una — white wave
Vala — chosen
Vanora — white wave

Winnifred, Wynnifred — white wave
Wynne, Wyn — fair
Ysbail — spoiled

MALE

Aberthol — sacrifice
Ab-Owen — son of Owen
Adda — Welsh form of Adam (of the red earth)
Addolgar — devout
Adwr — coward
Aedd — legend name (a king of Ireland)
Aethlem — meaning unknown
Ahasferus — meaning unknown
Alawn — harmony
Albanwr — from Scotland
Alun — legend name
Alwyn, Alwin — from Alwyn
Amathaon — legend name (son of Don)
Amerawdwr — emperor
Amhar — legend name (son of Arthur)
Amlawdd — legend name (father of Goleuddydd)
Amren — legend name (son of Bedwyr)
Amynedd, Amyneddgar — patient
Anarawd — legend name (father of Iddig)
Andreas — Welsh form of Andrew (manly)
Aneirin, Aneurin — myth name
Anfri — disgrace
Angawdd — legend name (son of Caw)
Anghrist — Antichrist
Angor — anchor

Anwar — wild
Anwas — legend name (father of Twrch)
Anwell, Anwyl, Anwyll, Anwill, Anwil — beloved
Anwir — liar
Anynnawg — legend name (son of Menw)
Anyon — anvil
Ap-Evan — son of Evan
Ap-Harry — son of Harry
Ap-Howell — son of Howell
Ap-Maddock — son of Maddock
Ap-Owen — son of Owen
Ap-Rhys — son of Rhys
Ardwyad — protector
Arglwydd — lord
Arian — silver
Arthur, Arthwr — bear hero
Arvel, Arval, Arvil — cried over
Avaon — legend name (son of Talyessin)
Awstin — august
Baddon — from Baddon
Baeddan, Badan, Badden — boar
Barris, Barrys — son of Harry
Beda — Welsh form of Bede (name of a priest)
Bedwyr — legend name (son of Pedrawd)
Bedyw — legend name (son of Seithved)
Beli, Beli Mawr — legend name

(brother-in-law of the Virgin
Mary)

Bendigeidfran — blessed raven

Berth — legend name (son of
Cadwy)

Berwyn — legend name (son of
Kerenhyr)

Beven, Bevyn, Bevin — youthful

Blathaon — legend name (son of
Mwrheth)

Bleidd — wolf

Brac — free

Brad — treason

Bradwen — legend name (son of
Moren)

Bradwr — traitor

Braen — corrupt

Bran — raven

Brannock, Brannoc — meaning
unknown

Brathach — legend name (son of
Gwawrddur)

Brian — legend name (son of
Turenn)

Broderick, ap-Roderick — son of
Roderick

Brynn — from the hill

Brys — legend name (son of
Brysethach)

Bwlch — legend name (son of
Cleddyv Kyvwlch)

Cadarn — strong

Caddock, Caddoc, Cadawg —
battle-sharp

Cadell, Cadel — spirit of the battle

Cadellin — legend name (father of
Gweir)

Cadman, Cadmon — warrior

Cadwallen — battle dissolver

Cadwgawn — legend name (son of
Iddon)

Cadwr — legend name (son of
Gwryon)

Cadwy — legend name (son of
Gereint)

Cadyryeith — well-spoken

Caer Llion — from Caerleon

Cai — rejoicer

Cain — clear water

Calcas — legend name (son of
Caw)

Caledvwlch — legend name
(Excalibur)

Cant — white

Caradawg, Caradog — legend
name (father of Eudav)

Carey, Caerau, Cary — from the
castle

Carnedyr — legend name (son of
Govynyon)

Cas — legend name (son of Seidi)

Casnar — legend name (a
nobleman)

Casswallawn, Caswallon — legend
name (son of Beli)

Caw — legend name

Cawrdav — legend name (son of
Caradawg)

Ceithin — legend name (uncle of
Lugh)

Clud — lame

Clust — legend name (son of
Clustveinydd)

Clyde, Clywd — loud-voiced

Cnychwr — legend name (son of
Nes)

Coch — legend name (son of Caw)

Coed — dwells in the woods

Conyn—legend name (son of Caw)

Corryn—spider

Cors—myth name

Craddock, Caradoc, Cradoc—beloved

Crist—Christian

Cubert—legend name (son of Daere)

Culhwch—legend name (son of Kilydd)

Culvanawd—legend name (son of Gwryon)

Custenhin—legend name (father of Erbin)

Cymry—from Wales

Cynbel, Cynbal—warrior chief

Cystennin—constant

Dadweir—legend name

Dafydd, Dewi—dearly loved

Dalldav—legend name (son of Cunyn Cov)

Daned—legend name (son of Oth)

Deverell, Deverril—from river bank

Dewi, Dewey—the Lord's

Digon—legend name (son of Alar)

Dillus—legend name (son of Eurei)

Dirmyg—legend name (son of Caw)

Drem—sight

Dremidydd—legend name (father of Drem)

Drew, Dryw—wise

Druce, Drywsone, Druson—son of Drew

Drudwas—legend name (son of Tryffin)

Drudwyn—meaning unknown

Drwst—legend name

Drych—legend name (son of Kibddar)

Drystan—Welsh form of Tristan (full of sorrow)

Duach—legend name (son of Gwawrddur)

Dwnn—meaning unknown

Dyffryn—meaning unknown

Dylan, Dilan, Dillie, Dillon—born near the sea

Dyngannon—legend name

Dyvynarth—legend name (son of Gwrgwst)

Dyvynwal—legend name

Dyvyr—legend name (son of Alun)

Dywel—legend name (son of Erbin)

Earwine, Erwyn, Earwyn, Erwin—white river

Edern—legend name (son of Nudd)

Edlym—legend name

Edmyg—honor

Ehangwen—legend name

Eiddoel—legend name (son of Ner)

Eiddon—legend name

Eiddyl—legend name

Eiladar—legend name (son of Penn Llarcan)

Einion, Einian—anvil

Eiryn—legend name (son of Peibyn)

Eivyonydd—legend name

Elidyr—legend name

Elphin—legend name (son of Gwyddno)

Emhyr—ruler

Emlyn — waterfall

Emrys — Welsh form of Ambrose (immortal)

Ennissyen — legend name

Erbin — legend name (son of Custenhin)

Ercwlff — Welsh form of Hercules (Hera's glory)

Ergyryad — legend name (son of Caw)

Erim — legend name

Ermid — legend name (son of Erbin)

Erwm — legend name

Eryi — from Snowdon

Eudav — legend name (son of Caradawg)

Eurosswydd — legend name

Eus — legend name (son of Erim)

Evan — young

Evrawg — from York

Evrei — legend name

Ewyas — legend name

Fercos — legend name (son of Poch)

Fflam — legend name (son of Nwyvre)

Fflergant — legend name (a king of Brittany)

Fflewdwr — legend name (son of Naw)

Ffodor — legend name (son of Ervyll)

Ffowc — of the people

Fotor — legend name

Fychan — small

Fyrsil, Fferyll — Welsh form of Virgil (bears the staff)

Gallgoid — legend name

Gamon — legend name

Gandwy — legend name

Garanhon — legend name (son of Glythvyr)

Garanwyn — white shank

Garnock, Garnoc, Gwernach — dwells by the alder-tree river

Garselid — legend name

Garwyli — legend name (son of Gwyddawg Gwyr)

Garym — legend name

Gavin, Gwalchmai — hawk of the battle

Gawl — myth name

Geraint — legend name (father of Cadwy)

Gilbert — legend name (son of Cadgyffro)

Gilvaethwy — legend name (son of Don)

Gleis — legend name (son of Merin)

Glew — legend name (son of Ysgawd)

Glewlwyd — legend name

Glinyeu — legend name (son of Taran)

Gloyw — legend name

Glyn, Glenn, Glynn — dwells in the glen

Glythvyr — legend name

Gobrwy — legend name (son of Echel Pierced Thighs)

Gogyvwlch — legend name

Goreu — legend name (son of Custenhin)

Gormant — legend name (son of Rica)

Goronwy — legend name

Gorsedd — from the mound

Govan—legend name (son of Caw)

Govannon—legend name (son of Don)

Govynyon—legend name

Gower, Gwyr, Gowyr—pure

Granwen—legend name (son of Llyr)

Greid—legend name (son of Eri)

Greidyawl—legend name

Griffin, Griffen, Gryphon, Gryphin—strong in faith

Griffith, Griffeth, Gruffudd, Grufydd—red-haired

Gruddyeu—legend name (son of Muryel)

Gruffin, Gruffen, Gruffyn—fierce lord

Grugyn—legend name

Gryn—legend name

Gusg—legend name (son of Achen)

Gwalchmei—legend name (son of Gwyar)

Gwales—legend name

Gwalhaved—legend name (son of Gwyar)

Gwallawg—legend name (son of Llenawg)

Gwallter—Welsh form of Walter (strong fighter)

Gwarthegydd—legend name (son of Caw)

Gwastad—legend name

Gwawl—legend name (son of Clud)

Gwawrddur—legend name

Gweir—legend name (son of Cadellin Silver)

Gwenwynwyn—legend name (son of Naw)

Gwern—old

Gwerthmwl—legend name

Gwevyl—legend name (son of Gwastad)

Gwiawn—legend name

Gwiffred—legend name

Gwilenhin—legend name (a king of France)

Gwilym—Welsh form of William (determined protector)

Gwitart—legend name (son of Aedd)

Gwlgawd—legend name

Gwlwlwyd—legend name

Gwlyddyn—legend name

Gwrddnei—legend name

Gwrddywal—legend name (son of Evrei)

Gwres—legend name (son of Rheged)

Gwrgwst—legend name

Gwrhyr—legend name

Gwri—legend name

Gwrtheyrn—meaning unknown

Gwryon—legend name

Gwyddawg—legend name (son of Menestyr)

Gwydre—legend name (son of Arthur)

Gwydyon—legend name (son of Don)

Gwyn, Gwynn—handsome (son of Nudd)

Gwyngad—legend name (son of Caw)

Gwynnan—legend name

Gwyr—from Gower

Gwys—legend name

Gwystyl — legend name (son of Nwython)

Gwythyr — legend name (son of Greidyawl)

Heilyn — legend name (son of Gwynn)

Hen Beddestyr — legend name (son of Erim)

Hen Was — old servant

Hen Wyneb — old face

Hetwn — legend name

Heveydd — legend name

Howel, Howell — attentive

Hu, Huw — Welsh form of Hugh (intelligent)

Huabwy — legend name (son of Gwryon)

Huarwar — legend name (son of Avlawn)

Hueil — legend name (son of Caw)

Hydd — deer

Iago — Welsh form of James (supplanter)

Iau — Welsh form of Zeus (life)

Iddawg — legend name (son of Mynyo)

Iddig — legend name (son of Anarawd)

Ioan, Iwan — Welsh form of John (God's gift)

Iona — legend name (a king of France)

Iorwerth — legend name (son of Maredudd)

Iustig — legend name (son of Caw)

Kay — fiery

Kei — legend name (son of Kynyr)

Keith — dwells in the woods

Kelli — from the wood

Kelyddon — legend name

Kelyn — legend name (son of Caw)

Kenehyr — legend name

Kenn, Ken — clear water

Kent — white

Kenyon — from Ennion's mound

Kethtrwm — legend name

Keudawg — legend name

Kevyn — from the ridge

Kian — legend name (father of Lugh)

Kibddar — legend name

Kilwich — myth name

Kilydd — legend name (son of Kelyddon)

Kim — leader

Kimball, Kimble — warrior chief

Kyledyr — legend name (son of Nwython)

Kynan — chief

Kynddilig — legend name

Kyndrwyn — legend name (son of Ermid)

Kynedyr — legend name (son of Hetwn)

Kynlas — legend name (son of Kynan)

Kynon — legend name (son of Clydno)

Kynwal — legend name (son of Caw)

Kynwas — legend name

Kynwrig — legend name

Kynwyl — name of a saint

Kynyr — legend name

Kyvwlch — legend name (son of Cleddyv)

Limwris — legend name

Llacheu — legend name (son of Arthur)

Llaesgymyn—legend name

Llara—meek

Llassar—legend name (son of Llassar Llaes)

Llawr—legend name (son of Erw)

Llawvrodedd—legend name

Llenlleawg—legend name

Llue—legend name

Llevelys—legend name (son of Beli)

Llewelyn, Llewellyn, Llyweilun—lion

Lloyd, Llwyd—one with gray hair

Lludd, Llundein—from London

Llwch—legend name

Llwyarch—legend name

Llwybyr—legend name (son of Caw)

Llwyd—legend name (son of Kil Coed)

Llwydawg—legend name

Llwydeu—legend name (son of Nwython)

Llwyr—legend name (son of Llwyryon)

Llwyrddyddwg—legend name

Llyn—from the lake

Llyr—from the sea

Lug, Luc—Welsh form of Luke (light)

Mabon—legend name (son of Modron)

Mabsant—legend name (son of Caw)

Madawg—legend name (son of Teithyon)

Maddock, Madawc, Madoc, Maddoc, Madog, Maddog—beneficent

Maddox, Maddockson,

Maddocson—son of Maddock

Mael—legend name (son of Roycol)

Maelgwyn—prince of the hounds

Maelwys—legend name (son of Baeddan)

Mallolwch—legend name (king of Ireland)

Manawydan—legend name (son of Llyr)

March—legend name (son of Meirchyawn)

Maredudd—legend name

Math, Mathonwy—myth name

Mawrth—Welsh form of Mars (god of war)

Maxen—legend name

Medyr—legend name (son of Medyredydd)

Meilyg—legend name (son of Caw)

Menw—legend name (son of Teirwaedd)

Mercher—Welsh form of Mercury (messenger of the gods)

Meredith, Meridith, Meredydd—guardian of the sea

Merin—legend name

Meurig—Welsh form of Morris (dark-skinned)

Mihangel—Welsh form of Michael (God-like)

Mil—legend name (son of Dugum)

Moesen—Welsh form of Moses (from the water)

Mordwywr—sailor

Moren—legend name (son of Iaen)

Morgan, Morcan, Morcar — dwells near the sea

Morgannwg — from Glamorgan

Morgant — legend name

Morthwyl — hammer

Morvran — legend name (son of Tegid)

Myrddin — Welsh form of Merlin (hawk)

Naw — legend name (son of Seithved)

Neb — legend name (son of Caw)

Neifion — Welsh form of Neptune (god of the seas)

Ner — legend name

Nerth — legend name (son of Cadarn)

Nerthach — legend name (son of Gwawrddur)

Neued — legend name (father of Tringad)

Newlin, Newyddllyn, Newlyn — dwells near the new pool

Nissyen — legend name (son of Eurosswydd)

Nodawl — legend name

Nudd — legend name

Nynnyaw — legend name (son of Beli)

Odgar — legend name (son of Aedd)

Odyar — myth name

Ofydd — Welsh form of Ovid (a Roman poet)

Ol — legend name (son of Olwydd)

Olwydd — tracker

Ondyaw — legend name (son of a French Duke)

Osla — legend name

Oswallt — Welsh form of Oswald (strength from God)

Oth — legend name

Owein, Owyn, Owen, Owin, Owain — young warrior

Padrig — Welsh form of Patrick (noble)

Panawr — legend name

Parry, Perry — son of Harry

Pebin — legend name

Pedr — Welsh form of Peter (rock)

Pedrawd — legend name

Peibyn — legend name

Peissawg — legend name (a king of Brittany)

Pembroke — lives in the headland

Pendaran — meaning unknown

Penkawr — myth name

Penllyn — from the lake's headland

Penn — from the peak

Penryn — legend name

Penvro — from Pembroke

Peredur — legend name (son of Evrawg)

Powell — son of Howell

Powys — legend name

Price, Prys, Preece — son of Rhys

Pryderi — myth name (son of Pwyll)

Prydwen — handsome

Puw — Welsh form of Pugh (son of Hugh)

Pwyll — son of Howell

Pyrs — Welsh form of Pierce (rock)

Ren, Ryn — ruler

Renfrew, Rhinffrew — dwells near the still river

Rheged — legend name (father of Gwres)

Rheidwn — legend name

Rheu — legend name

Rhioganedd — legend name (a prince of Ireland)

Rhisiart — Welsh form of Richard (strong ruler)

Rhobert — Welsh form of Robert (brilliant renown)

Rhun — legend name (son of Beli)

Rhuvawn — legend name (son of Deorthach)

Rhyawdd — legend name (son of Morgant)

Rhychdir — from the plow land

Rhyd — from the ford

Rhynnon — legend name

Rhys, Rice, Reece, Rees — ardent

Romney, Rumenea — dwells near the curving river

Sach — legend name

Sadwrn — Welsh form of Saturn (god of the harvest)

Sanddev — legend name

Sawyl — legend name

Sayer, Saer, Sayre, Sayers, Sayres — carpenter

Seissyllwch — legend name

Seith, Saith — seven

Seithved — legend name

Sel — legend name (son of Selgi)

Selyf — Welsh form of Solomon (peace)

Selyv — legend name (son of Kynan)

Siarl — Welsh form of Charles (manly)

Siawn — legend name (son of Iaen)

Siencyn — Welsh form of Jenkin (God is gracious)

Sinnoch — legend name (son of Seithved)

Sion — Welsh form of John (God is gracious)

Sior — Welsh form of George (farmer)

Steffan — Welsh form of Stephen (crowned with laurels)

Sugyn — legend name (son of Sugynedydd)

Sulyen — legend name (son of Iaen)

Syvwlch — legend name (son of Cleddyv Kyvwlch)

Tad, Tadd — father

Taffy — beloved

Taliesin, Talyessin — handsome

Tallwch — legend name

Taran — legend name

Tarawg — legend name

Taredd — legend name

Tarrant, Tarran, Taryn, Taren — thunder

Tathal — legend name

Tawy — legend name

Tegvan — legend name

Tegyr — legend name

Teir — legend name

Teirnon — legend name

Teirwaedd — legend name

Teithi — legend name (son of Gwynnan)

Teregud — legend name (son of Iaen)

Timotheus — Welsh form of Timothy (God-given)

Tomos — twin

Ton — legend name

Trachmyr — legend name

Trahern, Trahayarn — incredibly strong

Tremayne, Tremen — lives in the house by the rock

Trent, Trynt — dwells near the rapid stream

Trevelyan, Trevelian — from Elian's home

Tringad — legend name (son of Neued)

Tristan, Trystan — noisy

Tristram — sorrowful

Tryffin — legend name

Tudor, Tewdwr — God's gift

Twm — Welsh form of Tom (gift from God)

Twrch — legend name

Twrgadarn — tower of strength

Tywysog — prince

Uchdryd — legend name (son of Erim)

Unig — legend name

Uryen — legend name

Vaddon — from Bath

Vaughn, Vychan — small

Wadu — legend name (son of Seithved)

Waljan — chosen

Werbenec — meaning unknown

Wmffre — Welsh form of Humphrey (friend of the Huns)

Wren — ruler

Wrnach — legend name

Wynn, Wyn, Winn — handsome

Ynyr — legend name

Ysberin — legend name (son of Fflergant)

Ysberyr — legend name

Ysgawyn — legend name (son of Panon)

Ysgithyrwyn — legend name

Ysgonan — legend name

Yspadaden — myth name

Other

FEMALE

Abebi, Abebe — (Nigerian) asked for

Amira — (Yiddish) grain

Ardath — flowering field

Bethany — (Aramaic) house of poverty

Cari — (Turkish) flows like water

Carma — (Sanskrit) fate

Chanda, Chandra — (Sanskrit) dignified

Chasya, Chasye — (Yiddish) shelter

Deva — (Sanskrit) myth name

Hoshi — (Japan) star

Jayne — (Sanskrit) victorious

Kama — (Sanskrit) love

Kameko — (Japan) child of the tortoise

Lalita — (Sanskrit) pleasant

Lani, Loni — (Hawaiian) sky

Leilani — (Hawaiian) heavenly flower

Mandisa — (South Africa) sweet

Mariel — (Bavarian) bitter

Marigold, Marilla — flower

Martha, Marta, Marit — (Aramaic) lady

Maylea — (Hawaiian) wildflower

Mindel, Minna, Minah, Mirel, Mirka, Mirke — (Yiddish) bitter

Opal, Opel, Opalina, Opaline — (Sanskrit) jewel

Patty — (Aramaic) lady

Reina — (Yiddish) clean

Samantha — (Aramaic) listener

Sanura — (Swahili) kitten

Serophia — meaning unknown

Shayndel, Shayne — (Yiddish) beautiful

Sperancita — meaning unknown

Tabitha — (Aramaic) gazelle

Talitha, Taletha — (Aramaic) damsel

Tamary — palm tree

Tamika — (Japan) people

Tourmaline — (Singhalese) jewel

Upala — (Sanskrit) jewel

Veda — (Sanskrit) understanding

Vidonia — (Portuguese) vine branch

Xhosa — (South Africa) sweet

Zerlina — meaning unknown

MALE

Adon — (Phoenician) lord

Anbessa — a Saracen governor of Spain

Aquinas — saint name

Arvandus — meaning unknown

Ashur — (Semitic) warlike

Bardol, Bartol, Bardo, Bartel, Barta, Bartalan, Berti, Barnaby, Barthelemy, Bartley, Batt, Beartlaidh — (Aramaic) ploughman

Berchmans — meaning unknown

Becket — saint name

Borromeo — meaning unknown

Breindel, Breine — (Yiddish) blessed

Campion — meaning unknown

Cantius — meaning unknown

Dagan, Dagon — (Semitic) little fish

Declan — meaning unknown

DeWitt — (Flemish) blond

Dismas — meaning unknown

Ib — (Phoenician) oath of Baol

Konane — (Hawaiian) bright moon

Kyle — (Yiddish) victorious

Leib — (Yiddish) lion

Ligouri — meaning unknown

Loyola — meaning unknown

Mar — (Aramaic) lord

Namir — (Israeli) leopard

Parthalan, Parlan — (Aramaic) ploughman

Raisa, Raysel — (Yiddish) rose

Razi, Raz, Razial, Rachol, Rachel — secret

Riothamus — great king

Shamir — meaning unknown

Taj — (Urdu) exalted

Tarsicius — meaning unknown

Tevel — (Yiddish) dearly loved

Thady, Tadeo, Thaddeus — (Aramaic) praise

Thomas, Teoma — (Aramaic) twin

Velvel — (Yiddish) wolf

Vortigern — meaning unknown

Zelig — (Yiddish) blessed

Zindel — (Yiddish) defender of man

Index

Aage, 229
Aaron, 156
Aart, 29
Aase, 225
Abaigael, 150
Abaigeal, 150
Aballach, 43
Aban, 37
Abantiades, 202
Abarrane, 150
Abarron, 156
Abas, 202
Abasantis, 202
Abasi, 68
Abayomi, 68
Abba, 37
Abban, 177
Abbas, 37
Abbie, 150
Abboid, 113
Abbot, 76, 156
Abbotson, 156
Abbott, 76, 156
Abby, 150
Abd al Bari, 37
Abd al Hakim, 37
Abd al Jabbar, 37
Abd al Matin, 37
Abd al Qadir, 37
Abd al Rashid, 37
Abd al Sami, 37
Abd al'alim, 37
Abdalrahman, 37
Abdel, 37
Abdera, 127
Abd-er-Rahman, 37
Abderus, 138
Abdul, 37
Abdullah, 37
Abebe, 302
Abebi, 302
Abedabun, 215
Abegayle, 150
Abel, 156
Abelard, 123, 280
Abelia, 150
Abelie, 150
Abella, 103
Abellona, 127
Abellona, 60
Abellone, 127
Abeodan, 29
Abequa, 215
Abeque, 215
Aberfa, 289
Abertha, 289
Aberthol, 292
Aberto, 185

Abetzi, 217
Abey, 217
Abeytu, 217
Abhainn, 254
Abhaya, 167
Abhimanyu, 167
Abhirati, 164
Abia, 36
Abiageal, 173
Abichail, 150
Abigail, 150
Abijah, 156
Abimelech, 156
Abir, 36, 156
Abiram, 156
Abisha, 156
Abjaja, 167
Ablendan, 29
Abner, 156
Ab-Owen, 292
Abooksigun, 219
Abra, 36, 150
Abracham, 177
Abraham, 156
Abram, 156
Abramo, 156, 185
Abrecan, 29
Absalom, 156
Absyrtus, 138, 203
Abu Bakr, 37
Abubakar, 68
Abukcheech, 219
Abydos, 138
Acacia, 127
Academia, 188
Academicus, 203
Acair, 254
Acaiseid, 254
Acantha, 127
Acarnania, 188
Acarnanus, 203
Acastus, 138, 203
Acca, 27
Accalia, 188
Accalon, 43
Accius, 203
Ace, 29, 203
Acel, 107
Aceline, 103
Acennan, 29
Acestes, 138, 203
Acey, 29
Achaean, 203
Achaemenes, 203
Achaemenius, 203
Achaeus, 203

Achaius, 254
Achak, 219
Acharya, 167
Achates, 138, 203
Acheflour, 42
Achelous, 138
Acheron, 138, 203
Acheros, 203
Achilles, 138, 203
Achillides, 203
Achir, 167
Achivu, 203
Acidalia, 188
Acis, 138, 203
Acker, 76
Ackerley, 76
Ackerman, 76
Ackley, 76
Aconteus, 138
Acrisioniades, 203
Acrisius, 138, 203
Actaeon, 139, 203
Actaeonis, 203
Actaeus, 203
Acteon, 139
Actor, 203
Actoris, 203
Acwel, 29
Acwellen, 29
Ada, 72, 119, 277
Adabel, 277
Adah, 150
Adahy, 220
Adain, 289
Adair, 52, 113, 254
Adaira, 253
Adairia, 253
Adal, 119, 123, 277, 280
Adalard, 123, 280
Adalbeorht, 72
Adalbert, 123, 280
Adalbrechta, 72
Adalgar, 123
Adalhard, 123
Adalheida, 119
Adali, 119
Adalia, 119, 277
Adalie, 119, 277
Adalina, 277
Adaline, 277
Adalric, 123, 280
Adalrik, 123

Adalson, 76
Adalwen, 123
Adalwin, 123
Adalwine, 123
Adalwolf, 123
Adalwolfa, 119
Adam, 76, 156
Adamina, 188
Adamnan, 29, 177
Adamson, 76, 156
Adan, 174
Adar, 150, 156
Adara, 36, 127, 150, 173, 289
Adare, 177
Adbelle, 277
Adda, 72, 292
Addaneye, 76
Addergoole, 177
Addfwyn, 289
Addien, 289
Addiena, 289
Addis, 76
Addison, 76
Addney, 76
Addolgar, 292
Addy, 76
Ade, 42
Adeben, 68
Adeen, 174
Adel, 123, 277, 280
Adela, 103, 119, 277
Adelaide, 119
Adelajda, 242
Adelard, 280
Adelbert, 123, 163, 280
Adele, 103, 119
Adelhard, 123
Adelheid, 119
Adelheide, 119
Adelicia, 277
Adelina, 119, 262, 277
Adelinda, 119
Adeline, 119, 277
Adelita, 119, 262
Adelle, 119
Adelpha, 127
Adelphe, 127
Adelphie, 127
Adelric, 280
Adelyte, 119
Adena, 150
Adene, 150

Adenydd, 289
Aderet, 156
Aderrig, 177
Adette, 119
Adhamh, 113, 177, 254
Adharma, 167
Adi, 167
Adia, 72
Adiba, 36
Adil, 37
Adila, 36
Adin, 156
Adinam, 150
Adine, 150
Adio, 68
Adir, 156
Adiran, 49
Aditi, 164, 170
Aditya, 167
Adiv, 156
Adiva, 36
Adken, 76
Adkins, 76
Adkyn, 76
Adlai, 156
Adlar, 123, 280
Adler, 123, 280
Adley, 156
Admeta, 127
Admetus, 139
Admina, 151
Adnan, 37
Adne, 123
Adney, 76
Adny, 76
Adoette, 213
Adofo, 68
Adok, 203, 244
Adolf, 123, 244, 280
Adolph, 123, 273, 280
Adolpha, 119
Adolphina, 277
Adolphine, 277
Adolphus, 273, 280
Adom, 68
Adon, 156, 302
Adonia, 127
Adonis, 139
Adora, 188
Adorabella, 188
Adorabelle, 188
Adoracion, 262
Adoree, 188
Adoria, 188
Adorjan, 163

Adorlee, 103
Adras, 140
Adrasteia, 189
Adrastus, 139
Adreana, 183
Adri, 171
Adria, 189
Adrian, 119, 189, 203, 271
Adriana, 183, 262
Adriane, 119
Adriano, 185, 203, 267
Adrie, 63, 189
Adriel, 156
Adrien, 203
Adrienne, 103
Adrik, 203, 248
Adriyel, 156
Adsaluta, 50
Adsila, 215
Advent, 107
Adwr, 292
Adya, 164
Adyna, 289
Aea, 189
Aeacus, 139
Aeaea, 127
Aeccestane, 77
Aedd, 292
Aedon, 127
Aedre, 27
Aeetes, 139, 203
Aefentid, 27
Aefre, 27
Aegaea, 189
Aegaeus, 203
Aegates, 189
Aegelmaere, 77
Aegelweard, 77
Aegeria, 193
Aegeus, 139, 203
Aegides, 203
Aegileif, 225
Aegina, 127, 189
Aeginae, 189
Aegir, 229
Aegis, 139
Aegisthus, 139, 203
Aegyptus, 139, 203
Aeldra, 72, 76
Aelfdane, 76
Aelfdene, 76
Aelfraed, 72, 76
Aelfric, 77
Aelfwine, 72
Aelle, 29
Aello, 127
Aelwyd, 289
Aeneades, 203
Aeneas, 139, 203
Aenedleah, 76
Aenescumb, 76
Aengus, 52, 177, 254
Aeolia, 189
Aeolius, 203
Aeolus, 139, 203
Aerlene, 28
Aerwyna, 74

Aescby, 77
Aescford, 77
Aeschylus, 203
Aesclapius, 203
Aescleah, 77
Aesclin, 77
Aesctun, 77
Aesculapius, 139, 203
Aescwine, 77
Aescwyn, 77
Aesir, 229
Aesoburne, 77
Aeson, 139, 203
Aethelbald, 29
Aethelbeorht, 83
Aethelbeorn, 76
Aethelberht, 76
Aethelbert, 29, 76
Aethelflaed, 27
Aethelfrith, 29
Aethelhard, 76
Aethelhere, 29
Aethelisdun, 76
Aethelmaer, 76
Aethelmaere, 77
Aethelred, 29
Aethelreda, 74
Aethelstan, 30
Aethelstun, 76
Aethelthryth, 27
Aethelweard, 77
Aethelwine, 72
Aethelwulf, 29
Aethelwyne, 72
Aetheston, 76
Aethiops, 203
Aethlem, 292
Aethra, 127
Aethretun, 77
Aetna, 128
Aevar, 229
Affrica, 112
Afi, 229
Afra, 151
Afreda, 72
Afric, 50, 173
Africa, 50, 112, 173
Afrodille, 103
Agacia, 262
Agafia, 128, 246
Agalaia, 128
Agalia, 128
Agamedes, 139
Agamemnon, 139
Agastya, 167
Agata, 128, 173, 183, 262, 271
Agate, 128, 173
Agatha, 119, 128
Agathe, 103, 119
Agathi, 128
Agaton, 271
Agaue, 128
Agave, 128
Agda, 271
Age, 229
Agenor, 139, 203
Ager, 49, 156
Agestes, 138

Aggie, 161
Aghaderg, 177
Aghadreena, 173
Aghamora, 173
Aghamore, 177
Aghaveagh, 173
Aghavilla, 173
Aghna, 174
Aghy, 177
Agi, 161
Agiefan, 29
Agilberht, 29
Aglaeca, 29
Aglaral, 43
Aglarale, 43
Aglauros, 128
Aglaval, 43
Agna, 128
Agnek, 128
Agnella, 128, 183
Agnes, 128
Agnese, 128, 183, 262
Agnessa, 246
Agneta, 60, 128, 271
Agneya, 167
Agni, 171
Agnimukha, 167
Agoston, 163, 205
Agotha, 128, 161
Agoti, 161
Agrafina, 189, 246
Agrafine, 189
Agramant, 107
Agravain, 43
Agrican, 107
Agrippa, 203
Agrippina, 189
Agrippinae, 189
Agueda, 128, 262
Aguistin, 177
Agurtzane, 48, 262
Agyfen, 29
Agymah, 68
Ahalya, 164
Ahana, 174
Ahane, 177
Ahanu, 218, 219
Ahasferus, 292
Ahava, 151
Ahave, 151
Ahearn, 52, 177
Aheawan, 29
Ahebban, 29
Aherin, 113
Ahern, 52, 113, 177
Aherne, 113
Ahiga, 222
Ahiliya, 221
Ahisma, 164, 170
Ahmed, 37
Ahmik, 218
Ahote, 221
Ahreddan, 29
Ahren, 123
Ahriman, 107, 167

Ahtunowhiho, 220
Ahuda, 151
Ahura Mazda, 241
Ahuva, 151
Aibne, 254
Aichlin, 177
Aickin, 76
Aida, 72, 103, 183, 262
Aidan, 29, 52, 113, 174
Aideen, 174
Aiden, 52
Aidia, 262
Aidoios, 128
Aidrian, 177
Aife, 50
Aifric, 50, 173
Aiglentina, 103
Aiglentine, 103
Aigneis, 50, 112, 128, 174
Aiken, 29, 76
Aikin, 76
Ail, 254
Aila, 252
Ailat, 151
Ailbe, 52, 123
Ailbert, 254
Ailean, 113, 254
Aileana, 252
Aileen, 174, 252
Ailein, 254
Ailen, 113
Ailey, 174
Ailfrid, 177
Aili, 120, 174
Ailia, 174
Ailidh, 50
Ailill, 52
Ailin, 113, 177
Ailis, 50, 112, 120, 174
Ailisa, 174
Ailise, 174
Aillig, 254
Ailsa, 60, 151, 277
Ailse, 120
Ailsie, 151
Aimee, 103
Aimil, 112
Aimiliana, 277
Aimilionia, 277
Ain, 66, 76
Aina, 50, 271
Aindreas, 113, 140, 177, 254
Aindriu, 140
Aine, 50, 174
Aineislis, 177
Aingeal, 50, 174
Aingealag, 112
Aingeru, 49
Ainhoa, 48, 262
Ainhoe, 262
Ainmire, 177
Ainsley, 76
Ainslie, 76
Ainsworth, 76

Aintzane, 48, 262
Airavata, 167
Airdsgainne, 113
Airell, 52
Airla, 128
Airleas, 112, 113, 174, 177
Airlia, 128
Aisford, 77
Aisha, 36
A'ishah, 36
Aisle, 72
Aisley, 27, 77
Aislin, 174
Aisling, 174
Aislinn, 174
Aisly, 27
Aiston, 77
Aitan, 156
Aithne, 50
Aitziber, 48, 262
Aiya, 151
Aiyana, 213
Aja, 167
Ajax, 139, 203
Ajaya, 170
Akakia, 127
Akando, 218
Akantha, 127
Ake, 229, 273
Akecheta, 222
Akhenaten, 68
Akiba, 151, 156
Akibe, 151
Akiiki, 68
Akil, 37, 49, 68, 139
Akila, 66
Akilah, 36
Akilina, 190, 246
Akim, 156
Akins, 68
Akir, 254
Akira, 252
Akiva, 151, 156
Akker, 76
Akram, 37
Aksel, 123, 156
Akshamala, 164
Akshobhya, 167
Akub, 156
Akule, 218
Alabhaois, 177
Alacoque, 103
Alai, 113
Alaida, 189
Alain, 43, 107, 112
Alaine, 174
Alair, 203
Alajos, 280
Al'alim, 37
Alameda, 213, 262
Alan, 52
Alana, 112, 174
Alane, 50
Alanna, 50, 112, 174
Alano, 267
Alanson, 52
Alaois, 281

Alaqua, 213
Alard, 280
Alaric, 123, 280
Alarica, 119, 277
Alarice, 119
Alaricia, 277
Alarick, 123
Alarico, 267
Alarik, 123
Alasdair, 139, 254
Alastair, 139, 254
Alaster, 113
Alastor, 139
Alastrina, 50, 174
Alastrine, 50
Alastriona, 50, 174
Alawa, 214
Alawn, 292
Alayne, 112, 174
Alazne, 48, 262
Alba, 189
Alban, 177, 203
Albanact, 254
Albano, 203
Albanwr, 292
Albaric, 107
Alberic, 280
Alberich, 229
Alberik, 273
Albern, 76, 280
Albert, 76, 123, 163, 273, 280
Alberta, 72, 119, 161, 277
Alberte, 277
Alberteen, 72
Albertina, 72, 103, 119, 262, 277
Albertine, 72, 103, 119, 262, 277
Alberto, 267
Albertyna, 72
Albertyne, 72, 119
Albin, 203
Albin, 244
Albina, 189
Albinia, 183, 189
Albinka, 242
Albinus, 29, 203
Albion, 43, 203
Albiona, 42
Albracca, 103
Albrecht, 123
Albula, 189
Albunea, 189
Alburn, 76
Alburt, 76
Albus, 203
Alcaeus, 203
Alcamene, 189
Alcestis, 128
Alchfrith, 29
Alcibiades, 203
Alcides, 139, 203
Alcimede, 189
Alcina, 103, 128
Alcinoos, 139

Alcinous, 139, 203
Alcippe, 128, 189
Alcmaeon, 139
Alcmena, 189
Alcmene, 128
Alcott, 76
Alcuin, 281
Alcumena, 189
Alcyone, 128, 132
Alcyoneus, 139
Ald, 123
Alda, 119, 277
Aldan, 76
Aldea, 277
Alden, 29, 76
Alder, 76
Aldercy, 72
Aldfrith, 29
Aldhelm, 29
Aldin, 29
Aldis, 72, 76
Aldo, 76, 123, 185, 281
Aldona, 120, 242
Aldonsa, 262
Aldonza, 262
Aldora, 72, 128
Aldous, 76
Aldred, 29, 76
Aldric, 76
Aldrich, 107
Aldrich, 76, 281
Aldrick, 107
Aldrid, 76
Aldridge, 281
Aldrik, 76, 123
Aldtun, 76
Aldus, 76
Aldwin, 76
Aldwine, 76
Aldwyn, 29, 76
Aldys, 72
Alec, 139
Alecta, 128
Aleda, 72, 120
Aleen, 63
Aleeza, 151
Aleezah, 151
Alegria, 262
Alejandra, 262
Alejandrina, 262
Alejandro, 267
Alek, 248
Aleka, 128
Aleksander, 288
Aleksandr, 139, 244, 248
Aleksandra, 246, 287
Aleksandur, 139
Aleksi, 248
Aleksis, 248
Aleksy, 139, 244
Alemannus, 123
Alena, 128, 246
Alene, 50, 63
Aler, 76
Alera, 189
Aleria, 189
Alerio, 203

Aleris, 128
Alerissa, 128
Aleron, 107, 203
Alesandese, 48, 128
Alesia, 128
Alessandra, 183
Alessandro, 139, 185
Aleta, 72, 189, 262
Aletea, 262
Alethea, 128
Aletheia, 128
Alethia, 128
Aletia, 262
Aletta, 183, 189
Alex, 139
Alexa, 128, 161
Alexander, 139, 273
Alexandina, 128
Alexandra, 128, 161, 183, 246, 271
Alexandras, 139
Alexandre, 43, 107, 189
Alexandrea, 189
Alexandria, 189
Alexandriana, 189
Alexandrina, 189
Alexandrine, 103, 189
Alexandros, 139
Alexandrukas, 139
Alexei, 139
Alexei, 248
Alexia, 128
Alexina, 128, 189
Alexine, 128, 189
Alexio, 139
Alexis, 103, 128, 139, 189
Aleyn, 44
Alf, 229, 273
Alfarin, 229
Alfarinn, 229
Alfdis, 225
Alfgeir, 229
Alfons, 273
Alfonsa, 262, 277
Alfonsine, 119
Alfonso, 123, 267, 273, 281
Alford, 76
Alfred, 29, 76, 273, 277, 281
Alfreda, 262, 277
Alfredo, 76, 185, 267
Alfrid, 76
Alfrida, 72
Alfrieda, 277
Alfrigg, 229
Alfrothul, 229
Algar, 29
Alger, 29, 123, 281
Algernon, 107

Algiana, 277
Algiane, 277
Algoma, 213
Algot, 271
Algrenon, 107
Alhhard, 76
Alhmarric, 123
Alhraed, 72
Alhric, 76
Alhrick, 76
Alhrik, 76
Alhsom, 123
Alhwin, 123
Ali, 36
Alice, 50, 120, 277
Alicea, 277
Aliceson, 76
Alicia, 120, 128, 262, 271, 277
Alida, 63, 120, 189
Alik, 248
Alima, 36
Alina, 50, 63, 112, 128, 174, 242, 246, 277
Aline, 50, 63, 277
Alirick, 280
Alis, 44
Alisa, 277, 287
Alison, 76, 120, 174, 252, 277, 281
Alissa, 277
Alisz, 120, 161
Alita, 72, 103, 262
Alithia, 277
Alitza, 151
Alix, 139, 277
Alixandre, 43
Aliz, 120, 161
Aliza, 151
Alizah, 151
Alka, 170, 242
All, 76
Alla, 247
Allan, 52
Allard, 76, 280
Allegra, 103, 183
Allen, 52
Allene, 112, 174
Allete, 103
Allis, 277
Allison, 174, 277, 281
Allister, 113
Allochka, 247
Allona, 151
Allonia, 151
Allred, 76
Allsun, 174
Allura, 72
Allyn, 52, 112, 174
Allys, 277
Alma, 50, 174, 189, 262, 271
Almer, 77
Almeta, 60, 189
Almira, 36, 262

Almo, 76
Almund, 29
Almunda, 262
Almundena, 262
Almundina, 262
Alo, 221
Alodia, 27
Alodie, 27
Aloeus, 139
Aloin, 107
Alois, 123, 203
Aloisia, 120
Alon, 156
Alona, 48, 151, 262
Alonia, 151
Alonsa, 120, 262
Alonso, 267, 281
Alonza, 183, 277
Alonzo, 267, 281
Alosaka, 221
Aloyoshenka, 248
Aloys, 281
Aloysha, 248
Aloysia, 120, 277
Aloysius, 203, 281
Alpha, 128
Alphenor, 139
Alpheus, 139
Alphonsa, 277
Alphonse, 281
Alphonsine, 119
Alphonso, 123, 281
Alphonsus, 177
Alphonza, 277
Alphosina, 277
Alpin, 254
Alpina, 252
Alric, 280
Alrigo, 186, 281
Alrik, 123, 273, 280
Alroy, 113, 177, 203
Alsandair, 177
Alson, 76
Alsoomse, 214
Alston, 76
Alta, 189
Altair, 36, 37
Altaira, 36
Alter, 156
Altha, 72
Althaea, 128
Althaia, 128
Althea, 128
Altheda, 72, 128
Althia, 72
Altman, 123
Altmann, 123
Alton, 76
Altsoba, 217
Aluin, 107
Aluino, 267
Alula, 36
Aluld, 189
Aluma, 151
Alumit, 151
Alun, 292

Alura, 72
Alurea, 72
Alva, 63, 120, 156, 189, 203, 262
Alvan, 281
Alvar, 120, 203, 273
Alvara, 120
Alvarie, 120
Alver, 203
Alvera, 277
Alverna, 277
Alvernia, 277
Alvie, 120
Alvin, 123, 281
Alvina, 72, 277
Alvinia, 189, 277
Alvira, 277
Alvis, 229
Alviss, 229
Alvita, 189
Alvord, 76
Alvy, 123, 174
Alvyn, 281
Alwalda, 29
Alwin, 29, 123, 281, 292
Alwyn, 281, 292
Alyce, 277
Alycesone, 76
Alyda, 120
Alyosha, 139
Alyoshenka, 139
Alys, 50, 120, 277
Alysia, 128
Alyson, 174
Alyssa, 128, 277
Alzan, 36
Alzbeta, 58
Alzena, 36
Alzina, 36
Amabel, 189
Amabella, 103, 189
Amabelle, 103, 189
Amabilis, 189
Amadahy, 215
Amadea, 189
Amadee, 189
Amadeo, 185, 203, 267
Amadeus, 203
Amadina, 189
Amadine, 189
Amadio, 204
Amadis, 189, 203
Amado, 204, 267
Amaethon, 29
Amaia, 48, 262
Amal, 36
Amala, 36
Amalasand, 120
Amalasanda, 120
Amalea, 183, 189
Amalgith, 177
Amalia, 183, 262, 271, 277
Amalie, 189, 277
Amalija, 277
Amaliji, 247

Amalthea, 128
Amalthia, 128
Amalur, 262
Amalure, 262
Amanda, 189, 262
Amara, 120, 128, 189
Amaranda, 128
Amarande, 128
Amaranta, 262
Amarante, 103
Amarantha, 128
Amaravati, 164
Amare, 189
Amariah, 151
Amaris, 151
Amarisa, 151
Amarise, 151
Amarissa, 151
Amarna, 189
Amaryllis, 128
Amasa, 156
Amata, 103, 189, 262
Amathaon, 292
Amaury, 107
Amayeta, 216
Amba, 164
Ambar, 170
Amber, 36, 112
Ambert, 280
Ambi, 164
Ambika, 164, 170
Amblaoibh, 177
Ambra, 103
Ambre, 103
Ambrocio, 139
Ambros, 177
Ambrose, 139
Ambrosi, 185
Ambrosia, 128, 164
Ambrosine, 128
Ambrosio, 267
Ambrosius, 64, 273
Ambrotosa, 128
Ambrus, 139, 163
Amedee, 103
Ameerah, 36
Amelia, 189, 277
Amelie, 103, 277
Amelinda, 189
Amelita, 189
Amen, 68
Amenhotep, 68
Amenophis, 68
Amen-Ra, 68
Amerawdwr, 292
Ameretat, 167
Americus, 204
Amerigo, 204, 281
Amery, 123, 204, 281
Amethyst, 128
Amhar, 292
Amhlaoibh, 178, 229
Amhuinn, 112, 254

Ami, 103
Amialiona, 277
Amias, 204
Amichai, 156
Ami-el, 156
Amiel, 156
Amikam, 156
Amilia, 189
Amin, 37
Amineh, 36
Aminta, 189
Amiphitryon, 204
Amir, 36, 37, 156, 241
Amira, 36, 240, 302
Amiram, 156
Amita, 156
Amitabha, 167
Amite, 103
Amitee, 103
Amiti, 156
Amitola, 213
Amity, 103, 189
Amlawdd, 292
Amma, 167, 225
Ammar, 37
Ammi, 156
Ammitai, 156
Ammon, 68
Amnchadh, 177
Amnon, 156
Amon, 156
Amor, 262
Amora, 262
Amoretta, 189
Amorette, 189
Amorica, 72
Amorita, 189
Amory, 123, 204, 281
Amos, 156
Amphiaraus, 139, 204
Amphion, 139
Amphitrite, 128, 189
Amphitryo, 204
Amphitryon, 139, 204
Ampyx, 139
Amr, 44
Amram, 156
Amren, 292
Amrita, 164
Amritha, 164, 170
Amsden, 76
Amselmo, 281
Amser, 289
Amsi, 68
Amsu, 68
Amulius, 204
Amun, 68
Amund, 229
Amundi, 229
Amunet, 66
Amy, 103
Amyas, 204
Amycus, 139
Amymone, 128, 189

Amynedd, 292
Amyneddgar, 292
Amynta, 189
Amyntas, 189
An, 229
Ana, 151
Anaba, 217
Anabal, 112
Anabel, 189
Anabella, 189
Anacreon, 204
Anahid, 40, 189
Anahita, 164
Anais, 151
Anakausuen, 219
Anala, 170
Analise, 151
Anamari, 151
Anamarie, 151
Anand, 171
Ananda, 167, 170
Ananga, 167
Anant, 52
Ananta, 170
Anarawd, 292
Anastagio, 139, 185
Anastasia, 128, 247
Anastasio, 139, 267
Anastasios, 140
Anastasius, 139
Anastazja, 242
Anasuya, 164
Anasztaizia, 162
Anasztaz, 139
Anat, 66, 151
Anata, 151
Anate, 151
Anatie, 151
Anatol, 139, 259
Anatola, 128
Anatole, 139
Anatoli, 139
Anatolia, 128
Anatolii, 248
Anatolijus, 139
Anatolio, 139
Anaxagoras, 204
Anaxarete, 128, 189
Anaximander, 204
Anaximenes, 204
Anbessa, 302
Anbidian, 29
Ancaeus, 139
Ance, 151
Ancelin, 103
Ancelina, 103
Ancenned, 29
Anchises, 140, 204
Anci, 162
Ancil, 107, 281
Ancile, 204
Ancyra, 189
Andeana, 262
Ander, 49, 140, 229

Andera, 262
Andere, 48, 262
Anders, 61, 140, 273
Anderson, 140, 229, 256, 273
Andes, 189
Andettan, 29
Andoni, 204
Andor, 140, 163
Andraemon, 140
Andras, 225
Andraste, 50
Andrea, 60, 103, 128, 140, 185, 262
Andreana, 183, 189
Andreas, 123, 128, 273, 293
Andree, 103
Andrei, 248, 259
Andres, 140, 267
Andret, 44
Andrew, 140
Andria, 189
Andriana, 189
Andries, 140
Andrion, 203
Androgeus, 140
Andromacha, 189
Andromache, 128, 189
Andromeda, 128, 189
Andronicus, 204
Androu, 140
Andrusha, 248
Andrya, 248
Andrzej, 244
Andsaca, 29
Andsware, 27
Andswarian, 29
Andswaru, 27, 29
Andvaranaut, 229
Andvari, 229
Andweard, 29
Andwearde, 29
Andwyrdan, 29
Ane, 29, 151
Anechka, 247
Aneirin, 292
Anemone, 128, 189
Aneta, 151, 287
Anetta, 151
Aneurin, 292
Anevay, 213
Anezka, 58, 128
Anfeald, 29
Anfri, 292
Anga, 165
Angawdd, 292
Ange, 103
Angel, 128, 140, 189, 267
Angela, 103, 128, 183, 189, 262
Angeletta, 103
Angelette, 103
Angelia, 183, 262
Angelica, 189

Angelika, 103
Angeliki, 128
Angelina, 103, 128, 189, 262
Angeline, 103, 128, 189
Angelique, 103, 128
Angelita, 189
Angell, 140
Angelo, 140, 185, 267
Angeni, 213
Angerboda, 225
Angerbotha, 225
Angerona, 189
Angharad, 42
Angharat, 42
Anghard, 289
Anghrist, 292
Anghus, 52
Angilia, 103
Angirasa, 165
Anglesey, 76
Anglides, 42
Angor, 292
Angrboda, 225
Anguis, 204
Anguish, 177
Angus, 52, 113, 140, 177, 254
Anguysh, 44
Angwusnasomtaqa, 216
Angyalka, 162
Anhaga, 29
An-her, 68
Anhur, 68
Ania, 242
Anibal, 140, 267
Anica, 151, 262
Anice, 252
Anichka, 151, 287
Anicka, 58
Anieli, 242
Anika, 63, 151
Aniki, 151
Aniko, 151
Anila, 170
Aniol, 140
Anippe, 66
Anir, 44
Anish, 167
Anita, 151, 183, 262, 287
Anitchka, 247
Anitia, 262
Anitra, 151
Anius, 204
Anjelika, 189
Anka, 151, 242
Ankara, 189
Anke, 63
Anker, 61, 140
Anki, 63
Ankine, 40
Ankti, 216
Anku, 151
Anlicnes, 27
Anlicnisse, 27
Anlon, 177

Anluan, 177
Anmcha, 177
Ann, 76, 123, 151, 177
Anna, 29, 42, 76, 151, 189, 214, 247, 271
Anna Cristina, 271
Anna Perenna, 189
Annabel, 112, 252
Annabella, 112, 252
Annabelle, 112, 189
Annabla, 174
Annaduff, 177
Annali, 271
Annalie, 271
Annaliese, 151
Annalina, 271
Annalisa, 151
Annamari, 120
Annamarie, 151
Annan, 52
Annapurna, 165
Annar, 229
Anndra, 140
Anne, 151
Anneli, 271
Anneliese, 151
Annelise, 60
Annemarie, 120
Annemette, 60
Annemie, 63
Annette, 103, 151
Annie, 151
Annika, 271
Annike, 271
Annikka, 151
Annikke, 151
Annikki, 100, 151
Annis, 27, 128
Annona, 190
Annora, 151
Annorah, 151
Annot, 151
Annraoi, 281
Anntoin, 177
Annunciata, 190
Annuziata, 183
Annwfn, 50
Annwn, 50
Anny, 151
Annys, 128
Annze, 151
Anoki, 218
Anona, 190
Anora, 72, 151
Anoush, 40
Anpaytoo, 218
Anpu, 68
Anrid, 225
Ansa, 190
Anscom, 76
Anscomb, 76
Anse, 190
Ansel, 107, 281
Ansell, 107

Anselm, 281
Anselma, 225, 277
Anselmo, 267
Ansgar, 52, 230, 273, 281
Ansleigh, 76
Ansley, 76
Anson, 29, 123
Anstace, 128
Anstice, 128, 139, 140
Anstiss, 140
Antaeus, 140
Antal, 204
Antanas, 204
Antandra, 190
Antanelis, 204
Antanukas, 204
Ante, 204
Antea, 128
Antenor, 204
Anteros, 140, 204
Antfortas, 44
Anthea, 128
Anthia, 128
Anthony, 140
Anthor, 140
Anticlea, 128
Antigone, 129, 190
Antilochus, 140, 204
Antinko, 248
Antinous, 140
Antiope, 129
Antiphates, 140, 204
Antisthenes, 204
Antje, 151
Antoin, 204
Antoine, 204
Antoinetta, 190
Antoinette, 103, 190
Anton, 123, 140, 248, 267, 273
Antonetta, 271
Antonia, 183, 190, 262
Antonie, 120
Antonietta, 183
Antonin, 204
Antonina, 190, 242, 247, 262
Antonio, 185, 267
Antonius, 273
Antoniy, 204
Antony, 140
Antor, 44
Antosha, 248
Antranig, 40
Antropas, 129
Antti, 100, 140
Anttiri, 100
Antton, 49, 204
Anubis, 68
Anum, 68
Anumati, 165
Anunciacion, 262
Anwar, 292
Anwas, 292

Anwealda, 29
Anwell, 52, 292
Anwil, 292
Anwill, 292
Anwir, 292
Anwyl, 52, 292
Anwyll, 292
Anya, 247
Anynnawg, 292
Anyon, 52, 292
Anysia, 129
Anyuta, 151
Anzel, 281
Anzelm, 281
Anzety, 68
Aod, 52, 113
Aodh, 52, 113
Aodhagan, 113
Aodhan, 52
Aodhfin, 177
Aodhfionn, 177
Aodhan, 113
Aodhnait, 174
Aoibheann, 174
Aoidh, 254
Aoife, 151
Aoife, 174
Aonghas, 140
Aonghus, 52, 113, 177, 254
Ap Owen, 52
Apala, 165
Ap-Evan, 292
Apelles, 204
Apenimon, 218
Ap-Harry, 292
Ap-Howell, 292
Aphria, 50
Aphrodite, 129
Apirka, 112
Apis, 68
Ap-Maddock, 292
Ap-Owen, 292
Apollina, 103, 129
Apollinaris, 129
Apolline, 103
Apollo, 44, 140, 204
Apollodorus, 204
Apollonia, 129
Apollonis, 190
Apoloniusz, 140, 244
Aponi, 213
Aponivi, 221
Apophis, 69
Ap-Rhys, 292
April, 190
Aprille, 190
Apsaras, 165
Apsel, 123, 251
Apulia, 190
Aquene, 213
Aquilina, 190, 262
Aquiline, 190
Aquilino, 204, 267
Aquinas, 302
Aquitania, 190
Ar, 27

Ara, 36, 40, 129, 277
Arabella, 63, 120, 277
Arabia, 190
Araceli, 190, 262
Aracelia, 190, 262
Arachne, 129, 190
Aralt, 177
Aram, 156
Arama, 48, 262
Araminta, 151
Araminte, 151
Aranck, 219
Aranka, 162
Arar, 204
Ararinda, 120
Araris, 204
Aratus, 204
Arawn, 52
Arber, 107, 204
Arbor, 204
Arcadia, 190, 262
Arcanania, 190
Arcas, 140, 204
Arcelia, 262
Archaimbaud, 107
Archambault, 107
Archard, 29, 107, 123
Archemorus, 140
Archenbaud, 107
Archer, 76, 204
Archerd, 29
Archere, 76
Archibald, 29, 123, 281
Archibaldo, 267
Archimbald, 123
Archimedes, 204
Arcitenens, 204
Arctophylax, 204
Arctos, 204
Arcturus, 204
Arda, 72
Ardagh, 177
Ardal, 123, 177
Ardala, 174
Ardaleah, 76
Ardath, 151, 302
Ardea, 190
Ardeen, 72, 190
Ardel, 76
Ardelia, 72
Ardelis, 190
Ardell, 76
Ardella, 72, 190
Ardelle, 190
Arden, 44, 204
Ardene, 72, 190
Ardi, 72
Ardin, 204
Ardina, 190
Ardine, 72, 190
Ardinia, 190
Ardis, 190
Ardith, 27, 277
Ardkill, 177

Ardleigh, 76
Ardley, 76
Ardmore, 204, 281
Ardolf, 76
Ardolph, 76
Ardra, 50, 190
Ardwolf, 76
Ardwyad, 292
Ardyne, 72
Ardys, 72
Are, 123
Areille, 151
Arela, 50
Aren, 61, 123, 229
Arena, 129
Arend, 61, 123
Arene, 129
Ares, 140, 204
Areta, 129
Arete, 129
Aretha, 129
Arethusa, 129, 190
Aretina, 129
Argante, 42
Argel, 289
Argenta, 190
Argentia, 190
Argentina, 190
Argi, 48
Argia, 129
Argie, 129
Arglwydd, 292
Arglwyddes, 289
Argo, 140
Argoel, 289
Argolis, 190
Argos, 140
Argous, 190
Argraff, 289
Argus, 61, 140, 204
Argyle, 52, 254
Ari, 156
Aria, 73, 183, 277
Ariadna, 190
Ariadne, 129, 190
Arial, 289
Arian, 29, 290, 292
Ariana, 129, 190, 290
Ariane, 129
Arianrhod, 290
Arianrod, 27
Aric, 76, 123, 280
Aricia, 190
Aricin, 229
Arick, 123
Aridatha, 151
Arie, 156
Ariel, 151, 156
Ariela, 151
Ariellel, 151
Arienh, 50, 112
Aries, 204
Arietta, 72
Ariette, 72
Arif, 37
Arik, 76, 123, 280

Arild, 229
Arilda, 277
Arilde, 277
Ariobarzanes, 204
Arion, 140, 156, 204
Aristaeus, 140
Aristarchus, 204
Aristid, 140
Aristodeme, 190
Aristophanes, 204
Aristoteles, 204
Aristotle, 140
Arkadina, 247
Arkin, 229
Arkwright, 76
Arkyn, 229
Arlais, 290
Arlan, 52
Arlana, 50
Arledge, 76
Arleen, 50, 174
Arleigh, 77
Arlen, 52, 113, 177
Arlena, 174
Arlene, 50, 174
Arles, 251
Arleta, 50, 174
Arlette, 50, 174
Arley, 77
Arlice, 30
Arlie, 77
Arlin, 52
Arlina, 50
Arline, 50, 174
Arlo, 77, 267
Arlyn, 52, 177
Arlyne, 174
Arlys, 30
Arlyss, 30
Arman, 248
Armand, 107, 123, 244
Armandek, 244
Armando, 267, 281
Armanno, 185
Armen, 40
Armenia, 190
Armenouhie, 40
Armes, 290
Armida, 190
Armilda, 277
Armilde, 277
Armilla, 190
Armin, 281
Armina, 120
Armino, 281
Armod, 229
Armon, 281
Armonno, 281
Armstrang, 77, 254
Armstrong, 77, 254
Arn, 273
Arna, 225
Arnald, 123
Arnalda, 120

Arnaldo, 185, 281
Arnall, 123
Arnatt, 77
Arnaud, 107, 123
Arnbjorg, 225
Arnd, 123
Arndell, 77
Arndis, 225
Arndt, 123
Arne, 123, 190, 273
Arnell, 123
Arnet, 77, 123
Arnett, 77, 123
Arney, 123
Arngeir, 230
Arngrim, 230
Arnhold, 123
Arni, 123, 230
Arnlaug, 230
Arnljot, 230
Arno, 107, 123
Arnold, 123, 273, 281
Arnoldina, 277
Arnoldine, 277
Arnoll, 123
Arnon, 156
Arnora, 225
Arnot, 123
Arnott, 77, 123
Arnou, 107
Arnoux, 107
Arnt, 123
Arnthrud, 225
Arnwolf, 123
Aroghetto, 186
Aroldo, 281
Aron, 156, 244, 273
Aros, 230
Arpad, 163
Arpana, 170
Arrate, 48, 262
Arregaithel, 113, 254
Arridano, 107
Arrighetto, 281
Arrigo, 186, 281
Arrosa, 48, 190
Arrose, 190
Arruns, 204
Arsene, 140
Arsenio, 140
Arshavir, 40
Art, 52, 113, 177
Artair, 29, 254
Artaith, 290
Artaxiad, 40
Artegal, 177
Artemas, 140
Artemesio, 140
Artemia, 129
Artemis, 129
Artemisia, 129, 262
Artemus, 140
Arth, 29
Arthes, 290
Arthgallo, 44, 77, 177

Arthur, 29, 44, 52, 292
Arthwr, 292
Artur, 52, 113, 177, 244, 273
Arturo, 52, 186, 267
Artus, 107
Arub, 36
Aruba, 36
Arun, 167, 171
Aruna, 167, 170
Arundel, 77
Arundhati, 165
Aruns, 204
Arva, 190
Arvad, 156
Arvada, 60
Arvakl, 230
Arval, 204, 292
Arvalis, 204
Arvandus, 303
Arve, 230
Arvel, 292
Arvia, 190
Arvid, 230, 273
Arvil, 292
Arvin, 123, 281
Arwood, 84
Arwydd, 290
Arwyroe, 30
Arya, 165
Arye, 156
Aryeh, 156
Asa, 156
Asad, 37, 167
Asaf, 156
Asaph, 156
Asbiorn, 230
Ascalaphus, 140
Ascanius, 204
Ascencion, 262
Asclepius, 203
Ascot, 77
Ascott, 77
Ascra, 190
Asdis, 225
Asdza, 217
Ase, 225
Aselma, 112
Asenka, 151, 247
Asenke, 151
Asentzio, 49
Asfour, 37
Asfoureh, 36
Asgard, 230
Asgaut, 230
Asgeir, 230
Asgerd, 230
Asgre, 290
Asgrim, 230
Asha, 36, 241
Ashburn, 77
Ashby, 77, 251
Asher, 156
Ashford, 77
Ashia, 36
Ashiepattle, 230
Ashild, 225
Ashilda, 225
Ashilde, 225
Ashira, 151

Ashkii, 222
Ashley, 27, 72, 77
Ashlin, 77
Ashling, 174
Ashly, 77
Ashoka, 167
Ashraf, 37
Ashtaroth, 107
Ashton, 77
Ashur, 303
Ashwin, 77, 171
Ashwyn, 77
Asi, 230
Asia, 36, 190
Asim, 37, 69
Asima, 36
Asipatra, 167
Ask, 230
Askel, 230
Askell, 230
Asklepios, 139
Askook, 219
Askuwheteau, 219
Aslak, 230
Aslaug, 225
Asolf, 230
Asopus, 140
Aspasia, 129
Asrod, 230
Assa, 190
Assan, 178
Assana, 174
Assane, 174
Assim, 241
Asta, 129, 190, 225
Astarte, 66, 190
Astennu, 71
Asteria, 190
Asthore, 174
Astolat, 42
Astolpho, 107
Astra, 129, 225
Astraea, 129, 190
Astrea, 129
Astred, 225, 277
Astrid, 60, 225, 271, 277
Astrud, 225
Astryd, 225
Astryr, 225
Astyanax, 140, 204
Astynome, 190
Astyrian, 30
Asuncion, 262
Asura, 167
Asvald, 230
Asvor, 225
Asvora, 225
Asvoria, 277
Aswad, 37, 69
Asya, 151
Ata, 69
Atabulus, 204
Ata'halne', 222
Atalanta, 129, 190
Atalante, 129
Atalaya, 262
Atali, 271

Atalia, 151
Atalie, 151, 271
Atara, 151
Atarah, 151
Ate, 129
At'eed, 217
Atelic, 30
Atella, 190
Atemu, 69
Aten, 69
Atepa, 215
Atera, 151
Ateret, 151
Atgas, 290
Athaleyah, 151
Athalia, 151, 262
Athalie, 151
Athamas, 140, 205
Athan, 139
Athanasia, 129
Athanasios, 140
Athanasius, 139
Athangelos, 40
Athdar, 113, 254
Athdara, 113, 173
Athdara, 253
Athelstan, 30
Athelston, 76
Athelward, 77
Athemar, 76
Athena, 129
Athene, 129
Atherton, 77
Athilda, 72
Athmarr, 76
Athmore, 77
Athracht, 174
Atia, 36
Atilda, 72
Atira, 151
Atiya, 36
Atkinson, 76
Atkinsone, 76
Atlanta, 129
Atlantes, 107
Atlas, 140, 205
Atli, 230
Atman, 171
Atmore, 77
Atol, 30
Ator, 30
Atreides, 140
Atreus, 140, 205
Atrides, 205
Atropes, 129
Atropos, 190
Atsu, 69
Attalus, 205
Attewater, 77
Attewell, 77
Attewode, 77
Atteworthe, 77
Attheaeldre, 72
Atthis, 190
Attica, 190
Attie, 52
Attila, 163
Attis, 140, 205
Attkins, 76
Attmore, 77
Attor, 30

Attracta, 174, 190
Attwell, 77
Atty, 52
Atum, 69
Atwater, 77
Atwell, 77
Atwood, 77
Atworth, 77
Atyhtan, 30
Aubert, 107
Auberta, 277
Aubin, 107, 203
Aubina, 103
Aubine, 103
Aubrey, 77, 107, 281
Aubrian, 281
Aubyn, 203
Auctor, 44
Aud, 225, 230
Auda, 103, 225
Aude, 103
Audhild, 225
Audhilda, 225
Audhilde, 225
Audhumbla, 225
Audi, 72
Audley, 30
Audney, 225
Audolf, 230
Audra, 72
Audre, 72
Audrey, 27, 72, 277
Audric, 107, 123
Audrick, 123
Audris, 277
Audrisa, 277
Audumla, 225
Audun, 225, 230
Auduna, 225
Audwin, 123, 281
Audwine, 123
Audwyn, 281
Auerlio, 205
Aufidus, 205
Augeas, 205
August, 205
Augusta, 190
Augusteen, 174
Augustin, 205
Augustina, 190
Augustine, 190, 205
Augustus, 205
Augusty, 205
Augustyn, 244
Augwys, 44
Aulaire, 190
Auley, 178
Auliffe, 178, 229
Aulis, 190
Aura, 129, 190
Aure, 129
Aurea, 73, 190
Aurek, 244
Aureli, 244
Aurelia, 162, 190, 262
Aurelian, 205
Aureliana, 262
Aurelie, 190

Aurelien, 205
Aureline, 190
Aurelio, 267
Auria, 73
Aurick, 77, 123
Auriga, 205
Aurigo, 205
Aurik, 123
Auriville, 107
Aurkena, 262
Aurkene, 262
Aurnia, 174
Aurora, 190
Aurore, 190
Aurum, 190
Ausar, 69
Auset, 66
Auster, 140
Austin, 205
Austina, 190
Austine, 190
Autolycus, 140
Automatia, 190
Autonoe, 129, 190
Autumn, 73, 129
Auvita, 191
Avaldamon, 230
Avalloc, 43
Avalon, 42
Avang, 230
Avaon, 292
Avarair, 40
Avaro, 203
Avaron, 42
Avarona, 42
Avasa, 170
Avatar, 171
Avatara, 170
Avdotya, 247
Avedis, 40
Avelaine, 103
Aveline, 103
Avena, 190
Avenall, 107
Aveneil, 107
Avenelle, 107
Avent, 107
Avera, 151
Averell, 77
Averil, 30, 73, 77, 190
Averill, 30, 77
Averna, 191
Avernus, 140, 205
Avery, 30, 76, 77
Averyl, 73, 190
Avi, 156
Avice, 103
Avicenna, 38
Avichai, 156
Avichayil, 150
Avidan, 156
Avidor, 156
Aviel, 156
Avigail, 150
Avigdor, 156
Avilon, 42
Avimelech, 156
Avina, 190
Avinoam, 156

Aviram, 156
Avis, 73, 191
Avisha, 156
Avishai, 156
Avital, 156
Aviv, 156
Aviva, 151, 191
Avivah, 191
Avivi, 151
Avivit, 151
Avner, 156
Avniel, 156
Avonaco, 220
Avonmora, 174
Avonmore, 178
Avraham, 156
Avril, 73
Avryl, 73
Avsalom, 156
Avshalom, 156
Awan, 218
Awanata, 216
Awarnach, 44
Awel, 290
Awenasa, 215
Awendela, 214
Awenita, 214
Awiergan, 30
Awinita, 215
Awnan, 177
Awstin, 292
Axel, 61, 123, 156, 273
Axella, 151
Axelle, 151
Axenus, 205
Axton, 77
Aya, 103, 151
Ayalah, 151
Ayasha, 215
Ayashe, 215
Ayawamat, 221
Ayisha, 36
Ayita, 214, 215
Aylmar, 281
Aylmer, 77, 281
Aylsworth, 281
Aylward, 77, 281
Aylwin, 281
Aylwyn, 281
Aymon, 108
Ayn, 151
Ayodhya, 167
Ayrwode, 84
Ayska, 36
Azalea, 151, 191
Azar, 240
Azara, 240
Azaria, 156
Azarious, 156
Azaryah, 156
Azaryahu, 156
Azelia, 151
Azelie, 151
Azhar, 36
Azhara, 36
Azibo, 69
Aziel, 151
Azima, 36
Aziza, 36, 151
Aziza, 66
Azizah, 36

Azizi, 69
Azriel, 156
Azur, 240
Azura, 103, 240
Azzam, 38
ap-Roderick, 293

Baal, 69
Bab, 36, 50, 174
Baba, 69
Babafemi, 69
Babe, 174
Babette, 103
Babita, 129
Babu, 69
Bac, 254
Baccaus, 140
Bacchus, 205
Baccus, 140
Backstere, 78
Bacstair, 113
Badan, 292
Badden, 292
Baddon, 292
Badru, 69
Baecere, 30
Baeddan, 292
Baen, 254
Baerhloew, 77
Baethan, 178
Bagdemagus, 44
Baghel, 38
Bahir, 38
Bahira, 36
Bahiti, 66
Bahram, 241
Baibin, 129
Baibre, 174
Bailefour, 114
Bailey, 108
Bailintin, 178
Baillidh, 113
Bain, 113
Bainbridge, 77, 114
Bainbrydge, 77, 114
Bairbre, 129
Baird, 52, 114, 178, 254
Bairrfhionn, 52
Bairrfhoinn, 178
Baka, 170
Bakari, 69
Baker, 78
Bakula, 170
Balahadra, 167
Balara, 191
Balarama, 167
Balasi, 140
Balaza, 205
Balbas, 205
Balbina, 183, 191, 243
Balbine, 191
Balbo, 205
Baldassare, 186
Baldassario, 186
Baldemar, 123
Balder, 77, 230
Baldhart, 120
Baldhere, 77

Baldlice, 30
Baldr, 230
Baldric, 123
Baldrik, 123
Balduin, 61, 123
Baldulf, 44
Baldur, 230
Baldwin, 123, 281
Baldwyn, 123, 281
Balen, 44, 205
Balendin, 205
Balera, 191
Balere, 48, 191
Balfour, 114, 254
Balgair, 254
Balgaire, 254
Bali, 167
Balin, 44, 167
Baline, 205
Balint, 205
Balisarda, 108
Balki, 230
Ballard, 120
Ballas, 205
Ballinamore, 178
Ballinderry, 178
Balloch, 254
Balmoral, 254
Balmung, 230
Baltasar, 123, 273
Balthasar, 241
Baltsaros, 140
Bambi, 183
Ban, 44
Bana, 30
Banain, 114
Banaing, 77
Banan, 30, 178
Banba, 174
Banbhan, 178
Banbrigge, 77
Bancroft, 77
Bannan, 123
Banning, 30, 77, 114
Bannruod, 123
Banon, 290
Baptista, 129
Baptiste, 140, 183
Bar, 30
Barabal, 112
Barabell, 112
Baraka, 36
Barakah, 38
Baram, 156
Baran, 114, 281
Barbara, 129
Barbro, 271
Barclay, 30, 77, 254
Bard, 114, 230
Bardalph, 77
Bardan, 77
Bardaric, 77
Bardarik, 77
Bardawulf, 77
Barden, 77, 78
Bardene, 78

Bardi, 230
Bardo, 61, 303
Bardol, 303
Bardolf, 77
Bardolph, 77
Bardrick, 77
Bardulf, 77
Barend, 64
Barhloew, 77
Bari, 38
Barin, 281
Barkarna, 48
Barkarne, 48
Barlow, 77
Barna, 156
Barnabas, 156
Barnabe, 156
Barnaby, 156, 303
Barnard, 123
Barnett, 77
Barney, 123
Barnum, 77
Baron, 77, 281
Barr, 77
Barra, 52, 114
Barram, 178
Barran, 174
Barre, 77
Barret, 123
Barrett, 123, 281
Barrie, 108
Barrin, 281
Barris, 292
Barron, 77, 281
Barry, 52, 108, 114
Barrys, 292
Bart, 77, 156
Barta, 303
Bartalan, 163, 303
Bartel, 156, 303
Barth, 77
Barthelemy, 303
Bartholomeus, 64, 273
Bartholomew, 156
Barthram, 78
Bartleah, 77
Bartleigh, 77
Bartlett, 108
Bartley, 77, 156, 303
Bartol, 303
Bartoli, 267
Bartolo, 267
Bartolome, 267
Barton, 77
Bartram, 78, 281
Baruch, 140, 156
Baruti, 69
Barwolf, 77
Basha, 243
Basham, 129
Bashira, 36
Bashiyra, 36
Bashshar, 38
Basil, 52, 140
Basile, 140
Basilia, 129

Basilio, 140, 267
Basilius, 64, 273
Bast, 66
Baste, 140
Bastet, 66, 71
Bastiaan, 140
Bastien, 140
Batair, 114
Bathild, 120, 277
Bathilda, 120, 277
Bathilde, 120, 277
Bathsheba, 151
Batt, 303
Battista, 183
Battseeyon, 151
Battzion, 151
Batul, 36
Batula, 36
Batya, 151
Baucis, 129, 140
Baug, 230
Bautista, 183
Bav, 50
Bawdewyn, 30
Bawdewyne, 30
Bax, 78
Baxter, 78
Bay, 78
Bayard, 108, 281
Bayen, 30
Bayhard, 78
Bayley, 108
Bazyli, 140, 244
Beacan, 52
Beacher, 78
Beadu, 73
Beadurinc, 30
Beadurof, 30
Beadutun, 78
Beagan, 114
Beagen, 114
Beal, 44
Bealantin, 114
Bealohydig, 30
Beaman, 78
Beamer, 78
Bean, 254
Bearach, 52, 114
Bearchan, 52
Bearn, 30
Bearnard, 114, 178, 254
Bearrocscir, 27
Beartlaidh, 178, 303
Beata, 191, 243, 271
Beate, 191, 243
Beatha, 50
Beathag, 151
Beathan, 254
Beathas, 253
Beatie, 114
Beaton, 78
Beatrice, 183, 191
Beatricia, 183
Beatrisa, 262
Beatrix, 191
Beatriz, 191, 262

Beattie, 114
Beatty, 114
Beaufort, 108
Beaumains, 44
Beauvais, 108
Beb, 69
Bebeodan, 30
Bebhinn, 112, 114
Bebhinn, 174
Bebti, 69
Becan, 52
Beceere, 78
Beck, 78, 273
Becket, 303
Becky, 151
Beda, 73, 292
Bede, 30, 78
Bedegrayne, 42
Bedivere, 44
Bednar, 58
Bedrosian, 40
Bedver, 44
Bedwyr, 44, 52, 292
Bedyw, 292
Bee, 191
Beecher, 78
Behdeti, 69
Behrooz, 241
Behula, 165
Beinean, 205
Beinir, 230
Beinvenido, 267
Beircheart, 30
Beiste, 254
Beitris, 112
Bek, 78
Bekan, 230
Bel, 58
Bela, 58, 156, 162, 163, 170
Belakane, 42
Belda, 103
Beldan, 78, 281
Beldane, 78, 281
Belden, 78, 281
Beldene, 78
Beldon, 78
Beli, 292
Beli Mawr, 292
Belia, 58
Belinda, 183, 262
Belisarda, 103
Bell, 58, 108
Bella, 151, 162, 191, 262
Bellamy, 108
Bellance, 183
Bellangere, 44
Belle, 162, 191
Bellerophon, 141, 205
Bellinagar, 178
Bellinagara, 174
Bellinus, 30
Bellona, 191
Beltane, 108
Beltran, 267
Belus, 205
Bemeere, 78
Bemossed, 218

Ben, 156
Bena, 214
Ben-ami, 156
Ben-aryeh, 156
Benat, 49, 123
Bence, 205
Benci, 163, 205
Bendek, 244
Bendigeidfran, 52, 293
Bendik, 205
Bendyk, 244
Benecroft, 77
Benedek, 205
Benedetta, 183
Benedetto, 205
Benedict, 205
Benedicta, 191
Benedicte, 205
Benedicto, 267
Benedictson, 156
Benedikt, 273
Benedikta, 191
Benedikte, 205
Benen, 178, 205
Benes, 58
Benetta, 191
Bengt, 205, 273
Beniamino, 157, 186
Benigied Vran, 44
Benigna, 183, 191, 262
Benin, 205
Benita, 191, 263
Benjamin, 157
Benkamin, 156
Benke, 205
Bennett, 205
Bennu, 66
Benoic, 30
Benoit, 205
Benoni, 157
Benoyce, 44
Benroy, 156
Benson, 157
Bent, 61, 205
Bente, 191
Bentleah, 78
Bentleigh, 78
Bentley, 78
Benton, 78
Ben-tziyon, 157
Benvy, 174
Benwick, 30
Benzion, 157
Beolagh, 178
Beomann, 78
Beore, 78
Beorht, 78
Beorhthild, 73
Beorhthram, 78
Beorhthramm, 78
Beorhttun, 78
Beorn, 30
Beornet, 77
Beornham, 77
Beornia, 27
Beornwulf, 30
Beorthtraed, 73

Beowulf, 30, 273
Ber, 123
Bera, 225, 277
Berakhiah, 157
Berangari, 73
Berangaria, 103
Berchmans, 303
Berchtwald, 123
Bercilak, 44
Bercleah, 77
Berde, 61
Berdina, 120, 129
Berdine, 120, 129, 277
Berdy, 123
Berend, 123
Berengaria, 73
Berenice, 129
Beresford, 78
Beretun, 77
Berford, 78
Berg, 64, 123, 273
Bergdis, 225
Bergelmir, 230
Bergen, 251
Berggren, 251
Bergin, 251
Bergitte, 60
Bergren, 251, 273
Bergron, 273
Bergthor, 230
Bergthora, 225
Berinhard, 123
Berit, 50, 120, 271
Berkeley, 30, 77
Berkley, 77
Bern, 123
Bernadette, 103, 120
Bernadine, 277
Bernard, 123
Bernardina, 277
Bernardo, 123, 186, 267
Bernardyn, 123
Bernbe, 267
Bernd, 123
Berne, 123
Berneen, 174
Bernhard, 123
Bernia, 27
Bernice, 129
Bernlak, 44
Bernon, 123
Bernot, 123
Beroe, 129, 191
Beronika, 277
Berowalt, 123
Berrin, 123
Bersi, 230
Bersules, 44
Bert, 78, 281
Berta, 50, 120, 162, 271, 277
Berth, 290, 293
Bertha, 103, 120, 277
Berthog, 290
Berthold, 123

Berti, 303
Bertie, 30
Bertil, 273
Bertild, 277
Bertilda, 73, 277
Bertilde, 73, 277
Bertilla, 277
Bertille, 277
Bertin, 281
Bertina, 120
Bertine, 277
Berto, 267
Bertok, 281
Bertold, 281
Berton, 78, 281
Bertrade, 73
Bertram, 44, 78, 281
Bertrand, 108, 281
Bertrando, 186
Bertuska, 162
Bertwin, 281
Bertwyn, 281
Beruriah, 151
Berwick, 78
Berwyk, 78
Berwyn, 293
Beryl, 129
Bes, 69
Bestandan, 30
Bestla, 225
Besyrwan, 30
Beth, 254
Betha, 50
Bethany, 302
Bethel, 151
Betheli, 151
Bethia, 73
Bethsaida, 151
Bethseda, 151
Bethsheba, 151
Betia, 73
Betje, 63, 151
Betlic, 30
Betsy, 151
Betti, 151
Bettina, 151
Bettine, 151
Betty, 151
Betzalel, 157
Beula, 151
Beulah, 151
Bevan, 52
Beven, 293
Beverley, 73, 78
Beverly, 73, 78
Bevin, 52, 174, 293
Bevis, 108, 281
Bevyn, 52, 293
Bha, 165
Bhadraa, 165
Bhaga, 167
Bhagiratha, 165
Bhagwandas, 167
Bhaic, 254
Bhairavi, 165
Bhaltair, 254
Bharain, 113
Bharani, 171
Bharat, 171

Bharati, 170
Bhaskar, 167, 171
Bhavaja, 167
Bhavata, 167
Bheathain, 113
Bhikkhu, 167
Bhikkhuni, 165
Bhima, 167
Bhimadevi, 165
Bhishma, 167
Bhradain, 254
Bhraghad, 254
Bhreac, 254
Bhric, 254
Bhruic, 114
Bhu, 165
Bhudevi, 165
Biadhaiche, 114
Biaiardo, 186
Bialas, 244
Bialy, 244
Biana, 191
Bianca, 183, 191
Biast, 254
Bibiana, 191, 263
Bibiane, 191
Bibine, 191
Bibsbebe, 36
Bick, 78
Bickford, 78
Bicoir, 44
Biddy, 174
Bidelia, 174
Bidina, 174
Bidziil, 222
Biecaford, 78
Bienvenida, 263
Biford, 79
Bifrost, 225, 230
Bilagaana, 222
Bilko, 58
Bily, 58
Bimisi, 218
Binah, 157
Binean, 205
Bing, 123
Binga, 120
Binge, 120, 123
Bingen, 49
Binger, 205
Bink, 78
Binyamin, 156
Bionbyr, 231
Birch, 78, 79
Birche, 79
Bird, 79
Birde, 79
Birdhil, 78
Birdhill, 78
Birdie, 73
Birdoswald, 30
Birdy, 73
Birger, 230, 273
Birget, 272
Birgit, 50
Birgitta, 272
Birk, 78, 254
Birkett, 78
Birkey, 78
Birkhead, 78
Birkhed, 78

Birkita, 50
Birley, 78
Birney, 78
Birr, 178
Birte, 50
Birtel, 78
Birtle, 78
Bisgu, 27
Bishop, 78
Bitanig, 78
Bithynia, 191
Biton, 141
Bittan, 123
Bitten, 60, 123
Bittor, 49, 205
Bittore, 191
Bitya, 151
Bixenta, 48
Bjarne, 230
Bjarni, 230
Bjolf, 230
Bjork, 225
Bjorn, 230, 273
Bjornolf, 230
Blacey, 78
Black, 78
Blade, 78
Bladud, 44
Blaec, 78
Blaecleah, 78
Blaed, 78
Blagdan, 78
Blagden, 78
Blagdon, 78
Blaine, 52, 178
Blainey, 52
Blair, 50, 52, 114, 178, 254
Blaise, 44, 78, 205
Blake, 78
Blakeley, 78
Blakely, 78
Blakemore, 78
Blakey, 78
Blamor, 44
Blanca, 183, 263
Blanch, 103
Blanche, 103, 191
Blanchefleur, 103
Blancheflor, 42
Blancheflour, 42
Blanco, 267
Bland, 205
Blanda, 191
Blandford, 78
Blandine, 191
Blandon, 205
Blane, 52
Blanford, 78
Blanka, 191
Blar, 178
Blas, 120, 267
Blasa, 120, 263
Blase, 205
Blasia, 191
Blasius, 273
Blathaon, 293
Blathma, 178
Blathnaid, 174
Blayne, 52, 78

Blayney, 52
Blaze, 78
Bleecker, 64
Bleidd, 293
Blenda, 271, 278
Bleoberis, 44
Blessing, 73
Bletsung, 27, 73
Blian, 178
Bliant, 44
Blinne, 174
Bliss, 27, 30, 73, 78
Blithe, 73
Bliths, 73
Blodwen, 290
Blodwyn, 290
Blossom, 73
Blostm, 73
Bluinse, 174
Blund, 230
Bly, 214
Blyth, 78
Blythe, 27, 73, 78
Bo, 61, 273
Boadhagh, 52
Boadicea, 27
Boarte, 44
Boas, 157
Boaz, 157
Boc, 79
Bocleah, 79
Bocley, 79
Boda, 79
Bodashka, 288
Bodaway, 218
Boden, 30, 52
Bodgana, 243
Bodhi, 168
Bodi, 163
Bodiccea, 27
Bodicea, 27
Bodicia, 27
Bodil, 61, 225, 230, 273
Bodile, 225
Bodilla, 225
Bodmod, 230
Bodolf, 230
Bodvar, 230
Bodwyn, 44
Bodyn, 52
Boethius, 141
Bofind, 114
Bogart, 123
Bogdan, 157, 288
Bogdashka, 248
Boghos, 40
Bogna, 243
Bogohardt, 123
Bogumil, 244
Boguslaw, 244, 259
Bohdan, 157, 248, 288
Bohdanko, 288
Bohgana, 243
Bohort, 44
Bohous, 58
Bohumil, 58
Bohuslav, 259
Bolbe, 191

Boldizsar, 163
Boleslaus, 259
Bolli, 230
Bolodenka, 248, 259
Bolthor, 230
Bolton, 78
Bolverk, 230
Bomani, 69
Bona Dea, 191
Bonaventure, 205
Bond, 78
Bondi, 79
Bonie, 73
Boniface, 30, 205
Bonifacio, 205, 267
Bonifacius, 64
Bonifaco, 267
Bonifacy, 205
Bonnie, 73, 103, 191, 253
Bonny, 73, 103, 191, 253
Booth, 78, 230, 281
Boothe, 78
Bor, 230
Bora, 162, 191
Borbala, 162, 191
Bordan, 30
Borden, 30, 78
Boreas, 141, 205
Borg, 230, 274
Borghild, 225
Borghilda, 225
Borghlide, 225
Borgny, 225
Bori, 230
Boris, 248, 259
Boriska, 162
Borje, 274
Bork, 230
Borka, 162, 191
Borre, 44
Borromeo, 303
Bors, 44, 78
Borsala, 162, 191
Borsca, 191
Borska, 191
Borya, 248
Boryenka, 248
Borys, 244
Borysko, 259, 288
Boryslaw, 244
Bosworth, 78
Botewolf, 78
Both, 254
Bothain, 254
Bothan, 254
Bothe, 78, 230
Bothi, 230
Botilda, 225, 271
Botolf, 78
Botwolf, 78
Boudicca, 27
Boudicea, 27
Boulus, 38
Bourn, 79
Bourne, 79

Bow, 114
Bowden, 30, 52
Bowdyn, 30, 52
Bowen, 52, 114
Bowie, 114
Bowyn, 52, 114
Boyce, 281
Boyd, 52, 114
Boyden, 30, 52
Boyne, 114
Boynton, 52, 114, 178
Bozena, 58
Bozi, 151
Brac, 293
Brachah, 151
Brad, 78, 293
Bradach, 114
Bradaigh, 178
Bradamate, 103
Bradan, 78
Bradana, 253
Bradbourne, 78
Bradburn, 78
Brademagus, 44
Braden, 78, 254
Bradene, 78
Bradford, 78
Bradig, 79
Bradleah, 79
Bradley, 79
Bradly, 79
Bradwell, 79
Bradwen, 293
Bradwr, 293
Brady, 79, 114, 178
Bradyn, 78
Braemwiella, 79
Braen, 293
Bragi, 230
Brahma, 168, 171
Brahman, 168
Brahmaputra, 168
Braigh, 254
Brainard, 79, 281
Brainerd, 79
Braith, 290
Braleah, 79
Bram, 52, 64, 177
Bramwell, 79
Bran, 44, 52, 178, 293
Brand, 79, 231
Brandan, 52, 178
Branddun, 79
Brande, 63, 73
Brandeis, 124
Brandeles, 44
Brandelis, 44
Brander, 231
Brando, 186
Brandon, 79, 281
Brandr, 231
Brandubh, 178
Branduff, 178
Brandy, 63
Brangaine, 50
Brangoire, 44
Brangore, 44
Brangorre, 44

Brangwen, 290
Brangwy, 290
Branhard, 79
Brann, 52, 174
Brannoc, 293
Brannock, 293
Branor, 44
Branstock, 231
Brant, 79, 281
Brantley, 79, 281
Branwen, 42, 50
Branwenn, 290
Branwyn, 42
Braoin, 178
Brasil, 52
Brathach, 293
Brawleigh, 79
Brawley, 79
Braz, 205
Breac, 254
Breanainn, 52
Breandan, 52, 112, 114, 174, 178
Breanne, 174
Breasal, 52, 178
Brecc, 30
Bredbeddle, 44
Brede, 61, 231
Bredon, 52
Breeda, 50, 174
Breen, 178
Bregus, 290
Brehus, 44
Breindel, 303
Breine, 303
Bremusa, 191
Bren, 124
Brencis, 205, 248
Brend, 278
Brenda, 112, 174, 225, 278
Brendan, 52, 114, 124
Brendis, 124
Brendon, 114
Brengwain, 42
Brenius, 44
Brenna, 50, 174
Brennan, 52, 114, 178
Brennus, 44
Brent, 79
Brentan, 79
Breri, 44
Bresi, 231
Bret, 50, 52
Brett, 52
Bretta, 50
Breuse, 44
Brewster, 79
Brewstere, 79
Briallan, 290
Brian, 53, 231, 293
Briana, 50, 174
Brianna, 174
Brianne, 174
Briant, 53
Briareus, 141
Brice, 30, 53, 108, 254

Bricriu, 53
Bricta, 50
Brid, 50, 174
Bride, 50, 174
Bridger, 79
Bridget, 50
Briefbras, 44
Brietta, 50
Brigantia, 27
Brigetta, 272
Briggeham, 79
Briggere, 79
Brigham, 79
Brighde, 112
Brighid, 50, 174
Brigid, 50
Brigida, 263
Brigidia, 263
Brigitta, 50
Brigitte, 50
Brigliadoro, 108
Brimlad, 27
Brina, 50, 174
Brinton, 79
Briseis, 129
Brisingamen, 225, 231
Brit, 50, 225
Brita, 50, 225
Britannia, 191
Brite, 50, 272
Brites, 50
Britomartus, 53
Britt, 272
Britta, 50, 60, 225, 272
Brittany, 50
Britto, 79
Brlety, 58
Broc, 79, 254
Brochain, 254
Brochan, 254
Brock, 79
Brockley, 79
Brocleah, 79
Brocleigh, 79
Brocly, 79
Broderick, 79, 293
Broderik, 79
Brodie, 254
Brodrig, 79
Brodrik, 79
Brody, 178, 248
Broga, 30
Brogan, 30
Broin, 52
Brok, 79
Brokk, 231
Bromius, 205
Bromleah, 79
Bromleigh, 79
Bromley, 79
Bromly, 79
Bron, 30
Brona, 174
Brondolf, 231
Brone, 178
Bronislaw, 259
Bronson, 30
Bronwen, 290
Bronwyn, 290

Brook, 79
Brooke, 73, 79
Brooks, 79
Brookson, 79
Brooksone, 79
Brosca, 162
Broska, 162
Brothaigh, 114
Brougher, 79
Broughton, 79
Brown, 79
Bruce, 108, 254
Brucie, 103
Bruhier, 38
Bruin, 231
Brun, 30, 79
Bruna, 120, 183, 278
Brune, 120
Brunella, 103
Brunelle, 108
Brunetta, 183
Brunhild, 120, 225, 278
Brunhilda, 120, 225, 278
Brunhilde, 120, 278
Bruni, 231
Brunnehilde, 225
Bruno, 124, 186, 281
Brunon, 124
Brus, 114
Brutus, 79, 205
Bryan, 44, 53, 231
Bryana, 174
Bryanna, 174
Bryant, 53
Bryce, 30, 53, 191, 254
Brydger, 79
Bryggere, 79
Brygid, 50
Bryna, 174
Bryngerd, 225
Brynhild, 225
Brynhilde, 225
Brynja, 225
Brynjolf, 231
Brynn, 293
Brys, 108, 293
Buach, 178
Buadhachan, 114
Buagh, 178
Buan, 174
Bubona, 191
Bucer, 205
Buchanan, 254
Buciac, 59
Buck, 79
Buckley, 79, 178
Budd, 79
Buddug, 290
Buddy, 79
Buena, 263
Buidhe, 114
Buiron, 108
Bundy, 79
Burbank, 79
Burcet, 108

Burch, 79
Burchard, 79
Burdon, 79
Bureig, 79
Burel, 108
Burford, 79
Burga, 278
Burgeis, 79
Burgess, 53, 79
Burgha, 278
Burghard, 79
Burghere, 79
Burgtun, 79
Burhardt, 124
Burhbank, 79
Burhdon, 79
Burhford, 79
Burhleag, 79
Burhtun, 78, 79
Buri, 231
Burian, 248, 288
Burke, 281
Burkett, 108
Burkhart, 124
Burl, 79
Burleigh, 79, 281
Burley, 79, 281
Burly, 79
Burn, 79
Burnaby, 231
Burne, 79
Burneig, 78
Burnell, 108
Burnet, 79
Burnett, 79
Burney, 78, 79
Burns, 79
Burr, 231, 274
Burrell, 108
Bursone, 79
Burt, 78
Burton, 78, 79
Busby, 231, 254
Busbyr, 231
Buthaynah, 36
Butrus, 38
Bwlch, 293
Byford, 79
Byram, 79
Byrd, 79
Byreleah, 78
Byrle, 79
Byrne, 79
Byrnes, 79
Byron, 79, 108, 281
Byrtel, 78
Byrtwold, 30
Bysen, 28

Cabal, 44
Caca, 191
Cacamwri, 44
Cacanisius, 178
Cachamwri, 53
Caci, 112
Cacia, 191
Cacus, 205
Cadabyr, 79
Cadarn, 293
Cadawg, 293
Cadby, 79, 231

Cadda, 80
Caddaham, 80
Caddaric, 80
Caddarik, 80
Caddawyc, 80
Caddoc, 293
Caddock, 293
Cadel, 293
Cadell, 53, 293
Cadellin, 293
Cadena, 73
Cadence, 103, 191
Cadencia, 103
Cadenza, 183
Cadha, 253
Cadhla, 174, 178
Cadi, 290
Cadis, 129
Cadman, 30, 53, 293
Cadmon, 141, 293
Cadmus, 141, 205
Cador, 45
Caduceus, 205
Cadwallen, 293
Cadwallon, 30, 45
Cadwgawn, 293
Cadwr, 293
Cadwy, 293
Cadwyn, 290
Cadyna, 73
Cadyryeith, 293
Caecelius, 206
Caedmon, 30
Caedwalla, 30
Caeneus, 129
Caenis, 191
Caer Llion, 293
Caerau, 293
Caerleon, 45
Caersewiella, 80
Caesar, 61, 205, 274
Caesare, 141
Caethes, 290
Cafall, 44
Cafell, 290
Caffar, 178
Caffara, 174
Caffaria, 174
Caflice, 30
Cahal, 53
Cahir, 178
Cahira, 174
Cai, 45, 293
Caieta, 191
Cailean, 114, 254
Cailen, 114
Cailin, 174
Cailleach, 253
Caillen, 114, 254
Caillic, 253
Caimbeul, 114
Cain, 157, 178, 293
Caindale, 80
Cairbre, 53, 178
Cairistiona, 112, 191

Caiseal, 178
Cait, 112, 174
Caith, 178
Caitie, 174
Caitilin, 129
Caitlan, 174
Caitlin, 112, 129, 174
Caitlyn, 129
Caitrin, 129
Caitriona, 129
Caitryn, 129
Cajetan, 205
Cal, 80
Caladh, 254
Calais, 141, 205
Calandra, 129
Calandre, 103
Calandria, 263
Calantha, 103, 129
Calanthe, 103
Calbert, 80
Calbhach, 178
Calcas, 293
Calchas, 141, 205
Calcia, 191
Calder, 53, 80
Caldre, 80
Caldwell, 80
Caldwiella, 80
Cale, 80
Caleb, 157
Caledonia, 191
Caledvwlch, 293
Calendae, 191
Cales, 191
Caley, 114, 178
Calfhierde, 80
Calhoun, 114, 178
Calibor, 45
Caliborn, 45
Caliborne, 45
Caliburn, 45
Caliburnus, 45
Calida, 129, 191, 263
Caligula, 205
Calix, 205
Calla, 129
Callaghan, 178
Calldwr, 80
Calleo, 205
Calles, 45
Calli, 73, 129
Callia, 129
Callida, 191
Callie, 73, 129
Calligenia, 129
Callimachus, 205
Calliope, 129, 191
Callista, 129, 191
Calliste, 129
Callisto, 129, 191
Callixtus, 205
Callosus, 205
Callough, 178
Callula, 191
Callum, 254
Cally, 73
Calogrenant, 45

Calum, 53, 114
Calva, 191
Calvagh, 178
Calvert, 80
Calvin, 205
Calvina, 263
Calvino, 186, 267
Calvinus, 205
Caly, 178
Calybe, 191
Calyce, 191
Calydona, 191
Calypso, 129, 191
Cam, 254
Camber, 80
Cambeul, 254
Cambria, 73
Camdan, 254
Camden, 30, 114, 254
Camdene, 30, 114
Camdin, 254
Camdyn, 254
Camella, 191
Camelon, 45
Camelot, 42
Cameo, 184
Camero, 53
Cameron, 53, 114254
Camey, 53
Camhlaidh, 255
Camila, 263
Camilla, 191
Camille, 191
Camillus, 205
Camilo, 205, 267
Camlann, 45
Cammeo, 184
Camp, 254
Campbell, 108, 114, 254
Campion, 303
Camshron, 114
Camshron, 254
Canace, 129
Candace, 191
Candance, 129
Candice, 129, 191
Candida, 191, 263
Candide, 191
Canens, 191
Caniad, 290
Canice, 178
Canis, 205
Cant, 293
Cantabria, 191
Cantara, 36
Cantilena, 191
Cantius, 303
Cantor, 205
Cantrix, 191
Canute, 231, 281
Caoilfhionn, 50
Caoimhe, 174
Caoimhghin, 53
Caolabhuinn, 114
Caolaidhe, 114, 178
Caolan, 178
Caomh, 178

Caomhan, 114
Capaneus, 141
Capek, 59
Capeka, 58
Capita, 191
Cappadocia, 191
Caprice, 184
Capta, 191
Capucina, 103
Capucine, 103
Capys, 205
Car, 53
Cara, 50, 184, 192
Caradawc, 45
Caradawg, 293
Caradoc, 45, 53, 294
Caradog, 293
Caraid, 174
Caraidland, 254
Caramichil, 114
Carbry, 53
Carcer, 205
Cardea, 192
Cardew, 53
Carel, 108
Caren, 272
Caresse, 103
Carew, 53
Carey, 50, 53, 293
Cari, 302
Caria, 192
Caries, 192
Carilla, 263
Carin, 192
Carina, 103, 184, 192, 272
Carine, 103, 272
Carisa, 192
Carissa, 192
Carissima, 192
Carita, 192
Caritas, 192
Carla, 263
Carlatun, 80
Carleen, 174
Carleton, 80
Carletta, 263
Carlie, 114
Carlin, 114, 178
Carling, 112, 114
Carlino, 186
Carlisle, 80
Carlita, 263
Carlo, 108, 186
Carlomagno, 267
Carlos, 108, 267
Carlota, 263
Carlotta, 103, 184, 263
Carlton, 80, 254
Carly, 114, 278
Carlyle, 80
Carma, 302
Carmea, 192
Carmel, 50, 151, 157
Carmela, 151, 184, 263
Carmelide, 45

Carmelina, 151, 184
Carmeline, 151
Carmelita, 184, 263
Carmella, 151
Carmen, 151, 192, 263
Carmencita, 263
Carmenta, 192
Carmentis, 192
Carmi, 157
Carmia, 73, 192
Carmichael, 114, 254
Carmichail, 117
Carmin, 192
Carmina, 73, 263
Carmine, 73, 157, 205
Carmita, 73, 263
Carmya, 73
Carna, 192
Carnation, 103
Carneades, 205
Carnedyr, 293
Carney, 53, 114, 178
Carol, 73, 103, 114
Carola, 103
Carole, 103
Carolina, 73, 103, 184
Caroline, 73, 103, 253
Carolos, 108
Carolus, 108, 114
Carolyn, 73
Carona, 263
Carr, 53, 231, 255
Carrado, 45
Carraig, 114, 178
Carrick, 114, 178
Carrie, 73
Carrol, 53
Carroll, 53, 114, 178
Carrson, 251
Carson, 80
Carsten, 205
Carston, 205
Carswell, 80
Carter, 80
Cartere, 80
Carthach, 178
Carthage, 178
Cartimandua, 28
Cartland, 80
Carvel, 80
Carvell, 80
Carver, 80
Cary, 50, 53, 293
Carya, 192
Caryn, 192
Caryna, 192
Cas, 293
Caseareo, 141, 186
Casey, 53, 112, 114, 174
Cash, 205

Cashel, 178
Casidhe, 112, 114, 174
Casild, 263
Casilda, 263
Casimir, 244, 259
Casimiro, 267
Casnar, 293
Casper, 241
Casperia, 192
Cass, 205
Cassandra, 129, 192
Cassibellaunus, 80
Cassidy, 112, 114, 174
Cassie, 130
Cassiopeia, 130
Cassius, 205
Cassivellaunus, 53
Cassondra, 129
Casswallawn, 293
Casta, 130, 263
Castalia, 130
Caster, 80
Castor, 141, 205
Caswallan, 53
Caswallon, 293
Cat, 174, 255
Catalin, 48, 129
Catalina, 263
Catalyn, 129
Catarina, 129, 184
Catarine, 184
Cate, 28, 192
Cateline, 103
Catena, 192
Caterina, 184
Cath, 45, 290
Cathair, 53, 255
Cathal, 53, 178
Cathaoir, 53, 178
Cathaoirmore, 114
Catharina, 129
Cathasach, 112, 114, 174
Cathbad, 53
Catherin, 129
Catherine, 28, 129
Catheryn, 28, 129
Catheryna, 129
Cathleen, 130
Cathlin, 130
Cathlyn, 130
Cathmor, 114, 178
Cathmore, 114, 178
Cathryn, 28, 129
Catia, 129
Catlee, 174
Cato, 205
Caton, 205
Catori, 216
Catrin, 290

Catriona, 112
Cattee, 174
Catterick, 45
Catterik, 45
Catullus, 206
Catus, 205
Cauley, 231, 255
Cavalon, 45
Cavan, 114, 178
Cavana, 174
Cavell, 281
Cavillor, 206
Caw, 45, 293
Cawley, 231, 255
Cawrdav, 293
Cayle, 80
Ceallach, 112, 114, 180
Ceallachan, 178
Ceannfhionn, 114
Ceapmann, 80
Ceara, 112
Cearbhall, 108, 178
Cearbhallan, 114
Ceard, 255
Ceardach, 255
Cearnach, 114, 178
Cearo, 28
Ceasario, 186
Ceaster, 80
Ceastun, 80
Ceawlin, 30
Cebriones, 141
Cecil, 206
Cecile, 192
Cecilia, 192, 272
Cecilio, 186, 206
Cecilius, 64
Cecily, 192
Cecrops, 141, 206
Cedd, 30
Cedric, 53, 80
Cegluse, 192
Ceileachan, 114
Cein, 114, 178
Ceire, 174
Ceit, 112
Ceithin, 293
Celaeno, 130, 192
Celandina, 130
Celandine, 130
Celdtun, 80
Celek, 243
Celena, 130
Celeres, 206
Celesta, 192
Celeste, 192
Celestin, 206
Celestina, 192
Celestine, 192
Celestun, 206
Celeus, 141
Celia, 192
Celidon, 45
Celidone, 45
Celina, 130, 192
Celine, 192
Celinka, 243

Celistine, 206
Celosia, 130
Celsus, 178
Celyddon, 53
Cendrillon, 104
Cenehard, 80
Ceneward, 80
Cenewig, 80
Cenewyg, 80
Cenobia, 130, 263
Cenon, 141
Centaurus, 206
Cenwalh, 30
Ceolbeorht, 81
Ceolfrith, 30
Ceolwulf, 30
Cephalus, 141, 206
Cepheus, 141, 206
Cerberus, 141, 206
Cercyon, 141
Cerdic, 30
Cerelia, 184, 192
Ceres, 130, 192
Cerin, 114
Cermak, 59
Cermaka, 58
Cernach, 53
Cerny, 59
Cesar, 205, 267
Cesara, 263
Cesare, 141, 186
Cesario, 205
Cesaro, 267
Cestmir, 59, 259
Cestus, 130
Cetewind, 80
Ceto, 130
Cetus, 141
Ceyx, 141
Cezar, 205
Cha'akmongwi, 221
Chaba, 151
Chabah, 151
Chad, 30, 53, 80
Chadburn, 80
Chadburne, 80
Chadbyrn, 80
Chadwick, 80
Chadwik, 80
Chadwyk, 80
Chafulumisa, 69
Chagai, 157
Chaim, 157, 254
Chait, 255
Chaitra, 170
Chaka, 151
Chakra, 168
Cha'kwaina, 216
Chalciope, 192
Chalmar, 281
Chalmer, 255, 281
Chalmers, 255, 281
Chamunda, 165
Chana, 151
Chanah, 151

Chanan, 157
Chance, 80
Chancellor, 80
Chancey, 80
Chanda, 165, 302
Chandaka, 168
Chander, 171
Chandi, 165, 170
Chandler, 108
Chandra, 168, 170, 302
Changla, 170
Chankoowashtay, 222
Chanler, 108
Channa, 165
Channing, 108
Chanoch, 157
Chansomps, 219
Chantel, 103
Chapa, 218
Chapalu, 45
Chapin, 108
Chapman, 30, 80
Chappel, 108
Chappell, 108
Charis, 130
Cha'risa, 216
Charissa, 130, 192
Charity, 192
Charleen, 104
Charlene, 104
Charles, 108, 281
Charleton, 80
Charline, 104
Charlot, 108
Charlotta, 247
Charlotte, 103
Charlton, 80
Charmaine, 73, 104
Charo, 263
Charon, 141
Charraigaich, 114
Charumati, 165
Charybdis, 141, 192
Chas-chunk-a, 223
Chasidah, 151
Chasya, 151, 302
Chasye, 151, 302
Chatha, 69
Chatham, 80
Cha'tima, 221
Chattan, 255
Chatuluka, 69
Chatwin, 80
Chatwyn, 80
Chaucor, 206
Chaunce, 80
Chaunceler, 80
Chauncey, 80, 206
Chauncory, 206
Chava, 151
Chavatangakwunua, 221
Chaviv, 157
Chaviva, 151
Chavive, 151

Chavivi, 157
Chaya, 151
Chayim, 157
Chayka, 151
Chayton, 222
Che, 45, 157
Chedva, 151
Chela, 263
Chelinda, 42
Chelinde, 42
Chelsea, 28, 73
Cheney, 108
Chenoa, 214
Chenzira, 69
Cheops, 69
Chepe, 157
Chephzibah, 151
Chepi, 214
Chepito, 157
Cher, 104
Cheree, 104
Cheri, 104
Cherie, 104
Cherise, 104
Cherry, 104
Cheryl, 120
Cheslav, 248
Chesmu, 218
Chester, 80, 206
Cheston, 80
Chetwin, 80
Chetwyn, 80
Cheveyo, 221
Chhaya, 165
Chibale, 69
Chico, 267
Chigaru, 69
Chike, 69
Chilaili, 214
Chilton, 80
Chimalis, 214
Chimera, 141
Chinja, 168
Chione, 66
Chiquita, 263
Chiram, 157
Chiron, 141
Chisholm, 255
Chisisi, 69
Chitra, 170
Chitsa, 214
Chlodwig, 124
Chloe, 130
Chloris, 130
Chochmingwu, 216
Chochmo, 221
Chochokpi, 221
Chochuschuvio, 221
Chogan, 219
Choilleich, 114
Cholena, 214
Choni, 157
Choovio, 221
Chosovi, 216
Chosposi, 216
Choviohoya, 221
Chowilawu, 221
Chris, 141
Chriselda, 120
Christa, 130, 174

Christabel, 192
Christabella, 192
Christal, 253
Christel, 253
Christen, 130
Christian, 61, 130, 141, 174, 191, 205
Christiana, 130
Christiane, 130
Christiann, 205
Christiano, 141
Christiansen, 61
Christie, 255
Christien, 108
Christina, 191, 272
Christine, 130, 191
Christobel, 141
Christoffel, 141
Christoffer, 61
Christofferson, 61
Christoph, 141
Christopher, 141
Christophoros, 141
Christos, 141
Christy, 255
Chryse, 192
Chryseis, 130, 192
Chryses, 141, 206
Chrysogeneia, 192
Chrysonoe, 192
Chrysostom, 141
Chu'a, 221
Chuchip, 221
Chuma, 69
Chu'mana, 216
Chumani, 218
Chunta, 221
Churchill, 80
Churchyl, 80
Chu'si, 216
Chval, 59
Cian, 114, 178
Cianan, 178
Ciannait, 174
Ciar, 174
Ciara, 174
Ciarda, 112
Ciardubhan, 114
Ciarrai, 178
Cicero, 206
Ciceron, 206, 267
Cili, 162, 192
Cilla, 192
Cillian, 178
Cim, 73
Cimberleigh, 73
Cinderella, 104
Cingeswell, 80
Cingeswiella, 80
Cinnard, 114
Cinneide, 178
Cinneididh, 114
Cinnfhail, 114
Cinnia, 50

Cinnie, 50
Cinthia, 130
Cinwel, 80
Cinxia, 192
Cinyras, 130
Ciorstag, 112
Ciorstan, 112
Cipriana, 130, 263
Cipriano, 267
Ciqala, 220
Cira, 184
Circe, 130
Circehyll, 80
Cirilo, 141, 267
Cirio, 141
Ciro, 141, 142, 267
Cisco, 268
Claas, 141
Clach, 255
Cladian, 206
Clady, 60, 192
Claec, 78
Claefer, 73
Claeg, 80
Claegborne, 80
Claegtun, 80
Claennis, 28
Claiborn, 80
Claire, 104
Clamedeus, 45
Clancy, 178
Clara, 192
Clarabelle, 192
Clare, 192, 206
Clarence, 206
Clarensis, 206
Claresta, 73
Clareta, 192, 263
Clarette, 104
Claribel, 192
Claribella, 192
Claribelle, 192
Clarice, 104, 184, 192
Clarinde, 192
Clarine, 42, 192
Clarion, 45
Clariss, 184
Clarissa, 184, 192, 263
Clarissant, 42
Clarisse, 192
Clarita, 192
Claud, 206
Claudas, 45
Claude, 206
Claudette, 104
Claudia, 192, 263
Claudina, 184
Claudine, 104
Claudio, 206, 267
Claudion, 206
Claudios, 64
Claudius, 206

Claus, 141, 206
Clay, 80, 281
Clayborn, 281
Clayborne, 80
Claybourne, 80, 281
Clayburn, 80
Clayton, 80, 281
Cleantha, 73
Cleary, 114, 178
Cleirach, 114
Cleit, 255
Clem, 206
Clematis, 130
Clemence, 206
Clement, 206
Clemente, 206
Clementina, 104, 192, 263
Clementine, 192
Clementius, 64
Clennan, 255
Cleo, 130
Cleobis, 141
Cleon, 80
Cleopatra, 66, 130
Cletus, 141
Cleva, 73
Cleve, 80
Cleveland, 80
Clevon, 80
Cliantha, 130
Clianthe, 130
Cliff, 80
Clifford, 80
Cliffton, 80
Clifland, 80
Clifton, 80
Cliftun, 80
Clint, 80
Clinton, 80, 281
Clinttun, 80
Clio, 130
Clive, 80
Clodagh, 175
Clodius, 206
Clodovea, 263
Clodoveo, 267
Clonia, 192
Cloria, 130
Cloridan, 108
Clorinda, 184
Clorinda, 192
Cloris, 130
Clotho, 130, 192
Clotild, 278
Clotilda, 120, 278
Clotilde, 120, 278
Clover, 28, 73
Clovis, 108, 124
Clud, 293
Clunainach, 114
Cluny, 114, 178
Clust, 53, 293
Clustfeinad, 53
Clyde, 293
Clyffton, 80
Clyfland, 80
Clyftun, 80
Clymena, 130

Clymene, 130, 192
Clyte, 130
Clytemnestra, 130
Clytie, 130
Clyve, 80
Clywd, 293
Cnut, 30, 231
Cnute, 231
Cnychwr, 293
Cobhan, 115
Coch, 293
Cochava, 151
Cocheta, 214
Cochlain, 178
Cocidius, 53
Cocles, 206
Cocytus, 141
Codi, 73, 80
Codie, 73, 80
Cody, 73, 80
Coed, 293
Coeus, 141
Cofahealh, 81
Coghlan, 178
Coigleach, 114
Coilin, 114, 178
Coillcumhann, 114, 178
Coilleach, 114
Coinleain, 114
Coinneach, 53, 114, 178
Coira, 253
Coire, 115, 255
Coireall, 141, 178
Colan, 114
Colbert, 80, 281
Colby, 30, 81
Cole, 81, 141
Coleen, 112
Coleman, 81, 178
Colemann, 81
Colette, 104, 130
Coletun, 81
Colfre, 81
Colier, 81
Colin, 114, 255
Colina, 253
Colis, 81
Coll, 114
Colla, 178
Collatinus, 206
Colle, 115
Colleen, 112
Collette, 104
Collier, 81
Collin, 114, 178
Collis, 81
Collyer, 81
Colm, 114, 178
Colman, 178
Colmcilla, 175
Colmcille, 178
Colon, 206
Colquhoun, 255
Colt, 81
Colter, 81
Coltere, 81
Colton, 81
Colum, 114, 141

Columba, 192
Columbanus, 114
Columbine, 184
Columbo, 178
Colver, 81
Colvert, 81
Colvyr, 81
Colyer, 81
Colys, 81
Coman, 179
Comfort, 104
Comforte, 104
Comhghan, 114, 179
Comyn, 115, 179, 255
Comyna, 175
Con, 53, 112
Conaire, 115, 178, 179
Conall, 53
Conan, 53
Conant, 53
Conary, 178
Concepcion, 263
Concepta, 175
Conception, 192
Concetta, 184, 263
Conchetta, 263
Conchobar, 53
Conchobara, 175
Conchobarra, 175
Conchobarre, 175
Conchobhar, 179
Concordea, 192
Concordia, 192
Condan, 53
Condon, 53
Condwiramurs, 42
Congalie, 175
Conlan, 115, 179
Conlaoch, 53
Conleth, 179
Conley, 179
Conlin, 115
Conn, 53
Connacht, 179
Connal, 175
Connell, 53
Connie, 179, 192
Connla, 53
Connlaio, 179
Connlan, 115
Connolly, 179
Connor, 179
Conny, 179
Conor, 179
Conrad, 124, 281
Conradin, 124
Conradina, 120
Conradine, 120
Conrado, 124, 267
Conroy, 53, 115, 179
Conshita, 263
Consolacion, 263

Consolata, 184, 263
Constance, 192
Constancia, 192
Constansie, 184
Constant, 206
Constantia, 184, 192
Constantin, 186
Constantina, 184, 192
Constantine, 206
Constantino, 206, 267
Constantios, 206
Constanza, 184, 263
Constanze, 192
Constanzie, 184
Consuela, 192, 263
Consuelo, 263
Conway, 53, 115, 179
Conyn, 294
Cooey, 179
Cooley, 179
Coolie, 179
Cooney, 179
Cooper, 81
Coopersmith, 81
Cora, 130, 253
Coral, 130
Coralie, 104, 130
Coralin, 130
Coralina, 130
Coraline, 130
Corann, 53
Corazon, 263
Corbenic, 45
Corbin, 206
Corbmac, 179
Corcoran, 115, 179
Corcurachan, 115
Cord, 124
Cordelia, 50, 73, 290
Corella, 130
Coretta, 104, 130
Corette, 104, 130
Corey, 30, 115, 179, 255
Cori, 115, 179
Coridan, 141
Corin, 130
Corineus, 141
Corinna, 130
Corinne, 130
Corliss, 73
Cormac, 53, 115, 179
Cormack, 115
Cormic, 179
Cormick, 115, 179
Cornelia, 192
Cornelio, 206, 268
Cornelius, 179, 206
Corona, 170

Coronis, 130
Corradeo, 186
Corrado, 124, 186
Corryn, 294
Cors, 294
Corsen, 290
Cort, 108, 124, 231, 281
Cortie, 231
Corwan, 81
Corwin, 81
Corwine, 81
Corwyn, 81
Cory, 115, 179, 255
Corybantes, 141
Corydon, 141
Cos, 141
Cosette, 104
Cosima, 141
Cosimia, 130
Cosma, 130
Cosmas, 141
Cosmo, 141
Cotovatre, 42
Cottus, 141
Coughlan, 178
Court, 108
Courtland, 30, 81, 108
Courtnay, 30, 108
Courtney, 30, 108, 193
Covell, 81
Coventina, 28, 50
Covey, 179
Covyll, 81
Cowan, 115, 179
Cowbelliantus, 274
Cowen, 179
Cowin, 206
Cowyn, 179
Coyle, 115
Cradawg, 53
Craddock, 294
Cradoc, 294
Cragen, 290
Craig, 115, 255
Crandall, 81
Crandell, 81
Cranleah, 81
Cranley, 81
Cranly, 81
Crannog, 255
Cranston, 81
Cranstun, 81
Crawford, 81
Creag, 115
Creiddylad, 290
Creiddyladl, 42
Creighton, 81, 255
Creissant, 104
Creketun, 81
Creon, 141
Crescent, 104
Crescentia, 193
Cretien, 108, 141
Creusa, 130
Crevan, 179

Crichton, 81
Criostoir, 115
Crisdean, 115
Crispin, 206
Crispina, 193
Crist, 294
Cristiano, 205, 268
Cristin, 174, 191
Cristina, 263, 272
Cristiona, 191
Cristobal, 268
Cristoforo, 141, 186
Cristophe, 141
Crocale, 130
Croften, 81
Crofton, 81
Crogher, 179
Crohoore, 179
Crom, 254
Crombwiella, 81
Crompton, 81
Cromwell, 81, 255
Cronan, 115, 179
Cronus, 141
Crosby, 231, 281
Crosleah, 81
Crosleigh, 81
Crosley, 81
Crosly, 81
Crow-Hreidar, 231
Crowley, 179
Cruadhlaoich, 179
Crudel, 45
Cruim, 254
Crystal, 130
Csaba, 163
Csilla, 151
Ctesippus, 141
Cuanaic, 179
Cuartio, 268
Cuarto, 268
Cubert, 294
Cuchulain, 53
Cuilean, 115
Cuimean, 115
Cuini, 112
Cuinn, 53, 115, 179
Culain, 53
Culann, 53
Culbart, 80
Culbert, 80, 281
Culhwch, 45, 53, 294
Cullan, 115
Cullen, 53
Culley, 115
Cullin, 115
Cullo, 179
Culloden, 255
Cullodena, 253
Cullodina, 253
Cully, 115
Culvanawd, 294
Culver, 81
Cumania, 175
Cumhea, 179

Cumin, 255
Cumina, 253
Cumming, 255
Cundrie, 42
Cundry, 42
Cunningham, 255
Cupere, 81
Curadhan, 115
Curcio, 108, 268
Curney, 115
Curr, 115
Curran, 115
Currito, 267
Curro, 267
Curt, 108, 206
Curtice, 108
Curtis, 108
Custenhin, 294
Custennin, 45, 53
Cuthbeorht, 81
Cuthbert, 30, 81
Cutler, 81
CuUladh, 179
Cuyler, 179
Cwen, 28, 73
Cwene, 28
Cwentun, 81
Cy, 142
Cybele, 130
Cycnus, 141
Cym, 73
Cyma, 130
Cymbeline, 45
Cymbelline, 81
Cymberly, 73
Cymreiges, 290
Cymry, 294
Cynara, 130
Cynbal, 294
Cynbel, 294
Cynburleigh, 73
Cyne, 73
Cyneburhleah, 73
Cynegils, 30
Cyneheard, 30
Cyneleah, 81
Cyneley, 81
Cyneric, 30, 81
Cynerik, 81
Cynewulf, 30
Cynfarch, 45
Cynhard, 80
Cyning, 81
Cynn, 30
Cynric, 30, 81
Cynrik, 81
Cynthia, 130
Cynward, 80
Cynyr, 53
Cyprian, 141, 244
Cyprien, 193
Cyprienne, 193
Cypris, 130
Cyr, 141
Cyra, 130, 240
Cyrano, 142
Cyrek, 141, 244
Cyrena, 130
Cyrene, 130
Cyril, 141

Cyrilla, 130, 193
Cyrillia, 193
Cyrus, 142, 241
Cyryl, 141, 244
Cyst, 28, 30
Cystennin, 294
Cythera, 130
Cytherea, 130
Cytheria, 130
Czeslaw, 244
Czigany, 162

D'Arcy, 104, 108
D'Ary, 115
Dabi, 157
Dabir, 38
Dacey, 115
Dacia, 193
Dacy, 115
Dadweir, 294
Daedalus, 142
Daedbot, 28
Daegal, 31, 251
Dael, 73, 81
Daemon, 142
Daere, 290
Daesgesage, 73
Daeva, 165
Daffodil, 130
Dafydd, 294
Dag, 231
Dagan, 157, 303
Daganya, 151
Daganyah, 151
Dagfinnr, 251
Daghda, 50, 179
Dagian, 73
Dagmar, 60, 120, 272, 278
Dagna, 278
Dagny, 225
Dagoberto, 124
Dagomar, 120
Dagon, 303
Dagonet, 45
Daguenet, 45
Dagwood, 81
Dahlia, 225
Dahy, 179
Daibheid, 179
Daibhidh, 115
Daileass, 255
Daimh, 255
Daimhin, 115, 179
Dain, 231, 251
Daire, 179
Daisi, 104
Daisy, 28, 73
Daithi, 179
Dakarai, 69
Dakini, 165
Daksha, 168
Dakshina, 165
Dalbert, 81
Dale, 73, 81, 225, 281
Daley, 81
Daliah, 152
Dalila, 66, 152, 263
Dalis, 152

Dalit, 152
Daliyah, 152
Dall, 115
Dalla, 225
Dallan, 179
Dallas, 53, 115, 255
Dalldav, 294
Dalr, 225
Dalston, 31
Dalton, 81
Daly, 115
Dalyell, 255
Dalziel, 255
Damae, 142
Daman, 53, 179
Damara, 130
Damaris, 130
Damaskenos, 142
Damaskinos, 142
Damayanti, 165
Damek, 59
Damen, 142
Damh, 255
Damhlaic, 179
Damhnait, 175
Damia, 104, 130, 193
Damian, 142, 268
Damiana, 104, 193
Damiane, 104
Damien, 104
Damina, 193
Damita, 263
Damocles, 142
Damon, 179, 206
Damone, 193
Dan, 157
Dana, 50, 60, 175, 231, 251
Danae, 131, 152
Danaus, 142, 206
Danb, 231
Danby, 231
Dane, 61, 157, 231, 251
Daned, 294
Danel, 49, 157
Danele, 48, 152
Danelle, 152
Danetta, 152
Danette, 152
Dani, 157
Dania, 152
Danica, 259
Daniel, 157
Daniela, 152, 157
Daniele, 186
Danielle, 152
Danika, 259
Danil, 157
Danila, 152, 157
Danit, 152
Danita, 152, 263
Dannel, 281
Danny, 157
Dante, 186
Danu, 165
Danya, 152, 248, 288

Danylets, 288
Danylko, 288
Daphna, 152
Daphnah, 152
Daphne, 131, 152
Daphnis, 142, 206
Dar, 115, 157
Darach, 255
Daracha, 253
Darby, 115, 179, 231
Darce, 115
Darcy, 53, 104, 108
Darda, 162, 251
Dardanus, 142, 206
Dareh, 241
Darel, 28
Darelene, 28
Darelle, 28
Darerca, 175
Daria, 240, 263
Darice, 240
Dario, 268
Darioush, 241
Darius, 69, 241
Darlene, 28
Darline, 28
Darnell, 81
Daron, 115
Darragh, 179
Darrell, 81
Darren, 115
Darrick, 281
Darry, 115, 179
Darshan, 171
Darton, 81
Daru, 170
Darwishi, 69
Dary, 179
Darya, 240
Daryl, 28, 73, 81
Daryn, 115
Das, 168
Dasa, 168
Dasha, 247
Dasras, 168
Dasya, 168
Dave, 255
Daven, 251
Davet, 108
Davey, 157
Davi, 152, 157
David, 157, 274
Davida, 152, 193
Davide, 186
Davidson, 81, 255
Davidsone, 81
Davin, 157, 231, 251, 274
Davina, 152
Davinah, 152
Davinia, 152
Davis, 81, 255
Davitah, 152
Davite, 152
Davyn, 231
Dawn, 28, 73
Dawud, 38

Dayle, 73, 81
Dea Roma, 193
Deaglan, 179
Deagmund, 82
Dealbeorht, 81
Dealbert, 81
Dean, 81
Deana, 73
Deane, 73
Deanna, 73
Deanne, 81
Dearan, 115
Dearbhail, 175
Dearborn, 81
Dearbourne, 81
Deardriu, 112
Dearg, 53, 124, 255
Deasach, 115
Deasmumhan, 115
Debora, 152
Deborah, 152
Debra, 152
Dechtere, 42
Dechtire, 42, 51
Decima, 193
Decla, 175
Declan, 179, 303
Dedo, 206
Dedre, 175
Dedric, 281
Dedrick, 124, 281
Dedrik, 124, 281
Dee, 290
Deems, 81
Deen, 157
Deepa, 170
Deerward, 82
Defena, 73
Dehaan, 64
Deheune, 51
Deianira, 131
Deidameia, 193
Deidra, 112
Deiene, 263
Deikun, 263
Deina, 263
Deiphobus, 142, 206
Deira, 42
Deirdre, 51, 112
Delaney, 179
Delano, 115
Delbert, 81
Delbin, 131
Delbina, 131
Delbine, 131
Delcine, 263
Delfina, 131
Delfine, 131
Delia, 131, 290
Delicea, 193
Delicia, 193, 263
Deliciae, 193
Delight, 104
Delila, 152
Delilah, 152
Delit, 104
Della, 120, 131
Delling, 231
Dellingr, 231

Delma, 263
Delmar, 108, 206, 263, 268
Delmara, 263
Delmare, 104
Delmer, 108, 206
Delora, 193
Deloras, 193
Deloros, 193
Delphia, 131
Delphina, 131
Delphine, 131
Delphinus, 142
Delsin, 218
Delta, 131
Delwin, 281
Delwyn, 281
Deman, 31, 64
Demas, 131
Demason, 81
Demasone, 81
Demeter, 131
Demetre, 142
Demetri, 142
Demetria, 131
Demetrios, 142
Demetrius, 142
Demi, 104
Demodocus, 142, 206
Demogorgon, 142
Demonassa, 193
Demophon, 142
Demos, 131
Demothi, 218
Dempsey, 81, 115, 179
Dempster, 81
Den, 231
Dena, 73, 152, 214
Denby, 31, 231, 251
Dendera, 66
Dene, 81
Denes, 142
Denice, 104
Denis, 108
Denisc, 31
Denise, 104
Deniska, 248
Denley, 81
Dennet, 108
Dennis, 108
Denny, 231
Denton, 81
Denver, 81
Denys, 108, 142
Deoch, 51
Deogol, 31
Deoradhain, 179
Deorsa, 115
Deortun, 81
Deorward, 82
Deorwine, 82
Dera, 290
Derby, 231
Derebourne, 81
Derek, 124, 281
Derforgal, 175
Derforgala, 175

Derian, 31
Derimacheia, 193
Derinow, 193
Dermod, 115, 179
Dermot, 53, 115, 179
Dermott, 115
Deron, 157
Derora, 152
Derorice, 152
Derorit, 152
Derrick, 124
Derry, 115, 124
Derval, 175
Dervilia, 175
Dervla, 175
Dervorgilla, 175
Derwan, 81
Derward, 82
Derwen, 290
Derwin, 81, 282
Derwyn, 81, 282
Desdemona, 131
Desideria, 104, 263
Desiderio, 231, 268
Desirat, 104
Desirata, 193
Desire, 104, 108
Desiree, 104
Desma, 131
Desmon, 115
Desmona, 131
Desmond, 31, 53, 115, 179
Deucalion, 142, 206
Deunoro, 49
Deutsch, 124
Deva, 51, 165, 203
Devaki, 165
Devamatar, 165
Devan, 115
Devayani, 165
Deven, 168
Devent, 175
Devera, 263
Deverell, 294
Deverra, 193
Deverril, 294
Devi, 170
Devin, 53, 115
Devine, 179
Devisser, 64
Devlin, 115
Devlyn, 115
Devnet, 175
Devon, 31
Devona, 28, 51, 73
Devonna, 73
Devora, 152, 247
Devoria, 152
Devoss, 64
Devota, 193
Devries, 64
Devyn, 31, 53, 115
Devyna, 73

DeWitt, 303
Dewain, 54
Dewey, 294
Dewi, 294
Dewitt, 64
Dexter, 108, 206
Dextra, 193
Dezba, 217
Dezso, 206
Dharani, 165
Dhenuka, 168
Dhimitrios, 142
Dhoire, 255
Dhumavarna, 168
Dia, 131, 263
Diamanta, 104
Diamond, 82
Diamont, 82
Diana, 104, 193
Diane, 104, 193
Diantha, 131
Dianthe, 131
Diarmad, 115
Diarmaid, 115
Diarmid, 115
Dibe, 217
Dice, 131
Dichali, 218
Dick, 124, 281
Dickran, 41
Dickson, 82, 282
Dicra, 290
Didier, 108
Dido, 131, 193
Didrika, 120
Diederich, 124
Diega, 263
Diego, 268
Diella, 193
Dielle, 193
Diera, 28
Dierck, 124
Dierdre, 175, 290
Dieter, 124
Dietrich, 124
Dietz, 124
Difyr, 290
Digby, 231
Digna, 193, 263
Digne, 193
Digon, 294
Dike, 131
Dikesone, 82
Dikibyr, 231
Dikran, 41
Dilan, 294
Dillie, 294
Dillion, 53
Dillon, 115, 294
Dillus, 294
Dima, 249
Dimitra, 247
Dimitri, 249
Dimka, 259
Dina, 73, 152
Dinadan, 45
Dinah, 152
Dinas, 45
Dino, 81, 131
Dinsmore, 53
Diolmhain, 115

Diomasac, 115
Diomedes, 142
Dion, 142
Diona, 131
Dione, 131
Dionis, 263
Dionisa, 263
Dionizy, 244
Dionysia, 131, 193
Dionysie, 131
Dionysios, 142
Dionysius, 142
Dionysus, 142
Diorbhall, 112
Dioxippe, 193
Dirce, 131, 193
Dirck, 64
Dirk, 64, 124, 282
Dirmyg, 294
Dis, 206
Disa, 225
Discordia, 193
Dismas, 303
Diss, 225
Diti, 165
Div, 165
Diva, 51
Divone, 51
Divsha, 152
Divshah, 152
Divya, 170
Dixie, 104
Dixon, 82, 282
Diya al din, 38
Djoser, 69
Doane, 53, 82
Doba, 217
Dobhailen, 115
Dobieslaw, 244
Dobry, 244
Docila, 193
Docilla, 193
Dodek, 244
Dodinel, 45
Dohosan, 218
Dohtor, 28
Doire, 255
Doire-ann, 112
Doireann, 112, 174
Doli, 217
Dolius, 142
Doll, 131
Dollie, 131
Dolly, 131
Dolon, 206
Dolores, 263
Dolorita, 263
Doloritas, 263
Dolph, 273, 282
Dom, 206
Dome, 206
Domeka, 206
Domela, 193
Domele, 193
Domhnall, 54
Domhnull, 115, 255
Domhnulla, 112
Domiduca, 193
Domiducus, 206

Domiku, 206
Dominga, 263
Domingart, 45
Domingo, 268
Dominic, 206
Dominica, 175, 193
Dominick, 206
Dominico, 206
Dominika, 247
Dominique, 104, 193
Domino, 193
Domitiana, 193
Domitiane, 193
Domo, 206
Domokas, 206
Don, 28, 53
Dona, 184, 193
Donaghy, 54
Donahue, 115
Donal, 54
Donald, 53, 115
Donalda, 112, 251
Donall, 54
Donat, 54, 244
Donata, 184, 193
Donatello, 186, 206
Donatien, 108
Donato, 186, 206
Donel, 255
Donell, 255
Donella, 51
Donelle, 175, 193
Donia, 51, 112
Donica, 193
Donkor, 69
Donn, 179
Donna, 184, 193
Donnachadh, 255
Donnally, 54
Donnan, 179
Donnchadh, 115, 255
Donnchadh, 54
Donnelly, 54
Donner, 231
Donogh, 54
Donoma, 217
Donovan, 54
Dooley, 115
Doon, 175
Dor, 157
Dora, 131
Doralia, 131
Doralice, 131
Doralie, 131
Doralis, 131
Doran, 54, 142, 179
Dorbeta, 263
Dorcas, 131
Dordei, 131
Dordie, 131
Dore, 104
Dorea, 131
Doreen, 51, 104, 112, 131, 175
Doreena, 51
Dorek, 244

Dorelia, 131
Doren, 157
Dorene, 104, 112
Doretta, 131
Dorette, 131
Doria, 131
Dorian, 131, 142
Doriana, 131
Dorice, 131
Dorien, 131
Dorika, 162, 193
Dorinda, 131
Dorine, 104
Doris, 131, 193
Dorita, 131
Dorjan, 206
Dorkas, 131
Dorlisa, 131
Doroata, 243
Dorote, 193
Dorotea, 100, 193, 263
Doroteia, 263
Doroteya, 247
Dorothea, 61, 131, 193
Dorothee, 193
Dorothy, 131, 193
Dorottya, 162, 193
Dorran, 54
Dorte, 131
Dory, 104
Dougal, 31, 54, 179, 255
Doughal, 54
Doughall, 255
Doughlas, 54
Douglas, 31, 54, 179, 255
Doune, 82
Dour, 255
Dovev, 157
Dow, 179
Dowan, 179
Dowle, 179
Downeti, 175
Downett, 175
Doy, 53
Doyle, 53, 179
Draca, 82
Drake, 82
Draupnir, 225, 231
Drefan, 31
Drem, 54, 294
Dremidydd, 294
Dreng, 31, 231
Dreogan, 31
Drew, 31, 131, 294
Dridan, 82
Driden, 82
Drisana, 165, 170
Driscol, 54, 179
Driscoll, 54, 179
Driskell, 54
Dristan, 45
Druas, 45
Druce, 31, 54, 294

Drucilla, 193
Drud, 124
Drudwas, 294
Drudwyn, 45, 54, 294
Drugi, 124
Drummand, 255
Drummond, 54, 255
Drusilla, 193
Druson, 294
Drust, 45
Drwst, 294
Drych, 294
Dryden, 82
Drygedene, 82
Dryope, 131, 193
Drysi, 290
Drystan, 45, 294
Dryw, 294
Drywsone, 294
Du, 290
Duach, 294
Duana, 175
Duane, 54
Duartr, 231
Dubg, 179
Dubh, 255
Dubhagain, 179
Dubhain, 175
Dubhan, 179
Dubheasa, 175
Dubhgan, 115
Dubhghall, 179
Dubhglas, 255
Dubhloach, 115
Dubhthach, 115
Dubv, 54
Duci, 162
Duclea, 193
Dudek, 59
Dudley, 82
Dudon, 45
Duena, 263
Duer, 54
Duff, 54, 115, 255
Duffy, 54, 115
Dugald, 115
Dugan, 115
Duggan, 179
Dughall, 54, 115
Duhkha, 168
Duke, 206
Dulce, 263
Dulcia, 193
Dulcie, 193
Dulcina, 263
Dulcine, 193, 263
Dulcinea, 263
Dulcinia, 193, 263
Dulcy, 193
Dummonia, 42
Duncan, 54, 115, 255
Dunham, 54
Dunixi, 49, 142
Dunleah, 82
Dunleigh, 82
Dunley, 82
Dunly, 82
Dunmor, 255

Dunmore, 255
Dunn, 82
Dunstan, 82
Dunton, 82
Dunyasha, 247
Duran, 206
Durand, 206
Durandana, 104
Durant, 206
Durga, 170
Durin, 231
Durindana, 104
Durvasas, 168
Durward, 82
Durwin, 31, 82
Durwyn, 31, 82
Duscha, 247
Dushkriti, 168
Dustin, 282
Dustu, 220
Dutch, 124
Duvessa, 175
Dwayne, 54
Dwight, 64, 282
Dwnn, 294
Dwyer, 179
Dyami, 218
Dyani, 214
Dyaus, 168
Dyfed, 54
Dyffryn, 294
Dylan, 294
Dymitr, 244
Dymphna, 112, 175
Dympna, 175
Dymtrus, 288
Dyna, 193
Dynadin, 45
Dyngannon, 294
Dyre, 231
Dyrfinna, 225
Dyri, 231
Dyvynarth, 294
Dyvynwal, 294
Dyvyr, 294
Dywel, 294

Ea, 54
Eachan, 179
Eachann, 115, 142
Eachthighearn, 115
Eacnung, 28
Eada, 73
Eadaion, 120
Eadbeorht, 82
Eadbert, 31
Eadburt, 82
Eadda, 73
Eadelmarr, 82
Eadgard, 31
Eadger, 82
Eadgyth, 28, 73
Eadig, 31
Eadignes, 28
Eadlin, 28
Eadlyn, 31
Eadmund, 73, 82
Eadric, 82
Eadsele, 82

Eadward, 31, 82
Eadwardsone, 82
Eadweald, 82
Eadweard, 82
Eadwiella, 82
Eadwine, 73, 82
Eadwyn, 31, 82
Eagon, 179
Ealadhach, 115
Ealasaid, 112
Ealdian, 31
Ealdun, 82
Ealdwode, 82
Ealga, 175
Ealhdun, 82
Ealhhard, 82
Eallard, 82
Eallison, 82
Eamon, 31, 115, 179
Eamonn, 115
Eanan, 179
Eanruig, 115, 255
Ear, 255
Eara, 253
Earc, 179
Earh, 31
Earie, 253, 255
Earl, 31, 82
Earle, 31, 82
Earlene, 73
Earlson, 82
Earm, 31
Earna, 74
Earnan, 115, 179
Earnest, 124
Earnestyna, 74
Earric, 73
Eartha, 73
Earvin, 115
Earwine, 73, 82, 294
Earwyn, 73, 82, 294
Earwyna, 74
Easter, 28, 73
Eastre, 73
Eathelin, 73
Eathelreda, 74
Eathelyn, 73
Eaton, 82
Eatun, 82
Eavan, 175
Eawart, 83
Eban, 157
Ebba, 61, 73, 120, 272
Ebbe, 272
Eben, 157
Ebenezer, 157
Eberhard, 124
Eberhardt, 124
Eberta, 278
Ebissa, 31
Ebo, 69
Ebrill, 290
Eburacon, 54
Eburhardt, 124
Ecaterina, 131
Ecgbeorht, 82
Ecgfrith, 31

Echidna, 66, 131, 193
Echion, 142
Echo, 131
Echoid, 45
Eckerd, 124
Ecterine, 131
Ector, 45
Eda, 28, 59, 73, 82, 131, 225
Edan, 54, 152
Edana, 51, 112, 175
Edbert, 82
Edburga, 278
Edda, 63, 120, 225, 251
Eddis, 82
Eddison, 31
Eddy, 274
Ede, 73, 82131
Edeen, 253
Edel, 124
Edelina, 120, 278
Edeline, 120, 278
Edelmar, 82
Edelmarr, 82
Eden, 152
Edern, 45, 294
Ederyn, 231
Edfu, 69
Edgar, 31, 82
Edgard, 31
Edik, 249
Ediline, 120
Edina, 28, 73253
Edine, 253
Edingu, 124
Edison, 82
Edit, 28, 272
Edita, 28, 184
Edith, 28, 73, 278
Editha, 28
Editta, 184, 278
Edjo, 66
Edla, 28
Edlen, 73
Edlin, 28, 31, 73
Edlym, 294
Edlyn, 28, 31, 73
Edlynn, 28
Edlynne, 28
Edmanda, 73
Edmee, 28, 104
Edmond, 31, 82
Edmonda, 28, 73
Edmondo, 82, 186
Edmund, 31, 82
Edmunda, 28, 73
Edmundo, 268
Edmyg, 294
Edna, 51
Edoardo, 186
Edolia, 278
Edolie, 278
Edorta, 49
Edra, 73, 152, 278
Edrea, 73, 152, 278
Edred, 31

Edric, 31, 82
Edrigu, 49, 282
Edrik, 82
Edris, 28
Edrys, 28
Edsel, 31, 82
Edson, 31
Eduard, 82, 124, 249
Eduarda, 73
Eduardo, 186, 268
Edulica, 193
Edur, 49
Edurne, 48
Edvard, 82, 274
Edwald, 82
Edwaldo, 82
Edward, 31, 82, 124
Edwardson, 82
Edwige, 278
Edwin, 31, 82, 124
Edwina, 73
Edwy, 31
Edwyn, 31, 82, 124
Edyt, 28
Edyta, 243, 278
Edyte, 278
Edyth, 28, 73
Eeva, 100, 152
Efa, 290
Eferhard, 83
Eferhild, 73
Eferhilda, 73
Eferleah, 83
Effie, 131
Efnisien, 54
Efrat, 157
Efrayim, 157
Egan, 54, 115, 179, 282
Egbert, 31, 82, 282
Egberta, 73
Egbertina, 73
Egbertine, 73
Egbertyne, 73
Egeria, 131, 193
Egerton, 82
Egesa, 31
Egeslic, 31
Egesta, 193
Eggther, 231
Eghan, 54
Egidio, 142, 186
Egidius, 64
Egil, 231
Eginhard, 124
Eginhardt, 124
Egiodeo, 186
Eglantina, 104
Eglantine, 104
Egomas, 54
Egon, 115, 124, 179, 282
Egor, 249
Eguskina, 48
Eguskine, 48
Ehangwen, 294

Ehawee, 218
Eheubryd, 290
Ehren, 124
Ehud, 157
Eibhear, 82
Eibhlhin, 175
Eibhlin, 112
Eiddoel, 294
Eiddon, 294
Eiddyl, 294
Eideann, 112
Eideard, 82, 115
Eidothea, 131
Eigg, 255
Eigil, 231
Eikki, 100, 231
Eiladar, 294
Eileen, 175
Eileithyia, 131
Eilidh, 112
Eilif, 231
Eilig, 255
Eilinora, 175
Eilionoir, 112
Eilis, 175
Eily, 175
Eimar, 179
Eimhin, 179
Einar, 231
Einhard, 124
Einhardt, 124
Einian, 294
Einion, 54, 294
Einri, 282
Eir, 225
Eirene, 131, 193
Eiric, 253
Eirica, 253
Eirik, 231
Eiryn, 294
Eisa, 38
Eistein, 231
Eistir, 175
Eithna, 175
Eithne, 175
Eitri, 231
Eivyonydd, 294
Ejnar, 61
Ekadanta, 168
Ekaterina, 131, 247
Ekerd, 124
Ekhard, 124
Ektor, 45
Elaine, 42, 131
Elan, 157, 175, 218
Elata, 193
Elayne, 42
Elazar, 49, 157
Elazaro, 157
Elbert, 282
Elberta, 73, 278
Elberte, 73
Elbertina, 73, 263
Elbertine, 73
Elbertyna, 73
Elda, 28, 184, 278
Eldan, 82
Elde, 278
Elden, 82, 282
Elder, 82

Eldgrim, 231
Eldon, 82, 282
Eldora, 263, 278
Eldoris, 131
Eldred, 31, 282
Eldreda, 73
Eldrid, 31, 225
Eldrida, 28, 73
Eldride, 28
Eldridge, 282
Eldur, 82
Eldwin, 31
Eldwyn, 31
Eleanor, 104, 131
Eleanora, 131, 184
Eleanore, 131
Eleazar, 157
Electa, 193
Electra, 131
Elefteria, 131
Eleftherios, 142
Elek, 142, 244
Elekta, 193
Elemer, 282
Elen, 290
Elena, 131, 184, 263
Elene, 28, 184
Eleni, 131
Elenitsa, 131
Elenora, 184
Elenore, 184
Eleonora, 272
Eleora, 152
Elepheteria, 131
Elephteria, 131
Eleta, 104
Elethea, 73
Elethia, 73
Eleutherios, 142
Elfie, 74
Elfreda, 74, 278
Elfrida, 74, 278
Elfrieda, 74
Elga, 28, 247, 278
Elgar, 282
Elhanan, 157
Elhe, 179
Eli, 142, 157
Elia, 152
Eliana, 152
Eliane, 152
Elias, 157
Eliaures, 45
Elica, 120
Elida, 74
Elidor, 54
Elidure, 45, 82
Elidyr, 294
Elienor, 104
Eliezer, 157
Eligius, 206
Elihu, 157
Elijah, 157
Elin, 225, 272
Elinore, 104
Eliora, 152
Eliot, 108, 157
Eliott, 108
Elisa, 104, 263

Elisabet, 131, 152, 272
Elisabeth, 104, 131, 152
Elisabetta, 184
Elisavet, 152
Elisaveta, 152
Elise, 104
Eliseo, 157
Elisha, 157
Elishama, 157
Elisheba, 157
Elisheva, 152, 157
Elisia, 131
Elissa, 131
Elita, 74, 104
Elivina, 74
Eliza, 104, 152
Elizabeth, 42, 152
Elizabetta, 184
Elizaveta, 152
Elka, 152
Elkanah, 157
Elke, 152, 278
Elki, 221
Ella, 74
Ellama, 170
Ellard, 82, 282
Ellary, 282
Ellder, 82
Elle, 74, 225
Ellen, 31, 131
Ellenweorc, 28
Ellery, 124, 282
Ellette, 28
Elli, 152, 225
Ellice, 131, 152
Ellinor, 104
Elliot, 108, 255
Ellis, 157
Ellisif, 226
Ellison, 82
Ellwood, 82
Ellylw, 290
Elma, 131
Elmar, 282
Elmer, 31, 82, 282
Elmina, 278
Elmine, 278
Elmira, 74
Elmo, 186
Elmoor, 82
Elmore, 82
Elmyra, 74
Elne, 31
Elnora, 131
Eloina, 193
Eloine, 193
Eloisa, 104
Eloise, 104, 278
Eloisee, 104
Elora, 131, 152
Eloy, 124, 268
Elpenor, 142
Elphin, 231, 294
Elpida, 131
Elpide, 131
Elrad, 157
Elroy, 179

Els, 152
Elsa, 42, 120, 264, 272, 278
Elsdon, 82
Else, 61, 120
Elsha, 50, 120
Elsie, 120, 152
Elsje, 120
Elspeth, 152
Elsu, 218
Elsworth, 82
Elswyth, 28
Elthia, 73
Elton, 82
Eluwilussit, 219
Elva, 28, 74
Elvena, 74
Elvera, 193
Elvey, 82
Elvia, 28, 74
Elvie, 74
Elvin, 74
Elvina, 28, 74
Elvine, 74
Elvio, 206, 268
Elvira, 193, 264
Elvis, 231
Elvy, 82
Elvyne, 74
Elwald, 82
Elwell, 82
Elwen, 82
Elwin, 82
Elwine, 28
Elwira, 243
Elwold, 82
Elwood, 82
Elwyn, 82
Elwyna, 28
Ely, 124, 157
Elyse, 120
Elyta, 74
Elzbieta, 243
Elzira, 152
Ema, 264, 278
Embla, 226
Emelin, 278
Emelina, 278
Emeline, 278
Emer, 175
Emera, 194
Emeraude, 104
Emeric, 82, 282
Emerick, 82
Emery, 82, 124, 282
Emhyr, 294
Emil, 206, 274, 282
Emile, 206, 282
Emilia, 184, 264, 272
Emilian, 206, 282
Emilie, 120, 264, 278
Emiline, 278
Emilio, 268
Emily, 278
Emira, 194
Emlyn, 278, 295
Emma, 120, 272, 278

Emmanuel, 157
Emmanuele, 186
Emmanuella, 152
Emmanuelle, 152
Emmeline, 104
Emmilian, 244
Emory, 124, 282
Empanda, 194
Emric, 282
Emrik, 282
Emrys, 54, 295
Emunah, 152
Emyr, 45
Ena, 51, 175
Enan, 179
Enapay, 222
Enar, 231, 274
Enat, 175
Encarnacion, 264
Enceladus, 142
Enda, 179
Endora, 131
Endre, 142, 163
Endymion, 142
Enea, 142, 186
Eneas, 142, 268
Enerstina, 74
Enerstyne, 74
Eneuawg, 290
Engel, 28, 125
Engelbertha, 120
Engelbertina, 120
Engelbertine, 120
Engl, 51
Englbehrt, 124
Englebert, 124
Engleberta, 120
Engracia, 264
Engres, 45
Enid, 42, 51, 74, 290
Enide, 42
Enit, 74, 290
Enite, 42
Enkoodabaoo, 219
Enkoodabooaoo, 219
Ennea, 131
Ennis, 175
Ennissyen, 295
Enno, 124
Eno, 124
Enoch, 157
Enok, 61
Enola, 214
Enos, 177
Enrhydreg, 290
Enrica, 278
Enrichetta, 184
Enrico, 186, 282
Enrika, 278
Enriqu, 282
Enriqua, 264
Enrique, 268
Enriqueta, 264, 278
Entoria, 194
Eny, 175
Enya, 194

Enyd, 74
Enyeto, 218
Enygeus, 42
Enyo, 131, 194
Enzo, 186, 282
Eoforwic, 82
Eoghan, 115, 142, 179
Eoghann, 54, 115
Eoin, 54, 179
Eoin Baiste, 179
Eorl, 31, 82
Eorland, 82
Eorlland, 82
Eorlson, 82
Eos, 131, 194
Eostre, 28
Epeius, 142
Ephie, 132
Ephraim, 157
Ephram, 157
Ephrem, 157
Ephyra, 194
Epione, 194
Epona, 51, 194
Epopeus, 142
Equestris, 194
Eraman, 120
Eramana, 120
Erasmo, 268
Erasmus, 142
Erato, 131
Erbin, 45, 295
Erc, 179
Erchanbold, 124
Erchanhardt, 124
Ercole, 142
Erconberht, 31
Ercwlff, 295
Erdudvyl, 290
Erea, 51
Erebus, 142
Erec, 45
Erechtheus, 142
Erek, 45, 244
Erela, 152
Erelah, 152
Erembourg, 104
Erendira, 264
Erendiria, 264
Eres, 290
Ergyryad, 295
Erhard, 124
Erhardt, 124
Erian, 31
Eriantha, 131
Erianthe, 131
Erianthia, 131
Eriboea, 194
Eric, 231
Erica, 226, 278
Erich, 124
Erichthonius, 142, 206
Erick, 231
Erie, 51
Erigone, 131
Erik, 61, 231, 274
Erika, 162, 226, 272, 278
Erim, 54, 295

Erin, 51, 112, 115, 175
Erina, 51, 175
Erinyes, 131
Eriphyle, 132
Eris, 132
Erith, 152
Eritha, 152
Erkerd, 124
Erland, 82, 231, 274
Erleen, 73
Erlene, 28
Erlina, 28, 112
Erline, 28, 112
Erling, 82, 231, 274
Erma, 120, 278
Ermanno, 186, 282
Ermelinda, 278
Ermelinde, 278
Ermengardine, 104
Ermid, 295
Ermina, 194
Erna, 74, 120, 162, 226, 278
Ernan, 179
Ernest, 124
Ernesta, 264, 278
Ernestina, 120, 278
Ernestine, 120, 278
Ernestine, 74
Ernesto, 186, 268
Ernesztina, 162
Erno, 124
Ernst, 124, 274
Erp, 231
Erramun, 282
Errando, 124
Errapel, 124
Errita, 132
Errol, 206
Erroman, 282
Erromon, 49
Erskina, 253
Erskine, 255
Erssike, 162
Ertha, 73
Ervin, 163
Erwin, 82, 294
Erwina, 73, 74
Erwm, 295
Erwyn, 83, 294
Erwyna, 73, 74
Eryi, 295
Eryk, 231, 244
Erymanthus, 142
Erysichthon, 142
Erytheia, 132
Erzebet, 162
Erzsebet, 152
Erzsi, 162
Erzsok, 162
Esbjorn, 231, 274
Escalibor, 45
Escanor, 45
Escorant, 45
Esdras, 157

Eshe, 66
Eshkol, 157
Eskarna, 264
Eskarne, 264
Eske, 231
Eskil, 231, 274
Eskild, 61
Esma, 28, 264
Esme, 28, 264
Esmeralda, 132
Esmeraude, 104
Esmerelda, 132, 264
Esmond, 83
Esmund, 83
Espe, 194
Espen, 64
Esperanza, 104, 264
Essie, 194
Esta, 184
Estcot, 83
Estcott, 83
Este, 186
Esteban, 268
Estebana, 264
Estebe, 142
Estefan, 268
Estefana, 264
Estella, 194, 264
Estelle, 104, 194
Ester, 152, 264
Esteva, 264
Estevao, 142
Esther, 152, 240
Estmund, 83
Estra, 28
Estrela, 152
Estrella, 264
Esyllt, 290
Eszter, 152
Eszti, 162
Etain, 51, 175
Etan, 157
Etchemin, 219
Etel, 152, 162
Etenia, 214
Eteocles, 142
Eth, 179
Ethan, 157
Ethel, 152, 278
Ethelbald, 31
Ethelbert, 31, 83
Ethelda, 278
Ethelde, 278
Ethelind, 278
Ethelinda, 120, 278
Ethelinde, 120, 278
Ethelred, 31
Ethelreda, 74
Ethelwulf, 31
Etheswitha, 28
Ethna, 175
Ethne, 51
Etienne, 108
Etilka, 152, 162
Etelelooaat, 219
Etney, 175
Etor, 49, 142
Etta, 120, 278

Ettard, 42
Ettare, 42
Ettore, 142, 186
Etu, 218
Etzel, 231
Euadne, 194
Euandra, 194
Eubuleus, 142
Eudav, 295
Eudocia, 132
Eudokia, 132
Eudosia, 132
Eudosis, 132
Eudoxia, 132
Eugen, 124, 142, 274
Eugene, 142
Eugenia, 104, 132
Eugenio, 142, 186, 268
Eugenios, 142
Eugenius, 64
Eulalie, 104
Eulallia, 132
Eumaeus, 142
Eunice, 132
Eunomia, 132
Eupeithes, 143
Euphemia, 132
Euphemie, 132
Euphorbus, 206
Euphrosyne, 132
Eurayle, 132
Eurneid, 290
Eurolwyn, 290
Europa, 132
Eurosswydd, 295
Eurus, 143, 206
Euryale, 194
Euryalus, 143
Euryanassa, 194
Eurybia, 194
Eurycleia, 132
Eurydice, 132, 194
Euryganeia, 194
Eurylochus, 143
Eurymachus, 143
Eurymede, 194
Eurynome, 132, 194
Eurypylus, 143, 206
Eurystheus, 143, 207
Euryton, 143
Eus, 295
Eusebius, 143
Eustace, 143
Eustachy, 143
Eustacia, 194
Eustatius, 64
Eustella, 132
Eustis, 143
Euterpe, 132
Euzebia, 243
Eva, 61, 152, 247, 264, 272
Evacska, 152, 162
Evadeam, 45

Evadne, 132
Evalac, 45
Evan, 54, 255, 295
Evander, 207
Evangelia, 132
Evangeline, 132
Evania, 132
Evanna, 253
Evanth, 132
Evanthe, 132
Evasn, 142
Eve, 152
Evelake, 45
Eveleen, 175
Evelina, 51, 184, 247, 272
Eveline, 51
Evelyn, 51, 157
Ever, 82, 83
Everard, 83, 282
Everet, 82
Everhard, 82
Everhart, 64
Everleigh, 83
Everley, 83
Everly, 83
Evert, 82, 274
Evgenia, 132, 247
Evgenii, 249, 282
Evika, 152
Evike, 152, 162
Evin, 179
Evina, 253
Evita, 264
Evnissyen, 54
Evoy, 179
Evrain, 45
Evrard, 124
Evrawg, 45, 295
Evrei, 295
Evzen, 143
Ewa, 152, 243
Ewald, 83, 282
Ewan, 54
Eward, 124
Eweheorde, 83
Ewen, 54
Ewert, 83
Ewing, 83
Ewyas, 295
Ewyn, 54
Exaltacion, 264
Excalibur, 45
Eyfrod, 231
Eyjolf, 231
Eyota, 214
Eyou, 157
Eyslk, 290
Eystein, 231
Eyvind, 231
Ezechiel, 157
Ezhno, 218
Eznik, 41
Ezra, 157

Fabi, 249
Fabia, 184, 194
Fabian, 207, 274
Fabiana, 184, 194
Fabiano, 186, 207

Fabienne, 104
Fabio, 186, 268
Fabiola, 194
Fabiyan, 207, 249
Fabrice, 207
Fabrizio, 186, 207
Fabron, 207
Fabroni, 186
Fachnan, 179
Faddei, 249, 288
Fadey, 249, 288
Fadeyka, 249, 288
Fadeyushka, 288
Fadil, 38, 69
Fadilah, 36
Fadyenka, 282
Fae, 104
Faegan, 83
Faer, 83
Faerrleah, 83
Faerwald, 83
Fafner, 232
Fafnir, 232
Fagan, 83, 179
Fagen, 115
Fagin, 115
Fahd, 38
Fahey, 179
Fahy, 179
Fain, 83
Fainche, 175
Faing, 255
Fairfax, 31, 83
Fairlie, 83
Faith, 74, 194
Faithe, 74
Fakhir, 38
Faki, 69
Fala, 215
Falerina, 104
Fallamhain, 179
Fallon, 179
Fama, 194
Fanchon, 104, 278
Fanchone, 104
Fane, 83
Fanetta, 104
Fanette, 104
Fang, 255
Fani, 194
Fania, 194, 259
Fannie, 278
Fanny, 259, 278
Fantina, 104
Fantine, 104
Fanya, 259
Faodhagan, 115
Faoiltiarna, 175
Faolan, 115, 179
Faqueza, 264
Farah, 240
Faran, 31
Fardoragh, 179
Farica, 278
Farid, 38
Faridah, 36
Farideh, 240
Farika, 278
Faris, 38

Farlan, 255
Farlane, 255
Farleigh, 83
Farley, 83
Farly, 83
Farmon, 31
Farnall, 83
Farnell, 83
Farnham, 83
Farnley, 83
Farnly, 83
Farold, 83
Farquhar, 115
Farquharson, 255
Farr, 83
Farran, 38
Farrel, 54
Farrell, 54, 115
Farris, 143
Farrs, 83
Farruco, 268
Farry, 179
Fars, 83
Farson, 83
Faruq, 38
Fasolt, 232
Faste, 232
Fate, 132
Fatima, 36
Fatin, 36, 38
Fatina, 36
Fatinah, 36
Faula, 194
Faun, 104
Fauna, 104, 194
Faunia, 104
Faunus, 207
Faust, 186, 194, 207
Fausta, 184, 194, 264
Fauste, 194
Faustina, 194, 264
Faustine, 194
Fausto, 186, 207, 268
Favonius, 207
Favor, 104
Fawnia, 104
Faxon, 282
Fay, 104, 180
Faye, 104
Fayette, 104
Fayme, 104
Fayne, 83
Fayre, 74
Fayth, 74
Fe, 264
Fealty, 104
Feandan, 255
Fearbhirigh, 116
Fearchar, 255
Fearchara, 253
Fearcharia, 253
Fearcher, 115
Fearghall, 115
Fearghus, 54, 115
Fearnhamm, 83
Fearnhealh, 83
Fearnleah, 83

Feary, 180
Fedele, 207
Fedelm, 51
Federico, 186, 268
Federikke, 61
Fedor, 143, 249
Fedora, 132
Fedosia, 259
Fedya, 249, 282
Fedyenka, 249
Feenat, 175
Feich, 180
Feirefiz, 45
Fela, 243
Felabeorht, 74, 83
Felamaere, 83
Felan, 179
Felberta, 74
Felda, 120, 278
Felding, 83
Feldon, 83
Feldtun, 83
Feldun, 83
Feleta, 194
Felice, 194, 207
Felicia, 104, 194
Felician, 207
Felicienne, 104
Felicio, 186, 207
Felicitas, 194
Felicity, 104, 194
Feliks, 207, 244, 249
Felipe, 268
Felisa, 194, 264
Felisberta, 120
Felise, 194
Felita, 194
Felix, 31, 207, 268, 274
Felka, 243
Fell, 232
Felton, 83
Femi, 66
Fenella, 51, 175, 253
Fenice, 42
Fenrir, 232
Fenris, 232
Fenris-wolf, 232
Fenton, 83
Fenuku, 69
Fenyang, 69
Feodor, 143
Feodora, 247, 259
Feodras, 143
Feran, 31
Ferchar, 54
Fercos, 295
Ferda, 59
Ferdiad, 54
Ferdinand, 282
Ferdinando, 186
Ferenc, 163, 207
Fereng, 162, 278
Ferghus, 54, 115
Fergus, 54, 115, 255
Ferguson, 255

Fergusson, 255
Feri, 207
Ferika, 278
Ferike, 162, 278
Ferke, 207
Ferko, 163, 207
Fermin, 268
Fermina, 264
Fern, 74, 132
Fernald, 83
Fernanda, 278
Fernande, 278
Fernando, 268
Feroz, 241
Ferragus, 108
Ferran, 38
Ferrau, 108
Ferrex, 83
Ferris, 54
Ffanci, 290
Fferyll, 295
Fflam, 295
Fflergant, 295
Fflewdwr, 295
Ffodor, 295
Ffowc, 295
Ffraid, 290
Fia, 253
Fiach, 180
Fiachra, 180
Fiacra, 54
Fiacre, 54
Fiallan, 54
Fiamain, 54
Fianait, 175
Fianna, 51
Fibh, 255
Fidel, 207, 268
Fidele, 268
Fidelia, 194
Fidelio, 186, 207
Fidelis, 207
Fidelity, 194
Fides, 194
Fie, 255
Fielding, 83
Fiers, 249
Fifi, 104
Fifine, 104
Fifna, 152
Fifne, 152
Filbert, 83
Filberta, 74
Filburt, 83
Filia, 132
Filicia, 104
Filip, 249, 274
Filipa, 264
Filipina, 132
Filippa, 272
Filippio, 186
Filippo, 143, 186
Filips, 143
Filmarr, 83
Filmer, 83
Filmore, 83
Filomena, 132, 184, 194
Filomenia, 132
Filomina, 194
Fina, 152
Finan, 31

Finbar, 54, 180
Findabair, 51
Findlay, 115
Fineen, 180
Fineena, 175
Finella, 175
Fingal, 54
Finghin, 180
Fingula, 51
Finian, 54, 180
Finlay, 115
Finn, 54, 83, 115, 232
Finna, 175
Finnbar, 54
Finnbogi, 232
Finnin, 180
Finnobarr, 54
Finola, 175
Fiona, 51, 175
Fionan, 180
Fionn, 115, 175, 180
Fionnbarr, 180
Fionnghuala, 112, 175
Fionnlagh, 115
Fionnlaoch, 115
Fionnuala, 175
Fiorello, 186
Fiorenza, 184, 194
Firenze, 162
Firman, 31, 83
Firth, 255
Firtha, 253
Fisk, 274
Fiske, 83
Fitch, 83
Fitche, 83
Fitz, 83, 108, 282
Fitz Adam, 83
Fitz Gerald, 83, 282
Fitz Gibbon, 83
Fitz Gilbert, 83
Fitz Hugh, 83
Fitz James, 83
Fitz Patrick, 83, 282
Fitz Simon, 83
Fitz Walter, 83
Fitz Water, 83
Fitzadam, 83
Fitzgerald, 83, 282
Fitzgibbon, 83
Fitzgilbert, 83
Fitzhugh, 83
Fitzjames, 83
Fitzpatrick, 83, 282
Fitzsimmons, 83
Fitzsimon, 83
Fitzsimons, 83
Fitzwalter, 83
Fitzwater, 83
Fjall, 232
Fjarskafinn, 226
Fjorgyn, 226
Flainn, 180
Flamina, 194

Flaminia, 194
Flaminio, 268
Flanagan, 180
Flann, 115, 180
Flanna, 175
Flannagain, 180
Flannan, 180
Flavia, 184, 194
Flavian, 207
Flavio, 186, 207, 268
Flawiusz, 207, 244
Fleda, 278
Flede, 278
Fleischaker, 59
Fleming, 31, 83
Fleta, 74, 278
Fletcher, 108, 255, 282
Fleur, 104
Fleurette, 104
Flin, 115
Flint, 83
Flip, 143
Flita, 278
Flo, 214
Floinn, 180
Floki, 232
Flollo, 45
Flor, 194, 264
Flora, 194
Flordelis, 104
Floree, 42
Florella, 194
Floren, 207
Florence, 45, 194
Florencia, 264
Florentin, 207
Florentina, 194, 264
Florentine, 194
Florentino, 268
Florentyn, 207
Florentyna, 194
Florenza, 194
Florete, 42
Floria, 194
Florian, 207, 244
Florice, 194
Florida, 194, 264
Florinia, 264
Florinio, 268
Floris, 194
Florismart, 108
Florka, 162
Florus, 108
Flosi, 232
Floyd, 54
Fluonia, 194
Flynn, 115, 180
Flynt, 83
Flyta, 74
Fogartaigh, 180
Fogarty, 180
Fogerty, 180
Foley, 180
Folke, 282
Foma, 157, 249
Fonda, 74, 264
Forba, 180, 253
Forbes, 116, 255

Forbia, 253
Ford, 83
Forenza, 194
Forest, 83
Fornax, 194
Forrest, 108, 207
Forrester, 83
Forsa, 54
Forseti, 232
Fortun, 108
Fortuna, 184, 194, 264
Fortunata, 194
Fortune, 108, 194
Foster, 83, 207
Fotina, 278
Fotor, 295
Fowler, 83
Fraco, 268
Fraine, 83
France, 104
Frances, 278
Francesca, 184, 278
Francesco, 186
Franchot, 282
Franci, 278
Francine, 278
Francique, 278
Francis, 282
Francisca, 64, 264, 278
Francisco, 268
Franciscus, 282
Franciska, 162
Franciszk, 244
Franciszka, 243
Franco, 268
Francois, 282
Francoise, 278
Frang, 116
Frangag, 112
Frank, 282
Franklin, 282
Frannsaidh, 116
Frans, 61, 274
Franta, 59, 282
Frantisek, 282
Frantiska, 58, 278
Franz, 61, 124, 274, 282
Franze, 278
Franziska, 120, 278
Franziskus, 282
Fraomar, 31
Frasco, 268
Frascuelo, 268
Fraser, 255
Frashegird, 168
Frayne, 83
Freca, 83
Fred, 282
Freda, 278
Fredek, 163, 249, 274, 282
Frederek, 274
Frederic, 282
Frederica, 278
Frederick, 282

Frederik, 61
Frederika, 272
Fredi, 282
Fredrick, 282
Fredrik, 274, 282
Fredrika, 278
Freeland, 83
Freeman, 31
Freira, 264
Freki, 232
Fremont, 124
Freowine, 83
Fresco, 268
Frescura, 264
Frewen, 83
Frewin, 83
Frewyn, 83
Frey, 83, 232
Freya, 28, 226, 272
Freydis, 226
Freyne, 83
Freyr, 232
Freystein, 232
Freyvid, 232
Frici, 162, 282
Frick, 83
Frida, 226, 272, 278
Frideborg, 272, 278
Fridleif, 232
Fridolf, 83
Fridolph, 83
Friduwulf, 84
Fridwolf, 83
Frieda, 120, 226
Friedegard, 278
Friedegarde, 278
Friedel, 282
Friederika, 278
Friederike, 278
Friedhelm, 282
Friedrich, 124, 282
Frig, 251
Frigga, 226, 251
Frigyes, 282
Frika, 83, 226
Frikka, 226
Frimunt, 124
Frisa, 84
Fritjof, 272, 278
Frits, 282
Fritz, 61, 124, 282
Fritzi, 120, 278
Fritzie, 278
Frode, 232
Frodina, 278
Frodine, 278
Frodis, 226
Froille, 45
Frollo, 45
Fronda, 194
Fronde, 194
Fronia, 194
Frontino, 108
Fryda, 278
Fryderyk, 244, 282
Fugeltun, 84

Fugol, 31
Fukayna, 66
Fulaton, 84
Fulla, 226
Fuller, 84
Fullere, 84
Fulop, 143, 163
Fulton, 84
Fulvia, 184, 194
Funsani, 69
Furina, 194
Furrina, 194
Fusberta, 104
Fychan, 295
Fydor, 282
Fyfa, 253
Fyfe, 255
Fynballa, 175
Fynbar, 54
Fyodor, 249
Fyren, 31
Fyrsil, 295
Fytch, 83

Gaagii, 222
Gabhan, 116
Gabi, 157
Gabino, 268
Gabirel, 49
Gabor, 157, 163
Gabriel, 157, 268, 274
Gabriele, 152, 157, 186
Gabriella, 152, 184, 272
Gabrielle, 152
Gabrielo, 157
Gabrio, 268
Gad, 222
Gada, 168
Gadara, 40
Gadarine, 40
Gaderian, 31
Gadhi, 168
Gadhra, 180
Gadi, 38
Gadiel, 38
Gaea, 132
Gael, 180
Gaelan, 116
Gaelbhan, 116
Gaelle, 120
Gaetan, 108
Gaetana, 105, 184
Gaetane, 105, 184
Gaetano, 186
Gaffney, 180
Gahariet, 45
Gaheris, 45
Gahiji, 69
Gahmuret, 45
Gaho, 214
Gaia, 132
Gail, 74, 84
Gaile, 180
Gair, 116, 255
Gaira, 253
Gairbhith, 116
Gairbith, 180

Gais, 46
Gaizka, 49
Gajra, 168
Gal, 157
Gala, 105, 194, 226, 264, 272
Galahad, 45
Galahalt, 45
Galahault, 45
Galan, 31
Galantyne, 45
Galatea, 132, 194
Galatee, 105
Galatyn, 45
Galaway, 116
Galchobhar, 116
Gale, 74, 84, 180, 226
Galen, 116, 143
Galena, 264
Galenia, 264
Galenka, 152, 247
Galeno, 268
Galeron, 46
Galeun, 84
Gali, 152
Galia, 152
Galiana, 120
Galice, 152
Galiena, 120
Galiene, 42
Galila, 152
Galilah, 152
Galilahi, 215
Galina, 152
Galine, 247
Galinthias, 143
Galit, 152
Gall, 54, 116, 180
Galla, 105
Gallagher, 116
Gallehant, 46
Gallgaidheal, 116
Gallgoid, 295
Gallia, 105, 152
Galloway, 116
Galm, 232
Galochka, 152
Galt, 84
Galterio, 187
Galtero, 187, 268, 283
Galton, 84
Galvarium, 46
Galvin, 54, 116
Galvyn, 54
Galway, 116
Galya, 152, 247
Galyn, 116
Gamaliel, 157
Gamon, 295
Gan, 108
Gana, 152
Gandhari, 165
Gandwy, 295
Ganelon, 108
Ganesa, 170
Ganesh, 171
Ganet, 152
Ganger, 232
Ganice, 152

Ganieda, 43
Ganit, 152
Gannie, 116
Gannon, 116
Gano, 108
Ganya, 249
Ganymede, 143, 207
Gaothaire, 116
Gar, 31, 84
Gara, 180, 253
Garabed, 41
Garabi, 194
Garabina, 264
Garabine, 264
Garaden, 84
Garadin, 84
Garadun, 84
Garadyn, 84
Garafeld, 84
Garai, 69, 207
Garaitz, 48, 264
Garan, 290
Garanhon, 295
Garanwyn, 295
Garatun, 84
Garberend, 31
Garbhach, 116
Garbhan, 116, 180
Garbi, 194
Garbina, 264
Garbine, 264
Garcia, 268, 282
Garda, 278
Gardar, 232
Garde, 278
Gardell, 282
Gardener, 282
Gardi, 232
Gardiner, 84, 282
Gardner, 84
Gardotza, 264
Gare, 255
Garek, 282
Garet, 84, 232
Gareth, 31, 46
Garfield, 84
Gari, 278
Garia, 253
Gariland, 84
Garland, 84, 105, 108
Garm, 84, 232
Garman, 84
Garmangabis, 28
Garmann, 84
Garmon, 84
Garmond, 84
Garmund, 84
Garner, 282
Garnet, 84
Garnett, 84
Garnoc, 295
Garnock, 295
Garr, 31, 84
Garrard, 84
Garret, 282
Garrett, 31, 84, 232, 282
Garrick, 84, 282
Garrman, 84

Garroway, 84
Garrson, 84
Garselid, 295
Garson, 84
Garth, 232, 274
Garthf, 226
Garton, 84
Garuda, 168, 170
Garudi, 165
Garvan, 180
Garvey, 116, 180
Garvin, 84, 282
Garvyn, 84
Garwig, 84
Garwin, 84
Garwine, 84
Garwood, 84
Garwyli, 295
Garwyn, 84
Gary, 84
Garym, 295
Gascon, 108
Gaspar, 108, 241, 268
Gaspara, 264
Gaspard, 108, 268
Gaston, 108
Gatha, 165, 240
Gaukroger, 84
Gauri, 165, 170
Gaute, 232
Gauthier, 108, 282
Gautier, 108, 282
Gauvain, 46
Gav, 249
Gaven, 255
Gavenia, 253
Gavi, 157
Gavin, 255, 282, 295
Gavina, 253
Gavra, 152
Gavrel, 249
Gavriel, 157
Gavril, 249
Gavrila, 152, 259
Gavrilla, 152, 259
Gavrilovich, 249
Gawain, 46, 84, 255
Gawen, 84, 255
Gawl, 295
Gawyn, 84, 255
Gay, 74, 105, 278
Gayane, 40
Gayatri, 165
Gayeff, 249
Gayle, 74, 84
Gaylen, 116
Gayner, 116
Gaynor, 116
Gazit, 152
Gazsi, 163, 241
Gear, 116
Gearald, 116
Gearoid, 180, 282
Gearoidin, 175
Geary, 84
Geb, 69
Gechina, 48, 264

Gedaliah, 157
Gedalya, 157
Gedalyahu, 157
Gedeon, 157
Geela, 152
Gehard, 84
Geir, 232
Geirbjorg, 226
Geiri, 232
Geirleif, 232
Geirmund, 232
Geirolf, 232
Geirrid, 226
Geirrod, 232
Geirstein, 232
Gelasia, 132
Gelasius, 143
Gelban, 54
Geldersman, 64
Gellert, 282
Gelsomina, 61
Geltruda, 184
Gemma, 105, 184
Generosa, 264
Generoso, 268
Genetrix, 195
Geneva, 105
Genevieve, 51, 105, 120
Genevra, 184
Genevre, 105
Genius, 207
Genoveva, 120
Genowefa, 120
Gentza, 49
Geoff, 31
Geoffrey, 31, 108, 282
Geol, 84
Geordie, 143
Georg, 124, 143, 274
George, 143
Georges, 143
Georget, 143
Georgette, 105, 132
Georgia, 132
Georgiana, 132
Georgine, 132
Georgio, 186
Georgitte, 105
Geraghty, 180
Geraint, 31, 295
Gerald, 282
Geralda, 278
Geraldina, 120, 278
Geraldine, 120, 278
Geralt, 180
Geranium, 132
Gerard, 124, 282
Gerardo, 84, 186, 268
Geraud, 282
Gerd, 84, 226
Gerda, 121, 226, 272, 278
Gerde, 121, 278
Gerdie, 121, 226

Geremia, 157, 186
Gergely, 143
Gergo, 163
Gergor, 143
Gerhard, 124, 274
Gerhardina, 120
Gerhardine, 120
Gerik, 244
Gerlach, 124
Germain, 105, 108, 207
Germaine, 51, 105, 278
German, 268, 283
Germana, 105
Germane, 278
Germano, 108
Germund, 272
Gerold, 282
Geronimo, 186, 268
Gerrit, 84
Gerry, 84, 282
Gersham, 157
Gershom, 157
Gert, 283
Gerta, 278
Gerte, 278
Gertraud, 278
Gertraude, 278
Gertrud, 121, 272, 278
Gertruda, 121, 278
Gertrude, 121, 278
Gertrudes, 264
Gertrudis, 264
Gertrut, 121
Gervais, 282
Gervase, 84
Gervasio, 268, 283
Gervaso, 268
Gervazy, 283
Gervin, 116
Gerwalt, 120
Gerwalta, 120
Gerwazy, 244, 283
Geryon, 143
Gesnes, 46
Gest, 232
Gezana, 264
Gezane, 264
Ghebers, 241
Gheorghr, 143
Gherardo, 84
Ghislain, 124
Ghislaine, 121
Ghita, 132, 184
Ghleanna, 113
Ghoukas, 41
Giacomo, 157, 186
Gian, 157, 186
Giancarlo, 186
Giancinta, 132
Giancinte, 132

Gianina, 184
Gianna, 184
Giannes, 157
Gibbesone, 84
Gibson, 84
Gideon, 157
Gifford, 84, 108, 282
Giflet, 46
Gifre, 31
Gifuhard, 84
Gijs, 74, 84
Gil, 109, 157, 180, 268
Gila, 152
Gilah, 152
Gilal, 152
Gilala, 152
Gilamu, 282
Gilana, 152
Gilat, 152
Gilbarta, 253
Gilbert, 84, 282, 295
Gilberta, 121, 278
Gilberte, 278
Gilberto, 186, 268, 282
Gilbride, 180
Gilburt, 84, 282
Gilby, 232
Gilchrist, 180
Gilda, 51, 74
Gildan, 74
Gildas, 31, 46, 51, 54, 84
Gildea, 180
Gilen, 282
Giles, 143, 207
Gilford, 84
Gilfred, 282
Gilfrid, 282
Gili, 152, 157
Gilia, 152
Gilibeirt, 180
Gilit, 152
Gill, 109, 195
Gilleabart, 255
Gilleasbuig, 116, 124, 255
Gillecriosd, 256
Gille-Eathain, 116
Gillen, 282
Gilles, 143
Gilley, 180
Gilli, 157
Gillian, 195
Gillien, 195
Gillivray, 256
Gilmar, 84
Gilmer, 84, 282
Gilmore, 54, 116
Gilpin, 84
Gilroy, 54, 116, 207
Gils, 232
Gilvaethwy, 295
Gilvarry, 180
Gimle, 226, 232
Gimm, 31

Gina, 132
Ginebra, 51, 264
Ginerva, 51
Ginessa, 51, 264
Ginger, 195
Ginnungagap, 226
Gino, 186
Giolla Chriost, 180
Giollabrighde, 180
Giollabuidhe, 180
Giolladhe, 180
Giollamhuire, 116
Giollanaebhin, 116
Giollaruaidh, 116
Gionnan, 116
Giorgio, 186
Giorsal, 113
Giotto, 282
Giovanna, 152, 184
Giovanni, 157, 186
Girard, 46, 54, 282
Giraud, 282
Girelda, 278
Girflet, 46
Girisa, 170
Girish, 171
Girisha, 168
Girven, 116
Girvyn, 116
Gisa, 152
Gisel, 278
Giselbert, 84
Gisele, 278
Gisella, 162
Giselmaere, 84
Gisilberhta, 121
Gita, 165
Gitana, 264
Githa, 74
Gitta, 51, 162
Giuditta, 184
Giulia, 184
Giuliano, 187, 207
Giulio, 187
Giuseppe, 187
Giza, 152
Gizela, 243, 278
Gizi, 162, 278
Gizike, 278
Gizur, 232
Gizus, 278
Gjaflaug, 226
Gjallar, 232
Gjalp, 226
Gjerta, 61
Gjest, 232
Glad, 74
Gladwin, 84
Gladwyn, 84
Gladys, 195, 290
Glaedwine, 84
Glais, 46
Glaisne, 180

Glaleanna, 180
Glan, 290
Glasny, 180
Glauce, 132, 195
Glaucus, 143, 207
Gleann, 116
Gleda, 74, 290
Gleipnir, 232
Gleis, 295
Glen, 54, 113, 116
Glenda, 290
Glendon, 116
Glenn, 54, 113, 116, 295
Glenna, 113, 175
Glennis, 113
Glew, 295
Glewlwyd, 46, 295
Glifieu, 54
Glinyeu, 295
Glistenheath, 232
Gloria, 195
Gloriana, 74
Gloriane, 74
Glorianna, 74
Gloriosa, 195
Gloyw, 295
Glum, 232
Glyn, 54, 290, 295
Glynis, 113
Glynn, 295
Glynna, 175
Glynnes, 113
Glynnis, 113
Glythvyr, 295
Gna, 226
Gnup, 232
Gobha, 256
Gobinet, 175
Gobnait, 175
Gobnat, 175
Gobrwy, 295
Godalupe, 264
Goddard, 124, 282
Godewyn, 64
Godfredo, 268
Godfrey, 116, 124, 180, 282
Godfried, 124, 282
Godgifu, 74
Godiva, 74
Godofredo, 268, 282
Godric, 31
Godwin, 84, 283
Godwine, 31, 84
Godwyn, 283
Goewin, 290
Goffredo, 282
Gofraidh, 180
Gogarty, 180
Gogyvwlch, 295
Gold, 84
Golda, 74
Golden, 84
Goldie, 74

Golding, 84
Goldwin, 84
Goldwine, 84
Goldwyn, 84
Goldy, 74
Goleuddydd, 290
Golnar, 240
Goneril, 74
Gonerilla, 74
Goodwin, 84, 283
Goodwine, 84
Goodwyn, 84
Goraidh, 116, 256
Goran, 143, 274
Gorane, 264
Gorasgwrn, 290
Gorawen, 290
Gorboduc, 84
Gordain, 116, 256
Gordan, 116, 256
Gordana, 253
Gordania, 253
Gordie, 31
Gordon, 31, 84
Gordy, 31
Gore, 46
Goreu, 295
Gorin, 274
Gorka, 143
Gorlois, 46
Gormain, 180
Gorman, 116, 180
Gormant, 295
Gormghlaith, 175
Gormley, 175
Gormly, 175
Goronwy, 295
Gorre, 46
Gorrie, 180
Gorry, 180
Gorsedd, 54, 295
Gorvenal, 46
Gosheven, 218
Gota, 272
Gote, 272
Gothfraidh, 180
Gotilda, 272
Gottfrid, 282
Gottfried, 64, 124, 282
Gotthard, 64, 282
Gotzon, 49
Gotzone, 48, 264
Gouvernail, 46
Govan, 296
Govannon, 31, 296
Governayle, 46
Govert, 283
Govynyon, 296
Gow, 116, 256
Gowan, 256
Gower, 296
Gowyn, 84
Gowyr, 296
Graca, 195
Grace, 74, 195
Gracia, 74, 264
Graciana, 195, 264
Gracie, 74

Graciene, 195
Gracinha, 195
Gradasso, 109
Gradey, 116
Grady, 116, 180
Graeghamm, 84
Graegleah, 84
Graeham, 84
Graeme, 31, 207
Graent, 84
Grafere, 85
Graham, 31, 84, 207, 256, 283
Grahem, 31
Graine, 43
Grainne, 43, 113, 175
Gram, 31, 84, 207, 232
Granger, 84
Grangere, 84
Grani, 232
Grania, 51, 175
Granna, 175
Grant, 84, 207, 256
Grantham, 84
Grantland, 84
Grantley, 84
Granville, 109
Granwen, 296
Grata, 195
Gratia, 195
Gratian, 207
Gratiana, 195
Grayson, 84
Grayvesone, 84
Grazia, 184, 195
Grazina, 152
Grazinia, 152
Grazyna, 152, 243
Greagoir, 180
Gredel, 132
Greeley, 84
Greely, 84
Greger, 274
Gregoire, 143
Gregor, 64, 143, 256
Gregoria, 132, 195, 264
Gregoriana, 132
Gregorie, 143
Gregorio, 187, 268
Gregorior, 143
Gregory, 143
Gregos, 61, 143
Greguska, 59
Greid, 296
Greidyawl, 296
Greip, 226
Gremian, 31
Grendel, 31
Grenjad, 232
Grenville, 109
Gresham, 84
Greta, 132, 272
Gretal, 132
Gretchen, 121, 132

Grete, 132
Gretel, 132
Greyfell, 232
Grid, 226
Griffen, 296
Griffeth, 296
Griffin, 296
Griffith, 46, 296
Griffyth, 46
Griflet, 46
Grigor, 143
Grigori, 249
Grigorii, 249
Grigorov, 143
Grim, 232
Grima, 226
Grimbold, 31
Grimhild, 226
Grimhilda, 226
Grimhilde, 226
Grimkel, 232
Grimm, 32
Grimme, 32
Grindan, 32
Gringalet, 46
Gringolet, 46
Grioghar, 180
Griorgair, 256
Gris, 232
Grisandole, 43
Griselda, 121, 278
Griselde, 121, 278
Griseldis, 64, 278
Grisha, 249
Grisham, 84
Grishilde, 64
Grisjahilde, 121
Grissel, 278
Griswald, 124, 283
Griswalda, 121
Griswalde, 121
Griswold, 124
Grizel, 253, 278
Grizela, 253
Gro, 226
Groa, 226
Groot, 64
Grosvenor, 109
Grover, 85
Gruagh, 180
Gruddieu, 54
Gruddyeu, 296
Gruev, 143
Gruffen, 296
Gruffin, 296
Gruffudd, 296
Gruffyn, 296
Grufydd, 296
Grugyn, 296
Grushilda, 64
Gryfflet, 46
Gryn, 296
Gryne, 195
Gryphin, 296
Gryphon, 296
Gryta, 132
Grzegorz, 244
Guadalupe, 264
Gualterio, 268

Gualtiero, 187, 283
Guanhamara, 43
Guanhumora, 43
Gubnat, 175
Guda, 272
Gudbrand, 232
Gudbrande, 232
Gudlaug, 232
Gudmund, 232
Gudny, 272
Gudrid, 226
Gudrun, 61, 121, 226, 272
Gudruna, 121, 272
Guebers, 241
Guendolen, 74
Guenevere, 51
Guenloie, 43
Guennola, 51
Guerehes, 46
Guerin, 109
Guga, 168
Guglielmo, 187
Guglilmo, 283
Guida, 121
Guiderius, 46, 85
Guiditta, 152
Guido, 187, 207, 268
Guifford, 108
Guilaine, 121
Guilbert, 84
Guilerme, 282
Guilia, 195
Guilie, 195
Guilio, 143
Guillame, 282
Guillelmina, 184, 264
Guin, 116
Guinevere, 43, 51, 290
Guiseppe, 157
Guiseppie, 152
Guiseppina, 152
Guivret, 46
Gulab, 168
Gulielma, 184
Gullinbursti, 233
Gulltopp, 233
Gullveig, 226
Gungir, 233
Gunhilda, 226
Gunhilde, 226
Gunilla, 121, 272
Gunlaug, 233
Gunn, 256
Gunna, 253
Gunnar, 233, 274, 283
Gunnbjorn, 233
Gunnel, 121, 272
Gunner, 274, 283
Gunnhild, 226
Gunnhildr, 226
Gunnlaug, 233
Gunnlod, 226
Gunnolf, 233
Gunnvor, 226

Gunther, 233, 283
Gurgalan, 46
Guri, 157, 226
Gurice, 152
Gurion, 157
Gurit, 152
Guro, 226
Gurutz, 49
Gusg, 296
Gust, 64
Gusta, 64, 279
Gustaafa, 279
Gustaof, 283
Gustav, 274
Gustava, 264, 272, 279
Gustave, 207, 283
Gustavo, 268
Gustavus, 283
Gustel, 121, 195
Gustella, 195
Gustelle, 195
Gustha, 279
Gusztav, 207, 283
Guthr, 226
Guthrie, 116
Gutka, 243
Gutrune, 226
Guttorm, 233
Guusa, 279
Guy, 54, 109, 158, 207, 283
Guyapi, 218
Gvenour, 43
Gwaeddan, 290
Gwalchmai, 54, 295
Gwalchmei, 296
Gwales, 296
Gwalhaved, 296
Gwallawg, 296
Gwallter, 296
Gwanwyn, 290
Gwarthegydd, 296
Gwastad, 296
Gwawl, 54, 296
Gwawrddur, 296
Gwefl, 54
Gweir, 296
Gwen, 290
Gwenabwy, 291
Gwenddydd, 43
Gwendolen, 43, 51, 291
Gwendolin, 51
Gwendoline, 291
Gwendoloena, 43
Gwener, 291
Gweneth, 51
Gwenhwyfach, 43
Gwenhwyvar, 291
Gwenith, 51
Gwenledyr, 291
Gwenn, 51
Gwenn Alarch, 291

Gwenneth, 51
Gwenwynwyn, 296
Gwenyver, 51
Gwern, 54, 296
Gwernach, 55, 295
Gwerthmwl, 296
Gwevyl, 296
Gwiawn, 296
Gwidon, 207
Gwiffred, 296
Gwilenhin, 296
Gwilym, 283, 296
Gwitart, 296
Gwladys, 290
Gwlgawd, 296
Gwlwlwyd, 296
Gwlyddyn, 296
Gwrddnei, 296
Gwrddywal, 296
Gwres, 296
Gwrgwst, 296
Gwrhyr, 296
Gwri, 55, 296
Gwrtheyrn, 296
Gwryon, 296
Gwyddawg, 296
Gwydre, 296
Gwydyon, 296
Gwyn, 290, 296
Gwyndolen, 291
Gwyndolin, 51
Gwynedd, 291
Gwyneth, 291
Gwyngad, 296
Gwynham, 55
Gwynith, 51
Gwynn, 51, 296
Gwynnan, 296
Gwynne, 291
Gwyr, 46, 296
Gwys, 296
Gwystyl, 297
Gwythyr, 297
Gyala, 163, 207
Gyasi, 69
Gyda, 226
Gyes, 143
Gylda, 74
Gyldan, 74
Gymir, 233
Gymnasia, 195
Gynt, 233
Gyoergy, 143
Gyongy, 105
Gyorgy, 143
Gypsy, 74
Gyrd, 233
Gytha, 61, 74, 226
Gyuri, 143
Gyurka, 143, 163
Gyuszi, 163

Haaken, 233
Habib, 158
Habibah, 66
Hacket, 124
Hackett, 124
Hadar, 152, 158
Hadara, 152

Hadassah, 152
Haddad, 38
Hadden, 85
Haddon, 85
Haden, 85
Hadeon, 288
Hadley, 85
Hadon, 85
Hadrea, 195
Hadria, 195
Hadrian, 85, 274
Hadu, 121
Haduwig, 121
Hadwig, 279
Hadwin, 85, 283
Hadwyn, 85, 283
Haefen, 85
Haele, 85
Haemon, 143
Haesel, 74
Haestingas, 85
Haethowine, 85
Hafgan, 55
Hafgrim, 233
Hafleikr, 233
Hafnar, 233
Hafsah, 66
Hafthor, 233
Hagaleah, 85
Hagalean, 85
Hagan, 116, 179, 283
Hagar, 152
Hagaward, 85
Hagen, 233, 283
Hagley, 85
Hagly, 85
Hagop, 41
Hahkethomemah, 220
Hahnee, 218
Haidar, 168
Haidee, 132
Haig, 41, 85
Haimati, 165
Haine, 283
Haines, 283
Haji, 69
Hajna, 162
Hajnal, 195
Hakan, 218, 226, 272
Hakana, 272
Hakeem, 38
Haki, 233
Hakidonmuya, 216
Hakim, 38
Hakizimana, 69
Hakon, 233
Hal, 233, 283
Halag, 121
Halah, 36
Halbart, 85
Halbert, 85, 283
Halburt, 85
Halcyone, 132
Haldan, 283
Haldana, 226
Halden, 233, 283
Haldis, 226, 279
Haldisa, 279

Haldora, 226
Hale, 85, 283
Halebeorht, 85
Halette, 105
Haley, 180
Halford, 85
Halfrid, 121, 226
Halfrida, 121, 226
Halfrith, 74
Halfryta, 74
Hali, 143
Halifrid, 121
Halig, 32, 74
Haligwiella, 85
Halim, 38, 168
Halima, 66
Halimeda, 132
Halina, 132, 243
Halirrhothius, 143, 207
Halithersis, 143
Hall, 85, 233
Halla, 226
Hallam, 85, 283
Hallbjorn, 233
Halldis, 226
Halldor, 233
Halldora, 226
Halley, 85
Hallfred, 233
Hallfrid, 226
Hallfrita, 74
Hallgerd, 226
Hallgerda, 226
Hallie, 279
Halliwell, 85
Hallkel, 233
Hallstein, 233
Hallvard, 233
Hallveig, 226
Hallwell, 85
Hally, 279
Haloke, 217
Halona, 214
Halsey, 85
Halsig, 85
Halstead, 85
Halton, 85
Halvard, 233, 274
Halvdan, 233
Halveig, 226
Halvor, 233
Halwende, 32
Halwn, 55
Ham, 32
Hamadi, 69
Hamal, 38
Hamar, 233
Hamden, 39
Hamdun, 39
Hamelatun, 85
Hamia, 28
Hamid, 38
Hamilton, 85, 109, 256
Hamlet, 124
Hamlett, 124
Hamlin, 124, 283
Hammad, 38
Hammer, 233
Hamoelet, 124
Hamund, 233

Han, 124
Hanan, 158
Hananel, 158
Hanbal, 69
Hand, 85
Hane, 283
Hanes, 283
Hanford, 85
Hania, 221
Hanif, 69
Hanita, 170
Hank, 283
Hanley, 85
Hanly, 85
Hann, 124
Hanna, 38, 152, 272
Hannah, 152
Hanne, 61, 152
Hannela, 152
Hannele, 152
Hannelora, 121
Hannelore, 121
Hanno, 124
Hannraoi, 283
Hanraoi, 180
Hanrietta, 105
Hanriette, 105
Hans, 61, 124, 158, 233, 274
Hansel, 158, 274
Hansh, 171
Hantaywee, 218
Hanuman, 172
Hanz, 124
Hapi, 69
Hapu, 69
Haqikah, 66
Hara, 170
Harac, 90
Haraford, 85
Harailt, 256
Harakhty, 69
Haralambos, 143
Harald, 62, 233, 274
Haralda, 226
Harb, 38
Harbin, 109
Harcourt, 109
Hardar, 233
Hardbein, 233
Harden, 85
Hardie, 283
Hardin, 85
Harding, 85
Hardouin, 109
Hardtman, 124
Hardwin, 85
Hardwyn, 85
Hardy, 124, 283
Hardyn, 85
Hare, 85
Harel, 158
Harelache, 85
Harelda, 279
Harelde, 279
Hareleah, 85
Harford, 85
Hargrove, 85
Hari, 168, 172
Hariman, 124

Harimann, 124
Harimanna, 121
Harimanne, 121
Harimilla, 28
Haripriya, 168
Harischandra, 168
Hariti, 165
Harkahome, 220
Harlak, 85
Harlake, 85
Harlan, 85, 283
Harland, 85, 283
Harleigh, 85
Harley, 85
Harlow, 85
Harlowe, 85
Harm, 283
Harme, 283
Harmonia, 132, 195
Harmony, 195
Harold, 64, 233, 283
Harolda, 279
Harolde, 279
Haroun, 38
Haroun al Rachid, 38
Haroutyoun, 41
Harper, 85
Harpinna, 195
Harpocrates, 207
Harrell, 158
Harriet, 105. 279
Harrietta, 105, 279
Harriette, 105, 279
Harris, 85, 283
Harrison, 85
Harro, 283
Harrod, 158
Harry, 233, 274, 283
Hart, 85, 283
Harte, 283
Hartford, 85
Harti, 124
Hartley, 85
Hartman, 124
Hartmann, 124
Hartun, 86
Hartwell, 85, 283
Hartwig, 283
Hartwood, 85
Harun, 38
Harun al Rachid, 38
Harvey, 85, 124, 283
Hasani, 69
Hashim, 38
Hasin, 168
Hasina, 66
Hasione, 143
Haslet, 85
Haslett, 85
Hasna, 36
Hass, 283
Hassan, 38
Hassun, 219

Hastein, 233
Hastiin, 222
Hastimukha, 168
Hastin, 172
Hastings, 85
Hathor, 66
Hathor-Sakmet, 66
Hatshepsut, 66
Hattie, 279
Hatty, 279
Hauk, 233
Hausis, 214
Hausisse, 214
Havelock, 233
Haven, 85
Havyn, 85
Hawiovi, 221
Hawley, 85
Hawly, 85
Hay, 256
Haya, 152
Hayden, 85, 283
Haydon, 85, 283
Haye, 256
Hayes, 85
Hayle, 85
Hayley, 74
Hayward, 85
Haywood, 85
Hayyim, 158
Hazel, 74, 279
Heahweard, 86
Healhtun, 85
Heall, 85
Healleah, 85
Heallfrith, 74
Heallstede, 85
Healum, 85
Healy, 86
Heammawihio, 220
Heanford, 85
Heanleah, 85
Heardind, 85
Heardwine, 85
Hearne, 86
Hearpere, 85
Heartha, 279
Heath, 85
Heathcliff, 86
Heathclyf, 86
Heathdene, 85
Heather, 74
Heathleah, 85
Heathley, 85
Hebe, 132
Hebron, 46
Hecate, 132
Hector, 143, 207, 268
Hecuba, 132, 195
Hedda, 121, 279
Hedeon, 249
Hedia, 132
Hedin, 233
Hedvig, 61
Hedvige, 105
Hedwig, 121, 272, 279
Hedy, 132, 259, 279

Hedyla, 132
Hefeydd, 55
Hegarty, 180
Heh, 69
Hehet, 66
Hehewuti, 216
Heida, 121
Heidi, 121
Heidrun, 226
Heike, 283
Heikki, 100
Heikkinen, 100
Heilyn, 55, 297
Heimdal, 233
Heinrich, 124
Heinroch, 283
Hekja, 226
Hekuba, 132
Hel, 226
Hela, 226
Helain, 42
Helaku, 218
Helen, 132, 195
Helena, 132, 272
Helene, 121, 132
Helenka, 132, 247
Helenus, 143, 207
Helga, 121, 226, 247, 272
Helge, 226, 249
Helgi, 233
Helia, 132
Helice, 132
Helike, 132
Helios, 143
Helki, 216, 221
Helle, 132, 226
Hellekin, 46
Helli, 100, 132
Helma, 121
Helmar, 274
Helmer, 274, 283
Helmut, 124
Helmutt, 124
Heloise, 105
Helsa, 152
Helton, 85
He-lush-ka, 223
Hema, 170
Hemakuta, 168
Hemera, 132
Hemming, 274
Hen, 279
Hen Beddestyr, 297
Hen Was, 297
Hen Wyneb, 297
Henbeddestr, 55
Henderson, 256
Hendrik, 274, 283
Hendrika, 64
Henerik, 283
Hengist, 32
Henia, 279
Henicea, 195
Henie, 279
Heniuta, 243
Henka, 243, 279
Hennie, 279

Henning, 274, 283
Henning, 62
Henny, 279
Henri, 283
Henrich, 283
Henrick, 64
Henrietta, 105, 279
Henriette, 105, 279
Henrik, 62, 274, 283
Henrika, 132, 272, 279
Henriqua, 264
Henry, 109, 283
Henryk, 244, 283
Henson, 256
Henuita, 279
Henuite, 279
Henwas, 55
Heolstor, 32
Heorhiy, 288
Heorot, 32
Heort, 85
Heortwiella, 85
Heortwode, 85
Hephaestus, 143
Hephzibah, 152
Hepsiba, 152
Hepzibeth, 152
Heqet, 67
Hera, 132
Heraklesr, 143
Herbert, 274, 283
Hercules, 143, 207
Herdis, 226
Here, 132
Heremon, 180
Hererinc, 32
Heretoga, 32
Heribert, 283
Heriberto, 268, 283
Herjolf, 233
Herlbert, 86
Herlebeorht, 86
Herman, 283
Hermandina, 133
Hermandine, 133
Hermann, 274, 283
Hermes, 143
Hermia, 133
Herminia, 264
Herminius, 207
Hermione, 133
Hermippe, 195
Hermod, 233
Hermosa, 264
Hermund, 233
Hern, 86
Hernando, 124, 268
Herne, 55, 86
Hero, 133, 195
Heromin, 283
Herophile, 195
Herrick, 124, 233
Herryk, 233

Herschel, 158
Hershel, 158
Hersilia, 195
Hersir, 233
Herta, 121
Hertha, 74, 121, 279
Herthe, 279
Heru, 69
Herve, 85, 283
Herwin, 283
Herwyn, 283
Herzeloyde, 43
Hesione, 133
Heskovizenako, 220
Hesper, 133
Hespera, 195
Hesperia, 133, 195
Hesperie, 195
Hesperos, 143
Hester, 133, 240
Hestia, 133, 240
Hesutu, 221
Hetheclif, 86
Hetty, 240
Hetwn, 297
Hevataneo, 220
Heveydd, 297
Hevovitastamiutsto, 220
Hewett, 125
Hewitt, 125
Hewlett, 125
Hewlitt, 125
Hewney, 180
Heywood, 85
Hezekiah, 158
Hiamovi, 220
Hiatt, 86
Hibernia, 195
Hibiscus, 195
Hibiskus, 195
Hickey, 180
Hid, 86
Hida, 121
Hide, 86, 121
Hieremias, 158
Hiero, 180
Hieronim, 143, 244
Hieronymous, 207
Hietamaki, 101
Higgins, 180
Hilaeira, 133, 195
Hilaire, 105
Hilaria, 195
Hilario, 233, 268
Hilarion, 207
Hilary, 195, 207
Hild, 28, 74, 121, 226, 279
Hilda, 28, 74, 121, 226, 272, 279
Hildbrand, 125
Hilde, 74, 121, 226, 279
Hildebrand, 125, 283

Hildebrandt, 283
Hildegard, 121, 272, 279
Hildegarde, 279
Hildegunn, 226
Hildemar, 121
Hildemara, 121
Hilderinc, 32
Hildie, 74
Hildigunn, 226
Hildimar, 121
Hildireth, 121
Hildreth, 121
Hildur, 226
Hillary, 195, 207
Hillery, 207
Hilliard, 283
Hillock, 86
Hillocke, 86
Hilma, 121
Hilmar, 274
Hilton, 86
Hinrich, 283
Hinto, 220
Hinun, 218
Hiolair, 175
Hiordis, 226
Hipolit, 143
Hippocampus, 143, 207
Hippodameia, 195
Hippodamia, 133
Hippogriff, 143
Hippolyta, 133
Hippolyte, 133, 195
Hippolytus, 143
Hippolytusr, 143
Hippomenes, 144
Hippothoe, 195
Hiram, 158
Hiranyagarbha, 172
Hisolda, 175
Histion, 86
Hjalmar, 62, 274
Hlaford, 32
Hlif, 226
Hline, 88
Hlink, 88
Hlinka, 59
Hlisa, 32
Hlithtun, 88
Hlynn, 74
Hnedy, 59
Hobard, 125
Hobart, 125, 283
Hobbard, 125
Hod, 86, 158
Hoder, 233
Hodierna, 175
Hodr, 233
Hodsone, 86
Hodur, 233
Hoel, 46, 55
Hoenir, 233
Hofud, 233
Hogan, 116
Hogna, 233
Hogni, 233
Hoh, 125

Hohberht, 125
Hohnihohkaiyohos, 220
Hoireabard, 180
Hok'ee, 222
Holbrook, 86
Holcomb, 86
Holda, 121, 152
Holde, 121
Holden, 86, 283
Holdin, 86
Holdyn, 86
Holea, 74
Holgar, 62
Holger, 62
Holic, 59
Holle, 121
Holleb, 244
Hollis, 86
Holly, 74, 105
Holman, 283
Holmes, 86, 283
Holmstein, 233
Holt, 32, 86
Holwell, 85
Home, 256
Homer, 144
Homeros, 144
Homerus, 144
Honani, 221
Honaw, 221
Honbria, 74
Honbrie, 74
Hondo, 69
Honey, 74
Honi, 158
Honiahaka, 220
Honir, 233
Honon, 221
Honor, 175, 195, 264
Honora, 175, 195
Honorata, 195
Honoratas, 264
Honorato, 207, 268
Honore, 105
Honoria, 175, 195, 264
Honorina, 195
Honorine, 195
Honovi, 216, 218
Honza, 59
Hope, 74
Horace, 207
Horacia, 195
Horacio, 207, 268
Horae, 133
Horatia, 195
Horatio, 207
Horatius, 207
Horaz, 207
Hord, 233
Horemheb, 69
Hortencia, 195
Hortenciana, 195
Hortense, 195
Hortenspa, 243
Horton, 86
Horus, 69
Hosea, 158
Hoshi, 302

Hoskuld, 234
Hotah, 222
Hototo, 218, 220
Hotuaekhaashtait, 220
Houdain, 46
Houdenc, 46
Houerv, 85
Houghton, 86
Houston, 256
Hovan, 41
Hoven, 41
Hovhaness, 41
Hovsep, 41
How, 125
Howahkan, 222
Howard, 86, 283
Howe, 125
Howel, 46, 297
Howell, 297
Howi, 221
Howland, 86
Hraefnscaga, 86
Hrafn, 234
Hrani, 234
Hrapenly, 86
Hrapp, 234
Hrefna, 226
Hreidmar, 234
Hrifla, 234
Hrimfaxi, 234
Hring, 86
Hringham, 234
Hristun, 86
Hroald, 234
Hroc, 86
Hrocby, 86
Hrocesburh, 86
Hrodgeir, 234
Hrodny, 227
Hrolf, 234
Hrolleif, 234
Hromund, 234
Hrorek, 283
Hrosskel, 234
Hrothbeorhta, 74
Hrothberta, 74
Hrothbertina, 74
Hrothgar, 32
Hrothnerta, 74
Hrothrekr, 180
Hrusosky, 59
Hrut, 234
Hrycg, 86
Hrychleah, 86
Hrypa, 32
Hrypanleah, 86
Hrytherford, 86
Hu, 69, 297
Huabwy, 297
Huarwar, 55, 297
Huata, 216
Hubbard, 125
Hubert, 283
Huberta, 121, 279
Huberte, 279
Huberto, 283
Hud, 86
Hudak, 59
Hudson, 86
Hueil, 55, 297

Huetta, 74
Huette, 74, 105, 279
Huey, 86
Hugette, 105
Hugh, 86, 109, 283
Hughetta, 74
Hughette, 74
Hugi, 86, 234
Hugiberahta, 121
Hugiet, 74
Hugin, 234
Hugo, 268, 274, 283
Hugues, 283
Huguetta, 105
Hulbard, 125
Hulbart, 125
Hulbert, 125
Hulda, 121, 152, 227, 272
Hulde, 121
Huldiberaht, 125
Humayd, 39
Humbert, 283
Humberto, 268, 283
Hume, 256
Humfrey, 283
Humfrid, 274
Humfried, 283
Humility, 86, 195
Humita, 216
Humphrey, 125, 283
Hunbogi, 234
Hunfredo, 283
Hunfrid, 125
Hunfried, 125, 283
Hungas, 177
Hunig, 74
Hunt, 86
Hunter, 86
Huntingden, 86
Huntingdon, 86
Huntington, 86
Huntingtun, 86
Huntley, 86
Huntly, 86
Huon, 46, 55
Hurit, 214
Huritt, 219
Hurlbart, 86
Hurlbert, 86
Hurlee, 116
Hurley, 116, 180
Hurly, 116
Hurst, 86
Hurste, 86
Husain, 38
Husam al Din, 38
Husani, 69
Hutton, 86
Huw, 283, 297
Huxeford, 86
Huxford, 86
Huxley, 86
Huxly, 86
Huyana, 216

Hvergelmir, 227, 234
Hwaeteleah, 86
Hweolere, 86
Hwertun, 86
Hwistlere, 86
Hwitby, 86
Hwitcomb, 86
Hwitcumb, 86
Hwitford, 86
Hwithloew, 86
Hwitloc, 86
Hyacinth, 133
Hyacinthe, 133
Hyacinthusr, 144
Hyades, 133
Hyale, 195
Hyancinthe, 144
Hyatt, 86
Hydd, 297
Hyde, 86
Hydra, 133
Hygeia, 133
Hygieia, 133
Hylas, 144
Hyman, 158
Hymen, 144
Hyndla, 227
Hypate, 133
Hypatia, 133
Hyperion, 144
Hypermnestra, 133
Hypnos, 144
Hypsipyle, 133
Hyria, 195
Hyrieus, 144
Hyrna, 227
Hyrrokkin, 227

Iaera, 195
Iago, 268, 297
Iain, 116, 256
Iakovos, 158
Iamar, 36
Ian, 158, 256
Iantha, 133
Ianthe, 133
Ianthina, 133
Iaokim, 158
Iapetus, 144
Iarfhlaith, 180
Iasion, 144
Iasius, 133, 144
Iason, 144
Iau, 297
Ib, 303
Iban, 158
Ibernia, 175
Iblis, 43
Ibolya, 162, 195
Ibon, 283
Ibrahim, 38
Ibycus, 144
Ica, 133, 162
Icarius, 144
Icarus, 144
Icelos, 144
Ichabod, 158
Ida, 32, 121, 133, 175, 195, 279
Idaeus, 207

Idaia, 121
Idal, 87
Idalia, 133
Idalie, 121
Idalina, 279
Idaline, 279
Idas, 144
Iddawg, 297
Iddig, 297
Ide, 175, 279
Idelle, 279
Iden, 32, 55
Ider, 47
Idetta, 121, 279
Idette, 121, 279
Idla, 74
Idna, 121
Idogbe, 69
Idoia, 264
Idola, 133
Idomeneus, 144, 207
Idona, 227, 279
Idone, 279
Idun, 227
Iduna, 227
Idunn, 227
Idurre, 264
Ierna, 195
Ierne, 176, 195
Ife, 67
Ifield, 28
Ifig, 74
Ifor, 283
Igantia, 195
Igasho, 218
Igerne, 43
Ignac, 207
Ignace, 109
Ignacia, 195, 264
Ignacio, 187, 168
Ignatius, 144, 207
Ignazio, 187, 268
Igone, 48, 264
Igor, 249, 251
Igorr, 144
Igoryok, 249
Igraine, 43
Igrayne, 43
Iker, 49
Ikerne, 264
Ila, 105
Ilana, 152
Ilanit, 152
Ilari, 187, 207
Ilario, 187
Ilarion, 207
Ilarius, 207
Ilay, 133
Ilda, 279
Ilde, 74
Ildiko, 279
Ileana, 133
Ilia, 152, 195, 247
Ilias, 158
Iliona, 133, 195
Ilithia, 133
Ilithya, 133
Ilka, 133, 162, 259, 279
Ilke, 133, 279
Illan, 207

Illian, 207
Illias, 158
Illius, 207
Illugi, 234
Ilmarinen, 100
Ilon, 133
Ilona, 133, 162
Ilonka, 133
Ilsa, 279
Ilse, 120, 121, 152, 279
Ilu, 133
Iluminada, 264
Ilus, 207
Iluska, 133
Ilya, 249
Ilyse, 120
Im, 234
Imala, 214
Imanol, 158
Immaculada, 264
Immaculata, 195
Imogen, 195
Imogene, 195
Imogenia, 195
Imperia, 195
Imre, 163, 283
Ina, 195
Inachus, 144, 207
Inaki, 49, 207
Inay, 172
Ince, 207
Incendio, 268
Indeg, 291
Inder, 172
Indi, 170
Indra, 168, 170, 172
Indrani, 165
Indumati, 165
Ine, 32
Inek, 207
Inerney, 180
Ines, 133, 264
Inesa, 133
Inese, 133
Inez, 133, 264
Inferna, 195
Ing, 234, 251, 279
Inga, 61, 251, 272, 279
Ingaborg, 251, 272
Ingalill, 272
Ingall, 125
Ingalls, 125
Inge, 251, 272, 279
Ingeborg, 61, 227, 272, 279
Ingegard, 272
Ingel, 125
Ingelbert, 125
Ingelise, 61
Ingemar, 227, 234, 274
Ingemur, 234
Inger, 61, 234, 272, 279
Ingharr, 234
Inghean, 253
Inghinn, 253

Inghram, 234
Ingibjorg, 227
Ingigerd, 227
Ingimund, 234
Ingjald, 234
Ingmar, 234, 274
Ingolf, 234
Ingram, 234, 283
Ingria, 100, 279
Ingrid, 227, 272, 279
Ingrida, 227
Ingrit, 227
Ingunn, 227
Ingunna, 251
Ingvar, 251, 274
Iniga, 184, 195
Inigo, 49, 207
Ini-herit, 69
Inis, 175, 180
Iniss, 180
Injerd, 227
Inkeri, 100, 279
Innes, 180, 256
Inness, 55
Innis, 55, 180
Innocent, 86, 207
Innocenty, 207
Innocenzio, 187
Ino, 133
Inocencia, 264
Inocencio, 268
Inocenta, 264
Inocente, 268
Intercidona, 195
Inteus, 218
Intisar, 36
Intisara, 36
Intizara, 36
Inuus, 207
Invidia, 196
Inys, 180
Inyx, 196
Ioakim, 249
Ioan, 158, 297
Iobates, 144
Iola, 133, 291
Iolantha, 133
Iolanthe, 133
Iole, 133
Iomar, 116
Iomhar, 283
Ion, 144
Iona, 51, 133, 297
Ionanna, 152
Ione, 51, 133
Ionessa, 133
Ionia, 133
Ionna, 287
Ionnes, 158
Iorgas, 144
Iorwerth, 297
Iosep, 158
Ioseph, 158
Iov, 158, 249
Iphegenia, 133
Iphicles, 144, 208
Iphimedeia, 196
Iphinome, 196
Iphis, 144, 208
Iphitus, 144, 208
Ira, 158

Iratze, 264
Irena, 133, 247
Irenbend, 32
Irene, 133, 264
Irenke, 162
Irial, 180
Irina, 133, 247
Irini, 133
Irinia, 133
Iris, 133, 152
Irisa, 133, 247
Irma, 121, 196
Irmgard, 121
Irmigard, 121
Irmina, 121, 196, 264
Irmine, 121, 196
Irmuska, 121
Irta, 133
Irune, 264
Irus, 144
Irven, 55
Irvetta, 74
Irvette, 74
Irvin, 55, 256
Irving, 55, 86, 116, 256
Irvyn, 55
Irwin, 32, 86
Irwyn, 32, 86
Iryna, 133
Irynia, 133
Isa, 121, 279
Isaac, 158
Isaakios, 158
Isabel, 152, 265
Isabella, 43, 152, 184, 265
Isabelle, 152
Isadora, 133
Isadore, 133
Isadorer, 144
Isaiah, 158
Isaias, 158
Isak, 274
Isan, 121
Isane, 121
Isaura, 133
Isaure, 133
Isdernus, 46
Iseabail, 158
Iseabal, 113, 253
Isen, 32
Isenham, 86
Isha, 168
Isham, 86
Ishana, 168
Ishani, 165
Ishaq, 69
Ishvara, 168
Isi, 215
Isiah, 158
Isibeal, 152, 176
Isidora, 133, 265
Isidore, 144
Isidoro, 268
Isidoror, 144
Isidro, 268
Isidrro, 144
Isis, 67
Isleen, 176
Isleif, 234

Islene, 176
Ismene, 133
Ismenia, 176
Ismey, 176
Ismini, 133
Isobail, 113
Isobel, 253
Isold, 51, 121
Isolda, 51, 121, 291
Isolde, 43, 51, 291
Isole, 121
Isolf, 234
Isoud, 43
Isoude, 43
Isreal, 158
Isrod, 234
Issa, 69
Istaqa, 221
Istas, 214
Istu, 218
Istvan, 144, 163
Iswara, 172
Ita, 113, 175
Itai, 158
Ither, 46
Itsaso, 265
Ittamar, 158
Ituha, 214
Itxaro, 265
Iulia, 196
Iulius, 196
Iulus, 208
Iustig, 297
Iuwine, 32
Iva, 105, 152
Ivan, 144, 158, 249, 268, 288
Ivana, 152, 247
Ivane, 152, 247
Ivanetsr, 144
Ivankor, 144
Ivanna, 133, 152
Ivar, 251, 274, 283
Ive, 283
Iven, 109
Iver, 251, 256, 283
Ives, 86, 283
Ivey, 74
Ivor, 251, 283
Ivy, 74, 133
Iwan, 297
Iwdael, 87
Iwona, 243, 251
Ixaka, 49, 158
Ixidorr, 144
Ixion, 144
Iye, 218
Izaak, 158
Izabella, 152
Izar, 265
Izarra, 265
Izarre, 265
Izazkun, 264
Izett, 175
Izmirlian, 41
Izreal, 158
Izsak, 163
Izso, 152

Izusa, 214
Intelligent, 37

Jaakkina, 100
Jaantje, 153
Jaap, 158
Jabari, 69
Jabbar, 38
Jabir, 38
Jacinta, 133, 265
Jacintha, 133
Jacinthe, 133
Jacinto, 144, 268
Jack, 87, 158, 244
Jackson, 87
Jacob, 158
Jacoba, 153, 196
Jacobe, 158
Jacot, 158
Jacquelin, 109
Jacqueline, 105
Jacquenetta, 105
Jacquenette, 105
Jacques, 109
Jacy, 218
Jada, 279
Jade, 265
Jadriga, 279
Jadryga, 279
Jadwiga, 243
Jael, 153, 158
Jafar, 168
Ja'far, 38
Jafari, 69
Jaffa, 153
Jafit, 153
Jafita, 153
Jaganmata, 165
Jager, 87
Jagger, 87
Jago, 269
Jahi, 69
Jahnu, 168
Jaime, 269
Jaine, 153
Jaione, 265
Jake, 158
Jakinda, 265
Jakob, 62, 125, 274
Jakoba, 121, 153
Jakobah, 153
Jakobe, 121
Jakobie, 121
Jakome, 49, 158
Jaleh, 240
Jalil, 172
Jamal, 38
Jambha, 168
Jambhala, 168
James, 87, 158
Jamie, 158
Jamil, 38
Jamila, 36, 67
Jamilah, 36
Jamsheed, 241
Jan, 64, 153, 158, 244, 274
Jana, 58, 153, 176, 196, 243
Jancsi, 158
Jane, 153

Janecska, 243
Janek, 244
Janet, 153
Janetta, 153
Janette, 153
Jani, 101, 158
Janice, 153
Janie, 153, 158
Janina, 153
Janine, 153
Janis, 153
Janita, 153
Janka, 153, 162
Jankia, 158
Janko, 158
Janna, 165
Janne, 100, 153
Jannes, 158
Janos, 158
Jans, 153
Jansje, 153, 158
Januarius, 244
Janus, 208
Japhet, 125, 158
Jaquelina, 153
Jaqueline, 153
Jaquenette, 153
Jaques, 158
Jaquetta, 153
Jarda, 59
Jardena, 153
Jardina, 153
Jared, 158
Jarek, 244
Jarina, 133
Jarine, 133
Jarita, 165, 170
Jarlath, 180
Jarman, 125
Jarmann, 125
Jarngerd, 227
Jarnsaxa, 227
Jarold, 283
Jaroslav, 59
Jarvi, 101
Jarvis, 125, 283
Jasha, 249
Jasia, 243
Jasmine, 240
Jason, 144
Jasone, 265
Jasper, 87, 109, 158, 241
Jasunr, 144
Jatinra, 168
Javas, 168
Javier, 109
Javiera, 265
Javiero, 269
Jawhar, 38
Jay, 109, 125
Jaya, 170
Jayanti, 165
Jaye, 109, 125
Jayne, 153, 170, 302
Jayr, 144
Jean, 109, 158, 253
Jean Baptiste, 109
Jeanetta, 105

Jeanette, 105
Jeanne, 105
Jeannot, 158
Jed, 158
Jedi, 158
Jedidiah, 38, 158
Jedrik, 244
Jedrus, 244
Jefferson, 87
Jeffrey, 32, 109, 283
Jehane, 105
Jeirgif, 249
Jem, 158
Jemima, 153
Jemina, 153
Jen, 62
Jenci, 163
Jencir, 144
Jenda, 153, 158
Jendayi, 67
Jennifer, 51
Jenny, 51
Jennyfer, 51
Jennyver, 51
Jeno, 144
Jens, 62, 158, 251, 274
Jensina, 153
Jensine, 61, 153
Jeoffroi, 109
Jephtah, 158
Jeremi, 158
Jeremiah, 158
Jeremias, 158
Jeremie, 158
Jeremy, 158
Jermija, 249
Jeroenr, 144
Jerolin, 208
Jerome, 144, 208
Jeronimo, 269
Jerrold, 283
Jerusha, 153
Jervis, 283
Jerzy, 245
Jerzyr, 144
Jesper, 109, 274
Jessamina, 105
Jessamine, 105, 240
Jesse, 158
Jessica, 153
Jessie, 153, 158
Jesus, 269
Jesusa, 265
Jetje, 279
Jetta, 196
Jette, 196
Jewel, 105, 196
Jibade, 69
Jibril, 38
Jill, 74, 196
Jilt, 64
Jim, 158
Jimena, 265
Jimmy, 158
Jinny, 196
Jinx, 196
Jirair, 41
Jiri, 144
Jirina, 58

Jirka, 59
Jirkar, 144
Jivanta, 165
Jivin, 168
Joachim, 158
Joan, 153
Joanka, 243
Joanna, 105, 153
Joaquin, 269
Joaquina, 153, 265
Joaquine, 153
Job, 158
Jobina, 153
Jobyna, 153
Jocasta, 133
Jocelin, 153, 196
Joceline, 153
Jocelyn, 153, 196
Jocelyn, 74
Jocelyne, 74
Jochebed, 153
Jocheved, 158
Jock, 158
Jodie, 153
Joel, 158
Joella, 153
Joelle, 153
Joelliana, 153
Joelliane, 153
Joen, 62, 158
Jofrid, 227
Johan, 101, 125, 158, 274
Johann, 125
Johanna, 121, 153, 272
Johanne, 234
Johannes, 125, 234
Johfrit, 46
John, 158
Johnson, 256
Johnston, 256
Joka, 153
Joki, 101
Jokin, 158
Jokina, 153
Jokine, 153
Jola, 153
Jolan, 121
Jolanka, 121
Jolanta, 243
Jolgeir, 234
Joli, 121
Jolie, 105
Jolon, 218
Jon, 158
Jonam, 158, 274
Jonas, 158, 269, 274
Jonatan, 158
Jonathan, 158
Jonati, 153
Jone, 153
Joop, 158
Joosef, 101, 158
Joosep, 101
Jooseppi, 158
Joost, 208
Jopie, 158
Jord, 227

Jordan, 153, 158
Jordane, 153
Jore, 158
Joreid, 227
Joren, 62
Jorenr, 144
Jorge, 269
Jorgen, 62
Jorgenr, 144
Jorgr, 144
Jori, 158
Jorie, 158
Joris, 62
Jorisr, 144
Jorma, 101
Jormungand, 234
Jornr, 144
Jorund, 234
Jorunn, 227
Jory, 62, 158
Joscelin, 196
Josceline, 74
Joscelyne, 74
Jose, 153, 269
Joseba, 158
Josebe, 153
Josee, 153
Josef, 62, 125
Josefa, 265
Josefina, 265
Josep, 245
Joseph, 158
Josepha, 105, 153
Josephe, 105
Josephina, 153
Josephine, 105, 153
Josephus, 158
Josetta, 153
Josette, 105, 153
Josha, 168
Joshua, 158
Josiah, 158
Josias, 158
Josie, 153
Joska, 163
Jostein, 234
Josu, 158
Josue, 158, 269
Josune, 265
Jov, 158, 249
Jove, 208
Joxepa, 153
Joy, 105, 196
Joyce, 51, 196
Jozka, 59
Jozsa, 153
Jozsef, 163
Jozsi, 163
Juan, 158, 269
Juana, 153, 265
Juanita, 153, 265
Juanito, 269
Juci, 153, 162
Jucika, 153, 162
Jud, 158
Judah, 158
Judas, 158
Judd, 158
Jude, 158, 196
Judie, 153
Judit, 153, 272

Judith, 153, 196
Judy, 153, 158
Juga, 196
Jugalis, 196
Juha, 158
Jukka, 101, 158
Julcsa, 162
Jule, 105
Julen, 208
Julene, 196
Jules, 109, 208
Julesa, 196
Juli, 196
Julia, 105, 196, 272
Julian, 109, 144, 208, 269
Juliana, 28, 196
Julianna, 196
Julianne, 196
Julie, 105, 196
Julienne, 105
Juliet, 105, 196
Julietta, 105, 196
Juliette, 105, 196
Julinka, 196
Julio, 208, 269
Juliska, 162, 196
Julita, 105
Julius, 208
Juliusr, 144
Juliusz, 208
Jullian, 208
Jullien, 109, 208
Jumanah, 36
Jumoke, 69
June, 196
Junia, 196
Junius, 208
Juno, 196
Junus, 208
Jupiter, 208
Jurg, 249
Jurgen, 125
Jurgisr, 144
Jurma, 100
Jurre, 158
Jurrien, 158
Jussi, 101, 158
Justa, 196
Justin, 180, 208
Justina, 196
Justine, 196
Justus, 208, 274
Justyn, 208
Jutka, 153
Juturna, 196
Juventas, 196
Juverna, 196
Jynx, 196
Jyotis, 165
Jyotish, 168

Kaarl, 101
Kaarle, 101, 109
Kaarlo, 101, 109
Kabandha, 168
Kabir, 168, 172
Kachada, 221
Kachina, 214, 216
Kadar, 38
Kaden, 38

Kadin, 38
Kadir, 38
Kadmus, 144
Kadru, 165
Kadyriath, 46
Kaethe, 134
Kafele, 69
Kafka, 59
Kaga, 218
Kaherdin, 46
Kai, 217, 256
Kaia, 133
Kailasa, 165
Kaine, 116
Kairos, 133
Kaisa, 100, 134
Kaj, 144
Kajetan, 187
Kajika, 218
Kakar, 168
Kakawangwa, 216
Kakra, 67
Kal, 101
Kala, 168, 170, 172
Kalanit, 153
Kalara, 196
Kalare, 196
Kalari, 168
Kalevi, 101
Kalf, 234
Kali, 133, 168, 234
Kalie, 133
Kalika, 133
Kalil, 38
Kalila, 36
Kalinda, 170
Kalindi, 165
Kaliq, 38
Kaliska, 217
Kalki, 168
Kalkin, 168, 172
Kalle, 101, 109, 274
Kalliope, 133
Kalman, 109, 234
Kalonice, 133
Kalwa, 100
Kaly, 133
Kalyca, 133
Kama, 302
Kamal, 38, 172
Kamala, 165, 170
Kameko, 302
Kami, 168
Kamil, 38
Kamila, 36
Kamilah, 36, 67
Kamilka, 196, 243
Kamilla, 196, 243
Kamille, 196
Kamuzu, 70
Kanaka, 168
Kanake, 133
Kandake, 133
Kane, 55, 116
Kanelingres, 46
Kangee, 222
Kanika, 67

Kanishka, 168
Kansbar, 241
Kantha, 170
Kanti, 215
Kantu, 168
Kanya, 170
Kaphiri, 70
Kapil, 172
Kara, 134
Karayan, 41
Karcsi, 105, 109
Kardeiz, 46
Kardel, 38
Kare, 234
Kareef, 38
Kareem, 38
Karel, 64, 109, 259
Karen, 61, 134, 251, 272
Karena, 134
Kari, 105, 109, 234
Karif, 38
Karim, 38
Karimah, 36
Karin, 134, 272
Karka, 170
Karl, 62, 109, 125, 274
Karla, 105, 121, 272
Karlens, 109
Karli, 234
Karlis, 109
Karlitis, 109
Karlotta, 105
Karma, 165
Karmel, 158
Karmelit, 153
Karmelita, 153
Karmelite, 153
Karmia, 153
Karmit, 153
Karney, 55
Karol, 249, 259
Karola, 121, 162
Karolek, 249
Karolina, 105, 121, 162, 272
Karoline, 105, 121
Karoly, 105, 109
Karr, 234
Karsten, 144
Karthik, 172
Karu, 168
Karuna, 165
Kasa, 216
Kaseeb, 38
Kaseem, 38
Kasen, 134, 208
Kashi, 168
Kasi, 168, 170
Kasia, 134
Kasib, 38
Kasienka, 134, 243
Kasim, 38
Kasimer, 259
Kasin, 134
Kasiya, 70

Kaska, 134, 243
Kasma, 134
Kasmira, 259
Kasmo, 134
Kassia, 134, 243
Kat, 162
Katakin, 134, 162
Katalin, 162, 196
Katalyn, 196
Katarin, 134
Katarina, 133, 162, 247, 259, 272
Katarzyna, 134, 243
Katchen, 121
Kate, 134, 272
Kateb, 38
Katerina, 287
Katharina, 121
Kathe, 121
Katherina, 247
Katherine, 133, 272
Katheryn, 133
Kathleen, 176
Kathrine, 133
Katica, 134
Katie, 134
Katine, 243
Katinka, 134, 162
Katja, 134
Katla, 227
Katlyn, 196
Katoka, 134
Katri, 100, 134
Katrikki, 100
Katrina, 100, 133, 251, 272
Katrine, 61, 243, 272
Katrya, 287
Katus, 134
Katy, 134
Katya, 134, 243, 247
Katyenka, 247
Katyuska, 247
Kauldi, 208
Kavan, 180
Kaveh, 241
Kaven, 180
Kaveri, 170
Kavi, 168
Kawindra, 165
Kay, 46, 134, 256, 297
Kaya, 216
Kayne, 55, 116
Kaysa, 272
Kazatimiru, 259
Kazemde, 70
Kazimierz, 245
Kazmer, 244
Ke, 45
Keagan, 180
Keaghan, 55
Kealan, 180
Keallach, 180
Kealy, 180
Kean, 180
Keanan, 87, 180

Keane, 55, 87
Keara, 174, 176
Kearn, 116
Kearney, 55
Keary, 55, 180
Keavy, 176
Kedalion, 144
Kedar, 38, 168
Keefe, 116, 180
Keegan, 55, 116, 180
Keegsquaw, 215
Keelia, 51
Keelin, 50, 51
Keely, 51, 176, 180
Keenan, 87, 180
Keenat, 174, 176
Keene, 55, 87
Kees, 208
Keezheekoni, 215
Kefira, 153
Kegan, 55, 116
Kei, 46, 297
Keifer, 116
Keir, 55
Keith, 180, 256, 297
Kek, 70
Keket, 67
Kelan, 180
Kelby, 283
Kelcey, 283
Kelci, 227
Kelda, 227
Keldan, 234
Kele, 221
Kelemen, 163
Kelemon, 291
Keleos, 134
Kelilah, 153
Kell, 234
Kellach, 180
Kelleher, 180
Keller, 116
Kelley, 116
Kelli, 297
Kellie, 113
Kellman, 163
Kelly, 113, 116, 279
Kelman, 208
Kelsey, 227, 234, 283
Kelsig, 234
Kelula, 153
Kelvin, 55, 116
Kelvyn, 55
Kelwin, 55
Kelwyn, 55
Kelyddon, 297
Kelyn, 297
Keme, 219
Kemen, 49, 269
Kemena, 265
Kemina, 265
Kemp, 87
Kempe, 87
Ken, 87, 297
Kenan, 180
Kendal, 55

Kendall, 55, 87
Kendhal, 55
Kendra, 28
Kendrick, 32, 87, 116
Kendrik, 87
Kendryck, 32
Kendryk, 87
Kenehyr, 297
Kenelm, 87
Kenley, 87
Kenly, 87
Kenn, 297
Kennard, 87
Kennedy, 116, 180, 256
Kenneth, 55, 87
Kennocha, 51
Kenny, 180
Kenric, 32
Kenrick, 87
Kenrik, 87
Kenryk, 87
Kent, 32, 55, 87, 297
Kentigern, 55
Kenton, 87
Kenward, 87
Kenway, 32, 87
Kenyon, 116, 297
Kenzie, 256
Kepa, 134
Kepe, 134
Keran, 153
Kerani, 165
Kerbasi, 49, 283
Kerbasy, 283
Kerby, 283
Keren, 153
Keres, 134
Keriam, 113
Keril, 144
Kerk, 234
Kerman, 109
Kermeilde, 74
Kermichael, 116
Kermichil, 116, 256
Kermilda, 74
Kermilla, 74
Kermillie, 74
Kermit, 55, 116
Kermode, 55
Kern, 116
Kerne, 116
Kerr, 116, 234, 256
Kerrie, 74
Kerry, 55, 74, 113, 116, 180
Kerstan, 208
Kersten, 259
Kerstin, 272
Kerta, 279
Kerttu, 100, 279
Kerwen, 116
Kerwin, 55, 116, 180
Kerwyn, 55, 116, 180
Keryn, 153
Kesara, 265

Kesare, 265
Kesava, 170
Kesegowaase, 219
Keshi, 168
Kesi, 67
Kesin, 168, 172
Kestejoo, 219
Kester, 87, 144, 208
Kestorr, 144
Kethryn, 133
Kethtrwm, 297
Ketil, 234
Ketura, 153
Keudawg, 297
Kevan, 55
Kevay, 174
Kevin, 55, 116
Kevork, 41
Kevyn, 55, 116, 297
Key, 116
Khachig, 41
Khafra, 70
Khaldun, 38, 70
Khalfani, 70
Khalid, 38, 70
Khalidah, 36
Khalil, 38
Kharouf, 38
Khasa, 165
Khayri, 38
Khayyat, 38
Khentimentiu, 70
Khepri, 67, 70
Khnemu, 70
Khnum, 70
Khons, 70
Khoury, 38
Khristos, 144
Khrustina, 134
Khrystiyanr, 144
Khufu, 70
Kian, 180, 297
Kiara, 176
Kiarr, 234
Kiba, 153
Kibddar, 297
Kienan, 180
Kieran, 55, 116, 180
Kieron, 180
Kieve, 291
Kigva, 291
Kilby, 283
Kildaire, 181
Kildare, 181
Kilian, 55, 208
Killdaire, 181
Killian, 55, 180, 208
Kilwich, 297
Kilydd, 297
Kim, 32, 74, 87, 297
Kimama, 217
Kimball, 32, 297
Kimberly, 74
Kimble, 297
Kimbra, 74

Kimbro, 74
Kimbrough, 74
Kimi, 215
Kimimela, 218
Kin, 256
Kinden, 208
Kindin, 208
Kineks, 214
Kineta, 134
Kinetikos, 134
King, 87
Kingdon, 87
Kingsley, 87
Kingston, 87
Kingswell, 87
Kinnard, 116
Kinnat, 174, 176
Kinnell, 116
Kinneret, 153
Kinnette, 153
Kinnon, 256
Kinny, 256
Kinsale, 181
Kinsella, 181
Kinsey, 87
Kintan, 168, 172
Kiollsig, 234
Kip, 87
Kipp, 87
Kippar, 87
Kippie, 87
Kipr, 144
Kira, 196, 247
Kiran, 170
Kirati, 166
Kirby, 234, 283
Kirie, 196
Kiril, 249
Kirilr, 144
Kiritan, 168, 172
Kirk, 87, 234, 256, 284
Kirkjabyr, 234
Kirkkomaki, 101
Kirkley, 87
Kirkly, 87
Kirkwood, 87
Kirochka, 247
Kirsten, 61, 134, 196, 227, 251
Kirstie, 134, 196
Kirsty, 134, 196
Kirwin, 55
Kirwyn, 55
Kiryl, 249
Kirylr, 144
Kisa, 247
Kiska, 247
Kissa, 67
Kistna, 172
Kit, 134
Kitchi, 219
Kitr, 144
Kitty, 134
Kiva, 153
Kivi, 101, 153
Kiwidinok, 215

Klara, 196, 272
Klari, 196
Klarika, 196
Klarissa, 196
Klarisza, 196
Klarysa, 287
Klas, 274
Klaude, 208
Klaudi, 208
Klaudia, 196
Klaudius, 208
Klaus, 62, 125, 144
Klazina, 134
Kleef, 87
Klemenis, 208
Klemens, 208
Kleng, 234
Kleopatra, 134
Klepp, 234
Kliment, 208
Kneph, 70
Knight, 87
Knocks, 87
Knoton, 218
Knox, 87
Knud, 62, 234
Knut, 234, 251, 274
Knutr, 234
Kodran, 234
Koen, 125
Koenraad, 64, 125
Kohana, 222
Kohkahycumest, 220
Koko, 215
Kokyangwuti, 216
Kol, 234
Kolb, 41
Kolbein, 235
Kolbjorn, 274
Kolbyr, 235
Koldobika, 279, 284
Koldobike, 279
Kolenka, 249
Kolenya, 217
Kolete, 134
Kolette, 134
Kolfinna, 227
Kolgrim, 235
Kolichiyaw, 221
Kolina, 134
Koline, 134
Kolinka, 61
Kolinkar, 62
Koll, 235
Kolli, 235
Kollsvein, 235
Kolskegg, 235
Kolya, 144, 249
Konal, 235
Konane, 303
Konni, 125
Kono, 222
Konrad, 125, 274, 284
Konstancji, 208, 245

Konstantin, 208, 274
Konstantine, 249
Konstantinus, 208
Konstanty, 208
Konstanz, 208
Konstanza, 196
Konstanze, 196
Kontar, 70
Kontxesi, 48
Kopecky, 59
Kora, 134
Kord, 125
Kore, 134
Koren, 134
Korian, 41
Kornel, 208
Korneli, 208
Kornelia, 196
Kornelie, 196
Kort, 235
Korudon, 144
Kosey, 70
Kosma, 134
Kosmo, 134
Kosmosr, 144
Kosmy, 144
Kostas, 208
Kostenka, 249
Kostya, 249
Kosumi, 222
Kotari, 168
Kotkel, 235
Koto, 134
Kotori, 221
Kovar, 59
Kozel, 59
Kral, 59
Kramoris, 59
Krany, 59
Krasava, 58
Krasna, 58
Kratos, 144
Krejci, 59
Krelis, 208
Kriemhild, 227
Kriemhilda, 227
Krikor, 41, 144
Krischanr, 144
Kriska, 134
Krisoijn, 64
Krisr, 144
Krist, 274
Krista, 134
Kristar, 274
Kristel, 134
Kristell, 134
Kristen, 134
Krister, 274
Kristian, 144, 274
Kristin, 134
Kristina, 134, 272
Kristine, 61
Kristof, 163
Kristofer, 274
Kristofr, 144
Kristor, 144
Kristr, 144
Kriszta, 134, 162
Krisztina, 134, 162

Kritanta, 168
Krocka, 59
Krodha, 166
Krossbyr, 235
Krysia, 134
Krysta, 134, 243
Krystiyan, 288
Krystka, 243
Krystupasr, 144
Krystyn, 243
Krystynka, 243
Krzysztof, 245
Krzysztofr, 144
Ksana, 247
Ksanochka, 247
Ksathra, 241
Ksena, 153
Kuanbyr, 235
Kubas, 59
Kuckunniwi, 220
Kuhlbert, 125
Kuirilr, 144
Kulbart, 125
Kulbert, 125
Kumar, 168
Kumara, 168
Kumari, 166
Kumuda, 170
Kumudavati, 166
Kunagnos, 55
Kundegunda, 279
Kundegunde, 279
Kundry, 43
Kunegundy, 243
Kunigunde, 243
Kuno, 125
Kunti, 166
Kunz, 125
Kuonrada, 121
Kurt, 125
Kuruk, 222
Kurush, 241
Kusner, 59
Kuwanlelenta, 216
Kuwanyamtiwa, 216
Kuwanyauma, 216
Kveld, 235
Kvist, 235
Kwahu, 221
Kwatoko, 221
Kyla, 153
Kylan, 235
Kyle, 116, 303
Kyledyr, 297
Kyllikki, 100
Kyna, 113
Kynan, 297
Kynddilig, 297
Kyndrwyn, 297
Kyne, 87
Kynedyr, 297
Kyner, 46
Kynlas, 297
Kynon, 297
Kynthelig, 55
Kynthia, 134
Kynwal, 297
Kynwas, 297

Kynwrig, 297
Kynwyl, 297
Kynyr, 297
Kyra, 196
Kyran, 180
Kyrillos, 144
Kyrillosr, 144
Kyrk, 87
Kyrkwode, 87
Kyros, 145
Kyvwlch, 297

L'Angley, 109
La Reina, 265
La Roux, 105
La Vergne, 105
La Verne, 105
Laban, 158
Labhaoise, 176
Labhras, 208
Labhruinn, 116
Labrencis, 208
Lach, 87
Lache, 87
Lachesis, 134, 196
Lachlan, 256
Lachlann, 116
Laci, 259
Lacinia, 196
Lacko, 259
Laco, 59
Lacy, 208
Lad, 87
Lada, 59, 247
Ladbroc, 87
Ladd, 87
Ladde, 87
Ladislas, 259
Ladislav, 59
Ladon, 145
Laec, 87
Laefertun, 88
Laertes, 145
Laestrygones, 145
Laetitia, 176
Lage, 272
Lagmann, 235
Laibrook, 87
Laidley, 87
Laidly, 87
Laila, 36, 61, 100, 153
Laili, 153
Lailie, 153
Lailoken, 46
Laine, 87, 256
Lainie, 253
Lair, 253
Laird, 256
Laire, 253
Lairgnen, 55
Lais, 134, 168
Laiurenty, 208, 245
Laius, 145
Lajcsi, 284
Laji, 284
Lajila, 166
Lajos, 284
Lakeland, 181

Lakini, 170
Lakshmana, 168
Lakshmi, 166, 171
Lakya, 166
Lal, 172
Lala, 259
Lalage, 134
Lalasa, 171
Laleh, 240
Lali, 284
Lalia, 134
Lalita, 171, 302
Lalor, 181
Lamar, 125
Lamarr, 125
Lambart, 125
Lambert, 125, 284
Lamberto, 284
Lambi, 235
Lambrecht, 125
Lambret, 125
Lambrett, 125
Lamia, 134, 196
Lamond, 235
Lamont, 235, 251, 256
Lamorak, 46
Lamorat, 46
Lampetia, 134
Lampeto, 196
Lana, 134
Lanassa, 247
Lance, 109
Lancelin, 109
Lancelot, 46, 109
Landa, 265
Lander, 87, 145
Landers, 109
Landis, 109
Landmari, 125
Landon, 87
Landry, 32
Lane, 87
Lang, 32, 64, 235, 274
Langdon, 87
Lange, 32, 64
Langford, 87
Langlea, 87
Langley, 87, 109
Langston, 87
Langundo, 218
Lani, 302
Lanka, 171
Lansa, 221
Lanston, 87
Lanu, 222
Lany, 181
Laobhaoise, 279
Laochailan, 256
Laocoon, 145, 208
Laodamia, 134, 196
Laodegan, 46
Laoghaire, 181
Laoidheach, 113
Laoidhigh, 181
Laomedon, 145, 208

Lapidos, 158
Lapidoth, 158
Lapis, 67, 208
Lapu, 221
Lar, 32
Lara, 196, 247, 253
Laraine, 196
Larcwide, 32
Laren, 253, 256
Larena, 253
Larentia, 196
Lares, 208
Laria, 253
Larina, 61, 196
Larine, 61, 196
Larisa, 247
Larissa, 134, 196, 197
Larisse, 134
Lark, 74
Larke, 74
Larry, 64, 274
Lars, 62, 64, 208, 251, 274
Larson, 251
Lartius, 208
Larunda, 196, 265
Larz, 64, 274
Lass, 74
Lasse, 74, 145
Lassie, 74
Laszlo, 163, 259
Lateef, 70
Latham, 251, 284
Lathrop, 32, 87
Latika, 171
Latimer, 87, 109
Latinus, 208
Lativerna, 197
Latona, 196
Latonia, 196
Laudalino, 208
Laudegrance, 46
Laudine, 43
Laughlin, 181
Launcelot, 46, 109
Launder, 87
Launfal, 46
Laura, 196, 265, 272
Lauran, 208
Laureen, 196
Laurel, 105, 196, 208
Laurella, 196
Lauren, 105, 196, 208
Laurena, 196
Laurence, 208
Laurencho, 208
Laurencia, 265
Laurene, 105, 196
Laurent, 208
Laurentia, 196
Laurentij, 249
Laurentios, 208
Laurentzi, 208

Laurette, 105, 196
Laurica, 196
Laurie, 196, 208
Laurin, 196
Laurina, 196
Laurissa, 196
Lauritz, 62, 64, 208
Lauryn, 196
Lausanne, 43
Lavan, 158
Lavare, 196
Laveda, 196
Lavena, 51
Laverna, 105
Lavernia, 105
Lavetta, 196
Lavette, 196
Lavina, 196
Lavinia, 196
Lavra, 196, 287
Law, 87
Lawe, 87
Lawford, 87
Lawler, 116
Lawley, 87
Lawly, 87
Lawrence, 208
Lawrie, 208
Lawron, 208
Lawson, 87
Lawton, 88
Lay, 88
Layla, 67
Laylie, 153
Layton, 88
Lazar, 158
Lazaro, 269
Lazarus, 158
Lazlo, 259
Lazzaro, 158
Lea, 74, 134, 153
Leachlainn, 181
Leah, 74, 153
Leal, 88, 109
Leala, 105
Lealia, 105
Leamhnach, 116
Lean, 256
Leana, 253
Leander, 145, 208
Leandra, 197
Leandro, 145, 269
Leandros, 208
Leane, 256
Leanian, 32
Leannan, 116
Lear, 88
Learoyd, 284
Leary, 181
Leathan, 256
Leathlobhair, 181
Leax, 32
Leb, 158
Lechsinska, 243
Leda, 134, 196
Ledaea, 196
Ledyard, 284

Lee, 55, 74, 88, 181, 208
Legarre, 265
Legget, 109
Leia, 74
Leib, 303
Leicester, 88, 208
Leidolf, 235
Leif, 235, 274
Leigh, 55, 74, 88
Leighton, 88
Leila, 36, 176
Leilani, 302
Leira, 265
Leirioessa, 196
Leiriope, 196
Leis, 197
Leith, 55, 256
Leitha, 134
Leitis, 113
Leksi, 145
Lela, 196
Lelah, 196
Leland, 88
Lele, 88
Lelia, 134, 196, 279
Leman, 88
Lemuel, 158
Lemuela, 153
Len, 221, 284
Lena, 134, 197, 272
Lenci, 134, 162, 208
Lene, 227
Lenet, 197
Leneta, 197
Leng, 32
Lenis, 197
Lenita, 197
Lenmana, 216
Lennart, 275, 284
Lenno, 218
Lennon, 116
Lennox, 116
Lenore, 134
Lenusya, 247
Lenya, 249
Leo, 88, 208, 284
Leoarrie, 197
Leocadie, 109
Leod, 256
Leoda, 121
Leodegan, 46
Leodegrance, 109
Leodegraunce, 46
Leodora, 197
Leof, 32
Leoine, 197
Leola, 184, 279
Leoline, 197
Leoma, 197
Leon, 109, 208, 269
Leona, 105, 197
Leonaldo, 284
Leonard, 284

Leonarda, 105, 134
Leonardo, 187, 269, 284
Leonce, 109, 197
Leone, 105, 109, 187, 197, 208
Leonelle, 105, 197
Leonhard, 284
Leonid, 208
Leonidas, 208
Leonide, 208, 249
Leonides, 269
Leonie, 105
Leonita, 197
Leonlina, 197
Leonor, 265
Leonora, 134, 184, 265
Leonore, 134
Leontin, 197
Leontina, 197
Leontine, 197
Leontis, 208
Leontyne, 197
Leopold, 125, 284
Leopolda, 121
Leopoldina, 121
Leopoldine, 121
Leopoldo, 125
Leora, 134
Leorad, 284
Leota, 121
Leotie, 214
Leppa, 100
Lera, 265
Lerola, 197
Leroy, 109, 208, 284
Lesham, 153
Lesley, 51, 55, 113, 117
Leslie, 51, 55, 113, 117, 253, 256
Lester, 208
Leta, 197
Letha, 134
Lethe, 134, 145
Lethia, 134
Letitia, 197, 265
Letizia, 184
Letje, 105
Lettie, 197
Letty, 197
Letya, 105
Leucippe, 134
Leuconoe, 197
Leucothea, 134
Leucothia, 134
Leupold, 284
Lev, 59, 158, 208, 249
Levana, 197
Levene, 74
Leveret, 109
Leverett, 109
Leverna, 197
Leverton, 88
Levey, 158

Levi, 158
Levia, 153
Levina, 74
Levka, 208, 249
Levushka, 208, 249
Levyna, 74
Lew, 88, 208, 259
Lewanna, 153
Lewi, 158
Lewis, 284
Lewy, 125
Lexina, 134
Lexine, 134
Ley, 74
Leya, 166, 265
Leyati, 222
Leyman, 88
Leysa, 287
Lia, 134
Liam, 117, 284
Liana, 105, 265
Liane, 105
Libentina, 197
Liber, 208
Libera, 197
Libertas, 197
Liberty, 74
Libitina, 197
Libuse, 58
Lichas, 145, 208
Licus, 208
Lida, 197, 247
Lidia, 243, 247
Lidija, 247
Lidio, 145
Lidiya, 247
Lidmann, 32
Lidochka, 247
Lidoine, 43
Lidskjalf, 235
Liealia, 105
Lien, 64
Liesbet, 153
Liesbeth, 153
Lifton, 88
Ligia, 134
Ligouri, 303
Liisa, 100
Lil, 176
Lila, 134, 197, 240, 243
Lilac, 240
Lilah, 153
Lilch, 134
Lili, 113, 134
Lilia, 134
Lilian, 197
Liliana, 184, 197
Liliane, 197
Lilie, 153
Lilika, 197
Lilis, 134
Lilith, 153
Lilka, 243
Lilla, 134
Lillian, 197
Lillis, 134
Liluye, 217
Lily, 134, 153, 197
Lilybel, 197

Lilybella, 197
Lilybelle, 197
Lilybet, 197, 291
Lilybeth, 197
Lima, 197
Limentina, 197
Limwris, 297
Lin, 32, 75, 227
Lina, 36, 64, 134, 197, 272
Lincoln, 55, 88
Lind, 88, 121
Linda, 121, 197, 265
Lindael, 88
Lindberg, 125
Linddun, 88
Lindeberg, 125
Lindell, 88
Lindie, 121
Lindisfarne, 88
Lindleigh, 88
Lindley, 88
Lindly, 88
Lindsay, 74, 256, 284
Lindsey, 74, 284
Line, 88, 227
Linette, 28, 51, 105
Linford, 88
Link, 88
Linka, 162
Linleah, 88
Linley, 88
Linly, 88
Linn, 28, 32
Linne, 75
Linnea, 227
Linnette, 51
Lino, 208
Linton, 88
Lintun, 88
Linus, 145
Lionel, 46, 208
Lioslaith, 253
Liosliath, 117
Lipot, 284
Lipp, 145
Lippi, 145
Lippio, 145
Lippo, 101
Lir, 55, 88
Liriene, 105
Lirienne, 105
Liriope, 196
Lirit, 153
Lirita, 153
Lisa, 121
Lisabet, 153
Lisabette, 153
Lisavet, 153
Lisbet, 61
Lise, 61, 121, 153, 222
Liseli, 218
Lisette, 121
Lisimba, 70
Lisle, 109
Lissa, 74
List, 32
Lita, 197

Litonya, 217
Litton, 88
Liusaidh, 113
Liuz, 208, 245
Liv, 227
Livana, 153
Livia, 197
Livie, 197
Livingston, 88
Livingstone, 256
Liwanu, 222
Liza, 153, 162
Lizbet, 153
Lizbeth, 153
Ljotunn, 227
Ljudumilu, 259
Llacheu, 46, 297
Llaesgymyn, 298
Llamrei, 43
Llara, 298
Llassar, 298
Llawr, 298
Llawvrodedd, 298
Llenlleawg, 298
Llevelys, 298
Llew, 46
Llewellyn, 298
Llewelyn, 55, 298
Lloyd, 55, 298
Lludd, 46, 298
Llue, 298
Llundein, 298
Llwch, 298
Llwyarch, 298
Llwybyr, 298
Llwyd, 298
Llwydawg, 298
Llwydeu, 298
Llwyr, 298
Llwyrddyddwg, 298
Llychlyn, 46
Llyn, 298
Llyr, 55, 298
Llyweilun, 298
Loc, 46, 88
Lochlain, 181
Lochlann, 181
Locke, 88
Lockwood, 88
Locrine, 88
Lodema, 74
Lodima, 74
Lodmund, 235
Lodoiska, 243
Lodur, 235
Lodyma, 74
Loefel, 88
Loes, 279
Lofn, 227
Lofnheid, 227
Logan, 117, 256
Logestilla, 105
Loghan, 117
Logistilla, 105
Lohengrin, 46
Lohoot, 44
Lois, 279
Lojza, 59
Loki, 235
Lokni, 222

Loknoth, 172
Lola, 265
Loleta, 265
Lolita, 265
Lolitta, 265
Lomahongva, 216
Loman, 181
Lomasi, 214
Lombard, 208, 284
Lomsky, 59
Lomy, 59
Lon, 117, 208
Lona, 74
Lonato, 218
Longobard, 208
Loni, 74, 134, 302
Lonn, 117
Lootah, 222
Lopahin, 249
Lopold, 284
Lopolda, 284
Lopoldi, 284
Lopthaena, 227
Lora, 28, 196, 265
Loraine, 105, 121
Lorant, 163, 208
Lorcan, 181
Lorda, 265
Lore, 265
Loreca, 208
Lorelei, 121
Lorella, 197
Lorelle, 197, 279
Loren, 208
Lorena, 196
Lorenc, 208
Lorencz, 163, 208
Lorens, 274
Lorentz, 208
Lorenz, 125, 187, 274
Lorenzo, 187, 208, 269
Loretta, 28, 265
Loretto, 208
Lorilla, 197, 279
Lorimar, 88
Lorimer, 88, 208
Lorin, 208
Lorinda, 196
Lorine, 208
Lorineus, 88
Loring, 109, 125
Loris, 196
Lorita, 196
Loritz, 125, 208
Lorna, 196
Lorne, 208
Lorraine, 105, 121, 196
Lorrella, 279
Lorrimer, 208
Lot, 46, 158
Lothair, 109, 125, 284
Lothar, 125, 284
Lotharing, 125
Lotta, 272
Lotte, 121

Lotus, 67, 134
Lotye, 105
Lou, 279
Louella, 75, 197
Loughlin, 181
Louis, 109, 125, 284
Louisa, 279
Louisane, 121
Louise, 121, 279
Loukas, 208
Lourdes, 265
Louredes, 265
Louvel, 109
Lov, 74
Love, 74
Lovell, 88, 109
Lovisa, 121, 272
Lowe, 109
Lowell, 88, 109
Lowri, 291
Loxias, 145
Loyal, 109
Loyce, 121
Loyola, 303
Luana, 121
Luane, 121
Lubentia, 197
Lubmilla, 247
Lubomir, 245
Luboslaw, 245
Luc, 298
Lucaas, 208
Lucan, 32, 46, 187
Lucania, 197
Lucas, 117, 208
Lucca, 187
Luceria—, 197
Lucerna, 197
Lucerne, 197
Lucero, 269
Lucia, 184, 197
Lucian, 208
Luciana, 197
Lucianna, 184
Luciano, 187, 208
Lucie, 197
Lucien, 208
Lucile, 105
Lucilla, 197
Lucille, 105, 197
Lucina, 197
Lucinda, 197
Lucine, 40, 197
Lucio, 187, 208, 269, 275
Lucious, 208
Lucita, 265
Lucius, 46
Lucja, 243
Lucjan, 245
Lucrece, 197
Lucrecia, 265
Lucretia, 197
Lucrezia, 184
Lucy, 197
Lucyna, 243
Lud, 88
Luda, 247
Ludka, 243
Ludkhannah, 121

Ludlow, 88
Ludmila, 58, 247
Ludmilla, 259
Ludoslaw, 245
Luduvico, 125
Ludvik, 275
Ludwig, 125
Ludwik, 125, 245
Luell, 75
Luella, 75, 197
Luete, 121
Lufian, 32
Lufti, 38
Lug, 298
Lugaidh, 181
Lugh, 181
Lughaidh, 125
Luighseach, 176
Luigi, 125, 187
Luigina, 134
Luiginw, 125
Luijzika, 121
Luis, 125
Luisa, 184, 243, 265
Luise, 121
Luitpold, 284
Lujza, 121, 162
Luk, 208
Luka, 208, 249
Lukacs, 163
Lukas, 208, 275
Lukasha, 208, 249
Lukasz, 245
Luke, 208
Luken, 208
Lukene, 197
Luki, 125
Lukman, 70
Lukyan, 208, 249
Lulita, 279
Lulu, 214, 279
Lun, 181
Luna, 197
Lunden, 32
Lundie, 256
Lundy, 105, 256
Luned, 43
Lunet, 43
Lunete, 43
Lunetta, 185
Lunn, 181
Lunt, 235, 275
Lupe, 265
Luperca, 197
Lur, 265
Lurleen, 121
Lurlene, 121
Lurlina, 121
Lurline, 121
Lusila, 169
Luthais, 117, 256
Luther, 284
Lutz, 125
Luvena, 75
Luvina, 75
Luvyn, 75
Luxovious, 55
Luyu, 214
Luz, 265
Luzige, 70

Lyaksandra, 287
Lyaksandro, 288
Lycaon, 145
Lycomedes, 145
Lycoris, 134
Lycurgus, 145
Lycus, 208
Lydea, 134
Lydell, 88
Lydia, 134, 272
Lydon, 284
Lyfing, 88
Lyle, 109
Lyman, 88
Lyn, 28, 32, 75
Lynceus, 145
Lynd, 88
Lyndon, 88
Lynet, 28, 43, 51, 197
Lynette, 28, 43, 51, 197
Lynford, 88
Lyngheid, 227
Lynn, 28, 32, 75
Lynna, 28
Lynne, 28
Lynnette, 105
Lyonechka, 208, 249
Lyonene, 197
Lyones, 43
Lyonesse, 43, 51
Lyonet, 43
Lyonette, 105
Lyonors, 43
Lyonya, 208, 249
Lyra, 134
Lyris, 134
Lysander, 145, 209
Lysandra, 134
Lysanor, 43
Lysimache, 197
Lysippe, 197
Lyssa, 74
Lyting, 235
Lyuba, 247
Lyubochka, 247
Lyudmila, 247

Maat, 67
Mab, 176
Mabbina, 176
Mabel, 197
Mabelle, 197
Mabina, 51
Mabli, 291
Mabon, 46, 55, 298
Mabonagrain, 46
Mabsant, 298
Mabuz, 46
Mac, 55, 257
Mac Adhaimh, 117
Mac Ailean, 117
Mac Alasdair, 117
Mac Artuir, 117
Mac Asgaill, 117
Mac a'bhaird, 117

Mac
a'bhiadhtaiche,
117
Mac an Aba, 117
Mac an Bhaillidh,
117
Mac an Bharain,
117
Mac an
Bhreatannaich,
117
Mac an Tsagairt,
117
Mac an t-Saoir,
117
Mac Bheathain,
117
Mac Bhriain, 117
Mac Daraich, 117
Mac Ghille
Aindreis, 117
Mac Ghille
Mhicheil, 117
Mac Ghille-
bhuidhe, 117
Mac Ghille-
dhuibh, 117
Mac Ghille-
dhuinn, 117
Mac Ghille-
easpuig, 117
Mac Ghille-
laider, 117
MacAdam, 117,
256
MacAdhaimh,
117
MacAdhamh, 256
MacAilean, 117
MacAladair, 117
MacAlister, 256
MacAllen, 117
MacAllister, 117
MacAlpin, 256
MacAlpine, 256
MacAndrew, 256
MacArthur, 117,
256
MacArtuir, 117
MacAulay, 256
MacAuley, 181
MacAuliffe, 181
MacAuslan, 256
Macaire, 145
Macario, 269
Macartan, 181
Macawi, 218
MacBain, 256
MacBean, 256
MacBeth, 256
MacBride, 181
MacCallum, 256
MacCinfhaolaidh,
257
MacClennan, 256
MacColl, 256
MacCormack,
181
Maccus, 32, 55
MacDaibhidh,
255
MacDhuibh, 256

MacDomhnall,
256
MacDonald, 256
MacDonell, 256
MacDougal, 256
MacDoughall,
256
MacDubhgall,
256
MacDuff, 256
MacElroy, 181
MacEwen, 256
MacFarlane, 256
MacFie, 256
MacGillivray,
256
MacGowan, 256
MacGregor, 256
Macha, 176
Machair, 256
Machakw, 221
Machaon, 145
Machar, 256
Machara, 253
Machau, 159
Machk, 219
Machum, 159
MacInnes, 257
MacIntosh, 257
MacIntyre, 257
MacIver, 257
Macia, 243
MacKay, 257
MacKendrick,
256
MacKenzie, 257
MacKinley, 257
MacKinnon, 257
Mack, 55, 257
MackIntosh, 257
Macklin, 55
Macklyn, 55
MacLachlan, 257
MacLaine, 257
MacLaren, 257
MacLean, 117,
257
MacLeod, 257
MacMaureadhaigh,
181
MacMillan, 257
MacMurra, 181
MacNab, 117,
257
MacNachtan, 257
MacNair, 117
MacNaughton,
257
MacNeill, 257
MacNiall, 257
MacNicol, 257
MacPherson, 257
MacQuaid, 181
MacQuarrie, 257
MacQueen, 257
MacRae, 257
MacRay, 257
Mada, 176
Madailein, 176
Madalen, 153
Madalena, 265
Madalyn, 153

Madawc, 298
Madawg, 298
Maddalen, 122
Maddalena, 122
Maddalene, 122
Maddalyn, 122
Madden, 181
Maddoc, 298
Maddock, 55, 298
Maddockson, 298
Maddocson, 298
Maddog, 298
Maddox, 55, 298
Madel, 153
Madelaine, 153
Madeleina, 105
Madeleine, 105,
153
Madelena, 153
Madelene, 153
Madelhari, 122,
125
Madge, 134
Madhava, 169
Madhur, 171
Madie, 105
Madison, 88, 284
Madoc, 46, 298
Madog, 298
Madolen, 105
Madonna, 197
Mador, 46
Madora, 134
Madra, 75, 265
Madre, 75, 265
Madri, 166
Mads, 159
Madu, 70
Mady, 75, 121
Mae, 28, 153
Maed, 89
Maegth, 75
Mael, 298
Maeleachlainn,
181
Maelgwyn, 298
Maelisa, 181
Maelwine, 89
Maelwys, 298
Maera, 197
Maeret, 89
Maerewine, 89
Maertisa, 75
Maethelwine, 88
Maetthere, 89
Maeva, 227
Maeve, 51, 176
Maeveen, 51
Mafuane, 67
Magaere, 134
Magan, 32
Maganhildi, 122
Magar, 41
Magaskawee,
218
Magd, 121
Magda, 121, 153
Magdala, 153
Magdalen, 153
Magdalena, 153
Magdalene, 153
Magena, 214

Maggie, 134, 253
Maghnus, 209
Magna, 227
Magne, 235
Magnhilda, 122
Magni, 235
Magnild, 122,
227, 235, 275
Magnilda, 122,
227
Magnilde, 122,
227
Magnolia, 105
Magnor, 235
Magnus, 62, 209,
235, 275
Mago, 181
Mahadeva, 172
Mahadevi, 166
Mahakala, 169
Mahal, 214
Mahala, 153
Mahalia, 153
Mahamari, 166
Mahault, 64
Maheloas, 46
Maher, 181
Mahesa, 171
Maheshvari, 166
Mahieu, 109
Mahila, 166
Mahir, 38
Mahkah, 222
Mahmoud, 39
Mahmud, 39
Mahon, 181
Mahpee, 222
Mahu, 216
Mai, 214, 253
Maia, 134, 154,
197
Maialen, 153
Maibe, 67
Maible, 176
Maichail, 159
Maida, 28, 75
Maidel, 75, 153
Maidie, 75
Maighdlin, 176
Maiju, 100
Maikki, 100
Mailhairer, 109
Maille, 176
Mailsi, 176
Mainchin, 181
Mair, 291
Maire, 176
Mairead, 134,
176
Mairearad, 113
Mairghread, 113
Mairi, 113, 253
Mairia, 176
Mai-ron, 159
Mairona, 176
Mairtin, 209
Maisie, 253
Maitane, 75
Maite, 75, 265
Maitea, 265
Maitena, 75
Maiti, 176

Maitilda, 176
Maitilde, 176
Maitland, 88
Maj, 272
Maja, 272
Majeed, 241
Majella, 176
Majesta, 197
Majnoon, 241
Maka, 218
Makalani, 70
Makara, 171
Makarim, 36
Makarioa, 145
Makawee, 218
Makeen, 38
Maki, 101
Makimus, 209
Makin, 38
Makis, 159
Makkapitew, 219
Makkitotosimew,
215
Maks, 249
Maksimillian,
249
Maksym, 209,
245
Maksymilian,
209, 245
Makya, 221
Mal, 159, 181
Malache, 197
Malachi, 159
Malachy, 159,
181
Malagigi, 109
Malajit, 169
Malak, 153
Malcah, 153
Malcolm, 55, 117,
257
Malcsi, 162
Malduc, 46
Maledysaunte,
43
Malena, 272
Malene, 122, 272
Malgorzata, 243
Mali, 291
Malia, 218, 279
Malik, 38
Malika, 162
Malila, 217
Malin, 88, 272
Malina, 153
Malinda, 134
Malini, 171
Malkah, 153
Malkolm, 275
Mallaidh, 153
Malleville, 109
Mallolwch, 298
Mallory, 109,
122, 125, 209
Malloy, 181
Malmuira, 253
Malmuirie, 253
Malone, 181
Maloney, 117,
181
Malva, 134

Malvin, 55, 88, 117, 181
Malvina, 51, 134, 176, 197
Malvine, 134
Malvinia, 197
Malvyn, 55, 88
Malyn, 88
Mana, 197
Manaba, 217
Manal, 36
Manar, 36
Manara, 36
Manasses, 159
Manawydan, 298
Manda, 171, 197, 265
Mandara, 171
Mandek, 245
Mandel, 109, 125
Mandisa, 67, 302
Mane, 181
Manette, 105
Manfred, 88, 125, 275, 284
Manfrid, 88, 284
Manfried, 125
Manfrit, 125
Mani, 235
Mania, 197
Manipi, 218
Mankalita, 218
Manley, 88
Manly, 88
Mann, 32, 88
Manneville, 109
Manning, 88
Mannis, 117
Mannix, 181
Mannleah, 88
Mannuss, 181
Manoj, 169
Mansfield, 88
Mansi, 216
Mantel, 109
Manto, 197
Manton, 32, 88
Mantotohpa, 220
Manu, 70, 172
Manuel, 159, 269
Manuela, 153, 265
Manus, 117, 209
Manvel, 209
Manvil, 209
Manville, 109
Manya, 247
Maola, 176
Maoldhomhnaigh, 117
Maoli, 176
Maolmin, 113, 117
Maolmuire, 257
Maolruadhan, 181
Maoltuile, 117
Maonaigh, 181
Mapiya, 218
Maponus, 32
Mar, 235, 303

Mara, 153, 162, 185, 247
Maralah, 214
Marc, 209
Marcail, 253
Marcario, 145
Marceau, 209
Marcel, 209
Marcela, 265
Marcella, 106, 198, 279
Marcelle, 106
Marcellia, 106
Marcellin, 209
Marcellina, 198
Marcelline, 198
Marcello, 187
Marcellus, 209
Marcely, 209
March, 298
Marchland, 88
Marchman, 88
Marci, 209
Marcia, 198
Marcian, 209
Marciane, 198
Marcie, 198
Marcilka, 209
Marcinek, 245
Marco, 187, 209, 269
Marcos, 269
Marcsa, 162
Marcus, 117, 209
Marcy, 198
Marden, 88
Mardon, 88
Mare, 176
Marea, 185, 197
Maredud, 291
Maredudd, 298
Marek, 209, 245
Marelda, 122, 279
Marelde, 279
Maren, 153, 209
Marenka, 58
Margalo, 134
Margaret, 134, 176
Margareta, 134, 272
Margarete, 247
Margarethe, 61
Margaretta, 134
Margarid, 40
Margarita, 134, 265
Margaux, 106
Margawse, 43
Marged, 291
Margeret, 134
Margery, 106, 134
Margherita, 185
Margisia, 243
Margit, 272
Margo, 106
Margolo, 134
Margosha, 247
Margot, 106
Margred, 291

Marguerite, 106
Marhilda, 122
Marhildi, 122
Maria, 105, 122, 153, 185, 227, 265, 272
Mariadok, 46
Mariam, 36
Mariamne, 153
Marian, 105, 209
Marianna, 162, 247
Marianne, 105, 227, 247
Maribel, 153
Maribella, 153
Maribelle, 153
Marica, 197
Marid, 38
Marie, 105, 153
Mariel, 209
Marietta, 105, 185, 265
Mariette, 105, 153
Marigold, 302
Marika, 153, 162
Marilda, 122
Marilla, 302
Marily, 153
Marina, 197, 247
Marine, 197
Mariner, 56
Marinochka, 247
Marinos, 209
Mario, 187, 209, 269
Marion, 153, 209
Mariquita, 265
Maris, 46
Marisa, 265
Marisha, 153, 166, 247
Mariska, 153
Marisol, 265
Marit, 302
Marita, 272
Marius, 209
Marjan, 240
Marjolaina, 106
Marjolaine, 106
Marjori, 106
Marjorie, 134
Marjory, 134
Mark, 46, 209, 275
Markandeya, 172
Marketa, 134
Markos, 209
Markus, 209, 275
Marland, 88
Marlena, 153
Marlene, 153
Marley, 88
Marlis, 122
Marlisa, 122
Marlon, 109
Marlow, 88
Marlowe, 88
Marly, 88
Marmara, 134
Marmee, 134

Marmion, 109
Marnia, 197
Marnin, 159
Marpe, 197
Marpesia, 197
Marpessa, 135, 197
Marphisa, 106
Marquilla, 265
Marrok, 46
Mars, 209
Mars Leucetius, 32
Marsali, 113
Marschall, 88
Marsden, 88
Marsh, 88, 109
Marsha, 198
Marshal, 88, 109
Marshall, 88, 109
Marsil, 198
Marsila, 198
Marsile, 198
Marsilius, 109
Marsilla, 198
Marston, 88
Marsyas, 145
Marta, 243, 265, 272, 302
Martainn, 117
Martel, 209
Martella, 197
Martha, 153, 302
Marthe, 153
Martial, 209
Martin, 209, 269
Martina, 197, 272
Martine, 197
Martinek, 59
Martinez, 269
Martinien, 209
Martino, 209, 269
Martinus, 209
Marton, 209
Martuska, 162
Maruska, 58, 247
Marusya, 247
Marut, 172
Marveille, 106
Marvel, 106
Marvella, 106
Marvelle, 106
Marvin, 56, 284
Marvyn, 56
Marwan, 38
Marwin, 284
Marwood, 88
Marwyn, 284
Mary, 153
Marya, 259
Marynia, 287
Marysia, 243
Maryska, 287
Marzina, 243
Masha, 247
Masia, 243
Masichuvio, 221
Masika, 67
Maska, 219
Maskini, 70
Maslin, 109
Mason, 109, 284

Masou, 219
Masselin, 109
Massima, 185, 198
Massima, 198
Masson, 109
Masud, 70
Matai, 159
Matchitehew, 219
Matchitisiw, 219
Mate, 159
Matea, 153
Mateo, 269
Math, 257, 298
Mathe, 159, 257
Mathea, 153
Mather, 89
Mathers, 89
Matherson, 89
Matheson, 257
Mathew, 159
Mathews, 159
Mathia, 153
Mathild, 122, 279
Mathilda, 106, 122, 279
Mathilde, 106, 122, 135, 279
Matilde, 279
Matilda, 43, 106, 135, 272, 279
Matilde, 279
Matin, 38
Matoskah, 222
Matrika, 166, 171
Matro, 269
Mats, 275
Matsimela, 70
Matsya, 169, 172
Mattea, 153
Matteo, 187
Matteus, 275
Matthea, 153
Matthia, 153
Matthias, 159
Matthieu, 159
Mattias, 159, 275
Mattie, 106
Matty, 106
Matunaaga, 219
Matuta, 198
Matvey, 249
Matviyko, 288
Matwau, 219
Matxalen, 153
Matyas, 159
Matyash, 249
Matyidy, 243
Matz, 159
Maud, 106, 176, 279
Maude, 106, 176, 279
Maughold, 181
Maunfeld, 88
Maur, 145
Maura, 106, 176, 185, 198
Maure, 198
Maureen, 51,

106, 176, 198
Maurelle, 106
Maurice, 145, 209
Mauricio, 269
Maurina, 106
Maurine, 106, 176, 198
Maurita, 198
Mauritins, 209
Mauritz, 209
Maurizia, 185
Maurizio, 187
Mauro, 269
Maury, 209, 245
Maurya, 176
Maurycy, 245
Mausi, 214
Mava, 154
Mave, 176
Mavelle, 51
Mavie, 51
Mavis, 51, 106
Mavise, 106
Mavra, 198, 247
Mawrth, 298
Max, 209
Maxen, 298
Maxime, 198, 209
Maximilian, 209
Maximillian, 209
Maximos, 209
Maximus, 209
Maxina, 198
Maxine, 198
Maxwell, 32, 89, 257
May, 28, 153, 197, 253
Maya, 197
Mayah, 154
Mayda, 28, 75
Mayde, 75
Mayer, 209
Mayfield, 89
Mayhew, 109
Mayir, 159
Maylea, 302
Maynard, 125, 284
Mayo, 117
Mayor, 209
Maysun, 36
Maza blaska, 220
Mazel, 154
Mazentius, 209
Mbizi, 70
McCloud, 257
Mead, 89
Meadghbh, 51
Meadhbh, 176
Meadhra, 181
Meagan, 134
Mealcoluim, 257
Meara, 176, 181
Mearr, 176
Meda, 214
Medb, 51
Medea, 135, 198
Medesicaste, 198
Meditrina, 198

Medora, 134
Medoro, 109
Medr, 55
Medredydd, 55
Medrod, 46
Medus, 145
Medusa, 135
Medwin, 89, 284
Medwine, 89
Medwyn, 89, 284
Medyr, 298
Meeda, 176
Megan, 28, 134, 176
Megara, 134
Megedagik, 219
Meghan, 28, 134, 176, 291
Mehadi, 166
Mehemet, 39
Mehetabel, 154
Meheytabel, 154
Mehitabelle, 154
Mehrdad, 241
Mehtar, 169
Meht-urt, 67
Meilseoir, 159
Meilyg, 298
Meinhard, 125
Meinke, 125
Meino, 125
Meinrad, 125, 284
Meinyard, 125
Meir, 159
Meira, 154
Mela, 243
Melampus, 145
Melania, 135
Melanie, 135
Melanippe, 198
Melanippus, 145
Melantha, 135
Melanthe, 135
Melanthius, 145
Melantho, 135
Melborn, 89
Melbourne, 89
Melburn, 89
Melbyrne, 89
Melchior, 46, 181, 241
Melchoir, 159
Melcia, 279
Meldon, 89
Meldrick, 89
Meldrik, 89
Meldryk, 89
Meleagant, 47
Meleager, 145
Melecertes, 145
Melechan, 47
Meleda, 135
Melek, 36
Melena, 135
Meleta, 135
Meletios, 145
Meli, 218
Melia, 198
Meliadus, 47
Melicent, 279
Melina, 135

Melinda, 134
Meliodas, 47
Melisande, 106
Melisenda, 265
Melissa, 43, 135, 198
Melisse, 135
Melita, 135
Melka, 243
Melkedoodum, 219
Melker, 275
Melkorka, 227
Melleta, 135
Mellicent, 279
Mellisa, 135
Mellona, 198
Melodie, 106
Melosa, 265
Melosia, 265
Melpomene, 135
Melrone, 181
Melusina, 106
Melva, 51, 176
Melvern, 219
Melville, 55, 109
Melvin, 55, 89, 181
Melvina, 51
Melvyn, 55, 89, 181
Melwas, 47
Melyon, 47
Memdi, 214
Memnon, 209
Memphis, 67, 70
Menachem, 159
Menachema, 154
Menachemah, 154
Menassah, 159
Mendi, 265
Menelaus, 145
Menes, 70
Menglad, 227
Menkaura, 70
Menoeceus, 145
Mensah, 70
Mentor, 145
Menw, 55, 298
Menzies, 257
Meoquanee, 215
Mercede, 185
Mercedes, 198, 265
Mercer, 89, 109, 209
Mercher, 298
Merci, 106
Mercia, 28, 75, 291
Mercury, 209
Mercy, 75, 106
Meredith, 51, 291, 298
Meredydd, 291, 298
Merek, 284
Mererid, 291
Merestun, 88
Merewode, 88
Merewood, 88

Meridith, 298
Meriel, 36
Merin, 298
Meris, 197
Merise, 197
Merissa, 197
Merle, 109, 198
Merlin, 47, 55, 109
Merlina, 198
Merlion, 109
Merlow, 88
Merlyn, 55
Merna, 51, 176
Merolla, 198
Merope, 135
Merrell, 284
Merrick, 284
Merrill, 198, 284
Merritt, 89
Merry, 75
Mersc, 88
Mert, 67
Merta, 135, 198
Merte, 198
Mertice, 75
Mertise, 75
Merton, 32, 89
Mert-sekert, 67
Mertysa, 75
Merula, 198
Mervin, 89, 284
Mervyn, 89
Merwin, 284
Merwyn, 89, 284
Meryl, 36, 198
Mesha, 169
Mesi, 67
Meskhenet, 67
Mesrop, 41
Messena, 198
Messina, 198
Messinia, 198
Meta, 61, 198
Metabus, 209
Metanira, 135
Metea, 135
Methena, 106
Methina, 106
Metis, 135
Mettabel, 154
Mettalise, 61
Mette, 145
Meturato, 220
Meurig, 298
Mezentius, 145
Miach, 181
Miakoda, 214
Micah, 159
Michael, 159
Michaele, 154
Michaelina, 154
Michalin, 154
Micheala, 154
Micheil, 117
Michel, 109, 159, 187
Michelangelo, 187
Michele, 109, 159, 187
Micheline, 154

Michelle, 154
Michon, 159
Midas, 145
Mide, 176
Mielikki, 100
Mieze, 154
Migina, 217
Migisi, 215
Mignon, 106
Mignonette, 106
Miguel, 269
Mihaly, 159
Mihangel, 298
Mika, 159, 214
Mikael, 159, 275
Mikaela, 272
Mikel, 49, 159
Mikele, 154
Mikhail, 159, 249
Mikhalis, 159
Mikhos, 159
Mikkel, 62, 159, 235
Mikko, 159
Mikolai, 245
Mikolaj, 245
Mikolas, 49, 145
Mikolaus, 49
Miksa, 209
Mil, 298
Mila, 58, 247
Milada, 58
Milagritos, 265
Milagros, 265
Milagrosa, 265
Milap, 219
Milburn, 89
Milbyrne, 89
Milcah, 153
Mildraed, 75
Mildread, 113
Mildred, 28, 75
Mildri, 227
Mildrid, 75
Mildryd, 75
Milena, 247
Miles, 145, 181, 209
Milford, 89
Milia, 279
Milicent, 279
Milicente, 279
Milka, 58, 259
Millard, 109
Miller, 89, 209
Millicent, 106, 122, 279
Millicente, 106
Millman, 89
Milman, 89
Milo, 145
Milos, 181, 259
Miloslav, 59
Milton, 89
Milward, 89
Mimi, 106, 279
Mimis, 145
Mimiteh, 217
Min, 70
Mina, 64, 122
Minah, 302
Minal, 214

Minau, 240
Mindel, 302
Mindy, 122
Minerva, 135, 198
Minetta, 106
Minette, 106
Mingan, 219
Minka, 243, 279
Minkah, 70
Minna, 106, 122, 279, 302
Minne, 122
Minnie, 106, 279
Minninnewah, 220
Minny, 279
Minos, 145, 209
Minta, 135
Mintha, 135
Miolnir, 235
Mira, 135, 153, 166, 198
Mirabella, 106
Mirabelle, 106
Miranda, 198, 265
Mirande, 198
Mirari, 48, 265
Mireille, 106
Mirek, 59
Mirel, 302
Miren, 153
Mireya, 265
Miri, 153
Miriam, 40, 153
Mirias, 135
Mirilla, 198
Mirillia, 198
Mirit, 153
Mirjam, 100
Mirka, 58, 302
Mirke, 302
Mirna, 51
Miron, 159, 245
Miroslav, 59
Miroslava, 58
Misae, 217
Misenos, 209
Misenus, 209
Misha, 249
Mishe, 249
Mishenka, 249
Misi, 159
Miska, 159
Mista, 227
Misu, 222
Mitchel, 89
Mitchell, 89, 159
Mithra, 169
Mitra, 169, 240
Mituna, 217
Mitzi, 154
Mjolnir, 235
Mlynar, 59
Mnemosyne, 135
Mochni, 221
Modan, 235
Modesta, 198, 265
Modeste, 198, 209, 265

Modestus, 209
Modesty, 198
Modi, 235
Modig, 32
Modlen, 291
Modolf, 235
Modraed, 89
Modred, 47
Modron, 43
Moerae, 135
Moesen, 298
Mogens, 62, 64
Mogue, 181
Mohan, 172
Moibeal, 113, 253
Moina, 51, 176
Moira, 28, 51, 135, 176, 198
Moirae, 198
Moirai, 135
Moire, 28, 176, 253
Moireach, 253
Moises, 269
Mojag, 219
Mokatavatah, 220
Moketavato, 220
Moketaveto, 220
Moketoveto, 220
Moki, 221
Mokovaoto, 220
Molan, 181
Molara, 265
Molimo, 222
Molloy, 181
Molly, 153
Molner, 59
Molpe, 198
Moly, 135
Momus, 145
Momuso, 222
Mona, 135, 176, 185, 214, 222, 279
Monca, 176
Moncha, 176
Moncreiffe, 257
Moneta, 209
Mongwau, 221
Monica, 135, 198, 265
Monifa, 67
Monika, 135, 198, 272
Moniqua, 106, 135
Monique, 106, 135
Monohan, 181
Monroe, 117, 209
Montague, 109, 209
Montaigu, 109
Monte, 89
Montgomery, 89, 257
Month, 70
Monty, 89
Mooney, 181
Moor, 109
Moore, 109

Mopsus, 145
Mor, 51, 113, 176
Mora, 265
Morag, 113, 198
Morain, 181
Moran, 181
Moraunt, 47
Morcades, 43
Morcan, 299
Morcar, 299
Mord, 235
Mordecai, 159
Mordechai, 159
Mordrain, 47
Mordrayans, 47
Mordred, 47, 89
Mordwywr, 298
More, 89, 109, 176
Moreen, 51, 106, 176
Morel, 209
Morela, 243
Moreland, 89
Moreley, 89
Moren, 298
Morfinn, 117
Morfran, 55
Morgan, 43, 51, 56, 181, 291, 299
Morgan Tud, 47
Morgana, 43, 51, 106, 291
Morgance, 51
Morgane, 51
Morgannwg, 299
Morgant, 291, 299
Morgawse, 43
Morguase, 43
Morholt, 47
Moriah, 154
Moriarty, 181
Morice, 154
Moricz, 163
Morie, 209
Moriel, 154
Morise, 154
Morit, 154
Moritz, 209
Moriz, 249
Morland, 89
Morlee, 89
Morly, 89
Morna, 51, 176
Morogh, 257
Morold, 47
Morolt, 181
Morpheus, 145
Morrell, 209
Morrigan, 51
Morrin, 176
Morris, 89, 209
Morrisey, 89
Morrison, 89, 257
Morrissey, 181
Morse, 89
Morthwyl, 299
Mortimer, 209
Morton, 89

Morvan, 117
Morven, 56, 117
Morvin, 117
Morvran, 299
Morvudd, 291
Morvyn, 56, 117
Moryn, 56
Mosegi, 70
Moselle, 154
Moses, 159
Mosheh, 159
Mosi, 67, 70, 217
Moswen, 67, 70
Motavato, 220
Motega, 219
Motka, 249
Mottul, 235
Moukib, 38
Moulton, 89
Moya, 51, 176
Moyna, 51, 176
Mozes, 163
Mroz, 59
Msamaki, 70
Msrah, 70
Muadhnait, 113, 176
Muata, 222
Mudada, 70
Mudawar, 38
Mugain, 176
Muhammad, 38
Muhunnad, 39
Muir, 257
Muira, 253
Muircheartaigh, 181
Muire, 176, 253
Muireach, 117
Muireadhach, 181
Muireall, 113
Muireann, 176
Muirfinn, 257
Muirgheal, 176
Muirne, 176
Mukamutara, 67
Mukantagara, 67
Mukarramma, 67
Mukhtar, 39
Mukhwana, 70
Mukki, 219
Mukul, 169
Mulcahy, 181
Mulciber, 209
Mulconry, 181
Muminah, 67
Muna, 36, 216
Mundy, 181
Mungan, 117
Mungo, 56
Muni, 169
Munin, 235
Munir, 39
Munro, 209, 257
Munroe, 209, 275
Mura, 247
Muraco, 219
Murali, 172
Murchadh, 117, 181
Murdoc, 56, 257

Murdoch, 56, 257
Murdock, 56, 257
Murel, 176
Muriel, 36, 176
Murphey, 181
Murphy, 181
Murray, 56, 181, 257
Murrough, 181
Murry, 56, 181
Murtagh, 56
Murthuile, 117
Musa, 39, 70
Musadora, 135
Musetta, 106
Musette, 106
Musidora, 135
Muslim, 70
Mustanen, 101
Mut, 67
Muta, 198
Mychajlo, 288
Myfanawy, 291
Mykhaltso, 288
Myles, 145, 181, 209
Mylnburne, 89
Mylnric, 89
Mynogan, 56
Myra, 135, 198
Myrddin, 299
Myrilla, 198
Myrina, 198
Myrkjartan, 235
Myrlene, 198
Myrna, 51, 176
Myron, 145, 159
Myrta, 135
Myrtia, 135
Myrtice, 135
Myrtis, 135
Myrtisa, 135
Myrtle, 135
Myrtoessa, 198
Mythili, 171
Mytra, 135

Naal, 181
Naalnish, 222
Naalyehe ya sidahi, 222
Naamah, 154
Naaman, 159
Naamit, 154
Naava, 154
Naavah, 154
Nab, 257
Nabi Ulmalhamah, 39
Nabil, 39
Nabirye, 67
Nachman, 159
Nachton, 257
Nada, 36, 251, 259
Nadav, 159
Nadege, 259
Nadenka, 247
Nadetta, 122
Nadette, 122

Nadezhda, 247, 259
Nadia, 247, 259
Nadie, 215
Nadim, 39
Nadina, 122
Nadine, 106, 122, 259
Nadir, 39
Nadisu, 169
Nadiv, 159
Nadya, 259
Nadyenka, 247, 259
Nadyuiska, 259
Nadzia, 243
Naeem, 70
Naeemah, 67
Naenia, 198
Nafiens, 47
Naftali, 159
Naftalie, 159
Nagelfar, 235
Nahcomence, 220
Nahele, 219
Nahid, 240
Nahimana, 218
Nahiossi, 220
Nahum, 159
Naia, 198
Naiadia, 198
Naiara, 48, 265
Naiaria, 48
Naida, 198
Nailah, 67
Nainsi, 154, 176
Nairi, 40
Nairna, 253
Nairne, 253, 257
Najja, 70
Najjar, 39
Nalda, 265
Naldo, 269, 284
Nally, 181
Namid, 215
Namir, 303
Namo, 110
Nan, 154
Nana, 154
Nancsi, 154, 162
Nancy, 154
Nandin, 169, 172
Nandini, 171
Nanelia, 154
Nanelle, 154
Nanetta, 154
Nanette, 154
Nanine, 154
Nanna, 106, 154, 227, 273
Nannie, 154
Nanny, 154
Nanon, 106
Nansen, 275
Nantosuelta, 51
Nantres, 47
Naois, 56
Naomhan, 181
Naomi, 154
Napayshni, 222
Nape, 145

Napea, 198
Napia, 198
Napier, 89
Napolean, 145
Napoleon, 145
Nara, 75, 113, 169, 214
Narain, 172
Naraka, 172
Narayan, 172
Narcisa, 135, 265
Narcissa, 135
Narcisse, 145
Narcissus, 145
Narda, 198, 240
Nardia, 198
Narfi, 235
Narkis, 145
Narkissa, 135, 247
Narmada, 171
Narmer, 70
Narve, 64
Nascha, 217
Nascien, 47
Nascio, 198
Nashota, 214
Nasim, 39, 241
Nasser, 39
Nassor, 70
Nastas, 222
Nastasiya, 287
Nastunye, 287
Nastya, 247
Nata, 214, 243
Natal, 269
Natala, 185
Natalia, 198, 247, 265
Natalie, 106, 198
Natalii, 106
Natalio, 269
Natanael, 159, 269, 275
Nataniel, 269
Natascha, 247
Natasha, 135, 247
Natassia, 135, 247
Natesa, 171
Natesha, 172
Nathacha, 135
Nathair, 257
Nathaira, 253
Nathalie, 198
Nathan, 159
Nathanael, 159
Nathania, 154
Nathaniel, 159
Nathara, 253
Nathifa, 67
Nathrach, 257
Nathraichean, 257
Natia, 243
Natividad, 265
Natuche, 106
Natyashenka, 247
Naughton, 257
Naunet, 67
Nauplius, 145

Nausicaa, 135
Nautia, 198
Navit, 154
Naw, 299
Nawar, 36
Nawat, 219
Nawkaw, 223
Nayati, 219
Neacal, 117
Neal, 56
Neala, 51, 176
Nealcail, 257
Neale, 56
Nealie, 51
Neall, 117
Nealon, 56
Nearra, 75
Neason, 181
Neb, 299
Neb-er-tcher, 70
Nebt-het, 67
Nebula, 198
Nebulia, 198
Nechama, 154
Nechemya, 159
Nechtan, 32, 257
Neci, 163, 198
Nectarios, 146
Neda, 75, 259
Nediva, 154
Nedivah, 154
Neeheeoeewootis, 220
Neema, 67
Neerja, 171
Neese, 56
Nef, 125
Nefen, 125
Nefertari, 67
Nefertiti, 67
Nefertum, 70
Neff, 125
Nefin, 125
Nehama, 154
Nehemiah, 159
Nehru, 169
Neifion, 299
Neil, 56, 117
Neill, 56
Neith, 67
Neka, 219
Nekana, 265
Nekane, 265
Nekhbet, 67
Nelda, 28, 75, 176
Nelek, 209, 245
Neleus, 146
Nelia, 198, 265
Nelka, 243
Nell, 56, 135
Nella, 135, 198
Nellie, 135, 198
Nellis, 135
Nellwyn, 75
Nelly, 135, 198
Nelma, 135
Nels, 56, 275
Nelson, 56
Nelwin, 75
Nelwina, 75
Nelwyna, 75
Nemausus, 56

Nemesio, 209, 269
Nemesis, 135
Nemesus, 209
Nemo, 146
Nemos, 146
Nentres, 47
Neola, 135
Neoma, 135
Neomea, 135
Neomenia, 135
Neomi, 154
Neomia, 135
Neon, 209
Neorah, 154
Neotolemus, 146
Nephele, 135
Nephthys, 67, 70
Neptune, 209
Neptunine, 198
Ner, 299
Nerea, 48, 265
Nereus, 146, 209
Neria, 48
Nerian, 32
Nerice, 135
Neried, 135
Nerina, 135, 198
Nerine, 135, 198
Nerio, 198
Neris, 198
Nerissa, 135
Nerita, 135
Neron, 269
Nerth, 299
Nerthach, 299
Nerthus, 28, 227
Nesha, 247
Ness, 257
Nessa, 135, 247, 253
Nessan, 181
Nessia, 135, 253
Nesto, 269
Nestor, 146, 269
Nesya, 247
Net, 67
Neta, 154, 265
Nethanel, 159
Neto, 269
Nette, 279
Nettie, 279
Neued, 291, 299
Neuveville, 110
Neva, 265
Nevada, 198, 265
Nevan, 181
Neville, 110, 209
Nevin, 117, 284
Nevins, 117
Nevyn, 117, 181, 284
Newell, 89
Newland, 89
Newlin, 56, 299
Newlyn, 56, 299
Newman, 89
Newton, 32, 89
Newyddllyn, 299
Nexeu, 70
Neysa, 135
Ngozi, 70

Niabi, 217
Niall, 56, 117, 257
Niallan, 56
Niamh, 176
Nicanor, 269
Nicanora, 265
Nicea, 135
Nicholai, 259
Nicholas, 146
Nicholaus, 146
Nicia, 135, 185
Nick, 146
Nicodemus, 146
Nicol, 146
Nicola, 106, 135
Nicolaas, 64
Nicolai, 249
Nicolas, 146
Nicolaus, 146
Nicole, 135, 146
Nicoletta, 135
Nicolette, 106, 135
Nicson, 89
Nidawi, 217
Nidhogg, 235
Nidhug, 235
Nidra, 166
Niece, 56
Niel, 62
Niels, 62, 251
Nielsine, 61
Nieve, 265
Niewheall, 89
Nigan, 219
Nigel, 209
Nighean, 253
Nighinn, 253
Niichaad, 222
Nijlon, 215
Nik, 146
Nika, 247
Nike, 135
Niki, 135, 209
Nikita, 146, 249
Nikiti, 219
Nikki, 209
Niklas, 275
Niklaus, 146
Nikodem, 146, 245
Nikolaevna, 247
Nikolai, 146, 259
Nikolajis, 146
Nikolaus, 275
Nikolia, 135
Nikolos, 146
Nikson, 89
Nila, 169, 198
Nile, 67
Nilea, 198
Niles, 62, 101, 146
Nili, 154
Nilia, 198
Nilo, 146
Nilos, 146
Nils, 62, 146, 251, 275
Nimiane, 43
Nimue, 43
Nin, 154

Nina, 154, 214, 247, 265
Ninacska, 154, 162
Ninette, 106
Nineve, 43
Ninockha, 247
Ninon, 106
Niobe, 135
Niocol, 146
Niocole, 146
Nipa, 166
Nira, 154
Nireta, 135
Niria, 154
Nirit, 154
Nirveli, 166
Nishan, 41
Nishkala, 171
Nisien, 56
Nissa, 251
Nisse, 251
Nissim, 159
Nissyen, 299
Nisus, 146
Nit, 67
Nita, 154, 215, 265
Nitca, 247
Nithhogg, 235
Nitis, 219
Nitsa, 135
Nittawosew, 215
Nituna, 214
Nitza, 154
Nitzanah, 154
Niu, 70
Niut, 67
Nixen, 89
Nixi, 198
Nixie, 122
Nixkamich, 219
Nixon, 89
Niyol, 222
Nizam, 70
Nizana, 154
Njal, 235
Njall, 235
Njord, 235
Njorthrbiartr, 227, 235
Nkosi, 70
Nkrumah, 70
Nkuku, 70
Noach, 64, 159
Noah, 159
Noak, 275
Nobilus, 209
Noble, 209
Nodawl, 299
Nodens, 32
Nodin, 219
Nodons, 32
Noe, 159, 269
Noel, 106, 110
Noella, 106
Noelle, 106
Noga, 154
Noirin, 176
Nokomis, 215
Nola, 51, 198

Nolan, 56, 117, 181
Noland, 56, 117
Noleta, 198
Nolita, 198
Nona, 198
Nonna, 198
Nootau, 219
Nora, 135, 154, 198
Norah, 135, 154, 198
Norberaht, 122
Norbert, 235, 284
Norberta, 122, 227
Norberte, 122
Norberto, 235, 269, 284
Norcross, 89
Nordica, 122
Nordika, 122
Noreis, 110
Norice, 110
Norina, 198
Norine, 198
Norm, 110
Norma, 198
Norman, 110, 284
Normand, 110
Norn, 227
Norna, 227
Norris, 110, 284
Northclif, 89
Northcliffe, 89
Northclyf, 89
Northrop, 89
Northrup, 89
Northtun, 89
Northwode, 89
Nortia, 198
Nortin, 89
Norton, 32, 89
Norval, 257
Norvel, 32
Norville, 32
Norvin, 89, 284
Norvyn, 89, 284
Norward, 89, 284
Norwel, 89
Norwell, 89
Norwin, 89
Norwood, 89
Norwyn, 89
Nosh, 219
Noshi, 219
Noss, 227
Notcher, 284
Notker, 284
Notus, 146, 209
Nouel, 110
Nour, 39
Noura, 36
Nourbese, 67
Nova, 199, 216
Novak, 59
Novea, 199
Novia, 199
Nox, 135, 199
Noy, 154
Nuala, 175, 176

Nuallan, 113, 117
Nubia, 67
Nudar, 36
Nudara, 36
Nudd, 47, 299
Nukpana, 216, 221
Nulte, 181
Nulty, 181
Numa, 209
Numees, 215
Numeria, 199
Nun, 70
Nuna, 214
Nunciata, 199
Nuncio, 209
Nunzia, 199
Nunzio, 209
Nur, 39
Nureet, 154
Nureh, 36
Nuri, 159
Nurit, 154
Nurita, 154
Nuru, 67, 70
Nusa, 154, 162
Nusi, 154, 162
Nut, 67
Nuttah, 215
Nydia, 199
Nye, 89
Nyle, 32, 56, 89
Nympha, 135
Nyneve, 43
Nynnyaw, 299
Nysa, 135
Nyse, 135
Nyssa, 135, 251
Nysse, 251
Nyura, 287
Nyx, 135, 199

Oakden, 90
Oakes, 89
Oakley, 89
Oba, 70
Obadiah, 159
Obediah, 159
Obedian, 159
Obelia, 135
Obelie, 135
Obharnait, 176
Obiareus, 146
Oceanus, 146
Ocelfa, 89
Ocnus, 146
Octa, 32
Octave, 110
Octavia, 185, 199
Octavian, 209
Octavie, 199
Octavio, 209
Octavius, 209
Octha, 32, 47
Octobriana, 279
Ocumwhowurst, 220
Ocunnowhurst, 220
Ocvran, 47
Ocyale, 199
Ocypete, 135
Oda, 122, 227

Odahingum, 215
Odakota, 223
Odale, 89
Odam, 89
Odanodan, 181
Odar, 257
Odara, 253
Odaria, 253
Odayle, 89
Odbart, 125
Odbert, 125
Odd, 227, 235
Oddfrid, 227
Oddleif, 235
Oddnaug, 227
Oddny, 227
Oddvar, 235
Oddveig, 227
Ode, 67, 284
Oded, 159
Odeda, 154
Odede, 154
Odel, 32
Odele, 136
Odelet, 136
Odeletta, 106
Odelette, 106, 136
Odelia, 28, 279
Odelina, 28, 122
Odelinda, 28
Odell, 32, 89, 235
Odella, 28
Odelle, 136
Odelyn, 28
Odelyna, 28
Odessa, 136
Odette, 28, 122
Odgar, 299
Odharnait, 113, 117
Odhran, 181
Odi, 32
Odiana, 122
Odiane, 122
Odila, 122, 279
Odile, 122, 279
Odilia, 28
Odilo, 284
Odin, 32, 235
Odion, 70
Odo, 110, 284
Odom, 89
Odon, 32
Odra, 166
Odran, 117, 181
Odwolf, 89
Odwolfe, 89
Odwulf, 89
Ody, 32
Odyar, 299
Odysseia, 136
Odysseus, 146
Oedipus, 146
Oegelsby, 90
Oeneus, 146
Oengus, 177
Oenomaus, 146
Oenone, 136, 199
Ofer, 159
Offa, 32
Ofra, 154

Ofydd, 299
Ogaleesha, 223
Ogden, 90
Ogdon, 90
Ogelsby, 90
Ogelsvie, 90
Ogelsvy, 90
Ogier, 110
Ogilbinn, 257
Ogilvie, 257
Ogin, 214
Ohanko, 219
Ohanzee, 223
Ohcumgache, 220
Ohitekah, 223
Ohnicio, 176
Oidhche, 257
Oifa, 51
Oighrig, 136, 146
Oihane, 266
Oilbhe, 176
Oilell, 52
Oilibhear, 235
Oisin, 56
Oistin, 209
Okes, 89
Okhmhaka, 220
Okpara, 70
Oksana, 247
Oksanochka, 247
Oktobriana, 279
Ol, 299
Ola, 227, 235
Olabisi, 67
Olaf, 62, 235, 275, 284
Olathe, 214
Olaug, 227
Olav, 235
Olave, 235
Ole, 62, 235
Olechka, 247
Oleda, 75
Oleg, 249
Oleif, 235
Oleisia, 136
Olen, 235
Olena, 136, 247
Olenka, 247
Oles, 146, 245
Olesia, 243
Oleta, 75
Olethe, 199
Olethea, 199
Olethia, 199
Olezka, 249
Olga, 227, 247, 273, 279
Olin, 235
Olina, 136
Olinda, 122, 199, 266
Oliphant, 257
Olita, 75
Olithia, 199
Olive, 176, 199
Oliver, 110, 209, 236
Oliveria, 266
Oliverio, 209, 269

Oliverios, 209, 269
Olivia, 199, 266, 273
Olivie, 199
Olivier, 110, 209
Ollaneg, 90
Ollie, 209
Olliver, 209
Olney, 90
Olof, 235, 275
Olufemi, 67
Olvaerr, 236
Olvan, 209
Olvir, 236
Olwen, 52, 291
Olwina, 291
Olwydd, 299
Olwyn, 43, 52, 291
Olwyna, 291
Olya, 247
Olympe, 106, 136
Olympia, 106, 136, 185
Olyn, 235
Oma, 36, 199
Omar, 39
Omari, 70
Omawnakw, 221
Omer, 39
Ominotago, 215
Ommar, 39
Omorose, 67
Omparkash, 169
Omphale, 136
Omusa, 217
Ona, 154, 176, 199
Onatah, 216
Onawa, 214
Ondrus, 59
Ondyaw, 299
Onella, 136
Oney, 181
Onfroi, 110
Oni, 67
Onida, 214
Onit, 154
Onkar, 172
Onora, 113, 176
Onslow, 90
Onslowe, 90
Onufry, 245
Onund, 236
Onuris, 70
Ooljee, 217
Oona, 176
Oonagh, 176
Oota dabun, 215
Opal, 302
Opalina, 302
Opaline, 302
Opel, 302
Ophelia, 106, 136
Ophelie, 106, 136
Ophion, 146
Ophir, 159
Ophra, 154
Ophrah, 154
Oppida, 52
Oprah, 154

Ops, 199
Ora, 28, 75, 154, 199, 266
Orabel, 75
Orabelle, 75
Oracula, 199
Orah, 154
Orahamm, 90
Oralee, 154
Orali, 154
Oralia, 199
Oralie, 75, 199
Oram, 90
Oran, 56, 117, 181
Orane, 106
Oratun, 90
Orban, 209
Orbart, 125
Orbert, 125
Orbona, 199
Orcus, 209
Ord, 32
Ordalf, 122
Ordella, 122
Ordland, 90
Ordman, 90
Ordmund, 90
Ordsone, 90
Ordwald, 90
Ordway, 32
Ordwin, 75, 90
Ordwine, 90
Ordwyn, 75
Ordwyna, 75
Orea, 136
Orebjorn, 236
Oreias, 146
Orelia, 75, 199
Oren, 117, 159
Orenda, 216
Oreste, 146
Orestes, 146
Orford, 90
Orghlaith, 176
Orguelleuse, 43
Orham, 90
Ori, 159
Oria, 136, 185, 199
Orial, 199
Oriana, 52, 185, 199
Oribel, 199
Oribella, 199
Oribelle, 199
Orick, 90
Oriel, 106, 199
Orik, 90
Orin, 56, 118, 159
Orion, 146
Oris, 159, 199
Orithyia, 136
Orla, 176
Orlaith, 176
Orlaithe, 176
Orlan, 90
Orland, 90, 284
Orlanda, 266
Orlando, 187, 269, 284
Orlantha, 279

Orlanthe, 279
Orlee, 154
Orlege, 32
Orlena, 106, 199
Orlenda, 248
Orlene, 106, 199
Orlina, 106
Orlyg, 236
Orm, 236
Orman, 90, 284
Ormazd, 106
Ormeman, 90
Ormemund, 90
Ormod, 32
Ormond, 90, 284
Ormund, 90
Orn, 236
Orna, 154, 176
Ornah, 154
Ornat, 176
Orneet, 159
Ornet, 159
Ornetta, 154
Ornette, 154
Ornolf, 236
Ornora, 199
Ornoria, 199
Oro, 269
Orphe, 199
Orpheus, 146
Orquidea, 266
Orquidia, 266
Orran, 118
Orren, 118
Orrick, 90
Orrik, 90
Orrin, 118
Orsen, 90
Orson, 90, 110, 209
Ortensia, 199
Ortensiana, 199
Ortensie, 199
Orthros, 146
Orton, 90, 284
Ortrud, 279
Ortruda, 279
Ortrude, 279
Ortun, 90
Ortygia, 136
Ortzi, 49
Orva, 29, 75, 106
Orval, 90
Orvil, 90
Orville, 90, 110
Orvin, 32, 90
Orvyn, 32, 90
Orwald, 90
Orynko, 287
Orzora, 154
Orzsebet, 154, 162
Os, 90, 236
Osahar, 70
Osana, 266
Osane, 48, 266
Osaze, 70
Osbart, 90
Osbeorht, 90
Osbeorn, 90
Osberga, 29
Osbert, 90

Osborn, 90, 284
Osbourne, 90, 284
Osburga, 29
Osburn, 90
Osburt, 90
Oscar, 56, 236
Osckar, 56
Oseye, 67
Osgood, 236, 284
Osip, 159, 288
Osiris, 70
Osk, 227
Oskar, 56, 236, 275
Oskari, 101
Osker, 56
Osla, 47, 299
Osmar, 90
Osmarr, 90
Osmond, 90, 284
Osmont, 90
Osmund, 90, 284
Ospak, 236
Osraed, 90
Osred, 90
Osric, 32, 90, 284
Osrick, 90
Osrid, 90
Osrik, 90, 284
Osryd, 90
Ossian, 56, 181
Ostein, 236
Osten, 236
Osvald, 284
Osvif, 236
Oswald, 32, 90, 125, 284
Oswaldo, 284
Oswallt, 299
Osweald, 90
Oswell, 90
Oswine, 32
Oswiu, 32
Oswy, 32
Oszkar, 163
Ota, 284
Otaktay, 223
Oth, 299
Otha, 28
Othilia, 28
Othin, 235
Othman, 125
Othmann, 125
Othmar, 284
Otho, 125
Othomann, 125
Otik, 59, 284
Otilie, 122
Otis, 146
Otka, 58, 122
Otkatla, 227
Otkel, 236
Oto, 284
Otoahhastis, 220
Otoahnacto, 220
Otokars, 284
Otomars, 284
Otos, 146
Otrera, 199
Ottah, 70
Ottar, 236

Ottavia, 185
Ottavio, 209
Otthild, 122
Otthilda, 122
Otthilde, 122
Ottila, 122
Ottilia, 122
Ottilie, 28, 279
Ottillia, 279
Otto, 125, 275, 284
Ottokar, 125
Ottoway, 284
Otus, 146
Otway, 284
Otylia, 122, 243
Oubastet, 71
Ouray, 219
Ourson, 110
Outram, 284
Ovadiah, 159
Ovadya, 159
Ovaegir, 236
Ove, 52, 236, 275
Oved, 159
Ovia, 199
Ovid, 159, 209
Owain, 47, 299
Owein, 299
Owen, 56, 146, 299
Owin, 56, 299
Owney, 181
Owyn, 56, 299
Oxa, 33
Oxford, 90
Oxley, 90
Oxnaford, 90
Oxnaleah, 90
Oxnatun, 90
Oxton, 90
Oya, 217, 222
Oysten, 236
Oz, 90
Ozanna, 47
Ozi, 159
Ozur, 236
Ozzi, 159
Ozzie, 159

Paaveli, 101, 210
Paavo, 101, 210, 251
Pabla, 266
Pablo, 210, 269
Pacho, 269
Pachu'a, 221
Paciencia, 266
Paco, 219, 269
Pacorro, 269
Pacquita, 199
Padana, 194
Padarn, 47
Paddy, 210
Paden, 257
Padgett, 110
Padhraig, 210
Padma, 166, 171
Padraig, 181, 210
Padraigin, 176
Padriac, 181, 210
Padrig, 299

Padruig, 118, 257
Paegastun, 90
Paella, 90
Pafko, 59
Paganus, 209
Page, 33, 106, 110, 136
Paget, 110
Pahana, 221
Paien, 110
Paige, 33, 106, 110
Paili, 154, 176
Paine, 90, 209
Pajackok, 219
Paki, 71
Pakuna, 217
Pakwa, 216
Pal, 210
Palaemon, 146
Palamedes, 47, 146
Palash, 169
Palba, 266
Palban, 269
Palben, 49, 269
Pales, 199, 210
Palika, 210
Paliki, 162
Palinurus, 210
Pall, 154
Pallantia, 199
Pallas, 199
Pallaton, 219
Palma, 199
Palmer, 90, 210
Palmere, 90
Palmira, 199, 266
Palmyra, 199
Paloma, 266
Palomydes, 47
Palt-el, 159
Palti, 159
Pamela, 136, 199
Pamelina, 199
Pameline, 199
Pamella, 199
Pammeli, 199
Pamuya, 216
Pan, 146
Panagiota, 136
Panagiotis, 146
Panawr, 299
Panchika, 169
Panchito, 284
Pancratius, 146
Panda, 194
Pandara, 166
Pandareos, 146
Pandarus, 146, 210
Pandita, 171
Pandora, 136
Pandu, 169
Pani, 169
Pannoowau, 220
Panos, 146
Panphila, 136
Pansy, 106, 136
Pant, 47
Panteleimon, 146
Panthea, 136

Pantxike, 199
Panya, 67, 199, 248
Paola, 185, 199, 210
Paolo, 187
Papandrou, 140
Paphos, 199
Papina, 217
Paquita, 266
Paquito, 284
Parasha, 248
Parashie, 248
Parca, 199
Parcae, 199
Parcia, 199
Parfait, 110
Pari, 240
Paris, 146, 210
Parisch, 90
Park, 90
Parke, 90
Parker, 90
Parkin, 90
Parkins, 90
Parkinson, 90
Parlan, 181, 257, 303
Parle, 90
Parnall, 90
Parnassus, 210
Parnella, 106
Parounag, 41
Parr, 90
Parrish, 90
Parry, 299
Parsefal, 90
Parsifal, 47, 90
Parthalan, 118, 303
Parthenia, 136
Parthenie, 136
Parthenios, 146
Parttyli, 100
Parvaneh, 240
Parzifal, 47, 210
Pascal, 110, 159, 187
Pascala, 106
Pascale, 106
Pascaline, 106
Paschal, 159
Pasclina, 106
Pascual, 110, 187
Pasha, 136, 248
Pashenka, 249
Pasiphae, 136
Pasithea, 199
Pasquale, 110, 187
Passebreul, 47
Pastor, 210
Pastora, 266, 279
Pastore, 279
Pat, 219
Patamon, 219
Patholon, 181
Pati, 217
Patience, 106, 199
Patiencia, 199
Patientia, 199

Paton, 90, 210, 257
Patrice, 106, 199, 210
Patricia, 199, 266
Patricio, 210, 269
Patrick, 210
Patrik, 275
Patrizia, 185
Patrizio, 187, 210
Patroclus, 146, 210
Patryk, 210, 245
Patten, 90
Pattin, 90
Patton, 90
Patty, 302
Patwin, 219
Patxi, 284
Paul, 210
Paula, 199, 273
Pauleta, 199
Pauletta, 199
Paulette, 199
Pauli, 199, 210
Paulin, 210
Paulina, 199, 243, 248, 273
Pauline, 199, 248
Paulita, 199, 266
Pauloc, 90
Pauls, 210
Paulus, 210
Pauwau, 215
Pavaka, 169
Pavati, 216
Pavel, 210, 249, 259
Pavit, 169
Pavithra, 171
Pavla, 58, 199, 249, 287
Pavlina, 199
Pavlis, 210
Pavlov, 59, 249
Pavlus, 210
Pavlusha, 249
Pavlushka, 249
Pavlushshenka, 249
Pavlya, 249
Pawel, 210, 245
Pawelek, 210, 245
Pawl, 245
Pax, 75, 90, 199, 210
Paxon, 284
Paxton, 90, 284
Paxtun, 90
Pay, 219
Payat, 219
Payatt, 219
Payden, 90
Payne, 90, 209
Paytah, 223
Payton, 90, 210, 257
Paz, 154, 159, 266, 269
Paza, 154
Pazia, 154

Pazice, 154
Pazit, 154
Peace, 75, 199
Peada, 33
Peadair, 147
Peadar, 118
Pearce, 33, 91
Pearl, 199
Pearla, 199
Pearle, 199
Pearlina, 199
Pearline, 199
Pearroc, 90
Pearson, 91
Pebin, 299
Pedar, 62, 147, 251
Peder, 146, 275
Pedr, 299
Pedra, 266
Pedrawd, 299
Pedrine, 61
Pedro, 146, 269
Peg, 136
Pegasus, 146
Pegeen, 136
Peggy, 136
Peibyn, 299
Peigi, 113
Peirce, 91
Peirene, 199
Peisistratus, 146
Peissawg, 299
Pekar, 59
Pekka, 101, 146
Pelagia, 136
Peleus, 146
Peli, 210
Pelias, 146
Pelicia, 136
Pell, 90
Pellam, 47
Pellanor, 47
Pellean, 47
Pelleas, 47
Pelles, 47
Pellikita, 199
Pellinore, 47
Pellkita, 199
Pello, 146
Pellonia, 199
Pelltun, 90
Pelopia, 136
Pelops, 146
Pembroke, 299
Pemphredo, 136
Pemton, 90
Penarddun, 52, 291
Penates, 210
Penda, 33
Pendaran, 56, 299
Pendragon, 33, 47
Penelope, 136
Peneus, 146
Penina, 154
Peninah, 154
Penkawr, 299
Penleigh, 90
Penley, 90

Penllyn, 299
Penn, 90, 125, 299
Pennleah, 90
Penny, 136
Penrith, 33
Penrod, 125
Penryn, 299
Pensee, 106
Penthea, 136
Penthesilea, 136, 199
Pentheus, 146
Penthia, 136
Penton, 90
Penvro, 299
Peony, 136
Pepe, 269
Pephredo, 136, 210
Pepik, 59
Pepillo, 269
Pepin, 125
Pepita, 266
Pepperell, 110
Peppi, 125
Peppin, 110
Peppino, 187
Per, 146, 275
Perahta, 122
Perceval, 47, 90
Perchnosius, 275
Percival, 47, 90, 110, 210
Percy, 110
Percyvelle, 47
Perdita, 199
Perdix, 146, 199
Peredur, 47, 299
Peredurus, 47
Peregrina, 199
Peregrine, 199
Perekin, 90
Perfecta, 266
Pericles, 146
Periphetes, 210
Perke, 154
Perkin, 90
Perkins, 91
Perkinson, 91
Pernel, 90
Pernell, 90
Pero, 146, 200
Perpetua, 200
Perren, 110
Perrin, 110, 146
Perrine, 136
Perry, 33, 91, 110, 299
Perryn, 110
Persephone, 136
Persephonie, 136
Perseus, 146
Persis, 136, 200
Persius, 146
Pert, 56
Perth, 56
Pertras, 147
Pertunda, 200
Peru, 146
Pery, 91
Perzsi, 154

Perzsike, 154
Pesach, 159
Pesha, 136
Pessach, 159
Peta, 215
Petenka, 249
Peter, 146
Peterka, 59
Peterke, 146, 163
Petiri, 71
Petr, 146
Petra, 136, 200, 243, 273
Petrelis, 147
Petrina, 136
Petrine, 61, 136
Petronela, 243
Petronella, 136, 200, 273
Petronelle, 136
Petronia, 200
Petronilla, 122, 200
Petronille, 122
Petros, 146
Petrov, 59
Petrukas, 147
Petrus, 47
Petruso, 288
Petter, 146, 275
Petunia, 214
Petya, 249
Peverell, 110
Peyton, 90, 210, 257
Phaedra, 136, 200
Phaethon, 147
Phaethusa, 136
Phantasos, 147
Phaon, 147
Phebe, 136
Phedora, 136
Phelan, 56, 118, 181
Phelot, 47
Phelps, 91
Phemie, 136
Phemius, 147
Pheobe, 136
Pheobus, 147
Pheodora, 136
Pheredin, 47
Pherson, 257
Phiala, 176
Phila, 136
Philana, 136
Philander, 147
Philberta, 75
Philemon, 147
Philibert, 284
Philida, 136
Philina, 136
Philip, 91, 110, 147
Philipinna, 122
Philipp, 147
Philippa, 136
Philippe, 110, 147
Philippine, 122
Philips, 91

Philis, 136
Phillida, 136
Phillina, 136
Phillip, 91, 147
Phillipa, 106, 136
Phillipe, 110
Phillips, 91
Phillis, 136
Philo, 147
Philoctetes, 147
Philoetius, 147
Philomel, 136
Philomela, 136
Philomena, 136
Philomina, 136
Philothea, 136
Phineas, 147, 159
Phinees, 147
Phineus, 147
Phlegethon, 147
Phoebe, 136, 200
Phoebus, 210
Phoenice, 200
Phoenix, 136, 147
Phorbas, 147
Phorbus, 147
Phorcys, 147
Phrixus, 147
Phrygia, 200
Phylis, 136
Phyllis, 136
Phylo, 147, 200
Pia, 185, 200, 266, 273
Piaras, 118, 147
Piarres, 146
Picaworth, 91
Picford, 91
Pickford, 91
Pickworth, 91
Picus, 210
Pierce, 33, 91
Pierette, 136
Piero, 146, 187
Pierpont, 110, 210
Pierre, 110, 146
Pierrel, 90
Pierrepont, 110, 210
Pierretta, 106
Pierrette, 106
Pierro, 146
Piers, 33, 91
Pierson, 91
Piet, 147
Pieter, 147
Pietr, 147
Pietra, 185
Pietrek, 245
Pietro, 146, 187
Pilar, 266
Pili, 67, 71
Pilib, 147
Pilumnus, 200
Pinabel, 110
Pinga, 171
Pinochos, 159
Pinon, 219
Pio, 187, 210
Piotr, 146, 245

Pious, 210
Piper, 75
Pipere, 75
Piperel, 110
Pippa, 185
Pippen, 284
Pippin, 110
Pippino, 187
Pippo, 147
Piri, 200
Pirithous, 147
Piroska, 162, 200
Pirro, 147, 269
Pishachi, 166
Pista, 163
Pisti, 163
Pit, 91
Pitamaha, 169
Pitar, 169
Pithasthana, 166
Pitney, 91
Pitri, 169
Pittheus, 147
Pityocamptes, 147
Pius, 210
Pivane, 221
Pjotr, 259
Placid, 210
Placida, 200, 266
Placidia, 200
Placidio, 210
Placido, 269
Placyd, 210
Plat, 110
Plato, 147
Platon, 269
Platt, 110
Pleasure, 136
Pleoh, 33
Plexippus, 147
Pluto, 210
Plutus, 147, 210
Pluvius, 210
Podarge, 136
Podi, 284
Pol, 118, 210, 275
Polak, 59
Poldi, 163
Polemusa, 200
Polikwaptiwa, 216
Polites, 147
Poll, 154
Pollard, 284
Pollock, 91
Pollux, 147, 210
Polly, 154
Poloma, 215
Polycarp, 147
Polydamas, 147, 210
Polydeuces, 147
Polydorus, 147, 210
Polyeidus, 147, 210
Polyhymnia, 136
Polymestor, 147, 210
Polynices, 147
Polyphemus, 147

Polyxena, 136, 200
Pomeroy, 110
Pommeraie, 110
Pomona, 200
Pomonia, 200
Pompeia, 200
Pompilius, 210
Ponce, 269
Pontifex, 210
Pontus, 147
Poppy, 75, 200
Porfirio, 147, 269
Porfiro, 269
Porrex, 91
Porter, 110, 210
Porteur, 110
Portia, 75, 200
Portier, 110
Portumnus, 210
Posala, 217
Poseidon, 147
Poshita, 169
Potina, 200
Poul, 62, 210, 275
Powaqa, 216
Powell, 56, 299
Powwaw, 220
Powys, 299
Prabha, 171
Praenestins, 200
Pramlocha, 166
Prasutagus, 33
Praza, 59
Preben, 146
Predentia, 200
Preece, 299
Prentice, 91, 210
Prentiss, 91
Preostcot, 91
Preostun, 91
Preruet, 110
Prescot, 91
Prescott, 91
Presley, 91
Pressley, 91
Prestin, 91
Preston, 91
Prewitt, 110
Priam, 147, 210
Priapus, 147
Price, 299
Pridwyn, 43
Priestly, 91
Prima, 200
Primalia, 200
Primavera, 200, 266
Primeiro, 269
Primo, 187
Primrose, 200
Prince, 210
Prior, 91, 210
Priour, 110
Prisca, 200
Priscilla, 200
Priyamkara, 169
Procne, 136
Procris, 200
Procrustes, 147
Proctor, 210
Procurator, 210

Proinnseas, 279
Proinnsias, 284
Proinsias, 118
Prokopios, 147
Prometheus, 147
Prophyrios, 147
Proserpina, 200
Prosper, 210
Prospera, 200
Prosperia, 200
Prospero, 210, 269
Protesilaus, 147
Proteus, 147
Prudence, 200
Prudencia, 266
Pruet, 110
Pruie, 110
Pruitt, 110
Prunella, 106, 200
Prunellia, 200
Prunellie, 106
Pryderi, 56, 299
Prydwen, 299
Prydwyn, 43
Pryor, 91, 110, 210
Prys, 299
Psamtic, 71
Psusennes, 71
Psyche, 137
Ptah, 71
Ptaysanwee, 218
Ptolemy, 71
Publius, 210
Puebla, 266
Pueblo, 269
Pules, 215
Pumeet, 169
Pura, 266
Purdy, 172
Pureza, 266
Purisima, 266
Putnam, 33, 91
Puw, 299
Pwyll, 56, 299
Pygmalion, 147, 210
Pylades, 147
Pyn, 90
Pyotr, 249, 259
Pyramus, 147
Pyrena, 137
Pyrene, 137
Pyrenia, 137
Pyrenie, 137
Pyrrha, 137
Pyrrhus, 148
Pyrs, 299
Pyt, 91
Pythia, 137

Qadir, 39
Qaletaqa, 221
Qaseem, 39
Qasim, 39
Qeb, 71
Qeturah, 154
Qochata, 221
Quaashie, 71
Quaid, 181

Quarrie, 257
Quarry, 257
Quartus, 210
Queena, 75, 279
Queenie, 75, 279
Queeny, 279
Quenby, 251, 273
Quennel, 110
Quentin, 91, 210
Queran, 182
Querida, 266
Quesnel, 110
Quibilah, 67
Quies, 200
Quigley, 118, 182
Quimby, 236
Quin, 56, 182
Quinby, 251, 273
Quincey, 110
Quincy, 110, 210
Quinevere, 43
Quinlan, 118, 182
Quinn, 56, 118, 182
Quinta, 266
Quintina, 200
Quinton, 91, 210, 269
Quintus, 210
Quirinus, 210

Ra, 71, 75
Raanan, 159
Raananah, 154
Rab, 285
Rabah, 154
Rabhartach, 118
Rabi, 36, 39
Rabiah, 67
Rabican, 110
Rachel, 122, 154, 303
Rachele, 154, 185
Rachelle, 106
Rachol, 303
Rad, 91
Radbert, 91
Radbourne, 91
Radburn, 91
Radburt, 91
Radbyrne, 91
Radcliff, 91
Radcliffe, 91
Radclyf, 91
Radella, 75
Radford, 91
Radha, 171
Radilu, 259
Radinka, 259
Radley, 91
Radmilla, 259
Radmund, 91
Radnor, 91
Radolf, 91
Radolph, 91
Radorm, 236
Radoslaw, 245
Rae, 75, 251, 257
Raed, 91
Raedan, 33
Raedanoran, 91
Raedbora, 33

Raedburne, 91
Raedclyf, 91
Raedeman, 91
Raedford, 91
Raedleah, 92
Raedmund, 91
Raedpath, 92
Raedself, 75
Raedwald, 33
Raedwolf, 91
Rafa, 36
Rafael, 269
Rafaele, 187
Rafaello, 187
Rafal, 159, 245
Rafe, 91
Rafela, 154
Raff, 91
Rafferty, 118
Raghallach, 118
Raghnall, 118, 182, 284
Ragi, 236
Ragna, 228
Ragnall, 43
Ragnar, 236, 275
Ragnara, 273
Ragnarok, 236
Ragnfrid, 228
Ragnhild, 228, 273
Ragni, 228
Ragnild, 228, 280
Ragnilde, 228, 280
Ragnol, 284
Ragnor, 236, 275
Ragnorak, 125
Ragnvard, 275
Rahel, 243
Rahil, 154, 248
Rahimat, 39
Rahimateh, 36
Raibeart, 118
Raibert, 285
Raicheal, 176
Ra'id, 39
Raidne, 200
Raighne, 182
Raimondo, 187, 285
Raimund, 285
Raimunda, 266
Raimundo, 269, 285
Raina, 106, 280
Rainart, 125
Raine, 280
Rainer, 125, 236
Rainger, 110
Rainhard, 125
Raisa, 303
Raison, 106
Raissa, 106
Raja, 36
Rajak, 169
Raji, 169
Rajmund, 245, 285
Rajni, 171
Rajnish, 169
Rakel, 154, 273

Rakin, 39
Rakshasa, 169
Raktavira, 169
Raktim, 169
Rald, 126
Raleah, 91
Raleigh, 91
Raley, 91
Ralf, 91
Rally, 91
Ralph, 91, 284
Ralston, 91
Ram, 91, 284
Rambart, 125
Rambert, 125
Ramira, 266
Ramirez, 269
Ramiro, 269
Ramla, 67
Ramm, 33, 91
Ramon, 269, 285
Ramona, 266, 280
Ramone, 285
Ramsay, 91, 284
Ramsden, 91
Ramses, 71
Ramsey, 91, 257, 284
Ramya, 171
Ran, 171, 228
Rana, 36, 166, 228
Ranait, 176
Ranaldo, 284
Ranalt, 176
Rand, 33, 91
Randahl, 284
Randal, 91, 284
Randall, 91
Randi, 228
Randkin, 91
Randolf, 284
Randolph, 91, 284
Randson, 91
Randy, 91
Ranee, 171
Ranen, 159
Ranevskaya, 248
Ranfield, 91
Ranger, 110
Rani, 159, 171
Rania, 171, 228
Ranica, 154
Ranice, 154
Ranit, 154, 159
Ranita, 154
Ranjan, 169
Rankin, 91
Rannveig, 228
Ranon, 159
Rans, 91
Ransey, 91
Ransford, 91
Ransley, 91
Ransom, 91
Ransy, 91
Ranveig, 228
Ranya, 248
Raoghnailt, 253
Raonaid, 113, 154

Raonaild, 113
Raonull, 118
Raoul, 110, 284
Rapere, 92
Raphael, 159, 187
Raphaella, 154
Raquel, 154, 266
Rasha, 37
Rashad, 39
Rashid, 39
Rashida, 67
Rashidi, 71
Rashmika, 166
Rasia, 243
Rasine, 243
Raskogr, 236
Rasmus, 148
Rathnait, 176
Rathtyen, 291
Rati, 166
Ratna, 166, 171
Raud, 236
Raul, 269, 284
Raulo, 269
Rauthuell, 236
Ravana, 169
Ravati, 166
Ravelin, 182
Ravelyn, 182
Raven, 75, 91
Ravi, 169, 172
Ravid, 159
Ravyn, 75
Rawdon, 285
Rawiella, 92
Rawley, 91
Rawlins, 33m, 91
Rawls, 91
Rawson, 91
Ray, 110, 210, 251, 257
Raybourne, 91
Rayburn, 91
Raymond, 125, 285
Raymund, 285
Raynor, 236
Raysel, 303
Raz, 303
Razi, 303
Razial, 303
Raziya, 67
Re, 71
Read, 91
Reading, 91
Readman, 91
Reagan, 56
Reaghan, 52, 56
Reamonn, 285
Reave, 92
Reaves, 92
Reba, 154
Rebecca, 154
Rebekah, 154
Recene, 33
Rechavia, 159
Redamann, 91
Redding, 91
Redford, 91
Redley, 91, 92
Redman, 91

Redmond, 91, 285
Redmund, 91, 285
Redwald, 92
Reece, 300
Reed, 91
Rees, 300
Reeve, 92
Reeves, 92
Ref, 236
Regan, 52, 56, 75, 182
Regenfrithu, 92
Regenweald, 92
Reggie, 125
Reghan, 56
Regin, 236
Regina, 185, 200, 266
Reginald, 92, 125, 285
Reginberaht, 125
Regine, 200
Reginhard, 126
Reginy, 200
Re-Harakhty, 71
Rehema, 67
Reid, 91
Reidar, 236
Reider, 236
Reidhachadh, 182
Reidun, 228
Reina, 106, 266, 302
Reine, 106
Reiner, 125
Reinhard, 125, 126
Reinheld, 280
Reinhelda, 280
Reinhold, 285
Reist, 236
Reit, 137
Rekha, 171
Remedios, 266
Remi, 110
Remington, 92
Remus, 210
Remy, 110
Ren, 91, 299
Rena, 137, 154
Renata, 185, 200
Renate, 200
Renato, 210
Renaud, 284
Rendell, 284
Rendor, 163
Rene, 106, 110
Renee, 106, 200
Renella, 200
Renelle, 200
Renenet, 67
Reneta, 200
Renfield, 91
Renfred, 92, 285
Renfrew, 299
Renfrid, 92, 285
Renild, 280
Renilda, 280
Renilde, 280

Renita, 200
Renke, 125
Renny, 176, 182
Renshaw, 92
Renton, 92
Renweard, 33
Renwick, 285
Renwyk, 285
Renzo, 187, 210
Reod, 92
Reseda, 200
Reselda, 200
Reshef, 71
Resi, 137
Reta, 137
Reuben, 159
Reule, 110
Re'uven, 159
Reva, 200
Reve, 92
Reveka, 154
Revelin, 182
Rex, 210
Rexana, 200
Rexanna, 200
Rexanne, 200
Rexford, 92
Rexley, 92
Rexton, 92
Rey, 110, 269
Reyburn, 91
Reynard, 126, 236
Reynold, 285
Rez, 162, 163
Rezi, 137
Reznik, 59
Rezso, 285
Rhadamanthus, 148, 210
Rhan, 291
Rhawn, 291
Rhea, 137, 200
Rhea Silva, 200
Rheda, 29
Rhedyn, 291
Rheged, 33, 300
Rheidwn, 300
Rhesus, 148, 211
Rheta, 137
Rhete, 137
Rheu, 300
Rhiain, 291
Rhiannon, 52, 291
Rhianwen, 291
Rhianwyn, 291
Rhinffrew, 299
Rhioganedd, 300
Rhisiart, 300
Rhobert, 300
Rhoda, 137
Rhodantha, 137
Rhodanthe, 137
Rhode, 200
Rhodes, 92
Rhodia, 137
Rhodos, 200
Rhoecus, 148
Rhongomyant, 47
Rhonwen, 291

Rhosyn, 291
Rhun, 300
Rhuvawn, 300
Rhyawdd, 300
Rhychdir, 300
Rhyd, 300
Rhydderch, 47
Rhynnon, 300
Rhys, 300
Ria, 266
Riagan, 182
Rian, 182
Rica, 266
Ricadene, 92
Ricadonna, 185
Ricarda, 75, 122, 185, 266, 280
Ricardo, 126, 187, 269
Riccardo, 126, 287
Ricci, 226
Ricciardo, 187
Rice, 33, 300
Rich, 92, 125
Richael, 176
Richard, 92, 126, 285
Richman, 92
Richmond, 126, 285
Rickard, 126
Ricker, 92
Rickman, 92
Rickward, 92
Ricman, 92
Rico, 126, 269
Ricweard, 92
Riddhi, 166
Riddoc, 182
Riddock, 182
Rider, 92
Ridere, 92
Ridge, 92
Ridgeley, 92
Ridgely, 92
Ridley, 92
Ridpath, 92
Rigby, 92
Rigg, 92
Riggs, 92
Rigmor, 61, 273
Rigmora, 273
Rika, 226
Rikard, 125, 163, 275
Rikka, 100, 122, 280
Rikkard, 92, 101
Rikward, 92
Riley, 118
Rilla, 122
Rille, 122
Rilletta, 75
Rillette, 75
Rillia, 122
Rillie, 122
Rima, 37
Rimona, 154
Rina, 137, 154
Rinaldo, 187, 284
Rinan, 33

Rinc, 33
Rind, 228
Rinda, 228
Ring, 92
Rinna, 154
Rinnah, 154
Rio, 266
Riobard, 182
Riobart, 285
Riocard, 126
Riodhr, 236
Rioghbhardan, 118
Rioghnach, 176
Rion, 47
Riona, 176
Riordain, 182
Riordan, 118, 182
Riothamus, 303
Ripley, 33, 92
Risa, 59, 200
Rishi, 169
Risley, 92
Risteard, 118, 126
Risto, 101, 148
Riston, 92
Rita, 137, 266
Ritsa, 137
Ritter, 126
Ritza, 137
Riva, 106, 200
Rivalen, 47
Rivalin, 56
Rive, 106, 200
Rivka, 154
Riyad, 39
Ro, 33
Roald, 126, 275
Roan, 92
Roana, 266
Roano, 269
Roar, 236
Roark, 182
Rob, 285
Rob Roy, 257
Robby, 285
Robena, 253
Robert, 110, 285
Roberta, 75, 280
Robertia, 75
Roberto, 187, 269, 285
Robertson, 257
Robin, 285
Robina, 253, 280
Robine, 280
Robinet, 285
Robinetta, 106
Robinette, 106
Roch, 110, 122, 126, 243
Roche, 110
Rocio, 266
Rocke, 110
Rodas, 148, 269
Roderic, 285
Roderica, 122, 280
Roderick, 126, 285
Roderiga, 266

Roderigo, 269, 285
Roderika, 122
Rodes, 92
Rodhlann, 211
Rodman, 92
Rodney, 285
Rodolfo, 269
Rodor, 33
Rodrick, 285
Rodrigo, 269
Rodrigue, 285
Rodrik, 126
Rodwell, 92
Roe, 33, 92
Roesia, 106
Rogan, 182
Rogelio, 269, 285
Roger, 285
Rogerio, 285
Rognvald, 236
Rohais, 106
Rohana, 171
Rohin, 169
Rohini, 171
Roial, 107
Roibeard, 182, 285
Roibhilin, 182
Roibin, 182
Rois, 113, 176
Roland, 211, 275, 285
Rolanda, 122, 280
Rolande, 122, 280
Rolando, 285
Roldan, 270
Roldana, 266
Rolden, 285
Rolf, 91, 236, 275, 285
Rolfe, 91, 285
Rollanda, 280
Rollande, 280
Rollin, 285
Rollins, 285
Rollo, 285
Rolph, 285
Rolphe, 285
Roma, 185, 200
Romain, 110, 211
Romaine, 106
Roman, 249, 270
Romana, 106, 200, 266
Romania, 200
Romano, 187, 211, 270
Romelda, 280
Romelde, 280
Romeo, 187, 211, 270
Romhilda, 122
Romhilde, 122
Romia, 185
Romilda, 122, 280
Romilde, 122, 280
Romney, 92, 211, 300

Romochka, 249
Romola, 200
Romulus, 211
Ron, 47, 159
Rona, 154, 228
Ronald, 92, 257
Ronalda, 228, 280
Ronalde, 280
Ronan, 56, 182
Ronat, 52
Roni, 159
Ronia, 154
Ronit, 159
Ronli, 154
Ronnaug, 228
Ronson, 92
Rook, 92
Rooney, 118, 182
Roosevelt, 64
Roper, 92
Rorke, 182
Rory, 118, 182, 285
Ros, 113, 258
Rosa, 122, 185, 200, 273
Rosabel, 200
Rosabella, 200
Rosabelle, 200
Rosalba, 200
Rosaleen, 200
Rosalia, 185
Rosalie, 185
Rosalina, 200
Rosalind, 266
Rosalinda, 266
Rosalinde, 266
Rosaline, 200
Rosalyn, 200
Rosamaria, 266
Rosamonde, 106
Rosamund, 122, 280
Rosamunde, 280
Rosana, 154
Rosanne, 154
Rosario, 266
Roscoe, 236, 285
Rose, 106, 200, 253, 257
Rosel, 273
Roselin, 110
Roselle, 273
Roselyn, 110
Rosemaria, 106
Rosemarie, 106, 266
Rosemary, 200
Rosemond, 280
Rosemonde, 122
Rosemunda, 122
Rosetta, 185
Rosie, 200
Roslin, 110
Roslyn, 110, 266
Ross, 258, 285
Rosselin, 110
Rosselyn, 110
Rosswald, 126
Rostislav, 59, 259
Roswald, 126, 285

Roswalt, 126
Roswell, 126, 285
Rotger, 285
Roth, 126
Rothwell, 236
Rotland, 236
Rousse, 110
Roussel, 110
Rousset, 110
Rousskin, 110
Rouvin, 159
Roux, 106
Rover, 92
Rovere, 92
Row, 33, 92
Rowan, 92, 182
Rowe, 33, 182
Rowell, 92
Rowen, 182
Rowena, 29, 52
Roweson, 33
Rowin, 182
Rowland, 211, 285
Rowley, 92
Rowson, 33
Rowtag, 220
Rowyn, 182
Roxana, 240
Roxane, 106
Roxanne, 106, 240
Roxbury, 92
Roy, 56, 110, 118, 258
Royal, 110, 211
Royale, 107
Royce, 92, 110, 211
Royd, 236, 251
Royden, 92, 110
Royns, 47
Royse, 92
Roz, 243
Roza, 162
Rozalia, 162, 185, 243
Rozamond, 64
Rozene, 214
Rozmonda, 122
Rozomund, 122
Rozyczka, 243
R'phael, 159
Ruadhagan, 182
Ruadhan, 182
Ruadson, 33
Ruaidhri, 182, 285
Ruairidh, 118, 285
Ruanaidh, 118, 182
Ruarc, 182
Ruark, 182
Ruben, 159, 270
Rubetta, 200
Rubette, 200
Rubie, 107
Ruby, 107, 201
Ruck, 92
Rudd, 92
Ruddy, 92

Rudella, 122
Rudelle, 122
Rudger, 285
Rudiger, 126, 285
Rudolf, 285
Rudolph, 285
Rudra, 169
Rudrani, 166
Rudyard, 92
Rueban, 159
Ruelle, 110
Rufa, 266
Rufeo, 211
Ruff, 110
Ruffe, 110
Rufford, 92
Rufin, 211, 245
Rufina, 185, 201, 266
Rufine, 201
Rufio, 211, 270
Rufo, 270
Ruford, 92
Rufus, 211
Rugby, 92
Ruggero, 187, 285
Ruggiero, 285
Ruhdugeard, 92
Ruhleah, 92
Rui, 110
Rule, 110, 211
Ruma, 166
Rumenea, 300
Rumford, 92
Rumina, 201
Runa, 228
Runcina, 201
Rune, 92, 126, 275
Rungnir, 236
Runihura, 71
Runolf, 236
Ruodrik, 126
Ruomhildi, 122
Rupert, 126, 285
Rupetta, 122
Rupette, 122
Ruprecht, 126
Rurik, 249, 259, 275, 285
Rusalka, 58
Rush, 92, 110
Rushe, 110
Rushford, 92
Rushkin, 110
Russell, 33, 92, 110, 211
Russu, 100
Rust, 110
Rut, 273
Ruta, 100, 154
Rute, 100
Rutger, 126, 275, 285
Ruth, 154
Rutherford, 92
Rutland, 236
Rutledge, 92
Rutley, 92
Ruusu, 100, 200
Ruza, 58

Ruzena, 200
Ryan, 118, 182
Ryba, 59
Rybar, 59
Ryce, 33
Rycroft, 92
Ryder, 92
Rydge, 92
Ryence, 47
Rygecroft, 92
Rygeland, 92
Rygemann, 93
Rygetun, 93
Ryland, 92
Ryman, 93
Ryn, 299
Ryons, 47
Rypan, 33
Rysc, 92
Ryscford, 92
Ryszard, 126
Ryton, 93
Ryzard, 245

Saa, 71
Saadya, 159
Saba, 137
Sabah, 68
Sabana, 266
Saber, 110
Sabih, 39
Sabin, 211
Sabina, 201, 248, 266
Sabine, 201
Sabino, 211, 270
Sabinus, 211
Sabir, 39
Sabirah, 37
Sabola, 71
Sabra, 154
Sabria, 201
Sabrina, 75, 185, 201
Sach, 300
Sacha, 248, 249
Sachi, 169
Sacripant, 110
Sadbh, 176
Sadhbba, 176
Sadhbh, 176
Sadie, 154
Sadiki, 71
Sadiq, 39
Sadira, 37, 240
Sadwrn, 300
Saebeorht, 93
Saebroc, 93
Saeed, 241
Saeger, 93
Saehild, 228
Saehrimnir, 236
Saelac, 126
Saelig, 93
Saer, 300
Saeth, 291
Saeunn, 228
Saewald, 93
Saeweard, 93
Safa, 37
Saffi, 61, 137
Saffir, 291

Saffire, 47
Safford, 93
Safiya, 68
Safiyyah, 37
Saga, 228
Sage, 201
Saghir, 39
Sagira, 68
Sagirah, 37
Sagramour, 47
Sagremor, 47
Sahak, 41
Sahale, 219
Sahan, 169
Sahar, 37
Sahen, 169
Sahir, 39, 169
Sahkyo, 217
Said, 241
Saidah, 37
Saith, 300
Sajag, 169
Saka, 169
Sakari, 166
Sakeri, 159
Sakhmet, 68
Sakima, 219
Sakra, 166
Sakujna, 166
Salacia, 201
Salali, 215
Salama, 68
Salamon, 160
Salbatora, 266
Salbatore, 270
Saleem, 39
Saleen, 201
Salem, 39
Salena, 201
Salford, 93
Salhdene, 93
Salhford, 93
Salhtun, 93
Salih, 71
Salihah, 68
Salim, 39
Salina, 201
Saline, 201
Salisbury, 93
Sallie, 154
Sally, 154
Salmalin, 172
Salmoneus, 148, 211
Saloma, 154
Salome, 154
Salomeaex1, 154
Salomon, 270
Salton, 93
Salva, 201
Salvador, 211, 270
Salvadora, 266
Salvadore, 270
Salvator, 211
Salvatora, 266
Salvatore, 187, 270
Salvatorio, 187
Salvia, 201
Salvina, 201
Salvinia, 201

Samantaka, 169
Samantha, 154, 302
Samar, 37
Samara, 154
Sameh, 37
Samhaoir, 176
Sami, 39
Samia, 201
Samirah, 37
Samman, 39
Sampson, 159
Samson, 159, 275
Samuel, 159, 275
Samuela, 155
Samuka, 163
Samvarta, 166
Sanat, 172
Sanborn, 93
Sanbourne, 93
Sancha, 266
Sancho, 270
Sancia, 185, 201, 266
Sancta, 201
Sanddev, 300
Sander, 148
Sanders, 93, 148
Sanderson, 93
Sandhya, 166, 171
Sandon, 93
Sandor, 148, 163, 259
Sandra, 137
Sandrine, 137
Sandy, 258
Sanersone, 93
Sanford, 93, 94
Sangrida, 228
Sani, 222
Sanjiv, 169
Sanjna, 166
Sanson, 159
Santiago, 270
Santo, 187
Santon, 93
Santos, 270
Sanura, 68, 302
Sanuye, 217
Sanya, 166, 249
Sapphira, 137, 155
Sapphire, 137, 155
Saqr, 39
Sar, 33
Sara, 37, 154, 166, 266
Sarad, 172
Sarah, 154
Sarai, 155
Saraid, 177
Sarama, 166
Sarff, 291
Sargent, 110, 211
Sarika, 162
Sarisha, 171
Sarita, 154, 266
Sarlic, 33
Sarohildi, 122

Sarpedon, 148, 211
Sarsour, 39
Sarsoureh, 37
Sasa, 162
Sasha, 248, 249
Sashenka, 248
Saskia, 64
Sasson, 159
Sati, 166
Satinka, 214
Sativola, 56
Satordi, 110
Saturn, 211
Saturnia, 201
Saturnin, 270
Saturnina, 266
Satyavati, 166
Saubhari, 169
Saul, 159, 270, 275
Saunders, 93, 148
Saunderson, 93
Saura, 166
Sauville, 110
Savanna, 266
Savannah, 266
Savarna, 166
Saveage, 43
Savill, 211
Saville, 110
Savina, 201
Savitari, 166
Sawyer, 56, 93
Sawyere, 93
Sawyers, 93
Sawyl, 300
Saxan, 93
Saxe, 275
Saxon, 93, 285
Saxona, 75
Saxonia, 75
Sayer, 300
Sayers, 300
Sayre, 300
Sayres, 300
Sayyid, 39
Scadwiella, 93
Scaffeld, 93
Scand, 33, 93
Scandleah, 93
Scanlan, 182
Scanlon, 182
Scannalan, 182
Scarlet, 75
Scarlett, 75
Scead, 33
Sceadu, 33
Sceapleigh, 93
Sceley, 93
Scelflea, 75
Scelftun, 93
Sceotend, 33
Schaddoc, 93
Schlomit, 154
Schmaiah, 159
Schmuel, 159
Scholastica, 201
Schuyler, 64
Schyler, 64
Scilti, 56

Scirloc, 93
Scirwode, 94
Scolaighe, 182
Scot, 258
Scota, 177, 201
Scott, 93, 258
Scottas, 93
Scoville, 110
Scowyrhta, 33
Scrydan, 33
Scrymgeour, 258
Scully, 118, 182
Scur, 33
Scylla, 137
Seabert, 93
Seabright, 93
Seabrook, 93
Seaburt, 93
Seachnsaigh, 182
Seadon, 93
Seafra, 182
Seafraid, 182
Seager, 93
Seaghda, 182
Sealey, 93
Seamere, 33
Seamus, 182
Seana, 113, 177
Seanachan, 182
Seanan, 159, 182
Seanlaoch, 182
Searbhreathach, 182
Searlait, 107, 177
Searlas, 110
Searle, 110, 285
Searlus, 110
Season, 201
Seaton, 33, 93
Seaver, 33
Seaward, 93
Seb, 71
Sebak, 71
Sebasten, 148
Sebastene, 137
Sebastian, 148, 211
Sebastiana, 137, 185, 201
Sebastiane, 201
Sebastiano, 148, 187, 270
Sebastianus, 211
Sebastiene, 185
Sebastienne, 137
Seber, 33
Sebert, 93
Sebestyen, 148, 163
Sebille, 43
Sebo, 163
Secg, 93
Secgwic, 93
Sechet, 68
Secuba, 201
Sedge, 93
Sedgeley, 93
Sedgewic, 93
Sedgewick, 93
Sedgewik, 93
Seely, 93
Seema, 171

Seeton, 93
Sefton, 93
Sefu, 71
Segar, 93
Segenam, 220
Seger, 93
Segesta, 193
Segulah, 155
Segunda, 266
Segundo, 211, 270
Seifred, 285
Seigmund, 285
Seignour, 110
Sein, 270
Seina, 266
Seireadan, 182
Seissyllwch, 300
Seith, 300
Seithved, 300
Sekani, 71
Sekhet, 68
Sel, 300
Sela, 155
Selby, 93, 285
Selden, 93, 285
Seldon, 93, 285
Sele, 155
Seleby, 93
Selena, 137
Selene, 137
Seleta, 155
Selia, 137
Selig, 93, 126
Selik, 126
Selima, 154
Selina, 137
Selk, 68
Selma, 52, 68, 280
Selwin, 33, 93
Selwine, 93
Selwyn, 33, 93
Selyf, 300
Selyv, 300
Semadar, 155
Semele, 137, 201
Semira, 155
Semyon, 249
Sena, 201
Senalda, 266
Senapus, 110
Senen, 159
Senet, 110
Senior, 110
Sennet, 110
Senon, 270
Senona, 266
Senta, 122
Sente, 122
Senusnet, 71
Seoirse, 148
Seonaid, 113
Seorsa, 148
Seorus, 118
Seosaimhin, 177
Seosaimhthin, 177
Seosamh, 118, 159
Seosaph, 159
Seppanen, 101

Sept, 71
Septima, 201
Septimus, 211
Serafim, 159
Serafin, 159, 270
Serafina, 185, 266
Serafine, 155
Seraphim, 159
Seraphina, 155
Seraphine, 155
Serapis, 71
Serefina, 155
Seren, 291
Serena, 185, 201, 266
Serene, 201
Sereno, 211
Serenus, 211
Serge, 211, 249
Sergio, 187, 211
Sergios, 211
Sergius, 211
Sergiusz, 211, 245
Serguei, 211, 249
Serhild, 122
Serhilda, 122
Serihilda, 122
Serihilde, 122
Serilda, 122, 280
Serilde, 280
Serina, 201
Seriozha, 211, 249
Seriozhenka, 211, 249
Serle, 285
Serophia, 302
Serpuhi, 40
Serq, 68
Set, 71, 160, 275
Setanta, 56
Seth, 71, 159
Sethos, 71
Seton, 93
Seumas, 118
Sever, 33
Severi, 101
Severin, 93, 211
Sevti, 166
Sewald, 93
Sewall, 93
Seward, 33, 93
Sewati, 222
Sewell, 93, 285
Seweryn, 211, 245
Sextein, 93
Sexton, 93
Sextus, 211
Seymour, 93, 110, 285
Sguelaiche, 118
Shabaka, 71
Shabnan, 240
Shabouh, 241
Shada, 214
Shaddoc, 93
Shaddock, 93
Shadi, 217
Shadwell, 93

Shahdi, 240
Shahin, 240
Shaibya, 166
Shaitan, 169
Shaka, 169
Shakeh, 40
Shakini, 166
Shakir, 39, 71
Shakra, 166
Shaktar, 169
Shakti, 169
Shalom, 160
Shalott, 43
Shalya, 169
Shamba, 169
Shami, 169
Shamir, 303
Shamus, 182
Shanahan, 182
Shanata, 171
Shandley, 93
Shandy, 93
Shane, 159
Shani, 68
Shankara, 169
Shanley, 182
Shannon, 182
Shanta, 166
Shapa, 166
Sharada, 166
Sharama, 166
Sharif, 39
Sharifa, 68
Sharifah, 37
Sharon, 155
Shashenka, 249
Shashi, 166, 171
Shashida, 169
Shasti, 166
Shatrevar, 241
Shattuck, 93
Shaughnessy, 182
Sha-ul, 159
Shauna, 177
Shaw, 93, 258
Shawe, 258
Shawn, 93, 177
Shayndel, 302
Shayne, 302
Shea, 182
Sheary, 182
Sheehan, 182
Sheelah, 177
Sheena, 155
Sheffield, 93
Sheila, 177
Sheiling, 258
Sheiramoth, 155
Shelby, 33, 93
Sheldon, 33, 93
Shelley, 29, 33, 75, 93
Shelly, 29
Shelomo, 160
Shelton, 93
Shemariah, 154
Shemus, 182
Shepard, 33, 93
Shephard, 33
Shepherd, 93
Shepley, 93

Sheply, 33, 93
Sherard, 33
Sherborne, 93
Sherbourn, 93
Sherbourne, 93
Sherburne, 93
Sheridan, 56, 182
Sherlock, 93
Sherman, 93
Sheron, 182
Sherri, 75
Sherry, 75
Sherwin, 33, 94
Sherwood, 94
Sherwyn, 33, 94
Shesha, 169
Sheshebens, 215
Shet, 160
Shetan, 169
Shideezhi, 217
Shifra, 155
Shilah, 222
Shima, 217
Shimasani, 217
Shim'on, 160
Shimshon, 159
Shipley, 94
Shipton, 94
Shira, 155
Shiri, 155
Shiriki, 222
Shirley, 75
Shitala, 166
Shiva, 169
Shiye, 222
Shizhe'e, 222
Shoemowetochaw-
    cawewahcatowe,
    220
Sholeh, 240
Sholto, 118
Shoshana, 266
Shoushan, 40
Shraddha, 166
Shri, 166
Shu, 71
Shudra, 169
Shukura, 68
Shulamit, 154
Shuman, 216
Shunnareh, 37
Shura, 249
Shurik, 249
Shurochka, 249
Sian, 291
Siany, 177
Siarl, 300
Siawn, 300
Sibeal, 177
Sibley, 29, 33,
    137, 211
Sibyl, 137
Sibyla, 107
Sibylla, 64, 137,
    273
Sichaeus, 211
Sicheii, 222
Siddael, 94
Siddell, 94
Side, 201
Sidell, 94

Sidera, 201
Siderea, 201
Sideria, 201
Sidero, 201
Sidney, 94, 110,
    148
Sidonia, 107, 155
Sidonie, 107, 155
Sidra, 201
Sidwell, 56, 94
Siefried, 285
Siegfried, 126
Siencyn, 300
Sif, 228
Sifiye, 71
Sigebert, 33
Sigehere, 94
Sigfreda, 122
Sigfrid, 126, 285
Sigfried, 285
Sigfrieda, 122
Sigfriede, 122
Siggeir, 236
Sighle, 113
Sigifrid, 126
Sigifrith, 126
Sigilwig, 122
Sigismonda, 280
Sigismondo, 285
Sigismund, 285
Sigismunda, 280
Sigiwald, 126
Sigmond, 236,
    285
Sigmund, 285
Sign, 228
Signa, 201
Signe, 201, 273
Signia, 201
Signild, 273
Signilda, 273
Signy, 228
Sigrath, 228
Sigrid, 61, 228,
    273
Sigun, 228
Sigune, 43
Sigurd, 236, 275
Sigurdhr, 236
Sigvard, 236, 275
Sigvat, 236
Sigwald, 126
Sigwalt, 126
Sigyn, 228
Sihtric, 33
Sihu, 214, 216
Sijur, 236
Sike, 222
Sik'is, 222
Sikyahonaw, 221
Sikyatavo, 221
Sil, 211
Silana, 107
Silas, 211
Sile, 113, 177
Sileas, 253
Silio, 211
Silis, 113
Silka, 201
Silke, 201
Silkie, 201
Sill, 211

Silny, 59
Silos, 211
Silsby, 94
Silva, 201
Silvain, 211
Silvanos, 211
Silvanus, 211
Silver, 29
Silvester, 211
Silvia, 201
Silvio, 187
Silvius, 211
Sim, 118, 258
Sima, 253
Siman, 59
Simao, 160
Simcha, 155, 159
Simen, 160
Simeon, 148, 160
Simin, 240
Simon, 148, 160
Simona, 155, 185,
    266
Simone, 107, 155
Simpson, 160
Simson, 160, 275
Sina, 201
Sinai, 160
Sinclair, 211, 258
Sindri, 236
Sine, 113, 177
Sinead, 155, 177
Sineidin, 177
Sinfiotli, 236
Sinmora, 228
Sinnoch, 300
Sinobia, 137
Sinon, 148, 159,
    211
Sinopa, 215
Sinope, 201
Sinovia, 137, 248
Sinya, 248
Siobhan, 155, 177
Siodhachan, 182
Siolat, 118
Siomon, 160
Sion, 300
Sioned, 291
Sior, 300
Sippora, 155
Siran, 40
Sirena, 137
Sirina, 137
Sirpuhi, 40
Sirvat, 40
Siseal, 211
Sisika, 214
Sissel, 228
Sisyphus, 148,
    211
Sita, 166, 171
Sitala, 217
Sitara, 166, 171
Siti, 68
Sitsi, 217
Siubhan, 113, 253
Siusan, 113, 253
Siv, 228, 236
Sive, 176
Siwili, 219
Sixtus, 211

Skade, 228
Skagi, 236
Skah, 223
Skalla, 236
Skallagrim, 236
Skalm, 228
Skamelson, 275
Skamkel, 236
Skanda, 169
Skapti, 236
Skarp, 236
Skarphedin, 236
Skeat, 94
Skeet, 94
Skefil, 236
Skeggi, 237
Skelley, 118
Skelly, 118
Skelton, 94
Skena, 253
Skene, 258
Skereye, 237
Skerry, 237
Skete, 94
Sketes, 94
Skidbladnir, 237
Skinfaxi, 237
Skipp, 237
Skipper, 94
Skippere, 94
Skipton, 94
Skirnir, 237
Skorri, 237
Skrymir, 237
Skuld, 228
Skule, 237
Skuli, 237
Skum, 237
Skye, 64
Skyla, 64
Skylar, 64
Slade, 94
Slaed, 94
Slaibhin, 118
Slaine, 177
Slainie, 107
Slania, 107
Slanie, 107
Slansky, 59
Slany, 177
Slaton, 94
Slava, 259
Slaven, 118
Slavik, 250, 260
Slavin, 118
Slavochka, 259
Slayton, 94
Slean, 33
Slecg, 33
Sleipnir, 237
Sleven, 118
Slevin, 118
Slevyn, 118
Sloan, 56, 118
Sloane, 56, 118
Sluaghan, 118
Smedley, 94
Smedt, 64
Smetheleah, 94
Smid, 64
Smit, 64
Smith, 94

Smyth, 94
Smythe, 94
Snaebjorn, 237
Sneferu, 71
Snell, 33
Snor, 228
Snora, 228
Snorri, 237
Snotra, 228
Snowden, 94
Soasan, 273
Sobk, 71
Socorro, 266
Socrates, 148
Sofi, 137
Sofia, 137, 266
Sofie, 64
Sofiya, 287
Sofiyko, 287
Sofronia, 137
Sohrab, 241
Sokanon, 215
Sokw, 215
Sol, 211
Solaina, 107
Solaine, 107
Solana, 266
Solange, 107
Soledad, 266
Soledada, 266
Solita, 201
Solmund, 237
Solomon, 160
Solon, 137
Solona, 137
Solone, 137
Solonie, 137
Solveig, 228, 273
Solvi, 237
Solvig, 122
Soma, 163, 171
Somer, 111
Somerled, 118
Somerset, 94
Somerton, 94
Somerville, 111
Somhairle, 118
Somnus, 211
Sondra, 137
Sonechka, 248
Songan, 219
Sonia, 248
Sonja, 259, 273
Sonnehilda, 280
Sonnehilde, 280
Sonya, 248, 273
Sooleawa, 215
Sophia, 137
Sophie, 137
Sophronia, 137
Soraya, 240
Sorcha, 177
Soredamors, 43
Sorel, 111
Soren, 62, 111,
    237, 275
Sorina, 61
Sorine, 61
Sorley, 182
Soroush, 241
Soroushi, 240
Sorrell, 111

Sosanna, 177
Soterios, 148
Southwell, 94
Sowi'ngwa, 221
Soyala, 216
Spalding, 94
Spangler, 126
Spark, 94
Sparke, 94
Spear, 94
Sped, 94
Speed, 94
Spelding, 94
Spencer, 94
Spengler, 126
Spenser, 94
Sperancita, 302
Speranza, 185, 201
Spere, 94
Spes, 201
Sprague, 285
Sproul, 94
Sprowle, 94
Spurius, 211
Spyridon, 148
Squier, 94
Squire, 94
Srinath, 172
Sruthair, 182
Sruthan, 182
St. Alban, 94
Stacey, 137, 211
Stacie, 137
Stacy, 137, 211
Staerling, 94
Staffan, 275
Staffen, 148
Stafford, 94
Stamford, 94
Stamitos, 148
Stan, 94
Stanberry, 94
Stanburh, 94
Stanbury, 94
Stancliff, 94
Stanclyf, 94
Standa, 59
Standish, 94
Stanedisc, 94
Stanfeld, 94
Stanfield, 94
Stanford, 94
Stanhop, 94
Stanhope, 94
Stanislas, 260
Stanislaus, 260
Stanislav, 59, 260
Stanislava, 201
Stanislov, 250
Stanley, 94
Stanly, 94
Stannes, 260
Stansie, 184
Stanton, 94
Stantun, 94
Stanway, 94
Stanweg, 94
Stanwic, 94
Stanwick, 94
Stanwik, 94
Stanwode, 94

Stanwood, 94
Stanwyk, 94
Star, 75, 201
Starbuck, 94
Starkad, 237
Starkadhr, 237
Starla, 75
Starling, 94
Starr, 75, 94
Stas, 260
Stasia, 137
Stasio, 260
Stasya, 247
Staunton, 94
Stavros, 148
Steadman, 33
Steafan, 148
Stearc, 33
Stearn, 94
Steathford, 94
Stedeman, 94
Stedman, 33, 94
Steen, 285
Stefan, 148, 245, 250, 275
Stefania, 107
Stefano, 148, 187, 270
Stefanos, 148
Stefanya, 248
Steffan, 300
Stefina, 137
Stefinia, 137
Stefn, 33
Stein, 126, 237
Steinar, 237
Steinbjorn, 237
Steinolf, 237
Steinthor, 237
Steinunn, 228
Steinvorr, 228
Steise, 137
Stella, 201, 273
Stelle, 201
Sten, 275, 285
Stepan, 33
Stephan, 250
Stephana, 137
Stephania, 137, 248
Stephanie, 107, 137
Stephano, 148
Stephen, 148
Stephene, 137
Stepka, 250
Sterling, 94
Stern, 94
Sterne, 94
Stesha, 248
Steven, 148
Steverino, 148
Stevie, 137
Steward, 94
Stewart, 33, 94
Stewert, 33, 94
Stheno, 137
Stiabhan, 118
Stian, 237
Stig, 275, 285
Stigandi, 237
Stigols, 95

Stiles, 95
Stille, 64
Stilleman, 94
Stillman, 33, 94
Stillmann, 94
Stilwell, 33
Stimula, 201
Stina, 61, 273
Stinne, 61
Stirling, 94
Stoc, 94
Stock, 94
Stockard, 75
Stockhard, 75
Stockhart, 75
Stockley, 95
Stockwell, 95
Stocleah, 95
Stocwiella, 95
Stod, 95
Stodd, 95
Stoddard, 95
Stoffel, 148
Stok, 94
Stoke, 95
Stokkard, 75
Storm, 33, 75, 95
Storme, 95
Stormie, 75
Stormy, 75
Storr, 237
Stowe, 95
Strahan, 182
Strang, 33, 95
Stratford, 95
Strep, 137
Strephon, 137
Strephonn, 137
Strifebjorn, 237
Strod, 95
Strong, 95
Stroud, 95
Struan, 258
Struana, 253
Struthers, 182
Stuart, 33, 94
Sturla, 237
Styles, 95
Styr, 237
Styx, 137
Suada, 201
Suadela, 137
Subha, 171
Subira, 68
Sucki, 220
Sudi, 71
Sue, 155
Suelita, 266
Suffield, 95
Sugn, 56
Sugyn, 300
Suidhne, 182
Suileabhan, 182
Sulaiman, 39
Suletu, 217
Sulis, 29
Sullivan, 182
Sully, 95
Sulyen, 300
Suma, 68, 75
Sumarlidi, 237
Sumarville, 111

Sumernor, 95
Sumerton, 94
Sumertun, 94
Summer, 75
Sumner, 95, 111
Sunhild, 280
Sunhilda, 280
Sunhilde, 280
Sunki, 216
Sunn, 29
Sunniva, 29
Sunny, 75
Sunreet, 169
Sunukkuhkau, 220
Supriya, 171
Sur, 166, 171
Surtr, 237
Surya, 172
Susan, 155
Susana, 266
Susanna, 155
Susannah, 155
Susie, 155
Susy, 155
Sutcliff, 95
Sutclyf, 95
Sutekh, 71
Suthclif, 95
Sutherland, 237, 258
Suthfeld, 95
Suthleah, 95
Suthley, 95
Suthrland, 237
Suttecliff, 95
Sutton, 95
Suzanna, 155
Suzanne, 107, 122
Suzetta, 155
Suzette, 107, 155
Svaldifari, 237
Svan, 237
Svanhild, 228
Svanhile, 228
Svann, 237
Svante, 273
Svart, 237
Svartkel, 237
Svea, 273
Svec, 59
Svein, 237
Sven, 275
Svenbjorn, 275
Svend, 62, 237, 275
Svenhild, 228
Svenhilda, 228
Svens, 275
Sverting, 237
Sveta, 248
Svetla, 58
Svetlana, 248
Svewn, 237
Sveyn, 237
Swain, 95, 285
Swanhild, 228
Swanhilda, 228, 280
Swanhilde, 228, 280

Swayn, 95
Sweeney, 182
Swift, 33
Swinton, 95
Swintun, 95
Swithun, 33
Sybil, 177
Sybilla, 137
Sybyl, 137
Sybylla, 64
Sydney, 94, 107, 110, 148
Sylanna, 201
Syllis, 201
Sylva, 201
Sylvan, 211
Sylvana, 201
Sylvania, 201
Sylvanus, 211
Sylvester, 211
Sylvia, 201
Sylwia, 243
Symaethis, 137, 201
Symeon, 148, 160
Symington, 95
Symontun, 95
Syn, 228
Syna, 137
Synn, 33
Synne, 29
Synnove, 29
Syrinx, 137
Syver, 236
Syvwlch, 300
Szczepan, 245

Taaveti, 160
Taavetti, 101
Taavi, 101, 160
Tab, 95, 126
Tabari, 39, 71
Tabbart, 126
Tabbert, 126
Tabia, 68
Tabitha, 137, 302
Tablita, 216
Tabor, 111, 163, 270
Tabora, 266
Taburer, 95
Tacita, 201
Tad, 300
Tadd, 300
Tadeo, 270, 303
Tadewi, 217
Tadhg, 56, 118, 148, 182
Tadita, 217
Tadleigh, 182
Taffy, 300
Tag, 285
Tage, 62, 275, 285
Taggart, 118
Tahir, 39
Tahirah, 37, 68
Tahkeome, 220
Tahki, 215
Tahmelapachme, 220

Taicligh, 182
Taidgh, 148
Taidhg, 118
Taigi, 217
Taillefer, 111
Taima, 214, 219
Taini, 217
Taipa, 217
Tait, 29, 75, 95, 237, 251, 275
Taite, 29
Taithleach, 113, 118
Taj, 169, 303
Tajo, 270, 285
Takala, 216
Takchawee, 218
Takis, 148
Takoda, 223
Takouhi, 40
Takshaka, 169
Tal, 155
Tala, 214
Talaith, 291
Talar, 291
Talbot, 111
Tale, 68
Talebot, 111
Taletha, 302
Talia, 137, 155
Talibah, 37, 68
Taliesin, 47, 56, 300
Talitha, 302
Tallwch, 300
Talo, 101
Talon, 95, 111
Talora, 155
Talori, 155
Talulah, 215
Talus, 148
Talutah, 218
Talya, 155
Talyessin, 300
Tama, 214
Tamar, 33, 155
Tamara, 155
Tamarah, 155
Tamary, 302
Tamas, 160
Tamika, 302
Tamir, 39
Tamma, 155
Tamnais, 258
Tamtun, 95
Tanaquil, 201
Tandu, 169
Tanechka, 248
Taneli, 101, 160
Tangakwunu, 221
Tangerina, 75
Tangerine, 75
Tanguy, 56
Tangwen, 291
Tania, 248
Tanichka, 248
Tanner, 95
Tannere, 95
Tanni, 237
Tansy, 201, 216
Tantalus, 148

Tanton, 95
Tanya, 248
Tapani, 160
Tapati, 167
Tapio, 101
Tara, 113, 167, 177, 253
Tarafah, 39
Taraka, 167
Taran, 56, 300
Taraneh, 240
Tarawg, 300
Tarchon, 211
Taredd, 300
Taregan, 220
Taren, 138, 300
Tarian, 291
Tarif, 39
Tarik, 39, 71
Tarjei, 237
Tarleton, 95
Tarnkappe, 237
Tarpeia, 201
Tarran, 300
Tarrant, 300
Tarren, 291
Tarsicius, 303
Tarsuinn, 258
Tarub, 37
Taryn, 138, 300
Tass, 163
Tassos, 137
Tasunke, 220
Tasya, 248
Tatanka-ptecila, 221
Tate, 29, 75, 95, 219
Tathagata, 169
Tathal, 300
Tatiana, 248
Tatum, 75
Tatyana, 248
Tau, 71
Tauret, 68
Tavey, 211, 258
Tavia, 253
Tavis, 258
Tavish, 258
Taweel, 39
Tawy, 300
Taxiarchai, 148
Tayanita, 215
Tayib, 169
Taylor, 111
Taysir, 39
Tayt, 95
Tayte, 29, 75, 95, 237
Teadoir, 148
Teaghue, 56, 182
Teague, 56, 118, 148, 182
Teamhair, 177
Tearlach, 111, 118, 258
Tearle, 95
Tearley, 118
Tearly, 118
Teca, 162
Tecla, 137
Tedman, 33, 285

Tedmond, 95
Tedmund, 33, 95, 285
Tedra, 137
Tedre, 137
Teetonka, 223
Tefnut, 68
Tegid, 56
Tegvan, 300
Tegyr, 300
Tehuti, 71
Tehya, 214
Teimhnean, 118
Teir, 300
Teirnon, 300
Teirtu, 56
Teirwaedd, 300
Teithi, 56, 300
Tekla, 137, 273
Tekli, 243
Telamon, 148
Telegonus, 148
Telek, 245
Telemachus, 148
Telephassa, 201
Telephus, 148
Teleri, 291
Teles, 201
Telfer, 111
Telfor, 111
Telford, 111
Telfour, 111
Tellan, 33
Tellus, 201
Telutci, 222
Telyn, 291
Teme, 155
Temima, 155
Temira, 155
Temman, 33
Tempeltun, 95
Tempeste, 107
Templa, 201
Templeton, 95
Ten Eyck, 64
Tennyson, 95
Tentagil, 47
Teodor, 245
Teodora, 185
Teodoro, 270
Teodors, 148
Teodory, 243
Teodozji, 243
Teofile, 148
Teoma, 303
Teon, 33
Teos, 245
Teppo, 101, 160
Ter Heide, 64
Terceira, 266
Terciero, 270
Teregud, 300
Teremun, 71
Terence, 211
Terentia, 137
Teresa, 137, 185
Terese, 137
Teresia, 273
Teresina, 137
Tereus, 148
Teris, 182
Terisita, 137

Terje, 237
Terminus, 211
Terpsichore, 137
Terra, 201
Terran, 138
Terrell, 95, 285
Terrence, 118, 182, 211
Terrian, 138
Terriana, 138
Terrill, 95, 285
Terris, 95, 285
Terriss, 182, 285
Terrwyn, 291
Terry, 137, 211, 285
Terrys, 95
Tertia, 201
Tertius, 211
Teryysone, 95
Terza, 185
Tesar, 59
Tesia, 138, 243
Tess, 137
Tessa, 137
Tessie, 137
Tethys, 137, 201
Teucer, 148
Teuthras, 148
Teva, 253
Tevel, 303
Tevis, 258
Tewdwr, 301
Teyen, 96
Teyrnon, 56
Thabit, 71
Thacher, 95
Thacker, 95
Thackere, 95
Thaddea, 137
Thaddeus, 160, 303
Thaddia, 137
Thadina, 155
Thadine, 155
Thady, 303
Thain, 95
Thaine, 95
Thais, 137
Thalassa, 137, 201
Thaleia, 137
Thalia, 137
Thamyris, 148
Thanasis, 148
Thanatos, 148
Thane, 95
Thangbrand, 237
Thanos, 148
Thatcher, 95
Thaukt, 228
Thaumas, 148
Thaw, 95
Thawain, 95
Thaxter, 95
Thayer, 285
Thayne, 95
Thea, 137
Thearl, 95
Thecla, 137
Theda, 137, 248
Thedya, 248

Thegn, 95
Thekla, 137
Thelma, 137
Thelxepei, 201
Thelxiepeia, 201
Thema, 68
Themis, 137
Thenoma, 137
Thenomia, 137
Theobald, 285
Theoclymenus, 148
Theodora, 137
Theodore, 148
Theodoric, 285
Theodorus, 64
Theodosia, 137, 248
Theodosios, 148
Theodrekr, 148
Theodric, 285
Theodrik, 285
Theola, 137
Theomund, 33, 95, 285
Theon, 148
Theona, 137
Theone, 137
Theophane, 138
Theophaneia, 138
Theophania, 138
Theophanie, 138
Theophile, 148
Theophilia, 138
Theora, 138
Theore, 138
Theoris, 68
Thera, 138
Theresa, 137
Therese, 137
Thermuthis, 68
Theron, 148
Thersites, 148
Theseus, 148
Thetis, 138
Thia, 137
Thialfi, 237
Thibaud, 111
Thierry, 111, 285
Thilo, 285
Thir, 228
Thira, 138
Thirza, 155
Thisbe, 138
Thjalfi, 237
Thjodhild, 228
Thjodhilda, 228
Thokk, 228
Thoma, 160
Thomas, 160, 303
Thomasin, 155
Thomkins, 96
Thomsina, 155
Thor, 62, 237, 275
Thora, 61, 138, 229, 280
Thorald, 237
Thoraldtun, 95

Thorarin, 228, 237
Thorbert, 237, 285
Thorberta, 228
Thorbiartr, 228, 237
Thorbjorg, 228
Thorbjorn, 237
Thorburn, 237
Thord, 237
Thordia, 228
Thordis, 228
Thordissa, 228
Thorfinn, 237, 238
Thorfinna, 228
Thorgerd, 228
Thorgils, 238
Thorgrim, 238
Thorgunn, 228
Thorgunna, 228
Thorhadd, 238
Thorhall, 238
Thorhalla, 228
Thorhalli, 238
Thorhild, 228
Thorhilda, 228
Thoridyss, 228
Thorir, 229, 238
Thorkatla, 228
Thorkel, 238
Thorlak, 238
Thorleif, 238
Thorleik, 238
Thorley, 95, 285
Thormod, 238
Thormond, 95
Thormund, 95
Thorn, 95
Thorndic, 95
Thorndike, 95
Thorndyke, 95
Thorne, 95
Thornley, 95
Thornly, 95
Thornton, 95
Thorntun, 95
Thorolf, 238
Thororm, 238
Thorp, 95
Thorpe, 95, 285
Thorstein, 238
Thorsten, 285
Thorualdr, 237
Thorunn, 228
Thorunna, 228
Thorvald, 238
Thorvid, 238
Thoth, 71
Thrain, 238
Thrand, 238
Thrasi, 238
Thrasius, 211
Throst, 238
Thrud, 228
Thrym, 238
Thrythwig, 96
Thunder, 95
Thurayya, 37
Thurhloew, 95
Thurid, 228

Thurleah, 95
Thurleigh, 95
Thurlow, 95, 238
Thurmond, 95
Thurstan, 95
Thurston, 95, 251, 285
Thurstun, 95
Thutmose, 71
Thyestes, 149
Thyra, 61, 138
Tiarchnach, 182
Tibalt, 126
Tibault, 111
Tibbot, 182
Tibelda, 122
Tibelde, 122
Tibeldie, 122
Tiberia, 185, 201
Tiberio, 187
Tibor, 260
Tiebout, 64
Tiege, 148
Tienette, 138
Tier, 182
Tiernan, 56, 182
Tiernay, 56
Tierney, 182
Tifany, 138
Tiffany, 138
Tiffeny, 138
Tighearnach, 182
Tigris, 149, 201
Tigrisa, 201
Tigrisia, 201
Tihkoosue, 220
T'iis, 222
Tikva, 155
Til, 285
Tila, 95
Tiladene, 95
Tilda, 107, 273, 280
Tilde, 280
Tilden, 95
Tilford, 95
Tilian, 34
Till, 285
Tille, 280
Tillman, 95
Tillmann, 285
Tilly, 107
Tilman, 95, 285
Tilton, 95
Timandra, 201
Timin, 172
Timon, 149
Timothea, 138, 149
Timotheos, 149
Timotheus, 300
Timothia, 138
Timothy, 149
Timun, 149
Tina, 75
Tind, 238
Tintagel, 47
Tioboid, 118
Tiomoid, 149
Tiphanie, 138
Tiponi, 216
Tira, 171, 253

Tirell, 95, 285
Tiresias, 149
Tiridates, 41
Tirtha, 171
Tiryns, 201
Tisiphone, 138
Tis-see-woo-na-tis, 215
Tita, 202
Titania, 138
Tithonus, 211
Tito, 149, 187, 211, 270
Titos, 149
Titus, 149, 211
Tityus, 149
Tiu, 238
Tiva, 216
Tivadar, 148
Tivona, 155
Tiwesdaeg, 75
Tjasse, 238
Toba, 155
Tobiah, 160
Tobias, 160, 270, 275
Tobin, 160
Tobrecan, 34
Tobrytan, 34
Toby, 160
Tocho, 221
Todd, 258
Todor, 148
Toft, 95
Togquos, 220
Tohopka, 221
Toibe, 155
Toinette, 202
Toirdealbach, 113
Toirdealbhach, 118
Toireasa, 177
Tokala, 221
Tolan, 34
Toland, 34, 96
Tolek, 245
Tolenka, 250
Toli, 270
Tolinka, 217
Tolland, 96
Tolman, 96
Tolucan, 34
Tolya, 250
Toman, 59
Tomas, 118, 160, 270
Tomasina, 155
Tomasine, 155
Tomek, 160
Tomik, 59
Tomislaw, 245
Tomkin, 96
Tomlin, 96
Tommaso, 187
Tomos, 300
Ton, 300
Tonda, 59
Tonia, 202
Tony, 211
Tooantuh, 220
Topaz, 202

Tor, 47, 71, 237, 275
Tora, 229, 273, 280
Torald, 237
Torbert, 285
Torberta, 228
Torbjorn, 275
Torborg, 275
Tordis, 229
Tore, 275
Toreth, 291
Torfi, 238
Torgeir, 237
Torger, 237
Torgny, 238, 275
Torgunna, 228
Torht, 34
Torhte, 34
Toril, 229
Torin, 182
Torkel, 275, 285
Torlan, 291
Torley, 95
Tormaigh, 182
Tormey, 182
Tormod, 118, 285
Torn, 95
Torne, 229
Torney, 229
Torny, 229
Torquil, 285
Torr, 34, 96
Torra, 254
Torrad, 238
Torrance, 118, 182
Torrans, 182
Torrence, 182
Torrentem, 211
Torrey, 56
Torri, 292
Torsten, 275, 285
Tortain, 47
Torunn, 228, 229
Tory, 56, 182
Toryn, 182
Tosca, 202
Toscana, 202
Tosia, 137
Tostig, 96
Tosya, 250
Tote, 48
Totsi, 216
Toukere, 96
Tourmaline, 302
Tournour, 96
Toussaint, 111
Tova, 155
Tove, 229
Tovi, 160
Towley, 96
Townly, 96
Townsend, 96
Toxeus, 149
Trace, 34
Tracey, 34, 149
Trachmyr, 301
Tracy, 34, 137, 149, 211
Trahayarn, 301
Trahern, 56, 301

Traugott, 285
Travers, 111
Traviata, 185
Travis, 111
Treabhar, 182
Treacy, 182
Treadway, 96
Treasa, 177
Treasach, 182
Treasigh, 182
Tredan, 34
Treddian, 34
Tredway, 96
Treffen, 126
Treise, 177
Trella, 266
Tremaine, 56
Tremayne, 56, 301
Tremen, 301
Trennen, 126
Trent, 96, 211, 301
Treowbrycg, 96
Treowe, 96
Treoweman, 96
Tressam, 137
Treszka, 162
Tretan, 126
Trevelian, 301
Trevelyan, 301
Trevor, 56, 182
Trevrizent, 47
Trigg, 238
Trilby, 185, 273
Trillare, 185
Trina, 138, 273
Trind, 273
Trine, 138, 229, 273
Trinetta, 107
Trinette, 107
Tringad, 301
Trinity, 202
Trip, 96
Tripada, 170
Tripp, 96
Tripper, 96
Triptolemus, 149
Trisha, 171
Trishna, 167
Trisna, 167
Trista, 185, 202
Tristam, 211
Tristan, 47, 211, 301
Triste, 202
Tristram, 47, 211, 301
Triton, 149, 211
Trivia, 202
Trix, 202
Trixie, 202
Trixy, 202
Trofimoff, 250
Troilus, 211
Tron, 238
Trond, 238
Trophonius, 149
Tros, 211
Trowbridge, 96
Trowbrydge, 96

Troy, 111
Troyes, 111
Truda, 122, 229
Trudchen, 122
Trude, 122, 229
Trudel, 61
True, 96
Truesdale, 96
Truesdell, 96
Truitestall, 96
Truman, 96
Trumbald, 96
Trumball, 96
Trumble, 96
Trumen, 96
Trwyth, 56
Tryamon, 43
Tryffin, 301
Trygg, 238
Tryggr, 238
Trygve, 238
Trymian, 34
Trymman, 34
Tryn, 138
Tryna, 138
Tryne, 138
Trynt, 301
Tryp, 96
Tryphaena, 202
Tryphana, 202
Tryphena, 202
Trypp, 96
Trystan, 301
Tse, 222
Tsekani, 71
Tsidhqiyah, 160
Tsifira, 155
Tsiishch'ili, 222
Tuathal, 118
Tuccia, 202
Tucker, 96
Tuckere, 96
Tuder, 148
Tudor, 148, 301
Tuesday, 75
Tugenda, 122
Tuireann, 56
Tuketu, 222
Tulia, 202
Tulio, 211, 270
Tulley, 118
Tullia, 177, 202
Tulliola, 202
Tullius, 211
Tullus, 211
Tully, 118, 182,
    211
Tulsi, 167
Tum, 71
Tumaini, 71
Tunde, 162
Tunleah, 96
Tuomas, 101
Tuomas, 160
Tupi, 222
Tupper, 96
Tuppere, 96
Turannos, 149
Ture, 275
Turfeinar, 238
Turi, 56, 270

Turner, 96, 111,
    211
Turnus, 211
Turpin, 238
Turquine, 47
Turyahu, 160
Tusya, 250
Tutankhamun,
    71
Tutilina, 202
Tuvya, 160
Tuwa, 216
Tuxford, 238
Twain, 96
Twein, 96
Twiford, 96
Twigmuntus,
    275
Twitchel, 96
Twitchell, 96
Twm, 301
Twrch, 56, 301
Twrgadarn, 301
Twyford, 96
Twyla, 75
Txanton, 49, 211
Txomin, 49, 211
Tydeus, 149
Tye, 96
Tyeis, 111
Tyesone, 96
Tyg, 96
Tyla, 95
Tyler, 96
Tylere, 96
Tymek, 149
Tymon, 149
Tymoteusz, 149
Tyna, 75
Tynan, 118
Tyndareus, 149
Tyne, 75
Tynet, 138
Typhoeus, 149
Typhon, 71, 149
Tyr, 238
Tyra, 138, 253
Tyre, 211
Tyrell, 95
Tyrkir, 238
Tyro, 138
Tyrone, 149
Tyson, 96, 111,
    285
Tywysog, 301
Tzadok, 160
Tzefanyah, 160
Tzefanyahu, 160
Tzigane, 162
Tzilla, 155
Tzion, 160
Tzippa, 155
Tzivia, 155
Tziyona, 155
Tzuriel, 160
Tzvi, 160
Tzzipporah, 155

Uadjit, 68
Uaid, 182
Uaine, 182
Uald, 229, 280

Ualda, 280
Ualtar, 182
Uatchit, 68
Ubaid, 71
Ubel, 126
Ubert, 285
Uberto, 285
Uchdryd, 56, 301
Udale, 96
Udall, 96
Udayle, 96
Udela, 29
Udele, 29
Udell, 96
Udo, 286
Udolf, 96
Udolph, 96
Ufa, 71
Ugbjorn, 238
Ugo, 187, 285
Ugutz, 49
Uigbiorn, 238
Uileog, 285
Uilleam, 118
Uilliam, 285
Uisdean, 118,
    285
Uiseann, 211
Uisnech, 56
Uistean, 285
Uja, 170
Ula, 52
Uland, 285
Ulf, 238, 275
Ulfar, 238
Ulfmaerr, 238
Ulfred, 96
Ulger, 96
Uli, 122, 126
Ulicia, 177
Ulik, 285
Ulka, 122
Ull, 238
Ulla, 122, 273
Ullock, 96
Ullok, 96
Ulmar, 96
Ulmarr, 96
Ulmer, 238
Ulric, 285
Ulrica, 122, 280
Ulrich, 126
Ulrik, 62, 285
Ulrika, 273, 280
Ulrike, 122
Ulvelaik, 96
Ulysses, 149, 212
Ulz, 126
Uma, 167, 171
Umar, 39
Umarah, 39
Umayma, 68
Umi, 71
Umm, 68
Una, 52, 112,
    177, 202, 216,
    292
Unai, 49
Undina, 202
Undine, 202
Undinia, 202
Ungus, 177

Uni, 238
Unig, 301
Unika, 71
Unity, 177
Unn, 229
Unne, 229
Un-nefer, 70
Unwin, 96
Unwine, 96
Unwyn, 96
Uny, 177
Upala, 167, 302
Upchurch, 96
Upton, 34, 96
Uptun, 96
Upwode, 96
Upwood, 96
Ur, 71
Ur-Atum, 71
Ura, 238
Urania, 138
Uranus, 149
Urbain, 212
Urban, 212
Urbana, 202
Urbania, 202
Urbano, 270
Urbi, 68
Urd, 229
Uri, 160
Uriah, 160
Urian, 149
Urice, 155
Uriel, 160
Urien, 47
Uriens, 47
Urika, 217
Urit, 155
Urquhart, 258
Ursa, 138
Ursel, 138
Urselina, 202
Urseline, 202
Ursola, 202, 248
Ursula, 138, 202,
    248
Ursule, 202
Ursulina, 266
Urtzi, 49
Uryen, 301
Urzula, 202
Usenech, 56
Usha, 167, 171
Ushas, 167
Usi, 71
Usk-water, 57
Usoa, 266
Ustean, 285
Utathya, 170
Utgard-Loki, 238
Uther, 47, 182,
    285
Uthman, 71
Utina, 214
Uwaine, 47
Uwayne, 47
Uwe, 286
Uzumati, 222
Uzziah, 160
Uzziel, 160
Uzziye, 155

Vac, 167
Vach, 167
Vachel, 111
Vaclar, 260
Vacuna, 202
Vaddon, 301
Vaden, 111
Vadin, 172
Vadit, 155
Vaetild, 229
Vaetilda, 229
Vail, 96, 111
Vaino, 101
Vairocana, 171
Vaive atoish, 220
Vaiveahtoish,
    220
Val, 202, 212, 241
Vala, 292
Valara, 107
Valari, 202
Valarie, 202
Valborg, 275
Valborga, 122
Valbrand, 238
Valda, 229, 280
Valdemar, 126,
    275
Valdemarr, 126
Valdis, 229, 286
Valdislava, 259
Vale, 96
Valeda, 202
Valencia, 202
Valens, 212
Valentia, 202
Valentijn, 212
Valentin, 212,
    275
Valentina, 185,
    202, 248, 266
Valentine, 212
Valentino, 187,
    212
Valentyn, 212
Valera, 212
Valeraine, 107
Valere, 107
Valeria, 202
Valerian, 212
Valerie, 107
Valerii, 212, 250
Valerijs, 212
Valerik, 212, 250
Valerio, 187, 212
Valerius, 212
Valery, 202
Valeska, 248, 259
Valfrid, 275
Valgard, 238
Valgerd, 229
Vali, 238
Valiant, 96, 111
Valin, 172
Valkoinen, 101
Valkyrie, 229
Vallis, 111
Vallois, 111
Vallonia, 202
Valmiki, 170
Valonia, 202
Valora, 202

Valorous, 202
Valter, 276, 286
Valthjof, 238
Van, 64
Van Aken, 64
Van Eych, 65
Van Ness, 65
Vance, 96
Vanda, 122, 244
Vande, 122
Vandenberg, 64
Vanderbilt, 64
Vanderpool, 64
Vanderveer, 65
Vandrad, 238
Vandyke, 65
Vanechka, 250
Vanessa, 202
Vania, 138, 155, 248
Vanir, 238
Vanko, 149, 288
Vanna, 138, 155
Vannes, 96
Vanny, 138
Vanora, 292
Vanya, 248
Vanyusha, 250
Vappu, 101
Var, 229
Vara, 138
Varaza, 167
Varda, 155
Vardan, 111
Varden, 57, 111
Vardit, 155
Vardon, 57, 111
Vareck, 96
Vared, 155
Varek, 96
Vargovic, 59
Varian, 212
Varick, 286
Varik, 96, 286
Varina, 259
Varinka, 248
Varney, 57
Varouna, 171
Vartan, 41
Vartoughi, 40
Varun, 172
Varuna, 170
Varunani, 167
Varushka, 248
Varvara, 138, 248, 259
Varya, 248
Varyk, 96
Vas, 250
Vasek, 59, 260
Vashti, 240
Vasileios, 149
Vasilii, 250
Vasilis, 149
Vasilissa, 248
Vasin, 170
Vasistha, 170
Vasos, 149
Vassi, 250
Vassilissa, 248
Vassily, 250, 260
Vasu, 170

Vasuki, 170, 172
Vasya, 248, 250
Vasyl, 149
Vasylko, 149, 288
Vasyltso, 149
Vater, 286
Vatt, 276
Vaughn, 57, 301
Vavara, 138
Vavay, 202
Vayle, 96, 111
Vayu, 171
Ve, 238
Veda, 302
Vedas, 171
Vedetta, 107, 185
Vedette, 107, 185
Vedia, 273, 280
Vedis, 273, 280
Vega, 37, 202, 273
Vegard, 238
Vegeir, 238
Veit, 212
Velaug, 229
Velda, 280
Veleda, 280
Velief, 238
Velika, 248, 259
Vellamo, 100
Velouette, 75
Velvel, 303
Velvet, 75
Vema, 167
Venamin, 160
Vencel, 164
Venedictos, 212
Venessa, 138, 202
Venetia, 52
Veniamin, 160
Venilia, 202
Venita, 202
Venjamin, 160
Ventura, 266
Venus, 202
Vera, 202, 248
Veradis, 202
Veradisia, 202
Verbane, 202
Verbena, 202
Verbenae, 202
Verbenia, 202
Verbrugge, 65
Verda, 202
Verdad, 267
Verdandi, 229
Verddun, 111
Verel, 111
Verena, 122, 280
Verene, 122
Verge, 34
Vergil, 212
Verina, 122, 280
Verna, 202
Vernados, 126
Vernay, 111
Verne, 212
Verner, 276, 286
Verney, 111
Vernita, 202
Vernon, 111, 212

Vernus, 212
Verochka, 248
Veronica, 138, 202
Veronicha, 138
Veronika, 138, 202
Veronique, 107
Verrall, 111
Verrell, 111
Verrill, 111
Vertumnus, 212
Veryl, 111
Vespera, 202
Vesperia, 202
Vespira, 202
Vesta, 202
Vestar, 238
Vestein, 238
Veta, 202, 267
Veto, 270
Vevila, 177
Vevina, 177
Viator, 212
Vibald, 238
Vibeke, 61, 122
Vibishana, 170
Vic, 111
Vicenta, 267
Vick, 111
Vicq, 111
Victor, 212, 270
Victoria, 202
Victorien, 212
Victorin, 212
Victorina, 107
Victorine, 107
Victoro, 270
Victrix, 202
Victrixa, 202
Vicuska, 162
Vida, 155
Vidal, 270
Vidar, 238
Vidette, 155
Vidis, 280
Vidonia, 302
Vidor, 164, 212
Vifil, 238
Vigdis, 229, 280
Vigfus, 238
Vigilia, 202
Vignetta, 107
Vignette, 107
Vigrid, 238
Vigsterk, 238
Viho, 220
Vijay, 172
Vijaya, 171
Vika, 254
Viking, 239
Viktor, 164, 212, 250
Viktoras, 212
Viktoria, 162, 202, 273
Viktoryn, 212
Vilhelm, 62, 276, 286
Vilhelmina, 273, 280
Vilhelms, 286

Vilho, 286
Vili, 239, 286
Vilis, 286
Viljo, 101, 286
Villborg, 229
Villetta, 107
Villette, 107
Vilma, 248, 273, 280
Vilmos, 286
Vimka, 260
Vina, 167, 267
Vinata, 167
Vince, 212
Vincens, 212
Vincent, 212
Vincente, 212, 270
Vincentia, 202
Vincenzio, 187, 212
Vincenzo, 212
Vinci, 212
Vincien, 212
Vincze, 164, 212
Vineeta, 167
Vingon, 96
Vinn, 96
Vinnie, 212
Vinson, 96
Vinsone, 96
Vinzenz, 212
Viola, 202, 273
Violet, 185
Violetta, 107, 185
Viollette, 107
Vipponah, 220
Viradecthis, 29
Virag, 162
Virdia, 202
Virdis, 202
Virdisa, 202
Virdisia, 202
Virgil, 212
Virgilia, 202
Virgilio, 212, 270
Virginia, 185, 202, 267, 273
Virilis, 202
Virtus, 202
Visha, 170
Vishnu, 172
Vita, 202
Vital, 212
Vitale, 212
Vitenka, 212, 250
Vitia, 202
Vito, 187, 212, 270
Vittoria, 202, 267
Vittorio, 187, 212
Vitus, 212
Viva, 162
Viveca, 251
Vivek, 170
Viveka, 122, 248, 251, 273
Vivian, 202
Viviana, 185, 202
Viviane, 43
Vivien, 43, 212

Vivienne, 107, 202
Vivika, 167
Vladik, 250, 260
Vladimer, 260
Vladimir, 260
Vladimiru, 260
Vladislav, 250, 260
Vladislava, 260
Vladmir, 250
Vladmiri, 250
Vladsislas, 250
Vladya, 250, 260
Vlasta, 58
Vogel, 65
Vohkinne, 220
Voistitoevitz, 220
Voisttitoevetz, 220
Vokivocummast, 220
Volante, 185
Voleta, 107
Voletta, 107
Volker, 126, 286
Vollny, 126
Volney, 126, 286
Volodya, 250, 260
Volsung, 239
Volupia, 202
Volva, 229
Vor, 229
Vortigern, 47, 303
Vortimer, 47
Voshkie, 40
Vova, 260
Vrba, 59
Vrishni, 170
Vritra, 170
Vromme, 65
Vulcan, 212
Vyacheslav, 250, 260
Vyasa, 170
Vychan, 301

Wacfeld, 96
Wachiwi, 218
Wacian, 34, 96
Wacleah, 96
Wacuman, 96
Wada, 96
Wadanhyll, 97
Wade, 34, 96
Wadley, 96
Wadsworth, 96
Wadu, 301
Waed, 96
Waefreleah, 97
Waelfwulf, 34
Waer, 97
Waerheall, 99
Waeringawicum, 97
Waescburne, 97
Wafiyy, 39
Wagner, 126
Wahanassatta, 220

Wahchinksapa, 223
Wahchintonka, 223
Wahkan, 223
Wain, 97
Wainwright, 96
Wait, 96
Waite, 96
Wakanda, 218
Wake, 96
Wakefield, 96
Wakeley, 96
Wakeman, 96
Waki, 216
Wakiza, 219
Walborga, 122
Walbridge, 96
Walbrydge, 96
Walburga, 280
Walburgha, 280
Walby, 96
Walcot, 97
Walcott, 97
Walda, 122
Waldburga, 122
Waldemar, 126, 245, 286
Waldemarr, 126, 286
Walden, 97, 286
Waldhramm, 126
Waldifrid, 126
Waldmunt, 126
Waldo, 126, 286
Waldon, 97
Waldram, 286
Waldrom, 126
Waldron, 97, 126
Waleis, 75, 97
Walerian, 212, 245
Waleron, 245
Walford, 97
Walfred, 126
Walfrid, 126
Walidah, 68
Waljan, 301
Walker, 97
Wallace, 34, 97, 126, 258, 286
Wallache, 126
Waller, 97, 126
Wallis, 34, 75, 97, 286
Walmond, 126
Walsh, 97
Walt, 286
Walten, 126
Walter, 126, 286
Walthari, 126
Walther, 286
Walton, 97, 126
Walworth, 97
Walwyn, 97
Wamblee, 223
Wambleeska, 223
Wambli-waste, 221
Wamukota, 71
Wanageeska, 223
Wanahton, 223

Wanda, 122, 280
Wande, 122
Wandis, 280
Wandy, 122
Waneta, 214
Wanetta, 75
Wanikiya, 223
Wann, 34, 75
Wapi, 219
Waqi, 37
Waquini, 220
Ward, 97, 182, 286
Warda, 122
Warde, 97
Wardell, 97
Warden, 97
Wardley, 97
Ware, 34, 97
Wareine, 97
Waren, 126
Warenhari, 126
Warfield, 97
Warford, 97
Warian, 34
Waring, 212, 286
Warleigh, 97
Warley, 97
Warner, 126, 286
Warrane, 111
Warren, 97, 126, 286
Warrick, 97, 286
Warton, 97
Wartun, 97
Warwick, 97, 286
Warwyk, 97, 286
Washbourne, 97
Washburn, 97
Washburne, 97
Washington, 97, 286
Wasim, 39
Wat, 97, 286
Watelford, 97
Watford, 97
Watkins, 97
Watson, 97
Watt, 97, 286
Wattekinson, 97
Wattesone, 97
Wattikinson, 97
Wattkins, 97
Watts, 97
Wattson, 97
Wauna, 217
Waverly, 97
Wayland, 97
Wayne, 97
Wayte, 96
Wealaworth, 97
Weallcot, 97
Weallere, 97
Weard, 97
Weardhyll, 97
Weardleah, 97
Weatherby, 98
Weatherly, 98
Weayaya, 223
Webb, 97
Webbe, 97
Webbeleah, 97

Webber, 126
Webbestre, 97
Weber, 126
Webley, 97
Webster, 97
Weddell, 97
Weeko, 218
Wegland, 97
Weifield, 97
Weiford, 97
Weirley, 97
Welborn, 97
Welborne, 97
Welburn, 97
Welby, 97, 251
Welch, 97
Welcome, 75
Welda, 122
Weldon, 97, 286
Welford, 97
Welles, 97
Wellington, 34, 97
Wellington, 97
Wells, 97
Welsa, 75
Welsh, 97
Welsie, 75
Welton, 97
Wematin, 220
Wemilat, 219
Wenceslaus, 260
Wenceslava, 260
Wenda, 75, 280
Wende, 280
Wendel, 126, 286
Wendelin, 280
Wendelina, 280
Wendeline, 280
Wendell, 126, 286
Wendlesora, 98
Wenhaver, 43
Wenona, 214, 218
Wenonah, 218
Wentworth, 97
Weolingtun, 97
Weorth, 99
Werbenec, 301
Werhar, 286
Werian, 34
Werner, 126, 286
Weronikia, 244
Wes, 97
Wesley, 97
West, 97
Westbroc, 97
Westbrook, 97
Westby, 98
Westcot, 98
Westcott, 98
Westleah, 97
Westley, 97
Weston, 98
Westun, 98
Wetherby, 98
Wetherly, 98
Wethrby, 98
Wethrleah, 98
Wevers, 65
Weyland, 97

Weylin, 57
Weylyn, 57
Wharton, 98
Wheatley, 98
Wheeler, 98
Whelan, 182
Whistler, 98
Whitby, 98, 251
Whitcomb, 98
Whitelaw, 98
Whitfield, 98
Whitford, 98
Whitlaw, 98
Whitley, 98
Whitlock, 98
Whitman, 98
Whitmoor, 98
Whitmore, 98
Whitney, 29, 34, 98
Whittaker, 98
Whytlok, 98
Wiatt, 99, 111
Wicapi wakan, 215
Wicasa, 221
Wiccum, 98
Wicek, 212
Wicenty, 212
Wichamm, 98
Wichell, 98
Wickam, 98
Wickley, 98
Wicleah, 98
Wicus, 212, 245
Widad, 37
Wido, 122
Wiellaburne, 97
Wiellaby, 97
Wielladun, 97
Wiellaford, 97
Wiellatun, 97
Wienczyslaw, 245
Wies, 286
Wigburg, 64
Wigmaere, 99
Wigman, 99
Wihakayda, 218
Wikimak, 215
Wikitoria, 244
Wikta, 244
Wiktor, 245
Wiktorja, 244
Wikvaya, 221
Wilbart, 126
Wilbert, 98, 126
Wilbur, 34, 98, 126
Wilburt, 98, 126
Wilda, 29, 122
Wilde, 122
Wildon, 98
Wileen, 280
Wilford, 98
Wilfred, 98, 126, 286
Wilfrid, 34, 98, 126, 286
Wilfryd, 98
Wilhelm, 126, 286

Wilhelmina, 123, 280
Wilhelmine, 61, 123
Wilhelmus, 286
Wilhemina, 280
Wilhemine, 280
Will, 98, 286
Willa, 29, 75, 98, 280
Willaburh, 98
Willamar, 126
Willan, 34
Willaperht, 126
Willard, 98, 286
Willem, 286
Willesone, 98
Willette, 280
Willhard, 98
William, 98, 111, 286
Williamon, 126
Williams, 98
Williamson, 98
Willifrid, 126
Willimod, 126
Willis, 98
Willmar, 126
Willmarr, 126
Willoughby, 98
Wilmar, 126, 286
Wilmer, 126, 286
Wilmet, 280
Wilmod, 126
Wilmot, 126, 286
Wilna, 280
Wilny, 219
Wilona, 29
Wilone, 29
Wilpert, 126
Wilson, 98, 286
Wilton, 98
Wilva, 280
Wim, 286
Win, 98
Wincel, 98
Wincent, 212, 245
Wincent, 245
Winchell, 34
Windgate, 98
Windham, 99
Windsor, 98, 286
Wine, 34, 98
Winefeld, 286
Winefield, 98
Winefrith, 98
Winema, 214
Winetorp, 98
Winfield, 98, 286
Winfred, 98, 286
Winfreda, 280
Winfrid, 98
Winfrith, 98
Winfryd, 286
Wingate, 98
Winifred, 123, 280
Winifrid, 123, 280
Winifrida, 123
Winifride, 123
Winn, 98, 301

Winnie, 52
Winnifred, 292
Winola, 123
Winona, 218
Winslow, 98
Winslowe, 98
Winsor, 98, 286
Winston, 98
Winswode, 98
Wintanweorth, 97
Winter, 34, 98
Winthorp, 98
Winthrop, 98, 286
Winton, 98
Winward, 98
Winwodem, 98
Winwood, 98
Wira, 244
Wireceaster, 99
Wirke, 244
Wirt, 34
Wissian, 34
Wit, 65, 212, 245
Witashnah, 218
Withypoll, 75
Witt, 98
Witta, 98
Wittahere, 98
Wittatun, 99
Witter, 98
Witton, 99
Wlader, 286
Wmffre, 301
Wodeleah, 99
Woden, 34
Woglinda, 229
Wohehiv, 220
Wokaihwokomas, 220
Wolcott, 99
Wolf, 99, 286
Wolfcot, 99
Wolfe, 99, 286
Wolfgang, 126, 286
Wolfgar, 286
Wolfram, 286
Wolfric, 126
Wolfrick, 126
Wolfrik, 126
Woodley, 99
Woodman, 99
Woodrow, 99
Woodruff, 99
Woodward, 99
Woolcott, 99
Woolsey, 99
Worcester, 99
Worden, 97, 99
Wordsworth, 99
Worrell, 99
Worth, 99
Worthington, 34
Worton, 99
Wotan, 126
Woudman, 65
Wouter, 286
Wray, 239
Wregan, 34
Wren, 301

Wright, 34, 99
Wrnach, 301
Wryhta, 99
Wudoweard, 99
Wuhur, 286
Wulf, 34, 99
Wulfcot, 99
Wulffrith, 99
Wulfgar, 34, 99
Wulfhere, 34
Wulfsige, 99
Wulfweardsweorth, 99
Wurt, 34
Wuti, 216
Wuyi, 222
Wyanet, 214
Wyatt, 99, 111
Wybjorn, 239
Wyborn, 239
Wycliff, 99
Wyclyf, 99
Wylie, 34
Wyligby, 98
Wylingford, 98
Wylltun, 98
Wyman, 34, 99
Wymer, 99
Wyn, 292, 301
Wynchell, 34
Wynda, 254
Wyndham, 99
Wyne, 34, 98
Wynfield, 98
Wynfred, 286
Wynfreda, 280
Wynfrid, 98
Wynfrith, 98
Wynifred, 280
Wynn, 301
Wynne, 52, 57, 292
Wynnie, 52
Wynnifred, 292
Wynono, 219
Wynston, 98
Wynter, 98
Wynthrop, 98
Wynward, 98
Wynwode, 98
Wyrttun, 99
Wyth, 99
Wythe, 99

Xabat, 270
Xabier, 49
Xalbador, 270
Xalbadora, 267
Xalvador, 270
Xalvadora, 267
Xantha, 138
Xanthe, 138, 202
Xanthia, 138
Xanthus, 149, 212
Xanti, 49
Xarles, 111
Xavier, 39, 49, 270
Xavierra, 107
Xavierre, 107
Xenia, 138

Xeno, 149
Xenophon, 149
Xenos, 149
Xerxes, 149, 241
Xever, 270
Xevera, 267
Xeveria, 267
Xhosa, 302
Ximen, 160
Ximon, 49, 160
Ximun, 49, 160
Xuthus, 149
Xylia, 138
Xyliana, 138
Xylina, 138
Xylinia, 138
Xylon, 149
Xylona, 138

Yaakov, 160
Ya-akove, 155
Yachne, 155, 244
Yacoub, 39
Ya-el, 155
Yafeu, 71
Yaffa, 155
Yaffit, 155
Yagil, 160
Yago, 160, 270
Yahto, 223
Yahya, 71
Yair, 160
Yakov, 160, 250
Yale, 99
Yalena, 138, 248
Yalenchka, 248
Yalene, 138
Yama, 172
Yaman, 39
Yaminah, 68
Yamka, 216
Yamuna, 167
Yanamari, 48
Yanamaria, 267
Yanamarie, 267
Yancy, 219
Yanisin, 222
Yannis, 160
Yaphet, 160
Yardane, 160
Yardenah, 155
Yardley, 99
Yardly, 99
Yarema, 160
Yaremka, 160, 250
Yarkona, 155
Yaron, 160
Yaryna, 287
Yas, 222
Yasha, 250
Yasiman, 167
Yasin, 39
Yasir, 39
Yasmeen, 37
Yasmin, 37
Yasmina, 37, 167
Yasmine, 167
Yates, 99
Yavin, 160
Yazhi, 217
Yazid, 71

Yder, 47
Yechurun, 160
Yedda, 75
Yedidah, 155
Yedidiah, 160
Yedidyah, 160
Yeeshai, 160
Yehoash, 160
Yehonadov, 160
Yehor, 149
Yehoshua, 160
Yehuda, 160
Yehudi, 160
Yehudit, 155
Yelizaveta, 248
Yelizavetam, 155
Yelysaveta, 155, 287
Yeoman, 99
Yepa, 214
Yera, 48
Yerachmiel, 160
Yerik, 160, 250
Yermolay, 250
Yerucham, 160
Yervant, 41
Yeshaya, 160
Yetsye, 155
Yetta, 75
Yeva, 155, 287
Yevhen, 288
Yevheniy, 288
Yevtsye, 287
Yevunye, 155
Ygerne, 43
Yggsdrasil, 229
Yiftach, 160
Yigil, 160
Yigol, 160
Yiska, 222
Yisreal, 160
Yissachar, 160
Yitzchak, 160
Ymir, 239
Yngvar, 239
Yngve, 276
Yngvild, 229
Ynyr, 301
Yoana, 267
Yocheved, 155
Yoel, 160
Yo-el, 160
Yoki, 216
Yolanda, 107, 138, 267
Yolande, 107, 138
Yolanthe, 107
Yolette, 107
Yoman, 99
Yona, 155
Yonah, 160
Yonina, 155
Yonita, 155
Yordana, 155
York, 57, 99
Yoseba, 155
Yosebe, 155
Yosepha, 155
Yosephina, 155
Yoskolo, 219
Yosu, 49
Yovela, 155

Yrar, 239
Yrjo, 101, 149
Yrre, 34
Ysabel, 185
Ysabelle, 185
Ysbaddaden, 47
Ysbail, 292
Ysberin, 301
Ysberyr, 301
Yserone, 43
Yseult, 52, 107, 123
Ysgawyn, 301
Ysgithyrwyn, 301
Ysgonan, 301
Ysolde, 43
Yspadaden, 301
Yspaddaden, 57
Yuhudit, 155
Yul, 99
Yule, 99, 229
Yulene, 202
Yulenka, 202, 248
Yulenke, 202
Yuli, 49, 212
Yulia, 202
Yuliya, 202, 248
Yuma, 219
Yura, 149, 250
Yure, 149, 288
Yuri, 149, 250
Yurii, 149, 250
Yurik, 250
Yurochka, 149, 250
Yusef, 160
Yusuf, 39
Yuta, 155
Yves, 111
Yvet, 111
Yvette, 107
Yvon, 111
Yvonne, 107

Zabrina, 75
Zacarias, 270
Zachaios, 160
Zachariah, 160
Zacharias, 160
Zachary, 160
Zachery, 160
Zada, 37
Zadok, 160
Zadornin, 49
Zafir, 39
Zafirah, 37
Zagir, 40
Zagiri, 40
Zahavah, 155
Zahid, 39
Zahir, 39
Zahirah, 37
Zahra, 37, 68
Zahrah, 37
Zahur, 71
Zaid, 71
Zaida, 37
Zaira, 177
Zakarij, 260
Zaki, 39
Zale, 149

Zalika, 68
Zaliki, 68
Zaltana, 214
Zamora, 155, 267
Zandra, 138
Zane, 160
Zaneta, 155, 248
Zani, 160
Zanna, 155, 244
Zapotocky, 59
Zara, 37, 107, 155
Zarad, 160
Zarah, 155
Zarahlinda, 155
Zared, 160
Zarek, 149, 245
Zavrina, 75
Zayda, 37
Zayit, 160
Zayna, 37
Zdenek, 111
Zebadiah, 160
Zebediah, 160
Zebulon, 160
Zebulun, 160
Zedekiah, 160
Zeeman, 65
Ze'ev, 160
Zefiryn, 138, 244
Zehave, 155
Zehavi, 155
Zehavit, 155
Zehira, 155
Zehuva, 155

Zelda, 280
Zelde, 280
Zelenka, 58
Zeleny, 59
Zelia, 138
Zelig, 126, 303
Zelina, 138
Zelinia, 138
Zelotes, 149
Zelus, 149
Zemira, 155
Zemirah, 155
Zemora, 155
Zena, 138, 248
Zenaida, 138
Zenaide, 138
Zenas, 149
Zenda, 138, 240
Zene, 138
Zenechka, 248
Zenevieva, 52,
  248
Zenia, 138
Zenina, 138
Zenna, 138
Zeno, 149
Zenobe, 138
Zenobia, 37, 138
Zenochka, 248
Zenon, 149
Zenya, 248
Zephan, 160
Zephaniah, 160
Zephira, 138
Zephyr, 138
Zephyra, 138

Zephyrus, 149,
  212
Zera, 155
Zera'im, 155
Zerbino, 111
Zereld, 280
Zerelda, 280
Zerelde, 280
Zerlina, 302
Zerlinda, 155
Zero, 39
Zeroun, 41
Zesiro, 68
Zeta, 138
Zetes, 149
Zethus, 212
Zeus, 149
Zeuxippe, 202
Zeuxippus, 212
Z'ev, 160
Zeva, 138
Zevulun, 160
Zezili, 202
Zezilia, 202
Zhenechka, 250
Zhenya, 250
Zhorah, 250
Zibia, 155
Zibiah, 155
Zigana, 162
Zigor, 49
Zihna, 216
Zilla, 155
Zillah, 155

Zimra, 155, 160
Zimria, 155
Zindel, 303
Zinerva, 52, 248
Zinna, 177
Zippora, 155
Zipporah, 155
Ziska, 280
Ziske, 280
Zissi, 280
Zita, 138, 267
Zitkala, 215
Ziv, 160, 260
Ziva, 155
Ziven, 245, 250,
  260
Zivon, 250, 260
Ziyad, 71
Zoe, 138
Zoel, 138
Zoelie, 138
Zoelle, 138
Zofia, 138
Zofie, 138
Zohar, 155, 160
Zoheret, 155
Zoia, 138
Zoltan, 149
Zoltar, 149
Zondra, 138
Zophie, 58
Zora, 259
Zorah, 259
Zorana, 259
Zorian, 212
Zorion, 49

Zorya, 250
Zotikos, 149
Zoya, 138, 248
Zoyechka, 248
Zoyenka, 248
Zsa Zsa, 162
Zsiga, 286
Zsigmond, 286
Zsofia, 138, 162
Zsofie, 138
Zsofika, 162
Zsuska, 162
Zsuzsanna, 162
Zsuzsi, 162
Zuberi, 71
Zudora, 167
Zuhayr, 39
Zuka, 71
Zuleika, 37
Zuri, 107
Zuria, 107
Zurie, 107
Zuriel, 160
Zurina, 48, 267
Zurine, 48, 267
Zuzanny, 244
Zygmunt, 245,
  286
Zyphire, 138
Zyta, 138, 244
Zytka, 244